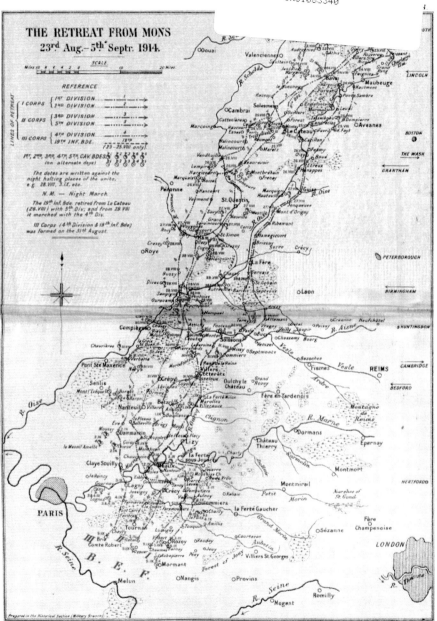

HISTORY OF THE GREAT WAR

MILITARY OPERATIONS

MACMILLAN AND CO., Limited
LONDON · BOMBAY · CALCUTTA · MADRAS
MELBOURNE

THE MACMILLAN COMPANY
NEW YORK · BOSTON · CHICAGO
DALLAS · ATLANTA · SAN FRANCISCO

THE MACMILLAN COMPANY
OF CANADA, LIMITED
TORONTO

SKETCH 1.

GENERAL THEATRE OF OPERATIONS (WESTERN FRONT).

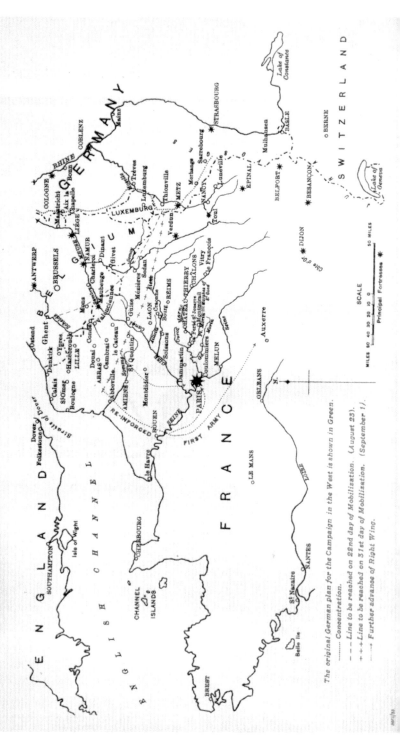

The original German plan for the Campaign in the West is shown in Green.

.... Concentration.
– – – Line to be reached on 22nd day of Mobilization. (August 23).
+ + + Line to be reached on 31st day of Mobilisation. (September 1).
——→ Further advance of Right Wing.

SCALE
MILES 50 40 30 20 10 0   50 MILES

★ Principal Fortresses

HISTORY OF THE GREAT WAR

BASED ON OFFICIAL DOCUMENTS

BY DIRECTION OF THE HISTORICAL SECTION OF THE
COMMITTEE OF IMPERIAL DEFENCE

MILITARY OPERATIONS

FRANCE AND BELGIUM, 1914

MONS, THE RETREAT TO THE SEINE, THE MARNE AND THE AISNE
AUGUST–OCTOBER 1914

COMPILED BY

BRIGADIER-GENERAL SIR JAMES E. EDMONDS

C.B., C.M.G., R.E. (Retired), p.s.c.

MAPS AND SKETCHES COMPILED BY

MAJOR A. F. BECKE

R.A. (Retired), Hon. M.A. (Oxon.)

The Naval & Military Press Ltd

in association with

The Imperial War Museum
Department of Printed Books

Published jointly by
The Naval & Military Press Ltd
Unit 10 Ridgewood Industrial Park,
Uckfield, East Sussex,
TN22 5QE England
Tel: +44 (0) 1825 749494
Fax: +44 (0) 1825 765701

www.naval-military-press.com
www.military-genealogy.com
www.militarymaproom.com

and

The Imperial War Museum, London
Department of Printed Books

www.iwm.org.uk

Printed and bound in Great Britain by
CPI Antony Rowe, Chippenham and Eastbourne

*In reprinting in facsimile from the original, any imperfections are inevitably reproduced
and the quality may fall short of modern type and cartographic standards.*

PREFACE

SINCE the original edition was compiled in 1920–21, the battlefields of 1914 have been visited by many parties of British officers, and much interesting information has been elicited on the ground. The volumes of the French and German official histories dealing with the period, besides numerous regimental histories, French, German and British, have been issued.[1] It was therefore thought desirable to carry out a thorough revision of the text, particularly as the portions of the original dealing with the French and German forces had been pieced together from various unofficial books, and were by no means complete. The maps and sketches have been revised accordingly, and some new ones added, notably a layered map of the Marne battlefield. No such revision of the other published volumes of the history will be necessary.

The opportunity has been taken to give in greater detail the information obtained during open warfare by the Royal Flying Corps ; for in the first volume of the official history " The War in the Air," the late Sir Walter Raleigh did not include sufficient for the purposes of military study. Further particulars also have been given of the destruction of bridges during the retreat : the work of collecting information from survivors was undertaken by Major-General Sir Reginald Buckland, Chief Engineer of the Fourth Army of the B.E.F., and occupied him two years—which gives some idea of the labour involved in this kind of work. A summary of his investigations was published in the *Journal of the Royal Engineers.*

J. E. E.

August 1933.

[1] The German Marne volume in 1926, the French Marne volume in 1933.

v

PREFACE TO THE FIRST EDITION

THIS history has been compiled with the purpose of providing within reasonable compass an authoritative account, suitable for general readers and for students at military schools, of the operations of the British Army in the Western theatre of war in 1914–1918. It is based on the British official records.

The present volume covers events from mobilization up to the middle of October 1914 only, a period of two and a half months, and is on a scale which to a large extent treats the battalion, squadron and battery records as the basis of the story. In succeeding volumes it will not be possible or desirable to adhere to this, and successively the brigade, division and even corps may become the unit of narrative. For this volume the scale adopted seems appropriate, in view of the importance of small units in the early operations, of the lessons to be derived from the study of the work of these units in open warfare, and of the desirability of leaving a picture of what war was like in 1914, when trained soldiers were still of greater importance than material, and gas, tanks, long-range guns, creeping barrages and the participation of aircraft in ground fighting were unknown.

The mass of documents to be dealt with was very great, and the difficulty has been not in obtaining information, but in compressing and cutting down what was available. The British records comprise not only the war diaries of every staff and unit engaged, with their voluminous appendices containing all orders, intelligence, etc., received and issued, and detailed reports of actions, but they include also the General Headquarters files, the Commander-in-Chief's diary, and practically every telegram and message despatched and received. These official documents have been supplemented by private diaries and papers which have been kindly lent, by regimental records, and by interviews with officers who took part in the operations.

On a modern battlefield, however, knowledge of events is extraordinarily local, and the transmission of information difficult; in addition important witnesses only too often become casualties. Though written orders and messages are absolutely reliable evidence of the matters with which they deal, war diaries and reports of actions, written up immediately after events, are liable to contain mistakes. Commanders and staffs are naturally more concerned in finding out and reporting the exact situation and condition of their troops and of the enemy, in sending up reinforcements, ammunition and supplies, and recording experience for future use than in the collection of historical matter. In fact, even officers well known to be specially interested in military history have confessed that during the war the idea of collecting or keeping material for its future historian never occurred to them. Many incidents deserving of record may therefore have escaped notice. It will greatly assist in the compilation of monographs or of a fuller official history in years to come, if readers who can supply further information or corrections will communicate with the Secretary of the Historical Section, Committee of Imperial Defence, 2 Whitehall Gardens, London, S.W.1.

The text and maps now presented are the result of the co-operative labours of the staff, past and present, of the Historical Section, Military Branch,[1] which, in collaboration with the Disposal of Records Department, War Office, is also charged with the sorting and arrangement of the

---

[1] Special assistance in compiling this volume has been rendered by Major A. F. Becke, Major F. W. Tomlinson, Captain G. C. Wynne and Mr. E. A. Dixon.

records dealing with operations overseas. This latter part of its work absorbed most of its energy and time until well on into 1921. The Branch did not obtain a permanent home until October 1919 ; thus a large amount of important material did not become available until it was unpacked and sorted after this date, and it was then found necessary to re-write an account of the initial operations already partly drafted.

The British Expeditionary Force in France in 1914 was not acting independently, and formed only a small part of the Allied Armies engaged ; it has therefore been necessary to include an account of the action of the French and Belgian forces sufficient to provide a proper framework for the British operations. As regards the Belgian Army, ample material for this purpose has been published by the Belgian General Staff. The French General Staff has not yet issued any history, but much information with regard to the French plans and operations has already been made public : officially in the reports of Parliamentary Enquiries, semi-officially by historians like M. Hanotaux, M. Engerand, M. Madelin and General Palat (*Pierre Lehautcourt*), and in the form of reminiscences and memoirs by actual participants, such as Generals Lanrezac, Galliéni, Dubail and Mangin. It was not, therefore, thought necessary to trouble the French General Staff except as regards the incident of the assistance rendered by General Sordet's Cavalry Corps at the battle of Le Cateau, when a copy of the war diary of the troops concerned was very courteously furnished. With this exception, it must be understood that for the French operations the only absolutely authoritative statements quoted are the orders, instructions, intelligence reports, etc., received officially by G.H.Q. from the French Grand Quartier Général.

The published German accounts of the early part of the war are very numerous, and they deal both with the decisions and orders of the higher commanders and the operations of many corps and even smaller fighting units. The most notable are the books of the three Army com-

manders, von Kluck, von Bülow and von Hausen, the
General Staff monographs "Lüttich-Namur" and "Mons,"
the official list of battles and engagements, with the
names of the formations, etc., present, entitled "Schlachten
und Gefechte," and the stories of participants like General
von Zwehl, General von Kuhl, Hauptmann Bloem (the
novelist) and Hofprediger Vogel.[1]   It was originally intended to give the accounts derived from German sources
in the form of notes at the end of each Chapter; but, after
consideration, it was decided that such an arrangement
might prove inconvenient, and that it was better as a
general rule to include them in the body of the Chapters,
as close as possible to the events in the British narrative to which they refer.   This arrangement, in view
of the difference of the character of the material, has
naturally caused breaks in the style and scope of the
story, but it makes the comparison of the two accounts
easier.

General Freiherr Mertz von Quirheim, the Director of
the German *Reichsarchiv*, Berlin, which has custody of
the war records, has been good enough to furnish material
in order to clear up a few points on which there seemed
insufficient information.

As separate histories of the Royal Air Force and the
Medical Services are being compiled, a detailed account
of their work has not been included in the narrative.

Two sets of maps have been prepared.   The one,
distinguished by the word " Sketches," sufficient for the
general reader, is bound in the volume ; the other, intended
for the use of students of war, is issued separately.   Except
the situation maps for the battle of the Aisne, which are
taken from the originals, the maps have been compiled
from data and sketches in the war diaries or furnished
by officers, or from French and German publications.

The typescript or proof sheets have been read by a
number of commanders and staff and regimental officers
who took part in the events narrated, and the compiler
has been greatly assisted by their advice and criticism,

[1] See List of Books, pp. xxv-xxix.

for which he tenders them his most sincere thanks. He is specially grateful to Mr. C. T. Atkinson, his predecessor in charge of the Branch, for advice and help at all times, which his intimate knowledge of the records made most valuable; and both to him and to Mr. W. B. Wood, the partner in the compilation of a book on an earlier war, for the reading and correction of the proof sheets.

J. E. E.

April 1922.

NOTES

THE locations of troops and places are given from right to left of the front of the Allied Forces, unless otherwise stated. Thus, even in the retreat to the Seine they are described from east to west. In translations of German orders they are left as in the original, but otherwise enemy troops are enumerated in relation to the British front.

The convention observed in the British Expeditionary Force is followed as regards the distinguishing numbers of Armies, Corps, Divisions, etc., of the British and Allied Armies, *e.g.*, they are written in full for Armies, but in Roman figures for Corps, and in Arabic for smaller formations and units, except Artillery Brigades, which are Roman; thus: Fourth Army, IV. Corps, 4th Division, 4th Infantry Brigade, 4th Cavalry Brigade, IV. Brigade, R.F.A.

German formations and units, to distinguish them clearly from the Allies, are printed in italic characters, thus: *First Army, I. Corps, 1st Division.*

The usual Army, and sometimes the Army List, abbreviations of regimental names have been used in the narrative; for example, "2/R. West Kent" or "West Kents" for 2nd Battalion The Queen's Own (Royal West Kent Regiment); "the Somerset" or "Somerset L.I." for The Somerset Light Infantry; K.O.Y.L.I. for the King's Own Yorkshire Light Infantry; K.R.R.C. for The King's Royal Rifle Corps. To avoid constant repetition, the " Royal " in regimental titles is often omitted: for instance, the Royal Warwickshire are called " the Warwickshire."

Abbreviations employed occasionally are :—
G.H.Q. for British General Headquarters.
G.Q.G. for French Grand Quartier Général (usually spoken as " Grand Q.G.").

xiii

O.H.L. for German *Oberste Heeresleitung* (German Supreme
Command). *N.B.*—"G.H.Q." in German means
Grosses Haupt-Quartier, that is the Kaiser's
Headquarters, political, military and naval, as
distinguished from O.H.L.

Officers are described by the rank which they held at
the period under consideration.

The accents in French and Belgian place names well
known to British troops have been omitted.

The meaning of *Reserve, Ersatz, Landwehr* as applied
to German formations is explained on pp. 21, 22. Of other
German terms used, *Jäger* and *Schützen* both signify
riflemen formed in special battalions ; *Abteilung* means
a group of three batteries of artillery ; a German artillery
brigade consists of two regiments each of two or three
Abteilungen.[1]

Pioniere : are the German field Engineers ; the word
cannot well be translated by " Engineers " or " Pioneers,"
as the men in the *Pioniere* units, although they have a
thorough training in field engineering, are not tradesmen
of the class found in R.E. Companies, and are only employed
on field duties ; besides, in Germany there was an " In-
genieur Korps," which had duties in the construction and
maintenance of fortresses.

Time in German narratives and orders, which in the
period dealt with was one hour earlier than British, has
been corrected to our standard, unless it is specified
" German time."

[1] *Abteilung* also means a mounted machine-gun battery with cavalry, as
opposed to the *M.G. Kompagnie*, which forms part of an infantry regiment
or *Jäger* battalion.

CONTENTS

INTRODUCTION

PAGE

THE ARMIES OF THE WESTERN ALLIED FORCES :
Great Britain 1
France 14
Belgium 18
GERMANY 20

CHAPTER I

THE OUTBREAK OF WAR 23
PROGRESS OF EVENTS 31
THE BRITISH ENTRY INTO FRANCE 48
Notes : I. Alleged German Troop Movements before Mobiliza-
tion 54
II. The Schlieffen Plan 56

CHAPTER II

22ND AUGUST 1914 :
First Contact with the Enemy 62
Note : German Uncertainty as to the Position of the B.E.F. . 68

CHAPTER III

THE BATTLE OF MONS, 23RD AUGUST 71
Note : The German Account of Mons 94

CHAPTER IV

THE RETREAT FROM MONS AND ACTION OF ELOUGES, 24TH
AUGUST 96
Notes : I. German Movements on the 24th August . . 114
II. Operations of the French Troops on the British Left,
20th-24th August 116

CHAPTER V

PAGE

THE RETREAT FROM MONS (*continued*), 25TH AUGUST . 118
Notes : I. Movements of the German *First* and *Second Armies*,
23rd-25th August 129
II. Movements of General Valabrègue's Group of Reserve
divisions, on British Right, 21st-25th August . 131

CHAPTER VI

THE RETREAT FROM MONS (*continued*), EVENING AND NIGHT
OF 25TH/26TH AUGUST :
Maroilles and Landrecies ; Solesmes . . . 132
Notes : I. Movements of the German *First Army* on 25th
August 149
II. First Belgian Sortie from Antwerp, 24th, 25th,
26th August 151

CHAPTER VII

THE BATTLE OF LE CATEAU, 26TH AUGUST. DAWN TILL NOON 152
Note : German Plans for the 26th August . . . 169

CHAPTER VIII

THE BATTLE OF LE CATEAU, 26TH AUGUST (*continued*).
NOON TO 5 P.M. 171

CHAPTER IX

THE CLOSE OF THE BATTLE OF LE CATEAU, 26TH AUGUST.
5 P.M. TO NIGHTFALL 186
THE RETREAT FROM THE BATTLEFIELD 197
THE I. CORPS ON THE 26TH AUGUST 200
Notes : I. German Accounts of Le Cateau . . . 204
II. General d'Amade's Force on the British Left, 26th
August 210

CHAPTER X

THE RETREAT (*continued*), 27TH-28TH AUGUST :
Smith-Dorrien's Force 212
Haig's I. Corps 219
General Situation, Night 28th/29th August . . . 229
Notes : I. Movements of the German *First* and *Second Armies*
after Le Cateau 233
II. Movements of the French Fifth Army from Charle-
roi to Guise 237
III. General Joffre's Congratulatory Telegram . . 238
IV. British Losses, 23rd-27th August . . . 238

CHAPTER XI

PAGE

THE RETREAT (*continued*), 29TH-31ST AUGUST :
29th August 239
30th August 242
31st August 246
Notes : I. Movements of the German *First* and *Second Armies*,
29th-31st August 250
II. The Battle of Guise, 29th-30th August . . 252

CHAPTER XII

THE RETREAT (*continued*), 1ST SEPTEMBER :
The Fight at Néry 255
The Rear-guard Action of Crépy en Valois . . . 259
The Rear-guard Actions of Villers Cottérêts . . 260
Notes : I. German Movements on 1st September . . 265
II. The Army of Paris 267

CHAPTER XIII

THE LAST STAGES OF THE RETREAT, 2ND-5TH SEPTEMBER . 268
Notes : I. Operations of the German *First* and *Second Armies*,
2nd-5th September 287
II. The Genesis of the Battle of the Marne . . 293

CHAPTER XIV

THE BATTLE OF THE MARNE :
6th September : The Return to the Offensive . . 295
The French on the 6th September 302
Notes : I. The German Right Wing on the 6th September . 304
II. The Despatch of General Joffre's Order for the
Battle of the Marne 306

CHAPTER XV

THE BATTLE OF THE MARNE (*continued*) :
7th September : The March to the Grand Morin . . 308
The French on the 7th September 313
Note : The German Right Wing on the 7th September . . 315

CHAPTER XVI

THE BATTLE OF THE MARNE (*continued*) :
8th September : The Forcing of the Petit Morin . . 318
The French on the 8th September 326
Note : The German Right Wing on the 8th September . . 328

CHAPTER XVII

PAGE

THE BATTLE OF THE MARNE (*concluded*) :
9th September : The Passage of the Marne and the Retreat
of the Germans 332
The French on the 9th September 344
Notes : I. The German Right Wing on the 9th September . 347
II. The Second Belgian Sortie from Antwerp, 9th-13th
September 356

CHAPTER XVIII

THE PURSUIT TO THE AISNE, 10TH-12TH SEPTEMBER :
10th September 358
The French on the 10th September 364
11th September : The Incline to the North-East . . 364
The French on the 11th September 366
12th September : The Advance to the Aisne . . 366
The French on the 12th September 372
Note : The German Retirement from the Battle of the Marne 373

CHAPTER XIX

THE BATTLE OF THE AISNE, 13TH SEPTEMBER :
The Passage of the Aisne 377
The French on the 13th September 391
Note : The 13th September on the German Side . . 392

CHAPTER XX

THE BATTLE OF THE AISNE (*continued*) :
14th September : The Fight for the Chemin des Dames . 395
The French on the 14th September 418
15th September : The Deadlock 419
The French on the 15th September 422
Note : The 14th-15th September on the German Side . . 423

CHAPTER XXI

LAST DAYS ON THE AISNE :
General Situation 428
Operations on the Aisne 439
Note : The German Strategy during the Battle of the Aisne . 453

CHAPTER XXII

THE " RACE TO THE SEA " AND THE TRANSFER OF THE B.E.F.
TO FLANDERS 456

GENERAL INDEX 577
INDEX TO ARMS, FORMATIONS AND UNITS . . 585

TABLE OF APPENDICES

PAGE

1. Order of Battle of the British Expeditionary Force, August and September 1914 471

2. Notes on the organization of some of the principal formations and units of the British Expeditionary Force in 1914 485

3. Order of Battle of the French Armies in August 1914 . 488

4. Notes on the organization of some of the principal French formations and units in 1914 490

5. Order of Battle of the Belgian Army in August 1914 . 492

6. Order of Battle of the German Armies in August 1914 . 493

7. Notes on the organization of some of the principal German formations and units in 1914 496

8. Instructions to Sir John French from Earl Kitchener, August 1914 499

9. The French plan of campaign, Plan 17 (translation) . 501

10. Sir John French's Operation Order No. 5, 1 P.M. 20th August 1914 (with march table and allotment of Army troops) 508

11. Sir John French's Operation Order No. 6, 11.55 P.M. 21st August 1914 513

12. Sir John French's supplementary instruction to Cavalry Division, 11.35 P.M. 21st August 1914 . . . 514

13. Sir John French's Operation Order No. 7, 8.25 P.M. 24th August 1914 515

14. Sir John French's Operation Order No. 8, 7.30 P.M. 25th August 1914 516

15. 4th Division Operation Order No. 1, 5 P.M. 25th August 1914 518

16. II. Corps Operation Order No. 6, 10.15 P.M. 25th August 1914 520

17. Sir John French's Operation Order No. 9, 8.30 P.M. 27th August 1914 521

18. Sir John French's Operation Order No. 10, 11.30 P.M. 28th August 1914 522

19. Sir John French's Operation Order No. 11, 9 P.M. 29th August 1914 524

20. Sir John French's Operation Order No. 12, 5.15 P.M. 30th August 1914 525

21. Sir John French's Operation Order No. 13, 8.50 P.M. 31st August 1914 527

22. G.H.Q. messages to I. Corps anticipating and confirming order to retire, 1st September 1914 . . . 529

PAGE

23. Correspondence with regard to halting on the Marne and the retreat behind the Seine (translation) . . 530

24. Sir John French's Operation Order No. 14, 7.30 P.M. 2nd September 1914 533

25. Sir John French's Operation Order No. 15, 11.50 P.M. 3rd September 1914 535

26. Le Général Commandant en Chef au Field Maréchal Sir John French, Commandant en Chef les forces Britanniques, 4th September 1914 537

27. Letter of Sir John French to Earl Kitchener, 7th September 1914 538

28. Sir John French's Operation Order No. 16, 6.35 P.M. 4th September 1914 540

29. Table giving length of daily marches (in miles) from 20th August to 5th September (both inclusive) . . 542

30. General Joffre's Instruction for the battle of the Marne (translation) 543

31. Sir John French's Operation Order No. 17, 5.15 P.M. 5th September 1914 545

32. Cavalry Division Operation Order No. 11, 5th September 1914 (with march table) 547

33. I. Corps Operation Order No. 10, 5th September 1914 . 548

34. II. Corps Operation Order No. 15, 5th September 1914 . 549

35. III. Corps Operation Order No. 7, 5th September 1914 . 551

36. Sir John French's Special Order of the Day, 6th September 1914 552

37. Sir John French's Operation Order No. 18, 9 P.M. 7th September 1914 553

38. Sir John French's Operation Order No. 19, 7.30 P.M. 8th September 1914 555

39. Sir John French's Operation Order No. 20, 8.15 P.M. 9th September 1914 556

40. Sir John French's Operation Order No. 21, 8.15 P.M. 10th September 1914 558

41. Sir John French's Operation Order No. 22, 6 P.M. 11th September 1914 560

42. General Joffre's Special Instruction No. 23 of 12th September 1914 562

43. Sir John French's Operation Order No. 23, 7.45 P.M. 12th September 1914 563

44. Sir John French's Operation Order No. 24, 6 P.M. 13th September 1914 565

45. Sir John French's Operation Order No. 25, 14th September 1914 567

46. Sir John French's Operation Order No. 26, 8.30 P.M. 15th September 1914 569

PAGE

47. Sir John French's Operation Order No. 27, 8.30 P.M.
16th September 1914 570

48. Sir John French's Operation Order No. 28, 3 P.M. 1st
October 1914 571

49. Sir John French's Operation Order No. 29, 11 A.M. 2nd
October 1914 573

50. Sir John French's Operation Order No. 30, 8 A.M. 4th
October 1914 575

51. Sir John French's Operation Order No. 31, 8.30 A.M.
5th October 1914 576

SKETCHES AND MAPS

SKETCHES

(Bound in Volume)

A. The Retreat from Mons . . . . *End-paper*

1. General Theatre of Operations (Western Front) *At beginning*

2. Concentration of the Armies (Western Front) . *Facing p.* 15

3. Operations 4th-22nd August (German Armies in Belgium) . . . . . ,, ,, 35

4. Operations of B.E.F., 23rd-28th August . . ,, ,, 51

5. The Eve of Mons, 22nd August . . . ,, ,, 63

6. The Eve of Le Cateau, 25th August . . ,, ,, 121

7. Le Cateau, 26th August . . . . ,, ,, 153

8. The Battle of Guise, 29th August . . ,, ,, 237

9. Operations, 28th August-5th September (Retreat of B.E.F.) . . . . ,, ,, 239

10. The German Advance, 17th August-5th Sept. . ,, ., 251

11. 1st September 1914 . . . . ,, ,, 255

12. The Marne, 5th September . . . ,, ,, 281

12A. General Joffre's Projects for the Counter-Offensive . . . . . ,, ,, 286

13. Operations, 6th-13th September (Advance of B.E.F.) . . . . . . ,, ,, 295

14. The Marne, 6th September . . . ,, ,, 299

15. The Marne, 7th September . . . ,, ,, 309

16. 8th September. Situation as known at German G.H.Q. . . . . . . ,, ,, 329

17. The Crisis, 9th September. The B.E.F. crosses the Marne . . . . . ,, ,, 333

18. The Marne. The German Retreat . . ,, ,, 359

19. The Aisne, 14th September . . . ,, ,, 377

20. The Aisne, 20th September . . . ,, ,, 439

21. The Extension of the Battle Line northwards, 15th September-8th October . . . ,, ,, 457

B. The Advance to the Aisne . . . . *End-paper*

MAPS

(In Separate Case)

Plate 1. Order of Battle of a German Cavalry Division and a German Corps in August 1914.

Map 1. The Concentration of the Armies (Western Front).

,, 2. Theatre of Operations (Western Front) 1 : 1,000,000.

,, 3. Mons to Compiègne, 1 : 250,000.

,, 4. Compiègne to Paris and Melun, 1 : 250,000.

,, 5. Situation, 17th-24th August.

,, 6. Battlefield of Mons, 1 : 100,000 (layered).

,, 7. Mons, Sunday, 23rd August.

,, 8. Action at Élouges, 24th August.

,, 9. B.E.F., night, 25th/26th August.

., 10. Battlefield of Le Cateau, 1 : 40,000 (layered).

,, 11. Le Cateau, 26th August.

,, 12. Actions at Fesmy and Étreux, 27th August.

,, 13. Retreat from Mons, 23rd-29th August.

., 14. Situation, 27th August (night).

,, 15. Situation, 28th August (night).

,, 16. Situation, 29th August (night).

,, 17. Situation, 30th August (night).

,. 18. Situation, 31st August (night).

,, 19. 1st September, 1 : 100,000.

,, 20. Situation, 1st September (night).

., 21. Situation, 2nd September (night).

.. 22. Situation, 3rd September (night).

,, 23. Situation, 4th September (night).

,, 24. Situation, 5th September (night).

,, 25. The Marne Battlefield, 1914 (layered).

,, 26. Situation, 6th September (night).

,, 27. Situation, 7th September (night).

., 28. Situation, 8th September (night).

,, 29. The Crisis of the Marne, 9th September (afternoon).

,, 30. Situation, 9th September (night).

,, 31. Situation, 10th September (night).

,, 32. Situation, 11th September (night).

.. 33. Situation, 12th September (night).

.. 34. Situation, 13th September (night).

,, 35. Battlefield of the Aisne, 1 : 100,000 (layered).

,, 36. Battle of the Aisne, 25th September 1914.

LIST OF BOOKS

TO WHICH MOST FREQUENT REFERENCE IS MADE

BAUMGARTEN-CRUSIUS : " Die Marneschlacht 1914." By General-major Baumgarten-Crusius. (Leipzig : Lippold.)
An account of the battle of the Marne and the events leading to it, founded on official records. It is written particularly from the point of view of the German *Third Army* by a Saxon general. This was the first German book which told the truth about the Marne.

BAUMGARTEN-CRUSIUS II. : " Deutsche Heerführung im Marne-feldzug 1914." By Generalmajor Baumgarten-Crusius. (Berlin : Scherl.)
A further contribution to the solution of the question of responsibility for the orders to retreat at the battle of the Marne.

BELGIAN GENERAL STAFF : " Military Operations of Belgium in Defence of the Country and to Uphold her Neutrality." (English translation : London, Collingridge, 1s. net.)
Report, compiled by the Belgian General Staff, for the period July 31st to December 31st, 1914.

BLOEM : " Vormarsch." By Walter Bloem. (Leipzig : Grethlein.)
One of the most graphic and dramatic accounts of war yet written. The author is a well-known German novelist, who was serving, as a Reserve Captain, in the *12th Brandenburg Grenadiers (III. Corps* of von Kluck's Army). He gives the story of his experiences from outbreak of war to the Aisne, where he was wounded on Chivres Spur.
There is an English translation : " The Retreat from Mons, 1914." (Peter Davies.)

BRANDIS : " Die Stürmer von Douaumont." By Oberleutnant von Brandis. (Berlin : Scherl.)
The author served in the *24th Regiment* of the *III. Corps* at Mons, Frameries, etc. He later took part in the capture of Fort Douaumont, Verdun ; this incident is commemorated in the title of his book.

BÜLOW : " Mein Bericht zur Marneschlacht." By Generalfeld-marschall von Bülow. (Berlin : Scherl.) Translated into French as " Mon rapport sur la bataille de la Marne." (Paris : Payot.)
A clear military narrative, with sketch maps, by the com-mander of the German *Second Army*, which includes the battle of the Aisne 1914.

xxvi MILITARY HISTORY OF THE GREAT WAR

ENGERAND : " La Bataille de la Frontière (Août 1914)." By
Fernand Engerand, *Député.* (Paris : Bossard.)
The author was " rapporteur " of the Parliamentary Commission which inquired into the loss of the Briey Basin. He
gives a summary of the report, with important documents as
appendices.

FALKENHAYN : " General Headquarters 1914–1916 and its Critical
Decisions." By General Erich von Falkenhayn. (English
translation, Hutchinson & Co., 21s.)
Von Falkenhayn was Prussian Minister of War in 1914 ;
but on 14th September he took over the duties of Chief of the
General Staff from von Moltke. The book deals mostly with
the successes of the Russian theatre of war, but contains much
of importance as regards decisions in the West.

F.O.A. (French Official Account) : " Les Armées Françaises dans la
Grande Guerre." Ministère de la Guerre : État-Major de
l'Armée-Service Historique. (Paris : Imprimerie Nationale.)
The first three volumes of " Tome I " cover the period from
the outbreak of war to 14th September 1914, the first volume
commencing with the pre-war plans, including Plan XVII. It
is a severely technical record, reinforced by a mass of documents,
there being seven volumes of these to three of text in the " Tome."
Both text and maps are inaccurate as regards the B.E.F. at the
Battle of the Marne.

GALLIÉNI : " Mémoires du Général Galliéni). Défense de Paris."
(Paris : Payot.)
A most valuable record. With Situation Maps.

G.O.A. (German Official Account) : " Der Weltkreig 1914 bis 1918.
Bearbeitet im Reichsarchiv. Die militärischen Operationen zu
Lande." (Berlin : Mittler.)
The first two volumes were published at the end of 1924,
and many more have since appeared. Those dealing with the
Western Front up to the end of October are the first, third,
fourth and fifth.
Although complete documents are not quoted, sufficient
data are published for the reader to form his own conclusions.
In the fifth volume the scale of the narrative is much reduced
and, generally speaking, the maps hardly reach the standard
of the text.

G.O.A. K.u.K. : The first volume, with appendices, of " Kriegs-
rüstung und Kriegswirtschaft," published in 1930.
A separate part of the German Official Account it deals with
" Preparations for War." That section devoted to military
preparations traces the increase of the German Army from
1875 to 1914.

HANOTAUX : " Histoire illustrée de la Guerre de 1914." By M. Gabriel
Hanotaux. Nine volumes published. (Paris : Gounouilhou.)
A beautifully illustrated work containing a large number
of official documents, which make it valuable. The twelfth
volume carries the narrative as far as the " Race to the Sea."

HAUSEN : " Erinnerungen an der Marnefeldzug 1914." By General-oberst Freiherr von Hausen. (Leipzig : Koehler.)
> A personal and historical account of the campaign up to the end of the battle of the Marne by the commander of the German *Third Army*, with numerous sketch maps and an order of battle of the German forces.

HEUBNER : "Unter Emmich vor Lüttich. Unter Kluck vor Paris." By H. Heubner, Hauptmann der Reserve und Professor in Wernigerode. (Schwerin : Bahn.)
> A very vivid account by a professor and Reserve captain, which ends at the Aisne 1914. He belonged to the *20th Infantry Regiment, 11th Infantry Brigade, 6th Division, III. Corps* of von Kluck's Army and was at Mons, the Ourcq, etc.

KLUCK : " Der Marsch auf Paris, und die Marneschlacht 1914." By A. von Kluck, Generaloberst. (Berlin : Mittler.) Trans-lated as " The March on Paris 1914." (Edward Arnold, 10s.)
> Von Kluck's own statement, with a very fine map showing the movements of the German *First Army*.

KUHL : " Der deutsche Generalstab in Vorbereitung und Durch-führung des Weltkrieges." By General der Infanterie H. von Kuhl. (Berlin : Mittler.)
> An account of the work of the Great General Staff in preparation for and during the war, specially valuable for the part dealing with the development of the German plan of campaign. The author was the Chief of the Staff to von Kluck and Crown Prince Rupprecht of Bavaria, and had served 22 years on the Great General Staff before the war.

KUHL'S " Marne " : " Der Marnefeldzug 1914." By General der Infanterie H. von Kuhl. (Berlin : Mittler.)
> Published January 1921.

LOHRISCH : " Im Siegessturm von Lüttich an die Marne." By Oberleutnant der Reserve Dr. H. Lohrisch. (Leipzig : Quelle und Meyer.)
> The author served in the *27th Infantry Regiment* of the *IV. Corps* in the early fighting, including Le Cateau.

" Lüttich-Namur " : " Der grosse Krieg in Einzeldarstellungen. Herausgegeben im Auftrage des grossen Generalstabes." (Olden-burg : Gerhard Stalling.)
> In the series of Great General Staff monographs. A very complete account of the capture of Liége and Namur.

" Marnedrama " : " Das Marnedrama 1914."
> This is also in the series of Great General Staff monographs. Published in 1928, in five volumes, it treats of the Battle of the Marne in much more detail than G.O.A. but as its manifest purpose is to glorify the officers and men of the old German Army its comments and claims will hardly bear investigation. The sketch maps, however, are of considerable value.

" Mons " : " Die Schlacht bei Mons."
> In the same series of Great General Staff monographs. There are excellent maps showing the German dispositions.

M.W.B. : Militär Wochenblatt. (Berlin : Mittler.)
The principal German military journal.

PALAT : " La Grande Guerre sur le Front Occidental." By General Palat (Pierre Lehautcourt). In fourteen volumes. (Paris : Chapelot.)
A valuable unofficial compilation, as regards the movements of the French. The sixth volume deals with the Battle of the Marne, and the seventh carries the story of the war on the Western Front to end of the " Race to the Sea," 1914. The maps are portions of the 1 : 80,000 with no troops marked on them.

POSECK : " Die deutsche Kavallerie in Belgien und Frankreich 1914." By Generalleutnant von Poseck. (Berlin : Mittler.)
The author was Chief of the Staff of the *I. Cavalry Corps*. It is a very valuable summary of the German cavalry operations, based on the official records, and has been translated in the United States.

" Regt. No. . . . " These are references to war histories of German regiments. Most of them are in the series " Erinnerungsblätter deutscher Regimenter," published by Gerhard Stalling, Oldenburg. The volumes vary in length and value : some give detailed accounts of the fighting with extracts from the reminiscences of combatants ; others merely reproduce the official war diaries.

" Schlachten und Gefechte " : " Die Schlachten und Gefechte des Grossen Krieges, 1914–1918. Quellenwerk nach amtlichen Bezeichnungen zusammengestellt vom Grossen Generalstab." (Berlin : Sack.)
An official list of battles compiled by the Great General Staff showing the formations, etc., engaged in each, and lists of the higher commanders, with excellent index.

STEGEMANN : " Geschichte des Krieges." Vols. I. II. and III. By H. Stegemann, a Swiss journalist. (Stuttgart : Deutsche Verlags-Anstalt.)
A good general account of the war from the German point of view.

TAPPEN : " Bis zur Marne." By Generalleutnant Tappen. (Oldenburg : Stalling.)
The author was head of the Operations Section of Supreme Headquarters until August 1916. His book gives considerable insight into the opening operations up to and including the Marne, but has led to a good deal of controversy in Germany.

VOGEL : " 3,000 Kilometer mit der Garde-Kavallerie." By Hofprediger Dr. Vogel. (Leipzig : Velhagen und Klassing.)
This is practically a picturesque diary of the operations of the *Guard Cavalry Division* from outbreak of war to May 1915, written by the Divisional Chaplain.

WIRTH : " Von der Saale zur Aisne." By Hauptmann der Landwehr A. Wirth. (Leipzig : Hesse und Becker.)
A small diary by an orderly officer attached to the Staff of the *13th Reserve Division* (*IV. Reserve Corps*) that fought at Le Cateau, etc.

" Ypres " . " Ypres 1914 " (Constable : 5s.), translation of " Die
Schlacht an der Yser und bei Ypern im Herbst 1914." (In the
same series as " Lüttich-Namur.")
Contains, besides an account of the First Ypres, a good
many details of the organization of the German Army.

Zwehl : " Maubeuge, Aisne, Verdun." By General der Infanterie
von Zwehl. (Berlin : Curtius.)
The author commanded the *VII. Reserve Corps*, captured
Maubeuge, and reached the Chemin des Dames ridge at the
Aisne just in time to prevent the British I. Corps from seizing
it. There is a good account of the battle and much else of
interest in the book.

INTRODUCTION

THE ARMIES OF THE WESTERN ALLIED POWERS

GREAT BRITAIN

EIGHTEEN HUNDRED AND SEVENTY-ONE, the year which saw the proclamation of the German Empire at Versailles, witnessed also the beginning of a new epoch in the history of the British Army. It was then that the first steps were taken to replace the old army of Peninsular model by a force raised and organized on modern lines : the system of purchase, under which officers of the cavalry and infantry bought their commissions in each successive regimental rank, was abolished ; short service was adopted, not so much with the idea of attracting recruits as of building up a reserve ; and regiments of infantry, except those which were already composed of more than one battalion, were grouped in pairs. Ten years later, in 1881, this grouping was made permanent, the old numbers were abolished and the infantry was reconstituted into double-battalion regiments with territorial titles on a territorial basis.[1]

The old Militia, Regular and Local, remained, as always, on a territorial basis. It was gradually drifting back to the function, which it had fulfilled during the Napoleonic wars, of a recruiting depot for the army, but without the ballot ; for the enforcement of the ballot had for a long time been suspended by an annual Act of Parliament.

Side by side with the Militia stood the Yeomanry Cavalry, first called into being by the threat of a French invasion in 1794–95. It had always attracted an excellent class of recruit, but its training was very limited, both in scope and duration.

Behind the Militia and Yeomanry were the Volunteers,

[1] An excellent account of the development of the Army will be found in " The Army Book of the British Empire " (H.M. Stationery Office, 5s.). It unfortunately stops at 1893.

chiefly infantry. They also had been first formed in 1794–95 ; but in 1806–7 they had been transformed into Local Militia, recruited by ballot without power of substitution, and subject to the same discipline as the Militia. After 1815 the Local Militia soon died out ; but in 1859 the Volunteers were revived on the original basis of 1794–95.

The best part of a generation, however, was needed for the new army system initiated in 1871 to settle down and bear fruit. The home battalion of a regiment was for years little more than a group of boys who, as they matured, were drafted out to the battalion on foreign service. Only in India was the real British Army of grown and fully-trained men to be seen.

In 1899–1902 the war in South Africa put the British military forces to a rude practical test. Never before had so many troops been sent overseas. The Regular Army was found to be too small for the work even when the Reserves had been called out, so that means to supplement it had to be improvised. The Militia and Yeomanry volunteered for foreign service almost to a man ; the Volunteer battalions sent a succession of companies to the Regular battalions of their regiments in South Africa, and formed special active service units ; finally the Overseas Dominions and Colonies enthusiastically raised and despatched contingents. The experience acquired in this war by all arms and by all branches of the Staff was soon to prove of the utmost value.

In February 1904 the office of Commander-in-Chief was abolished, and an Army Council was set up. It gave the Secretary of State a board of six advisers : four professional soldiers, each of them at the head of a great department, and two civilians, known as the financial and civil members. The duties of the Commander-in-Chief as regards inspection of troops were transferred to an Inspector-General of the Forces.

Next came the constitution of a General Staff, on principles which were established at a meeting of the Army Council on 9th August 1905. The Chief of the General Staff was authorized to proceed with its formation on 11th November 1905. Instructions for its organization were promulgated by a special Army Order of 12th September 1906. Such a body was a complete innovation in the British Army. The word " Staff " had been known for generations, but signified originally no more than the Department of the Commander-in-Chief as contrasted with

that of the Secretary of State for War—of the Horse
Guards as distinguished from the War Office. This Staff,
however, was an administrative one only ; there was no
such thing as a Staff at Headquarters charged with such
duties as are now associated with the name. Nor was the
Headquarters Staff at the Horse Guards consulted as to
military plans and operations. Its business was to provide such trained men as the Cabinet required, not to advise
as to their duties or their employment.

The General Staff came into being under the guidance
of Mr. (later Lord) Haldane, who became Secretary of
State for War in December 1905, and was charged with
the duty of reorganizing the land forces not only of the
country, but of the Empire.

The need of reform was urgent, for the Germans made
little concealment of their intention to enter the lists for
the domination of the world, and were not only perfecting
vast military preparations, but quietly insinuating themselves into the control of the most important financial and
commercial undertakings of their neighbours. They had
already established an elaborate system of espionage, and
were abusing the hospitality of friendly States by organizing
also a system of sabotage—that is to say, the destruction,
by secret agents introduced in time of peace, of such important means of communication as telegraph lines, railway junctions and bridges, and the like.[1] Hitherto our
ancient and glorious rival had been France ; but this new
enemy lay to the east and not to the south ; and the eyes
of those charged with the defence of the United Kingdom
were now turned towards the North Sea instead of across
the Channel.

There was now also a prospect that, in order to fulfil
our treaty obligations, it might become necessary to land
a force on the continent of Europe for the purpose of
protecting the integrity of Belgium, and to operate in
conjunction with the French and Belgian armies in case of
a German attack on France which should involve the violation of Belgian neutrality. Hitherto Britain had always

[1] An assurance has been received from the *Reichsarchiv* that neither in
the *Marine Archiv* (Navy Historical Section) nor in the Military Section
and the Espionage Section has anything of the nature of the sabotage
system mentioned in the text been discovered. Doubtless the arrangements detected in the Empire were the work of irresponsible individuals.
In any case, no harm was done in the United Kingdom ; for on declaration
of war all suspected German agents, except one who was absent from
England on a holiday, were arrested.

4 INTRODUCTION

depended upon a nominally voluntary army for service
abroad ; but the numbers which could thus be raised were
unlikely to be sufficient in an European war on a modern
scale ; and to combine a voluntary with a compulsory
system of recruiting at short notice seemed impracticable,
even if Parliament could have been brought to assent to
it. The problem presented to Mr. Haldane, therefore, was
how to reorganize the existing forces so as to raise them to
the highest point of efficiency, and to provide for their
rapid expansion in time of need.

In the reorganization of 1908 the first step was to build
up a General Staff which should be the brains of the army.
Special care was taken to separate its work, as a department
concerned with strategy and training, from that of the old
Headquarters Staff, whose duties were purely administrative. The instruction for officers of all branches of the
Staff was provided at the Staff College, Camberley, which
was greatly enlarged, and at the Indian Staff College at
Quetta, then recently founded by Lord Kitchener. From the
graduates of these institutions officers for the General Staff
and for the Adjutant-General's and Quartermaster-General's
Departments were chosen. For the technical instruction of
the Administrative Staff special arrangements were made
at the London School of Economics for selected officers,
including Staff College graduates, to be trained in such
matters as business management and railway organization.

The initial difficulty of providing a reserve of officers
was very great. Mr. Haldane turned to the universities
to supplement the military colleges at Sandhurst and
Woolwich by converting the Volunteer Corps which had
long existed at our older universities into Officers' Training
Corps.[1] In these, under the guidance of the General Staff
and with the concurrence of the university authorities,
practical military instruction was given not only to army
candidates but to many students who did not intend
entering the military profession as a career. Public
schools which possessed Volunteer Corps were invited
to convert them into contingents of the Officers' Training
Corps ; whilst universities and schools which did not pos-
sess such corps were encouraged to form them, and those
which did so were given the privilege of nominating a

[1] The idea of turning the University Volunteers into an Officers'
Training Corps was suggested by Lord Lovat and others just after the
conclusion of the South African War, but was not then taken up by the
authorities.

certain number of boys for admission to Sandhurst without further examination.

In the Regular Army one great need of the mounted branches was a reserve of horses to make good the deficiencies on mobilization. This was supplied by taking a census of all horses in the kingdom, and obtaining statutory power to requisition all which were suitable for military purposes.

In the Artillery there was an insufficiency of ammunition columns to meet the increased expenditure of ammunition due to the introduction of quick-firing guns. The Garrison Artillery Militia was therefore turned into a Special Reserve, to be used primarily in the formation of these columns; thirty-three Regular batteries, which had their full complement of guns but few men, were employed to train them. The general reserve of artillery was, by careful nursing, increased. By 1912 the number of batteries which could be mobilized for war had been increased from forty-two to eighty-one. The field artillery was gradually organized into brigades, each of three batteries and an ammunition column.

In the Infantry steps were taken to restore the observance of the system, generally called after Lord Cardwell, that for every battalion abroad at least one should be at home. The balance had been upset as a consequence of the South African War and our rapid Imperial expansion. By the withdrawal of certain colonial garrisons, the proportion was eventually established at eighty-four battalions at home—including nine of Guards that did not come into the Cardwell system—and seventy-three abroad.

The Army Service Corps, reorganized in 1888, had proved itself so efficient in South Africa that it needed little more than such changes in organization as were entailed by the introduction of motor transport. In 1900 the War Office had appointed a Mechanical Transport Committee, and by 1911 two schemes were in operation, viz. (a) the Provisional Subsidy Scheme, by which civil vehicles could be requisitioned for military purposes, until through (b) the Main Subsidy Scheme the number of vehicles built to the War Office specifications for private owners should suffice to supply the needs of the Army. Both schemes were employed to furnish the necessary vehicles on mobilization in 1914. In 1912 the transport of the divisions and the cavalry was reorganized. The horsed baggage and supply wagons were grouped into Train companies, leaving only first line or fighting trans-

port with regimental units. For each division there was
formed a divisional supply column of motor lorries, whose
business it was to bring up rations to a point where the
supply sections of the divisional Train could refill, and, if
possible, to take back sick and wounded.

In the Medical Services of the Army many important
changes were made in organization, training and administration.[1] They were due not only to the experience gained
in the South African War, but to the lessons learnt from
the Russo-Japanese War of 1904–5, and to the revision
of the Geneva Convention in 1906, which afforded a new
basis for the organization of voluntary aid. In the place
of the bearer companies and field hospitals each division
and the cavalry division were provided with self-contained
field ambulances, and a new echelon—the clearing hospital—
was introduced to facilitate the rapid evacuation of wounded,
which was to be the great feature of the new system. Motor
transport, though proposed in 1908, was only introduced
on a very meagre scale, sufficient for peace purposes. The
Army Nursing Service was put on a firm basis. Under
the auspices of an Army Medical Board, of which eminent
civilian specialists were members, sanitation, measures for
prevention of disease, inoculation, and the provision of
pure water, received special attention. To keep the
medical service in touch with the General Staff, officers of
the Royal Army Medical Corps were appointed to special
sections of the Directorates of Military Operations and
Military Training. The medical service of the Territorial
Force was organized similarly to that of the Regular Army,
and large provision made for the formation of hospitals in
time of war and the organization of voluntary aid.

The Militia was renamed Special Reserve, to indicate
what it had long been in practice—a depot for feeding the
Regular Army.

The Regular Army, or First Line, was reorganized
into an Expeditionary Force consisting of six divisions of
all arms and one cavalry division. Each of the six divisions comprised three infantry brigades, or twelve battalions
altogether, with divisional mounted troops, artillery,
engineers, signal service, supply and transport train, and
field ambulances. The total war establishment of each
division was thus raised to some 18,000 of all ranks and

[1] They will be found described in detail in " History of the Great
War, Medical Services, General History," and are therefore enumerated
here very briefly.

descriptions, of whom 12,000 were infantry, with 24 machine guns, and 4,000 artillery, with seventy-six guns (fifty-four 18-pdrs. ; eighteen 4·5-inch howitzers ; and four 60-pdrs.). The Cavalry Division comprised four brigades of three regiments each, and cavalry divisional troops, consisting of artillery, engineers, signal service and medical units.[1] The strength was some 9,000 of all ranks and 10,000 horses, with twenty-four guns (13-pdrs.) and twenty-four machine guns. Although the nucleus of one corps staff was maintained in time of peace, at Aldershot, and corps had been formed at manœuvres, it was not originally intended to have any intermediate echelon between General Headquarters and the six divisions. The decision to form corps was—in order to conform to French organization — made immediately on the formal appointment on mobilization of Field - Marshal Sir John French as Commander-in-Chief. Thus it happened that two out of the three corps staffs had to be improvised; even for each division four staff officers had to be found, as the Peace Establishment contained only two out of the six of the War Establishment. None the less, the organization of the Expeditionary Force was a great step forward in the preparation of the army for war.

The Yeomanry became the second line of cavalry, and was reorganized into fourteen brigades.

The Volunteers were treated according to the precedent of Castlereagh, who had invited them to convert themselves into Local Militia, on pain of disbandment. So, too, Mr. Haldane bade them either become Territorial troops or cease to exist. Mr. Haldane further reverted to the old policy of decentralization, and entrusted the raising and administration of the Territorial Force to the County Lieutenancies, renamed Territorial Associations, under the Presidency of the Lords Lieutenant. The only difference between the schemes of the two statesmen was that Castlereagh insisted upon compulsory personal service, under the ballot, for the Local Militia, whereas Mr. Haldane did not—or rather, in the prevailing temper of Parliament, could not—do the same for the Territorial Force. This force, whose establishment was something over 300,000 strong, was organized upon exactly the same lines as the Regular Army. Its units were grouped into fourteen divisions, commanded by major-generals of the Regular Army, with small Regular staffs.

[1] The 5th Cavalry Brigade was left independent.

The old Militia Garrison Artillery was replaced by Territorial Coast Artillery. The field artillery of Territorial divisions was armed with 15-pounder guns converted into quick-firers, and 5-inch howitzers used in the South African War ; its heavy artillery consisted of 4·7-inch guns. Thus none of its armament was modern.

So much for the reorganization of the Territorial Forces on paper. Unfortunately, before 1914, both Special Reserve and Territorial troops sank so far below their establishment as to cause some anxiety at headquarters ; but it was not doubted that many old Territorials would rejoin the force at the approach of danger, and this confidence proved to be well justified. It was not anticipated that the Territorials would be ready for the field in less than six months after mobilization ; but since they would have at least some training, and as their organization was identical with that of the First Line, they could be employed to reinforce the Regular Army, either by units or by complete divisions, as they became ready.

It had been Mr. Haldane's intention to make the County Associations the medium for indefinite expansion of the forces in case of need. The rough plans for such expansion were actually blocked out, some of the Associations possessing, in whole or in part, the machinery for carrying the plan into effect. But the scheme had not yet received statutory sanction, and had not been worked out in detail. Meanwhile, the County Associations justified Mr. Haldane's faith in them, and their zeal and ability were of the utmost value to the War Office and the country.

The first textbook issued after the South African War for the instruction of the army was " Combined Training," dated 1902, written by the late Colonel G. F. R. Henderson. This, in 1905, became Part I. of "Field Service Regulations." In 1909 the book was superseded by the issue of " Field Service Regulations—Part I. (Operations)," while " Part II. (Organization and Administration)" was published for the first time. These manuals dealt with the general principles governing the employment of the army in war.

Individual training—that is, the physical training, including route marching, bayonet fighting, musketry, signalling, scouting, and generally the education of the individual in his duties and the use of his arms—was carried on during the winter ; this gave place in the spring to the training by units, first of squadrons, companies and batteries; next of cavalry regiments, infantry battalions and artillery brigades; then of cavalry and infantry brigades, first alone and secondly in conjunction with other arms; and lastly of divisions; the whole culminated in inter-divisional exercises and army manœuvres.

The great feature of the training for the attack and counter-attack was combination of fire and movement. Ground was gained as the enemy was approached by rushes of portions of a battalion, company or platoon, under cover of the fire of the remainder and of the artillery. By this procedure, a strong firing line was built up some 200 yards from the enemy; when fire superiority had been attained an assault was delivered. An attacking force was divided into firing line and supports, with local reserves, and the advance was often made in parallel lines in extended order; but the form was essentially elastic and adapted to the ground, with the definite objects of maintaining control, utilizing such cover as was available, and presenting as difficult a target as possible to the enemy.[1]

Mobilization was regularly practised. Every winter certain units were brought up to war establishment in the prescribed manner, the reservists and horses required to complete them being represented by men and animals from other units. In 1910 one of the two Aldershot divisions was mobilized at the expense of the other and by volunteers from the 1st Class Army Reserve, and so was able to take part in the manœuvres at war establishment. Not only fighting units, but also such branches as the Ordnance and the Postal Service were represented at manœuvres, and their work was carried on under conditions approximating to those of active service.

All these reforms were pushed forward under the inevitable disadvantages which have ever hampered the British Army. Recruits were dribbling in at all times of the year. Trained instructors were being withdrawn for attachment to the auxiliary forces, and drafts of trained men were constantly leaving their battalions during the autumn and winter for India. The commanders, again,

---

[1] The soundness of the principle of the combination of fire and movement was abundantly proved during the war; but, as experience was gained, it was found that there was no rôle for " supports " of the kind laid down in the pre-war manuals; reinforcing a line already stopped by casualties merely meant increasing losses without corresponding gain; it became apparent that the proper employment of " local reserves " was to exploit local successes, and to fill defensively gaps in an attacking line that had been brought to a standstill.

could never tell whether their next campaign might not be
fought in the snows of the Himalayas, the swamps and
bush of Africa or the deserts of Egypt—a campaign in
Europe hardly entered into their calculations. It was
practically impossible for the General Staff to keep abreast
of the detailed information required as to possible theatres
of war. Nevertheless, British regimental officers, to use
their own expression, " carried on," although confronted
with two changes uncongenial to many of the older men
among them : the cavalry was trained to an increasing extent
in the work of mounted infantry, and was armed with a rifle
instead of a carbine ; and the Regular infantry battalions
were organized into four companies instead of eight.

In every respect the Expeditionary Force of 1914 was
incomparably the best trained, best organized, and best
equipped British Army which ever went forth to war.[1]
Except in the matter of co-operation between aeroplanes
and artillery, and use of machine guns, its training would
stand comparison in all respects with that of the Germans.[2]
Where it fell short of our enemies was first and foremost
in numbers ; so that, though not " contemptible," it was
almost negligible in comparison with continental armies,
even of the smaller States.[3] In heavy guns and howitzers,
high-explosive shell,[4] trench mortars, hand-grenades,[5] and

[1] For the Order of Battle and organization of the British Expeditionary
Force, see Appendices 1 and 2.
[2] The German General Staff in 1912 considered it an " ebenbürtiger
Gegner "—man for man as good as their own. (Kuhl, " Der deutsche
Generalstab," p. 87.)
[3] The following, which is translated from the German Admiralty
Staff's "Der Krieg zur See 1914–1918 : Nordsee," i. p. 82, is of interest
in this connection :
" The Supreme Command made no demands whatever on the Navy to
stop or delay the British transports. On the contrary, it seemed not to
place much value on the action of the efficient (wertvoll) but numerically
weak Expeditionary Corps. In any case, when at the beginning of the
war Frigate-Captain Heydel of the Operations Section was sent by the
Admiralty to inquire if the Army laid stress on the interruption of the
transport of troops, the Chief of the General Staff personally replied that
the Navy should not allow the operations that it would otherwise carry
out to be interfered with on this account ; it would even be of advantage
if the Armies in the West could settle with the 160,000 English at the
same time as the French and Belgians. His point of view was shared by
many during the favourable commencement of the offensive in the West."
[4] No high-explosive shells were provided for the 18-pdr. and 13-pdr.
field guns ; but for the 60-pdr. and 4·5-inch field howitzer a proportion of
the rounds carried in the field was high explosive : for the former 30 per
cent and for the latter one-third (2 shrapnel to 1 H.E.).
[5] There was a service hand-grenade, but it was a complicated one, with
a long shaft, which proved unsuitable in trench warfare, and a single one
cost £1 : 1 : 3.

much of the subsidiary material required for siege and trench warfare, it was almost wholly deficient. Further, no steps had been taken to instruct the army in a knowledge of the probable theatre of war or of the German army, except by the publication of a handbook of the army and of annual reports on manœuvres and military changes. Exactly the same, however, was done in the case of the armies of all foreign States. The study of German military organization and methods was specifically forbidden at war games, staff tours, and intelligence classes, which would have provided the best opportunities for such instruction.[1]

The last of the preparations for defence which requires mention here is the formation of the National Reserve, initiated by private enterprise in August 1910 with the approval of the Secretary of State for War and the Army Council. Its object was to register and organize all officers and men who had served in and left any of the military or naval forces of the Crown, with a view to increasing the military strength of the country in the event of imminent national danger. The National Reserve was divided into two classes:[2] one to reinforce existing units of the Regular Army, and the other to fill up vacancies in the Territorial Force, to strengthen garrisons, guard vulnerable points, or perform any other necessary military duties either as specialists or fighting men. By 1914, the National Reserve numbered about 350,000. On mobilization many of the members rejoined military and naval service; the remainder formed eventually the nucleus of the Royal Defence Corps.

As regards the other military Forces of the Empire, in 1907 there was a conference of Dominion Premiers in London, and the opportunity was seized to make the General Staff an Imperial one. Britain offered to train officers of the Overseas Dominions at the Staff Colleges, and to send out staff officers of her own as servants of the Dominion Governments. It was urged that there should be in all the forces of the Empire uniformity of armament

---

[1] Ignorance of the German Army proved a serious handicap in the early part of the campaign. British soldiers imagined that every German wore a spiked helmet, so that *Jäger*, who wore a kind of shako, and cavalrymen in hussar busbies and lancer caps were mistaken for Frenchmen or Belgians; machine-gun crews, carrying their weapons into action with the trestle legs turned back, were thought to be medical bearers with stretchers, and were not fired on.

[2] See "National Reserve Regulations," issued with Special Army Order, March 7, 1913.

and organization. The Dominions cordially welcomed these proposals. The Imperial General Staff was formed and unity of organization was established. The Dominions reserved to themselves the right of deciding whether to participate with their forces in the event of hostilities outside their own territories.

In India, the reorganization of the army on modern lines into nine divisions, six cavalry brigades and a certain number of independent brigades by Lord Kitchener in 1903, was designed to meet the Russian menace and make India independent of assistance from overseas for twelve months. As a consequence of the Anglo-Russian Agreement in 1907, and the state of Indian finances, this reorganization was never completed. The " Army in India Committee " of 1912–13 recommended that the field army should consist of seven divisions, five cavalry brigades and certain army troops, a force sufficient to deal with Afghanistan and the frontier tribes combined, till reinforcements could arrive. This was the authorized Field Army when war broke out in 1914, but even this had not been provided with all its mobilization equipment. No troops were maintained for the specific purpose of war outside the Indian sphere. Not till August 1913 was the Government of India invited to consider the extent to which India would be prepared to co-operate with the Imperial Forces in the event of a serious war between Britain and an European enemy. It was agreed that the Army Council might count upon two—possibly three—divisions and one cavalry brigade. Actually in 1914, as will be seen, two infantry divisions and two cavalry divisions were sent to France, a division to the Persian Gulf, the equivalent of the infantry of two divisions to Egypt, besides minor detachments, and all but eight battalions of British infantry were withdrawn from India, their places being filled by British Territorial troops. But no measures were taken to make India the Eastern military base of the British Empire by the provision of arsenals and the development of the industrial resources of the country for war purposes, except in certain minor items.[1]

The supreme direction of war in England, which originally lay in the sovereign, and was actually exercised

---

[1] Field artillery ammunition and rifles in small quantities, small-arm ammunition, certain vehicles, boots, saddles, harness.

by William III., passed after that monarch's death to the principal Ministers, and has remained with the Cabinet, or a group within the Cabinet, ever since. Up to 1904 no precedent had ever been set for the formation of a Council of War or of any standing advisory body for the Cabinet in naval and military matters in view of an outbreak of war.

In 1895, however, a Defence Committee of the Cabinet was formed which, after some changes in 1902, was finally turned by Mr. (later Lord) Balfour in 1904 into the Committee of Imperial Defence. It was then placed under the direct control of the Prime Minister, and a Secretariat was provided to record its deliberations and decisions, to collect information, to outline plans necessary to meet certain contingencies, and to ensure continuity of policy.

Much good work was done by the Committee in various directions. Full measures were thought out in 1909 for counteracting any hostile system of espionage and sabotage, the Official Secrets Act being amended in 1911 to give the Government greater powers. An amendment of the Army Act in 1909 also gave authority to billet troops in time of emergency. Lastly, the essential steps to be taken immediately upon the outbreak of war were all studied exhaustively, and a distribution of the consequent duties among the various departments, even among individual officials, was arranged in the minutest detail, so that there should be no delay and no confusion. The results of these preparations, and the regulations finally laid down, were embodied in a " War-book," and all essential documents were prepared beforehand, so that they might be signed instantly, the very room in which the signature should take place being fixed and a plan showing its exact position attached to the documents.

Altogether, Britain had never entered upon any war with anything approaching such forwardness and forethought in the preparation of the scanty military resources at the disposal of the War Office. The Committee of Imperial Defence was still, however, only an advisory body possessing no administrative or executive functions.

From 1911 onward the French and British Staffs had worked out in detail a scheme for the landing of the Expeditionary Force in France, and for its concentration in the area Maubeuge — Le Cateau — Hirson, but, though there was an " obligation of honour," there was no definite undertaking to send the whole or any part of this force to any particular point, or, in fact, anywhere at all.[1]

FRANCE

(Sketches 1 & 2; Maps 1 & 2)

For France the problem of defence against her eastern neighbour was a very difficult one. The frontier had no natural protection, both banks of the Rhine and the crest of the Vosges being in German hands, and the population of France was not only smaller than Germany's, but steadily sinking in comparison. She first sought to assist the solution of the problem by creating great fortified regions along her borders, alternating with selected gaps. Thus, from the Swiss frontier to Epinal there were roughly forty miles of fortification ; from Epinal to Toul a space of forty miles—the well-known Trouée de Charmes—was left undefended ; from Toul to Verdun was another forty miles of fortification ; and from Verdun to the Belgian frontier another gap of thirty miles. In second line were the second-class fortresses of Besançon, Dijon, Langres, Rheims, and Laon ; and in rear of them again the entrenched camps of

[1] The first steps in the elaboration of the British scheme were taken in 1906, as a result of a conversation between Major-Gen. (afterwards Lieut.-Gen. Sir James) Grierson, then Director of Military Operations at the War Office, and Colonel Huguet, then military attaché at the French Embassy in London. The studies were pursued by General Grierson and his successors, Major-Gen. (later Lieut.-Gen. Sir) J. Spencer Ewart and Br.-Gen. (later Field-Marshal Sir Henry) Wilson, with the authority of the Prime Ministers, Sir Henry Campbell-Bannerman and Mr Asquith, under the reserve that in no case should they constitute an engagement for the British Government.

Similar arrangements of a non-binding nature had been made between the Italian and German General Staffs for Italy to assist Germany in certain circumstances, by " strengthening the German Western Armies " by the despatch of an Army, and the holding of French forces, if only " small ones, to the Alpine frontier. The Italian fleet should, together " with the Austro-Hungarian, form a counter-weight to the French Medi- " terranean fleet." (G.O.A. i. p. 20.)

An account of the steps which led to the British General Staff being given permission by the Government to enter into relations with the French General Staff will be found in " The Quarterly Review " of April 1932, in an article, entitled " The Entente-Cordiale and the Military Conversations," by Major-Gen. Sir George Aston.

There was no arrangement with Belgium of any kind, her Government having made it clear that they would maintain strict neutrality, opposing with all the Belgian forces France or Germany, if either violated the frontier, or any third Power interested who might land troops in Belgium, or try to use Belgian territory as a base of operations. See the article " The Belgian Conversations of 1912 " by Professor Emile Cammaerts in " The Contemporary Review " of July 1933.

SKETCH 2.

THE CONCENTRATION OF THE ARMIES.

AUGUST 1914

Lyons and Paris. There were no modern fortifications on the Franco-Belgian frontier, but La Fère, Maubeuge, and Lille were defended by old-fashioned detached forts.

The steadily aggressive attitude of Germany justified the uneasiness of France. In 1887 Germany formed a Triple Alliance with Austria and Italy. In 1890 France responded by an Alliance with Russia. In 1891 Germany emphasized her hostile bearing by renewing the Triple Alliance; while in 1899 she rejected the Tsar's proposal for a limitation of armaments. In 1905, 1911, and 1912 she made important additions to her army, raising its strength to twenty-five active corps, as against the fifteen with which she had taken the field in 1870 ; and behind these twenty-five she had nearly an equal number of Reserve corps.[1] On 30th June 1913 the total number of men with the colours in peace was raised from 711,000 to 856,000 ; this not only made the army the readier for an *attaque brusquée*, so much dreaded by the French, but assured a substantial corresponding increase in the effectives of reserve formations.

France could only reply by reimposing the term of three years with the colours, which in 1905 she had reduced to two years. This signified an augmentation of 220,000 men to her peace strength. But, even so, France had at the outbreak of war, roughly speaking, only three millions and a half of trained men, whereas Germany had over five millions ;[2] and, moreover, Germany's reserve formations were more completely organized than those of the French.

The French Army in peace was composed of ten cavalry divisions ; twenty-one army corps, each corps area also furnishing in war a Reserve division[3] and certain Territorial brigades ; and a Colonial Corps.

On mobilization, according to the plan in force in

[1] See page 21.
[2] G.O.A., K.u.K., i. p. 219, puts the French trained strength at 5,067,000, and total available at 5,940,000!
F.O.A., i. (i.) p. 52, gives the theoretical mobilizable strength (with 680,000 reinforcements in the depots) for service in France at 3,580,000. This total does not take into account all of the coloured troops : including these the mobilizable strength realized was 3,683,000 (" Commission de l'Armée," p. 203, by General Pédoya, President of the Senate Commission of the Army during the war).
[3] The Reserve divisions were numbered by adding 50 to the army corps number up to the 71st : thus the I. Corps area provided the 51st Reserve Division. The word " Reserve " was dropped in June 1915, after which date the divisions were known by their numbers only. The XIX. Corps was in Algeria.

1914,[1] these forces formed five Armies, with seven divisions of cavalry, and a cavalry corps of three divisions. The Reserve divisions were grouped into pairs, threes, or fours, and allotted either to Armies or defences, or kept at the disposal of General Headquarters.[2]

Whilst the British and Germans had a clip-loading (5 cartridges) rifle, the French infantry had a magazine rifle with 8 cartridges in the butt; these fired it became a single-loader. On the other hand the French field gun was a true " Q.F.," with a rate of fire almost double that of the British or German; but, again, the French corps and divisions had no howitzers or heavy guns, and only a few groups of heavy guns of small range under Army control. In all a French Active corps had 28 battalions and 120 field guns; a German, 24 battalions, 108 field guns, and 52 howitzers (4·2 or 5·9-inch).

Map 2.   The zones of concentration selected in peace for the
Sketch 2. five Armies were, commencing as usual on the right:

First Army (General Dubail)—Region of Epinal.
Second Army (General de Castelnau)—Region of Nancy.
Third Army (General Ruffey)—Region of Verdun.
Fifth Army (General Lanrezac)—Between Verdun (exclusive) and Mezières, with a detachment east of the Meuse.
Fourth Army (General de Langle de Cary)—In general reserve in region Sainte Ménehould—Commercy.
On either flank was a group of Reserve divisions:
    On the right—a group of four Reserve divisions—Region of Belfort.
    On the left—a group of three Reserve divisions (General Valabrègue)—Vervins.

The French Staff in choosing the areas of concentration were in face of the following facts. At Metz there was an immense German entrenched camp touching the frontier, and connected by four main lines of railway with the heart of Germany. From this a sudden blow—the *attaque brusquée*—could be easily struck with all the force of perfect organization; it was imperative to take measures to parry it. On the other hand, the German school of strategy favoured envelopment from one or both flanks. This in a war with France signified, indeed, violation either

---

[1] Known as Plan XVII.; the text is given in Appendix 9. The earlier plans and the origin of Plan XVII. will be found in F.O.A., i., chapters i. and ii.
[2] For the Order of Battle and organization of the French Armies see Appendices 3 and 4.

of Belgian or of Swiss neutrality, or of both; but Germany was not likely to be squeamish about such matters. Such violation might not go beyond a peaceable passage of troops across a corner of the neutral territory, yet still might suffice for the aggressor's purpose of turning a flank.

To meet menaces so different in kind as direct attack in the centre and envelopment on the flanks, the French General Staff decided to take the offensive and to concentrate facing the Eastern frontier, trusting to fortifications and to covering troops to gain sufficient time to move the mass of the army elsewhere if required. It was intended to attack as soon as possible with all forces united : the First and Second Armies south of Metz, and the Fifth north of it ; the Third Army was to connect these two main attacks and arrange for the investment of Metz as they progressed. The employment of the Fourth Army depended on the action of the enemy ; if the Germans moved into Luxembourg and Belgium, it was to co-operate with the Fifth Army ; if the enemy merely covered the common frontier, it was to go to the support of the right attack. A detachment of the First Army (one corps and one cavalry division) was detailed in the plan to carry out a special operation on the extreme right in Alsace, with the object of holding any enemy forces which might attempt to advance on the western slopes of the Vosges, and of assisting in the removal of that part of the population which had remained faithful to France. It was hoped by the general offensive movement at any rate to dislocate the plans of the enemy, wrest the initiative from him, and, if he were moving through Belgium, strike a mortal blow at his communications.

No provision, it will be noticed, was made to meet an envelopment carried out through Belgium west of the Meuse, or to cover the gap between the western flank of the Fifth Army and the sea, in which there were only local Territorial troops and a few old fortresses incapable of offering serious resistance to any invader. The information at the disposal of the French General Staff appeared to indicate that the Germans would attack from Metz, and had not sufficient troops to extend their front west of the Meuse. Beyond arranging for an alternative concentration of the Fourth and Fifth Armies should the enemy enter Luxembourg and Belgium, there was no preparation against a wide enveloping movement.

On mobilization, General Joffre, *vice-président du Con-*

seil supérieur de la guerre et chef de l'État Major Général, was appointed *Commandant en Chef* of the French Armies, with General Belin as Chief of the Staff. The approximate strength of the Armies (with the Reserve divisions on the flanks included in the totals of the nearest Army) was, in round numbers, after certain exchanges had taken place (viz. the transfer of two corps and two Reserve divisions from Fifth Army to Fourth, of one corps from Second to Fifth, etc.) [1] :—

First Army	.	.	.	. 256,000 men
Second Army	.	.	.	. 200,000 ,,
Third Army	.	.	.	. 168,000 ,,
Fourth Army	.	.	.	. 193,000 ,,
Fifth Army	.	.	.	. 254,000 ,,

1,071,000 men

BELGIUM [2]

In 1914 the Belgian Army consisted of a Field Army organized in six divisions and a cavalry division, and fortress troops which formed the garrisons of Antwerp, Liége and Namur. Antwerp was the great fortress of Belgium, the final refuge and rallying point of her forces and population in case of invasion by a powerful enemy. Its defences originally consisted of a strong enceinte, *i.e.* a continuous inner ring of fortification, and a girdle of forts, some two miles from the town, finished in 1868. Though a second girdle of forts and redoubts outside the first had been gradually added from 1882 onwards, the line was incomplete, there were several gaps and intervals in it, and it was on the average only some eight miles from the town, an altogether insufficient distance under modern conditions. Nor was the construction of the forts, although improvements were in progress, capable of resisting modern heavy artillery; notwithstanding that the guns were protected by armour (cupolas and tourelles), the fact that they were inside the forts, which were conspicuously upstanding, and not in well concealed batteries outside, made them easy

[1] See footnote, page 40.
[2] The details of the operations of the Belgian Army are taken from the official account : " L'Action de l'Armée Belge. Période du 31 juillet au 31 décembre 1914," which has since been translated as " Military " Operations of Belgium. Report compiled by the Belgian General Staff " for the period July 31st to December 31st, 1914 " (London, Collingridge, 1s. net). For the Order of Battle see Appendix 5.

targets. The same remarks as regards construction apply to the defences of Liége and Namur ; these fortresses were " barrier forts and bridgeheads " on the Meuse ; they constituted the first line of Belgium's resistance, and were designed to guard the approaches into Belgium from the east and south-east, and hinder any force from crossing the Meuse either from France into Germany or Germany into France. They were never intended to be defended *à outrance* and depended on field troops for the defence of the intervals between the forts. At Huy on the Meuse between Namur and Liége there was an ancient fort, which at best might secure sufficient time for the destruction of the railway bridges and tunnel situated there.

The reorganization of the Belgian Army authorized by the Government in 1912, had barely begun to take effect. In accordance with this a force of 350,000 men was to be formed: 150,000 for the Field Army, 130,000 for the fortress garrisons, and 70,000 for reserve and auxiliary troops. But these numbers would not in the ordinary course have been available until 1926. Actually in August 1914 only 117,000 could be mobilized for the Field Army, and a smaller proportion for the other categories.

The six divisions were stationed in peace so that at short notice they could quickly confront any enemy, were he Germany, France, Great Britain or Holland: 1st Division around Ghent ; 2nd Division, Antwerp ; 3rd Division around Liége ; 4th Division, Namur and Charleroi ; 5th Division around Mons ; 6th Division, Brussels ; and Cavalry Division, Brussels. Thus the 1st Division faced England ; the 3rd, Germany ; the 4th and 5th, France ; and they were intended to act as general advanced guards as occasion arose and gain time for the movements of the other divisions to the threatened area.

On the ordinary peace footing only part of the recruit contingent was with the colours, so that in case of danger of war, the Belgian Army had first to recall men on unlimited leave, in order to raise its forces to " reinforced peace establishment," the ordinary strength of the units of the Continental Powers, and then to complete the numbers by mobilizing reservists. Thus not only was Belgium normally less ready than most nations, but she was in the throes of reorganization, and could not put into the field even as many men as the British Regular Army.

GERMANY [1]

From 1815 to 1860, the Prussian Army had practically remained stationary in numbers, with a peace strength of 150,000 men formed in eight Army Corps, maintained by a yearly contingent of 40,000 recruits, who served three years with the colours. One of the first acts of Wilhelm I. on coming to the throne in January 1860 was, in opposition to the wishes of his Legislature, to raise the annual contingent to 63,000, and the peace strength to 215,000. From thence onwards there was a steady increase of the Prussian military forces.

The war of 1866 made Prussia head of the North German Confederation, whilst Hesse-Darmstadt, Württemberg, Bavaria and Baden were bound to place their armies at the disposal of Prussia in time of war. In 1870, in addition to her original eight corps, she was able after arrangements with the other States to put into the field *the Guard, IX., X. (Hanoverian), XI.,* and *XII. (Saxon),* and *I. and II. Bavarian Corps,* and eventually the *XIII. (Württemberg)* and *XIV. (Baden),* with a war-strength of roughly 950,000.

The formation of the German Empire in 1871 made expansion still easier, for by the Constitution one per cent of the population could be in training under arms. The subsequent peace strengths were [2]:—

	Divisions.	Cavalry Brigades.	Officers.	N.C.O's.	Other Ranks.	One Year Volunteers.
1875 .	37	38	17,213	53,956	347,703	7,000
1882 .	37	38	18,134	57,694	369,580	9,000
1888 .	39	39	19,294	61,867	406,542	10,000
1890 .	43	45	20,285	65,001	421,982	8,000
1893 .	43	46	22,458	77,864	479,229	9,000
1898 .	43	46	23,176	78,237	479,229	9,000
1902 .	48	46	24,292	80,985	495,500	11,000
1910 .	48	46	25,722	87,071	504,446	13,145
1911 .	48	46	25,880	88,292	507,253	14,000
1912 .	50	51	27,267	92,347	531,004	14,350
1914, Aug.	50	55	30,459	107,794	647,793	16,000
(Sanctioned)	50	55	32,000	110,000	661,500	—

[1] For the Order of Battle and organization of the German Forces see Appendices 6 and 7.

[2] G.O.A., K.u.K., i. and tables in the Appendix volume.

The largest increase, it will be noticed, came after 1912. A project was put forward at the end of that year by the Chief of the General Staff, who stated, in view of the Balkan War, which had just broken out, that " the Army was not strong enough for the duties required of it "—which were to carry out the Schlieffen plan of campaign. The increase was

The approximate mobilizable strength was :—

Trained officers and men . . .	4,300,000	(5,020,700)[1]
Partially trained	100,000	—
Untrained	5,500,000	(5,474,000)
	9,900,000	(10,494,700)

The Army was organized into 25 Active army corps Plate 1.
(50 divisions)—the *Guard, I.* to *XXI.*, and *I., II., III.
Bavarian* ; and in each army corps district cadres were
provided to form certain Reserve divisions (32), *Ersatz*
divisions (7), *Landwehr* brigades and regiments (equivalent
to 16 divisions), from the supernumeraries in the depots.
There were also 11 cavalry divisions.

The plan on which this great force would be used on
the Eastern and Western fronts could only be surmised.
It will, so far as it is known, be given later [2] after the
opening moves of the campaign have been developed and
described.

Service in the German Army was divided into :—
service in the Active (or Standing) Army (two years,
but three in the cavalry and horse artillery) ; service
in the Reserve (five years, but four in the cavalry and
horse artillery) ; service in the *Landwehr* (eleven years).
The *Landsturm* included youths between 17 and 20, too
young for service in the Army, and trained and untrained
men between 39 and 45, who were thus over the ordinary
military age.

The original *Reserve corps* which took part in the August
offensive were formed mainly of Reserve men supernumerary to the requirements of the Active Army, with
some *Landwehr* ; but the *Guard Reserve Corps* contained
an Active division, and others, *e.g.* the *V., VI., VII.* and
IX., each contained an Active brigade, as the Active corps
of these numbers had each in peace time an extra brigade ;
others had similarly an Active regiment. Soon after
declaration of war, additional Reserve divisions and corps
were built up of volunteers (mainly youths under full
military age and men not yet called up, etc.), with a sub-

sanctioned by the *Reichstag* in June 1913. In the spring of 1914 a decision
was made to introduce complete universal service, no one escaping it, in
1916. This would probably have doubled the strength of the German
Army.
[1] The figures in brackets are from G.O.A., K.u.K., i. p. 219 ; the original
ones were calculated before the war by the British Intelligence Branch.
[2] See page 56.

stantial nucleus of about 25 per cent of trained men of the older classes.[1]

The *Ersatz* brigades and divisions of 1914 were not formed from untrained men of the *Ersatz Reserve*,[2] but from trained men supernumerary to the numbers required for the Active and Reserve formations. They were organized like the Reserve formations but had not the full establishment of machine guns, cavalry, or artillery, and were entirely without field kitchens, medical units, train and ammunition columns. They were therefore not equivalent to other brigades and divisions in open warfare.

The *Landwehr* units were formed of men who had completed seven years with the Active Army and Reserve, and were under 39 years of age.

As the war went on, the significance of the various classifications largely disappeared, and Active, Reserve, *Ersatz* and *Landwehr* divisions contained men of all categories.

The French were at the outbreak of war dressed in their peace-time old-fashioned uniforms — the infantry in blue, with red trousers, and képi ; the officers conspicuous by reason of their shorter coats ; " horizon-blue " was not introduced until 1915. The Belgian infantry wore dark blue, with blue-grey trousers, adopting khaki in 1915. The Germans wore " field-grey," with a cover of that colour on the spiked helmet or other cavalry or *Jäger* head-dress. The British were of course in khaki, and wore the flat peaked cap.

[1] " Ypres 1914," p. 5.
[2] This consisted of men temporarily unfit, or fit and liable for military service but not called up for training either because they were supernumerary to the annual contingent, or for family reasons, or on account of minor physical defects.

CHAPTER I

THE OUTBREAK OF WAR

(Sketches 1, 2, 3, 4 & 5 ; Maps 1, 2 & 5)

THE record of the negotiations and of the diplomatic correspondence and conversations which took place after the
assassination of the Archduke Franz Ferdinand of Austria
and his Consort at Serajevo on the 28th June 1914 until
the outbreak of war is available in an official publication.[1]
In this work the efforts of the British Government to bring
about mediation and their determination to take no step that
would contribute to precipitate war are made abundantly
clear. It is therefore unnecessary here to allude to diplomatic proceedings, except to show how military preparations
were affected by them.

On the 27th July, the British Government judged the
situation to be sufficiently serious to warrant them in
countermanding the dispersal, then in progress, of the
Home Fleets at the end of the exercises at sea which had
followed a test mobilization. At 5 P.M. on the 28th, on
which day Austria-Hungary declared war on Serbia, the
First Fleet was ordered to proceed to its preliminary war
station in the North ; [2] on the 29th, at 2 P.M., the
Government further ordered the precautionary measures

[1] " British Documents on the Origin of the War," xi., edited by G. P.
Gooch and Harold Temperley (H.M. Stationery Office). As narratives
and as commentaries on these documents should be read : " The History
" of Twelve Days, July 24th to August 4th 1914. Being an Account of the
" Negotiations Preceding the Outbreak of War, based on Official Pub-
" lications," by J. W. Headlam (T. Fisher Unwin), and " The Outbreak
" of the War 1914–1918 : A Narrative based mainly on British Official
" Documents," by Professor Sir Charles Oman (H.M. Stationery Office).
[2] The naval precautions taken will be found fully described in " The
History of the War : Naval Operations," i., by Sir Julian Corbett.
   According to the protocol in Document No. 10855 of the official diplomatic papers of the Austro-Hungarian Ministry of Foreign Affairs, published in eight volumes under the title of " Österreich-Ungarns Aussen-
politik vor der Bosnischen Krise 1908 bis zum Kriegsausbruch 1914,"

arranged by the General Staff to meet an immediate prospect of war, to be put in force. These affected the Regular troops only, and included the recall of officers and men on leave and furlough, and the manning of all coast defences.

The Belgian Government decided to place their Army upon its " reinforced peace footing." [1]

On the same day, the 29th, the British Ambassador at Berlin was asked by the German Chancellor to give assurance of England's neutrality if Russia should attack Austria and an European conflagration were to ensue. To this significant enquiry Sir Edward Grey, the Minister for Foreign Affairs, responded on the 30th by a refusal to entertain the proposal. Russia on this day issued orders for the mobilization of her four Southern Armies; and Germany threatened that she would begin mobilization unless Russia ceased hers. News was also received of the Austrian bombardment of Belgrade. In order to avoid the possibility of a frontier incident the French Government ordered that no individual, no patrol, should under any pretext pass a line between Hussigny (on the Luxembourg frontier, east of Longwy) and Delle (on the Swiss frontier, south-east of Belfort), described by a precise enumeration of localities. This line was on an average 10 kilometres inside the frontier.[2]

---

on the 27th July Count Berchtold, the Foreign Minister, told Kaiser Franz Joseph, in order to induce him to sign the declaration of war against Serbia, that, " according to a report from the *IV. Corps*, Serbian troops " have fired from Danube steamers on the troops near Temesvar, and, on " this being replied to, a general action developed. Hostilities are there- " fore actually opened."

In the draft of the declaration of war this incident was given as one of the principal causes of its despatch. Count Berchtold, having obtained the Kaiser's signature, struck out the paragraph, reporting to him on the 29th (Document No. 11015) that he had done so, as "the reports of the " fighting near Temes Kirbin have not been confirmed. On the contrary, " only an isolated report of trifling firing near Gradiste [equally false]." Herr Emil Ludwig in " July 1914 " asserts, with regard to the outbreak of war, that in Germany, " of the 23 documents susceptible of falsification, " the Government falsified 18," but " the worst liar was Count Berchtold."

[1] See page 19.

[2] F.O.A. i. (i.) p. 76. This particular order was repeated on 31st July with the addition :—

" This prohibition applies to the cavalry as well as to the other arms. " No patrol, no reconnoitring party, no post, no individual, must be east " of the said line. Anyone who crosses it will be liable to court-martial. " It is only permitted to transgress this order in case of a very definite " attack." (*Idem*, p. 81.) The restriction was withdrawn at 2 P.M. on the 2nd August on account of German violation of the French frontier. (*Idem*, p. 85.)

At 1 P.M. on the 30th July the " Berlin Lokalanzeiger " issued a special number (*Extrablatt*), announcing that mobilization had been ordered. The statement was soon contradicted, but it had been telegraphed to Petrograd and at 6 P.M., before contradiction arrived, Russia ordered general mobilization.[1] On the 31st Austria followed suit, and decreed the full mobilization of her forces, whereupon Germany made a formal proclamation of " Imminent Danger of War " (*drohende Kriegsgefahr*), which enabled measures similar to those of the British " Precautionary Period " to be taken.[2] At the same time Germany presented an ultimatum to Russia to the effect that, unless she ceased mobilization within twelve hours, Germany herself would mobilize upon both frontiers. Significantly, Turkey also ordered mobilization on the 31st July.[3] Sir Edward Grey, on the same day, sent an identic request to Germany and France enquiring whether they would respect Belgian neutrality. France immediately answered with an unequivocal affirmative; Germany, however, sent only an evasive reply ; and on the 1st August both France and Germany ordered general mobilization.

The beginning of mobilization in France raised a serious

[1] See Renouvin, " Les origines immédiates de la Guerre," p. 146 ; General Danilov (Quartermaster General of the Russian Army), " Russland in Weltkrieg 1914–15," pp. 25-6 ; General Suchomlinov (War Minister), " Erinnerungen," pp. 365-7.

[2] On the proclamation of *drohende Kriegsgefahr*, the following precautionary measures had to be taken in all Army Corps districts :—
Protection of important railway structures :—bridges, tunnels, etc.
Recall from leave of all members of the Active army.
Recall of troops, if away, to their garrisons.
Control of railway and other traffic.
Execution of the measures laid down for protection of the frontier.
Move of garrisons of active troops and fighting equipment to the islands of the North Sea coast.
In addition, in the frontier districts :—
Guard of railway lines ; defence of large bridges and important railway junctions, air-ship sheds and establishments important to aircraft and radio-telegraphy against attempts at demolition, including attacks by aircraft ; removal of sick into the interior of the country.
" If a hostile attack is made before definite mobilization, or it is evident " that such an attack is imminent, the Army Corps commanders must take " all necessary measures to remove inland from the threatened districts and " protect all men liable to service, and all men found fit for military service, " as well as all serviceable horses. They must also, as far as possible, " remove all material resources from reach of the enemy, particularly " depots of supplies, the monies of the State, petrol. In case of necessity " measures must be taken to destroy them." (Kindly furnished by the *Reichsarchiv*.)

[3] The " 1st day of mobilization " was the 3rd August. The secret treaty of alliance between Turkey and Germany was signed at Berlin on the 2nd August.

1 Aug. question for Great Britain. There was, it is true, no
1914. definite agreement or understanding that she should send
assistance to France, and the British Government was free
to decide, untrammelled, for peace or war. But a scheme
had been elaborated, in the event of certain contingencies,
between the General Staffs of the two countries ; and an
essential point in this scheme was that the first movement
of the British advanced parties, stores and so forth, should
begin on the first day of mobilization. Assuming this coincidence of movement and mobilization, it was reckoned
that six divisions—or four, if six could not be spared—
one cavalry division and one cavalry brigade could be
transported from Great Britain to concentration areas
between Avesnes and Le Cateau, and would be ready to
advance thence on the fifteenth day after the order for
mobilization had been issued.

That the British mobilization, if it should take place at
all, would be later than the French was now obvious. The
British General Staff therefore suggested that measures
might be taken to ensure that, if mobilization should come
after all, movement to France of the advanced parties,
which could be warned at once, should be simultaneous
with the issue of the order for it. Another important
measure was the guarding of the lines of railway to the
ports of embarkation. This duty had been assigned to
certain units of the Territorial Force ; but these were
about to proceed to camp for their annual training ; and,
unless the orders for that training were cancelled, there
might be delay in the despatch of the Expeditionary Force.
The Government considered, however, that the countermanding of the orders for Territorial training would be
construed as not less menacing than the order for mobilization itself ; and they shrank from any measure which might
seem to extinguish the last hope of peace.

At 12 noon on the 1st August, the German ultimatum
to Russia expired, and a general conflagration became
inevitable.[1] The Cabinet at 2 P.M. on the 2nd cancelled
the orders for Territorial training and at 6 P.M. those

[1] The German declaration of war was delivered by the Ambassador at
Petrograd, Count Pourtalès, at 7 P.M on the 1st August ; he at the same
time demanded his passports (Kautsky's " Die deutsche Dokumente zum
Kriegsausbruch," iii. pp. 50 and 83, which is confirmed by the Russian
Orange Book). The Russian Foreign Minister, M. Sazonov, said to him,
" You could have prevented war by a word ; you would not do so. In
" all my efforts to preserve peace, I received not the slightest help from
" you."

for the Army manœuvres, but still issued no orders for mobilization.[1] The Navy was quite ready for active service, and the French Ambassador was given the assurance that " if the German fleet comes into the Channel or through " the North Sea to undertake hostile operations against the " French coasts or shipping, the British Fleet will give all " the protection in its power." Beyond this conditional promise of naval intervention the Cabinet would not go without consulting Parliament. Parliament was consulted on the following day, the 3rd August ; but in the meanwhile a most momentous event had occurred.

2 Aug. 1914.

Faithful to the obligations imposed upon her by treaty, Belgium on the 1st August had ordered her forces to be mobilized, and was preparing to resist violation of her territory from any quarter whatsoever ; but at seven o'clock in the evening of the 2nd the German Minister at Brussels presented a Note to the Belgian Government, requesting a reply within twelve hours. This Note had been drawn up by the Great General Staff as early as 26th July, and despatched under seal to the German Minister at Brussels on the 29th, with orders that it was not to be opened pending further instructions. It set forth that the German Government had certain intelligence of the intention of the French forces to march on the Meuse by Givet and Namur, and, in view of this attack, requested free and unresisted ingress for the German troops into Belgian territory. The Belgian Government replied that they would repel any attempt either of France or Germany upon Belgium ; and they also declined the help of France against any German encroachment until they should have made formal appeal to the Powers, Prussia among them, which had guaranteed Belgian neutrality.

Sketch 1. Map 2.

Other important events on the 2nd August were that German troops crossed the Polish frontier, broke also into France at four different points,[2] and entered the territory of Luxembourg.[3]

[1] At 10 A.M. on the 2nd the leaders of the Unionist party despatched by special messenger to the Prime Minister a letter assuring the Government " of the united support of the Opposition in all measures required by " England's intervention in the war."

[2] They are enumerated in F.O.A. i. (i.), p. 83, which adds that " at " Petit Croix German cyclists fired on French custom house officers."
According to the *Reichsarchiv* : " There were transgressions of the " frontier by small detachments, contrary to the will of the High Command."

[3] By the treaty of 1867 Prussia guaranteed the perpetual neutrality of Luxembourg ; by the Convention of 1902 Germany re-insured the neutrality and contracted that the railways in the Grand Duchy which she exploited should not be used for the transport of her troops.

Sir Edward Grey had no accurate information as to the exact nature of the German ultimatum to Belgium when he met the House of Commons on the 3rd August. He was aware, however, of the crude fact that an ultimatum had been tendered, and, whilst coming down to the House, he had been informed that King Albert had telegraphed to King George invoking England's diplomatic intervention to safeguard the integrity of Belgium. He presented, in due order, the course of action he had pursued and the motives dictating it. The House of Commons, as it followed him, applauded his decision not to commit the country to armed intervention on account of the Serbian quarrel, but approved the conditional promise of the Fleet's aid to France, and grew enthusiastic when it heard that England would be true to her engagements to uphold the integrity of Belgium.

No resolution followed upon the speech of the Secretary of State for Foreign Affairs. After the adjournment which followed it, towards 7 P.M., he was able to read to the House full information, received from the Belgian Legation, of the German Note that had been presented in Brussels. It left no doubt that a German attack was about to take place, if indeed it had not already begun.

The immediate measures taken were to announce that a moratorium would be proclaimed and that the Government would undertake the responsibility of maritime insurance. The Territorial Force was embodied and the Naval Reserves were called out. It was now clear that our mobilization must take place at least three days later than the French, and that, even so, movement could not be simultaneous with it. The Government, however, reckoned that by this delay they had gained more than they had lost by securing the unanimity, or approximate unanimity, of the nation and the benevolence of neutrals.

On the 3rd August, at 6.45 P.M., Germany declared war on France, making alleged violation of her frontier by patrols and of her territory by aviators a pretext.[1] Italy,

---

[1] These allegations have since been admitted to have been false. See M. Poincaré's " The Origins of the War," pp. 3 and 4.
    G.O.A., i., p. 104 f.n. 2 and p. 105 f.n. 1, revives the charges, although Freiherr von Schoen, German Ambassador in Paris in 1914, in his book translated as " The Memoirs of an Ambassador," p. 201, has declared the alleged air attacks to be " merely the product of highly overwrought im-" agination." He adds : " How such false reports could have been given " the weight of facts in our responsible quarters, and of such momentous " facts, is inconceivable."

though a member of the Triple Alliance, declared that she
would maintain her neutrality in the impending struggle.
Meanwhile Germany, unhampered by moral considerations, completed her arrangements for the invasion of
Belgium. On the morning of the 4th August, she declared
war on Belgium, and two of her cavalry divisions passed the
frontier : in the afternoon the heads of infantry columns
also entered Belgium.

Early in that same afternoon of the 4th August Sir
Edward Grey telegraphed to the British Ambassador at
Berlin instructing him to ask for his passports if no satisfactory answer were given regarding the observance of
Belgium's neutrality by 12 midnight (11 P.M. Greenwich
mean time). At 4 P.M. the British Government gave
orders for the mobilization of the Army. At 12.15 A.M.
on the morning of the 5th August, the Foreign Office issued
the following statement :

Owing to the summary rejection by the German Government of the request made by His Majesty's Government for
assurances that the neutrality of Belgium will be respected,
His Majesty's Ambassador at Berlin has received his passports
and His Majesty's Government have declared to the German
Government that a state of war exists between Great Britain
and Germany as from 11 P.M. on the 4th August.

On the 5th and 6th August, two meetings, attended
by the principal Ministers, including Lord Kitchener, who
was at home on leave from Egypt and became Secretary
of State for War on the 6th, and by the leading members
of the Staffs of the Navy and Army of Britain, were
assembled to consider the conduct of the war. The exact
state of affairs at the moment was that Great Britain,
France and Russia were at war with Germany ; that
Belgium had been wantonly attacked but was making a
better defence than had been expected ; that Austria was
at war with Serbia only ; and that Italy was neutral. The
main military questions to be decided were the employment
and disposition of the Expeditionary Force, questions
which were complicated by the delay in mobilization. It
was determined first that the Force, less the 4th and 6th
Divisions, should embark for the continent. In order to
reduce the chance of a German landing in force interfering
with this move, the Secretary of State decided that the 18th
Brigade of the 6th Division, then at Lichfield, should move
to Edinburgh, and two brigades of the 4th Division should

proceed to Cromer and York, in each case accompanied by some artillery. The 11th Brigade of the 4th Division was already at Colchester. Five cyclist battalions and eventually the Yeomanry Mounted Division were also sent to the East coast. The rest of the 6th Division was to remain in Ireland.

Then came the final decision as to the destination of the Expeditionary Force. In view of the attack on Belgium, had the British contingent been of a size adequate for independent operations of a substantial character, there would have been much to be said in favour of making Antwerp the base of its military operations; but as it was so small, and as Antwerp, owing to part of the Schelde being Dutch territorial waters, would have to be reached overland after disembarkation at Ostend and other ports, and as operations in the north might involve separation from the French, the suggestion was not followed. There remained the area already considered with the French, namely, that around Le Cateau and Avesnes. Certain military opinion, however, was against a concentration of the British forces in any area in advance of Amiens. Finally, after discussion as to the expansion of the army, it was agreed to leave the decision with our Allies, the French;[1] and the council broke up after passing three resolutions, namely—*First*, to embark ultimately five (1st, 2nd, 3rd, 4th and 5th), but for the present only four (1st, 2nd, 3rd and 5th) of the divisions and the Cavalry Division (plus the extra brigade) of the Expeditionary Force, to commence on the 9th; *Secondly*, to bring home the Imperial troops from South Africa; *Thirdly*, to transport two Indian divisions to Egypt, but no further, and to urge the Government of India to send a division to capture Dar es Salaam in German East Africa.

Through the efforts of Colonel Huguet, who as intermediary travelled backwards and forwards between Paris and London, it was settled that the Expeditionary Force should proceed to the zone selected in peace time by the

[1] According to Maréchal Joffre's official report to a Parliamentary Commission d'Enquête : " The directions for concentration did not " mention the place eventually reserved for the British Army. . . . Our " military arrangements with England had in fact a character which was " both secret and contingent (*éventuel*), and made it improper to mention " them in such a document. . . . In the event of its arrival, its employment " was looked for at the place which should be logically reserved for it, on the " left of the line of the French Armies, which it would thus prolong." " La préparation de la guerre et la conduite des opérations," par Le Maréchal Joffre, p. 21.

French Staff, with some slight modification, but according 4 Aug.
1914. to the British time table. General Joffre's request, that at least one British division should be sent over as rapidly as possible to take its place in the line, Lord Kitchener refused on the grounds that any alteration of the plan of transport would cause confusion and, in the end, delay.

To Field-Marshal Sir John French, who had been selected to command the Expeditionary Force, special instructions as to his co-operation with the French were issued by the Secretary of State for War.[1]

Lieut.-General Sir Douglas Haig was appointed to command the I. Corps ; Lieut.-General Sir James Grierson, the II. Corps ; Lieut.-General W. P. Pulteney, the III. Corps ; and Major-General E. H. H. Allenby, the Cavalry Division. The six divisions were to be commanded by Major-Generals S. H. Lomax, C. C. Monro, H. I. W. Hamilton, T. D'O. Snow, Sir C. Fergusson and J. L. Keir.

PROGRESS OF EVENTS

At 4 P.M. on the 4th August, as already stated, the order for mobilization of the Expeditionary and Territorial Forces was issued by the British Government, the 5th August being declared " the first day of mobilization." As a matter of fact, mobilization occurred at an extremely awkward moment, for the 3rd August had been Bank Holiday and, as usually is the case in the middle of summer, Territorial units were in the act of moving to various camps for their annual training when the orders cancelling it arrived. Hence arose the question whether the existing time-tables for concentration should stand, or whether the movements by railway should be postponed. The Cabinet decided for a short postponement, and gave orders, as already mentioned, that the embarkation of the Expeditionary Force should not begin until the 9th, although " the advanced parties " were to proceed on the 7th. Meantime the mobilization of the various units proceeded with the smoothness which had been anticipated. In all essentials everything went " according to plan " ; and even the task of collecting 120,000 horses was accomplished within twelve days. Embarkation was conducted upon the principle that every train-load should be a complete unit or subdivision of a unit, so that upon arrival in France after its passage, it should be self-contained and in possession

<hr>

[1] Appendix 8.

of enough transport to go straight into a rest-camp or into another train. The ports of embarkation were as follows :

Southampton—all troops in Great Britain; Avonmouth—motor transport and petrol; Newhaven—stores and supplies; Liverpool—frozen meat and motor transport; Glasgow—a few details ; and Dublin, Cork and Belfast for the 5th and 6th Divisions.

The ships were also divided into classes : (1) personnel ships ; (2) horse and vehicle ships ; (3) motor transport ships ; (4) store ships.

Sketch 1. The ports of disembarkation in France were : Havre,
Map 2.   Rouen and Boulogne.

In the five days of greatest activity 1,800 special trains were run in Great Britain and Ireland ; on the busiest day of all, eighty trains, containing the equivalent of a division, were run into Southampton Docks ; the daily average of ships despatched was thirteen, with an average daily tonnage of about 52,000 tons gross. At first the transports were despatched singly as they were ready, both by day and by night ; for, as yet, there was no menace by German submarines, and the measures taken by the Navy gave absolute security.[1] Everything went regularly and smoothly, and the official programme was carried out to the letter ; but there was little margin to spare.

To his embarking troops, H.M. the King sent the following message :—

" You are leaving home to fight for the safety and honour " of my Empire.

" Belgium, whose country we are pledged to defend, " has been attacked, and France is about to be invaded by " the same powerful foe.

" I have implicit confidence in you, my soldiers. Duty " is your watchword, and I know your duty will be nobly " done.

" I shall follow your every movement with deepest " interest and mark with eager satisfaction your daily " progress ; indeed, your welfare will never be absent from " my thoughts.

" I pray God will bless you and guard you, and bring " you back victorious."

Meanwhile the situation in Belgium [2] and on the French

[1] See " Naval Operations," i. p. 72 *et seq.*
[2] The Belgian Official Account has been published serially in the " Bulletin Belge des Sciences Militaires," but no doubt will shortly be available in book form.

frontier was developing rapidly. When during the night 4-5 Aug. of the 3rd/4th August, it became clear that the Germans 1914. intended to advance through Belgium, with or without permission, the Belgian Staff at once took the measures necessary for the defence of their country's neutrality against Germany. The 3rd Division, supported by the Map 1. fortifications of Liége, was to check the German advance ; and, under cover of the 3rd Division, the 1st, 2nd, 5th and 6th Divisions were to move to the line of the river Gette, the Cavalry Division and detachments from Liége and Namur screening the movement. This position covered a considerable part of Belgium, Brussels and the communications with Antwerp. The concentration began on the 4th August, and by the morning of the 6th the Belgian Army was in position two marches west of Liége, in the area Tirlemont (1st Division), Perwez (5th Division), Louvain (2nd Division) and Wavre (6th Division).

On the morning of the 4th, when German cavalry crossed the Belgian frontier and moved upon Visé, north of Liége, it found the bridge over the Meuse broken, and the western bank held by Belgian troops. Two regiments were then pushed northward to Lixhe (3 miles north of Visé), where they crossed the river by a ford. The Belgians, finding their left threatened, thereupon fell back on Liége. By evening the heads of six small German columns of all arms which had crossed the frontier were nearly two miles into Belgium. Further concentrations were also reported to the south ; and it became evident that a very large army threatened invasion along the lines of advance guarded by the fortress of Liége and by the 3rd Division.

Liége [1]

On the 5th August, the Germans, having bridged the Meuse at Lixhe, pushed forward patrols to Tongres (about ten miles N.N.W. of Liége), and the commander-in-chief of the invading troops, General von Emmich (*X. Corps*), demanded free passage through Liége. This being at once refused, he attempted to seize the place by a *coup de main*. His troops consisted of six infantry brigades (at frontier peace strength) provided by the *III., IV., VII., IX., X.* and *XI. Corps*, each with a squadron of cavalry, a battery of artillery, a battalion of *Jäger* (Rifles), and cyclists attached to it.

---

[1] See " La Bataille de Liége " (Belgian Official Account) and " Lüttich-Namur."

Two of the six batteries had field guns, and the other four, field howitzers. Besides this force, General von Emmich had at his disposal two heavy mortar batteries and General von der Marwitz's cavalry corps, comprising the *2nd, 4th* and *9th Cavalry Divisions*.

After an unsuccessful attempt had been made to kidnap the commandant of Liége, General von Emmich gave orders for a night attack. His general plan was to make a demonstration against the forts with a few companies, and to send the six brigades through the intervals between the forts to secure the town and citadel, and then to fall upon the forts from the rear. This attack was delivered soon after nightfall in five columns; one from the north; one from the north-east (two brigades which took different routes); one, the central column, from the east; and two from the south. The first two columns, for the most part, lost their way, and fell back after suffering heavy losses, though one battalion penetrated into Liége and was there captured. Of the two southern columns, one halted, having casualties so severe as to forbid further progress, and the other was seized with panic, the men firing upon each other. The central column met with serious resistance, the brigadier and the commander of the leading regiment being killed. It was on the point of falling back when Major-General Ludendorff, who, as Deputy Chief of the General Staff of the *Second Army*, was with General von Emmich watching the operations, came up and, taking command, pushed on. He was specially interested, for he had planned these very operations in peace when Chief of the Operations Section of the Great General Staff. After giving his men a rest, he renewed the attack in the forenoon of the 6th, and advanced until his leading troops were within a mile of Liége. Though unsupported by the other columns, he decided to make a dash for the citadel, and on advancing found practically no opposition. The Belgian Staff, anticipating that the 3rd Division might be surrounded, had withdrawn it to the Gette; so the Germans found themselves in possession of the town of Liége.

The true siege of the fortress then began. Marwitz's cavalry corps worked round to the western side of the defences, and the German artillery shelled the forts. On the 12th, 42-cm. howitzers were brought up, and the last of the forts fell at 8.30 A.M. on the 16th. General Leman, the commandant, was taken unconscious from under a heap of wreckage and made prisoner. Liége was lost, but by

SKETCH 3.

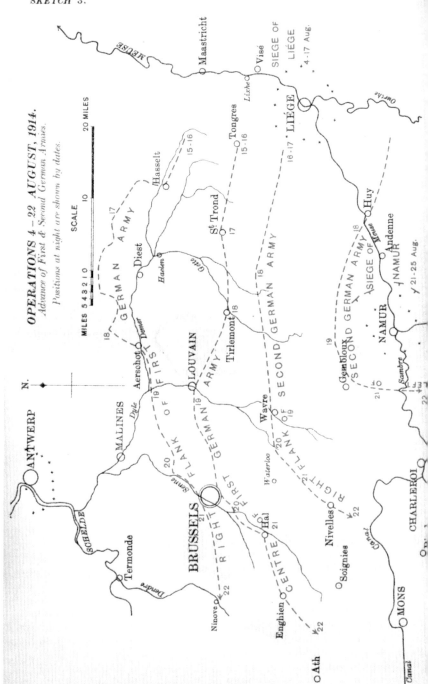

OPERATIONS 4–22 AUGUST, 1914.
Advance of First & Second German Armies.
Positions at night are shown by dates.

SCALE

MILES 5 4 3 2 1 0   10   20 MILES

LIÉGE   35

delaying the German advance it had rendered transcendent 10-20Aug.
service to the cause of Belgium's Allies.[1]   1914.

Whilst the siege was in progress, on the 10th, German Sketches
cavalry and *Jäger*[2] appeared before the line of the Gette, 1 & 3.
and gradually extended their front northwards as far as Maps 1, 2
Hasselt (18 miles north-east of Tirlemont) and Diest & 5.
(12 miles north of Tirlemont). On the 12th six German
cavalry regiments, with three horse-batteries and two
Jäger battalions attacked the line of the Gette at Haelen, a
little to the south-east of Diest, and made some progress,
but were ultimately driven back by the Belgians, with
appreciable loss, after ten hours of sharp fighting.

German troops, however, continued to pour into Belgium, and by the 17th the space between the Meuse, the
Demer and the Gette was occupied by them in strength,
in spite of the fact that the Belgian Army, assisted by the
Garde Civique, had systematically obstructed the roads
and destroyed the bridges. The right flank of the line of
the Gette was already threatened, and columns to support
the turning movement were passing the Meuse at Huy,
where the bridge, blown up by the Belgians, had been repaired. On the 18th, the Germans again attacked and
carried Haelen, and also entered Tirlemont. They then
fell upon the front and left flank of the Belgian 1st Division,
and only by hard fighting were held at bay. The Gette
position was now evidently in imminent danger. It was
certain that the German *II.*, *IV.* and *IX. Corps*, covered

[1] The time gained to the Allies would appear to have been about four or
five days. According to Kluck (pp. 10-19), his three leading corps were
on the line Kermpt—Stevort—Gorssum, forty miles (say three marches)
west of Aix la Chapelle, on the night of the 17th. They had begun to
arrive in the concentration area north-east of Aix on the 7th. Had
Liége offered no opposition and had they at once marched off into Belgium,
there seems no reason why the *II.*, *III.* and *IV. Corps* should not have
reached the above line on the 10th, and completed concentration there
on the 12th or 13th—four or five days earlier than was the case. The
six composite brigades and cavalry corps which attacked Liége were
available to cover the concentration. Even on the 10th August the German
Supreme Command hoped to commence the advance on the 13th, five
days earlier than was possible (Bülow, pp. 11, 12). According to post-war
German publications however, *e.g.* " Graf Schlieffen und der Weltkrieg "
by Foerster, the German time-table made the armies reach the line Thionville—Sédan—Mons, on the 22nd day of mobilization (23rd August), and Sketch
they were actually slightly ahead of it ; but this is accounted for by the
hasty retreat of the French Armies after the first contact. Belgian opinion
is that at least four days were gained (" Bulletin Belge des Sciences Militaires," Sept. 1921). See also Note II. at end of Chapter.
[2] It must be borne in mind that a German cavalry division was a
mixed force of all arms, with two or more *Jäger* (Rifle) battalions included.
(See Plate 1.)

36   THE OUTBREAK OF WAR

by the *2nd* and *4th Cavalry Divisions* were opposite the
Belgian left between Diest and Tirlemont ; whilst the
Guard, X. and *VII. Corps* were marching against the
Belgian right on a front from Jodoigne (7 miles S.S.W.
of Tirlemont) to Namur. It was also known that the
Active corps were being followed by Reserve formations,
namely, in the *First Army* by the *III., IV.* and *IX.
Reserve Corps* ; in the *Second Army* by the *Guard, VII.*
and *X. Reserve Corps* ; and in the *Third Army* by the
XII. Reserve Corps. The French and the British, as will be
seen, were neither of them yet at hand to render assistance ;
and it was hopeless for the Belgians to think of contendng
against odds of four or five to one. Accordingly, on the
evening of the 18th, the five Belgian divisions were skilfully
drawn off from the Gette north-westward to Antwerp, and
on the 20th entered the lines of that fortress without
being seriously molested. There, on the flank of the Germans if they advanced westward, and in their rear if they
should turn southward, the Belgian Army remained—an
effective menace to the enemy.[1]

Namur [2]

Further to the south, about Namur, where the Belgian
4th Division was stationed, German cavalry patrols were
in touch with the Belgian cavalry to the north of the
fortress on the 5th August, and to the south-east of it on
the 7th. But it was not until nearly a fortnight later that
the main bodies of the enemy approached ; meanwhile,
on the 19th, the garrison had been joined by the Belgian
8th Brigade which, finding itself completely isolated at
Huy, had blown up the bridge over the Meuse there and
fallen back on Namur. On that day the *Guard Reserve
Corps* of the German *Second Army* appeared on the north

[1] According to Hausen, the commander of the *Third Army* (" Marneschlacht," p. 244, f.n.), the *III. Reserve Corps* and *IX. Reserve Corps*
were originally detailed to push forward to the coast " direction Calais,"
but this order was cancelled when the Belgian Army went into Antwerp,
and both corps were sent to watch the fortress. Later, in early September,
the *XV. Corps* was detained near Brussels on account of a sortie being
expected from Antwerp. These three corps were absent from the Battle
of the Marne, though the *IX. Reserve and XV. Corps* reached the Aisne in
time to oppose the Allied advance. There were further employed at
Antwerp : the *4th Ersatz Division* (sent from the *Sixth Army*), the *1st
Ersatz Reserve Division*, a *Matrosen* division, the *26th* and *37th Landwehr
Brigades*, besides heavy artillery and engineers.
[2] See " La Défense de la Position Fortifiée de Namur " (Belgian official
work), and " Lüttich-Namur."

of the fortress, and the *XI. Corps*, consisting of the *22nd* 5-23 Aug.
and *38th Divisions*, of the *Third Army*, on the south-east, 1914.
the whole under the command of General von Gallwitz.
With these troops was a large proportion of heavy artillery,
including four batteries of Austrian 30·5-cm. mortars and
one battery of Krupp's 42-cm. howitzers.

On the 20th August, the Germans drove in the Belgian
outposts, but this time instead of attempting a *coup de main*,
waited for their heavy guns which on the 21st opened fire
on the eastern and south-eastern forts. The Belgian commandant was powerless either to keep these monster howitzers at a distance or to silence them by counter-batteries.
Before evening two of the principal forts had been very
seriously damaged ; within another twenty-four hours both
were practically destroyed. Two Belgian counter-attacks
on the 22nd August failed ; and by the evening of the 23rd
the northern and eastern fronts had been laid bare, and
five out of the whole circle of nine forts were in ruins. At
midnight the 4th Division and the mobile garrison withdrew southwards, losing 5,500 men but just escaping the
clutches of the enemy who was closing round the fortress ;
so they made good their escape into France, whence later
they rejoined the main Belgian Army at Antwerp.

Thus for eighteen days the Belgians had faced the
German invasion, delaying the hostile advance during a
most critical period, and gaining time which was of price-
less value to the Allies. In addition to this great strategic
advantage, the fact that the first German operations
against fortresses, conducted under the conditions obtaining in modern warfare, were so rapidly successful gave
warning to the French to readjust their conceptions of the
defensive value of their fortified front, and reorganize it on
lines calculated to counter the effect of bombardment by
heavy howitzers.

The Operations of the French [1]

(Sketch 2 ; Maps 1, 2 & 5)

On the 2nd August, the day of the presentation to Sketch 2.
Belgium of the German ultimatum, the French Commander-

[1] F.O.A., i. (i.) pp. 87, 93, 134 ; also General Joffre's statement to the
Parliamentary Commission d'Enquête : Défense du bassin de Briey ; the
very lucid commentary on this Commission, by its *rapporteur*, M. Fernand
Engerand, entitled " La Bataille de la Frontière " ; and the official publication " Quatre Mois de Guerre : Rapport sur l'ensemble des opérations
du 2 août au 2 décembre 1914."

in-Chief decided to use "the alternative concentration "areas" for the Fourth and Fifth Armies, so as to interpolate the former in the general line, and extend the left wing further towards the north.

Map 1. On the 3rd, in view of the German violation of Luxembourg territory, General Joffre ordered Sordet's cavalry corps to push forward next day to the east of Mezières, but telephoned to its commander and to the Army commanders insisting "on the imperious obligation" not to cross the frontier; "if there are incidents," he said, "they must "only arise and develop on French territory." On the evening of the 4th, twenty-four hours after the German declaration of war and twelve hours after German cavalry had advanced into Belgium, King Albert authorized the French to enter his territory for the purpose of ascertaining the direction of advance of the Germans and of delaying their columns. General Sordet crossed the frontier on the 6th and moved first towards Neufchateau (36 miles east of Mezières). Then, striking north, he eventually arrived within nine miles of Liége; but, finding that the Belgian field troops had been withdrawn from the area of the fortress, he retired on the 10th in the direction of the Meuse. Valuable information was obtained by him as to the enemy's movements from an officer who was captured on the 9th, but otherwise the intelligence gained in the strategic reconnaissance was negative; neither did the latter achieve its secondary object of delaying the enemy's advance; for, owing to the resistance of Liége, no important columns of German troops had at the time entered the area explored.

To fill the gap between the French Fifth Army and the Belgian troops defending Namur, a French infantry regiment was sent on the 8th to occupy all the bridges on the Meuse north of Dinant and gain touch with the Belgians; and the I. Corps extended its protective troops along the Meuse from Mezières to Givet. On the 13th the whole I. Corps was sent northwards "to oppose any attempts of "the enemy to cross the Meuse between Givet and Namur." On the 15th, in conjunction with General Mangin's 8th Brigade (specially detailed to support the cavalry corps), it repulsed an attempt of Richthofen's cavalry corps (*Guard* and *5th Cavalry Divisions*) to cross near Dinant.

Between the 6th and 8th August, it became certain that an enemy force containing units belonging to five different army corps was operating against Liége; but the main

group of the German Armies appeared to the French
General Staff to be around Metz, in front of Thionville and
in Luxembourg. The enemy was thus, it was thought, in
a position either to advance westwards if Liége fell, or if
Liége held out to wheel southwards, pivoting on Metz. A
decision was therefore made by General Joffre, and communicated to the French Armies on the 8th August,[1] to the
effect that his intention was to bring the Germans to battle
with all his forces united, as in the original plan, with his
right extended to the Rhine. If necessary, the left of the
line would be held back, so as to avoid the premature
engagement of one of the Armies before the others could
come to its assistance. If, however, the enemy's right
were delayed in front of Liége, or turned southwards, the
left would be advanced. General directions were issued as
to the objectives and zones of action for the Armies, the
Fifth being ordered to remain concentrated so as to be in
a position either to prevent an enemy passage of the Meuse
between Mouzon (20 miles above Mezières) and Mezières,
or to cross itself between those two places. The instructions ended with an order to make all preparations so that
the movement could be carried out on receipt of a telegram,
and to render the offensive crushing (*foudroyante*).

On the 13th General Joffre came to the conclusion that
the enemy was wheeling south towards the Third, Fourth
and Fifth Armies on the Upper Meuse, and it was too late
for them to seek battle beyond that river " under good
" conditions." He directed them to be prepared to counter-
attack. He paid no heed to the view of General Lanrezac
(Fifth Army), that the enemy wheel was of a much wider
nature.

Meantime in Alsace, " to facilitate the attack of the
" main Armies," the small offensive—outlined in the original
plan—was commenced on the extreme right by a detachment of the First Army, consisting of the VII. Corps
and 8th Cavalry Division. This detachment crossed the
frontier on the 6th August. After its advanced guard had
reached Mülhausen, it found itself in the presence of
superior forces, and was withdrawn. On the 14th the offensive was renewed with a stronger force, called the Army
of Alsace, consisting of the VII. Corps, and the Alpine
and three Reserve divisions, under General Pau. On the
same date the First and Second Armies began their forward

[1] In Instruction No. 1, dated 8th August 1914, 7 A.M. F.O.A., i. (i.)
Annexe No. 103.

movement across the frontier. For the Armies on the left only certain precautions were ordered. But during the afternoon of the 15th, news came from the Belgian Army that 200,000 Germans were crossing the Meuse below Visé, and from the I. Corps of the attack at Dinant ; the Grand Quartier Général (G.Q.G.) in consequence ordered the Fifth Army to hand over to the Fourth Army its right corps (II.) and Group of Reserve divisions, which were guarding the Meuse in touch with the I. Corps, and take the rest of its forces northwards across the Belgian frontier into the angle of the Meuse and the Sambre to the region of Mariembourg (24 miles north by west of Mezières) or Philippeville (33 miles north of Mezières), " to act in concert " with the British Army and the Belgian forces against the "enemy forces in the north." G.Q.G. placed Sordet's cavalry corps and Valabrègue's Group of Reserve divisions, then at Vervins (36 miles west of Mezières), under the Fifth Army, and also ordered to it two recently arrived African divisions and the XVIII. Corps, originally in the Second Army, from the general reserve.[1]

In order to leave the Third Army entirely free to concentrate its attention on offensive operations the duty of masking Metz was given to a new force, the Army of Lorraine, composed of three Reserve divisions from the Third Army and three others sent up for the purpose ; General Maunoury, who had originally been on the Italian frontier, was given command of it. There was thus a general taking of ground to the left.

The French general plan of operations now began to take definite shape as cumulative evidence showed that the main German advance was in progress through Belgium. Map 2. The situation as it presented itself to G.Q.G. on the 16th August was as follows :

In the north, seven or eight German army corps and four cavalry divisions are endeavouring to pass westwards between Givet and Brussels, and even beyond these points.

[1] To make the changes clear, they are enumerated together here :
The Third Army was reinforced by one Reserve division, and then by two more.
The Fourth Army took over from the Fifth Army : II. Corps ; XI. Corps ; 52nd and 60th Reserve Divisions (leaving it the 51st) ; a cavalry division ; and the Moroccan Division from the IX. Corps of the Second Army.
The Fifth Army, to make up for this, received the 37th and 38th Divisions from Africa ; the XVIII. Corps from the Second Army ; and General Valabrègue's Group of three Reserve divisions. So that the corps it now contained were the I., III., X. and XVIII., with the 37th Division added to the III. and the 38th to the X.

In the centre between Bastogne and Thionville there were Aug, 1914, thought to be six or seven army corps, and two or three cavalry divisions,

South of Metz, the Germans appeared to be on the defensive.[1] General Joffre's intention now was to make the principal attack with the Third and Fourth Armies through Luxembourg and Belgian Luxembourg, so as to strike at the flank and communications of the enemy forces which had crossed the Meuse between Namur and the Dutch frontier, and if possible attack them before they could deploy for battle by wheeling south. To support this offensive the First and Second Armies were to make only a secondary attack between Metz and the Vosges, for the purpose of holding the enemy, who seemed to be gradually shifting westwards and might otherwise be able to take in flank the French Armies attacking in Luxembourg. Lastly, the left wing, consisting of the Fifth Army, the British Army when it should arrive, and the Belgian Army, was to move up so as to hold in check any German forces which might advance from the Meuse, and so gain sufficient time to allow the attack of the Third and Fourth Armies to become effective. In order to give weight to the attack, the Third and Fourth Armies were somewhat strengthened.[2]

In brief, General Joffre's first object was to break the enemy's centre ; that done he intended to fall with all available forces on the right or western wing of the German Armies.

The instructions which he sent out on the 20th were as 20 Aug. follow :   1914.

To General Ruffey :

" The Third Army will begin its offensive movement

---

[1] The German Order of Battle was given as follows :

" Two Armies of the Meuse under the orders of General von Bülow
" are operating in front of the Fifth Army ; one comprises the *VII., IX.*
" and *X. Corps*, the *2nd* and *9th Cavalry Divisions* ; the other is said to
" be formed of the *III., IV., VI.* and *XI. Corps* and two cavalry divisions,
" *Guard* and *5th.*

" There is no precise information of the great concentration in Belgium
" and Belgian Luxembourg. It is believed that there is in Belgian Luxem-
" bourg one Army commanded by General von Heeringen, including the
" *Guard, XII.* and *XIX. Corps* and a cavalry division ; and between
" Luxembourg and Thionville a fourth Army under General von Eichhorn,
" in which are grouped the *VIII., XVI.* and *XVIII. Corps,* and the *3rd*
" and *6th Cavalry Divisions.*"

This, except for the commanders' names, was not far from the mark ;
but there is no mention of the Reserve corps. (See page 36.)

[2] See footnote on previous page.

20 Aug. " to-morrow in the general direction of Arlon. . . . The
1914. " mission of the Third Army is to counter-attack any
" enemy force which may try to gain the right flank of the
" Fourth Army."

To General de Langle of the Fourth Army, he telegraphed :

" I authorize you to send strong advanced guards of
" all arms to-night to the general line Bertrix—Tintigny
" to secure the debouchment of your Army beyond the
" Semoy. . . . The general direction of the movement will
" be Neufchateau."

The positions on the morning of the 20th indicate the
preliminary movements which had been made for the
purpose. They were :

The Army of Alsace had reached Mülhausen.

The First and Second Armies were across the frontier in front
of Lunéville and Nancy, from near Sarrebourg to Delme,
about thirty-six miles north-west of Sarrebourg.

The Army of Lorraine was observing Metz.

The Third and Fourth Armies were close up to the Belgian
frontier, astride the river Chiers, from near Longwy to
Sedan, ready to cross the river Semoy.

Map 5.

The Fifth Army was disposed :

The I. Corps and 8th Infantry Brigade on the Meuse,
near Dinant, facing east, with

The 51st Reserve Division marching up from the south
to act as a link between the French Fourth and Fifth
Armies.

The X. and III. Corps, each with an African division
attached to it, lay in depth close up to the Sambre near
Charleroi, facing north.

The XVIII. Corps was echeloned to the left rear on
the line Gozée—Thuin (6 miles and 9 miles south-west
of Charleroi).

General Valabrègue's two remaining Reserve divisions
were on the left of the XVIII. Corps and north-east of
Maubeuge, on the east of the gap into which General Joffre
intended the British Army should move.

Further to the west and beyond the space to be occupied
by the British, were three Territorial divisions under
General d'Amade, sent up on the 14th, the 84th near Douai,
the 82nd near Arras, and the 81st between Hazebrouck
and St. Omer.

It will be observed that the front of the Fifth Army
under General Lanrezac along the Meuse and Sambre

formed a salient, with its apex just short of the Belgian 20-21Aug.
fortress of Namur, on which by the evening of the 20th 1914.
the Germans were closing. Consequently, any failure of
his right to hold its ground on the Meuse would place his
centre and left in a very dangerous situation, and render
them liable to be cut off.

On the 20th, however, before the general advance had
begun, misfortunes had already overtaken the French.
According to the bulletins originally issued : " The First
" and Second Armies, tired by several days of marching and
" fighting, came up against strongly organized positions,
" armed with powerful artillery, whose fire was admirably
" prepared and corrected by aeroplanes." This, however,
was not quite the case. The Germans (*Sixth Army*) had
at first withdrawn before the Second Army, and the latter,
with the XX. Corps under General Foch on the left, had
on the 18th followed in pursuit. Early in the morning of
the 20th the enemy had come forward again and attacked
the Second Army in front and left flank ; it had been
compelled to retire and the First Army had to conform to
its movements. The actions in which the First and Second
Armies were engaged are known as the battles of Sarrebourg
and Morhange (25 miles north-west of Sarrebourg).[1]

On the 21st August, in spite of this reverse to the
French right wing, the Third and Fourth Armies crossed
the frontier and advanced from ten to fifteen miles into
the difficult Ardennes country, an area of rough hills and
deep river valleys, covered by forests broken only by
narrow belts of pasture land. Aeroplanes could see nothing,
the cavalry could not get forward, and in the defiles,
which the roads through the villages and forests constitute, the French columns ran literally at right angles
into German columns belonging to the Armies of the
German Crown Prince and Duke Albert of Württemberg,
numerically slightly superior to them,[2] which were crossing
their front. After fighting the actions known as the battles

---

[1] It may be added here that an attempted pursuit of the Second Army
by the Germans received a serious check on the 25th ; for, in spite of the
reverse, the French First Army returned to the offensive and struck them
in flank. After some indecisive fighting, the situation of the French
First and Second Armies became stabilized on a line in France, just inside
the frontier.

[2]   *French.*   *German.*

Third Army	.	.	. 168,000	Fifth Army	. .	. 200,000
Fourth Army	.	.	. 193,000	Fourth Army .	.	. 180,000
			361,000			380,000

44 THE OUTBREAK OF WAR

21 Aug. 1914. of Virton and of the Semoy,[1] having suffered heavy losses, particularly in officers, the Third and Fourth Armies were compelled to fall back towards the Meuse. The attempt to break in the German centre before the right wing could deliver its blow against the Allied left wing had thus failed, owing to the French having neglected to adapt their method of advance to the nature of the ground (an advance by bounds from the edge of one open belt to another does not appear to have been considered) ; to their having been caught in column in narrow defiles and thus unable to use their artillery with effect ; and to their line of advance having brought them head-on to the broadside of the German columns. Thanks however to a premature enveloping attack attempted by the German Crown Prince the reverse was less serious than it might otherwise have been.

As regards the French Fifth Army, General Lanrezac had considered it inadvisable to advance simultaneously with the Armies on his right. He preferred to wait until his reinforcements should have arrived, which would not be until the 23rd ; [2] until the Fourth Army should have cleared the gorges of the Semoy and shortened by its advance the eastern face of the salient which the front of the Fifth Army presented to the enemy ; and until the British Army should similarly have come up on his left. As will presently be seen, Sir John French's force on the 21st was approaching the line of the Mons—Condé canal. The general situation in which it was about to play its part may be thus summarized :—

The French First and Second Armies were retiring after the battles of Sarrebourg and Morhange ;
The Third and Fourth " had failed, and the reverse seemed serious " ;
The Fifth Army was in a salient about to be attacked by two German Armies ;
Namur was on the point of falling (the last fort surrendered on the 25th) ; and
The Belgian Army had been driven into Antwerp.[3]

---

[1] There are vivid accounts of these actions in Commandant Grasset's " Ethe," " Virton " and " Neufchateau."
[2] See page 40.
[3] The French tactical doctrine—infantry attack head down, regardless of fire and of artillery support—had proved so totally unsuited to modern warfare that on 24th August the following note was issued to all the French Armies over General Joffre's signature :—
" It has been noticed in the information collected with regard to the

Operations of the Germans [1]

Leaving only three Active corps and three Reserve 17 Aug. divisions, assisted by a cavalry division, one *Ersatz* division 1914. and *Landwehr* formations, some 250,000 men in all, on her Sketch 1. Eastern frontier, where she had the co-operation of the Maps 1 Austro-Hungarian Army, and the *IX. Reserve Corps* (until & 2. the 23rd August) and *Landwehr* formations in Schleswig to guard against a possible landing, Germany had assembled the rest of her available mobile troops on her Western frontier in seven Armies,[2] with Generaloberst von Moltke as Chief of the General Staff and practically in command.

By the evening of the 17th August these Armies were concentrated, ready to move, on a long front extending from the fortress of Strasbourg to the Dutch frontier north of Liége. This front ran through Sarrebourg, Metz and Thionville ;[3] up the centre of the Duchy of Luxembourg (the neutrality of which had been violated on the 2nd August), to Liége ; and then to the north-west of this fortress, where the northernmost German Army, Kluck's,

---

" actions which have so far taken place that attacks have not been carried " out with close co-operation between the infantry and the artillery.
" Every combined operation includes a series of detailed actions aiming " at the capture of the points d'appui.
" Each time that it is necessary to capture a point d'appui the attack " must be prepared with artillery, the infantry must be held back and not " launched to the assault until the distance to be covered is so short that " it is certain the objective will be reached. Every time that the infantry " has been launched to the attack from too great a distance before the " artillery has made its effect felt, the infantry has fallen under the fire of " machine guns and suffered losses which might have been avoided.
" When a point d'appui has been captured, it must be organized imme- " diately, the troops must entrench, and artillery must be brought up."
[1] See G.O.A., i., and Note II. at end of Chapter.
[2] For Order of Battle, see Appendices 6 and 7. In round numbers (G.O.A. i. p. 69), 1,600,000 ; excluding 4 cavalry corps and the covering troops in Upper Alsace :

First Army	.	.	.	.	320,000 men
Second Army	.	.	.	.	260,000 ,,
Third Army	.	.	.	.	180,000 ,,
Fourth Army	.	.	.	.	180,000 ,,
Fifth Army	.	.	.	.	200,000 ,,
Sixth Army	.	.	.	.	220,000 ,,
Seventh Army	.	.	.	125,000 ,,

1,485,000 ,,

In addition 6½ mobile *Ersatz* divisions (say another 100,000 men), which would be ready on the 12th day of mobilization.
[3] The continuous fortifications round and connecting these two latter places formed the so-called Moselle Position.

17 Aug. was deployed facing the Belgians on the Gette. In order
1914. to reach the far side of the neutral barrier formed by the
projecting peninsula of Dutch Limbourg, behind which it
had been assembled, Kluck's Army had defiled in three
columns through Aix la Chapelle. The Supreme Command
(*O.H.L.*) orders directed the Armies of Kluck (*First*) and
Bülow (*Second*), acting together under the latter general,[1]
to deal with the Belgian Army, to force it away from
Antwerp and to reach the line Namur—Brussels. The
First Army was to detail a detachment to mask Antwerp,
and by holding back its right provide against a British
landing on the coast. Hausen's (*Third*) Army was to
gain the line of the Meuse from Givet to Namur. Namur
was to be attacked and taken as soon as possible by the
left of the *Second* and the right of the *Third Army*.
Meanwhile, the *Fourth* and *Fifth Armies* were to conform
so that the whole five Armies on the right might carry out
a gigantic wheel, first to the line Thionville—Brussels, and
then in a south-westerly direction, Thionville still remaining
the pivot.

The *Sixth* and *Seventh Armies*, under the senior Army
commander, Crown Prince Rupprecht of Bavaria, were
given as their principal task the protection of the left flank
of the five wheeling Armies. How they could do so, said
the instructions, depended on the action of the enemy.
If the French, based on their fortress line, remained on
the strategic defensive, Crown Prince Rupprecht was to
take the offensive, " advance against the Moselle below
" Frouard (5 miles below Nancy) and the Meurthe, hold
" fast the French troops [First and Second Armies] as-
" sembled there and hinder their transfer to the French
" left wing." If, on the other hand, the French moved
against his front in superior numbers, and he had to give
ground, he was to retire to a prepared position on the
Nied, which was flanked by Strasbourg and Metz. If the
left flank of the wheeling Armies did not seem to be
threatened, part of the *Sixth* and *Seventh Armies* might be
withdrawn via Metz to take part in the fighting on the left
bank of the Moselle.[2]

[1] The order of the 17th August which placed Kluck under Bülow was
cancelled on the 27th, but reissued on the 10th Sept.
[2] Crown Prince Rupprecht had begun a retirement on 14th August,
under the second case, keeping in touch with the outer defences of Metz ;
but by the evening of the 17th the French Second Army in its advance
had exposed " a long-spread and visibly thin flank towards Metz, which
" invited a blow," and the mass of that Army was crowded together

The strategic objective was to outflank the French by the west and drive them eastwards against the Swiss frontier. 17 Aug. 1914. To give sufficient weight to the blow which was to crush the Allies' left, roll up the line from the westward and, in conjunction with the advance of the *Third, Fourth* and *Fifth Armies*, push the entire line of battle south-east towards neutral territory, five of the ten cavalry divisions and twenty-six out of the total of the whole seventy-two divisions on the Western Front were allotted to the two Armies under General von Bülow.[1]

To summarize the initial movements of the two belligerents, we find that the French offensive carried out by the Armies of Dubail and de Castelnau on the 14th August south of Metz " was counter-attacked by the " German *Sixth* and *Seventh Armies* and failed tactically " : the general strategic advantage too remained with the Germans ; for their 345,000 men, including the detachments in Upper Alsace, contained about 456,000 French. The offensive of the Armies of Ruffey and de Langle de Cary north of Thionville, commencing on the 21st August, encountered the German *Fourth* and *Fifth Armies*, which had begun on the 17th to wheel forward to the line Thionville—Givet, so that two Armies met two Armies of about equal strength ; yet the French suffered a number of small disasters.

The result of the above operations was distinctly, but not decisively, in favour of the Germans. This however was not all. Their dispositions left three Armies, Hausen's, Bülow's and Kluck's, comprising in all thirty-four divisions, free to deal with Lanrezac's Army of ten divisions, the tiny British Army of four divisions, and the almost equally small Belgian Army of six divisions—thirty-four divisions against twenty, covering a frontier destitute of natural Map 5.

---

between Morhange and Sarrebourg. Rupprecht therefore issued orders, although Moltke was in favour of letting the French come further, for a " lightning and surprise attack," with the result already recorded. (Bavarian Official Account, " Die Schlacht in Lothringen.")

[1] The density of the different German Armies on the original front on the 17th August is of interest :

First Army front	18 miles, about 18,000 men per mile.					
Second	,,	20	,,	,,	13,000	,,	,,
Third	,,	15	,,	,,	12,000	,,	,,
Fourth	,,	30	,,	,,	6,000	,,	,,
Fifth	,,	40	,,	,,	5,000	,,	,,
Sixth	,,	70	,,	,,	3,100	,,	,,
Seventh	,,	35	,,	,,	3,500	,,	,,

obstacles, guarded only by obsolete fortresses, and with the shortest and most direct route to Paris behind it.

The first step in the German plan had therefore been successful, as regards its objectives ; the line laid down for the first stage of the wheel on Thionville had been reached, and Liége and Namur had been taken ; it was unsuccessful only in that the Belgian Army had not been forced away from Antwerp, which it entered, after rear-guard fighting, on the 20th. Surprise has sometimes been expressed that the Germans did not push at least detachments to the Channel ports in August 1914, when there was no force available to oppose them except some French Territorial units. It would appear that they had intended to do so, but the necessity of investing the Belgian Army in Antwerp absorbed the two corps, *III. Reserve* and *IX. Reserve*, which had been selected for that purpose. Besides, when the opening phase of the campaign was going so nearly according to plan, and there seemed a certainty of winning the war in a few days by a defeat of the French in a super-Sedan in the open field, it would have been strategically unjustifiable to divert a single man to seize a section of coast, which, like Italy after the battle of Austerlitz, must have fallen to the invaders without serious conflict directly the main decision had been gained.

THE BRITISH ENTRY INTO FRANCE

12 Aug.   On the 12th August, the Commander-in-Chief, retain-
Sketch 1. ing only a small party of his immediate staff with him,
Map 2.   despatched General Headquarters (G.H.Q.) from London
to Southampton. They crossed to Havre on the 14th, and proceeded by rail early on the 16th, reaching Le Cateau late that night.

On the 14th August, Sir John French himself, with his party, left London. He arrived at Amiens soon after 9 P.M. An hour later, General Valabrègue's chief staff officer came to report that his group, the 53rd and 69th Reserve Divisions, was entrenching south of the Oise between Vervins and Hirson, as a second line to the French left.

On the following days, 15th, 16th and 17th August, the Commander-in-Chief proceeded to visit, in succession, the French Minister of War at Paris, General Joffre at the Grand Quartier Général (G.Q.G.) at Vitry le François, and General Lanrezac at Fifth Army Headquarters at Rethel.

From them he learned in some detail the disposition of the French forces in the angle formed by the Sambre and the Meuse, south-west of Namur.[1] General Lanrezac's Army was then rapidly concentrating in the area south of Charleroi, the I. Corps, on the right, being already massed between Namur and Givet ; the head of the III. Corps was at Philippeville, and that of the X. Corps at Bohain, midway between St. Quentin and Le Cateau. The XVIII. Corps was expected to begin arriving in the area between Bohain and Avesnes on the 18th and 19th. General Valabrègue's divisions were in position, as already stated above, south of Avesnes. General Sordet's cavalry corps was advancing again, this time north-east, from Charleroi and, if driven back, would pass to the left of the British Army. The task of that Army was to move northward and form the extreme left of the French advance.

Throughout this period, that is to say between the 12th and 17th August, the British troops had been passing across the Channel and disembarking on French soil. All was ready for their reception, and the welcome given to them by the inhabitants was enthusiastic. On the 14th and following days the corps and divisions began to move up by train to the areas of concentration, which were Sketch 3. arranged so that the army was assembled in a pear-shaped area between Maubeuge and Le Cateau, about twenty-five miles long from north-east to south-west, and averaging ten miles wide. The cavalry was at the north-eastern end, ready to join hands with the French Fifth Army.

In detail, the areas were :   Map 3.

Cavalry : East of Maubeuge, Jeumont, Damousies, Cousolre.
    Divisional Headquarters, Aibes.
II. Corps : East of Landrecies. Headquarters, Landrecies.
    3rd Division : Marbaix, Taisnières, Noyelles.
    5th Division : Maroilles, Landrecies, Ors.
I. Corps : East of Bohain. Headquarters, Wassigny.
    1st Division : Boué, Esqueheries, Leschelles.
    2nd Division : Grougis, Mennevret, Hannappes.

The Royal Flying Corps, taking the field in war for the first time, assembled four squadrons, with 105 officers, 755 other ranks, and 63 aeroplanes at the aerodrome of Maubeuge ; it also formed an aircraft park at Amiens.

---

[1] As neither General Lanrezac nor Sir John French could speak or fully understand the other's language, a good personal accord was not, unfortunately, established between them at their meeting. See Lanrezac's "Le Plan de Campagne français," pp. 91-2 ; French's " 1914," pp. 36-7.

The concentration was virtually complete on the 20th, that is six days late according to French reckoning, owing to the various delays which have been enumerated. One sad incident marred the progress to the scene of action, namely the death of Lieutenant-General Sir James Grierson, commanding the II. Corps, who expired suddenly in the train on the morning of the 17th. Sir John French asked that Sir Herbert Plumer might take General Grierson's place ; but the Secretary of State for War decided to send Sir Horace Smith-Dorrien.

On the 19th August, G.H.Q. was informed that the 4th Division would be despatched from England immediately ; and it was settled that the 2/Royal Welch Fusiliers, 1/Scottish Rifles, 1/Middlesex and 2/Argyll and Sutherland Highlanders, which had been employed on the Lines of Communication, should be formed into the 19th Brigade, under Major-General L. G. Drummond. On the same day the Flying Corps carried out its first reconnaissances from Maubeuge northward towards Brussels, and north-west over Tournai and Courtrai. No large bodies of troops were seen. On the 20th the cavalry was pushed forward as far as Binche on the north without encountering any enemy. But an aerial reconnaissance that day observed a column of troops stretching through Louvain as far as the eye could reach. This was a column of the German *First Army.* Diverting one of his corps, the *III. Reserve,* followed later by the *IX. Reserve Corps* and the equivalent of five divisions,[1] to follow the Belgian forces towards Antwerp, Kluck was pressing westward. On this day, the 20th, his troops entered Brussels. It was a fateful day in many respects, for during its course the main Belgian Army retired into Antwerp, the Germans approached within decisive range of Namur, and General Joffre gave his orders for the general advance.

In this great movement, the outline of which has already been given, the British were to advance on the left of the Fifth Army north-east, by way of Soignies, in the general direction of Nivelles. If Kluck wheeled southward from Brussels, it was not anticipated that his right would extend much beyond Mons. If, therefore, the British were in line about this place, they would be ready, when once General Lanrezac had passed the Sambre, to wheel eastward and envelop the right of the Germans. To make this envelopment the more certain, General Sordet's cavalry

---

[1] See f.n. 1, page 36.

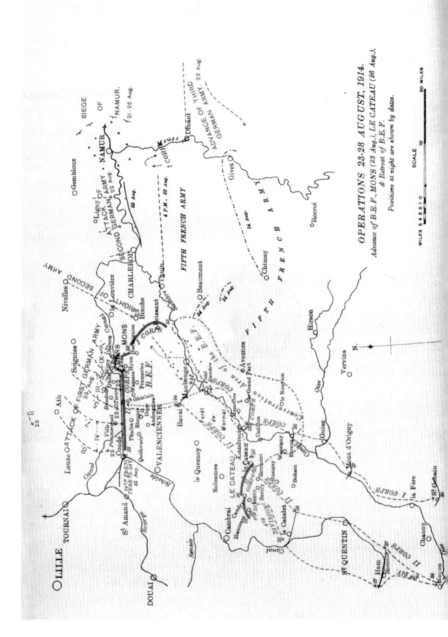

OPERATIONS 23-28 AUGUST, 1914.

Advance of B.E.F., MONS (23 Aug.), LE CATEAU (26 Aug.),
& Retreat of B.E.F.

Positions at night are shown by dates.

MILES 5 4 3 2 1 0   SCALE   10   20 MILES

corps, which had on this day fallen back across the Sambre 20 Aug.
to Fontaine l'Évêque (midway between Charleroi and 1914.
Binche), was directed to take position beyond the left of
the British. Still further to the west, the three French
Territorial divisions, under the command of General
d'Amade, were to push gradually forward.[1]

The initiative seemed to be passing into the hands of Sketches
the Germans, and it was urgent to ascertain by aerial and 4 & 5.
other reconnaissance what use, if any, they were making of Maps 2
it. Meanwhile, in pursuance of General Joffre's plan, & 3.
G.H.Q. on the evening of the 20th issued orders [2] for a
movement northward during the three ensuing days.
An attached march table gave the approximate positions
to be reached each day. The general effect of these
orders when executed would be that the 23rd August
would find the Army aligned on a front, roughly facing
north-east, from Estinne au Mont (near Binche) on the
south-east, to Lens, eight miles north of Mons, on the north-
west, with the Cavalry Division (Major-General E. H. H.
Allenby) on the left, while the 5th Cavalry Brigade
(Br.-General Sir P. W. Chetwode), having covered the
right flank during the movement, would find itself finally
in advance of the right front. The daily moves were to be
as follows :

The 5th Cavalry Brigade was to proceed on the 21st
to the neighbourhood of Binche, the right of the line, and
there remain ; the Cavalry Division, moving on the left
of the 5th Cavalry Brigade, was to march level with it on the
21st, and on the 22nd proceed to Lens, the left of the line,
where it would halt astride the road that connects Mons and
Ath. Covered by the cavalry, the rest of the Army was
to advance.[3]

On the 21st the II. Corps to the line Goegnies—Bavai ; the
I. Corps to the line Avesnes—Landrecies.

On the 22nd the II. Corps north-westward to the line from
Mons westward to Thulin ; the I. Corps north-eastward to the
line Hautmont—Hargnies.

On the 23rd the II. Corps was to wheel eastwards, so that one
division would be in rear of the other, with the front east of
Mons between Spiennes and St. Denis ; the I. Corps was to
incline north-eastward and come up on the right of the II.,

---

[1] For further information as regards General d'Amade's force, see
Note II. at end of Chapter IV.
[2] Appendix 10.
[3] The positions of troops are always given from right to left, unless
otherwise stated.

on a line from Estinne au Mont westward to Harmignies (immediately south-east of Spiennes).

21 Aug. The morning of the 21st broke thick and misty, render-
1914. ing aerial reconnaissance impossible until the afternoon.
The cavalry moved northwards early, and after reaching
Villers St. Ghislain (six miles south-east of Mons) heard
that German cavalry was in force five miles to the northward. A patrol which entered Mons found a similar report
current there. The 2nd Cavalry Brigade (Br.-General
H. de B. de Lisle), after crossing the Condé canal east of
Mons, occupied a line on both banks from Maurage to
Obourg. Patrols of the 9th Lancers and 4th Dragoon
Guards sighted German patrols in the vicinity of the two
bridges east of Mons, those of Nimy and Obourg ; but
contact was not established. Information from peasants,
however, pointed to the movement of considerable forces
southward from Soignies (10 miles north-east of Mons).

The II. Corps followed the cavalry to a line level with
and west of Maubeuge, the 3rd Division, on the right, to
the line Bettignies—Feignies—La Longueville, and the 5th
Division, on the left, to the line Houdain—St. Waast—
Gommegnies. Sir Horace Smith-Dorrien reached Bavai
from England at 4 P.M. and took over command of the
corps. The outposts of the 9th Brigade on this evening
overlooked the old battlefield of Malplaquet, and were
found by the Lincolnshire Regiment which, together with
the Royal Scots Fusiliers, had fought in the action, two
hundred years before.

The I. Corps simultaneously moved up to the line from
Avesnes to Landrecies, about ten miles behind the front
of the II., the 1st Division on the right, and the 2nd on
the left. The day was sultry and many of the reservists
suffered in consequence ; a considerable number of men
were still feeling the effects of inoculation, and all found the
hard irregular surface of the cobbled roads extremely trying
for marching. In the afternoon the weather cleared and
the Flying Corps was able to carry out reconnaissances.
Map 5. It reported a large body of cavalry with some infantry
and guns south-east of Nivelles. This intelligence was
confirmed, and the formation identified as the German
9th Cavalry Division, by a British intelligence officer who
was in Nivelles when the division entered, but escaped by
motor. The presence of two more cavalry divisions was
ascertained ; one of them, the 2nd, had pushed parties

far to the westward, which had reached the line Ghent— Audenarde, being evidently intended to explore the area as far as the sea. The other division, supposed to be the *4th*, was between Charleroi and Seneffe.[1] These three cavalry divisions formed the German *II. Cavalry Corps* under General von der Marwitz.[2] The main German line was reported as extending south-east from Grammont, through Enghien, Nivelles, Genappes and Sombreffe to Charleroi. It is now known that from right to left—that is to say from north-west to south-east—the order of the German corps was *IV.* (with *II.* echeloned behind it), *III., IX., VII., X.* and *Guard Corps,* with four Reserve corps in rear of them. The Allied High Command was correctly informed as to the actual number of German corps in Belgium ; but it could do no more than forecast the scope of the movement in progress. Part of Kluck's cavalry at least, and possibly some of his infantry had begun a wheel south-westwards from Brussels. Whether he intended to continue in that direction or sweep further westwards, it was as yet impossible to judge on the available information. On the British right, General Lanrezac's Army was in contact with infantry of the German *Second Army* along the whole line of the Sambre on either side of Charleroi, from Tamines to Pont à Celles, so that hard fighting in that quarter on the morrow was almost certain. There seemed every chance that it might spread further to the west.

At 2.45 P.M. G.H.Q. ordered the cavalry to close the line between the French left and Mons : the 5th Cavalry Brigade to take up a line from the left of General Sordet's cavalry corps at Fontaine l'Évêque to Péronnes, in front of Binche, and the Cavalry Division to prolong that line to the canal at Boussoit (five miles east of Mons) with another brigade, the 3rd (Br.-General H. de la P. Gough). Thence patrols were to be pushed out north and north-east. Operation orders, issued from G.H.Q. shortly before midnight,[3] directed that the march table issued on the 20th would hold good for the 22nd, with two modifications : the outposts of the II. Corps, instead of having

---

[1] The *4th Cavalry Division* was on the line mentioned about midday on the 20th, and on the 21st was moving westwards from Soignies towards Ath ; otherwise identifications were quite correct. Poseck, Map.

[2] The corps, after concentrating near Ath, was sent north-westwards towards the coast, in front of the right flank of the *First Army*, to look for the British army. Poseck, p. 35.

[3] Appendices 11 and 12.

their right on Mons, were now to hold an angle with Mons in the apex—that is from Givry north-westward to Nimy and thence westward along the canal to Pommeroeul ; and as soon as they had relieved the Cavalry Division, the latter was to move westward to a position in echelon behind the left, in the area comprised within the triangle Thulin —Quiévrain—Baisieux, with outposts along the line of the canal from the left of the II. Corps to Condé. It was still the intention that the British Army should take the offensive.

NOTE I

ALLEGED GERMAN TROOP MOVEMENTS BEFORE MOBILIZATION

Some further information with regard to the Potsdam Conference of the 5th and 6th July 1914 has been published in " Stenographische " Berichte über die öffentlichen Verhandlungen des Untersuchungs- " ausschusses der verfassunggebenden deutschen Nationalver- " sammlung," the shorthand reports of the Commission ordered by the German National Assembly to take evidence on matters affecting critical periods of the war. One of the terms of reference was : " It is to be ascertained what political and military proceedings took " place in Berlin or Potsdam on the 5th and 6th July 1914."

In the evidence there given, General von Falkenhayn states that the Kaiser, on the afternoon of the 5th, warned him that the Army should be ready for all emergencies. Admiral Capelle and Admiral Behnke, temporary Chief of the Staff, Admiralty, were similarly warned ; these two officers then arranged to make such " intellectual " preparations " (intellektuele Vorbereitungen) as were possible without arousing suspicion. Admiral Behnke then describes what was done:— the mobilization orders, etc., were carefully gone through and got ready, steps were taken for the immediate preparation of ships and auxiliary vessels, all ships filled up with fuel, the movements of ships arranged in accordance with the situation, etc.

No evidence of the exact military measures taken was asked for or given at the Commission. An article in the " Revue Militaire " Générale " of September 1919, however, gives a large number of extracts from captured German diaries and interrogations of prisoners which tend to shew that mobilization orders were issued secretly some days before the 31st July ; men on leave were recalled, the brigades on the frontiers intended for the surprise of Liége were brought up to war strength by the recall of reservists, and Landsturm battalions were formed on 31st July to replace active troops in guarding the frontier, railways, etc. There would thus seem no room for doubt that in a variety of ways Germany gained a most valuable start of several days on her opponents.

The above three paragraphs appeared in the original edition. The Reichsarchiv, however, states with reference to them that no mobilization took place in Germany before the 1st August and that the Landsturm in the frontier districts was called out on the same date, not on the 31st July : the troops employed against Liége were at peace strength [in 1913 the peace strength of the infantry battalions of the frontier regions had been raised from 663 to 800]. Movements of men and troops were those made in consequence of the proclamation of " Imminent Danger of War."

The *Reichsarchiv* official history of the German railways in the war (" Das deutsche Feldeisenbahnwesen," i., p. 28) reads as follows :

" As the political situation became acute, the Imperial Chancellor " von Bethmann-Hollweg, on the 28th July put into force, in the " areas near the frontier and in the Berlin railway district, ' the " ' augmented railway protection,' provided for times of political " tension. It affected principally the guarding of the more important " bridges, tunnels and other engineering structures on the lines " required for mobilization and deployment, and was carried out " by railway employees, assisted by the normal machinery of public " safety, and, so far as the watching of bridges from the water, by the " conservancy authorities.

" On the same day the recall was ordered of all bodies of troops " absent from their garrisons which on mobilization should be ready " to leave ' at once ' or ' at short notice ' for the duty of frontier " protection or for certain definite special tasks. The return of all " other troops absent on marches or at training grounds followed " on the evening of the 29th. On this day also orders were issued " for the military guarding of the larger bridges and engineer struc- " tures on the railways and waterways in the frontier areas.

" On the 30th July the state of ' Alert ' for the German fleet " was ordered ; this required the provision of a few trains for the " Active troops detailed for the protection of the North Sea islands. " On the proclamation of ' Imminent Danger of War ' at 1 P.M. on " the 31st July, all the measures settled on in times of peace for the " military guarding of the railways came into force."

General von Moser (commander of the *53rd Brigade*) in his " Kampf und Siegestage 1914 " (Mittler, Berlin, 1915), page 1, says :

" On the 29th July early the order ' Return to Garrison ' reached " us on the troop training ground, where we had assembled on the " previous day for regimental and brigade training. On the 1st " August ' Last Preparations for taking the Field.' On the 2nd " August (first day of mobilization) the brigade, reinforced by a " squadron and 3 batteries, left at 9 A.M. on frontier protection duty."

The regimental history of the *1st Jäger Battalion*, " Im Yorckschen Geist," pages 5–6, contains the following :

" It was a relief to everyone from the company commander to " the youngest rifleman when on the 30th July the commanding " officer, Lieut.-Colonel Modrow, suddenly paraded the battalion on " the barrack square, announced the state of ' Imminent Danger " ' of War ' [not publicly proclaimed until next day], and in glowing " words reminded officers, N.C.O.'s and men of their oath and their " duty to their country. With heavy heart, he at the same time " bade farewell to the battalion. He was entrusted with the com- " mand of the *59th Reserve Infantry Regiment*. Major Weigeit " succeeded him in command of the battalion. The companies were " on the spot clothed and equipped for war. Every man received " 150 rounds of ammunition. . . . In exactly two hours the battalion " was ready to march off. . . . The four companies marched about " 2 P.M. to occupy the line of obstacles (*Hindernislinie*) which ran " parallel to the frontier, a few kilometres east of Ortelsburg, through " the thick woods, and was intended, in case of war, to offer the

" first resistance to the Russian advanced troops. . . . The machine-
" gun company and cyclist company remained in Ortelsburg in
" alarm quarters at the disposal of the battalion commander. Here,
" as in the blockhouse line in front, an always increasing state of
" nervous tension soon made itself observed."

In the market place of Treis, on the Moselle, a place visited by
British officers during the occupation of the Rhineland, is a War
Memorial to 302 men of the village, on which appears the words :
" Auf dieser Stelle traten an 31.7.14 abends um 8½ Uhr unsere
" ersten Kämpfer ein." (" On this spot our first fighting men fell
" in at 8.30 P.M. on the 31.7.14.")

If the date is correct these men " fell in " two days before the
first day of mobilization.

In the captured papers of Captain von Papen (in 1914 German
military attaché at Washington) was found a letter from a bank,
the Disconto-Gesellschaft, Potsdam branch, signed " R. Mimel,"
dated 25th July 1914 (postmark, Potsdam 7 P.M. of same day), in
which occurs the sentence : " We have never before seen such
" preparations for war as are being made at present." [1]

NOTE II

THE SCHLIEFFEN PLAN [2]

The strategical conception underlying the initial deployment of
the German Armies on the Western Front, and the invasion of
Luxembourg, Belgium and France, were founded on what is known
as the " Schlieffen Plan." Field-Marshal Graf Alfred Schlieffen
became Chief of the Prussian General Staff in 1890, in almost immediate succession to Moltke the elder, Graf Waldersee having held
the post for a little over one year between them. Just before vacating
office in favour of Moltke the younger, in December 1905, Schlieffen
drew up a Memoir (*Denkschrift*) for the benefit of his successor. He
had already, ten years earlier, departed from the basis of Moltke
the elder's plan in the event of a two-front war, which was to attack
Russia and stand on the defensive in the Western theatre. The Memoir
has never been published in extenso : only extracts from it are given
in the German Official Account ; but some other parts of it have
been disclosed by authoritative writers.[3] In 1905 Russia having

[1] The first financial war measure appears to have been taken on 18th
June 1914, when the President of the *Reichsbank*, " with special emphasis,"
recommended the directors of the leading Berlin banks to increase the
cover of their foreign securities by 10 per cent. From 2nd July en-
deavours were made to increase the gold reserve by " drawing in and
" holding foreign capital." " Financial readiness " was not officially
ordered until 31st July when " Imminent Danger of War " was declared.
(G.O.A., K.u.K., i. pp. 472-7.)
[2] See G.O.A., i. pp. 49-69, and Bredt, Moltke, Kuhl, Tappen, Baumgarten-Crusius, Foerster's " Graf Schlieffen und der Weltkrieg," Rochs'
" Schlieffen."
[3] Notably by Dr. J. V. Bredt, Member of the *Reichstag* and of its
Committee which enquired into the loss of the war, in his " Die belgische
" Neutralität und der schlieffensche Feldzugsplan." There is a mass of
literature on the subject.

only just emerged from the Manchurian war, Schlieffen in his plan
" dealt exclusively with a war against France and England " (G.O.A.).
The object was the annihilation of the French Armies and any British
troops that might be with them ; and the whole resources of Germany
were to be devoted to this single purpose. If, however, it turned
out to be necessary to fight on the Eastern Front as well as on the
Western, ten divisions, Schlieffen wrote, drawn " proportionately "
from the Groups of Armies allotted to the latter, should be detailed.

He calculated that $26\frac{1}{2}$ corps, 14 Reserve corps, 8 new *Ersatz*
corps and 11 cavalry divisions were required to ensure success.[1]
The actual mobilization strength at the time he wrote was $23\frac{1}{2}$ corps,
20 Reserve divisions not organized in corps (except one),[2] and 11
cavalry divisions ; but he indicated how the balance could gradually
be raised. By 1914 the numbers had increased to 26 corps, $13\frac{1}{2}$
Reserve corps, $6\frac{1}{2}$ *Ersatz* divisions (not corps) and 11 cavalry divisions.
In this interval, however, the French Army had also increased ;
Russia, too, had grown strong again ; and although only 9 divisions,
not 10, were allotted by Moltke to the Eastern Front, " in the end,
" the relative strength turned out to be more unfavourable than the
" Memoir had assumed." (G.O.A.) In fact, in August 1914 Moltke
had for the Western Front $20\frac{1}{2}$ divisions less than Schlieffen had
counted upon.

Schlieffen divided his forces into two unequal wings, in the
proportion of 7 to 1, on either side of the great fortified area of
Metz—Thionville. The larger mass, after deploying on the general
line Crefeld—Metz, was to make the gigantic left wheel already
mentioned, not only across Belgium, but across " South Holland "
and the so-called " Limburg Appendix," the narrow 40-mile-long
strip of Dutch territory which projects southwards and covers part
of the Belgian frontier against Germany.[3]

To condense what is known of the plan : by the 22nd day of Sketch 1.
mobilization (23rd August in 1914), the five Armies of the right
wing were expected to reach the line Thionville—Sedan—Mons—
Ghent ; by the 31st day (1st September), the line Thionville—
Rethel—La Fère—Amiens.[4]

Then—provision having been made for the investment of Antwerp,
" where the English may have landed "—whilst the other Armies of
this wing held their ground, or advanced methodically by siege
methods (the *Second Army*, in particular, digging in on the line of
the Oise or of the Oise—Aisne, thus covering Paris on the north),
the *First Army*, always trying to outflank the French by the west,

---

[1] *Landwehr* and *Landsturm* formations are omitted.
[2] The *Guard Reserve Corps* consisted of 1 Active and 1 Reserve division.
[3] Moltke's " Erinnerungen," p. 17. Captain van Voorst, of the
Netherlands General Staff, in " Over Roermund," has stated that in 1914
maps were issued to formations of the German *First Army* showing the
routes to be followed through Dutch territory south of Grave—Hertogen-
bosch—Tilburg—Turnhout. It is worth looking at Map 2 to see where
the routes thus delimited would bring a German Army : it is to Antwerp,
behind the Belgian Army deployed on the frontier, and to the Channel
coast ports.
In view of possible violation of their frontier, the Netherlands Government ordered the railway bridges in the Appendix to be prepared for
demolition on 26th July 1914.
[4] This was actually accomplished in 1914, the time lost by the Belgian
resistance having been regained by the rapid retirement of the French.

was to sweep over the lower Seine, past the west of Paris and round by the south. It was to be followed by six *Ersatz* corps, which would complete the investment of the capital. When they were in position, the *First Army*, reinforced by every division which could be spared from other Armies, possibly by part of the left wing brought round by train, was " to advance eastwards and drive the French by attack " on their left flank against their Moselle fortresses, against the Jura " and against Switzerland. The essential for the execution of the " operation as a whole is the formation of a strong right wing, by " whose assistance the battles will be won, and the enemy forced " to give ground again and again by a relentless pursuit." (G.O.A., i. p. 58.) " Everything was risked on the strength and rapidity of " the first blow." (General von Seeckt in a lecture delivered in 1928.)

If the French advanced to the attack, even broke into Alsace-Lorraine, so much the better for the success of the German plan ; it would in fact be " a kind service " (*Liebesdienst*) if they did so, for they would walk, as they did, into the trap set for them. Indeed, unless they advanced there could not be a " Cannæ " and it was with this battle of annihilation, on which he had written a book, in his mind that Schlieffen drafted his plan.

There was to be no ultimatum to Belgium or to Holland. The right of the German Armies was at first to deploy on the Dutch-Belgian frontier without any notification. This would give a hint of the German intentions, and it was assumed that the French would take counter-measures. In Schlieffen's opinion these could only be the occupation of the natural defensive position along the Meuse south of Namur. Thus the French would be the first to violate Belgian neutrality. (Bredt, p. 52.)

In any case, Schlieffen appears to have thought that there would be no difficulty in obtaining permission from the King of the Belgians, Leopold II., to traverse his territory ; he would make a protest and accept monetary compensation.[1] Similarly, " he did not consider " it out of the question, in view of the political situation [in 1905, " that is soon after the S. African War] that Germany on outbreak " of war against England would have no difficulty in obtaining " permission by an amicable arrangement with the Netherlands " Government, for the German Army to cross the Dutch province " of Limbourg (Maestricht, Roermund). Then the [Belgian] fortress " of Liége could be avoided by passing north of it, and quickly " brought to surrender by threatening it from the rear." (Bredt, p. 53.)

To the German left wing Schlieffen assigned no more than 3½ corps, 1½ Reserve corps and 3 cavalry divisions, in addition to the war garrisons (2 Reserve divisions) of Metz and Strasburg, 3½ *Landwehr* mixed brigades on the Upper Rhine, and one brigade in Lower Alsace. This small force was not, however, to stand on the defensive : 3 corps, a Reserve corps and the 3 cavalry divisions " were from the " outset to be employed in an attack on Nancy " (G.O.A., i. p. 59) ; their business was to attract as many French troops as possible. If the French did not counter-attack, two corps were to be shipped off by train to the right wing in Belgium (G.O.A., i. p. 60). Other versions, however, speak of an attack by the left wing taking place

[1] The Germans issued a proclamation on entering Belgium promising to pay for everything in " minted gold." The proclamation is in " Lüttich-Namur," pp. 14-15.

at some later stage of the proceedings in order to bring about a
" colossal Cannæ." Schlieffen's biographer, Dr. Rochs, states the
Field-Marshal " kept the plan [of thus using the left wing] in his
" eye in order to execute it in the course of the campaign, and thus
" achieve the complete rounding up of the Franco-British forces."
We shall see that Moltke attempted to do so.

It was easier to sketch out such an academic plan of campaign,
with complete contempt of the enemy and neutrals, than to carry
it out in the field, and the unfortunate Moltke was forced to make
modifications in it.[1] In the period that the changes were made,
1908–9, Colonel Ludendorff was head of the Operations Section of
the Great General Staff. (Bredt, p. 50, f.n. 44.)

First, Moltke gave up the idea of marching through Holland, " in
" order not to force the Netherlands also into the ranks of our
" enemies." (Moltke, p. 17.)[2] It was not expected that Belgium
would offer armed opposition to a march across her territory. But
the dropping of the plan of entering Holland forced the extreme
German right, the *First* and *Second Armies* to pass between Aachen
(Aix la Chapelle) and the southern end of the Limburg Appendix.
To ensure the rapid passage of this defile it was necessary to gain
possession of Liége as quickly as possible. It was most important
not to give the Belgians time to put the fortress in a state of defence
and destroy the important railway bridges near it. Moltke feared
that this could not be done by an " accelerated artillery attack "
and therefore decided to take Liége by a *coup de main* carried out
by frontier troops on peace establishment, without mobilization,
immediately on outbreak of war. " For the execution of this *coup*
" *de main* two days and the following night were allowed in the
" appreciation." (Bredt, p. 54.) If this failed, it was left to the
commander of the *Second Army* to decide whether to try again
with stronger forces, or proceed to " accelerated siege methods."
How long these might take is not stated in the scheme.[3]

The other and more important change was as regards the strength
of the left wing. In view of the increased importance of the industrial
areas, particularly those of the Saar and Rhine valleys, Moltke could
not leave them unnecessarily exposed to enemy attack. It is also
stated (Bredt, p. 50) that an additional reason for his not abandoning
Alsace was the expectation that the Italians might take part on
the German side ; in fact, their General Staff had made arrangements
to do so. As their troops would be brought to Upper Alsace, it was
necessary to hold that province with at least two corps (the *Seventh
Army* had three). If the Italians did not arrive, then the transport
of the corps to the right wing could be taken up. Trains to transport
seven corps were in fact collected as a railway reserve, beginning

[1] Schlieffen drew up his plan before aeroplanes were in practical use or
air reconnaissance behind the adversaries' lines was thought of. There is
no hint that Moltke and his assistants ever took into consideration the
fact that their foe might obtain information from the air which would
enable him to recognize and to stultify their plan.
[2] The German Government, too, wanted to keep Holland neutral so
as to be able to obtain world supplies through her ports.
[3] As the 5th August was the " first day " of the *coup de main* and the
last forts fell on the 16th, and the German Armies were mobilized, deployed
and ready to move in 7 days, the loss of time occasioned by the resistance
of Liége would appear to be at least four days. (See above, page 35.)

on the tenth day of mobilization. They were assembled in three sections ; the first behind the left wing, the second on the middle and lower Rhine, and the third in the Munster—Cassel area. (G.O.A., Railway Vol. i. p. 41.)

In any case, in 1909 Moltke raised the strength of the left wing from 5 to 8 corps. It is claimed by the German Official Account that by so doing he altered the proportion of 7 to 1 to about 3 to 1 (actually 60½ divisions to 16, excluding *Landwehr*), and thereby missed the point of the Schlieffen plan, which was a strong right wing. This does not appear to be quite fair on Moltke ; for he had to consider altered circumstances and his allotment of the extra strength to the left wing was intended to be a temporary measure at the outbreak of war.

After the defeat and retreat of the French First and Second Armies on the 20th August, six or even more divisions, to restore the Schlieffen balance, could, from the operations viewpoint, have been transferred from the left to the right wing ; but this was not practically feasible beyond Aix la Chapelle, owing to the destruction of the Meuse railway bridges and other demolitions carried out by the Belgians. Not until the 24th August could trains run past Liége, and then only by a deviation with 1 in 30 gradients, which required four locomotives for a train, two in front and two behind. The whole of the railway communications of the *First*, *Second* and *Third Armies* were compelled to pass over this one route until the 2nd September, when the Huy—Namur route became available for the *Third Army*. (G.O.A., Railway Vol. i. pp. 82-3.) " The Thionville— " Libramont—Namur section, so important for the transfer from " the left to the right wing, was opened to traffic on the 8th September " up to the destroyed Meuse bridge at Namur. The restoration of " the bridge was not accomplished until the last days of September." (Kretschmann, " Eisenbahnen," p. 37.) Not until the 5th September was it possible to begin the transport of troops from the left wing via Aix la Chapelle, Liége, Brussels.[1]

In consequence of the transport difficulties of sending the troops from left to right as planned (Tappen, pp. 13-15), and of the easy defeat of the French Third and Fourth Armies on the 21st August and their retreat—followed as it was by that of the Fifth Army and the B.E.F., as will be seen—Moltke appears to have jumped to the conclusion that the moment had arrived to carry out the second part of the Schlieffen plan. When in the early afternoon of the 22nd, Major-General Krafft von Dellmensingen, Crown Prince Rupprecht's Chief of the Staff, enquired on the telephone of Lieut.-Colonel Tappen, the head of the Operations Section O.H.L., whether troops would now be transferred to the right wing, the latter gave the astonishing order from Moltke, " Pursuit direction Epinal," and the explanation, " There are still strong forces in the Vosges, " they must be cut off." [2] It was hoped that the French, like the Belgian, frontier fortifications would be easily destroyed and overrun, and that the " operation in co-operation with the movements of the

---

[1] The *XV. Corps*, sent first, was delayed at Antwerp as the result of a Belgian sortie, and was not in the line of battle until the 14th September on the Aisne.

[2] Moltke, p. 434, says of this : " the pursuit came to a stop on the " Meuse, and the break-through (*Durchstoss*) planned between Epinal and " Nancy did not succeed."

" right wing would be the first stage of the surrounding of the " enemy's Armies as a whole, which, if successfully carried out " must, according to the views then held, bring about the end of the " war in a very short time." (Tappen, p. 15.) Thus the " Cannæ," the double envelopment dreamed of by Schlieffen was to be accomplished. It may fairly be said that Moltke failed, not by " watering down " the Schlieffen plan, as sometimes averred, but by trying to carry it out in its entirety, in the spirit of its originator, without the forces necessary for so vast an operation.

There was no doubt of the certain success of the Schlieffen Plan in the minds of the Prussian General Staff. In the negotiations with the Austro-Hungarian General Staff before the war, in 1908–9, the Germans laid down as the basis of the common plan that only twelve or thirteen German divisions would be employed in East Prussia in the first instance (only ten were actually thus employed in August 1914) : " Austria-Hungary, for the rest, must carry on " the conflict alone with Russia until a decision against France has " been obtained, which will be sought with all speed. This accom-" plished, there will be a mass transport to the East of important " German forces, which will be engaged there, in co-operation with " those of Austria-Hungary, to obtain a decision against Russia."

When Conrad enquired of Moltke when this decision against France and this transfer of troops might be expected to take place, he was informed " between the 36th and 40th day of mobilization " (" Aus Meiner Dienstzeit 1906–1918," i. pp. 369-70, by Feld-Marschall Conrad von Hötzendorf). Later on this was slightly modified, and Conrad was informed, " if France takes the offensive, " the decision is expected on the 21st day of mobilization ; if she " fights behind her frontier defences, on the 28th day. After this " decision the forces to operate against Russia should arrive there " about the 41st day of mobilization " (idem, p. 374).

CHAPTER II

22ND AUGUST 1914

FIRST CONTACT WITH THE ENEMY

(Sketches 4 & 5 ; Maps 2, 3, 5 & 6)

Maps 2 & 3. AT dawn on the 22nd August C Squadron of the 4th Dragoon Guards (2nd Cavalry Brigade) pushed out two officer's patrols from Obourg, on the canal, north towards Soignies ; one of these found a German piquet on the road, fired on it, and drove it off. This was apparently the first shot of the war fired by the British on the continent. Later a troop of the same squadron advanced to meet a body of German cavalry which was moving south along the road from Soignies towards Mons, turned it back near Casteau, and pursued it until checked by fire.[1] The 4th killed three or four of the enemy and captured three more, who proved to belong to the *4th Cuirassiers* of the *9th Cavalry Division.* Further to the east, the 3rd Cavalry Brigade found all clear for two miles north of the canal within the triangle Gottignies—Roeulx—Houdeng ; but here again the peasants reported the enemy to be in strength to the north, at Soignies and north of La Louvière (eleven miles east of Mons). Still further east patrols of the 5th Cavalry Brigade early found contact with the enemy in the direction of La Louvière and reported German troops of all arms to be advancing from the north, and the French to be retiring across the Sambre. General Sordet's 3rd Cavalry Division passed through the British 5th Cavalry Brigade soon after, on its march westward ; but it was not until nearly 10 A.M. that a German detachment of all arms [2] came in contact with two squadrons of the Scots Greys (5th Cavalry Brigade), which were holding

[1] German accounts also record this as the first contact. "Mons," p. 17.
[2] Of the *13th Division.* See page 70.

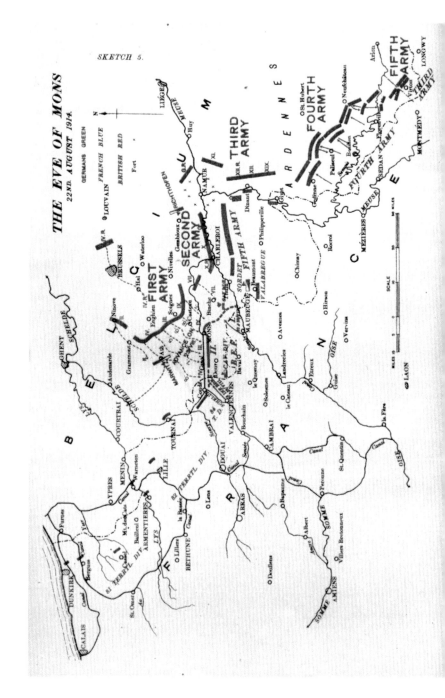

SKETCH 5.

THE EVE OF MONS
22ND AUGUST 1914.

GERMANS GREEN
FRENCH BLUE
BRITISH RED
Fort ×

the bridges over the Samme at Binche and Péronnes, facing east. The enemy made little effort to force the passage, though he shelled the Greys heavily but ineffectively, and kept up a fairly accurate rifle fire. The 3rd Cavalry Brigade, in support of the 5th, remained about Bray, two miles in rear, whence D and E Batteries R.H.A. fired a few shells. At 2 P.M. the Greys slowly drew off, having apparently, by sheer superiority of marksmanship, inflicted some thirty or forty casualties at the cost of one officer wounded. A troop of the 16th Lancers, which had been sent to their support, gave chase to a hostile patrol on the way, and came suddenly upon a party of *Jäger* on the hill immediately to the west of Péronnes. The troop rode straight over the *Jäger*, charged through them again on the return journey, at a cost of only one man wounded and three horses killed, and then left them to E Battery R.H.A., which had unlimbered to cover its return. Altogether, the cavalry was heartened by its work on this day, being satisfied that it was superior to the German horsemen, both mounted and dismounted, alike with rifle and with sword.

The cumulative effect of the encounters during the day on the British cavalry commanders was the conviction that German infantry in great force was in close support of the German cavalry. They had made reports in that sense on the previous day, and they were now more than ever confirmed in their opinion. Aerial reconnaissance during the forenoon did not tend to shake this view. One aviator landing at Beaumont (about 12 miles east of Maubeuge) to take in petrol, learned from General de Mas-Latrie, the commander of the French XVIII. Corps, that General Sordet, on his march westwards to the left flank of the Allied Armies, had on the 21st encountered German infantry north of the Sambre canal, and had been compelled to fall back. This accounted for his movement southward to Binche. Later, another British aeroplane (which returned to the aerodrome at 1.10 P.M.) reported the northern part of Charleroi and many other towns and villages near it to be in flames, and on its return westward was fired at by an infantry brigade between Ath and Enghien. A third aeroplane had a similar experience, the observer being wounded. The sum total of these observations was to the effect that brigades of German infantry, probably amounting to a corps in all, filled the roads south of Grammont, that a cavalry division was at

Soignies, and that the general front of this corps and cavalry division extended, facing south-west, from Lessines to Soignies,[1] no part of them being west of the Dendre canal, excepting a party of mounted troops which had been seen at Peruwelz, immediately to the north of Condé. Their further advance, if the direction were maintained, would bring their left (east) flank to Mons.

Sketch 5. Meantime, the British I. and II. Corps were advancing. Maps 3 & 5. In view of the situation, both corps started an hour and a half before the time which had been originally ordered. The 1st Division, moving at 4 A.M., reached its selected halting places—north and south-west of Maubeuge—at Bettignies, St. Rémi Mal Bâti, Limont Fontaine, between 3 and 5 P.M. But shortly before 3.30 P.M. Sir Douglas Haig received orders for the I. Corps to continue its advance. The result of the morning's reconnaissances had shown G.H.Q. that if the Cavalry Division were withdrawn, as already ordered, to the left of the line, the 5th Cavalry Brigade would be too weak to cover the large gap between the right of the II. Corps and the left of the French XVIII. Corps on the Sambre, and that consequently the I. Corps must be hurried up to its support. Accordingly, between 5 and 7 P.M. the 1st Division resumed its march, but did not reach its billets until far into the night, the 2nd and 3rd Brigades entering Villers Sire Nicole and Croix lez Rouveroy, some eight to ten miles south-west of Binche, between 9 and 10 P.M., whilst the 1st (Guards) Brigade on the right did not arrive at Grand Reng until 2 to 3 A.M. on the 23rd. This was a long march, which tried the troops severely.

About noon the 2nd Division, which had started at 5 A.M., halted in depth at La Longueville, Hargnies, and Pont sur Sambre, which lie on a north and south road passing west of Maubeuge. Its head was thus some six miles south-west of the rear of the 1st Division. The 2nd Division also received orders to resume its march; but they were subsequently cancelled, since the German advance had apparently ended for the day, and there was no immediate necessity to make such a call on the troops.

The whole movement of the I. Corps was covered on the west by a flank guard of the divisional cavalry, which traversed the Forest of Mormal.

In the II. Corps, the 3rd Division moved off at 7 A.M.,

---

[1] The troops in question were, commencing on the west : *IV. Corps, III. Corps* and *9th Cavalry Division.*

and the 5th, in three columns, at 6 A.M.; the former 22 Aug.
reached its billets around Mons, in the area Nimy—Ghlin 1914.
—Frameries—Spiennes, at about 1 P.M., and the latter, Sketches
on its left, the line of the Mons canal from Jemappes west- 4 & 5.
ward to Bois de Boussu, one or two hours later. The Map 6.
troops again suffered much from the cobbled roads, and
the march, though not long, was extremely trying. The
first outpost line taken up by the 3rd Division, consequent
upon the reports of the engagement of the 5th Cavalry
Brigade, was from Givry (6 miles south-east of Mons) to
the edge of Mons. Later in the afternoon, however, the
line was thrown forward in a wide sweep eastwards,
through Villers St. Ghislain, St. Symphorien, the bridge
at Obourg, and the bridge at Lock 5, to Nimy. The 8th
Brigade took the right of this line, the 9th the left, and the
7th was in reserve some five miles in rear at Frameries
and Ciply—the village around which Marlborough's army
had bivouacked on the night before the battle of Malplaquet. On the left of the 3rd Division, the 13th Brigade
of the 5th Division occupied the line of the canal from
Mariette to Les Herbières, and the 14th Brigade from Les
Herbières to Pommeroeul. The total front round Mons
held by the II. Corps was over twenty miles.

Thus the two corps were approximately in the positions
assigned to them in G.H.Q. orders of the 20th August. The
I. Corps was only a short distance from its intended
position ; but the cavalry was now about to move due
west, and a wheel of the II. Corps to the north-east up to
Lens had still to take place. For the moment the line of
the Mons canal, now held by the outposts of the II. Corps,
was the left of the British front ; with the I. Corps' front
it formed a salient angle, not a straight line.

A broad belt of woodland extended along the whole
length of the front north of the canal, capable of screening
the approach of the enemy to within two miles, or even
less, of the British piquet line. Around Mons itself the
canal forms a pronounced salient (the " Mons Salient " as
it will be called), which was ill-adapted to prolonged and
serious defence. On appreciating the situation, 3rd Division headquarters, which had been warned of the possibility of an attack by German advanced guards, decided
that in this quarter the outposts should not be reinforced
in case of attack, and ordered the preparation of a second
line position in rear, which will presently be described.
Meanwhile, as the II. Corps came up, it became possible

gradually to collect the Cavalry Division. Originally it had been intended that the division should move westward at noon ; but this, in view of the German menace about Binche, had been considered inadvisable. At 4 P.M., however, General Allenby gave the order to withdraw westward. The main body of the 5th Cavalry Brigade remained near Estinne au Mont (south-west of Binche), leaving the Scots Greys in position at Estinne au Val, a couple of miles to the north-west. At 6.30 P.M. this brigade, having first put the bridges over the Samme into a state of defence, went into billets between Binche and Merbes Ste. Marie. As the Cavalry Division drew off, it was followed by a German airship. After a most painful march westward behind the II. Corps, along some fourteen miles of cobbled street through the dreary squalor of an interminable mining village, it reached its billets at Elouges, Quiévrain and Baisieux, on the left of the Army, between midnight and 3 A.M. of the 23rd.

Maps 3 & 5.
In the course of the afternoon the Flying Corps made further reconnaissances towards Charleroi, and ascertained that at least two German army corps—one of them the *Guard Corps*—and the *Guard Cavalry Division*, were attacking the French Fifth Army on the line of the Sambre.[1] In the evening, the observers returned with very grave news, which was confirmed in detail, later, by Lieut. E. L. Spears, the British liaison officer with General Lanrezac, and by an officer of the Fifth Army Headquarters sent by that general. The French centre had been driven back, and the X. Corps had retired to the line St. Gérard (13 miles E.S.E. of Charleroi)—Biesme—Gerpinnes, from five to ten miles south of the river ; the III. Corps had likewise fallen back nearly the same distance, to a line from Gerpinnes westward to Jamioulx ; the XVIII. Corps on the left, however, remained in its original position, still echeloned to the rear, between Marbaix and Thuin.[2] General Sordet had moved southward from Binche, and was halting his cavalry corps for the night at Bersillies l'Abbaye (9 miles south of Binche), striking well to the rear of the British Army before moving west. General Valabrègue's two Reserve divisions were near Avesnes,

---

[1] The attack was made by the *Guard, X., X. Reserve* and *VII. Corps* (east to west). The advance on the previous day up to the Sambre had been led by the *Guard Cavalry Division* and the *Guard* and *X. Corps*.
[2] A good account of these events will be found in " Le 10ᵉ Corps à la bataille de Charleroi," by Colonel Lucas.

twenty-five miles south of Mons, preparing to march north- 22 Aug.
east towards Beaumont—Cousolre, in rear of the gap 1914.
between the Allied Armies.[1] The British on the Mons
canal, therefore, were some nine miles northward of the
main French line ; moreover, the 1st Division, when it came
up to its destination about Grand Reng, would be fully nine
miles from the left flank of the French XVIII. Corps. To
fill the gap there were no troops available, except the 5th
Cavalry Brigade and Valabrègue's two Reserve divisions ;
unless we include Sordet's cavalry, which was still in
the neighbourhood, though moving fast away from it.
Further, nine miles of the British line from the Mons
Salient to Rouveroy (9 miles south-east of Mons), was held
by no more than one infantry brigade, the 8th.

The enemy's main bodies were now reported at various
points in dangerous proximity. Twenty thousand men of
all arms, presumed to be part of the German *VII. Corps*,
were known to be moving southward from Luttre, about
eight miles north of Charleroi. Thirty thousand more
(supposed to be the *IV.* or the *III. Corps*, but actually
the *VII. Reserve*) were reported about Nivelles, and the
IX. Corps was bivouacking for the night south-east of
Soignies.[2] Yet another large body of all arms, reckoned
to be another corps, the *II.*, was moving west through
Ladeuse, about five miles south of Ath. Further, the
German *9th Cavalry Division* had been identified, with its
head at Peruwelz, and other cavalry, probably divisional,
was known to be north of Mons.[3] The inhabitants of Les
Herbières informed the Scottish Borderers that twelve
Uhlans had ridden into their village on the 21st, and that
some two hundred Germans were close at hand. Finally
an air report was brought into Maubeuge, and at once
taken personally to G.H.Q. by Br.-General Sir David
Henderson, that a long column, estimated at a corps, was
moving westward on the Brussels—Ninove road, and at
the latter town had turned south-west towards Grammont. This was later identified as the German *II. Corps*

---

[1] For the movements of General Valabrègue's Group see Note II. at end
of Chapter V.

[2] The *III.* and *IV. Corps* were to the west of the *VII. Reserve* and
IX., near Soignies and south-west of Enghien, respectively.

[3] On the night of 22nd/23rd Marwitz's three cavalry divisions were
concentrated around Ath, preparatory to moving north-westwards towards
Courtrai and the coast. The extreme left of the *9th Cavalry Division*, not
its head, had approached Peruwelz during the 22nd. Marwitz was looking
for a British advance from the coast, that is the west, not from the south.
Poseck, p. 31.

of the *First Army*. There were also signs of a strong force (*III. Corps*) moving down the great chaussée on Soignies ; it was endeavouring to hide itself from observation by keeping under the trees which bordered the road.

As the situation disclosed itself, the British Commander-in-Chief, whilst still hoping that offensive action might be possible, began to realize, in view of the isolated position of his force, the necessity of being prepared for any kind of move, either in advance or retreat. The air report that a corps was moving on the road Brussels—Ninove—Grammont seemed to give warning of a very ambitious enveloping movement to the south-west. In any case Kluck's advance made it impossible to expect that the British would be able to reach Soignies without opposition. Taking all these facts into consideration, Sir John French, after consultation with Major-General Sir A. Murray, his Chief of the General Staff, announced about 10 P.M. to the senior General Staff officers of the two corps and the Cavalry Division (Br.-Generals J. Gough, G. T. Forestier-Walker and Colonel J. Vaughan), who had been summoned to Le Cateau to receive orders for the next day's operations, that, owing to the retreat of the French Fifth Army, the British offensive would not take place. To a request of General Lanrezac, brought by a staff officer about 11 P.M., that the English should attack the flank of the German columns which were pressing him back from the Sambre, Sir John French felt that it was impossible to accede, for it would mean exposing his own left flank to an enemy at least twice his strength ; but he agreed to remain in his position on the canal for twenty-four hours. At the suggestion of the II. Corps, he ordered the I. Corps to take over by 6 A.M. on the 23rd the portion of the outpost line of the II. Corps which lay east of Mons. Accordingly the 2nd Division which, as we have seen, had remained in its original billets, moved forward at 3 A.M. on the 23rd, but it was too late to relieve the II. Corps before fighting commenced.

NOTE

German Uncertainty as to the Position of the B.E.F.
on 23rd August 1914

From the many sources of information now available, it would appear that the fog of war on the German side, in spite of superiority in aircraft, was very much more intense than on the British.

In the first place, Kluck laboured under the misapprehension [1] Aug. 1914. that the B.E.F. had landed at Ostend, Dunkirk and Calais. The Great General Staff had expected that it would do so ; [2] but the measures taken by the French to prevent espionage were so good that no information as to the real landing-places reached the Germans. Thus their accounts say : [3] " As regards the arrival of this " Force [the B.E.F.], the information was unreliable, and as regards " its line of advance, there was none whatever. Even a message " from the Supreme Command dated 20th August, which arrived at " *First Army Headquarters* on the evening of the 21st, ran : ' Dis- " ' embarkation of the English at Boulogne and their employment " ' from direction of Lille must be reckoned with. The opinion here, " ' however, is that large disembarkations have not yet taken " ' place. . . .' It was only on the 22nd August that an English " cavalry squadron was heard of at Casteau, 6 miles north-east of " Mons,[4] and an aeroplane of the English 5th Flying Squadron which " had gone up from Maubeuge was shot down. The presence of the " English on our front was thus established, although nothing as " regards their strength." [5]

What is more convincing perhaps than even this statement is the opening paragraph of Kluck's operation orders for the 23rd August,[6] issued at Hal at 8.30 P.M. on the 22nd ; all that he could tell his corps commanders was : " A squadron of British cavalry " was encountered to-day at Casteau, north-east of Mons, and a " British aeroplane, coming from Maubeuge, was shot down near " Enghien." Kluck's uncertainty, however, was still great, and he was so obsessed with the idea that the British would appear on his flank that on 23rd August, the actual day of the battle of Mons, hearing from Marwitz's cavalry corps, which he had sent towards the coast, that troops were detraining at Tournai, he halted his Army for two hours—8.30 to 10.30 A.M.—and prepared to wheel westwards. In Kluck's own words : " A report reached Army " Headquarters that a detrainment of troops had been in progress " at Tournai since the previous day. It seemed therefore not un- " likely that strong British forces were being sent forward through " Lille. The heads of the advanced guards of the corps were therefore " halted on the road Leuze—Mons—Binche to enable preparations

[1] Kluck, p. 33.
[2] Kuhl, " Generalstab," p. 91.
[3] General von Zwehl writing in the " Militär Wochenblatt," Nos. 35, 36, 37 and 38 of September 1919, in an article entitled " The Operations of Field Marshal French against the *First Army* and the *VII. Reserve Corps*." Kluck, p. 34, and Bülow, p. 21, also give the Supreme Command message.
[4] This belonged to the 4th Dragoon Guards, as mentioned at the beginning of Chapter II.
[5] The German navy had not been helpful in the matter. On 1st August the Chief of the Admiral Staff wrote to the Commander-in-Chief of the Fleet. " All information indicates that England intends to send the " Expeditionary Force, which has been assembled in Essex (*sic*), to the " Dutch and Belgian ports." On the 8th, " the naval command had " ' definite ' information that the transport of the B.E.F. to Calais and " eastwards (Dunkirk, Ostend and Zeebrugge) was ' in full swing.' " Nothing was heard in Germany of the mass of the Expeditionary Force " crossing the Channel in the middle of August." Schäfer's " Generalstab und Admiralstab," pp. 33-4.
[6] Kluck, p. 34.

" to be made for the Army to wheel westwards. . . . Eventually,
" however, it was reported that only a French infantry brigade was
" at Tournai, and that it was retiring on Lille. The Army, therefore,
" continued to advance."

The German General Staff monograph " Mons " adds that by the
detrainment at Tournai " the still unsolved question as to where the
" British principal forces would be met was made yet more difficult
" to answer. In relation to the landing-places of the British, their
" detrainment near Lille was not unlikely." It continues that, in
the course of the forenoon, information as to the presence of the
B.E.F. on the canal became more and more definite. " A captured
" private letter announced the presence of a strong British Army
" south of Mons. The nearest division of the *Second Army*, the *13th*
" *Division*, reported that a British cavalry brigade had been driven
" from Péronnes in a south-westerly direction.[1] . . . In the early
" morning, aeroplane reconnaissance had given no results in conse-
" quence of the prevailing fog."

On the arrival of the *2nd Battalion* of the *12th Grenadier Regiment*
(*III. Corps*), at Baudour, 2 miles north of the Mons canal, about
noon on the 23rd August, the cavalry reported [2] that there was no
enemy within fifty miles, and shortly afterwards two hussars, covered
with blood, galloped past shouting that the enemy had occupied the
line of the canal in front. A third limped past, dragging his blood-
stained saddle, and reported " in front, in the village, there they
" are ! "

The German General Staff account states that " reconnoitring
" parties were unable to reach the bridges [of the canal]. Whenever
" they tried to penetrate between the numerous widely scattered
" farms . . . they were received with fire from invisible riflemen."
It was thus in complete ignorance of the strength of the British that
Kluck advanced to the canal ; as he says, there " might have been
" only cavalry " in front of him.[3]

[1] It was two squadrons of the Royal Scots Greys. See page 62.
[2] Bloem, p. 116.
[3] Just as Bülow on the 22nd August at Charleroi thought that he was
only opposed by cavalry and weak infantry detachments when he had the
French Fifth Army in front of him. Bülow, pp. 21, 22.

CHAPTER III

23RD AUGUST

(Sketches 3, 4 & 5 ; Maps 5, 6 & 7)

THE ground on which the British Army had taken up its Map 6.
position was a narrow belt of coalfield which extends
roughly for rather more than twenty miles westwards from
Maurage (6 miles east of Mons) along the Mons canal, and
has an average breadth, from the canal southward, of two
miles. South of this belt the country gradually rises to a
great tract of rolling chalk downs, cut into by many streams
and with numerous outlying spurs. Every inch of this
territory has in bygone days seen the passage of British
armies ; name after name is found upon British colours,
or is familiar in British military history.

On the ground occupied by the I. Corps—that is to say,
roughly from Givry northward to Spiennes, thence westward almost to Paturages and thence southward again
to Quévy le Petit—the chalk comes to the surface ; and
there is even a little outcrop of it within the salient or
loop of the canal around Mons. This small area is cut up
by wire fences, market gardens, and the usual artificial
features which form the outskirts of a provincial town ;
and it is noteworthy that across this tangle of enclosures
no fewer than seven different roads diverge from Mons
north-east and north-west to as many bridges. At the
base of the salient the ground rises gradually from north
to south, for fifteen hundred to two thousand yards, till
it culminates in three well-marked features. The first of
these is Mount Erebus, a round hill immediately to the
south of Mons ; the second is a great whale-backed hump,
about a thousand yards long from north to south, very
steep upon every side except the eastern, and crowned by

71

two summits, Mont Panisel on the north and Bois la Haut on the south, the whole called by the latter name. The third is the height known as Hill 93, which lies south-east of Bois la Haut and is divided from it by a shallow valley. This last hill was of considerable tactical importance, since from it and from Bois la Haut observation and cross-fire could be brought to bear upon the ground east-ward about St. Symphorien. But Bois la Haut was in parts thickly wooded, and consequently from its northern end, where there were hospital buildings, there was little field of fire.

West of Mons the line of the canal is straight, and the actual borders are clear; the ground on both sides of it is cut up by a network of artificial water-courses, chequered by osier-beds, for a breadth of a mile or more. But the opening up of the coal-measures has turned much of the country immediately south of this watery land into the hideous confusion of a mining district. The space occupied by the II. Corps in particular, within the quadrangle Mons—Frameries—Dour—Boussu, was practically one huge unsightly village, traversed by a vast number of devious cobbled roads which lead from no particular starting-point to no particular destination, and broken by pit-heads and great slag-heaps, often over a hundred feet high. It is, in fact, a close and blind country, such as no army had yet been called upon to fight in against a civilised enemy in a great campaign.

At 5.30 A.M. the Commander-in-Chief met the commanders of his two corps and of the cavalry division in the chateau at Sars la Bruyère, when he issued orders for the outpost line to be strengthened, and for the bridges over the Mons canal to be prepared for demolition.[1] The conference over, the Field-Marshal, at 9.15 A.M. proceeded to Valenciennes. The 19th Brigade had just detrained there and was marching to occupy the left flank of the outpost line on the canal. This would thus extend nearly to Condé, where it was understood from a French staff officer that Territorial troops would take it up.[2] The local situation,

[1] The G.O.C. II. Corps, foreseeing the imminence of an attack, had already, at 2.30 A.M., sent an order to his two divisions to prepare the bridges for demolition. At 8.53 A.M. he issued a further order directing them to be destroyed on divisional order in the event of a retirement being necessary. All the barges in the canal were sunk by small gun-cotton charges. A full description of the work done will be found in " The Royal " Engineers Journal " for March 1932, " Demolitions carried out at Mons " and during the Retreat 1914," by Major-General Sir R. U. H. Buckland.

[2] The 84th Territorial Division subsequently arrived.

therefore, seemed satisfactory. For the rest, there was 23 Aug.
intelligence of fighting between German cavalry and French 1914.
Territorial infantry about Tournai, though no information
as to its results.

In describing the general disposition of the troops it Sketches
must be remembered that, as the Army had halted whilst 4 & 5.
in the course of wheeling or forming to face towards Map 7.
Nivelles, the front of the I. Corps was already turned north-
eastward, whereas the II., upon the wheeling flank, still
mainly faced to the north. The general front, therefore,
formed an obtuse angle, the I. Corps being on the right half
of the south-eastern arm, and the II. Corps round the apex
and along the western arm. The south-eastern arm from
Peissant to Mons was about ten miles long, and the arm
along the canal from Mons to Condé, seventeen miles.

The I. Corps was extended, roughly speaking, from the
Sambre to the Haine ; the 1st Division (Major-General
S. H. Lomax) being on the right, with the 3rd Brigade
(Br.-General H. J. S. Landon) in front between Peissant
and Haulchin (about four miles) ; the 1st (Guards) Brigade
(Br.-General F. I. Maxse) in rear of its right at Grand Reng
and Vieux Reng ; and the 2nd Brigade (Br.-General E. S.
Bulfin) in rear of its left at Villers Sire Nicole and Rouveroy.
The 2nd Division (Major-General C. C. Monro) was on its
way to take up the line on the left of the 1st Division from
Haulchin to Harmignies (another four miles), and meanwhile the vacant place was filled by the 5th Cavalry Brigade.
In the II. Corps, the ground in front of the right of the outpost
line of the 3rd Division (Major-General H. I. W. Hamilton)
was commanded by the great bluff of Bois la Haut. This
hill was reconnoitred for occupation by the batteries of the
XL. Brigade R.F.A., which were billeted immediately behind
it at Mesvin, and had been secured on the night of the 22nd-
23rd by sending forward the 2/Royal Irish Regiment, of the
8th Brigade, to connect with the I. Corps at Harmignies, and
hold the villages of Villers St. Ghislain and St. Symphorien.
The 1/Gordon Highlanders and 2/Royal Scots of the
8th Brigade (Br.-General B. J. C. Doran) were in position
near the Harmignies road from Hill 93 to the north-east
corner of Bois la Haut. The front from Bois la Haut
northwards to the apex of the Mons Salient, two miles, was
held as an outpost line by the 4/Middlesex. Rough entrenchments had been thrown up during the afternoon of
the 22nd, but were still unfinished when darkness fell. On
the left of the 4/Middlesex, the 9th Brigade (Br.-General

F. C. Shaw) held the line of the canal from the Nimy bridges on the western face of the Mons Salient, as far as the bridge of Mariette, six miles, with the 4/Royal Fusiliers, 1/Royal Scots Fusiliers and 1/Fifth Fusiliers.[1] The remaining battalion, the 1/Lincolnshire, was a mile south-west of Mons at Cuesmes. The 7th Brigade (Br.-General F. W. N. McCracken) was in reserve about Ciply, two miles south of Mons. The rest of the artillery of the 3rd Division was held for the present mostly in reserve—XXIII. Brigade R.F.A. north of Ciply, and XLII. R.F.A., together with the 48th Heavy Battery, at Nouvelles (1½ miles east of Ciply). The XXX. Howitzer Brigade was still on its way from Valenciennes.

Passing westward to the 5th Division (Major-General Sir C. Fergusson), the 13th Brigade (Br.-General G. J. Cuthbert) was posted, with a three-mile front, on the left of the 9th, the 1/Royal West Kent covering the bridges which span the canal immediately east of St. Ghislain, with four guns of the 120th Field Battery in close support on the tow-path. On the left of the West Kent, who had dug themselves excellent trenches by the railway bridge, the 2/King's Own Scottish Borderers, with the machine guns of the 2/King's Own Yorkshire Light Infantry, occupied the canal up to, but not including, the railway bridge at Les Herbières, with one company entrenched on the road north of that bridge. The two remaining battalions of the 13th Brigade were held in reserve in St. Ghislain, in rear of the centre of the brigade front.

On the left of the 13th Brigade, the 14th (Br.-General S. P. Rolt) occupied the line of the canal from the railway bridge of Les Herbières westward to Pommeroeul road bridge, a front of 2½ miles. The 1/East Surrey were on the right, holding the railway bridge itself, with one company pushed across to the north bank. From the foot-bridge south of La Hamaide, the 1/Duke of Cornwall's Light Infantry prolonged the front to Pommeroeul bridge. Here again a platoon, together with the machine-gun section, was sent across the canal to form a bridgehead upon the north bank. The machine guns were posted to sweep the straight length of road towards Ville Pommeroeul ; but a clear view northward was obstructed by rolling stock on the railway, which crosses the road about a mile to north of the canal. As the Haine stream, which was unfordable

[1] Two companies of the 1/Fifth Fusiliers were in the line, the remainder of the battalion was in brigade reserve with the Lincolnshire.

and had few bridges, passed about a mile behind this part 23 Aug.
of the line, the Duke of Cornwall's had orders to hold the 1914.
canal as an advanced position only, and to retire when
necessary to a second position, which the 15th Brigade
(Br.-General Count Gleichen) was directed to prepare
behind the Haine. The 2/Suffolk and 2/Manchester, the
remaining battalions of the 14th Brigade, were in reserve.
The 15th Brigade was divided, part preparing a position
on the Haine, with the rest in reserve further to the rear
near Dour. From Pommeroeul westward the 4th Cavalry
Brigade was responsible for the two remaining crossing-
places east of Condé, at Lock 5 and St. Aybert, until the
19th Brigade should come up, and these two points were
accordingly occupied by the Carabiniers. All troops were
warned to expect an attack early next morning.

The selection of positions along the part of the line held
by the 5th Division was a matter of the greatest difficulty,
the ground being a wilderness of deep ditches, straggling
buildings, casual roads and tracks, and high slag-heaps.
These last seemed to offer points of vantage, which were
generally found to be non-existent when their summits had
been explored, as they were commanded by some other
slag-heap ; while certain of them, which seemed to promise
all that could be desired, were found to be so hot that men
could not stand on them. The artillery was even more
embarrassed than the infantry : the officers had great
difficulty in finding suitable positions for batteries or even
for single guns, and were equally at a loss to discover good
observation posts. The general policy followed was to
push batteries or sections of batteries up to the infantry
line for close defence, and to keep the mass of the artillery,
including the heavy battery, on the left, where the guns
could cover all open ground in anticipation of a turning
movement round that flank. Altogether, the ground was
such as to baffle the most skilful and sanguine of British
gunners. Fortunately, on the enemy side, the conditions were almost identical ; and, except on the east,
where the ground was more open, the Germans could make
little use of their overwhelming superiority of numbers ; for
they were about to match eight divisions against four, and
actually in the infantry fight six against two extended
along a front of 13 miles. In fact, the line of the II. Corps
was so thin that it was little better than an outpost line, a
chain of small groups, lying on the canal bank, almost invisible, as is shown in a photograph taken by a machine-

gun officer during the battle from his flanking gun. Not without good reason was provision made for a retrenchment across the rear of the Salient and for occupying a position in rear of the canal, roughly Frameries—Wasmes—Dour, should a strong attack develop.

23 Aug.
1914.
Sketches
3, 4 & 5;
Maps 5
& 7.
The morning of Sunday the 23rd broke in mist and rain, which, about 10 A.M., cleared off and gave place to fair weather. Church bells rang, and the inhabitants of the villages near the canal were seen in their best attire going to worship as if war was utterly distant from them. Trains were running towards Mons crowded with the usual holiday makers. The mounted troops of both armies however were early astir. Those of the British 1st and 2nd Divisions, reconnoitring east of Mons towards the bridges of Binche, Bray, Havre and Obourg, soon encountered small parties of the enemy. Near Obourg they were pressed back, and at 6 A.M. the German cavalry exchanged shots with the 4/Middlesex. About the same time, other parties of German horse approached the Royal Fusiliers in the apex of the Salient, and two officers of the German *3rd Hussars*, the corps cavalry of the *III. Corps*, were made prisoners. Another patrol, towards Nimy, came in sight of the Scots Fusiliers, who killed one man, and identified his uniform as that of the cavalry regiment of the *IX. Corps*. Further west, two German patrols were caught in ambush, near Ville Pommeroeul between 6.30 and 7 A.M., and two prisoners were taken, one a dragoon, the other a hussar: an indication of the presence of two more regiments, both of the German *9th Cavalry Division*. The mounted troops of the British 5th Division crossed the Canal near the posts of the K.O.S.B. and of the West Kent; and both battalions pushed a reserve company forward to secure their retreat. That of the West Kent, " A " Company, advanced to the road-junction south of the village of Tertre ; that of the Scottish Borderers to a pond about half a mile north of Les Herbières road bridge. Each side was feeling for the other in expectation of the coming shock.

There could be little doubt where the first blow would fall. The Germans were completing a wheel from east to south, and immediately opposite to the eastern, or standing flank of Kluck's Army lay the Mons Salient. Before 9 A.M. German guns were in position on the high ground north of the canal, and very soon shells were bursting

thickly along the whole line of the Middlesex and the
Royal Fusiliers. One German battery commander boldly
unlimbered his guns in the open, and began firing at a
range of 1,500 yards ; but he was speedily compelled to
shift his ground by the machine guns of the Middlesex.
By 9 A.M. German infantry was pressing on to engage
the Middlesex about Obourg and, as the hostile movement
from north-east to south-west developed itself, troops,
all apparently of the *IX. Corps*, gradually spread around
the entire curve of the Salient from Obourg to Nimy.
By 10 A.M. the company in Obourg was heavily engaged
and, indeed, hard pressed ; and, shortly afterwards, the
machine-gun section of the Royal Irish joined that of the
Middlesex. Meanwhile, the Royal Fusiliers were cease-
lessly shooting down Germans, who at first came on in
heavy masses, but, being caught by the rapid fire of the
Fusiliers in front and by the machine guns of the Middlesex
and Royal Irish in flank, soon abandoned this costly method
of attack. They then began working across the front in small
parties, in order to form for a fresh effort under cover of the
woods. The British troops in the Salient had orders to make
" a stubborn resistance " ; the Middlesex and the Royal
Fusiliers, therefore, defended themselves with tenacity, and
until past 11 A.M. were still holding their original positions.

As the southward wheel of Kluck's Army progressed,
the attack gradually spread westward along the line of the
canal. The right of the German *IX. Corps* did not appear
to extend beyond Nimy ; [1] and it was not until 11 A.M.
that the *III. Corps*, which was next on the right of it,
came into action about the bridge of Jemappes, 2 miles
west of Mons. German shells fell in Jemappes itself, in
rear of the Scots Fusiliers ; the infantry almost simultaneously advanced in heavy lines. The forward post of
the Scots Fusiliers north of the canal was thereupon withdrawn, and, as the Germans came nearer, they were met by
a fire of rifles and machine guns which effectually checked
their progress. After a pause they came on again, taking
shelter behind the northern bank of the canal, and actually
closed to within two hundred yards of the bridge at Lock
2, west of Jemappes, when they were compelled by the
accuracy of the British fire once more to fall back. [2]

---

[1] This is now known to be correct (see Sketch 3 in " Mons ").
[2] Hauptmann (Professor) Heubner, of the *20th Infantry Regiment,
5th Division, III. Corps*, who witnessed the attack at Jemappes, in his

At Mariette, 3½ miles west of Mons, still in the 9th Brigade area, German shells found the bridge immediately, and a column of infantry in fours came swinging down a country road immediately to the east. It was promptly stopped by the fire of a small party, under a corporal, which occupied a house in the angle between this road and the waterway. The enemy then tried an advance down the main road ; but this had been obstructed by a wire entanglement immediately north and west of the bridge, and by a barricade immediately south of it ; the Fifth Fusiliers too were well and skilfully disposed, under good shelter, on both flanks of the road, both in advance and in rear of the bridge. Under a withering fire from three sides, the Germans pressed on to the wire, only to be brought to a standstill, and then driven back with heavy loss.

They now brought up two field guns within half a mile of the canal, and opened fire with high-explosive shell upon the defenders of the bridge : not without effect, for a shell bursting in the occupied house on the east side of the road killed the whole of the little garrison. But, instead of grey-coated soldiers, a number of little Belgian girls came down the road, and the Fifth Fusiliers naturally ceased their fire.[1] Thereupon, the Germans swarmed forward and, flooding over to the western side of the main road, were able to establish themselves within two hundred yards of the canal, whence they could bring an oblique fire to bear upon the defenders of the barricade. The advanced party of the Fifth on the north side of the bridge was then withdrawn ; but the Germans were still far from being masters of the passage of the canal at Mariette ; and the Fifth Fusiliers for the moment held their own with no great difficulty and without serious loss.

Further to the left, in the 13th Brigade area, " A " Company of the West Kent, at the cross roads south of Tertre, which was in support of the 5th Division mounted troops, was warned by the cyclists of the advance of the enemy in

book " Unter Emmich vor Lüttich, Unter Kluck vor Paris," pp. 69 and 74, speaks of the " numerous wounded " of the regiment which attempted to storm the railway and factory ; and at the end of the day says " that " they [the English], in any case, fought bravely and obstinately is proved " by the heavy losses that our German troops suffered here."
    [1] Evidence of Captain B. T. St. John, commanding the company of the Fifth Fusiliers which held Mariette Bridge. It is not suggested that the enemy drove them deliberately in front of him. In many cases inhabitants were caught between the two hostile lines.

force. This company had found a fair field of fire ; but the
line of retreat to the canal was difficult, the ground being
cut up by many deep ditches and barbed wire fences. As
far as time permitted, passages had been cut through the
wire, so that during its retirement the company might not
mask the fire of the main body on the canal ; but the
preparations were scarcely completed before a small party
of the cyclists came at top speed down the road from
Tertre and reported that the Germans had brought up guns
to drive them from the village. The leading German
infantry regiment, the *Brandenburg Grenadiers* of the *5th
Division* of the *III. Corps*, had, in fact, moved southward upon Tertre from Baudour, and the battalion
which was at its head had encountered considerable resistance from the cyclists. Five minutes after this alarm
had reached the West Kent company (that is to say at
about 11.10 A.M.), this German battalion debouched from
Tertre and moved southward, the bulk of the men being in
massed formation on the eastern side of the road to St.
Ghislain, with parties in extended order upon either flank.
They were met by a shattering fire of rifles and machine
guns, and were seen to suffer heavily. The commander of
the German regiment then made a regular attack with the
support of artillery, deploying his two remaining battalions
to the right and left of the first. By the German account,
the Brandenburgers suffered some loss in the village of
Tertre from the British artillery, presumably from the
guns of the 120th Battery on the canal. Meanwhile " A "
Company commander received a message from the divisional
cavalry, a squadron of the 19th Hussars, which had gone
out in the direction of Hautrage, north-west of Tertre,
asking him to cover its retirement ; and accordingly he
clung to his position, while three German battalions, a
German battery and a German machine-gun company all
came into action against him. The pressure soon became
so strong that he began gradually to withdraw by succession
of platoons, the men behaving with the greatest steadiness
and firing with great effect as the enemy came within
closer range. The rearmost platoon, in fact, fought its
way out with the Germans within a hundred yards of it
in front and upon both flanks. Eventually about half of
the company rejoined the battalion on the canal, the
remainder having been killed or wounded, and left, inevitably, to fall into the enemy's hands. This was the
fate of the company commander, Captain G. D. Lister,

and of one of his subalterns; but his men had made a magnificent fight and inflicted far heavier losses than they received.

Having cleared this advanced party out of their way, the *Brandenburg Grenadiers*, covered now by the fire of four or five field batteries, swarmed forward over the maze of wire fences and boggy dykes against the main positions of the West Kent and the Scottish Borderers on the canal. The four guns of the British 120th Battery were soon compelled to withdraw, apparently about noon ; [1] though, later on, the remaining section found a position upon a slag-heap, further to the south and east, and came into action with considerable effect. But the positions of the British infantry were so well chosen and concealed that the German artillery failed to discover them, and hence the progress of the German infantry was both slow and costly. In any case, the attack upon the bridge of St. Ghislain was stopped while still three hundred yards distant from the canal by the accurate fire of the West Kent, the machine guns of the K.O.Y.L.I., and the half company of the K.O.S.B., on the left of the bridge, who all alike had excellent targets, and took advantage of them to the full, with little loss to themselves. The Germans imagined that they were everywhere opposed by machine guns only, not realizing the intensity of British rapid fire. [2]

In this area, the enemy attack spread westward towards noon to the bridges of Les Herbières, where the *52nd Infantry Regiment* contrived, with great skill, to pass men by driblets over the road into the reedy marshes alongside the canal, and even to send one or two machine guns with them. Reinforcements of the 2/Duke of Wellington's and 2/K.O.Y.L.I. were called up about 2 P.M. in

---

[1] See page 74.

[2] A full and dramatic account of the attack of the *Brandenburg Grenadier Regiment* is given in " Vormarsch," by Walter Bloem, the novelist, who, as a reserve officer, was commanding one of the companies. He states that he lost all five of his company officers and half his men. The battalion commander said to him in the evening, " You are my sole " and only support . . . you are the only company commander left in the " battalion . . . the battalion is a mere wreck, my proud, beautiful " battalion ! " And the regiment was " shot down, smashed up—only a " handful left." Bloem adds, " Our first battle is a heavy, unheard of heavy, " defeat, and against the English, the English we laughed at." The regiment was withdrawn a quarter of a mile as soon as it was dark, and spent an anxious night, for, as the colonel said, " if the English have the slight- " est suspicion of our condition, and counter-attack, they will simply run " over us." " Vormarsch " has been translated under the title of " The " Advance from Mons 1914 " (Peter Davies).

closer support of the Scottish Borderers, the former suffering a few casualties from shell fire ; but their services were
not required, for the German attack had already come to a
standstill.

At the railway bridge of Les Herbières the Germans—
of the *6th Division* of the *III. Corps*—began by bringing a
machine gun into action in a house about half a mile from
the barricade put up by the East Surrey (14th Brigade).
This was instantly silenced by one of the East Surrey
machine guns ; the Germans, thereupon, searched all the
houses round the railway bridge with shell, in the hope of
locating it. They then tried to push forward in small
columns, but were stopped short by rifle and machine-
gun fire, which also dispersed a group of German staff
officers a thousand yards away and further to the east.
The enemy then plied the East Surrey defences with
shrapnel and machine-gun fire for half an hour, causing
no casualties, but disabling one machine gun ; after which,
about 1.30 P.M., he attacked with two battalions of the
52nd in mass, which advanced across the open at a range
of six hundred yards. Such a target was all that the
British could wish for : another company of the East
Surrey had by this time joined the one astride the embankment, and three platoons of the Suffolk had also come up
to cover their left flank. Rapid rifle fire, combined with
long bursts at selected objects from the remaining machine
gun at the barricade, mowed down large numbers of the
enemy and scattered the rest. At this point, therefore,
the Germans were decisively repulsed with very heavy
loss, at the cost of trifling casualties to the East Surrey.

Thus far, seven miles west of Mons, the German attack
had spread during the forenoon and the early afternoon ; the
line of the infantry of the *III. Corps* did not extend further
westward, while that of the *IV. Corps* had not had time to
complete its wheel to the south, so that the 1/Duke of
Cornwall's L.I. at Pommeroeul had not yet come into
action.

Throughout the forenoon and the early afternoon, Map 7.
that is to say, until 2 P.M., all had remained quiet opposite
the I. Corps, which it will be remembered faced north-
east. Between 11 A.M. and 12.30 P.M. the 2nd Division
had reached its destination, and the 6th Brigade took
position on the left of the corps between Vellereille le Sec
and Harmignies, with the 4th (Guards) Brigade in rear

of it about Harveng, and the 5th still further to the rear
at Genly and Bougnies. The 3rd and 6th Brigades now
therefore held the front of the I. Corps. About 2 P.M.
German guns at some point between Binche and Bray,
3½ miles to the north-east, opened fire upon the ridge of
Haulchin, against the left of the 3rd Brigade. About half
an hour later German cavalry [1] was seen moving across
the British front north-west from Bray towards St. Symphorien. The 22nd and 70th Field Batteries, which were
unlimbered about Vellereille le Sec, were able to shell these
parties with good effect, but in return were heavily shelled
by batteries which they were unable to locate. The 4th
(Guards) Brigade was pushed forward to extend the line
of the 6th from Harmignies north-west along the road to
Mons, and various battalions, coming under artillery fire in
the course of the afternoon, suffered a few casualties. But
heavy firing could be heard to the north about Mons.
About 3 P.M. a message from Major-General H. I. W.
Hamilton reported a serious attack on the 3rd Division,
and asked for assistance. Though the situation on the
right of the I. Corps was not yet clear, for the Germans
were still shelling the 3rd Brigade severely, General Haig
directed that two battalions of the 4th (Guards) Brigade
should take over the defence of Hill 93 from the 3rd
Division, and thus afford it some relief. The news brought
in by the 1st and 2nd Division cavalry at 3 P.M., that
the French east of the I. Corps had been obliged to fall
back a little, might well cause some anxiety; but the more
pressing danger lay on the left of the I. Corps in the vicinity
of Mons. In every other sector of the line the British
were holding their own with ease, and were punishing all
attempts to force the passage of the canal with severity;
but in the Salient, the weakest and most critical point of
the line, the situation was not so satisfactory.

Map 7.   We left the 4/Middlesex of the 8th Brigade, and the
4/Royal Fusiliers of the 9th between 11 A.M. and noon
making " a stubborn resistance " on the curve from Obourg
to Nimy, north-east of Mons. Br.-General Doran (8th
Brigade) had early given orders to the 2/Royal Irish,
whose companies had covered the ground in front of Hill
93 and Bois la Haut during the night, to assemble north
of the latter hill, and by noon the entire battalion was
collected there. Just about that time, the Middlesex at

[1] The *16th Dragoons* (see " Mons ").

Obourg, finding that Germans were nearly in rear of them, began to fall back westward through the Bois d'Havre, the wood just south of Obourg, and the enemy artillery began to shell the main line of the 8th Brigade, south-east of Mons, with shrapnel, but without much effect ; for it could not see the position of the Royal Scots along the Harmignies—Mons road, and the majority of the Gordon Highlanders were hidden from view. Infantry then advanced by rushes obliquely across the front of these two battalions, heading for Hill 93 and offering excellent targets. The rifles of both battalions were soon effectively employed, whilst the machine guns of the Royal Scots, thrown slightly forward in a quarry about the centre of the line, poured in a deadly enfilade fire. The 49th Battery also contributed to the enemy's discomfiture by firing shrapnel from Bois la Haut. Thus, in this quarter the enemy was brought to a complete standstill three hundred yards from the British trenches.

23 Aug. 1914.

Within the Salient the conditions were very different. The Germans shortly after noon succeeded in passing the canal west of Obourg, and in reaching the railway ; then, taught by hard experience, they abandoned massed formation and advanced in extended order. At 12.30 P.M. the Royal Irish were ordered to reinforce the Middlesex and moved off in the direction of Hill 62 under heavy fire of artillery and machine guns, which so delayed them that it was nearly 1.30 P.M. before they deployed on the left of the Middlesex. Anything in the nature of a local counter-attack to relieve the situation was out of the question, owing to wire fences and other obstacles. Far from gaining ground, the Royal Irish could only just hold their own. They now shifted their machine guns, which had previously been massed with those of the Middlesex, to the extreme right of their own front. They had not long been there when a body of Uhlans debouched from a wood about six hundred yards east of them : instantly fire was opened from both rifles and machine guns. The German horsemen turned about but, as they retired, were caught in flank by the fire of some of the Middlesex falling back from Obourg. This, however, though satisfactory, was but an incident if the *IX. Corps* was attacking in earnest, and every minute went to show that this was the case.

The situation of the Royal Irish and the Middlesex was precarious in the extreme ; for they were not in a well concealed position which the German artillery could not exactly locate, or with a good field of fire before them. On the contrary, their ground was under good observation from the heights on the north of the canal; and the German batteries,[1] having complete ascendency, kept them under heavy fire. Under the protection of this fire, the enemy infantry slowly gained ground by sheer weight of numbers, although not without loss. Shortly after 2 P.M. the machine-gun section of the Royal Irish tried to come into action on the road about three hundred yards north of Bois la Haut, but one gun was at once disabled and had to be abandoned. Returning to the original position, the remaining gun again came into action, but called down upon itself a concentrated fire of guns and machine guns, which disabled it immediately and killed or wounded every man of the section. The machine guns of the Middlesex were also in trouble; for the Germans had brought up at least six of these weapons against them, and the officer in command of the section had been wounded, though he still remained in charge of his men. By 3.15 P.M. the German infantry, in great force, was within a furlong of the Royal Irish and working round both flanks; so, after consultation with Lieut-.Colonel C. P. A. Hull of the Middlesex, Major S. E. St. Leger who was in command decided to withdraw the Royal Irish some fifteen hundred yards southward to the northern slopes of Bois la Haut. The right of their line moved first, meanwhile the re- mainder were collected into two bodies : one by Colonel Hull on the northern slopes of Hill 62, and the other at its north-eastern corner. The latter helped greatly to cover the retreat, which was conducted methodically and in good order. Finally the battalion rallied on the left of the left company of the Gordons whose line now extended almost to the cross roads north of Bois la Haut, the time being then about 4 P.M. The shelling was still very heavy, and the cross roads themselves were swept by machine guns from the east, though some buildings at that point and the ground west of the cross roads gave some protection from bullets. A section of the 49th Battery unlimbered on the left of the Royal Irish and, though greatly exposed, gave them some support.

The Middlesex fell back about the same time as the Royal Irish, between them and the 9th Brigade in Mons,

---

[1] Of the *18th Division* between St. Denis and Masières, 3 miles north- east of Mons.

though, being more widely extended, they were less easily re-formed. One company, on leaving the Bois d'Havre, which lies south of Obourg, entered the deserted rifle pits of the Royal Irish and there for a time stood fast. But the retreat of both battalions was facilitated by the fate of the first German attack upon the hill of Bois la Haut itself. This attack was opened by about a company of German infantry, which, with scouts in front of it, emerged gradually from a wood against the left centre company of the Gordons. The Highlanders allowed the scouts to advance and held their fire until greater numbers appeared; then they opened rapid fire at five hundred yards' range, and in a few minutes stopped the attack with heavy loss. Thereby a short respite was gained, which enabled the retiring battalions to settle down in their new positions.

Earlier, at 2 P.M., the Royal Fusiliers, in obedience to Br.-General Shaw's (9th Brigade) orders, withdrew southwards from Nimy, the supporting companies covering the retirement of the advanced companies with peace-time precision. Their losses did not greatly exceed one hundred; and after re-forming in Mons the battalion moved southward again to Ciply.[1] The Lincolnshire had been employed since noon in barricading the three roads which lead from Mons to the south; but the Germans did not follow the Royal Fusiliers very closely, and when at last they tried to debouch by the main road from Mons, they were met by a destructive fire from the Lincolnshire at the barricade and by a few shells from the 109th Battery at close range. Unable to make any progress, they turned westward, leaving the Lincolnshire to retire at their leisure by Mesvin upon Nouvelles, 3 miles south of Mons.

Owing to the close proximity of the enemy only the bridge over the canal to the north-west of Mons was blown up in this sector, although charges were laid. An officer of the 57th Field Company R.E. was taken prisoner at the Nimy bridge and all the work was done under sniping. One charge which had been placed in position was removed by a shell.

West of the Salient, about 3 P.M the Scots Fusiliers (9th Map 7. Brigade) likewise fell back, by order, through Jemappes

[1] Lieut. M. J. Dease (who died of wounds) and Private S. F. Godley of the 4/Royal Fusiliers were awarded the V.C. for the manner in which they fought the machine guns. All the men of two crews were killed or wounded.

upon Frameries, 3 miles from the canal. Here, since two of the three bridges had not been destroyed, from lack of an "exploder" to fire the charges, the Germans followed hard after, and there was sharp fighting among the slag-heaps. Some of the Fusiliers, firing from the houses, used their weapons with special effect ; but two companies seeking a route between the slag-heaps suffered much from machine guns which the Germans had instantly brought forward, and for a time were in serious difficulties, the ground being most unfavourable either for defence or for the co-operation of artillery. About 4 P.M., however, the two reserve companies of the Fifth Fusiliers, the left of the 9th Brigade, whose orders to retire from Mariette had reached them rather late, struck in from the west upon the flank of the Germans, and, after some fighting, enabled the Scots Fusiliers to extricate themselves and to re-form in Frameries. The German guns were sufficiently far advanced to shell the position of the South Lancashire (7th Brigade), a mile north of the village, but only one or two small parties of enemy infantry approached it. The forward companies of the Fifth Fusiliers meanwhile stuck to their position on the canal, in spite of the command to retire, in order to cover the engineers who were preparing the bridge of Mariette for destruction. Despite the remarkable coolness and gallantry of Captain T. Wright, R.E.,[1] who swung himself forward, hand over hand, under the bridge to connect the charges, the work could not be completed, though he made a second attempt after being wounded in the head. It was not until 5 P.M. when the sappers had withdrawn, after collecting all their gear, that these two companies of the Fifth retired towards Frameries. The Germans made no effort to press them and, in fact, did not immediately cross the bridge.

Further to the left, the 13th Brigade still held its position on the canal, though the fire of the German artillery steadily increased in the course of the afternoon. The enemy, indeed, pushed forward three batteries to within twelve hundred yards of the canal about St. Ghislain, and smothered the 13th Brigade with shells, but did remarkably little damage. Indeed, it was not until about 6 P.M., when guns were brought up within close range and destroyed the

---

[1] Captain Wright, who was killed on the Aisne, 14th September, received the V.C. for this service. Lance-Corporal C. A. Jarvis, 57th Field Company, R.E., also received it for working 1½ hours under heavy fire and successfully firing the charges at Jemappes station bridge.

barricade over Les Herbières road bridge that the Scottish 23 Aug.
Borderers withdrew to the southern bank. The East 1914.
Surreys (14th Brigade) withdrew their advanced parties
from north of the canal about the same time. The battalion then retired by alternate companies to the position
ordered near Thulin, south of the Haine. Nevertheless in
this quarter the Germans were unable to make the slightest progress, and, indeed, at dusk the West Kent were still
holding their position north of the canal.[1] Parties of the
17th Field Company R.E. remained near the bridges in
this sector until 1.30 A.M. on the 24th, when, after all the
infantry had withdrawn, they blew up the railway and
road bridges at St. Ghislain, and the three bridges to the
west.

On the left of the East Surreys the Duke of Cornwall's
L.I. were left wholly undisturbed until 4.45 P.M. when a
mass of German cavalry coming down the road from Ville
Pommeroeul was driven back headlong by machine-gun
and rapid rifle fire. Immediately afterwards, the advanced
parties were recalled to the southern bank of the canal ; the
bridge was blown up by the 59th Field Company R.E., and
the adjacent bridges near Pommeroeul by the 1st Field
Squadron R.E. ; and then all fell back across the Haine
to the second position.

On the extreme left, the 19th Brigade relieved the
Cavalry Division between 2 and 3 P.M., the 1/Middlesex
and the Cameronians taking the line up to Condé. Soon
after 5 P.M. an attack was made upon Lock 5, when
the enemy contrived to mount a machine gun in a house
commanding the buildings. The lock bridge was therefore
blown up by the 1st Field Squadron R.E., but the 1/Middle-
sex, though it abandoned the buildings, continued to hold
its own without difficulty and with trifling loss. The two
bridges at St. Aybert, further west, were destroyed at
3 A.M. on the 24th, after all the cavalry parties had come in.

Such, therefore, was the condition of affairs west of Map 7.
the Salient whilst the 2/Royal Irish and 4/Middlesex were
defending their second position north of Bois la Haut ; the
facts most important to them were, that the Germans, in
consequence of the retirement, by order, of the 9th Brigade,
were defiling through Mons, and, though checked for a
time at its southern border, had nearly reached Frameries,
3 miles south-west of the town. About 5 P.M. the main

[1] See page 80, f.n. 2.

body of the Royal Irish was again forced to retire. By that time the men of the Middlesex who had occupied the rifle pits of the Royal Irish, many of their rifles being so clogged with sand as to be useless, were overwhelmed by the attacking swarms of Germans. Then came the turn of their machine-gun section which, with the water boiling furiously in the jackets of the guns, fired away its last rounds of ammunition into the masses of the enemy, and was then overpowered. Having no other position in rear which offered any field of fire, the main body of the Royal Irish re-formed west of the northern end of Bois la Haut, their withdrawal being assisted by the left company of the Gordons. Here the 4/Middlesex passed through them and, taking the first road to the westward, marched towards Hyon ($\frac{1}{4}$ mile west of Bois la Haut) on their way to Nouvelles, their place in the second position. The Royal Irish started back along the same road, but had not proceeded far before they found the enemy ahead of them little more than a hundred yards away. Cramped between the steep slope of Bois la Haut and a tangle of buildings on the other side of the road, they could not deploy ; the battalion was obliged to turn northward and to work round the hill to its south-eastern angle. Here the guns of the 6th Battery, expecting an attack every minute, were disposed in a semi-circle, and the Royal Irish, together with a platoon of the Gordons which was acting as escort to the battery, entrenched themselves about the guns, facing north, west, and south. The enemy followed them up, but, being in no great strength, did not venture to attack.

Meanwhile, the 23rd Battery had received orders to retire from the summit of Bois la Haut, and selected as its route a sunken lane leading due south into the main road to Hyon. Proceeding that way, the head of the battery had reached a point within a hundred yards of the main Hyon road, when the leading teams and drivers were all shot down by German infantrymen, who had come through Mons and were hidden behind a barricade at right angles to the end of the lane. The gunners went forward to engage the enemy with rifles, and, being joined by the battery escort of the Gordon Highlanders, drove the Germans back into Hyon with some loss. The enemy's barricade was then occupied, and a second barricade thrown up a little east of it ; some adjoining buildings were placed in a state of defence ; and, while all ranks gave themselves to the task of clearing the lane, the major in command of the battery went off to find Br.-General Doran (8th Brigade). Although the light had now begun to fail, the 23rd Battery was still in an unenviable situation. Moreover, the Germans seemed bent upon pinning the 8th Brigade to its ground; for between 7 and 8 P.M. they launched a general attack, without any preliminary bombardment, against the whole front of the Gordons and Royal Scots along the Harmignies—Mons road. The attenuated line of the Royal Scots had since 4 P.M. been reinforced by two companies of the Irish Rifles [1] from the 7th Brigade, and the entire front blazed into a burst of rapid fire, which cut the Germans down by scores and brought them instantly to a complete standstill.[2] They then drew off, and some of them assembling about the cross-roads north-east of Bois la Haut, they were dispersed anew by the fire of the little party of the Royal Irish installed there. Still, the general situation of the 8th Brigade was insecure; on its front the enemy, as he had just demonstrated, was in force, and in its rear parties had penetrated through Mons as far as Hyon.

To review the British line from the Salient westward, as it stood at nightfall : of the 3rd Division, the position of the 8th Brigade has just been described; it was the apex of the new front. The 7th and 9th Brigades were entrenched on its left between Nouvelles and Frameries three miles from the canal ; the guns had been withdrawn from Erebus to the vicinity of Frameries for the night. Of the 5th Division, on the left of the 3rd, in the 13th Brigade the West Kent were still in their position on the canal, with orders to retire three miles south-east to Wasmes at midnight. They had lost little more than a hundred men ; from five to six hundred yards to their front the *Brandenburg Grenadiers*, who had suffered heavy loss, were entrenched in the marshy meadows on the north bank. On the left of the West Kent, the K.O.S.B. had just withdrawn their advanced companies from the north of the canal, and had repulsed, with great slaughter, an attempt of the Germans to debouch in mass from a wood opposite the left of their main line. The bridges over the canal on

23 Aug. 1914.

Map 7.

---

[1] The 2/R. Irish Rifles had been attached about 2.30 P.M. to the 8th Brigade and had relieved the Royal Scots on Hill 93.
[2] The *75th Regiment* lost 5 officers and 376 men in this attack. See " Mons," pp. 33, 34.

their front were ready for demolition, and the K.O.S.B. were also preparing to march to Wasmes, some of the K.O.Y.L.I. coming forward to cover the movement. There was no sign of pursuit by the Germans, though even demolished bridges are not impassable for an enterprising infantry. Opposite Les Herbières the East Surreys and the remainder of the 14th Brigade had joined, or were in the act of joining, the Duke of Cornwall's L.I. in the second position south of the Haine. Here the enemy, after suffering severely while passing the canal from the machine guns of the D.C.L.I. and the Manchester, was firing away an immense amount of ammunition with very little result. On the extreme left, the 19th Brigade was in position on the bank of the canal.

Thus it will be observed that there was no uniformity of movement from the outpost line on the canal to the main position in rear : the characteristic obstinacy of the British infantry, which has always fought on without much regard to what was happening in other parts of the field, was thus early made manifest, in spite of the efforts of the Staff to co-ordinate the withdrawal. The 13th Brigade did not attempt to retire until night, though the brigades to the right and left of it had fallen back in the afternoon. The 19th Brigade also stood fast. As a result of the retirement of the two divisions from the outpost line on the canal to the position south of Mons, the left of the 3rd Division remained as heretofore on the road between Frameries and Cuesmes, but the right of the 5th Division extended no further than to the road from Quaregnon to Paturages ; between the inner flanks of the divisions there was a gap, almost entirely covered by houses, of some two miles. This gap had been foreseen by II. Corps headquarters, and more than one message passed early in the afternoon between General Smith-Dorrien and G.H.Q. and the Staff of the I. Corps with reference to using the 5th Brigade (Br.-General R. C. B. Haking) to fill it, as this brigade was close at hand in reserve near Genly, in rear of Frameries. As a first measure, General Smith-Dorrien ordered the 1/Bedford from the 15th Brigade to Paturages, and, later on, three battalions of the 5th Brigade arrived from the I. Corps, in compliance with his request. Two battalions of the 4th (Guards) Brigade had moved up late in the evening to Hill 93, and were in touch with the Royal Scots, thus completing the junction between the I. and II. Corps.

The only thing which still remained in doubt was the 23 Aug.
fate of part of the 8th Brigade and the artillery with it. 1914.
At 9 P.M. orders were issued by Br.-General Doran to fall
back to the new position at Nouvelles. The party of the
Royal Irish at the cross-roads, having clung to their little
stronghold till 10 P.M., joined the Gordons, bringing with
them one of the battalion machine guns, which had been
repaired from the wreck of the other. The 6th Battery
guns were man-handled to the foot of Bois la Haut, where
the teams were hooked in. These guns and the Royal
Irish were the first to move off, about 11 P.M. Meanwhile
the 23rd Battery had been working hard to clear the lane
and extricate its guns. Interference by a strong German
patrol soon after dark was stopped without serious difficulty, and by 10 P.M. the road was free and the battery
ready to march. Shortly afterwards the battery commander returned, having walked through some German
troops, and by his orders, shortly before midnight, the
battery drove off as noiselessly as possible—the Germans
being within three hundred yards of it—eastward to the
Beaumont road and thence, by Spiennes, to Nouvelles.
Then the Gordon Highlanders marched off, the Royal Scots
opening fire to drown the tramp of men and the clatter of
vehicles. Finally the Royal Scots withdrew, company by
company, and before 3 A.M. on the 24th the whole of the
8th Brigade, together with the three batteries attached to
it, was safe in Nouvelles. The two Guards battalions and
the Royal Irish Rifles left Hill 93 shortly after 2 A.M.

Altogether, the British commanders were not ill-
satisfied with the day's work. The unsatisfactory position
on the canal had been imposed upon them fortuitously ;
but it had been held for a sufficient time, and had been
evacuated, without great difficulty or disaster, in favour
of a second position only a mile or two in rear. The men,
too, were in high spirits, for they had met superior numbers
of the most highly renowned army in the world and had
given a good account of themselves.[1] The total casualties
amounted to just over sixteen hundred of all ranks, killed,
wounded and missing. The whole of these, except forty,
were sustained by the II. Corps, and practically half of
them by two battalions of the 8th Brigade in the Salient.[2]

[1] It may be of interest to note that the strength of the 3rd and 5th
Divisions, those principally engaged at Mons, was just under 36,000 ;
the strength of the British Army at the battle of Waterloo was 31,585
(Wellington Despatches, xii. pp. 485-7).
[2] The 4/Middlesex had lost over 400 and the 2/Royal Irish over 300.

The only loss of artillery was that of two guns of the 120th Battery, which could not be removed from their exposed position on the canal at St. Ghislain.

The general result of the action was that the German advance was delayed a whole day. Kluck's orders for the 23rd August had directed the *III.* and *IV. Corps* to " occupy the rising ground on the southern side of the canal," whilst the *IX. Corps* was to advance via Mons to the north and north-western front of Maubeuge. The positions prescribed for the 23rd were actually the limits of advance on the 24th.[1] Judged by the units whose casualties are now known, the enemy losses must have been very heavy. And this is confirmed by the behaviour of the Germans as it grew dusk. The success in the Salient against the 8th Brigade was not exploited. Nor did any enemy appear elsewhere to take advantage of the gaps in the British line or to embarrass the retirement. As at the close of a manœuvre day, German bugles, to the astonishment of the British troops near the canal, were heard to sound the " Cease fire," repeating it along the line unit by unit, and then, after some little singing at one place, all was quiet. But the enemy showed his nervousness and fear of a night attack by the constant discharge of illuminating flares, which the British soldier then saw for the first time.

Sketch 4.
Maps 3 & 5.

There was no real anxiety at G.H.Q., therefore, except as regards events in the French Fifth Army further east. During the day the Flying Corps had reported fighting about Charleroi, two powerful German columns moving south-westward from Charleroi and from Luttre, and a heavy engagement at Thuin, the left of the French Fifth Army.[2] A report which came to hand soon after 5 P.M.

---

[1] See Note at end of Chapter.

[2] The following message was dictated by Sir John French to Colonel G. M. W. Macdonogh and telephoned by the latter at 3.10 P.M. to Lieutenant Spears (liaison officer) at Philippeville for communication to General Lanrezac, in reply to the latter's enquiry for information as to the British action :

" I am waiting for the dispositions arranged for to be carried out, " especially the posting of French cavalry corps on my left.

" I am prepared to fulfil the rôle allotted to me when the Fifth Army " advances to the attack. In the meantime I hold an advanced defensive " position extending from Condé on the left through Mons to Erquelines, " where I connect with the two Reserve divisions south of the Sambre.

" I am now much in advance of the line held by the Fifth Army, and " feel my position to be as forward as circumstances will allow, particularly " in view of the fact that I am not properly prepared to take offensive " action till to-morrow morning, as I have previously informed you.

" I do not understand from your wire that the XVIII. Corps has as " yet been engaged and they stand on my inner flank."

stated that Tournai appeared to be in the enemy's hands, 23 Aug. and that a long column of all arms was moving southward 1914. through Ladeuze (13 miles west of Soignies), Grosage and Neufmaison towards Ville Pommeroeul.[1] The conclusion to which this intelligence tended was, that the enemy would probably continue to develop his attack during the night and upon the following day.   At 8.40 P.M. this conclusion was embodied in a message from Sir John French to the II. Corps : " I will stand the attack on the ground now " occupied by the troops. You will therefore strengthen " your position by every possible means during the night."

Further information, however, which arrived from French Fifth Army Headquarters during the evening and just before midnight—when Lieutenant Spears brought the news that General Lanrezac had decided to order a retreat to begin at 3 A.M. next morning—led the British Commander-in-Chief to decide that his position in advance of the general line was strategically untenable, and that an immediate retirement was necessary. He thereby escaped, to use the enemy's words, a " veritable wasps' nest "[2] and his action fell in with the wishes of General Joffre, official notification of which reached him next day shortly after 1 P.M. in two messages.

The first message was to the effect that the French commander had decided that his Fifth Army should manœuvre in retreat and rest its left on the fortress of Maubeuge, and its right on the wooded *massif* of the Ardennes, remaining in liaison with the British Expeditionary Force by means of cavalry. The second pointed out the desirability of delaying the advance of the enemy between Maubeuge—Valenciennes, and gave Cambrai as the general direction of retirement for the British if the enemy should appear in superior force, with their right on Le Cateau, and their left on the water line Denain—Bouchain—Arleux. G.H.Q. informed General Joffre that the British Force was falling back slowly to the position Maubeuge—Valenciennes, and that, if driven from this, it would act in accordance with his wishes.

The reason for these messages was sufficiently cogent. As a result of his operations on the 23rd, General de Langle de Cary had ordered a general retirement of the French Fourth Army on the 24th to the line Montmédy—Sedan— Mezières, that is, the line of the Chiers and Meuse. In consequence of the failure of the Fourth Army to get

---

[1] The German *IV. Corps*.   [2] Lieut.-General von Zwehl.

forward, General Lanrezac's right flank on the Meuse was not only exposed to attack, but his right rear was actually attacked by the German *Third Army* from the east, whilst the German *Second Army* advanced against his main force near Charleroi from the north. On the night of the 23rd/24th, therefore, General Lanrezac ordered the French Fifth Army to commence retiring before daybreak south of the general line Givet—Philippeville—Beaumont—Maubeuge, with its left, the XVIII. Corps, about Solre le Château, 22 miles south-east of Mons. General Valabrègue, hearing of the attack on the XVIII. Corps near Thuin on the 23rd, had assembled his Reserve divisions that night near Cousolre, 10 miles due east of Maubeuge. There was therefore not only a considerable gap between the Allied forces, but the French were preparing a retirement which might increase it.

NOTE

THE GERMAN ACCOUNT OF MONS

The monograph " Die Schlacht bei Mons," published by the German General Staff at the end of 1919, gives a very clear account of the fight, with excellent maps showing the attacks of the different Sketches corps. According to this, 3½ divisions (the *17th*, *18th*, *6th* and part 4 & 5. of *5th*) of the *First Army* attacked the British 3rd Division, and 2½ Map 5. (part of *5th*, the *7th* and *8th*) the British 5th Division.

The *IX. Corps* (*17th* and *18th Divisions*) attacked south-west towards Mons on the front Villers Ghislain—Nimy. On its right came the *III. Corps* (*6th* and *5th Divisions*) against Jemappes and Les Herbières and, further west, as far as Lock No. 5, the *IV. Corps* (*7th* and *8th Divisions*). At nightfall the *VII. Corps* of the *Second Army*, on the left of the *IX.*, had got no further than Binche, and the *II. Corps*, on the right of the *IV.*, was some 15 miles north of Condé, still marching southwards heading for that town, with the *II. Cavalry Corps* on its right facing westwards towards Tourcoing—Roubaix— Lille.

It was part of the *17th Division* artillery (six batteries) behind Villers Ghislain, and possibly some of the *VII. Corps* artillery, covered by the *16th Dragoons* and a *Fusilier* battalion, which fired on the I. Corps as related in the narrative.

The German account is frank enough ; it states : "Well en- " trenched and completely hidden, the enemy opened a murderous " fire . . . the casualties increased . . . the rushes became shorter, " and finally the whole advance stopped . . . with bloody losses, " the attack gradually came to an end." As soon as it got dark the Germans gladly stopped.

In the *17th Division* the *75th* (*Bremen*) *Regiment* lost 5 officers and 376 men in one attack. This division made no attempt to advance after dusk fell.

In the *18th Division* at the beginning of darkness the brigades dug in on the line which they had reached, and bivouacked. The *6th Division* got across the canal, but towards 7 P.M. all attempts to advance failed, and the division went into bivouac. " Fighting posts, pushed a few hundred yards out, protected the " tired troops." The *5th Division* failed to get across the canal. One of its regiments, the *12th Brandenburg Grenadiers*, whose attack on the West Kent has been referred to, had lost " 25 officers and far more than " 500 N.C.O.'s and men," when " the summer night settled on the " blood-stained battle-field and with its shade gave a protecting " curtain against the hostile fire." It was this division whose singing was heard : to cheer themselves, the men sang " Deutschland über " alles." The *IV. Corps* did not cross the canal during the battle. Some patrols managed to get over after midnight, but " up to 9 P.M. the " enemy fire was as strong as ever."

Kluck, according to the General Staff account, " after the stub- " born defence of the enemy, especially opposite the *III. Corps*, " expected that the British would offer energetic resistance again " next day on the high ground south of Mons. He therefore resolved " to continue the attack next day enveloping the left flank, with the " intention of cutting off the enemy's retreat to the *west*." [1] The *II. Cavalry Corps* was ordered south to assist. Kluck, in his version of his orders, adds " The attack will be so directed as to force the " enemy into Maubeuge."

The German Official Account of the battle ends with the words :— " A decision had seemingly not been obtained. Only the en- " velopment of the British by the right wing of the Armies could " lead to this. Whether the German leaders could manage to carry " out this manœuvre, in time, against the left wing and left flank " of the British was now of vital importance for the result of the " great battle, not only to the *First Army*, but to the whole German " front."

The attempt was to fail on the 24th, and fail again on the 26th at Le Cateau, and the final result was to be the envelopment of the German right itself by the Allied left wing.[2]

[1] Kuhl's " Marne," p. 70, confirms this.
[2] It may be recalled that on this day, the 23rd August, began the battle of Tannenberg, which ended on the 31st with the complete defeat of the Russian Second Army (General Samsonov) ; also the battle of Krasnic, the first of the encounters of the long struggle in Galicia between the Russian Armies of the South-West front and the Austro-Hungarians, which ended on the 11th September with the retreat of the latter.

CHAPTER IV

THE RETREAT FROM MONS AND ACTION OF ELOUGES

24TH AUGUST

(Sketches A & 4 ; Maps 2, 3, 5, 6, 7, 8 & 13)

Sketches THE night of the 23rd/24th August passed without serious
A & 4. disturbance of any kind from the enemy ; and at dawn on
Maps 6 the 24th the Army occupied a line facing roughly north-
& 7. east, seventeen miles long, with the centre some three
miles south of Mons. The positions from right to left
were :—

I. CORPS :
   1st Division . . . . Grand Reng, Rouveroy, Givry.
   5th Cavalry Brigade . . Givry.
   2nd Division :
      6th Brigade. . . . Harmignies.
      4th do. . . . . Harveng.
      5th do. . . . . Paturages.
         2/Connaught Rangers . Bougnies.

II. CORPS :
   3rd Division :
      8th Brigade. . . . Nouvelles.
      7th do. . . . . Ciply.
      9th do. . . . . Frameries.
   5th Division :
      1/Bedford (15th Bde.) . Paturages.
      13th Brigade
      1/Dorset (15th Bde.) } Wasmes.
      14th Brigade . . Hornu—Bois de Boussu.
      15th do.
         (less two battalions) . Champ des Sarts—Hornu.
      19th Brigade . . . {Thulin, Elouges, Audregnies,
      Cavalry Division . . . { Quiévrain.

96

The bulk of the Army had been subjected to great 24 Aug. fatigue. The 1st Division, though scarcely engaged, had 1914. been hurried into its place by a forced march during the night of the 22nd/23rd and had been under arms for eighteen hours before it could billet or bivouac. Of the II. Corps, the 8th Brigade had been fighting all day, and the greater part of it obtained no rest until the early morning of the 24th. The 9th Brigade did not get into billets at Frameries until late. The 13th Brigade did not reach its assigned position much before daylight on the 24th, and the 14th Brigade was little earlier. The 15th Brigade fared better, though it did not settle down until midnight. The 19th Brigade had only just left the train at Valenciennes, when it was hurried up to take over a sector of the outpost line. Altogether, the circumstances were very trying for the reservists, who formed 60 per cent. of the infantry, and were for the most part still out of condition.

Shortly after 11 P.M. on the 23rd the senior General Staff Map 3. officers of the I. and II. Corps and of the Cavalry Division had been summoned, in view of a possible retirement, to G.H.Q. at Le Cateau. There about 1 A.M. the Chief of the General Staff explained to them that it was the intention of Sir John French to make a general retreat southwards of about eight miles to an east and west line, previously reconnoitred, from La Longueville (five miles west of Maubeuge) westward through Bavai and four miles beyond it to the hamlet of La Boiserette,[1] a front of about seven miles. He instructed the General Staff officers that the corps were to retire in mutual co-operation, the actual order of retirement to be settled by the two corps commanders in consultation. Br.-General Forestier-Walker left immediately by motor car, as telegraphic communication between G.H.Q. and II. Corps headquarters, thirty-five miles off, was interrupted ; but Br.-General J. E. Gough was able to send off a message, which reached General Haig about 2 A.M., with the additional information that the I. Corps was to cover the retirement of the II., the cavalry simultaneously making a demonstration, and that the roads through Maubeuge were not open to the British. G.H.Q. further suggested that the left of the I. Corps should receive particular attention, and that the line from Bonnet (six miles north of Maubeuge) westwards to Blaregnies should be firmly established before the

---

[1] Misspelt La Bois Crette on some maps.

II. Corps was withdrawn. Actually, it was nearly midday on the 24th before the corps commanders found opportunity to meet and arrange how these suggestions should be put into practice.[1]

Map 6.   To carry out G.H.Q. orders the I. Corps detailed a special rear guard, composed of the 5th Cavalry Brigade, J Battery, the XXXVI. and XLI. Brigades R.F.A., and the 4th (Guards) Brigade (Br.-General R. Scott-Kerr), under the command of Br.-General H. S. Horne, R.A., of the corps staff. It was to concentrate at Bonnet and make an offensive demonstration at daybreak, so as to delay the enemy's leading troops whilst the 1st and 2nd Divisions fell back.

To save time, General Haig motored to 1st and 2nd Division headquarters and in person issued orders for them to retire by two roads on Feignies and Bavai. The main body of the 1st Division marched off at 4 A.M., unmolested, except by a little ineffective shelling, and by a few small bodies of cavalry, which were roughly handled and dispersed by infantry and artillery fire. The 2nd Division followed at 4.45 A.M. and was equally undisturbed. Even the rear guard was not really troubled : [2] the 4th (Guards) Brigade retired by successive echelons from Harveng and Bougnies to a position two miles back between Quévy le Petit and Genly, pursued only by heavy but innocuous bursts of shrapnel. The 5th Cavalry Brigade covered the ground on the left of the Guards from Vellereille le Sec westward, through Harmignies and Nouvelles, to Ciply, under similar ineffective shelling. There was no real pressure from the enemy on the rear guard.

The main bodies of the divisions reached their destinations at Feignies, La Longueville and Bavai between 9 and 10 P.M., with no further mishap than the loss of tools and other articles which had been unloaded by the regimental transport and could not be re-loaded in time. None the less, the men were extremely fatigued ; they had had little rest for over sixty hours ; the country was close and cramped, and the day had been exceedingly hot ; there had been constant deployments and much labour on entrenching—inseparable from a retreat—so that the men suffered

[1] They met at the cross-roads near Bonnet, Sir John French being there with General Haig at the time.
[2] As will be seen in the account of the German operations on the 24th, no orders were issued for pursuit in this part of the field till 8 A.M.

greatly from weariness and want of sleep. Yet one bat- 24 Aug.
talion commander records on this date : "We had marched 1914.
" 59 miles in the last 64 hours, beginning the march in
" the middle of an entirely sleepless night and getting only
" 8 hours altogether during the other two nights. Many
" men could hardly put one leg before another, yet they all
" marched in singing. The other battalions of the brigade
" did not arrive till long after dark, but they also marched
" in singing."

The comparative ease with which the I. Corps was able Maps 3, 6,
to withdraw was far from reassuring, for it might indicate & 7.
that the Germans intended to make a decisive turning
effort further west, as, indeed, was their plan. Soon after
6 A.M. an aeroplane, which had been sent out at dawn,
brought information not calculated to diminish the anxiety
of the Commander-in-Chief : a column, from five to ten
miles long, had been seen at 4.30 A.M. moving south from
Leuze towards Peruwelz, having changed direction, at
Leuze, off the road that runs westward from Ath to
Tournai. This could hardly mean anything less than a
German division,[1] and its line of march from Peruwelz to
Condé would carry it to the west of the extreme western
flank of the British Army. Nothing, however, was known
of this at 4 A.M. at the commencement of the British
retreat, and the first movements of the II. Corps were
naturally made in complete ignorance of it. General
Smith-Dorrien, in pursuance of the Commander-in-Chief's
original orders, had made his dispositions before dawn to
withstand another German attack on the ground on which
his corps had spent the night. These dispositions proved
of advantage for gaining time when the instructions to
retire arrived ; for, before the II. Corps could retreat, it
was imperative that the roads should be cleared of all
transport and impedimenta, and the orders to that effect
did not filter down to the brigades of the 3rd Division
before 4.30 A.M. Meanwhile, before dawn, the Germans
had already opened a heavy bombardment against the
right of the II. Corps ; within an hour the fire extended
westwards along the whole length of the line, and by
5.15 A.M. a general infantry attack was rapidly developing.
At 5.30 A.M. the commander of the 3rd Division became
aware that the main body of the I. Corps was retiring, and
sent a staff officer to reconnoitre a second position further
to the south. Half an hour later he despatched orders to

[1] It was the *II. Corps* (see " Mons," Sketch 2).

the 8th Brigade, the right of his line, to withdraw from Nouvelles.[1]

Beyond the shelling, which did no damage, the 8th Brigade had been little troubled ; the German infantry did not show itself at all ; and at 8 A.M. the brigade began its march southward upon Genly. The 7th Brigade about Ciply, and the 9th Brigade at Frameries, when they began to move in their turn, did not escape quite so easily. The Germans were evidently bent upon holding them to their ground for a time, and about 6 A.M. launched their infantry in dense waves to the attack. They were thrown back with heavy loss, the 109th Battery finding excellent targets in the masses of the enemy visible behind the front line. Having thus cleared the air, about 9 A.M. the 9th Brigade fell back, in perfect order, through the town of Frameries, where there was some sharp fighting before the troops got clear of the streets, and marched southward upon Sars la Bruyère. The 7th Brigade held on for a little longer, and the South Lancashire were enfiladed by machine guns from the slag-heaps about Frameries, and lost between two and three hundred men before this brigade also was with-

---

[1] The following message from the II. Corps to the 5th Division gives a good idea of the situation about 7 A.M. :

To 5th Division.   From II. Corps.
G. 313.   24th [August 1914].

First Corps are retiring from the line Peissant—Haulchin—Harmignies to positions at Villers Sire Nicole and Quevy le Petit aaa Sixth Infantry Brigade moving to position about cross roads one mile west of Harveng aaa All these positions are to cover retirement of Third Division when that becomes necessary aaa Fifth Cavalry Brigade to Harveng with detachment and battery at Harmignies aaa Third Division right flank will probably fall back to Harveng early aaa When Third Division is forced to retire or ordered to retire it will take up position about Sars la Bruyere aaa Your retirement will have to be more or less simultaneous and you should at once send to reconnoitre a position if possible about Blaugies and Montignies sur Roc or where you can find it aaa Your roads of retirement will be those described to Colonel Romer [General Staff of 5th Division] and in addition that through Blaugies and Erquennes to Hergies but not through second *I* of Pissotiau [that is west of the Blaugies—Erquennes—Hergies road] which belongs to Third Division aaa If you feel yourself sufficiently strong where you are you might send a brigade or less back to your next position to prepare it aaa We cannot tell when Third Division will have to retire to Sars la Bruyere but hope that it will at least not be for two or three hours.

G. F. W. [FORESTIER-WALKER],
                                              B.G.
7.15 A.M.
Copy handed to Col. Maurice [G.S. 3rd Division].
One by tel.
One by officer.

drawn towards Genly. The Germans made no attempt 24 Aug.
to press them ; indeed, they handled the 3rd Division on 1914.
this day with singular respect. The division had, in fact,
though it was not appreciated at the time, inflicted on
them very heavy losses.

It was in the section immediately to the west of Maps 6
Frameries that serious fighting was first experienced. The & 7.
right of the 5th Division at Paturages, in the midst of the
sea of mining cottages, was held by three battalions of the
5th Brigade, and one, the Bedfordshire, of the 15th. The
German guns opened a bombardment before dawn, and
continued it steadily for some four hours, though to little
purpose. The enemy infantry meanwhile fell upon a company of the Bedfordshire near Paturages, and a very lively
fight followed without definite result. Meanwhile, further
to the west, the Dorsetshire (15th Brigade, but detached
with the 13th) were well entrenched along the railway to
the north-west of Wasmes, with two guns of the 121st
Battery dug in near their extreme left.[1] Still further to
the left, in the 13th Brigade, the 2/K.O.Y.L.I. was coming
into position with the 37th Howitzer Battery level with it.
The 2/Duke of Wellington's, which was shortly to relieve
the 1/Dorset, and the 1/R. West Kent were in Wasmes ;
the 2/K.O.S.B. was on the left at Champ des Sarts. The
1/Norfolk and 1/Cheshire of the 15th Infantry Brigade,
together with the 119th Battery, were ordered to Dour
(two miles south-west) as divisional reserve. The XXVII.
Brigade R.F.A. (less the 119th Battery) was about Champ
des Sarts ; the VIII. Howitzer Brigade (less the 37th
Battery) to the right and in advance of it ; and the
XXVIII. Brigade R.F.A. was to the left of it, to the north
of Dour.

In this sector of the line the enemy began operations
at dawn by bombarding the northern edge of St. Ghislain
for two hours, after which he pushed his patrols forward
and ascertained that the place had been evacuated by the
British.[2] The infantry [3] then crossed the canal by some
of the foot-bridges still left standing, and a battalion and
a half, hastening through the deserted streets, deployed

[1] The trenches alongside them were never occupied, so that the guns
were completely en l'air.
[2] Writing of the advance through St. Ghislain on the 24th, Hauptmann
Bloem (p. 153) writes : " Truly, our artillery shot famously this night and
this morning " ; and he says that the town looked " as if it had been
visited by a whirlwind."
[3] 5th Division.

from the southern edge of Hornu, the next village, opposite Champ des Sarts. The two advanced guns of the 121st Battery, which had opened fire, were quickly compelled to retire by the enemy's machine guns; but the Dorset and the 37th Battery brought the German advance to an abrupt standstill with considerable loss.

At 9 A.M. the three battalions of the 5th Brigade on the right of the 5th Division at Paturages, in accordance with their orders from the I. Corps, began to withdraw by Culot and Eugies southward upon Sars la Bruyère. Roused at 4 A.M. the Worcestershire and the H.L.I. had dug in on the front line, whilst the Oxfordshire L.I. entrenched a position in rear to cover retirement. Though under shell fire no German infantry had attempted to close with them, but their retirement at once brought trouble upon the denuded right flank of the II. Corps, where stood the Bedfordshire. A detachment of the Dorset filled the vacant place for the moment, and the resistance was for the time maintained; for the Germans were evidently less concerned to drive the British back than to hold them to their ground.

None the less, they were not content to be checked at the exits of Hornu. Again and again they tried to debouch, but without success, the 37th Battery working great havoc among them. It seems that the Germans must have lost heavily, for the *Brandenburg Grenadiers*, though exhausted and thinned by the engagement of the previous day, were hastily called up to reinforce the firing line.[1] Meanwhile, the German artillery had for some time been shelling Wasmes furiously, causing some loss in the 13th Brigade both to the Duke's and to the West Kent; but the former, as already related, was withdrawn to relieve the Dorset, and shortly afterwards two companies of the West Kent were also shifted eastwards to fill a gap between the Duke's and the K.O.Y.L.I. The German guns then turned with fury upon the British batteries, and the

---

[1] Of the approach to Hornu, Hauptmann Bloem says (p. 156) that his battalion was fired on by gun and rifles whilst it was in column of march, and the regimental adjutant brought him the order : " The *52nd* in front " are heavily engaged and require reinforcement at any cost. Haste is " imperative." Bloem cannot believe his observer when he reports " Herr " Hauptmann, the enemy is retiring." " What—what do you say—the " enemy is retiring. You mean he is advancing." . . . " In the thick " masses everybody rushes forward, Grenadiers and Fusiliers, men of all " companies mixed up . . . we jump into the English trenches. . . . " Suddenly something awful happens." They were heavily shelled by their own artillery.

XXVII. Brigade R.F.A. at Champ des Sarts was com 24 Aug. pelled to shift its ground.   But here, once again, the enemy 1914. did not seriously press the attack of his infantry.

On the front of the 14th Brigade, on the left of the 13th, all was quiet.   Still further to the west, the 19th Brigade had received orders from G.H.Q. at midnight to fall back to Elouges, six miles south-east, and at 2 A.M. it began its march upon that village by Hensies and Quiévrain.   At the same hour, the French 84th Territorial Division evacuated Condé and commenced its retirement towards Cambrai.   At dawn the Cavalry Division, which was in rear of the left, began to move : General Allenby, finding that the Germans were in great strength on his left, decided to withdraw some distance, and sent a message to Sir Charles Fergusson to that effect ; but, on hearing from him that the 5th Division was to hold its ground, agreed to cover its left flank.   A squadron of the 9th Map 8. Lancers, feeling its way forward to Thulin, the left of the II. Corps, found the enemy at the northern edge of the town and engaged him.   Meanwhile, the 2nd Cavalry Brigade (Br.-General H. de B. de Lisle) had taken up a position south of the main highway to Valenciennes and astride the road from Thulin to Elouges ; the 1st Cavalry Brigade (Br.-General C. J. Briggs) was on the railway to its left ; the 3rd (Br.-General H. de la P. Gough) to the left rear of the 1st near a sugar factory about a thousand yards south-east of Quiévrain, and the 4th (Br.-General Hon. C. Bingham) at Sebourg, about five miles further south. There they remained until the 19th Brigade had been withdrawn, when it came under General Allenby's command and was halted at Baisieux, two miles south-west of Elouges, to the vicinity of which the 1st Cavalry Brigade also retired.   Meanwhile, the advanced squadron of the 9th Lancers was delaying the march of the Germans from Thulin, and inflicting some loss upon them, though all the time falling back upon its main body.   About 6 A.M. German guns opened fire upon that main body from the neighbourhood of Thulin, and about 7 A.M. German infantry and artillery—of the 7th Division of the IV. Corps—were seen moving westward along the highway to Valenciennes.   One party turning southward, came down the road towards Elouges in column of route, and, after suffering severely from the rifles of the 18th Hussars and 9th Lancers upon either side of it, deployed and advanced upon a wide front.

Thereupon, General Allenby, ordering the road Elouges
—Audregnies—Angre—Roisin (five miles south of Elouges)
to be left open for the retreat of the 5th Division, about
9 A.M. began to withdraw his troops slowly southward.
Though he had sent three officers, one of them in a motor
car, to ascertain whether the 5th Division had begun its
retirement, not one of these messengers had yet returned.
Accordingly, he made his dispositions for retreat with due
precautions for the safety of the left flank of the Army.
The 19th Brigade was directed to fall back and take up a
position at Rombies (three miles south-west of Baisieux
and about seven south of Condé), and then the Cavalry
Division began to withdraw, by successive brigades, in
the same direction.   In order to delay the enemy's advance
to the utmost, the 2nd Cavalry Brigade, which formed the
rear guard, utilized the sunken roads, mineral railways
and slag-heaps which crossed and dotted the ground
between the Mons—Valenciennes road on the north and the
villages of Elouges and Audregnies on the south.   It was
supported by L Battery R.H.A., which was in position in
the middle of the area behind the railway between Elouges
and Quiévrain.   The brigade was very heavily shelled as
it retired, but fortunately little harm was done, and here
also there was no real pressure from the enemy.   By 11.30
A.M. the very last parties had come in, and the 2nd Cavalry
Brigade was moving through Audregnies upon Angre, the
18th Hussars bringing up the rear.

Maps 6   So much for the first moves of the great retreat.   The
& 7.   succeeding hours of the 24th August likewise passed without serious trouble on the right of the Army.   General
Horne's rear guard had, as related, taken up a position on
a front of three miles facing north-east, with its right on
the road from Mons to Maubeuge, about a mile north of
Bonnet, its left near Genly.   About 10.30 A.M. the 8th
Brigade came in on its western flank.   The 7th Brigade,
assembling at Genly from Ciply and Nouvelles, passed
through the 8th on its way to Blaregnies, where it—or,
at any rate, some part of it—halted and faced about.
About 11 A.M. the 5th Brigade [1] likewise joined the 8th
on the western side, forming up in depth from Eugies to
Sars la Bruyère.   The 9th Brigade made its way, as indeed
from the direction of the roads was inevitable, to the same

[1] That is to say, the three battalions which had been at Paturages.
The remaining battalion (2/Connaught Rangers) was with the 4th (Guards)
Brigade.

point; there the 3rd Division, together with General 24 Aug. Horne's rear guard, waited until far into the afternoon. 1914. There was no pressure whatever upon them. Indeed, at 11 A.M. General Horne reported that the special responsibility of his rear guard was at an end, and that he proposed to return his troops to their divisions. But, soon after 1 P.M., a message came in to I. Corps headquarters from the II. Corps that the retreat of the 5th Division on the left was delayed, and that meanwhile the 3rd Division would stand fast. Sir Douglas Haig directed his rear guard to conform with the movements of the 3rd Division; it accordingly remained in its position, little troubled or threatened, but stationary.

The retirement of the 5th Division had been delayed Maps 6 by the fact that it had to be carried out in the close pre- & 7. sence of the enemy. The Dorsetshire and Bedfordshire had been left at Paturages covering the right of the 13th Brigade, which was engaging the enemy issuing from the southern exits of Hornu. After the withdrawal of the 5th Brigade on their right, it was evident that these two battalions could not maintain themselves in such a position for long, and at 10.30 A.M. Br.-General Count Gleichen began the somewhat awkward operation of withdrawing them westward through Paturages. It was none too soon. The first line transport of the Dorsetshire, retiring by La Bouverie on its way to Blaugies, six miles north of Bavai, was caught in an ambush by the Germans,[1] but managed to extricate itself with little loss; then at 11 A.M. the Bedfordshire on the right (south of the railway line from Wasmes to Frameries), and the Dorsetshire on the left began their movement south-west across the rear of the 13th Brigade, towards Petit Wasmes and Warquignies. They had some sharp fighting, in which British marksmanship seems to have told its usual tale, before they could clear themselves from the streets. Part of the Bedfordshire, acting as escort to the divisional artillery, struck due south from Warquignies, and made its way to St. Waast lès Bavay;[2] the remainder marched to Athis, west of Blaugies, and the bulk of the Dorsetshire to Blaugies itself, where both halted, the time being about 2 P.M.

About 11 A.M., Sir Charles Fergusson had received a message from the II. Corps, giving him discretion to fall

[1] Part of the *20th Regiment* of the *6th Division*, it appears, had pressed on (see " Mons "), between Frameries and Paturages.
[2] On some maps St. Waast la Vallée, two miles west of Bavai.

back as soon as the troops on his right had retired ; finding that they had already gone and that the enemy was working round his right flank, he proceeded to follow their example. The 13th Brigade was holding its own with no great difficulty, though the enemy was shelling the 2/Duke of Wellington's on the right and inflicting considerable loss ; he was however doing little mischief to the 2/K.O.Y.L.I., and still refrained from any serious infantry attack. The 14th Brigade, on the left of the 13th, remained in comparative quiet, the 2/Manchester, part of which had been moved up to the left of the K.O.Y.L.I., alone being under heavy artillery fire. This brigade began the withdrawal by successive battalions, and formed up at Blaugies to cover the retreat of the 13th Brigade. The latter then fell back. The VIII. Howitzer Brigade withdrew at once ; the XXVIII. Brigade R.F.A. left a section of each battery behind to support the infantry rear guards. The operations seem to have proceeded with little or no interference from the German infantry. One enemy battery did, indeed, come into action in the open at three thousand yards' range, but was quickly silenced. Only in one quarter does the German infantry appear to have advanced in earnest. By some mishap, the order to retreat did not reach the 2/Duke's, which accordingly remained in position, with a battery of the XXVII. Brigade R.F.A. close to it. About 11.30 A.M., exactly the time when the order should have affected the Duke's, the Germans suddenly concentrated very heavy fire upon this battery from guns which they had brought up to close range. A sharp fight followed during the next hour and a half, and it was only the rifles of the infantry that saved the British battery. About 1 P.M. the Germans debouched in thick skirmishing formation followed by dense masses from the Boussu—Quiévrain road on the left front of the British battalion, but were greeted by such a rain of bullets from rifles and machine guns at 800 yards, and such a salute from the battery, that they stopped dead. Under cover of this final stroke, the guns limbered up and the battalion withdrew south-west into Dour. The Duke's had suffered heavily, their casualties reaching nearly four hundred of all ranks, but they had driven back six battalions.[1] By 2 P.M. the 13th and 14th Brigades were assembled at Warquignies and Blaugies, respectively, ready to continue

---

[1] *66th* and *26th Regiments* of the *7th Division* (see " Mons," Sketch 5). A German infantry regiment contained three battalions.

their retreat to their places in the new position: St. Waast (2 miles west of Bavai) and Eth (4 miles west and a little north of St. Waast).

But the 5th Division was not destined to march so far to the south-west as Eth. Hardly had the 13th and 14th Brigades begun their retreat, when Sir Charles Fergusson became aware that the withdrawal of the cavalry and 19th Brigade had been premature, and that his left flank was seriously threatened by German forces of considerable strength advancing due south between Thulin and Condé.[1] At 11.45 A.M. he sent an urgent message to the Cavalry Division to come to his assistance, and at the same time placed the 1/Norfolk and 1/Cheshire, together with the 119th Battery, all of which were still in reserve near divisional headquarters at Dour, under the command of Lieut.-Colonel C. R. Ballard of the Norfolk Regiment. The first orders given to this officer were to advance north and counter-attack. Accordingly, he moved his troops northward for half a mile till a staff officer came up and directed them to be moved westward into position along the Elouges—Audregnies—Angre road, down which, as we have seen, the rear guard of the Cavalry Division had already retired. Thither, accordingly, they marched. General Allenby had received General Fergusson's message about noon, and responded instantly by sending back the 2nd and 3rd Cavalry Brigades to the vicinity of Audregnies, which brought them within a couple of miles of Colonel Ballard. The 18th Hussars, who had just quitted their position of the forenoon, returned; L Battery came up next at a rapid trot, and halted just to the west of Elouges; whilst the 9th Lancers formed up by the road immediately to north of that village, with the 4th Dragoon Guards in rear. Simultaneously, the 3rd Cavalry Brigade, which was nearing Rombies, faced about and, hastening back, occupied a position on the ridge immediately west of Audregnies.

The scene of action was an irregular parallelogram, bounded on the north by the great highway from Mons to Valenciennes, on the east by the Elouges rivulet, on the south by the road from Elouges to Audregnies, and on the west by the valley of the Honnelle: a space, roughly speaking, about three thousand yards from north to south, by five thousand from east to west. From south to north the ground forms a perfect natural glacis, at this time

[1] The whole IV. Corps.

covered with corn-stooks. Across the parallelogram runs
the railway from Elouges to Quiévrain, for the most part
sunk in cutting and bordered upon each side by a quickset
hedge. About a thousand yards to the south, a mineral
railway runs parallel with it for about half its length, and
then comes to an abrupt end in a group of cottages. More
or less parallel to the Honnelle, the old Roman road,
famous under the name of the Chaussée Brunehaut, runs
straight as an arrow north-west from Audregnies, cutting
the great highway about a thousand yards east of Quiévrain.
Upon this road, about a mile and a quarter north of Audregnies, stood a sugar-factory, and, immediately to the
east of it, a cluster of high slag-heaps.

It was now about 12.30 P.M. Colonel Ballard's force
was just taking up its ground, facing nearly west, the
Norfolk with their right resting on the railway from
Elouges to Quiévrain, and the Cheshire on their left,
carrying the line to the northern outskirts of Audregnies,
and securing touch with the cavalry. All had, so far, been
comparatively quiet, when a sudden burst of fire, both of
guns and rifles, from the north-west, gave warning that the
Germans were opening their attack. It developed in
two distinct parts, one from Quiévrain, the other from the
Bois de Déduit and Baisieux south-east upon Audregnies.
Br.-General de Lisle (2nd Cavalry Brigade), galloping to the
9th Lancers, instructed the commanding officer to deliver,
if necessary, a mounted attack northwards in order to take
the German advance in flank ; whilst L Battery, finding
no suitable forward position near, wheeled about and
galloped south, coming into action behind the railway just
to the east of Audregnies.

Lieut.-Colonel D. G. M. Campbell ordered the 9th
Lancers to advance, which they did at the gallop in column
of squadrons, with two troops of the 4th Dragoon Guards
echeloned to their left rear. Crossing the sunken road
from Baisieux to Elouges at a point where it ran level with
the ground, they galloped on, speared a couple of German
scouts near the road, and caught sight of a few more taking
cover among the corn-stooks ; then, their advance checked
by the fire of nine batteries, they hesitated. Some dismounted by the sugar-factory, others swept round to the
right and back towards Audregnies, and a great number,
retiring along the mineral railway towards Elouges, rallied
there upon the 18th Hussars. Simultaneously, a squadron
of the 4th Dragoon Guards galloped down a narrow lane

ELOUGES

towards Baisieux, in order to seize a house at the end of it, 24 Aug.
and thus cover a further advance upon Quiévrain. On its 1914.
way the squadron was shattered by heavy fire of rifles and

The advance of the 2nd Cavalry Brigade seems to have
German attack, and so gained time for Colonel Ballard's
for there was not a moment to spare for digging—but in
Brigade and covered by the guns of D and E Batteries in
Baisieux. About 12.45 P.M. the action became serious, with
had at least seven batteries in action about a mile north
and, under the protection of their shells, the main body of
Quiévrain and Baisieux, into the open. L Battery now had
the chance for which every gunner prays ; no sooner did
Battery was not to be silenced, and forbade, under heavy

Colonel Ballard's infantry, likewise, with a perfect
which was in position south of Élouges, not less so. The

[1] All four regiments, twelve battalions, of the *8th Division* were

fire of the German artillery was heavy, but its shell, for the most part, went over. The 119th Battery answered the German guns with considerable effect, the Norfolks found excellent targets in the German infantry, who strove to swarm out of Quiévrain, while the Cheshire brought both rifles and machine guns to bear with great exerution upon the masses which were endeavouring to debouch from the Bois de Déduit. The 3rd Cavalry Brigade, which was spared all artillery fire, likewise held its own successfully south of the infantry, before Baisieux, and, with the help of D and E Batteries, effectually barred the way against the Germans at that point. The baffled enemy then tried a movement still further to the south by Marchipont, but was stopped by the 5th Dragoon Guards, who had come up, from the 1st Cavalry Brigade, on the left of the 3rd Cavalry Brigade. Everywhere the Germans were checked. The first of Kluck's enveloping movements had been, in fact, completely and victoriously foiled.

There were, however, disquieting signs of a still wider turning movement further to the west about Quarouble (three miles south-west of Quiévrain), where a mass of German infantry, thought to be the flank guard of an army corps,[1] could be seen moving steadily to the south. Accordingly, shortly after (about 2.30 P.M.) Colonel Ballard gave the order to retire.

Maps 3 & 6. About the same hour the troops to the eastward were also set in motion to resume the retreat. The 3rd Division marched from Genly—Sars la Bruyère for Bavai en route for the villages to the south-west of that town ; General Horne's rear guard, on its right, moved last of all, not until about 4.30 P.M. The main body of the 5th Division struck south from Blaugies through Athis upon Bavai and St. Waast, its place in the selected position ; the Cavalry Division also prepared to withdraw, the 1st Cavalry Brigade moving up to Onnézies to cover the first rearward Map 8. bound of the 3rd Cavalry Brigade to Angre. Meanwhile, the effect of the advance of the Germans [2] to the east of Colonel Ballard's flank guard was beginning to be felt, and the 119th Battery, between the fire of the three German batteries, and of a machine gun at much closer range, was suffering considerably. One section, the first that had come into action, fired at the hostile infantry

---

[1] Actually the three battalions of the *36th Regiment* of the *IV. Corps.*
[2] The *7th Division* of the *IV. Corps.*

until it was within eight hundred yards, and then withdrew. The four remaining guns were brought off by the
battery commander, Major E. W. Alexander, one at a time,
with the help of a party of the 9th Lancers.[1] The Norfolk
then fell back in two parties under a continuous hail of
shrapnel bullets, leaving a hundred of their wounded
behind them at Elouges. Most unfortunately, both the
second in command and the adjutant were wounded at
this critical moment, and thus one platoon in an advanced
position received no orders to retire.

Colonel Ballard sent to the Cheshire three separate
messages to fall back, not one of which reached them.
The major of L Battery also did not receive orders, but
seeing no sign of the Norfolk and having fired away nearly
the whole of his ammunition, was meditating withdrawal
when the brigade-major of the 2nd Cavalry Brigade arrived
and directed him to bring his battery out of action. The
guns were thereupon run down close under the screen of
the railway hedge ; the limbers were brought up one by
one at a gallop from Audregnies ; and the battery limbered
up and got away without further mishap. The party of
the 4th Dragoon Guards in the house by the lane then
retired also ; and they, together with L Battery and the
main body of the 2nd Cavalry Brigade, moved off south-
westward upon Ruesnes. The Cavalry Division had meanwhile fallen back towards St. Waast and Wargnies, the
4th Cavalry Brigade being further to the west between
Saultain and Jenlain.

The Cheshire, together with a small party of the Norfolk,
were thus left alone. Lieut.-Colonel D. C. Boger, commanding the former, was unaware of the general retreat of the
force, so that he was at a loss to know what was expected
of him. The Germans were now pressing forward rapidly
upon both flanks, and about 4 P.M., while making dispositions to meet the movement, he was disabled by three
wounds. Shortly before this, part of the reserve company
of the Cheshire at Audregnies had been ordered by a staff
officer to fall back, and, after vainly striving to rejoin the
fighting line—which was rightly forbidden—made its way
to Athis. As the Germans came closer, the main body

---

[1] Major Alexander received the V.C. for " handling his battery against
" overwhelming odds with such conspicuous success that all his guns were
" saved, notwithstanding that they had to be withdrawn by hand by him-
" self and three other men." Captain Francis Grenfell, 9th Lancers, also
received the V.C. on this day for gallantry in action and for assisting to
save the guns of the 119th Battery.

of the Cheshire fell back to the Audregnies road, where they were fired on by two machine guns placed in a dip in the ground, a couple of hundred yards away. These were promptly silenced by the machine guns of the Cheshire, and a little party of men charged forward with the bayonet to dislodge the enemy from this point of vantage. The Germans turned at the sight of them, and during this short respite the opportunity was taken to draw off a small part of the battalion across country to Audregnies wood, which they reached under heavy fire, thence making their way to Athis. But the Germans, seeing how few were their assailants, returned to the attack, and there was nothing left for the remainder of the Cheshire, mere handful though they were, but to fight to the last. They still had ammunition and could keep up rapid fire, and, by this time separated into at least three groups, they continued to defend themselves desperately until nearly 7 P.M. Then at last, surrounded and overwhelmed on all sides, they laid down their arms. Of the main body on the Audregnies road, only forty remained unwounded. Their captors were the *72nd Regiment*, belonging to the German *IV. Corps*.

The troubles of the small parties which had escaped were not ended on the battlefield. The enemy broke in from Dour during their retreat, and cut off a few men, and at Athis only one hundred could be assembled. The indefatigable gunners of the 5th Division artillery came into action along the line Blaugies—Athis—Montignies, and again further to the south at Houdain, and this enabled the survivors of the flank guard to reach their bivouac at St. Waast at 9 P.M., utterly worn by hunger, fatigue and hard fighting, but still unvanquished. They had held off from the main body of the 5th Division the pursuit of a whole German corps, but at heavy cost. The 119th Battery had lost thirty officers and men ; the Norfolk over two hundred and fifty officers and men ; whilst of the Cheshire, who in the morning had mustered nearly a thousand, only two officers and two hundred men answered their names at St. Waast.

The total losses on the 24th August were greater than on the 23rd, and amounted to roughly 250 in the Cavalry Division, 100 in the I. Corps, 550 in the 3rd Division, 1650 in the 5th Division and 40 in the 19th Infantry Brigade.

Thus ended the first day of the retreat. All circumstances considered, although the casualties were consider-

able, the operations had not been unsuccessful. The
5th Division had, indeed, been called upon not only to
defend six miles of front, but also, with the help of the
cavalry and of the 19th Brigade, to parry Kluck's enveloping attack, and it had triumphantly accomplished its task.
The flanking battalions to the east and west had, it is true,
suffered much, but only one had been actually overwhelmed ; not a single gun had been lost ; and the enemy
had been very severely punished. Our troops were still
confident that, when on anything like equal terms, they
were more than a match for their opponents ; the one
trouble which really oppressed them was want of sleep.
Long after nightfall the battalions of the 3rd Division were
passing the cross roads in Bavai, the men stumbling along
more like robots than living soldiers, unconscious of everything about them, but still moving under the magic impulse
of discipline and regimental pride. Marching, they were
hardly awake ; halted, whether sitting or standing, they
were instantly asleep. Yet these men on the eastern flank
of the corps had done little fighting and endured little pressure during the day. Worse was it on the western flank,
where cavalry and infantry had had hard fighting from
dawn till dusk, and many a man had been for over twenty-
four hours without sleep or food. And this, it must be
borne in mind, was only the beginning of the retreat.

The general disposition of the Army on the night of the Sketches
24th/25th, on a line east to west through Bavai, was :— A & 4.
Maps 3
& 13.

5th Cavalry Brigade .	.	. Feignies.
I. Corps :		
1st Division	. .	. Feignies, La Longueville.
2nd Division .	.	. Bavai.
II. Corps :		
5th Division .	.	. Bavai, St. Waast.
3rd Division .	.	. St. Waast, Amfroipret,
		Bermeries.
Cavalry Division⎱	.	. St. Waast, Wargnies,[1]
19th Brigade ⎰	.	. Jenlain, Saultain.

It will be observed that in the course of the day's march,
the 3rd and 5th Divisions had changed places, the latter
being now on the right and the former on the left of the
II. Corps. This manœuvre was intentional and carried

---

[1] The 2nd Cavalry Brigade was much broken up. Headquarters, with
L Battery, ½ squadron of 4th Dragoon Guards, 1½ squadrons of 9th Lancers,
and one squadron of 18th Hussars, were at Ruesnes.

out in accordance with orders issued for the purpose. The whole Army was inclining westward, in order to clear Maubeuge, and since the 3rd Division was able to begin its retirement considerably before the 5th, it could without difficulty proceed to the westward of Bavai, and thus shorten the retreat of the 5th Division by permitting it to fall back due south instead of south-west, and so to drop into its place on the right of the II. Corps. This movement not only eased the immediate task of the 5th Division, but relieved it from its difficult position upon the threatened western flank ; it was carried out without any collision, in fact without the divisions seeing each other.

NOTE I

GERMAN MOVEMENTS ON THE 24TH AUGUST 1914

Maps 3
& 6.

The German accounts of the 24th August are somewhat meagre. Kluck (according to the German Official Account) ordered the " continuation of the attack " to begin at 4 A.M. : the *II. Corps*, which was deeply echeloned behind the right, to close up to the front line ; and the *IV. Reserve Corps* to push up behind the right flank. Both corps were to move at 1 A.M. and reach Condé and Ligne (west of Ath). The directions given to the other corps were : *IX. Corps*, right on Bavai ; *III. Corps*, left on Bavai ; *IV.* on Wargnies le Grand (6 miles west of Bavai) and westwards. Marwitz's cavalry corps, moving on Courtrai, was, by Bülow's orders, implored to turn south on Denain (25 miles west of Bavai) and cut off the retreat of the British. At 10.30 A.M. the cavalry corps was put under Kluck, and ordered to Valenciennes via Denain ; but it was delayed at Tournai by the action with French Territorial troops (which it had mistaken for British), and at night, after a 25-mile march, was still about 10 miles short of Denain.

All that Kluck himself has to say about the day is : " After heavy " fighting, the leading troops reached a line (west to east) Onain— " Élouges—Dour—Genly—Harveng. The British force, estimated at " from two to three divisions, was driven back towards a line Curgies " —Bavai." He does not explain why his attempt at envelopment failed, why such a very short advance—only three and a half miles from the canal—was made, or why his corps halted in the middle of the afternoon. His staff officer, Kuhl,[1] states frankly " the enemy " put up a lively resistance with rear guards so that we only ad- " vanced slowly." Kluck adds : " After the severe opposition " offered by the British Army in the two-days battle Mons—St. " Ghislain, a further and even stronger defence was to be expected " on the line Valenciennes—Bavai—Maubeuge," and he then quotes four pages from Sir John French's despatch.

The German General Staff monograph, " Mons " gives a few details—some of which have been noticed in footnotes—and explains the absence of the *IX. Corps* from the fighting. The orders for its

[1] Kuhl's " Marne," p. 72.

advance were not issued until about 8 A.M., and immediately after- 24 Aug.
wards " an aviator brought news from which it appeared that the 1914.
" enemy had left only weak infantry and artillery on the line Ciply—
" Nouvelles—Givry, that numerous small columns were in retreat
" to the south and south-west, and that the enemy's artillery was
" in lively action with our own. At 9 A.M. the enemy's fire ceased,
" and the advancing infantry encountered no more resistance, as the
" enemy had apparently marched off in great haste."
    Nothing therefore could have been more successful than the with-
drawal of the I. Corps and 3rd Division. The heavy losses inflicted
on the Germans on the 23rd had not been without important results.
    The sketch maps in the monograph show that in the German
III. Corps the *6th Division* attacked Frameries and Paturages, and
the *5th Division* Hornu and Boussu. Towards 5 P.M. this corps halted
for the night.
    The German regimental accounts of the fighting at Frameries
are so greatly to the credit of the British Expeditionary Force, that
they are worth recording here.
    The attack on the Lincolnshire and South Lancashire was made
by a whole German division—the *6th* of the *III. Corps.* There is
a detailed story of the action by Captain von Brandis of the *24th*
(Brandenburg) Regiment.[1] He says :—
    " Our artillery is to prepare the assault. . . . A continuous
" stream of gun and howitzer shell thunders out, hurtling and
" howling over our heads, and bursting in dust and smoke on the
" edge of the village [Frameries]. No human beings could possibly
" live there. At 7 A.M. six companies of the regiment advance to
" the attack. We remain impatiently in reserve. . . . If we thought
" that the English had been shelled enough to be storm-ripe, we were
" fairly mistaken. They met us with well-aimed fire."
    His company was then sent up to reinforce. As it reached the
firing line, the men shout " Vorwärts " expecting to carry it with
them, but no one rose. " There were only dead and wounded to
" be seen. Tommy seems to have waited for the moment of the
" assault. He had carefully studied our training manuals, and
" suddenly, when we were well in the open, he turned his machine
" guns on." It was however only rapid rifle fire. The assault failing,
the village was shelled again, and the attack renewed with larger
forces. Eventually the Germans entered Frameries and found no
defenders there.
    " Up to all the tricks of the trade from their experience of small
" wars, the English veterans brilliantly understood how to slip off
" at the last moment." Of the casualties he says : " Our battalion
" alone lost three company commanders, and, besides, every second
" officer and every third man."
    Captain Liebenow[2] of the *64th Regiment,* of the same brigade
as Brandis, states that his battalion at Frameries lost " the adjutant,
" every fourth man and, of three companies, every lieutenant."
    Captain Heubner,[3] of the *20th Regiment,* states : " many of our
" companies had heavy losses in the attack on Frameries. . . . As
" on the previous day, the English again vanished without leaving
" a trace (*spurlos*)."

[1] In his book " Die Stürmer von Douaumont."
[2] In a letter to " The Times Literary Supplement," 4th September 1919.
[3] In his book " Unter Emmich vor Lüttich, Unter Kluck vor Paris."

In the *IV. Corps*, the *7th Division* moved through Thulin towards Elouges and the *8th*, swinging westwards, came through Quiévrain and Quiévrechain towards Audregnies and Angre, and thus, as related, struck the 5th Division flank guard. They halted in the afternoon : the *7th Division* near Elouges and the *8th* at Baisieux and northwards. No details of the fighting are given in the German account, but it is mentioned that the " British resistance was quickly " broken." This statement is not borne out by time and space : it is sufficient commentary on it to remark that through a long summer's day these two divisions made an average advance of only three miles.

Map 5.   Kluck's orders for the 25th, issued at 8 P.M., were : " Enemy's " main position is believed to be Bavai—Valenciennes. The *First* " *Army* will attack it with envelopment of the left flank, *II. Cavalry* " *Corps* against the enemy's rear." He " was of the opinion that " he had so far had only to deal with advanced portions of the British " Army—two or three divisions—which had now withdrawn on to " what was supposed to be their main position." [1]

NOTE II

The Operations of the French Troops on the British
Left between 20th and 24th August [2]

Maps 2   G.Q.G. instructions to General d'Amade, who took up his head-
& 3.   quarters at Arras on 18th August 1914, were : " To establish a " barrier between Dunkerque and Maubeuge, in order to protect the " railway communications from possible raids by enemy cavalry." He was also to extend the inundations of the Scarpe, the Schelde and the Rhonelle by opening the canal sluices, and to occupy the old forts of Maulde, Flines, Curgies, Condé and Le Quesnoy.

In accordance with these instructions General d'Amade, on the 20th August, disposed his three Territorial divisions (" de campagne " —*i.e.* excluding the Territorial divisions " de place," such as the 34th Territorial Division at Lille) as follows :—

Map 5.   81st from the sea to the Lys ;
                          82nd from the Lys to the Scarpe ;
                          84th from the Scarpe to the Sambre.

Map 3. The main line of defence for the 84th was : northern edge of Bois l'Evêque (north-east of Le Cateau)—Solesmes—Villers en Cauchies —Estrun—Sensée Canal ; its advanced line being Maubeuge— Mecquignies—Wargnies—Valenciennes—junction of Schelde and Scarpe.

On the 22nd, on the advance of the British Army west of Mau-beuge, the 84th Division closed in on its left about Valenciennes, clearing the British front, and advanced to Condé. It then formed along the Schelde from Condé north-westwards to Maulde.

On the night of the 22nd/23rd the 88th Territorial Division left Choisy le Roi, near Paris, in twenty-two trains, and detrained on the morning of the 23rd at Seclin and Templeuve, near Lille. It

---

[1] G.O.A., i. p. 430.   [2] See F.O.A., i.

was then ordered to march at once towards Cysoing (8 miles south-   23-24Aug.
east of Lille) and then to retake Tournai, which some German cavalry   1914.
had entered on the 22nd.[1] The main body of the division reached   Map 2.
Cysoing early on the 24th, and at 9 A.M. was suddenly subjected to
a heavy artillery fire (by Marwitz's cavalry corps) from about Tournai.
As the division had no artillery, it eventually retired towards Templeuve and Arras, after delaying the enemy some hours.

After the German attack at Mons on the 23rd, General d'Amade   Map 3.
reconstructed his line. At 2 A.M. (24th) the 84th Division retired
from Condé through Valenciennes towards Cambrai and Marquion.
During the morning of the 24th, the rear guard of the division in
position near Fresnes (two miles south of Condé) was attacked and
badly shaken. On the 25th, as will be seen, the division, still on the
left of the British, was attacked when near Haspres and became
disorganized.

Lille was evacuated on the 24th by order of the Ministry of   Map 2.
War,[2] and the 82nd Division took up the line La Bassée—Corbehem.
The 81st Division conformed to this move and was allocated the
area between Aire and the sea. Thus, a barrier between the British
left and the sea was still maintained.

[1] This cavalry patrol left again within a few hours.
[2] For an account of this incident see General Percin's " Lille."

CHAPTER V

THE RETREAT FROM MONS (*continued*)

THE 25TH AUGUST

(Sketches A, 4 & 6 ; Maps 2, 3, 9, 10 & 13)

Sketch 4.
Map 3.
AFTER a visit to the I. Corps and to General Sordet at Avesnes, Sir John French, on his return to G.H.Q. at Bavai in the afternoon of the 24th August, received further information of the retreat of the French Third and Fourth Armies and of the continuation of the retirement of the Fifth. Valabrègue's Group of two Reserve divisions, immediately to the right of the British, had fallen back south of Maubeuge.[1] The XVIII. Corps of the Fifth Army, next on the right, had been attacked early, and had fallen back in good order to a line from Solre le Chateau (about ten miles south-east of Maubeuge) south-eastward to Clairfayte.

As to the western flank, the Field-Marshal had been informed that two French Reserve divisions, the 61st and 62nd (General Ebener's Group), had been sent from Paris to Arras to reinforce General d'Amade, who would thus have six divisions—some 80,000 men, without counting the garrison of Lille, 25,000—to hold a line, some 70 miles long, through Douai, Béthune and Aire to the sea. What enemy forces were before d'Amade was still unknown ; but German troops—presumably part of the *IV. Corps*— had actually been seen marching south between Valen-
Map 2. ciennes and Bavai, and the Flying Corps in the evening reported that a large column of two divisions, ·in all probability the German *II. Corps*, moving west from Ath and Grammont, had wheeled southward at 10 A.M. at Lahamaide (5 miles north-west of Ath) and Ladeuze (4 miles south of Ath) ; also that at 4.40 P.M. one of these divisions

---

[1] For the movements of this group, the nearest French troops on the right of the B.E.F., see Note II. at end of Chapter.

118

had halted at Lignc (3 miles west of Ath) to allow the other to pass it. Cavalry was known to be as far west as Tournai. The British Staff was informed that Cambrai had been entrenched, and would be held by the French, while to the west of Cambrai the strong line of the Sensée would be occupied. From the small numbers available and the nature of d'Amade's troops, it could not be hoped that they would keep off for very long any serious German pressure upon the British western flank. 25 Aug. 1914.

The British Commander-in-Chief judged from the method and direction of the German attacks on the 24th that Kluck was endeavouring not only to turn the left flank of the British force, but to press it back on to the old fortress of Maubeuge,[1] which lay to its right rear, offering asylum just as Metz had presented its shelter to the French in 1870 during the battle of Gravelotte. Sir John French was not, however, inclined to be thus tempted, and, as the left of the French XVIII. Corps was already ten miles in rear of the British right, he decided to continue the retreat on the 25th some fifteen miles further, to a position in the neighbourhood of Le Cateau.

The routes for this retirement of the British Force presented some difficulty. Bavai is the crossing place of two ancient highways, the Chaussée Brunehaut, running from south-east to north-west, and another, known simply as the Roman road, running from south-west to north-east; in the southern angle enclosed between them lies the Forest of Mormal. This was then a compact and well-cared-for block of woodland, mostly oak and beech, with an extreme length of nine miles and an average breadth of from three to four. On its western side the Roman road forms its boundary for some seven miles; from east to west several fair roads, one main road and a railway cross it; in addition, the Bavai—Pont sur Sambre and the Englefontaine—Landrecies roads run respectively just north and south of it; but there is no road through it from north to south : the numerous forest tracks shown on the map were narrow and unmetalled, or at best had only a thin layer of unrolled stones ; they had, however, proved good going for the divisional cavalry of the I. Corps in the march northwards.[2] With the uncorrected maps Map 3. Map 10.

---

[1] This was actually the case. Kluck's orders for the 24th ran : " The " attack is to be so carried out that the enemy will be thrown back on " Maubeuge and his retreat to the west cut off " (Kluck, p. 45).

[2] See page 64.

then at the disposal of the British, a commander might well hesitate before involving his columns, with an enemy on their heels, in so large and blind a mass of trees.[1]   Just east of the forest runs the Sambre, with many loops and windings, with a general course south-west to north-east, but without, as might have been expected, a main road following the line of its valley : the Maubeuge—Leval—Landrecies road, the nearest to the river, was from half a mile to two miles east of it.   Consequently, if the river were crossed (and circumstances dictated that it must be crossed by the I. Corps as close to Maubeuge as possible), it must be recrossed before that corps could be re-united with the II.

The situation presented to the British Commander-in-Chief was, through the mere accident of topography, most embarrassing.   To pass the whole of his Army to the west of the forest would mean, practically, a flank march across the front of an enemy greatly superior in numbers and already threatening his western flank ; to pass entirely to the east of it was impossible owing to the proximity of the French.   Sir Douglas Haig was communicated with on the subject of avoiding the forest, and at 5.45 P.M. on the 24th he wrote to the Commander-in-Chief that he would be able to march at 5 A.M. on the 25th along the roads near the Sambre, and therefore could leave the Roman road to the II. Corps.   He added that his march would bring the head of his corps as far as Landrecies.

The Commander-in-Chief decided therefore to divide the British Force, and send the I. Corps east and the II. Corps west of the forest, and at 8.25 P.M. he issued orders for the retirement, with a notification that the exact positions to be occupied at Le Cateau would be pointed out on the ground.[2]   The movement was to be commenced so that all rear guards would be clear of the Bavai —Eth road by 5.30 A.M. on the 25th.   In the G.H.Q. operation orders the Roman road, Bavai—Montay (just north-west of Le Cateau) was made the boundary between the I. and II. Corps and assigned to the II. Corps ; thus the I. Corps was responsible for the Forest of Mormal.

Maps 3 & 13.

[1] The leading German corps avoided crossing the forest from north to south.   The *III. Corps* sent advanced guards by two of the transverse roads from west to east to secure the eastern edge ; the *IV. Corps* also sent a column from west to east by the road south of the forest to Landrecies, as will be seen.   The *IX. Corps* crossed it with infinite precautions by the main road from Berlaimont from east to west, two days after the battle of Le Cateau.   The next corps to the east, the *X. Reserve* (at Etreux on the 27th), with Richthofen's cavalry corps, moved well to the east of the forest.
[2] Appendix 13.

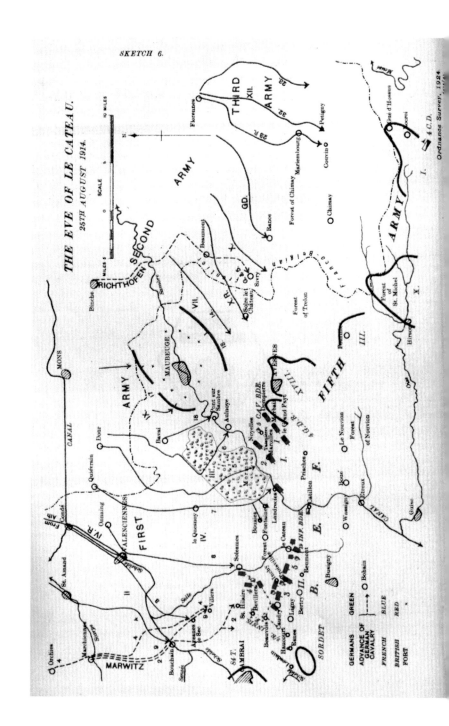

SKETCH 6.

THE EVE OF LE CATEAU.
25TH AUGUST 1914.

SCALE
MILES 5   0   5   10 MILES

Ordnance Survey, 1924.

GERMANS

ADVANCE OF
GERMAN CAVALRY

FRENCH   BLUE
BRITISH   RED
FORT   ×

GREEN

The various orders for moving the Force south-west- 25 Aug. wards may be summarized as follows :— 1914.

I. Corps : to move in two columns, and billet in villages on the route.

1st Division : to cross the Sambre at Hautmont and proceed thence southward by Limont Fontaine, Ecuelin and Monceau to Dompierre and villages beyond.

2nd Division : to cross the Sambre at Pont sur Sambre and Berlaimont, and billet in the area from Leval south-west to Landrecies.

5th Cavalry Brigade (attached I. Corps) : to cover the above movements, follow the march of the 2nd Division and billet in the area from Leval northward to Bachant.

II. Corps : to fall back west of the Forest of Mormal to the line Le Cateau—Caudry—Haucourt, by three roads.

Cavalry Division (with 19th Brigade attached) :

Two brigades, with II. Corps divisional cavalry attached, under a special commander, to cover the retreat of the II. Corps ; two brigades, with the 19th Brigade, under G.O.C. Cavalry Division, to guard the western flank.

In the course of the 22nd/23rd the 4th Division, having been relieved of its duties on the east coast of Great Britain by Yeomanry mounted brigades, Territorial cyclists and other units, had crossed the Channel to the ports of Havre, Rouen and Boulogne, and by the 24th eleven battalions of infantry and one brigade of artillery, the bulk of the combatants, had arrived by train at Le Cateau and the neighbouring stations. They were ordered to move forward and occupy a position at Solesmes to assist the retirement of the II. Corps. Major-General T. D'O. Snow subsequently received orders to withdraw, when the time should come, to the left of the II. Corps on the Le Cateau position.

In the right centre of the I. Corps the 5th Cavalry Maps 3 Brigade, in the early hours of the 25th, took over the out- & 13. posts of the 2nd Division from La Longueville to Bavai, Sketch 6. which had been attacked, though not in force. A troop was sent out eastwards to gain touch with the outposts of the 1st Division, and it ascertained that the French 53rd Reserve Division was retiring upon Hautmont, the very place selected for the 1st Division to cross the Sambre. From Feignies to Hautmont the 1st Division was confined to a single, narrow, high-banked, dusty road, and when the river had been passed at the allotted bridge the French

53rd Reserve Division and part of the 69th shared with it the road from Hautmont to Dompierre and Marbaix.[1] The weather was extremely hot, and the march, broken as it was by constant checks owing to the number of troops on the road, was greatly distressing to soldiers already much worn by fatigue and want of sleep. Otherwise the column was little disturbed, except by occasional bullets from German patrols, and the division reached its billets, in a line of villages west of Avesnes : the 1st (Guards) Brigade at Dompierre, the 2nd at Marbaix, which was shared with the French 53rd Reserve Division, and the 3rd at Le Grand Fayt.

Map 9.

The 2nd Division, moving to Noyelles—Maroilles—Landrecies, south of the Forest of Mormal, on the west of the 1st, had a better road from La Longueville to its bridges at Berlaimont and Pont sur Sambre ; the rear guard, supplied by the 6th Brigade, was only followed by dismounted cavalry and but little pressed, although it also encountered trouble, for Maroilles was the supply re-filling point of the French 53rd and 69th Reserve Divisions ; and no one could tell the British Staff which roads the supply columns would use after re-filling. Moreover, the tail of General Sordet's cavalry corps was using the road from Maroilles to Landrecies on its way to Le Cateau, and this meant further congestion. However, the 4th (Guards) Brigade duly reached Landrecies about 4 P.M., and the 6th Brigade reached Maroilles about 6 P.M. ; the 5th was detained till evening to guard the passages of the Sambre from Pont sur Sambre to Sassegnies (west of Leval) until it could be relieved by French troops, and did not reach Noyelles till midnight.

Sir Douglas Haig soon after 2 P.M had established his headquarters at Landrecies, where a message despatched from G.H.Q. soon after 3 P.M. reached him with the information that the II. Corps was occupying the Le Cateau position from Caudry to Inchy, including, temporarily, the I. Corps' part of Inchy, and asking him when he would be able to

[1] General Palat, in an article entitled " Le Maréchal French et le Général Lanrezac " in the " Anglo-French Review," November 1919, stated that the mistake was the I. Corps' and that it got on the roads assigned to the Reserve division ; but no allotment of roads as between the British and the French can be traced before a memorandum dated 10 A.M. on the 26th. F.O.A. does not mention the collisions. Similar mishaps as regards allotment of roads between Armies occurred on the German side, according to General Baumgarten-Crusius in his " Marneschlacht," due to there being no intermediate commander between Supreme Headquarters and the Armies, as there was later on in the war.

take his place in a defensive line, which had been partially prepared by civil labour, from Inchy south-eastward to St. Benin (1¾ miles south of Le Cateau).[1] His answer was urgently requested, since the orders for the 26th depended upon it.

General Haig realized that the situation was serious, for, about noon, the Flying Corps had reported German columns to be closing on Bavai. Meantime, his chief General Staff officer, Br.-General J. E. Gough, had gone to G.H.Q. and returned with instructions, in accordance with which he ordered the march of the I. Corps to be resumed south-westwards at 2 A.M. on the 26th : that of the 1st Division to St. Martin (5 miles south of Le Cateau), the 2nd to Bazuel (2 miles south-east of Le Cateau), the whole movement to be covered by the 5th Cavalry Brigade. Orders, issued at 7.30 P.M. by G.H.Q., were, however, received subsequently, and they directed that the retirement was to be continued a little further and that the I. Corps was to go on to Busigny (7 miles south-west of Le Cateau). The II. Corps (with the 19th Brigade), moving in echelon, was to fall back in the general direction of La Sablière (a wood just south of Busigny)—Prémont— Beaurevois (3 miles east of Le Catelet). The 4th Division, on the left was to reach the area Beaurevoir—Le Catelet.[2] The reason of the change was that, in view of the reports received of the further retirement of the French on his right and of the strength of the enemy on his own immediate front, Sir John French had decided that he could not stand on the Le Cateau position, but must continue the retreat on St. Quentin and Noyon.

The II. Corps had made every preparation for a very early start on the 25th in its retirement south-west from Bavai to the Le Cateau position ; but owing to the passage of General Sordet's cavalry corps from east to west across

---

[1] Thus ran the message to the I. Corps. The front allotted to the II. Corps seems very narrow. But some other message must have been sent to the II. Corps : for the diary of the latter for the 25th reads, 4.30 P.M., " Halt orders issued [they are attached to the diary] for the occupation of " the portion of the defensive position allotted to the II. Corps :

" 5th Division, Montay—Ruemont road (inc.) [this is the Roman " road, west of Le Cateau, the road which was the II. Corps boundary on " the 25th] to Troisvilles (inc.).

" 3rd Division, Troisvilles—Audencourt—Caudry (inc.)."

It was a wider and more suitable front than that mentioned in the G.H.Q. message to the I. Corps.

[2] Appendix 14.

its line of retreat, the roads to the south were blocked, and there was much difficulty in getting the whole of the transport into motion by midnight, the hour fixed in orders. The process was not, in fact, accomplished without the delay of a full hour, with the result that the fighting troops were also that much behind their time. The 5th Division was allotted the Roman road, immediately west of the Forest of Mormal ; the 14th Brigade formed its rear guard. The 3rd Division was to march to the west of the 5th Division on two roads as follows :

> 9th Brigade via Gommegnies (three miles north-east of Le Quesnoy)—Salesches—Vendegies au Bois ;
> 8th Brigade via Wargnies le Petit—Le Quesnoy—Salesches—Viesly ;
> 7th Brigade, general rear guard.

The 19th Brigade and the Cavalry Division were to move still further west by Villers Pol, Ruesnes, Vertain, Romeries and Solesmes, thus passing a couple of miles west of Le Quesnoy ; their function was to cover the rear and protect the western flank of the II. Corps.

It will be remembered that the 4th Division had been ordered to occupy a position in the vicinity of Solesmes to assist the retirement of the II. Corps, though not actually under its orders. The infantry and such of the artillery of the division as had arrived accordingly marched northward from their detraining stations at 1 A.M. to carry out the rôle assigned to them.

The main body of the 5th Division moved off at 3 A.M., but the rear guard was obliged to push some way northward towards Bellignies (3 miles north-west of Bavai), to cover the withdrawal of its guns from St. Waast through Bavai : a flank march, though short, across the enemy's front, which the nature of the country made inevitable. There was a brush with German troops about Breaugies (just south of Bellignies) and a second encounter near Bavai, where the guns of the XV. Brigade R.F.A. came into action with good effect. By 6.30 A.M.—just one hour late—the bulk of the rear guard had crossed the road Bavai—Eth, when, dropping into the Roman road, it was no further troubled ; the Germans followed it up at no great distance, but never pressed the pursuit.

Further to the west, the main bodies of the 3rd Division moved off at 5 A.M., the rear guard taking up a line from the Roman road westward through Bermeries to Wargnies le Petit, where its left was in touch with General Allenby's command. The ground on the west flank of the British, over which the Cavalry Division was working, is cut into a series of ridges by four streams, which flow in a north-westerly direction into the Upper Schelde between Bouchain and Cambrai. Across this ground from north-east to south-west runs the straight line of the Bavai—Cambrai road, and from north to south the Valenciennes—Solesmes —Le Cateau road. The 1st and 2nd Cavalry Brigades were extended from Wargnies beyond Jenlain, with the 3rd and 4th Cavalry Brigades to their left rear between Maresches and Préseau, all on the first ridge ; and the 19th Brigade, again to the left rear, on the next ridge between Sepmeries and Quérénaing.

The operations which now ensued on the west flank may be summarized as a running fight during which the Germans closed in, following the II. Corps and Cavalry Division, so that at night their advanced troops were practically in contact with the British.

The 7th Brigade, the rear guard of the 3rd Division, began its retirement upon Le Quesnoy without seeing any sign of the enemy except a few horsemen ; a reconnaissance pushed north-west to Famars, on the outskirts of Valenciennes, could also find nothing of him. On the other hand, bodies of French Territorial troops, belonging to General d'Amade's 84th Territorial Division, originally at Condé, were met retreating southward from Valenciennes, which indicated the evacuation of that town, and the prospect of increasing pressure from the enemy on the west. Reports from the Flying Corps pointed to the same conclusion : the head of a very large column—apparently a corps (the *IV.*)—had been seen at Quiévrechain (5 miles north-east of Valenciennes) at 7.30 A.M. Another column of cavalry and guns, three miles in length (evidently two regiments, part of the *II. Corps*), was moving south from Somain (12 miles west of Valenciennes), and its head had reached Bouchain (11 miles south-west of Valenciennes) at 6 A.M. Lastly, between 9 and 10 A.M. the divisional cavalry reported that parties of the enemy, presumably cavalry, were on the road between Haspres and Saulzoir (9 miles south by west of Valenciennes), and that they had passed along the main road from Valenciennes to Cambrai and struck south from the neighbourhood of Denain. The British cavalry was in position, well covered, and just keeping contact with the enemy ; but the menace to the western flank of the force and to the retreating French Territorials caused the 3rd and 4th Cavalry Brigades to be sent westwards to Quérénaing and beyond it to Verchain, thus covering the second ridge already referred to. The 1st Cavalry Brigade also moved north of them in the same direction, through Artres (4 miles south of Valenciennes) where it was heavily, though ineffectively, shelled.

At the same time, the 19th Brigade was moved by General Allenby south-west over the third ridge to Haussy in the valley south of it. At Quérénaing French gendarmes reported the information that large German forces were moving south-east from Bouchain, and this news was confirmed by the sound of heavy firing about Avesnes le Sec (3 miles south-east of the last-named village), and only four miles from the 19th Brigade. The 16th Lancers were therefore sent, about noon, to Haspres and Saulzoir to help the French Territorials ; but from Saulzoir they were driven back by artillery fire and withdrew south-eastwards to rejoin the 3rd Cavalry Brigade. Meanwhile, the 2nd Cavalry Brigade, left alone in the north, had fallen back southward, not very hard pressed, first to a line between Villers Pol and Le Quesnoy, and then, in succession, to Ruesnes, Capelle sur Ecaillon and Vertain, east of the 19th Brigade.

The troops of the 4th Division had been in position since 5 A.M. immediately to the south of Solesmes : the 11th Brigade on the right, on the spur to the south-east of the town ; the 10th Brigade on the left, near the farm of Fontaine au Tertre (two miles south-west of Solesmes) ; and the 12th Brigade, in reserve, in rear at Viesly. It was of the utmost importance that Solesmes should be strongly held, for upon it the principal highways from the north-east, north and north-west, all converged ; the more so as, soon after noon, a huge mass of British transport was struggling to pass through it by roads which were already seriously congested by crowds of refugees. These, with every kind of vehicle from six-horse farm wagons to perambulators, everywhere delayed the marching troops, and made it impossible for motor cars carrying staff officers to pass the columns.

The further operations of the cavalry had all the characteristics of a prolonged rear-guard action.[1] Eventually

---

[1] General Allenby's opponents on this day, Marwitz's cavalry corps, spent the night of the 24th/25th :—*2nd* and *9th Cavalry Divisions* at Marchiennes (16 miles north of Cambrai and about the same distance

the 1st, 3rd and 4th Cavalry Brigades under increasing shell 25 Aug. fire from the enemy, fell back along the third of the ridges 1914. between the Selle and the Harpies. The French 84th Territorial Division was found retreating southward across this ridge, and liaison was arranged with it; but at one time the pressure upon the British cavalry seemed so heavy that the 19th Brigade was brought up on to the ridge from Haussy and deployed, in order to relieve it. The Germans, however, were checked with no great difficulty; the 19th Brigade, between 2 and 3 P.M., then resumed its way southward to Solesmes, while the bulk of the cavalry and horse artillery, having for the time-being shaken off the enemy, was collected and massed to the east of Vertain (3 miles north-east of Solesmes). Here, between 3 and 4 P.M., they were suddenly assailed by a storm of German shells from the north-east as well as from the north; whereupon the Cavalry Division, being cramped for space, moved across country by brigades and still smaller bodies, after detailing rear guards to cover the passage of the infantry through Vertain and Solesmes. The 3rd Cavalry Brigade drew off south-east, leaving behind the greater part of the 4th Hussars with instructions to gain touch with the I. Corps; part of the 2nd Cavalry Brigade, including its headquarters, took the same route; the 1st Cavalry Brigade fell back to the high ground immediately south-east of Solesmes; the 4th, with other portions of the Cavalry Division, remained in the vicinity of that town.

Meanwhile, the rear guard of the 3rd Division (7th Brigade) was gradually coming in from Le Quesnoy to Solesmes, and by 5.45 P.M. its head had reached the point where the roads from Romeries, Vertain and Vendegies meet immediately to the north of Solesmes. There the 1/Wiltshire and 2/South Lancashire halted and deployed, whilst the 3/Worcestershire occupied a covering position to the south of Solesmes between the 10th and 11th Brigades. The 2/Irish Rifles and a section of the 41st Battery, the rear

from the British flank), and the *4th Cavalry Division* at Orchies (4 miles north of Marchiennes). The corps orders for the 25th were for " an " overtaking pursuit," and the divisions were given as their respective objectives the three towns lying to the south-west, one behind the other : Le Cateau, Solesmes and Haspres. This line of march brought them in on the flank of the British, but too late to be effective. It is claimed that charges were made against the French Territorials ; but, except for " a street fight " in Haspres, about 3 P.M., " after which the *9th Cavalry Division* spent the night there," the *II. Cavalry Corps*, according to the German records, employed only artillery fire against the British. (Poseck, pp. 51-55.)

party of the rear guard, having been warned of strong German forces moving on Le Quesnoy, were following the rest of the 7th Brigade slowly on account of the units in front taking every precaution and continually halting; they were at this time at Pont à Pierres, on the main road, a couple of miles to the north-east of Romeries. The 19th Brigade about the same time was passing west of Solesmes, through St. Python, and beginning to make its way up the Selle valley by Briastre and Neuvilly towards Le Cateau. The 4th Cavalry Brigade, together with the detachments of other mounted troops near Solesmes which had joined it, fell back by St. Python south-west upon Viesly, soon after the Wiltshire and South Lancashire (7th Brigade) had been deployed. By 6 P.M., or soon after, these two battalions were the only troops covering Solesmes, whilst the 4th Division still held its original position on the high ground to the south of that town, with orders from G.H.Q. to cover the retirement of

Map 9. the 3rd Division, Cavalry Division and 19th Brigade.

The stifling heat of the day had about 5 P.M. given place to a thunderstorm; the light therefore began to fail very early and the rain streamed down in torrents. Through this downpour, between 6 and 7 P.M., the remainder of the 3rd Division, drenched to the skin, hungry and weary, marched into their billets on the Le Cateau position : the 8th Brigade to Audencourt and the 9th to Inchy.

The main body of the 5th Division came in earlier, between 3 and 5 P.M., on the right of the 3rd : the 13th Brigade between Le Cateau and Troisvilles, and the 15th, west of it, to Troisvilles. The march along the Roman road had been most trying, for the sun beat fiercely upon the interminable length of the straight, white, dusty road, and under the tall trees of the Forest of Mormal there was not a breath of air to relieve the stifling heat. The 13th Brigade was delayed for some time just outside Le Cateau to allow six regiments and a cyclist battalion of General Sordet's cavalry corps to pass under the railway bridge on their way westward. As soon as the rear guard, the 14th Brigade, which had been little troubled, came in between 5.30 and 6.30 P.M., the D.C.L.I. and half of the East Surrey [1] were sent to the east of Le Cateau to establish connection with the I. Corps, while the Suffolk and the Manchester were diverted a little westward to the other side of the Selle

---

[1] The two remaining companies under Major H. S. Tew had been misdirected on the evening of the 24th, and had spent the night at Eth, from which place they marched by Ruesnes, Vertain and Solesmes to Viesly, where they arrived between 5 and 6 P.M.

valley astride the Roman road just south of Montay. Here, 25 Aug with two batteries of the XXVIII. Brigade R.F.A., they 1914. entrenched in order to keep the Germans at a distance upon that side.

As darkness began to close in, the 7th Brigade, the 4th Division, and half of the Cavalry Division were still engaged, or in position to engage, with the enemy near Solesmes ; the 19th Brigade and the remainder of the Cavalry Division were still far from their halting places for the night ; the 5th Division and part of the 3rd Division had, however, reached their destinations on the Le Cateau position. From front and left flank, the Germans appeared to be closing in, but at a respectful distance without affording the British the satisfaction of seeing the results of their good shooting. It would indeed have alleviated the fatigue of the men, tired out as they were with deployments upon rear-guard positions which were never attacked, had they had more fighting ; but the Germans never really came within rifle shot and rarely gave even the guns a target.

The air reports which arrived at G.H.Q. during the day and were summarized in the afternoon gave, correctly, German columns near Bavai and Le Quesnoy, with a third between them (*6th, 7th* and *5th Divisions*), and one entering Valenciennes (*8th Division*). This information was passed to the two corps and the Cavalry Division. A later summary made up at night showed the first three columns further advanced—the head of one column being half-way between Le Quesnoy and Landrecies—a great collection of troops near Valenciennes (*IV. Reserve Corps* and *3rd Division*) and a western flanking column (cavalry) moving through Orchies, with numerous advanced parties to the south. Some infantry was moving on Solesmes. This very accurate picture does not seem to have been communicated to the corps or divisions, or to the cavalry.

NOTE I

MOVEMENTS OF THE GERMAN *FIRST* AND *SECOND ARMIES* FROM 23RD TO 25TH AUGUST 1914

Until the 27th August inclusive, the German *First* and *Second* Map 3. *Armies* were both under the orders of Bülow, the commander of the Sketch 6. *Second Army,* and they appear to have had no other directions from Supreme Headquarters than those issued on the 18th August :
" The *First* and *Second Armies,* combined under the command ' of Generaloberst von Bülow, will have their advanced guards across

" the Brussels—Namur railway by the 20th August, when they
" will wheel southwards "—that is they were to continue the great
wheel pivoting on Thionville laid down in the initial directions.[1]
    On the 23rd August, after the battles of Charleroi [2] and Mons,
Bülow, in his instructions for the 24th, directed the *First Army* to
continue the attack on the British and " to send the *IX. Corps* round
" the west side of Maubeuge as soon as possible, with the *II. Corps*
" in echelon behind it, in order to envelop the left flank of the French
" Fifth Army." This, he says, could not be carried out because the
British offered " renewed " resistance on the 24th.
    The German *Second Army*, with Richthofen's *I. Cavalry Corps*,
continuing the pursuit of the French Fifth Army on that day,
reached in the evening an east and west line between Dinant and
Maubeuge, and detailed the *VII. Corps*, the right of its line, to
watch the south-eastern side of the French fortress. Marwitz's
II. Cavalry Corps was sent towards Tournai and Denain " to attack
" the British left flank."
    On the 25th, the *First Army* continued the attack against the
British, hoping to envelop their left wing ; " but the enemy, by a
" cleverly executed retirement, evaded the *First Army*, in spite of
" the latter's brilliant marching performances." [3]
    The *Second Army* continued the pursuit of the French, but in a
south-westerly direction, so that at night the heads of its four corps
were roughly on a south-east and north-west line passing through
Solre le Chateau. Maubeuge was invested by the *VII. Corps* on
the south-east and by the *IX. Corps* (of the *First Army*) on the
north-west, and at the suggestion of the *First Army*, a double
envelopment of the British was to be attempted :
    " Strong portions of the *14th Division* were, if possible, to advance
" round the south of Maubeuge against the rear of the British, in
" the direction of Aulnoye," and " the *I. Cavalry Corps* was also
" ordered to push forward in a westerly direction via Aulnoye to
" hinder the retreat of the British." But neither infantry nor cavalry
got within a march of Aulnoye and, in any case, the British were six
miles south of that place on the evening of the 25th August.
    Thus it was that on this day the British were not in contact with
the German *Second Army* ; of their collision with the *First Army*
the next chapter will tell.
    The German Official Account of this part of the operations ends
as follows :—" Air reconnaissance up to 4 P.M. gave the following
" surprising [and incomplete] picture. ' At Solre le Chateau and
" ' south-west of Valenciennes, artillery fights ; retiring enemy of
" ' all arms on the road Maubeuge—Le Cateau, and on the railway
" ' alongside heavy traffic, direction Le Cateau.' The hopes which
" shortly before had been based at Army Headquarters on the
" advance of the *First Army* did not seem likely to be fulfilled ; it
" appeared that the British had managed to extricate themselves
" from the threatening envelopment by the *First Army* ; the artillery
" fire meant rear-guard actions." The accounts go on to describe the
expectations derived from the reported " demoralization of the
French."
    On this day General von Gallwitz, who was in charge of the

---

[1] Kluck, p. 9.   [2] See page 46.
[3] The movements of the *First Army* are further described on page 149
et seq.

siege of Namur (with the *Guard Reserve* and *XI. Corps*, the inner 21-25Aug, flank corps of the *Second* and *Third Armies*), was able to report that, 1914. except for a few forts on the south-west front, the fortress was in his hands. So there was every prospect of these corps becoming available in the near future.

NOTE II

MOVEMENTS OF GENERAL VALABRÈGUE'S GROUP OF RESERVE DIVISIONS OF THE FRENCH FIFTH ARMY, IMMEDIATELY ON THE RIGHT OF THE B.E.F.

The following were the movements of General Valabrègue's Group, 21st-25th August. They are of interest, as this group was the nearest French formation of all arms to the right of the British Forces.

On the 22nd August, General Valabrègue still had his head- Map 3. quarters at Avesnes (10 miles south of Maubeuge). On the evening of the 21st, the 69th Reserve Division commenced a movement northeast on Beaumont and Cousolre (13 miles and 10 miles east of Maubeuge, respectively). On the 22nd at 9 P.M. the group received orders not to go so far east, but to march northwards towards the Sambre, so as to have its left on the fortress of Maubeuge, and its right on the road Solre sur Sambre—Beaumont, facing north-east. Its march was much impeded by the crowds of refugees on the roads.

On the 23rd the orders to the group were slightly changed : it was to go further northwards and prevent the passage of the Sambre near Solre sur Sambre ; for this purpose it was to take up a position south of the river between Montignies and the Bois de Jeumont, 69th Reserve Division on the right, 53rd Reserve Division on the left, headquarters at Solre le Chateau (10 miles south-east of Maubeuge). These orders were in course of execution, when news came of the attack on the British at Mons. Towards 5 P.M. it also became known that the left flank of the French XVIII. Corps had been attacked near Thuin, and that it was necessary to support it. The 69th Reserve Division was then ordered north-eastwards towards Thirimont—Bousignies (both two miles to the north of Beaumont) and the 53rd, on its left, towards Cousolre, the result of which was to widen the gap between the Group Valabrègue and the British Expeditionary Force.

On the 24th, after an engagement in which the 53rd Reserve Division took part, the Group Valabrègue retired, moving past the east and south fronts of Maubeuge. On the 25th it continued its retreat by Dompierre to the north-west of Avesnes. It was thus abreast of and in touch with the British, in fact, as already related, it came into collision on the roads with the I. Corps. The 53rd Reserve Division, as will appear later, supported that corps when attacked at Maroilles.

CHAPTER VI

THE RETREAT FROM MONS (*continued*)
EVENING AND NIGHT OF THE 25TH/26TH AUGUST 1914

(Sketches A, 4 & 6 ; Maps 3, 9 & 10)

MAROILLES AND LANDRECIES ; SOLESMES

Sketches WITH the close of day in the I. Corps area, stories brought
4 & 6. by refugees began to circulate in the villages in which the
Map 9. British were settling down, of the approach of the Germans
towards Maroilles and Landrecies, near which places lay the
two main passages over the Sambre at the southern end
of the Forest of Mormal. Although Sir Douglas Haig had
not had the forest searched, he had taken precautions
against a hostile attack from it upon his western flank
during his retreat : the bridge over the Sambre, which lies
to the north-west of Maroilles and carries the road from Le
Quesnoy south-eastward through the forest by Locquignol
to Maroilles, was guarded by a troop of the 15th Hussars :
another troop watched a lock bridge some two miles
farther down the river. Infantry was to relieve the cavalry
at night : at Maroilles the passages of the Sambre were to
be held by the 6th Brigade, and those near Landrecies by
the 4th (Guards) Brigade. On the right of the I. Corps were
General Valabrègue's Reserve divisions. From all reports,
the enemy was not within striking distance,[1] and so little
were the rumours believed that an officer of the 15th
Hussars was denied permission by the local civil authorities to destroy some wooden buildings, which obstructed
his view near Maroilles bridge, on the ground that no
Germans were anywhere near him. Suddenly, about 5.30
P.M., there was a panic amongst the inhabitants of Landrecies, caused by cries that the Germans were upon them.

---

[1] According to the statements of German officers, the enemy seems to
have been equally unaware of our presence at Landrecies and Maroilles
(see page 133, f.n. 2).

The troops promptly got under arms, and two companies of the 3/Coldstream took post at the road-junction near the railway about half a mile to the north-west of the town. Mounted patrols were sent out, but without finding any enemy. At Maroilles half an hour later (about 6 P.M.) German parties [1] engaged the two detachments of the 15th Hussars, but were easily held at bay for an hour, when the assailants of the road bridge brought up a field gun and, creeping forward under cover of the very buildings which the British officer had wished to destroy, compelled the troop to fall back. As it retired towards Maroilles, it was met by a company of the 1/Royal Berkshire which was coming up in relief. The infantry took post by the Rue des Juifs about a mile to the south-east of the bridge. The Germans challenging in French succeeded in enticing a British officer forward and making a prisoner of him ; but they made no further advance and presently retired.

In Maroilles itself there was for a time such a congestion of supply lorries and of refugees with their vehicles, that the three remaining companies of the Royal Berkshire could march off only after considerable delay to the support of the company at the Rue des Juifs. When these companies at last came up, they found that the enemy had retired, and accordingly pushed on to recover the lost bridge. The only access to this, however, was by a causeway over marshy ground, and the enemy having barricaded the bridge and put his field gun into position, the Royal Berkshire failed to drive him from it. After a total loss of over sixty men, it was decided to make no further attempt to recapture the bridge until daylight, and to be content with forbidding advance along the causeway.

Meanwhile at Landrecies also there had been fighting, the seriousness of which was at the time somewhat exaggerated. The cavalry patrols returned with the report that all was clear, and the 4th (Guards) Brigade was confirmed in its belief that the alarm at 5.30 P.M. had been a false one. Subsequent events proved that the rumour of the near presence of Germans was true.[2]

---

[1] The force which came to Maroilles was the *48th Regiment* of the *5th Division*, *III. Corps*, the advanced guard of the *5th Division*. See Sketch 6.

[2] The advanced guard of the German *7th Division* (*IV. Corps*)—an infantry brigade (the *14th*) with a battery—had marched from Le Quesnoy past the south of the forest towards Landrecies for the purpose of billeting there, entirely ignorant of the presence of the British. On discovering the town was occupied, the vanguard crept along the hedges and corn-stooks, and entrenched themselves parallel to the road not five hundred yards from

At 7.30 P.M. No. 3 Company of the 3/Coldstream was on piquet, on the road, with a machine gun upon each flank, and wire entanglements a short distance ahead. Wheels and horses were heard approaching along the road ; [1] the sentry challenged. The challenge was answered in French ; a body of men loomed through the darkness, and the officer in command advanced to question them. He was answered always in French, but in the course of the parley the supposed Frenchmen edged themselves up closer to the piquet, and then, suddenly and without the slightest warning, lowered their bayonets and charged. In the first moment of surprise, they knocked down the officer, seized the right-hand machine gun and dragged it ten yards, but a few seconds later they were swept away by a volley from the piquet, and the machine gun was recovered.

The piquet was at once reinforced ; and the rest of the 4th (Guards) Brigade turned out, the 2/Grenadiers coming up to the support of the Coldstream along the road from the railway northwards. Charge after charge was made by the enemy without gaining any advantage, and at 8.30 P.M. German artillery opened fire upon the town and upon the piquet. This fire was accurate, but the German infantry-men shot far too high and accomplished little, until, having by means of incendiary bombs set light to some straw-stacks in a farmyard close to the British, they apparently realized for the first time, by the light of the flames, that their way was barred only by a single thin line.[2] There-upon they tried, but unsuccessfully, to enfilade the Guards. The engagement went on until past midnight when a howitzer of the 60th Battery was hauled up by hand to within close range and with its third round silenced the German guns. This seems to have decided the issue, and the enemy drew off. The losses of the 3/Coldstream were

---

the line of the two advanced companies of the 3/Coldstream. They even loopholed a garden wall still closer to those companies. The original report that the German force was part of the *IX. Corps* appears to have been due to an identification received by wireless from the Eiffel Tower, Paris. For the German movements on the 25th see Note I. at end of Chapter.

[1] This, according to the story of a German general who was present, was the regimental transport which had been ordered to trot past the column to get to the billets.

[2] Lance-Corporal G. H. Wyatt, 3rd Coldstream Guards, dashed at and extinguished the burning straw, though the enemy was only 25 yards distant. For this and a further act of bravery at Villers Cottérêts on 1st September, he received the V.C.

LANDRECIES 135

one hundred and twenty ; those of the Germans, according 25 Aug. to their official casualty lists, were 127.[1] 1914.
By about 4 A.M. on the 26th, all was again quiet on the line of the I. Corps. But, as it was impossible in the dark to discover the scope of the attack, the information sent back to G.H.Q. from the I. Corps was somewhat alarming. At 10 P.M. there was telephoned " Attack heavy "from north-west can you send help?" Thereupon G.H.Q. directed General Smith-Dorrien to move to the assistance of the I. Corps, at any rate to send the 19th Brigade. He was forced to reply, " much regret my troops are quite " unable to move to-night. The 19th Brigade could not " reach Landrecies in a useful state." On this being repeated to General Haig, he decided at 12.30 A.M. on the 26th, after a consultation with General Lomax, to move the 1st Division at 6 A.M. via Marbaix and Grand Fayt to the neighbourhood of Favril to support the left of the 2nd Division. At 1.35 A.M. he reported to G.H.Q., " situation " very critical," and that he was putting in every available man on his left. A little later he suggested that the troops near Le Cateau should assist by advancing straight on Landrecies. There is at this point a gap in the records, but it would appear from what followed that General Haig must have been told by Sir John French that, in view of the direction of the enemy's attack, he must retire southwards, not south-west. At 3.45 A.M., the Commander-in-Chief informed General Smith-Dorrien, " enemy appears " to be working round south of Landrecies. G.O.C. 4th " Brigade doubts if he can move south. My orders of " last night [7.30 P.M.] hold good as far as you and Snow " [4th Division] are concerned," and he now gave the II. Corps the Le Cateau—Busigny road, previously allotted to the I. Corps, thus directing the latter more south than south-west. Just before 5 A.M., through the French

[1] The following information was obtained from Berlin in 1921 :
The German forces involved in the fighting at Landrecies consisted of the *14th Infantry Brigade* (Major-General von Oven) of the *IV. Corps*, containing the *27th* and *165th Regiments*, one squadron *10th Hussars*, and the *4th Field Artillery Regiment.* Of these the *165th Regiment* and three batteries were only employed in the later stages of the fight.

Casualties : *27th Regt.*—1 officer, 32 men killed,
4 officers, 65 men wounded ;
165th Regt.—3 men wounded,
2 men missing ;
10th Hussars—1 man wounded ;
4th Field Artillery Regt.—3 officers and 16 men killed ;
total casualties, 127.

Mission at G.H.Q., he called on his French neighbours, General Lanrezac and General d'Amade, and General Sordet (cavalry corps) for help, making clear, as will be narrated under the operations of the 26th, that the I. Corps was retiring south, if not south-eastward.[1]

Map 9.
Sketch 6.

The labours of the II. Corps lasted to as late an hour on the night of the 25th/26th as those of the I. Corps. All through the evening the stream of transport flowed slowly and uneasily through Solesmes, and shortly before dark the Germans closed more resolutely on the South Lancashire and Wiltshire (7th Brigade), the rear guard of the 3rd Division before that town ; they brought their artillery up to close range, though pushing forward only small bodies of infantry. When darkness fell, however, they went into bivouac.[2] This enabled the two battalions to be

[1] The messages sent off at 5 A.M. are Nos. 630 and 631 in F.O.A. i. (ii.) Annexes i. The one to General Lanrezac runs (those to Generals d'Amade and to General Sordet are similar) :—
" The I. Corps was sharply attacked this night [night of 25th/26th] in " its cantonments between Landrecies and Le Cateau, and is retreating, " if it can, on Guise, southwards [Guise is 17 miles due south of Landrecies] " if not south-eastwards in the direction of La Capelle [15 miles south-east " of Landrecies]."
" The cavalry division, cantonned at Catillon [5 miles south-east of " Le Cateau] is going to retire on Bohain ; the II. Corps and 4th Division, " cantonned in the zone Caudry—Le Cateau, are going to retire on the " line Le Catelet—Beaurevoir. The next day, the general movement of " retreat will be continued on Péronne.
" In these circumstances, Field-Marshal French asks you to help him " by receiving the I. Corps until it can rejoin the main body of the British " forces."
[2] The action at Solesmes looms somewhat large, as so often in an unsuccessful fight, in the German records, the title of " The Battle of " Solesmes—Le Cateau " being given officially to the fighting on the 25th and 26th. The history of the 153rd Regiment (pp. 51-2) states that the regiment, with a battery, formed the advanced guard of the 8th Division marching south on Solesmes. It ran unexpectedly into the British on the heights north of the town about dusk, the divisional cavalry not having reported the presence of any enemy. After a rapid deployment, all three battalions (only two companies following in second line) attacked about 7 P.M. ; but in the dusk, in enclosed country, confusion resulted and, two battalions of the 93rd Regiment coming up on the right (see page 40 of its history), the Germans fired on each other. To stop this the manœuvre bugle call of " The whole will halt " was sounded, followed by the " Com- " manding Officers " call. It was proposed to make a bayonet attack at 9 P.M., but this was abandoned on account of the existence of wire fences, and the two regiments lay down where they were. This was perhaps fortunate for them, for they would have found in Solesmes only a portion of the 72nd Regiment, of the 8th Division, which had entered and settled down in the north-west corner of the town, without having seen any British (" Regt. No. 153," p. 52). Soon after this General von Kluck himself had arrived in the town, having selected it as his night quarters, only to retire to Haussy, a couple of miles back. (Kluck, p. 55.)

SOLESMES 137

withdrawn, much scattered, indeed, and with the loss of 25 Aug.
several small detachments cut off by the enemy, but with- 1914.
out further mishap.[1] The infantry of the 4th Division
meanwhile stood fast on the heights immediately south of
Solesmes, while the mass of transport and troops disen-
tangled itself on the roads leading south and south-east
upon Caudry and Le Cateau. The 3rd Cavalry Brigade
(less the 4th Hussars), with the headquarters and portions
of the 2nd, pushed on through the congested streets of Le
Cateau to Catillon, where it halted for the night between
10 and 11 P.M. The 1st Cavalry Brigade bivouacked in
the fields south of Le Cateau, with the exception of the
5th Dragoon Guards, which retired after dark to Inchy and
thence shortly before midnight to Troisvilles, west of Le
Cateau, their horses utterly exhausted. The 19th Brigade,
together with two companies of the Scots Fusiliers which
had lost connection with the rear guard of the 9th Brigade,
marched into Le Cateau at 10 P.M. and bivouacked in the
central square and at the goods station. The bulk of the
7th Brigade retired to Caudry, but the Irish Rifles and the
41st Battery, the last party of the rear guard, only reached
Le Cateau about 10 P.M., when, finding they could not
rejoin their brigades direct, owing to the rapid advance of
the enemy, they passed southward to Maurois. There
they bivouacked in the grey dawn of the 26th. At least
one detachment of the Wiltshire, having with some difficulty avoided capture, also found its way into Le Cateau
in the early hours of the 26th. The masses of troops,
guns and transport at dusk and for many hours afterwards
pressing through the northern entrance to the town created
most alarming congestion. The British alone would have
sufficed to crowd it, but besides the British a considerable
body of French chasseurs marched in from Valenciennes.
The mile of road from Montay to Le Cateau falls very
steeply and becomes a defile, and here infantry, cavalry,
guns and wagons, in places all three abreast, were jammed
together in what seemed irremediable confusion. Had the
Germans pushed on, even with a small force supported by
guns, they might have done terrible damage ; for one or
two shells would have sufficed to produce a complete block
on the road. The rear parties of the Suffolk and Manchester
(14th Brigade), rear guard of the 5th Division, had been

[1] Both infantry brigades of the German *8th Division* (*IV. Corps*) and
the *4th Cavalry Division* had casualties at Solesmes on 25th August (see
" Schlachten und Gefechte ").

withdrawn at dusk, and there would have been nothing to stop an enterprising enemy. The Germans, however, were no less weary than the British, and they had also gained sufficient experience of British rapid fire to make them cautious. They had gone into bivouac here as at Solesmes ; and though at dusk they were in force only five miles away,[1] they left the British free to disentangle themselves at their leisure. The process was long and tedious, and until a late hour Viesly was as hopelessly blocked as Solesmes had been.

Though the infantry of the 4th Division had been unmolested since dusk, except by one or two cavalry patrols which were quickly driven off, it was not free to begin to move off until 9 P.M. During its detention near Solesmes the remainder of its divisional artillery, except the heavy battery, had been detraining, and the 2/Royal Inniskilling Fusiliers, which had not come up with the 12th Brigade, arrived at Ligny, where it took over guard of the divisional transport. In view of the flank march that the division would later have to make to its new position on the left of the Le Cateau line, two companies of this battalion were in the afternoon sent as a western flank guard to occupy
Map 10. Bévillers and Beauvois. A hasty reconnaissance of the new ground had been made on the 24th, at the suggestion of G.H.Q., by Br.-General J. A. L. Haldane (10th Brigade) and Lieut.-Colonel A. A. Montgomery (G.S.O. 2) ; and they selected a good reverse-slope position, or, as it was then called, " back position," covering Haucourt.

At 5 P.M. the 4th Division issued warning orders for the march to and occupation of the position.[2] A G.H.Q. alteration, sent out at 6.40 P.M., reduced the length of front to be held, and made it from Fontaine au Pire to Wambaix, that is to say about three miles. General Snow's orders directed that the 11th and 12th Brigades should hold the front line, with the 10th in reserve at Haucourt, whilst the artillery should assemble at Ligny.

The artillery (with the exception of the XXXII. Brigade, which was with the rear guard) arrived fairly early in the evening ; the 12th Brigade moved off from the heights above Solesmes soon after 9 P.M. ; the 11th, an hour later, before which time the German guns shelled and set on fire the eastern portion of Briastre (2 miles south of Solesmes),

---

[1] The *7th Division* spent the night in Bousies, Fontaine, and adjoining villages.
[2] Appendix 15.

at the west corner of which the brigade was assembled.
The 10th Brigade, which could not move until the 3rd
Division had got clear of Briastre, started at midnight. As
the three brigades marched off south-west rain was falling
heavily and the darkness was only relieved on the northern
horizon by the red glow of villages fired by the enemy.
Instructions from G.H.Q., received in the afternoon, in-
timated that the retirement would probably be continued
at 7 A.M. next morning, but it was on the position defined
in General Snow's orders that the troops of the 4th Division
stood when the first shots were fired in the early morning
of the 26th.

The head of General Sordet's cavalry corps had passed
through Ligny, behind the Le Cateau position, in the course
of the day, and the corps bivouacked for the night near
Walincourt. Its arrival on the western flank of the British
was, perhaps, the one cheerful feature in a gloomy situation.

To summarize the situation : at 7.30 P.M. the British Map 3.
Commander-in-Chief, after having established his head- Sketch 6.
quarters at St. Quentin at 6 P.M., had issued definite orders for
the retreat to be continued ten to fifteen miles to the south-
west on the morrow,[1] to a line Busigny—Le Catelet, facing
a little west of north. Communications from General Joffre
admitted that his attempt at the offensive had failed, and
that his intention was to retire to the line Laon—La Fère—
St. Quentin, and from this position to take the offensive
again. Later information which arrived during the evening
was not reassuring. There seemed little time to lose. The
Germans were in touch with the British at several places,
and had considerable forces within a few miles of them.
They were known to be pushing troops with all speed
towards the western flank of the British, where General
d'Amade's six Reserve and Territorial divisions guarded
the long line to the sea. The I. Corps had already been
struck at Maroilles and at Landrecies, the II. had been
engaged in a definite rear-guard action at Solesmes ; and
it was not difficult to guess what these blows might portend.
Sir Douglas Haig's troops stood to arms all night, losing
the rest of which they were so much in need ; and it was
feared that the attack at Landrecies might mean that the
Germans were already in force across the southern end of
the Forest of Mormal, between Landrecies and the Roman

[1] Page 123 and Appendix 14.

road.[1] It will be remembered that on the afternoon of the 25th General Haig had issued instructions for the I. Corps to march at 2 A.M. south-westwards to the right of the Le Cateau position.[2] These orders he had changed on receiving those of the Field-Marshal to continue on to Busigny ; but the events of the night had caused him to decide, with at least Sir John French's knowledge, to retreat southwards on Guise. For the G.O.C. II. Corps a decision was more difficult.

Map 9.   Only a sketch would give an idea how the various units
Sketch 6. of the II. Corps had been jostled between the barrier of the Forest of Mormal, which edged them away to the west, and the pressure of the enemy on the western flank, which bore them back towards the east. To General Smith-Dorrien the true situation did not reveal itself until late at night. At 10.15 P.M. he too had issued orders for the renewal of the retreat towards the line La Sablière—Beaurevoir prescribed by Sir John French's 7.30 P.M. order which he had received at 9 P.M. : the transport was to start at 4 A.M. and the main bodies at 7 A.M.[3]

Meantime the divisions of his corps, acting on his previous order, were in readiness on or near the Le Cateau position : the 3rd Division, under orders issued at 9.42 P.M., was to stand to arms at 4 A.M. and be prepared to occupy the sections of the position allotted in case of attack ; two and a half infantry brigades of the 5th Division were bivouacking on a line across the Troisvilles—Le Cateau roads, with the remaining two battalions posted on the high ground north-east of Le Cateau to connect with the I. Corps as originally arranged. This division had orders to stand to arms at 3.30 A.M.

G.H.Q. orders for the continuance of the retreat, and for the Cavalry Division to cover it on the north and west,[4] did not reach General Allenby at his headquarters at Beaumont (on the west side of Inchy) until after 11 P.M. Shortly after their receipt, Lieut.-Colonel G. K. Ansell of the 5th Dragoon Guards came in to report that his regiment and the 4th Division had safely withdrawn from the high ground north of Viesly, which overlooks Solesmes, and that the enemy was in possession of it. Now it was this high ground and the ridges abreast of it that the cavalry must occupy to cover the initial stages of the retirement from the

[1] The German *7th Division* was there, with the *5th Division* in rear of it.
[2] See page 123.   [3] Appendix 16.   [4] Appendix 14.

Le Cateau position, and as General Allenby had not suffi- 26 Aug.
cient force—in fact, only the 4th Cavalry Brigade—under 1914.
his hand to recapture it, he proceeded at once to General
Smith-Dorrien's headquarters at Bertry. There he explained the situation, and expressed the opinion that, the
Germans being so close, unless the troops of the II. Corps
and 4th Division could march " before daylight," the
enemy would be upon them before they could start, and
it would be necessary to fight. General Smith-Dorrien
thereupon at 2 A.M. sent for General H. I. W. Hamilton,
commanding the 3rd Division, whose headquarters were
close at hand, and asked him if it was possible to get on
the move during the hours of darkness. His reply was
that many units of the division were only just coming in,
and he did not think that he could get them formed up
for retreat before 9 A.M. General Allenby further said
that his division was too much scattered and exhausted to
be able to give useful assistance in covering the retreat
next day. General Smith-Dorrien, after a full discussion
of the situation with Generals Allenby and Hamilton,
reluctantly came to the decision that he must stand his
ground. To do this he must ask the commanders of the
Cavalry Division and of the 4th Division to place themselves under his orders ; with them and with the II. Corps
—that is to say, with the whole of the British troops in the
line from Catillon westwards—he would strike the enemy
hard, and, after he had done so, continue the retreat.
Whether he could withdraw his troops after such a stand
would depend on the pressure and weight of the German
attack. Several German cavalry divisions, and the head
of a division of the German *IV. Corps* were already before
him, the British I. Corps had been attacked by another
corps, and further forces were known to be hurrying up.
Much would obviously depend on breaking off the action
before the overwhelming numbers of the enemy became
effective. To guard his flanks he had to depend upon the
weary and sorely tried Cavalry Division, with some possibility
of assistance on the western flank from General Sordet's
equally weary cavalry corps, and on the eastern flank from
the I. Corps, should it not be held fast itself. Help from
this quarter, however, appeared unlikely, and indeed Sir
Douglas Haig had asked for assistance from the II. Corps.
The situation, in short, seemed to him one that could
be saved only by desperate measures. General Allenby
promptly accepted the invitation to act under his com-

mand ; there was no doubt that General Snow of the 4th
Division would do likewise when the request reached him.
A lengthy message was despatched by II. Corps at
3.30 A.M. to G.H.Q. St. Quentin, by motor car, where it
was received about 5 A.M., informing Sir John French in
detail of the decision taken. At 5 A.M. another message
was sent asking that General Sordet might be told that
the II. Corps was not retiring.

A written reply to the first message was prepared at
once, between 5 and 6 A.M., but it was not sent until 11.5
A.M. as it was found that G.H.Q. could communicate with
the II. Corps by a railway telephone line. General Smith-
Dorrien was accordingly summoned from his quarters in
Bertry to the railway station, where, shortly after 6 A.M.,
Major-General H. H. Wilson, the Sub-Chief of the General
Staff, spoke to him and gave him the gist of the G.H.Q.
reply.[1] Subsequent to this conversation the 4th Division
was warned at 6.55 A.M. by G.H.Q. that the II. Corps
might not be able to continue the retirement at the time
arranged, and that it was to cover Sir H. Smith-Dorrien's
left flank. The written reply sent by G.H.Q. to General
Smith-Dorrien—despatched after a further message had
come in from the II. Corps, timed 9.10 A.M., reporting that
Caudry was being heavily attacked, but that the 7th
Brigade was still holding its own—was signed " C. in C,"
and ran as follows :—

" Your G971 received. News from I. Corps reassuring
" also 4 divisions of French Territorials in area Cambrai—
" Villers—Campeau—Douai—Croisilles. Thus left seems
" fairly secure. An intercepted German message says
" German *Guard Cavalry Division* [2] about Solesmes were
" asking for reinforcements at 8.25 A.M.
      " If you can hold your ground the situation appears
" likely to improve. 4th Division must co-operate.

---

[1] Sir Horace Smith-Dorrien spoke, " putting the matter squarely," to
General Wilson, who said to him that his " voice was the first cheerful
" one he had heard for days," and " if you stand to fight there will be
" another Sédan." To this the commander of the II. Corps replied that
" it was impossible to break away now, as the action had already begun,
" and that he could hear the guns firing as he spoke." (See " Recollections
" of Sir Horace Smith-Dorrien " in the *Army Quarterly*, October 1930, by
his signal officer, Br.-General A. Hildebrand, who accompanied him to the
telephone, and the " Foreword " to " The Advance from Mons 1914 "
(translation of Bloem's " Vormarsch "), written by Br.-General Sir J. E.
Edmonds, to whom General Smith-Dorrien spoke on the matter at 2 P.M.
during the battle.)
      [2] The *9th Cavalry Division* was near Solesmes ; the *Guard Cavalry
Division* was thirty miles further to the east.

" French troops arc taking offensive on right of I. Corps. 26 Aug.
" Although you are given a free hand as to method this 1914.
" telegram is not intended to convey the impression that
" I am not as anxious for you to carry out the retirement
" and you must make every endeavour to do so."
The die having been cast, it remained only for General
Smith-Dorrien to inform his subordinates. As General
H. I. W. Hamilton had been present at the conference,
this was easy as regards the 3rd Division ; to Sir Charles
Fergusson he went himself about 4 A.M. and whilst he was
discussing the situation the commander of the 5th Division
drew his attention to the fact that formed bodies, the rear
guard (2/R. Irish Rifles) of the 3rd Division, were still
coming in, dead beat.   The actual orders to stand fast,
which were conveyed by two staff officers in a motor car,
reached 5th Division headquarters shortly afterwards.   A
staff officer was sent to the 4th Division, but did not arrive
at Haucourt until 5 A.M., only a short time before the
division became engaged.   The news that meanwhile had
come in to II. Corps headquarters was not reassuring.   At
2.30 A.M. General Smith-Dorrien heard that the Germans
had occupied Cambrai ; and at 3.45 A.M. that they were
working round to the south of Landrecies.   These details
were neither of them true ; but, true or false, they could
not affect his resolution.[1]
Seeing that many of the brigades had only lately come
in, it was inevitable that the divisional commanders should
have considerable difficulty in communicating the order to
stand fast to the brigadiers, owing to the uncertainty of
their whereabouts : General Shaw of the 9th Brigade,
being in Beaumont, received the order through General
Allenby at 3.30 A.M. ; the 7th and 8th Brigades, having
stood to arms at 4 A.M., were actually on the position and
improving trenches when fired on at 6 A.M.   There is no
record either of the order to continue the retirement at
7 A.M., issued by the II. Corps at 10.15 P.M., or of the
later order not to retire, reaching them.   Of the 5th
Division, Count Gleichen of the 15th Brigade, being
nearest to divisional headquarters, heard at 5 A.M., and
the other two infantry brigadiers about 6 A.M.

We left the 4th Division hungry, wet and weary after Map 9.
its hurried journey by night to Le Cateau, its equally Sketch 6.

[1] Actually, the French 84th Territorial Division was in occupation of
Cambrai and its northern approaches.

hurried march to Solesmes, and a long wait in position without supplies,[1] marching through the darkness to take its place on the extreme left of General Smith-Dorrien's line between Fontaine au Pire and Wambaix, with its reserve at Haucourt. The first of the troops to reach their destination, about 1 A.M., were the headquarters and two companies of the 2/Inniskilling which had left Ligny shortly before midnight to secure Esnes (5 miles south-east of Cambrai). There they found a small party of General Sordet's cavalry which had barricaded the western approaches to the village. The two remaining companies of the battalion, it will be recalled, had been detached as a flank guard to Beauvois and Bévillers (both about four miles north-east of Esnes) on the afternoon of the 25th. Just after darkness fell, the outposts before Bévillers were suddenly aware of a troop of German horse, which came within thirty yards of them before it was recognized to be hostile, and was followed by six motor lorries full of *Jäger*. The Inniskillings opened rapid fire, with what effect could not be seen, but the enemy retired in haste. The two companies remained in their positions until 3 A.M. when, by order of their brigadier, they marched for Longsart (just north-west of Haucourt). Meanwhile, the advanced guard of the 12th Brigade—two companies of the Essex—which had moved from Béthencourt at 10 P.M., reached Longsart about 3.30 A.M., and the 2/Lancashire Fusiliers came in a little later. Both parties entrenched themselves on the plateau just to the north-west of the hamlet. The 1/King's Own reached the eastern end of Haucourt shortly after 4 A.M. and halted there, General Sordet's rear guard riding through the village during the halt. The two remaining companies of the Essex, which had been left at Béthencourt as rear guard under Lieut.-Colonel F. C. Anley, remained there until recalled at 3 A.M., and then marched via Ligny and Haucourt to Esnes, where they arrived two hours later. Towards 5 A.M. the flank-guard companies of the Inniskillings came in to Longsart. Thus by 5 A.M. the whole of the 12th Brigade had reached its allotted ground.

The 11th Brigade was not so fortunate in reaching without mishap the position assigned to it. It was about 2.15 A.M. before the head of its column arrived at Fontaine au Pire, the march having been delayed by a serious block of 3rd Division transport at Viesly, which brought the brigade

---

[1] " Cookers " had not been issued to the 4th Division as they had to the other divisions.

to a standstill for some time.   The 1/Hampshire was leading,
followed by the 1/East Lancashire, two companies of the
1/Somerset L.I., the 1/Rifle Brigade (one company and a
platoon being with the brigade transport to give assistance),
the transport, and the rest of the Somerset L.I. as rear
guard.   Fontaine au Pire and Beauvois north of it, form
one long straggling village a mile and a half in length, and
it was intended, on reaching the road fork near the far end
of the houses, to take the right to Cattenières, which passes
north of the " Quarry ", called " Carrière " on the French
1:80,000 map then in use, which marked the top of the ridge
on which position was to be taken.   Not an inhabitant
could be found of whom to make enquiries, and a mistake
was made.   A street to the right in Fontaine au Pire, immediately before the turning to Cattenières, was followed,
and it led out to a mud track between pasture fields, with
barbed wire on either side of it.   The brigadier, who was
near the head of the column, decided therefore to halt and
rest the brigade where it stood and wait for daylight, the
two leading battalions being already well down the track,
and the rest of the column in the streets of the long village,
the rear still in Beauvois.   The Rifle Brigade was ordered
to furnish outposts, and moved to the open fields in front,
pushing out one company down the slope to cover the ground
between Beauvois and Cattenières.   The leading portion
of the Somerset L.I. covered the transport near the southern
end of Beauvois.   The other units sought what resting
places they could, some in houses, some in fields recently
tenanted by cattle, whilst others were lucky enough to find
corn in stooks on which to bed down.   The portion of the
transport which had entered the lane was in the course of
time turned round so that the whole of it could be got clear
by taking the road from the centre of Fontaine au Pire
southwards to Ligny, two and a half miles away across the
Warnelle ravine.   The rear guard of the Somerset went
on towards Ligny to occupy a covering position there, and
the detachment of the Rifle Brigade with the transport,
which had become rear guard and had remained some time
at the northern end of Beauvois, rejoined its battalion.
    Towards daylight, in accordance with custom at train-
ing and manœuvres, the brigade stood to arms preparatory
to moving back to its assigned sector just behind the
ridge.   In the faint light of early morning parties of the
Rifle Brigade on outpost saw hostile cavalry and artillery
advancing from the north on Cattenières, and almost im-

mediately the enemy opened an indiscriminate and ineffective rifle fire from the north and north-west backed by a few shell. The transport was at once got on the move, the German skirmishers who were pushing in towards Fontaine au Pire being held off by the cooks and brakesmen, and by the Somerset. The whole of it reached Ligny safely, and during the day retired by stages to Serain (6 miles south of Ligny), where it arrived late in the afternoon.

As it had grown light, about 4 A.M., the senior officer with the East Lancashire (the lieutenant-colonel and second-in-command having gone to a brigade conference), seeing the exposed position of the battalion, drew it back, first a couple of hundred yards clear of the wire to the open fields, and then to the ridge. When the Germans opened fire on the transport, he formed his men up in battle position, with two companies in reserve. The Hampshire were also moved back about 4.30 A.M., and then, by Br.-General A. G. Hunter-Weston's order, took position on the left of the East Lancashire, astride the railway leading to Cambrai. The Somerset L.I. (half-battalion) and the Rifle Brigade, helped by fire from the East Lancashire, gradually fell back fighting, somewhat intermixed in consequence, but with the Rifle Brigade mostly on the right of the line, the front of the two battalions being astride and to the west of the Ligny—Fontaine au Pire road. The half battalion of the Somerset L.I. was ordered back from Ligny to support its forward companies ; but on the left there were too many troops in the front line, and the East Lancashire, except one company, were withdrawn into reserve in the hollow behind the right centre.

The 10th Brigade, the last of the troops of the 4th Division to leave the Solesmes position, also had some difficulty in finding its way in the dark night. It moved, with its transport leading, via Viesly, Béthencourt and Beauvois, where the head of the column turned southwards, as the 11th Brigade had done, to Fontaine au Pire. Here the divisional commander, who was at the moment with the 11th Brigade, told Br.-General Haldane to pass through that brigade and to continue on to Haucourt. The 11th Brigade, having already taken a turn to the right, the wrong one as it happened, the 10th Brigade transport took the next turning, and at 3.40 A.M. arrived at a village whose name it could not discover until daylight, when a board inside the railway station revealed it as Cattenières, in front of the outpost position of the 4th Division, as was at

once realized. Firing was already heard, and the transport 26 Aug.
was hastily got on the march for Haucourt, its tail being 1914.
fired into shortly after it had cleared Cattenières. The
infantry of the brigade—there was a considerable gap
between it and the transport owing to the latter moving
faster—had not followed the vehicles. With the Seaforth
as rear guard and the R. Irish Fusiliers as west flank guard,
marching by country tracks until Beauvois was reached,
the column, after one mistake at a turning near Beauvois
—corrected by receiving fire—marched straight through
Fontaine au Pire at the first streak of dawn without turning off, and by 4.30 A.M. had arrived at Haucourt, where
the men threw themselves down and slept, hoping that,
being in reserve to the division, they might have a little rest.
A French cavalry patrol returning shortly before 5 A.M.
reported that the front was clear, but there was no means
of verifying this except by using the horses of field officers
and the Staff, for reasons which will appear.

Thus, by 5 A.M. on the 26th, the infantry of the 4th
Division had to all intents occupied the position assigned
to it for the night of the 25th/26th, with its firing line near
the crest of the ridge, in order to obtain a field of fire, and
the rest under cover on the short, sharpish reverse slope
which falls to the Warnelle stream behind it. It was a good
position for action, though hardly for a rear-guard action,
in view of the long, gradual and exposed slope from the
stream up to Ligny which must be crossed in retirement.
On the right there was a gap of nearly two thousand yards
between the Rifle Brigade and the 3/Worcestershire of the
3rd Division about Caudry. There was also a gap of
nearly three-quarters of a mile between the 11th and the
12th Brigades, but the 10th Brigade, in reserve south of
the Warnelle, near Haucourt, covered this, the R. Dublin
Fusiliers and R. Warwickshire being east of the village
and the Seaforth and R. Irish Fusiliers behind it. The
artillery was not in battle position, as its commander, Br.-
General G. F. Milne, was with divisional headquarters and
therefore expected to resume the retirement at 7 A.M.

Though complete in field artillery and infantry, the
4th Division was as yet without its divisional cavalry[1] and

---

[1] A deplorable order had been issued on the 24th by G.H.Q. withdrawing the divisional squadron (A of the 19th Hussars) of the 5th Division
from it. With B Squadron, the divisional cavalry of the 4th Division,
which had just arrived, it was sent to reinforce the Cavalry Division.
Thus—one of the two squadrons formerly allotted to divisions having
been withdrawn for the same purpose early in 1914—the 4th and 5th

cyclists, heavy battery, engineers, the greater part of its signal company,[1] train, ammunition column and field ambulances. Hence there were no mounted troops to furnish patrols or covering parties, no 60-pdrs. to mow down the enemy before deployment as was to be done with such striking effect by the heavy battery of the 5th Division on the right, no engineers to superintend working parties, very limited means of attending to wounded, no means of removing them, and, above all, no means of controlling from divisional headquarters the general movements of some fifteen thousand men extended along a front of five miles, except by the use of mounted officers and orderlies. The ground on which the 4th Division lay, on the left of the British line, was open fields under cultivation, with some of the crops, notably beetroot and clover, still ungathered, soaked by the rain of the previous night, and in many places churned into deep mud by the passage of men, horses, guns and vehicles ; over such a surface horses, already none too fresh, were soon exhausted by a few hard gallops.

The 4th Division did not receive the 7.30 P.M. order to continue the retreat on Le Catelet until midnight, when a copy was brought by Colonel W. H. Bowes from G.H.Q. Divisional orders were prepared but were not issued to the brigades, for they were all on the move. At 5 A.M. officers were sent out to ascertain the positions of the

Divisions were left without trained " eyes," except in so far as mounted officers, the cyclist companies, and Yeomanry detachments eventually sent to replace the cavalry, could furnish them. The absence of the divisional cavalry squadron was a cause of heavy loss to the 4th Division on the morning of Le Cateau, as will be seen, and hampered both divisions gravely in the retreat to the Seine and the advance to the Aisne. The other divisional troops (less the 60-pdr. battery) mentioned in the text as being absent reached St. Quentin early on the 26th, and the O.C. Signal Company sent a message to the 4th Division, timed 8.10 A.M., which reached General Snow during the morning, saying " detained here by " order of G.H.Q." Formed in a column, under Lieut.-Colonel H. B. Jones, the C.R.E. of the 4th Division, these divisional troops were soon after ordered by G.H.Q. to retire. They waited south of the Somme until the main body of the division reached them on the 28th. Half a squadron North Irish Horse reported to 4th Division headquarters on the evening of the 25th, and was sent to assist the flank detachment of the R. Inniskilling Fusiliers at Bévillers. During the night, however, it lost touch with the 4th Division and fought at Caudry on the 26th with the 3rd Division, not returning to the 4th until late on the 28th.

[1] No. 1 Section (for divisional headquarters) was absent. It contained three cable detachments with telephone equipment, motor cyclists, push cyclists, mounted men, heliographs and other means of communication. It formed the exchange centre of the division for the despatch and receipt of messages.

troops, and it was intended to issue the orders as soon as 26 Aug. the officers reported, should the situation permit retire- 1914. ment. It was almost immediately after this that Captain B. Walcot arrived from General Smith-Dorrien to announce his decision to stand and to request that the 4th Division would cover his flank. General Snow agreed to do so, and at 5.30 A.M. sent messages to his brigades to take up the positions already ordered, and to the 11th Brigade to get in touch with the 3rd Division. Shortly after this the officers who had carried the order returned reporting, to use the words of one of them, Captain H. J. Elles, that the infantry was already " at it hammer and tongs."

NOTE I

The Movements of the German *First Army* on the 25th August 1914

General von Kluck's book and the special sketch-map for the Map 3. 25th/26th August which he has provided make it perfectly clear Sketch 6. how there came to be collisions between the British and the Germans at Maroilles, Landrecies and Solesmes on the night of the 25th/26th.

On the evening of the 24th August he issued operation orders in the expectation that the British Army would accept battle on the line Maubeuge—Bavai—Valenciennes, making his plans for a " Cannae " on a small scale. His *IX. Corps* was to attack against Bavai, that is against General Haig, and guard against any interference from Maubeuge ; the *III. Corps* against St. Vaast—Wargnies, that is against General Smith-Dorrien ; the *IV. Corps* was to envelop the British western flank ; and the *II. Cavalry Corps* was to work round in rear of the British and cut off their retreat " westwards." He had asked that a division of the *VII. Corps* and the *I. Cavalry Corps* might be sent from Maubeuge to close on the British right. With the *II. Corps* only a march in rear and close to Condé, and the *IV. Reserve Corps* following on, " the envelopment of the British " Army, provided it stood, seemed certain."

The *First Army* Staff appears to have been considerably misled by air reports. Those of the evening of the 24th and early morning of the 25th gave " the impression of a general retreat on Maubeuge " :[1] columns were converging on Bavai, and the roads from Le Quesnoy to the south and south-west, as well as the main roads through the Forest of Mormal were reported clear of troops. At 7.15 A.M. orders were sent out by motor car for the *II., III.* and *IV. Corps* to wheel southwards on Aulnoye, Landrecies and Le Cateau, and the *II. Cavalry Corps* to advance to the area north-west of Guise. " It was " hoped to cut off the British and then turn against the left flank of " the French."

At 9 A.M., however, the " surprising air report " arrived that long columns were moving from Bavai on Le Cateau by the Roman

[1] Kuhl's " Marne," p. 73.

road and that numerous small columns were crossing the Selle, north and south of Solesmes. " The enemy was marching in an " almost opposite direction to what was supposed earlier in the " morning." Fresh orders were rapidly sent out to attack the British and prevent their further retreat : the *II. Cavalry Corps* was to head them off, the *III. Corps* to make its right (west) column stronger, the *IV. Corps* to march with its right wing on Solesmes— Le Cateau, with the *II. Corps* west of it. The *IX. Corps* was to continue opposite Maubeuge covering the movement.

In accordance with these orders, the *IX. Corps* wheeled south-
Map 9. eastwards from Bavai and commenced investing Maubeuge.[1] The *III. Corps*, passing over the old front of Smith-Dorrien's corps, St. Vaast—Wargnies, in two divisional columns, pushed its advanced guards through the Forest of Mormal south-eastwards by the two good roads which lead to Berlaimont and Maroilles. At night the *5th Division* billeted and bivouacked in the forest, along the high road Maroilles—Le Quesnoy, in the area Hachette (near the bridge over the Sambre 2 miles N.N.W. of Maroilles)—Locquignol—Joli-metz :[2] and the leading troops of its advanced guard came in contact with the 1/Royal Berkshire of the 6th Brigade, as already related.[3] The *6th Division* halted north of the *5th Division*, with half its troops on either side of the forest : the *11th Brigade* and part of the divisional troops in the area, west of the forest, between Villereau—Gommegnies—Amfroipret and the border of the forest ; the *12th Brigade* and the rest of the divisional troops in the area, east of the forest, La Grande Carrière—Aymeries—Berlaimont—Sassegnies.

The *IV. Corps*, marching due south, also advanced in two columns, one via Le Quesnoy and then past the south-west boundary of the Forest of Mormal to Landrecies, and the other via Valenciennes to Solesmes. Thus they came in contact with the British 2nd[4] and 3rd Divisions. The *II. Cavalry Corps* billeted four to eight miles east of Cambrai, around Avesnes lez Aubert.
Map 3.   Of the German *Second Army*, as already noticed, the *VII. Corps* was detailed to invest the eastern side of Maubeuge. The *X. Reserve Corps* was near Solre le Chateau on the night of the 25th/26th August, with the *I. Cavalry Corps* on its left near Sivry, and the *X. Corps* beyond it.

---

[1] There is a good account of the investment of Maubeuge by the *IX. Corps* on the 25th August, the blocking of the roads, construction of entanglements, etc., in Tepp's " In Siegessturm nach Paris."
[2] This information was obtained in Berlin on January 1922.
[3] See page 133. The *III. Battalion* of the *48th Regiment* was in action at Maroilles (" Regt. No. 48," p. 16).
[4] The following extract from a book by Oberleutnant Dr. Lohrisch, published in 1917, entitled " Im Siegessturm von Lüttich an die Marne," throws a little light on Landrecies. His battalion (*I. of the 27th Regiment*) marched forward on the 25th via Le Quesnoy to Bousies (four miles north-west of Landrecies), where it halted for the night. He continues : " Our advanced guard stumbled on the enemy at Landrecies, and the *II.* " and *III. Battalions*, which were billeted at Robersart and Fontaine au Bois " (south-east of Bousies), and two of our companies were sent forward in the " direction of the little town. . . . At 5.45 A.M. (on the 26th) the regiment " was ordered to capture Landrecies, as the tired troops sent forward the " night before, on account of difficulties caused by the darkness and ignor- " ance of the ground, had been compelled to stop their operations."

Thus it was that on the evening of the 25th, the German *II.* 25 Aug.
Cavalry Corps and *IV.* and *III. Corps* were close enough to the 1914.
British to be able to strike in force at Le Cateau in the early morning, Map 9.
whilst the *IV. Reserve, II., I. Cavalry, X. Reserve,* and *X. Corps*
were within a march of the field, with parts of the *IX.* and *VII. Corps,*
drawn from the investment of Maubeuge, available in case of need.

NOTE II

First Belgian Sortie from Antwerp, the 24th, 25th
and 26th August

During the 24th, 25th and 26th August the Belgian Army, in 24-26Aug.
order to assist the French and British troops fighting on the Sambre 1914.
and on the Mons canal, made a sortie against the German corps Map 2.
observing Antwerp, with a view to detaining them there, and, if
possible, acting against the German communications passing through
Louvain and Brussels.

On the 24th a reconnaissance was made, and on the 25th four
divisions, with a fifth division and the cavalry division in reserve,
attacked southwards from Malines towards the gap between Louvain
and Brussels. Good progress was made, and the fight continued on
the 26th, when information from Paris of the withdrawal of the
French and British forces having been received, and also of the
intention of General Joffre to resume the offensive at a later date, it
was decided to adopt a similar course and retire into Antwerp.

As will be seen, the second Belgian sortie took place during the
Battle of the Marne.

CHAPTER VII

THE BATTLE OF LE CATEAU—26TH AUGUST
DAWN TILL NOON

(Sketch 7 ; Maps 3, 10 & 11)

Sketch 7.
Map 10. THE 26th August, the anniversary of Crécy, dawned hot and misty, with some prospect that the historic weather of A.D. 1346 would be repeated, and the certainty that in an almost similarly desperate situation, the stout hearts of our island race would again triumph over superiority of numbers, and rob the enemy of what he considered an easy prey.

Although in the first instance it was the intention of G.H.Q. to occupy a position in the neighbourhood of Le Cateau, a subsequent order had directed the retreat to be continued.[1] It was upon the original understanding, however, and in expectation that the I. Corps would be in touch with the right flank of the II. Corps, that the disposition of the troops on the ground was made by General Smith-Dorrien. Officers had been sent ahead to reconnoitre the position, but most of the units did not come on to it until dark, and heavy rain had interfered with the observation of those which reached it earlier in the day. Moreover it was difficult to identify places by the map ; for the only one then available was the French uncontoured hachured map of the 1 : 80,000 scale, to which British officers were not accustomed. When the troops stood to arms about 4 A.M. under orders to continue the retreat, there was a heavy ground mist, so that, though the troops were approximately in position, there was little opportunity, or apparent necessity, to rectify the line and choose the best ground to repel a determined attack by superior numbers.

The town of Le Cateau lies deep in the narrow valley

---

[1] See page 123.

LE CATEAU

WEDNESDAY, 26TH. AUGUST 1914.

SKETCH 7.

Ordnance Survey. 1924.

of the river Selle, surrounded on all sides by open cultivated country, with never a fence, except in the immediate
vicinity of the villages, and hardly a tree, except along the
chaussées.   The river, though small, is unfordable.   The
heights on the east, crescent shaped, slightly overlook those
on the west, the highest ground of which is roughly a ⊣
in plan : the head (the Reumont ridge), running north
to south, from Viesly to Reumont, and the stalk (the Le
Cateau position or Caudry ridge) east to west from Le
Cateau to Crèvecœur.   The reverse or south side of the
Caudry ridge drops sharply to the Warnelle stream, with
higher undulating country behind it, dotted with villages
and woods, admirably suited to cover a retirement, once
the long slope from the stream up to the edge of the
higher ground marked by Montigny and Ligny had been
passed.   The front or north side is broken by a succession
of long spurs running northwards ; the western end drops
to the Schelde canal.

Except for this canal with its accompanying stream,
and the Selle river with its tributary the Rivierette des
Essarts, the country was free for the movement of troops
of all arms, and, from its open character, generally suited
to defensive action, though there were numerous small
valleys up which enterprising and well-trained infantry
could approach unseen.   Beetroot and clover covered
part of the ground, but the other crops had mostly been
cut and partly harvested.   Here and there were lines of
cattle, picketed Flemish fashion, in the forage patches.
Crops had been held so sacred at British manœuvres that
there was occasionally hesitation before troops, particularly
mounted troops, would move across them.

The town of Le Cateau on the right of the line of the
II. Corps was at 4.40 A.M. still full of British transport,
though the long columns, after protracted delay owing
to the passage of General Sordet's cavalry corps across
them, had for hours been pushing south-westwards along
the Roman road.   The 19th Brigade, placed under the
II. Corps by G.H.Q. orders of the previous night, had not
yet received any message postponing the retreat, as its
headquarters could not be found in the dark ; it was
delayed nearly two hours in starting by the congestion in
the streets, and had hardly got clear—being the last
troops to leave the town—when shortly after 6 A.M. the Map 11.
first German scouts made their appearance in Le Cateau.
There was some firing, but the scouts were easily kept at a

distance, and the brigade eventually pursued its march to Reumont with hardly a casualty. The 1/D.C.L.I. and half of the 1/East Surrey (14th Brigade), which had bivouacked on the heights to the east of Le Cateau, and had likewise received no orders to stand fast, were at this time formed up in column of route by the railway bridge near the south-eastern corner of the town, facing west and ready to march off at 6.30 A.M. The remainder of the 14th Brigade had meanwhile occupied a position immediately to the west of Le Cateau : the Suffolk across the centre of the spur—which for convenience may be called the Montay spur—which runs from the Reumont ridge north-eastward to Montay, the remaining one and a half battalions south of them. Next to the 14th Brigade, but separated from it by a small valley between spurs, came the K.O.Y.L.I. of the 13th Brigade, with the XV. Brigade R.F.A. and the 37th Howitzer Battery in close support on the right, and the XXVIII. Brigade R.F.A. in close support on the left. West of the K.O.Y.L.I., the Scottish Borderers of the same brigade occupied the next ridge of rising ground ; and west of them again, the 15th Brigade prolonged the line to the road that leads from Troisvilles to Inchy, with the XXVII. Brigade R.F.A. in rear of it to the east and south-east of Troisvilles. Of the rest of the artillery of the 5th Division, the 61st Howitzer Battery and 108th Heavy Battery took up positions of observation about a mile to the north of Reumont, while the 65th Howitzer Battery unlimbered to the south-west of Troisvilles. In reserve near Reumont was the 19th Brigade, as orders to halt there reached it soon after it left Le Cateau.

The battalions of the 14th Brigade which lay west of Le Cateau did not receive their counter-orders to stand fast until about 6 A.M. ; those to the east of the town never received them at all. Hence the 5th Division was in a manner surprised, and compelled to accept battle in positions which were being held with a view to slipping away under cover of rear guards. The Suffolk in particular, who lay immediately to the west of Le Cateau, were badly placed for a general action : there was much dead ground on every side ; the field of fire was for the most part limited and could nowhere be called really good; while small valleys and sunken roads at sundry points gave hostile infantry every opportunity of concealing their approach. The battalion, in common with the other troops of the 5th Division, made shift to throw up such entrenchments as it could with its

"grubbers," no better tools being obtainable. The
XXVII. R.F.A. had time to dig in its batteries ; the
XV. Brigade for the most part had to be content to mask
its guns with corn-sheaves.

But the serious difficulties in which the 5th Division
became involved during the action of the 26th August
arose not so much from the lack of preparation of the
position, as from the belief that the I. Corps would be on
its right, and hold the high ground east of Le Cateau,
whence an enemy could rake a considerable portion of the
line.   The risk that this ground would fall into German
hands had to be accepted by Sir Horace Smith-Dorrien
when, late indeed but as early as in the circumstances it
was possible to come to a decision, he resolved to stand and
fight.

Passing to the dispositions of the 3rd Division, the 9th
Brigade took up the line from Troisvilles westward to
Audencourt.   The brigadier, as has been told, had received
timely notice of General Smith-Dorrien's intentions and,
bringing his battalions early into position, enabled them
to improve some mathematically straight trenches which
had been hastily begun by French civilians, and to dig
themselves fair shelter.   The XXIII. Brigade R.F.A. was
in close support on the reverse side of the ridge, with two
sections dug in on the forward slope, one of the 107th
Battery to the right front, and one of the 108th Battery
on the left rear of the Lincolnshire, the left of the brigade.
About a thousand yards to the south of these batteries was
the 65th Howitzer Battery (5th Division), and about five
hundred yards to the west of them the 48th Heavy Battery.

Next on the left of the 9th Brigade stood the 8th Brigade,
holding Audencourt and the ground thence westward to
Caudry.   This brigade also was partly dug in, having taken
in hand at dawn the work of improving and extending some
trenches made by French civilians.

The 7th Brigade occupied Caudry and its vicinity.
The right of the position along the ridge to the north-east
of the town was held by the 1/Wiltshire ; an enclosure near
Point 129, just north of the town, by the 2/South Lancashire
and the 56th Field Company R.E. ; and the remainder of
the line along the north and north-western outskirts by the
3/Worcestershire.   The battalions of the 7th Brigade were
very weak, many men having lost their way in the dark
during the retirement from Solesmes.   The Irish Rifles,
indeed, had not yet rejoined, being still at Maurois with the

41st Battery. A divisional reserve was formed of men collected from first line transport, signal sections, etc.

Of the rest of the 3rd Division artillery, the XL. Brigade R.F.A. was in readiness south-west of Audencourt; two batteries of the XLII. Brigade R.F.A. at the north-eastern corner of Caudry; a section of I Battery R.H.A. (of the Cavalry Division) at the north-western corner; and the XXX. Howitzer Brigade just south of the buildings of Caudry facing north-west. Speaking generally, the 3rd Division was better posted and more fully prepared for action than either the 5th Division on its right or the 4th on its left, having received earlier warning of what was expected of it.

Between Caudry and Fontaine au Pire there was a gap; this, however, was of no importance, since it could be swept by crossfire from the two villages; and at Fontaine au Pire itself the rear guard of the 11th Brigade was still bickering with the advanced parties of the enemy. Its main body, as already described, was aligned from the east of the "Quarry" south-west towards the Warnelle ravine; and by this time the King's Own had crossed the ravine from Haucourt, and was halted in mass near the cross roads five hundred yards north-east of Longsart, thus filling the gap between the 11th and 12th Brigades.

In reserve to General Smith-Dorrien's force there were nominally the Cavalry Division and the 19th Brigade; orders were issued for the 2nd and 3rd Cavalry Brigades to proceed to Bazuel and Mazinghien (2 miles east by south and 4 miles south-east of Le Cateau respectively), to guard the right flank; whilst the 1st Cavalry Brigade was to take post at Escaufourt, about four miles south-west of Le Cateau. The 4th Cavalry Brigade, which had moved at midnight to Inchy, fell back to Ligny, as desired, at dawn. But the orders to the cavalry were for the most part difficult to execute, for only the 3rd and 4th Cavalry Brigades were more or less complete and concentrated, and they were at opposite ends of the line. As it happened, however, part of the 1st and 2nd Cavalry Brigades, as well as the 3rd Brigade, were in the vicinity of Le Cateau and thus, it was hoped, available to cover the gap between the I. and II. Corps.

Map 11. Very soon after 6 A.M., while the morning mist was
Sketch 7. still thick, about a dozen German batteries opened fire from the vicinity of Forest (3 miles N.N.E. of Le Cateau)[1]

[1] These were batteries of the *7th Division*.

THE RIGHT OF THE LINE

THE RIGHT OF THE LINE   157

upon the troops immediately west of Le Cateau, thereby ^{26 Aug.}
putting a stop to entrenching except so far as it could be ^{1914.}
carried on by the men lying down, with their " grubbers." ¹
The Duke of Cornwall's L.I. and two companies of the
East Surrey were, as mentioned, waiting in column of
route in Le Cateau, by the railway bridge in the Faubourg
de Landrecies when, at 6.30 A.M., exactly the time that
they should have moved off, rifle fire was opened upon
them from the windows of the neighbouring houses.²
Several men fell ; but the detachment, under the covering
fire of the signal section and some of the headquarters of
the 14th Brigade, was rapidly led back through a succession of wire fences to the high ground above the south-
eastern corner of Le Cateau. Here the six companies
formed a firing line, north and south, athwart the cross
roads just to the south of the Faubourg de France. How
the Germans had contrived to reach the south-eastern outskirts of Le Cateau without being seen, is unknown ; ³ but
the fact remains that, when the action opened, the Germans
were in the town on the flank of the II. Corps, with every
prospect of cutting off the detachment of the 14th Brigade
which lay on the east of the town, and of pouring through
the gap between the I. and II. Corps. They lost no time,
in fact, in following up that detachment, which, however,
under cover of a counter-attack by the half-battalion of
the East Surrey, fell back south-east by successive companies along the road towards Bazuel, repelling simultaneous attacks against its front and its right flank. A
mile from Bazuel portions of the 1st Cavalry Brigade,
followed by the 5th Lancers of the 3rd with D Battery,
came to its help ; ⁴ with their support the D.C.L.I. and

---

¹ A Note on the German plans for the 26th is given at end of this
Chapter. Some account of the battle from the German side will be found
in a Note at end of Chapter IX.
² The account in the history (pp. 63-72) of the *72nd Regiment*, which
was concerned, is rather different. As advanced guard of the *8th Division*,
it started early from Solesmes ; on the " point " nearing Le Cateau a
cavalry officer, sent on ahead, galloped back, wounded in the arm, shouting
" the exits are occupied." Pushing on, the leading half-battalion was
fired on from houses and the railway embankment. Fire was opened on
a train which was leaving the station, which the regiment heard from
prisoners contained " higher Staffs and probably General French." In the
course of the battle the *72nd* was cut off from its division by the advance
of the *7th Division* into the gap between them.
³ The 5th Division had been deprived of its divisional squadron two
days before, but still had a cyclist company for patrolling. See page 147,
f.n. 1.
⁴ The 3rd Cavalry Brigade was proceeding to St. Souplet. See below.

East Surrey soon after 8 A.M. began to move westward to
rejoin their brigade. The Germans, favoured by the mist,
had by this time worked up the valley of the Selle southward from Le Cateau, for about a mile, with no very clear
idea, probably, of what was going forward, when they were
caught by the counter-attack on their eastern flank, and
retired to the south edge of Le Cateau.[1]

Meanwhile fresh German batteries [2] had opened fire
from a concealed position near Rambourlieux Farm (2
miles W.N.W. of Le Cateau) against the troops between
Le Cateau and the Roman road, now the right of the
British line, and practically enfiladed the whole of them
with most destructive effect. The British guns replied as
well as they could with nothing but the flashes to guide
them ; for, though the German aeroplanes were active in
this quarter of the field, British machines were not employed in aid of the artillery. The infantry, having no
targets as yet, was obliged to endure the bombardment
passively, though comparatively early in the day—that is
to say, soon after 8 A.M.—German skirmishers climbed to
Point 150 on the summit of the Montay spur, and began
firing at the British gunners. Upon these, and also upon
a concealed German machine gun on the Cambrai road the
left company of the Suffolk opened fire ; but there was
some doubt as to the situation, for it never occurred to
any of the officers that the high ground immediately to
the east and west of Le Cateau would be left open for
occupation by the enemy. Of the fight that was going
forward in the valley of the Selle they could see nothing
nor, in the roar of the battle, hear anything.

The D.C.L.I. and the East Surrey were, as a matter of
fact, progressing slowly but steadily westward in spite of
considerable opposition ; although two companies of the
former became separated from the rest of the detachment
and losing touch turned to the south-west upon St. Benin.
Some confusion was caused during the movement by the
presence of Germans dressed in what appeared to be
khaki,[3] which more than once misled the battalions as to the
action they should take in order to rejoin their division.
However, D Battery and the southern half-battalion of
the D.C.L.I. succeeded in enfilading the German troops

---

[1] Where they remained until the *7th Division* came into action on their
left. (G.O.A., i. p. 520.)
[2] Of the *8th Division*.
[3] Probably *Jäger*, who wore a uniform of greenish-grey hue, and
shakoes, not spiked helmets.

in the valley, and the enemy withdrew to the eastward, to all appearances pretty severely punished. The greater number of the D.C.L.I. and East Surrey then moved south-west on Escaufourt, though one party, while still 500 yards short of St. Benin, turned westward, and made for Reumont, where 5th Division headquarters were established. The bulk of the D.C.L.I. arrived at Escaufourt between 11 A.M. and noon, and found that they had cut their way through the Germans at the comparatively small cost of two hundred casualties, and this number in the course of the following days was reduced to one-half by the return of missing men. The half-battalion of the East Surrey made its way to Maurois, beyond Reumont and the 1st and 3rd Cavalry Brigades retired with great deliberation due south up the valley towards St. Souplet. The first turning movement of the Germans on the eastern flank—attempted, it is true, in no great strength—had thus been foiled.

During this period the troubles of the troops immediately to the west of Le Cateau were increasing. About 10 A.M. the Germans brought guns up to the summit of the heights east of the town, and the devoted batteries and battalions of the 5th Division on the high ground between the town and the Roman road, were now enfiladed from both flanks. The 11th Battery man-handled two guns round to the east and replied effectively to the German fire ; but the concentration of a superior number of German guns, probably the artillery of the *7th* and *8th Divisions*, and very soon of the *5th Division* also, upon the exposed batteries of the XV. and XXVIII. Brigades R.F.A. caused considerable losses : salvos of shells crashed down on gun after gun in succession, but the gunners stood to their work, and the supply of ammunition never failed. The Suffolk and K.O.Y.L.I., the front line of the 14th and 13th Brigades, were also assailed by an unceasing storm of shrapnel and high-explosive shell, but vied with the artillery in steadiness. At 9.45 A.M. the Argyll and Sutherland Highlanders, of the 19th Brigade, who had been ordered forward from Reumont, arrived on the right rear of the Suffolk ; two companies dug themselves such cover as they were able with their " grubbers " on the ridge, while the rest remained in the hollow to the west of them. About 10 A.M. the firing line at last had a target, as German battalions began to advance in thick masses along a front of over two miles from the valley of the Selle

to Rambourlieux Farm.[1]   The 11th Battery, man-handling
a second section round to the right, fired upon them in the
valley at pointblank range with great execution.   Before
long, every officer of this battery had fallen, and so many
men that only enough were left to work a single gun.   But
that single gun never ceased firing ; and the other batteries,
nearly all of which had suffered heavily, showed the like
indomitable spirit.   From Reumont also the 108th Heavy
Battery burst its sixty-pounder shells among the hostile
infantry with beautiful precision, tearing great gaps in
their swarming ranks and strewing the ground with killed
and wounded.

But losses did not stop the German infantry of 1914.
The gaps were instantly filled, and the advance of the
enemy in the valley, though retarded, was not brought to
a standstill.   Parties reached a little copse upon Montay
spur, and strove to enfilade the Suffolk from the north ;
but they were checked mainly by a machine gun of the
K.O.Y.L.I. posted on the Roman road.   Further to the
west, the Germans made less progress.   From the region
of Rambourlieux Farm, profiting by past experience, they
came forward in small bodies, at wide intervals, and
taking cover behind the corn-stooks which covered the
fields ; but, though they attacked again and again, they
were driven back by the shrapnel of the artillery.   In the
zone allotted to the 37th and 52nd Batteries and the
XXVIII. Brigade R.F.A. the Germans came on in close
formation, and suffered very heavily.   The first target of
the 122nd Battery was a platoon in line, with the men
shoulder to shoulder, which emerged from a fold in the
ground.   The battery commander gave the order " one
round gun fire," and every man of the Germans fell.   At
each subsequent effort of the enemy in this direction,
much the same scene was repeated and each gathering
line of Germans was laid low.

Nevertheless, though the machine gun of the K.O.Y.L.I.
checked every attempt of the enemy to approach the
Suffolk in force, it was possible for small parties of Germans
to creep up into a cutting on the Cambrai road on their
flank, and to enfilade them both with rifles and machine
guns.   Every attempt of these parties to build up a firing

---

[1] This was the attack of the *7th Division*, with the *14th Brigade* on
both sides of the Forest—Le Cateau road and *13th Brigade* on both sides
of the Forest—Montay road (see Lohrisch).   The orders of the *14th Brigade*
were to envelop the British right.   " Regt. No. 66 " (1930 edition), p. 25.

linc in advance of the cutting was, however, foiled by the steady marksmanship of the Suffolk and by the shells of the 52nd Battery. The left company of this battalion had besides a very fair field of fire over the ground to the north-east, and forbade any hostile progress in that quarter. But the German machine guns could be neither discovered nor silenced ; and the Suffolk, except on their extreme left, which was protected by a sunken road, were falling fast under their fire. Lieut.-Colonel H. L. James of the Manchester had already pushed forward one company and a machine gun to the right rear of the Suffolk, pro-longing their line to the south ; shortly after 11 A.M., judging the position to be critical, and being unable to find the brigadier, he ordered two more companies of his battalion to advance and reinforce the Suffolk. At the same time, he called upon the Argyll and Sutherland Highlanders and 1/Middlesex, of the 19th Brigade, to support him.

The two companies of the Manchester accordingly moved forward under fire of artillery, rifles and machine guns, but, in spite of more than one check, succeeded in reaching the trenches of the Suffolk. The left company seems to have suffered less than the other, and on reaching the left company of the Suffolk found that it was not needed. The remainder, who bore more to the right, were thrown back more than once ; eventually, however, a portion reached the right centre of the firing line. Ammuni-tion for the Suffolk machine guns began to fail at this point ; it was vital to replenish it before the enemy could further develop his attack from the east. Major E. C. Doughty, who had succeeded to the command of the battalion upon the fall of Lieut.-Colonel C. A. H. Brett early in the day, with a small party managed to bring up a few bandoliers, but he fell desperately wounded at the moment of his arrival. Meanwhile, two half-companies of the Highlanders from the low ground, once again facing a storm of fire, rushed through the wreck of the 11th Battery into the right section of the trenches of the Suffolk and, though at heavy loss, brought them at least some assistance. It was about noon. Two German guns, reported to be " heavy," [1] now reached the summit of the Montay

[1] Probably 4·2-inch field howitzers with telescopic trails, enabling them to be used for direct fire. Heavy howitzers (each German corps took into the field 4 batteries, each of four 5·9 howitzers) were brought up on other parts of the field against Caudry (" Regt. No. 153," p. 54) and against Troisville and Audencourt (" Regt. No. 93," p. 44).

spur and opened fire at close range. The last gun of the 11th Battery was silenced, and the Suffolk and Manchester, together with their reinforcement of Highlanders, were in a worse plight than ever. Nevertheless, after nearly six hours of incessant fire, the troops on the right of the British line, which rested on Le Cateau, still stood firm. The German infantry was steadily increasing in numbers on their front and, despite all efforts, was drawing steadily nearer; their right flank was open; they were searched with fire from front and right and left; strong columns, betokening the approach of the German *III. Corps*, were closing in upon the right flank. It mattered not : they had been ordered to stand. The I. Corps, for whose coming they waited, might be late, as Blücher had been at Waterloo ; but, until it should come, there must be no giving way. Nor did they yield the ground until the divisional orders for retirement reached them some hours later.

Map 11.
Sketch 7.   On the left of the K.O.Y.L.I. the 2/Scottish Borderers (13th Brigade) and the Bedfordshire and Dorsetshire (15th Brigade) were for the present hardly engaged. They saw nothing of the enemy but distant columns advancing upon Inchy from the north-east, which were observed to be caught by shell fire and forced to deploy. With the 9th Brigade, on the left again, the situation was nearly similar. The German guns [1] opened upon it soon after 6 A.M. before the men had completed the trenches begun overnight, but with so little effect that they were able to continue digging themselves in and, thus sheltered, suffered trifling loss. There was no sign of any infantry attack — no rifle fire, indeed, except that of a few skirmishers with here and there a machine gun—and it was pretty evident that the enemy had no idea for the present of any attack upon this portion of the line. On the other hand, German troops,[2] working up the valley from Béthencourt and from the wood just to the east of it towards Inchy, were heavily shelled by the guns of the 6th Battery and of the XXIII. Brigade R.F.A. Some small parties, nevertheless, contrived to make their way into Beaumont and Inchy, only to be greeted by the lyddite shells of the 65th Howitzer Battery ; all their efforts to build up a firing line in front of these twin villages were foiled by the deadly marksmanship of the British.

[1] Probably of the *4th Cavalry Division.*
[2] The *4th Cavalry Division.* (Poseck, p. 63.)

THE RIGHT CENTRE 163

Against the line of the 8th Brigade around Audencourt 26 Aug. 1914 the German guns came into action rather later than against the 9th Brigade ; but the German infantry showed itself almost immediately afterwards, trickling down in thin lines towards the Cambrai road, with its machine guns clearly visible. Its advance was, however, cautious, and three British platoons which had been pushed out to the north of the Cambrai road were able to rejoin the brigade without being seriously pressed. It was not until about 9 A.M. that first the 4/Middlesex to the east of Audencourt, and later the machine guns of the Royal Scots, in the country road just to the north of it, opened fire upon parties of Germans which had crossed the Cambrai road. Even then the engagement in this quarter throughout the forenoon was no more than desultory. The headquarters of the brigade and the whole of its transport were in Audencourt itself, and there seemed no immediate menace to their security. Masses of German infantry were indeed assembling upon the Cambrai road under a devastating fire from the British artillery ; but the 8th and 9th Brigades had a good field of fire, and there was little temptation to the enemy to waste strength in attacking them, when immediately to their left lay Caudry, forming a decided salient in the British line.

Upon Caudry the German shells fell very heavily from an early hour, and bullets were whistling down the streets even before the fall of the shells. Up to 6 A.M. and even later the units of the 7th Brigade were still under the impression that the retreat would be resumed ; but the enemy's movements soon banished any such idea ; for about 7 A.M. the German riflemen [1] moved against both flanks of the village with vigour, pouring a very heavy fire in particular upon the Worcestershire on the left. So pertinacious was the onset that reinforcements were summoned from the 8th Brigade ; in consequence about 8.30 A.M. two weak companies of the Royal Irish came up and took post in a railway cutting which skirts the eastern flank of the village. Half an hour later, at 9 A.M., the Irish Rifles and the 41st Battery ended their wanderings of the night by rejoining the brigade.[2] The battalion entrenched itself about a thousand yards south of Caudry near Tronquoy, while the guns unlimbered to its right rear. Thus until noon the 7th Brigade contained the Germans without difficulty, so that they gained little or

---

[1] The *9th Cavalry Division* and three *Jäger* battalions. (Poseck, p. 59.)
[2] See page 155.

no ground ; it seemed probable that here, as on the rest of the British centre, they were husbanding their strength until their main effort against both flanks of the British should produce its effect.

Map 11.
Sketch 7. On the left wing, in the 4th Division, no orders had been issued for the retirement to be continued ; those sent out on the previous evening to occupy the Haucourt position still held good [1] and were confirmed as soon as General Smith-Dorrien's message reached divisional headquarters at 5 A.M. But, as on the right, the general action opened with misfortune for the British. Until 6 A.M., or thereabouts, the rear guard of the 11th Brigade on the right of the division continued exchanging shots with the enemy to the north of Fontaine au Pire, when it gradually withdrew, the 1/Rifle Brigade coming in last of all and taking position in the hollow road which runs southward from Beauvois to Ligny. A platoon of *Jäger*, which was imprudent enough to advance in pursuit through Fontaine au Pire, was annihilated by the accurate fire of a detachment of the 1/Hampshire. After that the enemy made no further attempt to follow up the 11th Brigade.[2] Meanwhile, in the 12th Brigade, which was on the left of the 11th, the Lancashire Fusiliers and two companies of the Essex Regiment had from 4 A.M. onwards been preparing a position near Longsart and doing what digging was possible with their " grubbers." The King's Own had been delayed on the march, but towards 5 A.M. were seen approaching over the hill from Haucourt.

French cavalry patrols, as already related, had been understood to report the front to be clear ; and the 4th Division had no divisional cavalry or cyclists to verify the French observations. Suddenly, shortly after 6 A.M., two French troopers riding towards Cattenières were seen to turn and gallop at top speed to the south-west; immediately afterwards devastating fire of machine guns, after opening on the outpost at the railway crossing north of Wambaix, swept down upon the King's Own. The battalion on arrival on the right of the brigade had halted in quarter-column—that is, the companies were in line one behind the other at six paces distance—arms had been piled, the officers had fallen out and were in a group on the right front ; some of them and most of the men had lain down. At the moment that

---

[1] See page 148.
[2] This enemy was the *2nd Cavalry Division*, with two *Jäger* battalions. (Poseck, p. 55.)

fire was opened, the rear company was moving off to the left to extend the line ; it was caught, as were most of the men of other companies who were standing up, and Lieut.-Colonel A. M. Dykes was killed.   The regimental transport, which was just arriving with rations, turned and stampeded, knocking over the brigadier and his brigade-major.   The companies were at once ordered to lie down and all men who could safely use their rifles opened fire at about eight hundred yards range upon the German machine guns, with immediate effect.   Five minutes later, however, two or three German batteries came into the open between Wambaix and Cattenières railway station, unlimbered, and speedily picking up the range, poured upon the unlucky King's Own a storm of shells, which thinned their already depleted ranks still further.   Two companies of the War-wickshire from the reserve, by direction of a staff officer, swarmed up the hill to extricate them, but were swept back upon reaching the crest with very heavy loss.   For some twenty minutes this storm of shells burst over the King's Own, after which the fire of guns and machine guns slackened, and the survivors of the battalion moved away to their right into the shelter of a country lane, running east and west, from which they opened fire with such effect that the machine guns were smothered.   A few men from the rear of the mass, who had sought shelter in the ravine, rallied and rejoined their comrades ; and the King's Own, though reduced by some four hundred casualties, recovered them-selves with commendable rapidity.

The Germans then turned their fire upon portions of the right wing of the Lancashire Fusiliers, to the west of the King's Own ; and soon German mounted men came out into the open, only to give place to a considerable body of infantry [1] in the space between Wambaix and Cattenières. The Lancashire Fusiliers brought their two machine guns into action, and though one of these became jammed at once, the other did good execution.   But the enemy, having a far greater number of machine guns—it was estimated that they had twenty-three in this quarter of the field alone at this time [2]—and being consequently able to use them with greater freedom, now crept away to the left flank of the Lancashire Fusiliers, and enfiladed them with deadly

26 Aug. 1914.

---

[1] Dismounted men of the *2nd Cavalry Division* and *Jäger*. (Poseck, p. 56.)

[2] Twenty-one, according to Poseck, p. 56 : the guns of the *4th M.G. Abteilung* and two *Jäger* battalions.

effect. Two companies of Inniskilling Fusiliers had
already come up from Longsart to prolong the line of the
Lancashire Fusiliers, one upon the eastern and the other
upon the western flank; but the latter was at once engaged with German dismounted cavalry. There were signs
also of the development of a hostile attack upon the front
and western flank of Esnes, where the two remaining companies of the Inniskilling Fusiliers were already disposed
for defence. Against them, across a cornfield that had
recently been cut, advanced the *7th Jäger*, in open order,
apparently without any suspicion that a foe was near. As
soon as the Inniskillings opened fire the Germans took cover
behind the corn-stooks. These availed them little, and
after a time they ran back, leaving forty-seven dead in front
of one of the companies when its commander in the lull that
ensued went out to count them. Thus for at least an hour
and a half the 12th Brigade held its own against the *2nd
Cavalry Division* and two *Jäger* battalions, backed by
artillery and numerous machine guns.

At length about 8.45 A.M. the German progress towards
Wambaix, round the left flank of the advanced line, had
gone so far that a retirement seemed to Br.-General H. F. M.
Wilson imperative. The King's Own on the right were the
first to be sent to the south side of the Warnelle ravine;
to cover this movement, two companies of the Warwickshire (10th Brigade) were ordered to deliver a counter-attack
from Haucourt upon the ridge to the north of Longsart.
The 1/Hampshire, of the 11th Brigade, pushed forward two
platoons to protect the Warwickshire's right flank, whereupon a German battery moved up and unlimbered close
to the railway station just south of Cattenières. The
Hampshire men, after taking the range, opened rapid fire
at a thousand and fifty yards, and within a minute the
battery turned and galloped away to seek shelter. This
little incident, though a triumph for British musketry, could
not of course affect the main issue. The Warwickshire
again reached the crest of the ridge, and so gained some little
respite for the King's Own, but they suffered severely from
the fire of artillery and machine guns and were forced to fall
back. The Lancashire Fusiliers, covered by the fire of two
companies of the Essex on the Haucourt—Esnes road, were
the last to go; not without difficulty, for the Germans were
within three hundred yards of them. They rallied on the
ridge to the south. The company of the Essex on their
immediate left had retired a little earlier; but that of the

Inniskillings on the right withdrew with them, with the exception of the left platoon, which remained where it had fought, amid a circle of German dead, with not a single man unwounded. The withdrawal of the 12th Brigade across the valley to the line Ligny—Esnes was now practically accomplished.

Meanwhile, the artillery of the 4th Division had come into action. At 5.30 A.M., immediately on the issue of the divisional operation orders sent out on receipt of General Smith-Dorrien's message, the C.R.A., Br.-General G. F. Milne, ordered his brigades to reconnoitre positions : the XXXVII. (Howitzer) and XXXII. Brigades R.F.A. to the east of the Iris stream, and the XIV. and XXIX. to the west of it ; the two last at once to take up positions of readiness south-east of Esnes. Shortly afterwards, they came into action : the XXXII. and XXIX. Brigades detailed to co-operate with the 11th Brigade, and the XIV. with the 12th Brigade.

The XXXII. Brigade was brought into action as rapidly as possible, as the 11th Brigade was asking for artillery support to divert from it some of the German gun fire to which it was being subjected. The 27th Battery un-limbered in the open to the west of Ligny, the 134th in a covered position on higher ground immediately to the south-west of the village, with the 135th, also under cover, to the left rear of the 27th.

The XXIX. Brigade took up its position south-east of Haucourt. Of the XIV., the 68th Battery came into action at once just south-west of the village, the 39th three-quarters of a mile in rear, with the 88th in the valley-head to the east of St. Aubert Farm. The XXXVII. (Howitzer) unlimbered in the Iris valley, but did not open fire from this position. The heavy battery, as already noted, was not present.

The fire of the XIV. Brigade gained time for the 12th Brigade to rally ; and then the enemy came on, against the Lancashire Fusiliers, just as the British would have desired —in bunches, firing from the hip. A burst of rapid fire from a hastily formed line speedily brought the advance to a standstill, and the Lancashire Fusiliers took advantage of the lull to re-form on a better position a short distance in rear. The German artillery now redoubled its fire ; but between 9.30 and 10 A.M. the worst of the surprise attack was over, and Br.-General Wilson was able to reconstitute his line along a front from Ligny through Haucourt to

Esnes, already occupied by part of the 10th Brigade. Br.-General J. A. L. Haldane, warned to secure the left flank of the division, indeed of the whole B.E.F., moved the R. Irish Fusiliers to a ridge south-east of Esnes, marked by St. Aubert Farm and Point 137, and later despatched the Seaforth to take a position in echelon to the Fusiliers. On this ridge the new position of the two brigades assumed the shape almost of a semicircle, with its convex side to the enemy. The units were very much mixed, and it is impossible to say precisely where parts of them were placed.

By 11 A.M. the firing in this quarter of the field had died down. The German attack, delivered by a force of cavalry and *Jäger*, with a very powerful backing of artillery, had been repulsed, although the 12th Brigade had been forced back to the south side of the Warnelle ravine, and had suffered heavy casualties, chiefly owing to the mishap to the King's Own. The cavalry and the cyclists of the 4th Division, had they been available, would undoubtedly have prevented this surprise. Even as things were, the division had succeeded in holding its own. Moreover, if the Germans hoped to pin it to its ground, they had failed; for there was nothing now to prevent the 4th Division from continuing its retirement if it so desired.

During this period the 11th Brigade became isolated to a certain extent, on its left owing to the retirement of the 12th Brigade and, on its right, by the distance which separated it from the 7th Brigade ; but it held on with the greatest tenacity. Its position, it may be recalled, was on the Caudry plateau to the north of the Warnelle ravine, astride the " Quarry " knoll and extending thence south-west across the railway to the edge of the plateau, its general front being towards the north-west. Before part of this front, notably on the northern slope of the " Quarry" knoll, there was a natural glacis, but further to the west the field of fire was bad. The enemy, of course, avoided the glacis, and preferred to work round both flanks of the brigade and attack along the line of the railway from the west and from the southern margin of Fontaine au Pire from the north-east. But though the Germans brought up battery after battery, until the line of their guns extended from Wambaix to the north of Fontaine,[1] and swept the plateau with them and with machine guns, the bombard-

---

[1] The artillery of the *IV*. *Reserve Corps* was sent up ahead of its infantry, and the whole of its batteries came into action between 11.10 and 11.30 A.M. to assist the *Cavalry Corps*. ("Res. F.A. Regt. No. 7," p. 28.)

mcnt was not followed by the advance of infantry in large 26 Aug. bodies. After a time the East Lancashire were compelled 1914. to retire from the northern slope of the " Quarry " to a sunken road upon the southern slope, and there they remained. The Rifle Brigade and two companies of the Somerset Light Infantry, on the right of the East Lanca-shire, also held their ground, though heavily shelled. They were rewarded occasionally by the sight of German infantry striving to advance over the stubble, and seized every opportunity of cutting them down by rapid fire.

More than once small parties of the 11th Brigade were forced out of the more exposed positions by the rain of shrapnel ; but they always reoccupied them, or were re-placed by supports from the Warnelle ravine.   Once the Hampshire, on the left of the line, essayed a counter-attack, but it proved too costly.   The Germans dealt with it by fire, and then waited ; they had an overwhelming force of artillery ; they had brought forward their machine guns with much skill ; and they might reasonably reckon that the 11th Brigade would soon retire and abandon the position without bitter fighting, or, better still, cling to it too long, and be surrounded.   Here, therefore, as on the remainder of the left wing, there was a deadlock.

So far General Smith-Dorrien had held his ground successfully for some six hours ; and, except immediately west of Le Cateau, his line was not only unbroken but unshaken.   Even there the enemy had not immediately pressed home the advantages which he had gained.   But the situation was rapidly growing more serious.   To that critical point we must now return.

NOTE

GERMAN PLANS FOR THE 26TH AUGUST 1914

" The *First Army* orders for the 26th were based on the two ideas " of continuing the pursuit south-westwards by forced marches, and " of widening the front.   Report was made to the Supreme Command " that the intention was ' to bar the retreat of the enemy between " ' Cambrai and St. Quentin.' "   (G.O.A., i. p. 521.)

The situation as it appeared to the Germans at night is fully Map 3. disclosed by Kluck's operation orders issued at 10.50 P.M. on the 25th August.   In them he ordered " the continuation of the pursuit " of the beaten enemy " in a general south-westerly direction :—his right, the *II. Corps*, via Cambrai on Bapaume ;   the *IV. Reserve Corps* (then at Valenciennes) starting early, via Vendegies to Cattenières ; the *IV. Corps* via Caudry and Montay to Vendhuille ;   the *III. Corps* via Le Cateau to Maretz. The *IX. Corps* was still in rear observing the western front of Maubeuge and protecting the lines of communication against sorties from the fortress ; it was to send any troops it could spare after the *III. Corps*. " The commander of the " *II. Cavalry Corps* had reported that on the 26th he wished to " continue the pursuit on Bohain (10 miles south by west of Le " Cateau). With this the *First Army* agreed."[1]   It was Kluck's intention to envelop the British on both flanks.   From his own account, he seems to have been under a complete misconception of the situation in the morning.   He thought, when it was found that the British were not retiring, that they were holding a more or less north and south position (he ordered " the *IV. Corps* to envelop " the northern ; the *III. Corps* the southern flank of the position "), and were trying " to draw off in a westerly direction " ; and he lost sight of the I. Corps altogether.   Possibly, the extension of the British front westwards by the newly arrived 4th Division helped to mislead him.   Further, that front at nightfall on the 25th had been established by contact on the line Landrecies—Solesmes facing north-east ; and the move of the 4th Division from Solesmes during the night, practically in contact with the Germans, was south-west. Possibly he thought the whole force was following the same direction. This, of course, fitted in with his preconceived idea that the British Expeditionary Force was based on Ostend, Dunkirk and Calais.

In the German *Second Army*, Bülow also issued operation orders that " on the 26th the pursuit of the beaten enemy should be con- " tinued in a south-westerly direction with the greatest possible " energy."   As he had to leave the *VII. Corps* to observe the eastern side of Maubeuge, the *X. Reserve Corps* now became his right.   This corps only reached Marbaix on the 26th and did not get into contact with the British until it struck the rear guard of the I. Corps, the 1st (Guards) Brigade, at Étreux on the 27th.

---

[1] The orders in Poseck, p. 55, are for the *II. Cavalry Corps* to move due south against the great Roman road :
2nd Cavalry Division, with *4th* and *7th Jäger*, via Carnières—Esnes (practically Wambaix).
9th Cavalry Division, with *3rd*, *9th* and *10th Jäger*, via Beauvois.
4th Cavalry Division, via Caudry (due south of Quiévy).

CHAPTER VIII

THE BATTLE OF LE CATEAU, 26TH AUGUST (*continued*)

FROM NOON TILL 5 P.M.

(Sketch 7 ; Maps 3, 10 & 11)

SHORTLY after noon the situation of the Suffolk and of the batteries supporting them, on the right of the line, became serious under the German enfilade fire. The 108th Heavy Battery, in action well behind the right flank, had silenced one troublesome group of guns near Croix ; but, despite this piece of good shooting, the hostile artillery still far outmatched the British.[1] Reserves there were none, except the four battalions of the 19th Brigade ; of these the Cameronians and Royal Welch Fusiliers, in view of the enemy's movement on Ligny, had at 10 A.M. been moved away westwards to Montigny, behind the left flank of the II. Corps ; a part of the Argyll and Sutherland Highlanders had already been thrown into the fight ;[2] and only the remainder of this battalion, together with the 1/Middlesex, was available on the right. By the orders of Major-General L. G. Drummond, commanding the brigade, two half-companies of the Argylls, with the battalion machine

Sketch 7.
Maps 10
& 11.

---

[1] Apparently the greater part of the artillery of the German *5th* and *7th Divisions* was in action against the 5th Division. " F.A. Regt. No. 18 " (*5th Division*), p. 21, states that the division deployed for action about 11 A.M. and one of its artillery brigades " had to be given up to the *IV.* " Corps, which was engaged in a hard fight," whilst one battery of the other brigade was attached to the *6th Division*. The regimental commander was wounded. " Regt. No. 26 " (*7th Division*), pp. 57-8, gives the interesting information that the artillery of the *5th Division* about 12.25 P.M. fired on one of its own battalions and on other infantry of the *IV. Corps*, because " troops of the *III. Corps* put up artillery screens, painted black-white-red " on the rear side, in order to make clear their position to the artillery. " As our corps did not show their screens, the *III. Corps* artillery believed " it had the enemy in front of it." The fire received was " heavy and loss- " bringing." The regiment was also fired on by its own corps artillery, " which did not suppose the attackers had got so far forward."

[2] See page 161.

guns, were now sent up the track which ran over the ridge
to the right rear of the Suffolk ; and the 1/Middlesex moved
forward into position upon the right of the Highlanders.
The only reassuring feature in the situation of the 5th
Division was that the Germans were not pushing their way
up the valley of the Selle past the right flank of the 14th
Brigade with the rapidity and vigour that might have been
expected.   Whether the German *III. Corps* had been slow
in following its advanced troops, or, as it came upon the
field, had been diverted from Le Cateau westward, in
support of the frontal attack on the 14th and 13th Brigades,
was unknown.[1]   In any case, the detachment of the Argyll
and Sutherland Highlanders, seeing no German troops in
the valley, turned its machine guns at long range on to
the ridge east of Le Cateau.   This drew the fire of the
German artillery, which put both the machine guns out of
action.   But, at the moment, the danger lay not in the
east but in the north.   About noon, General Smith-
Dorrien again visited 5th Division headquarters, and discussed with Sir Charles Fergusson the question of holding
on or retiring.   As the Germans were so near, it was thought
that a counter-attack would be necessary to disengage, and
the decision to retire was, temporarily, postponed.

    Shortly before 1 P.M., Sir Charles Fergusson from his
lookout in Reumont village could see that the right of his
division was shaken and might shortly give way, and he
reported in that sense to corps headquarters.   A little
later he added that a German division [2] was working round
his right from Bazuel.   Finally at 1.20 P.M. he suggested
that unless material assistance could be sent to him he had
better begin retiring.   It seems to have been about this
time, during a lull in the German fire, that the teams of the
11th Battery came up to the guns, and got five of them
away, that of the sixth being shot down.   The teams of
the 80th and 37th Batteries also came forward, and brought
away five of the guns and four of the howitzers ; another
howitzer as will be seen was recovered later on.   But these
three batteries were saved at the cost of the teams of the

---

[1] For what had happened to the German *III. Corps*, see Note I. at
end of Chapter IX.
    [2] This was thought to be the head of the *5th Division* of the *III. Corps*,
but must have been the *165th Regiment* of the *7th Division* (in the same
brigade as the *27th*).   This regiment went over the high ground east of
Le Cateau, deployed south of the Le Cateau—Maubeuge railway and then,
about 4 P.M., turned towards Honnechy, which it reached as the last British
were leaving the village (p. 25 of its history).

52nd, whose guns had consequently to be abandoned. The
gunners of this battery were ordered to retire, but a few remained and managed to keep one gun in action. Somewhat later, the teams of the 122nd Battery galloped up through the line of the West Kent, in brigade reserve, who stood up and cheered them loudly as they dashed between their trenches and onward down the slope towards their guns. As they came within view of the enemy, they were struck by a hurricane of shrapnel and of bullets from the machine guns in the Cambrai road ; but still they went on. The officer in charge of the teams was killed, and one team shot down in a heap before the position was reached ; but two guns of the 122nd Battery were carried off without mishap. A third was limbered up, but the horses went down instantly. It was an extraordinary sight : a short wild scene of galloping and falling horses, and then four guns standing derelict, a few limbers lying about, one on the skyline with its pole vertical, and dead men and dead horses everywhere. It was then decided to abandon the remaining guns, as also those of the 124th and 123rd Batteries, which were in an even more exposed position, the breech-blocks being first removed and the sights smashed. Altogether, twenty-four field guns and a howitzer were lost in this part of the field ; considering that the batteries were practically in the firing line, it is astonishing that any were rescued ; the feat redounds to the eternal honour of the officers and men of the 5th Division artillery.

It was now about 2 P.M. At 1.40 P.M., in response to the 1.20 P.M. message, General Smith-Dorrien had placed his two remaining battalions, the Cameronians and the Royal Welch Fusiliers, at Sir Charles Fergusson's disposal, ordering them to move from Montigny to Bertry, and asking him to hold his ground at any rate a little longer, so as to allow the preliminary movements of the retirement to take effect ; he was to begin the withdrawal of the 5th Division as soon as he should think fit : after which the 3rd and 4th Divisions were to follow in succession. General Smith-Dorrien had already summoned to his headquarters the G.S.O.1 of the 4th Division—to which he was, about midday, connected by signal cable—to receive orders. These were to the same effect as those given to the 5th Division. Roads were allotted for the retirement to the north-west of St. Quentin, when it should take place, as follows :—

Map 3.   To the 5th Division and 19th Brigade :
(1) via Bertry—Maretz, and thence the Roman road to
    Vermand ;
(2) via Reumont—Maurois—Busigny—Bohain—Bran-
    court—Joncourt—Bellenglise.
To the 3rd Division, via Montigny—Clary—Elincourt—
Malincourt (east of the Church)—Beaurevoir—Gouy—Bony—
Hargicourt—Jeancourt.
To the 4th Division, via Selvigny—Malincourt (west of the
Church)—Aubencheul—Ronssoy—Templeux—Roisel.
To the Cavalry, any roads west of the 4th Division.

Sketch 7.   The pressure upon the British line immediately west
Map 11.   of Le Cateau now became severe, and it seemed clear that
the Germans were preparing for a great effort. Before
the teams of the 122nd Battery advanced, three platoons
of the Argyll and Sutherland Highlanders had twice made
gallant attempts to reach the trenches of the Suffolk,
but had been beaten back with severe loss by artillery
and machine-gun fire. They rallied under the protection
of the 59th Field Company R.E., which gave up its trenches
to them and lay down in the open. So intense, in fact,
was the machine-gun fire upon the whole ridge to the rear
of the Suffolk that the Highlanders had to abandon the
line which they had taken up, and move further down
the slope towards the valley of the Selle. Meanwhile, the
German battalions were steadily gaining ground ; in fact,
as the last gun team of the 5th Division artillery was driving off, as described above, they were only four hundred
yards from it, and were only kept back for a time by a party
of the Manchester, which, with the machine-gun detachment, offered so stout a resistance as to gain a few minutes'
respite. During this brief interval, Captain D. Reynolds
of the 37th Battery, having obtained permission to call
for volunteers, came galloping down with teams to rescue
the two howitzers which had been left on the ground.
The German infantry was then within two hundred yards,
yet by the gallantry and devotion of this little party both
howitzers were limbered up ; and though one team was
shot down before it could move, the other galloped off
with its howitzer and brought it safely away.
        This episode was the last gleam of light upon this gloomy
corner of the field.[1] Between 2.30 and 2.45 P.M. the end came.
The Germans had by this time accumulated an overwhelm-

---
[1] It gained the Victoria Cross for Captain Reynolds and for Drivers
Luke and Drain. Captain Reynolds was killed by gas near Ypres, 1916.

ing force in the shelter of the Cambrai road, and they now 26 Aug.
fell upon the Suffolk and Manchester from the front, right 1914.
flank and right rear. The turning movement, however,
did not at once make itself felt, and the two battalions and
the Argylls with them opened rapid fire to their front with
terrific effect, two officers of the Highlanders, in particular,
bringing down man after man and counting their scores
aloud as if at a competition. The Germans kept sounding
the British " Cease fire " and gesticulating to persuade the
men to surrender, but in vain. At length a rush of the
enemy from the rear bore down all resistance. The Suffolk
and Manchester and their Highland comrades were overwhelmed. They had for nine hours been under an incessant bombardment, and they had fought to the very
last, covering themselves with undying glory.

Meanwhile orders had been issued about 2 P.M.[1] by
Sir Charles Fergusson for the retirement of the 5th Division
to begin, but these do not appear to have reached any
battalion much before 3 P.M. It was comparatively easy
to communicate with brigades, but nearly impossible to get
messages to the firing line, as the fighting there was almost
hand-to-hand, and the ground in rear was swept by shell
fire. Further, the 14th Brigade was handicapped by the
loss of its signal section, which had been practically destroyed in the early morning fighting in Le Cateau. As a
result no orders at all reached Lieut.-Colonel R. C. Bond
and the companies of the K.O.Y.L.I. in the firing line.
The survivors of the Suffolk and the Manchester (14th)
and the Argylls (19th) had drifted back towards Reumont ; thus the right of the K.O.Y.L.I., which faced
eastwards, became heavily engaged with German infantry
advancing over the ridge which the Suffolk had held.
First two battalions in dense masses swept over the crest
and down the beetroot-field on its western slopes. The
Yorkshiremen—five platoons with two machine guns—
allowed them to move well down the slope and then opened
rapid fire, which drove the enemy back with heavy loss to
the reverse side of the ridge. Meanwhile, the Duke of
Wellington's and West Kent (13th Brigade) had begun to
retire from the right rear of the K.O.Y.L.I., as did also
the East Surrey, conforming to the movement of the West
Kent; whilst the Scottish Borderers (13th) on the other flank
of the brigade were also beginning to fall back. When,

[1] No records or messages of this period are available, as the 5th Division
headquarters wagon was hit and blown up in Reumont.

therefore, shortly after their first advance, the Germans re-appeared on the crest of the ridge, they could outflank the right of the K.O.Y.L.I. This they proceeded to do, pro-gressing slowly and warily, after the lessons which they had received, throwing out troops wide to the south-east so as completely to envelop the K.O.Y.L.I.'s right rear. The five platoons and the machine guns once again found a good target at five hundred yards range and took full advantage of it ; but the Germans now pressed home their attack on the main front of the battalion from the Cambrai road, and on its left flank from the ground vacated by the Scottish Borderers. Although the left, by sheer marks-manship, was able to prevent the enemy from planting machine guns on the last-named ground, its occupation by increasing numbers of the enemy, who at once opened a destructive enfilade fire, could not be prevented. A desperate effort was made to reinforce this flank, but nearly every man sent forward was shot down ; and the enemy now set himself systematically to roll up the attenuated line of Yorkshiremen from left to right. In spite of the gallant efforts of Major C. A. L. Yate,[1] who commanded the firing line, the end came soon afterwards. The company with him had lost over sixty men killed outright and many wounded, and the other companies had suffered equally ; when therefore about 4.30 P.M. the final rush of the enemy took place, the survivors were overpowered and made prisoners. That night the 2/K.O.Y.L.I. mustered only 8 officers and 320 rank and file, but it had held up the Germans at the only point where they penetrated into the British position, and thus gave the rest of the 5th Division a clear start in their retirement.

Whilst the advance of the enemy through the gap im-mediately to the west of Le Cateau had thus been delayed by a single battalion, the progress of his outflanking move-ment to the east of the town was also checked. Three platoons of the Argyll and Sutherland Highlanders, it will be remembered, had moved down the western slope of the valley of the Selle ; here they found the 59th Field Com-pany R.E. ; and in the course of time, half the 1/Middle-sex, with two companies of the 1/Scots Fusiliers (which had joined the 19th Brigade on the night of the 25th from the 9th Brigade reserve) prolonged the line to the right.

---

[1] Major Yate was awarded a posthumous V.C. He escaped from his prison camp in Germany and was found near Berlin with his throat cut.

Towards 3 P.M. German troops [1] were seen advancing 26 Aug.
westwards over the spur on the eastern side of the valley ; 1914.
whereupon the Middlesex, Highlanders and Royal Engineers opened fire at fifteen hundred yards range, and
effectually turned them back.   Thus the Germans were
held for a time both to the east and west of Le Cateau, and
General Smith-Dorrien's dispositions, now in progress, to
cover the retreat on this side had ample time to take effect.
The long valley that runs up from Le Cateau southwards
to Honnechy had been since 9 A.M. under the observation
of the 1st Cavalry Brigade and E Battery, posted between
Escaufourt and Honnechy, these troops having retired to
that position, where they found L Battery in action, at
the close of their first engagement with the enemy about
Bazuel.   At 1.15 P.M. the D.C.L.I., and the two companies
of the East Surrey which were with them, were ordered
from the reserve of the 5th Division [2] to Honnechy ; about
2 P.M. the 2/Royal Welch Fusiliers and 1/Scottish Rifles
of the 19th Brigade, General Smith-Dorrien's only corps
reserve, now at the disposal of the 5th Division, were
directed to march from Bertry, and to post themselves on
the left of the Duke of Cornwall's at Maurois ; and the
1/Norfolk was sent back from the " Tree " on the Sunken
Road to Reumont.   Lastly, a section of the 108th Heavy
Battery was ordered to take up a position near Honnechy ;
though one gun was unfortunately upset going through a
gateway with a little bridge over a ditch and had to be
abandoned, the other safely reached the place assigned to
it.   By 3 P.M., or very little later, the whole of these troops
were in position behind the right flank : it only remained
to be seen how vigorously the enemy would follow up his
success.   At 3.47 P.M. the II. Corps reported to G.H.Q. by
a telegram, received at 3.50 P.M., that the retirement had
begun.
    Towards 3.30 P.M. Germans again showed themselves
on the eastern side of the Selle, this time in extended order,
so that the rifles and machine guns of the party of Argyll
and Sutherland Highlanders had not the same chance
against them as before.   But, as they advanced, they were
met by the shells of E and L Batteries, and, after working
their way south for a time, took shelter under cover of
the railway embankment, and there came to a temporary
standstill.   The 1/Middlesex on the Highlanders' right
next withdrew up the valley of the Rivierette des Essarts

[1] The *165th Regiment* (see page 172, f.n. 2).   [2] See page 159.

towards Reumont ; and the Argylls, being warned that the
Germans were crossing the Roman road in their left rear,
fell back to the spur which runs south-east from Reumont,
where they found a mixed body of Manchesters and other
units deployed, and took up position alongside them.   The
Germans had by this time—about 4.30 P.M.—brought up
guns to engage the British batteries near Escaufourt and
were advancing up the valley of the Rivierette des Essarts;
but their losses were heavy and their progress slow.   An
aeroplane detected the position of E and L Batteries, but
the consequent German fire does not appear to have done
any great damage.   There was no sign of German cavalry
hurrying forward in masses to the pursuit, and there
seemed to be a good prospect that darkness would fall
before the enemy could close with the rear guards retiring
from the valley of the Selle.[1]

Immediately to the west of Le Cateau in the 13th
Brigade area, the enemy had equally failed to press his
advantage ; the shells of the 61st Howitzer Battery and
108th Heavy Battery constantly broke up the German
infantry when it tried to reassemble and re-form.   The
2/Duke of Wellington's was certainly heavily shelled as
it retired, but suffered little harm, though the battalion
became widely scattered.   The West Kent fell back slowly
and methodically, and their rear guard saw nothing to
shoot at except a German company which showed itself
for a few minutes passing eastward through the abandoned
guns of the XV. Brigade R.F.A. more than a thousand
yards away.   Between 4.30 and 5 P.M. this rear guard
retired in extended order without molestation even by
artillery.   The Scottish Borderers withdrew in the same
way, though the order to retire unfortunately did not
reach the greater part of one company, which was surrounded and captured.   Near the " Tree " on the Sunken
Road at least one company halted for the best part of an
hour, and fired with great effect upon German infantry
nine hundred yards to its right.   Between 4.15 and 5 P.M.
the battalion fell back by successive companies to Troisvilles, and then turned to cover the retreat of the 15th
Brigade which was falling back in perfect order.   Thus on
the right of the line, the most critical point of all, things
had not gone altogether ill in the first and most difficult
stage of the retreat.

[1] No orders for pursuit were issued by Kluck until 8.13 P.M., and these
directed the line Esnes—Caudry—Reumont to be crossed at 4 A.M. next day.

Until a little past noon, on the right centre of the line, the Bedfordshire and Dorsetshire in the firing line of the 15th Brigade, the left of the 5th Division, saw little or nothing of the enemy, except at a distance ; and even then they could perceive only small parties on the Cambrai road (which at this point except for one small house offered no shelter to the enemy) bringing up what appeared to be stretchers—but actually were machine guns carried by their folding legs. As soon as the real nature of their burdens was discovered they were engaged by the machine guns of the Dorsetshire, and the detachments, one of which endeavoured to take shelter in the small house, shot down [1] before they could come into action. Later on the German infantry showed itself in front in greater force, but was so hotly received by the Bedfordshire and Dorsetshire, as well as by the batteries of the XXVII. Brigade R.F.A. that it would not venture upon a definite attack. Soon after 3 P.M. the order to retire was received by the 15th Brigade, and it was calmly and systematically obeyed. The 119th Battery was withdrawn first, and moved back to the spur just south of the " Tree " on the Sunken Road. About 3.30 P.M. the Bedfordshire and Dorsetshire fell back slowly in succession covered by the machine guns of the latter, and, together with the 121st Battery, faced about again at the south-eastern angle of Troisvilles. Germans had not yet crossed the Cambrai road on their front, having been checked by the rifle fire, at long range, of the right company of the Fifth Fusiliers (9th Brigade); but the enemy's artillery now concentrated a very heavy fire upon Trois-villes from the north and north-east, and, gradually finding the range, compelled this company, as well as the Scottish Borderers on its right, to retire once more. The 121st Battery was only limbered up with difficulty, but the Dorsetshire, well covered by their machine guns, got back to the southern end of Troisvilles with little loss. A German aeroplane now appeared over their heads, dropping smoke signals, and the German gunners guided by these put down a barrage of shrapnel on every road and track leading to the south. The Scottish Borderers, who had taken the road towards Reumont, were diverted from it to the open country further west. The Dorsetshire and the Bedfordshire broke into small parties and, passing

26 Aug. 1914. Sketch 7. Map 11.

---

[1] Three infantry regiments of the *8th Division* were endeavouring to reach the road on the front Inchy and east of it—Caudry, mainly against the 3rd Division.

through the barrage with little or no damage, headed south across country towards Maurois. Bedfordshire, Dorsetshire, Cheshire (15th Brigade reserve) and Scottish Borderers all entered the Roman road near Reumont or Maurois without the slightest pressure of German cavalry or infantry upon their rear. Only on their right—towards Le Cateau—had the enemy pushed on in any force; and his advance there had been delayed as has already been described.

The withdrawal of the 5th Division from a broad and scattered front on to a single road at right angles thereto naturally brought as a consequence a thorough mix-up of all units—except in the case of the 15th Brigade, which entered it as a formed body. This state of affairs the Staff, as will be later narrated, took steps to remedy as soon as possible ; but the enemy was too close for any immediate attempt at re-forming to be made. There was, to quote one eye-witness, " confusion, but no disorganiza- tion ; disorder, but no panic " ; while another has exactly caught the scene by saying that it reminded him of a crowd leaving a race meeting and making its way earnestly towards a railway station.

Sketch 7.   On the left of the 15th Brigade in the 3rd Division
Map 11. sector, the 9th had been perfectly secure. The enemy had established himself on the southern edge of Inchy, but had been unable to advance a yard further ; and, though Br.- General F. C. Shaw's battalions had had little opportunity of using their rifles, the XXIII. Brigade R.F.A. had inflicted very severe loss on the German infantry. Soon after 3 P.M. the brigadier observed that the troops on his right were retreating ; though it was plain that the Germans were not following them in any strength, he was relieved when orders reached him, at 3.30 P.M., to conform with the movement. Pushing up the Royal Fusiliers from the reserve to the north-western edge of Troisvilles, he brought away nearly all his wounded, after which he withdrew deliberately in succession the Fifth Fusiliers, the two companies of the R. Scots Fusiliers and the Lincolnshire with very trifling loss. The German skirmishers lining the southern edge of Inchy tried hard to hinder the movement, but were silenced by the advanced sections of the 107th and 108th Batteries. Although the Fifth Fusiliers, before they could reach the shelter of a hollow near Le Fayt, had to cross a thousand yards of open ground, the German artillery scarcely fired a round at them. As the last party of the Lincolnshire

came abreast of the advanced section of the 108th Battery, 26 Aug. the officer in command, having fired off his last round of 1914. ammunition, disabled and abandoned his guns. This and the other advanced section had done great work, but at the cost of four 18-pdrs. The retreat was then continued methodically, without pressure from the enemy, and the battalions re-formed as soon as they reached sheltered ground. The XXIII. Brigade R.F.A. was collected at Bertry. The 9th Brigade took position on the ridge between Bertry and Montigny to cover the retreat of the rest of the 3rd Division ; its casualties amounted to hardly one hundred and eighty.

The course of events west of the 9th Brigade is less easy Sketch 7. to describe. From noon onwards there was a lull in the Map 11. German fire, and advantage was taken of this to reinforce the troops at Caudry with half a company of the Irish Rifles. Some of the 12th Brigade likewise seized the opportunity to recross to the north side of the Warnelle ravine in order to bring in their wounded, but they were driven back by a steady fire from the enemy before they could collect many of them. Then about 1.40 P.M. the German guns opened fire once more with increased violence and in much greater numbers,[1] concentrating in the first instance chiefly on Caudry, while simultaneously German infantry advanced against the junction of the Royal Scots and Gordon Highlanders immediately to the north of Audencourt. They failed however to gain any ground, being met by an accurate fire on their front and effectively enfiladed, at a range of six hundred yards, by the left company of the Gordons. At Caudry itself the enemy was more successful. About 2 P.M. he began a bombardment of the village with heavy guns, the first shell of which stunned Br.-General F. W. N. McCracken and wounded his brigade-major. The brigadier was understood to order a retirement, and Caudry was evacuated, so that German infantry was able to enter and occupy it.[2] About the same time large parties of enemy infantry[3] developed a strong attack from the north-west against the half-battalion of the Inniskilling

[1] See page 161, f.n. 1.
[2] The bombardment of the village was by 5·9-inch howitzers. " Regt. No. 153," p. 56 (f.n.), quotes the text of the first edition of this volume, and says that nothing is known in the *8th Division* of any infantry entering Caudry. But the British account, of the counter-attack which retook all but the northern part of the village, is circumstantial, and the presence of Germans in Caudry is supported by the evidence of the 11th Brigade.
[3] This was the advanced guard of the *7th Reserve Division*, which got up at 2 P.M. (see page 184, f.n. 1).

Fusiliers which covered the western flank at Esnes. They were met by rapid rifle and machine-gun fire, supported shortly after by artillery. The answering German fire was wholly ineffective, and the Inniskillings were able to check this attack completely. Nevertheless, the situation was not reassuring; for it was clear that fresh German infantry, the herald of another corps, had come up, and that, if it failed to break in on the north side of Esnes, it would work round to the left flank and rear.

Meanwhile, between 2.30 and 3 P.M. the 3/Worcestershire (7th Brigade) counter-attacked at Caudry, reoccupied the southern portion of the village and pushed advanced posts to the north and north-east. But the northern part of the village was not recovered, and the Germans had already made the 11th Brigade sensible of their presence on its right flank. Br.-General A. G. Hunter-Weston, naturally assuming that Caudry had been finally lost, decided to withdraw the 11th Brigade across the Warnelle ravine to a position before Ligny. The guns of the 135th Battery were brought forward and entrenched in and round Ligny for close defence ; and then, the 1/Rifle Brigade, with a platoon of the East Lancashire, being left at the " Quarry " as rear guard, the remaining battalions of the brigade were shortly after 3 P.M. drawn off into the low ground of the ravine whilst a perfect tempest of shrapnel raged above and behind them. As they came into sight of the Germans again, on the slope just below Ligny, the enemy redoubled his fire, inflicting considerable loss, and when at last the rear guard withdrew from the " Quarry," the German infantrymen[1] sprang up from their concealed positions and rushed forward in pursuit. Their ranks were instantly torn and mangled by the British guns ; but they speedily rallied and continued the advance regardless of losses. Before the 11th Brigade could be completely re-formed, they swarmed forward to the attack of Ligny. Met by shrapnel and rapid fire, they turned, unable to persist against the hail of bullets. Reinforced, they advanced again, only to suffer still more heavily ; for the British were now better prepared to receive them. They fell back again, too severely punished to find heart for a third attempt, and the 4th Division was left in undisputed possession of Ligny. These actions hardly came to a complete end before 5 P.M.

It was during this turmoil on his left that shortly after

[1] The *3rd*, *9th* and *10th Jäger* and *19th Cavalry Brigade*, according to Poseck, pp. 59, 60.

3 P.M. General Hubert Hamilton rode down from Bertry
to Lieut.-Colonel W. D. Bird, who was with his battalion
of Irish Rifles at Troncquoy, and directed him to take
command of the 7th Brigade, since Br.-General McCracken
had been stunned by a shell, and to withdraw the troops
from Caudry under cover of the Irish Rifles and two field
batteries. Colonel Bird made his dispositions accordingly,
and by 4.30 P.M. the companies which had reoccupied it
were practically clear of the village. At that hour the
troops in Audencourt, on the east of Caudry, suddenly fell
back. About 3.30 P.M. the 8th Brigade had received its
instructions to retire, but there had been difficulty and
delay in communicating orders to the various units, and
it is certain that some of them received none at all. The
4/Middlesex and the Royal Scots, with the exception of a
detached party of the latter on the immediate right of the
Gordons, were withdrawn without much difficulty. The
party above named, together with the bulk of the Gordons,
and two companies of the Royal Irish, having no orders to
move, remained in their positions. Three platoons of the
Gordons, however, heard of the order to retire, and managed to get away, as also did the reserve companies of the
Royal Irish. These last were obliged to fight hard to
extricate themselves and the batteries of the XL. Brigade
R.F.A. ; [1] but three guns of the 6th Battery were lost, the
teams being shot down by a lucky salvo whilst in the act of
withdrawing. Two platoons of the Royal Irish also were
cut off from their main body, but contrived to make good
their retreat independently. Meanwhile since 2.30 P.M.
Audencourt had been furiously bombarded by 4·2-inch
and 5·9-inch howitzers, and the vehicles and horses of
8th Brigade headquarters, and the whole of the brigade
machine guns and transport were lost. The enemy, however, made no attempt to advance. The 41st Battery,
working with Colonel Bird, opened fire on the glacis east
of Caudry, as soon as our troops were clear of it ; but, so
far as can be gathered, there was at the time not a single
German upon this ground. Half an hour later, however, at
5 P.M. the German infantrymen did swarm forward, toiling
painfully up a gentle slope through beetroot which reached
to their knees. Whether they expected opposition or not
is hard to say, but they were met by the rapid fire of
the Gordon Highlanders and Royal Scots, who shot them

---

[1] Their adversaries were two brigades of the *9th Cavalry Division*, the
three of the *4th* (Poseck, pp. 61, 62), and the right of the *93rd Regiment*.

down at a range of from four to six hundred yards with the greatest coolness. One subaltern of the Royal Scots reckoned that he hit thirty to forty of them himself. The Germans were unable to gain an inch of ground ; for the best part of an hour they swayed backwards and forwards in front of these few isolated groups, probably exaggerating their strength both in men and machine guns, but completely at a loss how to clear them out of the way.

The rest of the 8th Brigade, having re-formed in dead ground, took the road to Montigny, and Colonel Bird, after waiting for fully twenty minutes without seeing a sign either of retreating British or advancing Germans, led back the 7th Brigade soon after 5 P.M. by the same road, without the slightest interference on the part of the enemy.

Map 3.   Thus by 5 P.M., roughly speaking, the whole of the II. Corps had begun its retreat and its rear guards were all in position, and the moment had come for the 4th Division, which was on its left, to move off. There was no time to lose. For, although the right of the division was for the moment secure after the double repulse of the German attack upon Ligny, masses of the *IV. Reserve Corps* [1] were now arriving from the direction of Cattenières—Wambaix.

Sketch 7.   The appearance of Sordet's cavalry in the left rear of
Map 11.   the 4th Division now provided a most opportune diversion. General Smith-Dorrien had naturally counted on this co-operation, and General Sordet, having visited Sir John French at 9 A.M., was fully conversant with the situation. His corps on the night of the 24th/25th had bivouacked near Avesnes—Dompierre, and on the 25th moved more than thirty miles across the line of march of the B.E.F. in order to reach its left flank. It arrived late at night in the neighbourhood of Walincourt, about ten miles west by south of Le Cateau, men and horses dog-tired and soaked with rain. Of its three divisions, the 5th halted for the night in and about ʃEsnes, the 1st at Lesdain and the 3rd at Le Bosquet (3 miles south-west of Esnes). The corps moved out to the south of Cambrai on the morning of the 26th in observation of the ground on the left rear of the British and of the southern exits from Cambrai.

---

[1] The *7th Reserve Division*; see Hauptmann Wirth's " Von der Saale zur Aisne." He states that the advanced guard of the division reached the Cambrai high road north of Cattenières about 2 P.M. The guns had been sent on ahead and were already in action. (See page 168, f.n. 1.) He adds that the German " cavalry had been thrown on the defensive and several regiments were cowering under cover behind the houses."

There, about 1 p.m., General Sordet received the following 26 Aug.
message from Colonel Huguet of the French Mission at 1914.
G.H.Q.[1]: " General Joffre requests that you will not
" only cover the left of the British Army, but do more Map 3.
" and intervene in the battle with all the forces at your
" disposal." At 1.30 p.m., therefore, General Sordet issued
orders for his three divisions to recross the Schelde, the
5th at Crèvecœur, the 3rd at Masnières, and the 1st at
Marcoing, sending reconnaissance parties ahead.[2] Towards 4 p.m., when the divisions of the German *IV. Reserve Corps* [3] were crossing the front of the French cavalry,
the artillery of the latter came successively into action
and took the Germans in flank, whilst cyclists engaged
them with success near Séranvillers (2 miles north-west of
Esnes). It was this gun fire which was heard by General
Smith-Dorrien about 4.30 p.m. as he was moving south
from Bertry to his new headquarters at St. Quentin, and,
not knowing whether the sound came from French or
German artillery, he had a bad moment. Then, galloping
up to some high ground near Maretz, he was able to satisfy
himself that it could only come from French 75's.[4] Further,
beyond the left of the French cavalry, it was known that
troops of General d'Amade were in and about Cambrai.[5]
All, therefore, seemed well, and the British left flank secure.[6]

[1] F.O.A., i. (ii.) p. 49. The message is recorded as telephoned at
12.10 p.m.
[2] " Historique du Corps de Cavalerie Sordet," pp. 77-9.
[3] The *22nd Reserve Division* had followed the *7th*, and advanced on its
right.
[4] The action was broken off by General Sordet at 6.30 p.m. and the
cavalry corps retired so as to cover the British left ; it reached the area
north-west of Villers Fauçon (15 miles south by west of Cambrai), with
the horses completely exhausted. [F.O.A., i. (ii.) p. 40.]
[5] See Note II at end of Chapter IX.
[6] Lieut.-Colonel F. G. Anley, commanding 2/Essex Regiment on the
left of the line, received two direct reports from the French cavalry, one
about ten minutes before the attack opened, and another about noon,
both saying that the French were maintaining their position. He, most unfortunately, failed to get either of these messages through to 12th Brigade
headquarters.

CHAPTER IX

THE CLOSE OF THE BATTLE OF LE CATEAU

(Sketches A, 4, 6 & 7 ; Maps 3, 4, 9, 10, 11 & 13)

5 P.M. TO NIGHTFALL

Sketch 7.
Map 11.

THE party of the Argyll and Sutherland Highlanders (19th Brigade),[1] together with the 59th Field Company R.E. and a collection of scattered men, last mentioned as being on the right, was deployed upon the spur that runs south-eastward from Reumont. The Royal Welch Fusiliers, Cameronians (both of the 19th Brigade, from Montigny), D.C.L.I. and half the East Surrey (14th Brigade), Norfolk (15th Brigade) and one 60-pdr. of the 108th Heavy Battery were in rear of it, between Maurois and Honnechy. The Bays (1st Cavalry Brigade), with E and L Batteries, were at Escaufourt, E Battery being in action against the guns which were endeavouring to cover the advance of the German infantry up the valley of the Rivierette des Essarts. This infantry now extended across the Roman road on the High-landers' left front, and, advancing in open order with company columns in rear, was engaged by the party at a thousand yards range. The enemy made no great progress, for the party had plenty of ammunition, and there was no im-mediate reason why it should fall back. After a time, however—about 5.30 P.M.—Lieut.-Colonel B. E. Ward of the 1/Middlesex (19th Brigade) led his own battalion, which had been halted east of Reumont in the valley of the Rivierette des Essarts, and the various detachments on the spur near by, towards Reumont and the Roman road, detailing the Highlanders to act as his rear guard. The whole, therefore, moved off in succession, skirting Reumont, where German shells were now falling thickly ; the rear guard had no sooner quitted its position than the German

[1] See page 176.

artillery searched the deserted spur with a hail of shrapnel.
A company and a half of the Norfolk, sheltered in a quarry
to the south-west of Reumont, were now left as the troops
nearest to the enemy ; for about this time the cavalry and
horse artillery also began to fall back slowly from Escaufourt towards Busigny (6 miles S.S.W. of Le Cateau),
leaving the passage up the valley towards Honnechy open
to the enemy. The Norfolk opened fire at a range of about
1,800 yards on the German infantry in extended order to
the north-east, and in due time retired to the edge of
Honnechy, passing as they went through a company of the
R. Welch Fusiliers, which had been deployed to take over
rear guard from them.

From this point the Norfolk companies had a clearer
view of German columns, both of infantry and artillery,
advancing on the road up the valley of the Rivierette,
preceded by lines of skirmishers. They engaged them at
long range, and the solitary 60-pdr. of the 108th Heavy
Battery, having no shrapnel left, opened fire with lyddite.
Major G. H. Sanders commanding the 122nd Field Battery,
having followed his two remaining guns to Reumont, collected two ammunition wagons, unlimbered south of the
village, and also opened fire on the enemy columns.

The Germans had by this time advanced up the valley
to the point where the road from Reumont to St. Souplet
intersects that from Le Cateau to Busigny ; but there, to
the great surprise of the Norfolk, they stopped and showed
themselves no more.[1]

It was now fully 6 P.M. A drizzling rain had just set
in, and the light was beginning to fail early. The enemy's
pursuit seemed to die away. His guns did indeed shell the
position of the R. Welch Fusiliers ; but, instead of heavy
masses of infantry, small parties of cavalry now hovered
about the front, feeling their way forward and provoking
constant little bursts of fire from the British rear guards,
which in the meanwhile continued to fall back in succession
as the Roman road gradually became clear for them. The
congestion on that road was considerable, for it was packed

---

[1] It appears from regimental histories that two battalions of the *7th
Division* reached Honnechy just in time to exchange shots with the British
rear guard. The troops of the division then received orders to halt and
clear the road for the *III. Corps* to pursue. But the leading battalion of
this corps did not reach Honnechy until midnight (" Leib Gren. Regt.
No. 8," p. 62). Kluck states truly that " the latter [*III.*] *Corps*, ordered
" to march on Maretz, did not get further than Honnechy on the 26th,
" so that the attempted enveloping movement failed."

with infantry, guns, transport and ambulances of the 5th Division and the 19th Brigade in no fixed order, just as each unit had happened to strike the highway.   There was some confusion, but the men marched on steadily and in silence. A few units—the 1/Middlesex and a number of scattered men under Lieut.-Colonel H. P. Moulton-Barrett of the Argyll and Sutherland Highlanders—made their way by two parallel tracks, east of the Roman road, to Busigny, where the 3rd Cavalry Brigade was in position to cover them, and thence turned westward into the Roman road.   At 7 P.M. or a little later, German cavalry patrols ran into parties of the 11th and 19th Hussars north of Busigny, and men of the former regiment were shelled while crossing the railway near Busigny station.   The Duke of Cornwall's L.I., the two companies of the East Surrey which were with them, the R. Welch Fusiliers and the Cameronians moved back steadily from position to position and arrived at Maretz, almost without firing a shot ; the Cameronians waited at Maretz until 9.30 P.M. without seeing a sign of the enemy. Hostile pursuit, worthy of the name, had ceased after 6 P.M. ; in fact, contact was practically lost as darkness fell. The whole of the 5th Division and the 19th Brigade were now in retreat along the Roman road ; their right flank, which had been exposed all day, was no longer threatened.

The narrative left the 3rd Division with two companies of the Royal Irish, some of the Royal Scots and the greater part of the Gordon Highlanders still occupying their original ground in front of Audencourt, having received no orders to retire, and successfully arresting any German advance ; the 9th Brigade was in a covering position between Bertry and Montigny (2 miles south of Caudry) ; and the bulk of the 7th and 8th were in orderly retreat on Montigny.   These two latter formations passed through the 9th Brigade and marched away to Clary, making south-westwards for Beaurevoir (13 miles south-west of Le Cateau) by way of Elincourt and Malincourt.   Not a German, not even a cavalry patrol, followed them ; and not a shell was fired at the 9th Brigade, which at 6 P.M. became the rear guard to the 3rd Division.   Evidently the enemy was wholly occupied with the detachments—not a thousand strong, all told—which had not retired from the original fighting line. At 6 P.M., after an hour spent in vain and costly attempts to break through the Gordons, his fire died down, but began again twenty minutes later, as he tried to work round the

Map 3.

Sketch 7.
Map 11.

Map 3.

right of the Royal Scots. This was however foiled by the oblique fire of the right company of the Gordons, across the front of the Royal Scots ; and at 6.45 P.M. the Germans once again concentrated a heavy howitzer bombardment upon Audencourt. As darkness came down the firing died away into occasional fitful bursts ; but at 8.30 P.M. the German guns once more heaped shells upon Audencourt, not a little to the wonder of the 3rd Division, which, from the heights south of Clary some six miles away, watched the projectiles bursting over its deserted position with grim satisfaction. Thus the British centre had been withdrawn, from under the very eyes of the Germans, with very little difficulty and no serious loss.

26 Aug. 1914.

In the 4th Division the infantry brigadiers received their orders to retreat about 5 P.M., the 10th Brigade being detailed as rear guard. At that hour the German *Jäger* to the immediate front of the line were still quiescent from the effects of their repulse before Ligny ; but the volume of hostile artillery fire had continued steadily to increase, and the turning movement round the western flank of Esnes had been renewed and pressed until the Inniskillings had been forced back to the western fringe of the village. The units of the 10th and 12th Brigades were so intermixed that the transmission of orders was exceedingly difficult ; but the sound of General Sordet's guns about Crèvecœur ($2\frac{1}{2}$ miles west of Esnes) gave assurance that the division could retire without fear of serious attack on its western flank. The R. Irish Fusiliers and Seaforth Highlanders were already in position behind this flank, south-west of St. Aubert Farm, and, with the 4th Cavalry Brigade further east near Selvigny, were thus ready to cover the first stage of the retreat. Artillery support was also close at hand, for, meantime, Br.-General Milne, having had early warning of the intention to break off the action, had made general arrangements for the retirement of the artillery to a succession of covering positions. After the heavy attack on Caudry about 2 P.M. the XXIX. Brigade R.F.A. had retired to a position in the Iris valley between Caullery and Selvigny (2 miles S.S.W. of Ligny), and the XIV. Brigade had moved back about the same time to another one immediately north of Selvigny. About 4 P.M. the 35th (Howitzer) Battery had been ordered back behind the railway, so as to be prepared to cover the retirement of the remainder of its brigade, which was ready to do the same

Sketch 7. Map 11.

service for the XXXII. Brigade, still south-west of Ligny. At 4.30 P.M. orders were given for the brigade ammunition columns to get clear and join the route of the main column at Walincourt (3 miles S.S.W. of Ligny). About 5 P.M. the 31st and 55th (Howitzer) Batteries were withdrawn to the south of Selvigny, where the 35th Battery joined them.

It is difficult to ascertain which of the infantry was the first to be withdrawn ; but it seems that part of the 12th Brigade, the Essex and the two forward companies of the Inniskillings, moved off soon after 5 P.M., halting and facing about on the road between Selvigny and Guillémin. The Lancashire Fusiliers, half of the Dublin Fusiliers (10th Brigade), and part of the King's Own appear to have started rather later, though half of the King's Own, receiving no warning to retire, remained in position at Haucourt. The rest of the Inniskillings slipped away from Esnes in small parties, just as the infantry of the *7th Reserve Division* penetrated to the western houses of the village, and retreated upon Walincourt in good order. The enemy artillery searched the road with shrapnel, but the British columns moved on either side of it and escaped all damage.

The 11th Brigade and the remainder of the 12th, much scattered, held their positions until 6 P.M. or even later. The 135th Battery (XXXII. Brigade R.F.A.), which was in close support of the infantry near Ligny, was so exposed that its withdrawal seemed impossible, and orders were actually issued that the guns should be abandoned ; but the battery commander, Major C. H. Liveing,[1] decided to try and save his guns and, withdrawing them and their wagons by hand, brought all of them except one wagon safely away. To the west of Ligny the position of the 27th Battery (XXXII. Brigade R.F.A.) was even worse ; nevertheless, the gunners, taking advantage of every lull, had succeeded in running back four guns and limbers to the sunken road in rear when increase in the German artillery fire compelled them to abandon the remaining two. The battery then formed up and awaited its opportunity : eventually it made a dash to the south-west, and, though it was pursued by German shells, got its four guns safely away.[2]

Of the 11th Brigade, Lieut.-Colonel E. H. Swayne of the Somerset L.I. brought away with him what survived of two companies ; the rest of the battalion under Major

---

[1] He was awarded the D.S.O.

[2] The battery commander, Major H. E. Vallentin, received the D.S.O., and two sergeants and five gunners, the D.C.M.

C. B. Prowse, having become separated from him, remained 26 Aug.
fighting at Ligny until a late hour. The East Lancashire 1914.
withdrew in three distinct bodies, two of which united at
Clary. The main body of the 1/Rifle Brigade made its
way to Selvigny and took up a covering position there,
whilst another party, with scattered men of other regiments,
came later to the same village with Br.-General Hunter-
Weston. Last of all the Hampshire retired, about 7 P.M.,
and overtook the rest of the brigade on its way to Serain
(4 miles south of Selvigny), where it passed the night. Of
the 10th Brigade, only the Seaforth Highlanders and the
Irish Fusiliers were under Br.-General Haldane's hand.
Half of the Warwickshire and a good number of the Dublin
Fusiliers were still in Haucourt, and the remainder were
dispersed in various directions, some as escort to guns,
others in small isolated bodies.

As with the rest of Sir Horace Smith-Dorrien's force,
the enemy not only did not pursue the 4th Division, but
did very little even to embarrass the retreat. The 1/Rifle
Brigade, the rear guard of the 11th Brigade, and the composite party with it, finding the roads blocked in every
direction, bivouacked at Selvigny, within two miles of the
battlefield, and the Irish Fusiliers and Seaforths were
almost level with them on the east, at Hurtevent Farm.
The remainder were directed on through Walincourt, by Map 3.
way of Malincourt—where a divisional column of march
was made up with the artillery—and Aubencheul, to Vendhuille (2 miles north-west of Le Catelet). German shells,
as we have seen, followed the British as long as they were
within sight and range, and caused a few casualties, though
not many ; the guns also bombarded the evacuated positions with great fury until dark ; but the cavalry and
infantry made no attempt to press on. In fact, Smith-
Dorrien's troops had done what G.H.Q. feared was impossible. With both flanks more or less in the air, they
had turned upon an enemy of at least twice their strength ;
had struck him hard, and had withdrawn, except on the
right front of the 5th Division, practically without interference, with neither flank enveloped, having suffered
losses certainly severe, but, considering the circumstances,
by no means extravagant.[1] The men after their magnificent

---

[1] The total losses, after the stragglers had come in, were 7,812 men
and 38 guns, including one 60-pdr. abandoned (for details see Note IV.
at end of Chapter X.).
General von Zwehl stated in the *Militär Wochenblatt* of the 30th

rifle-shooting looked upon themselves as victors; some indeed doubted whether they had been in a serious action. Yet they had inflicted upon the enemy casualties never revealed, which are believed to have been out of all proportion to their own; and they had completely foiled the plan of the German commander and of O.H.L.

The suggestion has been made that the battle might have been avoided if G.H.Q. had ordered General Smith-Dorrien to continue his retreat and had detailed the 4th Division as rear guard to cover the movement. It will, however, be recalled that only the infantry and field artillery of the 4th Division were present on the field. Without cavalry, heavy battery, cyclists, engineers and signal company, it would have been difficult for Major-General Snow to carry out a step-by-step retirement in the face of the very superior number of German troops —three cavalry divisions and the *IV. Corps*—who were immediately available to deal with opposition. There is a consensus of opinion among the officers of the 4th Division that, had not the II. Corps stayed to fight, the division, whether appointed rear guard or not, would have been destroyed.[1]

It has also been suggested that General Smith-Dorrien might have ordered the retirement during the lull in the fighting about 1 P.M. Withdrawal might have been begun then with the greatest ease; but in the several hours of daylight which remained the real direction of retirement would have been noticed by the enemy; in the middle of the day his units were not only fresher but were not yet disorganized as a result of heavy fighting, and in all probability there would have been a close and disastrous pursuit.

Could the 5th Division have stood until dusk, or had the I. Corps given some assistance, there might have been fewer losses; for the missing were largely made up of

September 1919 that the prisoners taken, who included wounded, were 2,600; and this is confirmed by Kluck. The surprise of the King's Own in the early morning and the capture of the 1/Gordon Highlanders, about to be described, added a considerable portion to the total casualties, and might have been avoided.

[1] Until his death, General Sir Horace Smith-Dorrien was the guest at the annual dinner of the 4th Division. At the first at which he was present, Lieut.-General Sir Thomas Snow thanked him on behalf of the members of the division for saving them from death or captivity on the 26th August 1914.

wounded left on the ground, and of parties which did not
receive the order to retire.

In the circumstances, General Smith-Dorrien was fully
justified in his decision to fight, and he was wise in delaying
the retirement to the latest moment compatible with the
safety of his force.

A number of air reconnaissances were made for G.H.Q.
during the fighting, but the reports were not forwarded
to Sir Horace Smith-Dorrien. One airman, however, made
a forced landing near him, and reported three German
batteries in action near Forest. For the first time airmen
were used for liaison : about 11.30 A.M. one machine was
sent to find where General Haig was, and, descending near
a cavalry patrol, was able to do so ; another was sent to
General Smith-Dorrien, who used the aviator to discover
whether there was any menace to his left flank, where all
was found well, and, later, to examine his right. After
this, at 3 P.M., the general sent him back to G.H.Q. to
report that the 5th Division had been unable to withstand
a most determined artillery bombardment, and was retiring,
but would get away somehow.

The air reports for the day, owing no doubt to the Map 3.
retirement of G.H.Q. from St. Quentin to Noyon at 3.30
P.M., were not summarized : indeed, it is not certain when
or where they were received. They were valuable both
positively and negatively. The earliest one, 7.45–10.30
A.M., reported a British battle line formed, and on its left
rear a French infantry division (really cavalry) in bivouac
near Gauzeaucourt, and a cavalry division moving westward ; further, no sign of any enemy west of a line through
Cambrai—Le Catelet. The next reconnaissance (8.15–9.45
A.M.) reported a column, without stating nationality—
it was the 4th (Guards) Brigade—moving from Landrecies
on La Groise ; German columns moving south on Engelfontaine and Solesmes ; a mixed force (it must have been
part of Marwitz's cavalry corps) near Carnières ; and Le
Cateau clear of troops but on fire. A third reconnaissance
(9.55–11.15 A.M.) discovered troops marching south from
Valenciennes (*II. Corps*), but found the roads to the north,
except for transport, and to the east, clear, and at 11 A.M.
a division (*7th Reserve*) approaching Carnières ; the
airman landed at Bertry, and gave this information to
Sir Horace Smith-Dorrien. A fourth reconnaissance (11
A.M.–1.40 P.M.) reported shells bursting along the whole
battle front, and Caudry partly in flames. The airman

saw what was a brigade of the German *6th Division* moving down the western side of the Forest of Mormal ; he reported Le Quesnoy full of troops, and dropped a bomb on a mass of transport ; he found Valenciennes and roads leading into it clear. A fifth reconnaissance (3.30–5.18 P.M.) observed shells bursting on Troisvilles, and Caudry on fire, and reported that one battery just east of Audencourt was all that could be seen of British troops on the battlefield : but along the ridge north of the Le Cateau—Cambrai road there was visible a line of German infantry in close forma-tion (local reserves no doubt) : and one German infantry regiment, moving south-west of Estournel (probably part of the *22nd Reserve Division*), was outflanking the British left : later it was added that behind the British line re-tirement appeared general but orderly, and mainly down the Roman road : the final entry at 5.18 P.M. was that no infantry could now be seen engaged, but there was a good deal of artillery fire, principally from the Germans.

These reports, combined with what was known of the British troops and of the previous moves of the Germans, should have given G.H.Q. a fairly clear picture of the situation.

Sketch 7. There can be little doubt that the comparative
Maps 2 ease with which the first stages of the retreat were ac-
& 11. complished was due to the tenacity of the units which, having received no order to retire, clung with all their strength to the positions they had been ordered to hold. The story of the Suffolk and the K.O.Y.L.I. has already been related ; it now remains to tell that of the isolated detachments of the 3rd and 4th Divisions. Some time after dark, firing having ceased, it became known to Lieut.-Colonel F. H. Neish of the Gordons that an order had been shouted or signalled by two staff officers to different parts of the line for the 8th Brigade to retire, and that a signal to retire had been seen by one of his own junior officers ; but that the order had not reached his own regiment, the company of the Royal Scots which lay on its right and two companies of the Royal Irish on its left. At 7.45 P.M. Brevet-Colonel W. E. Gordon, V.C., of the Gordon Highlanders, being the senior officer in army rank, assumed command of the whole of these troops ; but at 9.20 P.M. Colonel Neish sent an officer and two men to Troisvilles to obtain orders, if possible, from the headquarters of the 3rd Division. This officer not returning within the

allotted time of two hours—he had fallen into the hands 27 Aug. of the enemy at Troisvilles—Colonel Gordon assembled 1914. his force towards Caudry at midnight, and at 12.30 A.M. marched off, quite undisturbed, through Audencourt. All was quiet in the village, and at 1.30 A.M. the head of the column reached Montigny. Here a light was seen in a cottage, and the occupants reported that early in the morning the British troops had moved on Bertry and Maurois. A man was ordered to guide the party through Montigny on to the road to Bertry, which he did ; and at 2 A.M. the head of the column reached the cross roads to the south-west of Bertry. Here three shots were fired, and after a few minutes' delay, during which the advanced guard endeavoured to ascertain the nationality of the post, there was a heavy outbreak of rifle fire. The men were extended, and answered it. Orders were then given for the column to move back along the road to Montigny. But in the darkness the road south-westward to Clary was taken instead, and the column came upon a field gun which was trained to fire down the highway. This gun was rushed and taken before it could be discharged, and a mounted German officer near it was pulled off his horse, but the rear of the column now received rifle fire from the south and south-west. Once again the men were extended and replied, but the fire from the front and rear showed them pretty clearly that they were trapped. The head of the column now made an effort to force its way into Clary, and stormed a house on the outskirts of the village, in which were a number of German officers. The enemy, however, was by this time thoroughly alarmed. Firing began on all sides, and after fighting against hopeless odds for the best part of an hour longer, the Gordons, and the parties with them, were overpowered. Their captors were the *66th Regiment* (*IV. Corps*), which had engaged the 13th Brigade near Le Cateau.[1]

Of the Gordon Highlanders about five hundred were taken, but a few escaped, and a handful of them actually made their way through the German lines to Antwerp,

[1] " Regt. No. 66 " (pp. 37-9) confirms this account. It states that the fight at Clary lasted an hour. " A hurricane of fire was directed on " the British. . . . Their losses were frightful," and there were " consider- " able losses on the German side." Seven hundred prisoners of ten or eleven different regiments, including artillery, are said to have been captured. The *72nd* arrived from Troisvilles after the fight, at 7.30 A.M. ; its history (p. 73) speaks of " uncounted bodies of Highlanders, who had " been surprised in the early morning, lying along the road."

whence they were sent back to England. The fortune of war was hard upon the 1/Gordons. For the time they practically ceased to exist as a battalion, but by their gallant resistance to all German attacks between 5 P.M. and dark on the 26th August they had rendered incalculable service to the 3rd Division and to the Army at large.

Further to the west, isolated parties of several battalions of the 4th Division remained behind about Haucourt and Ligny. Two companies of the Dublin Fusiliers under Major H. M. Shewan, and two of the King's Own under Major R. G. Parker, holding fast to their trenches north and east of Haucourt, were attacked soon after nightfall, but succeeded in beating off the enemy ; and another party of the Dublin Fusiliers, attracted by the sound of the firing, moved up in time to shoot down a number of the retreating Germans. Major Shewan, and Major A. J. Poole of the Warwickshire, who had also remained behind on the east of Haucourt with three to four hundred men of his battalion, then consulted together as to what should be done, since the enemy had apparently moved round both their flanks. Major Poole, being familiar with the ground, undertook to lead the party southward across country, and at 11 P.M. the march began. About the same time Major Parker and his party of the King's Own started southward independently, and succeeded in making good their retreat. Major Poole, steering for Selvigny, struck the village of Caullery. Here he was joined at dawn of the 27th by another platoon of the Dublin Fusiliers under Lieutenant R. F. H. Massy-Westropp, who had retired at dusk from his trenches in the road between Ligny and Haucourt and, finding his retreat threatened by a party of Germans in a farm, had promptly attacked them, driven them away and gone on his way unmolested. These, together with his own party and some of the Irish Fusiliers who were with them, Major Poole later led on in the track of the 4th Division. The Dublin Fusiliers, however, lost touch of him in the darkness, and drifted into Ligny at 2 A.M. on the 27th, where they made a short halt to find food. The men dropped down on the road, and instantly fell asleep. After a time, the march was resumed southward upon Clary, but near the entrance to the village they were fired on from the east and, signalling to ascertain whether the aggressors were friend or foe (for in the dim light there was abundant room for error), were told to join them as quickly as possible. The column accordingly advanced, and was at once swept by machine-gun fire from front and flank.   The men were deployed, 27 Aug. and then ordered to retire by small groups mutually sup- 1914. porting each other.   Eventually, the Dublin Fusiliers reached Ligny with about two hundred men, comprising soldiers from nearly every battalion of the 3rd, 4th and 5th Divisions—and even two men of the 1st Division—who had drifted together upon the nucleus under Major Shewan. First they struck out south-east, but finding Germans on every side, turned north-west, and after many wanderings and more than one sharp engagement, eventually seventy-eight officers and men came through the German lines into Boulogne.   The remainder of Major Shewan's party seems to have been killed or taken to a man.

On the whole, therefore, it appears that of these three detachments which may have numbered in all two thousand men, about one half escaped and rejoined the Army sooner or later.   These details may be considered trivial, but they are a testimony to the courage and resource of the officers and men of the old army.   Moreover, these detachments had done far better work than they imagined.   Though a mere handful scattered along some eight thousand yards of front, they had prevented the enemy for several hours from advancing along the whole of that line.   The perpetual bombardment of vacated positions, and in particular that of Audencourt which was repeated an hour after dark, is plain evidence that the Germans were exceedingly suspicious of what might be before them.   Beyond question, they had suffered very heavily—as indeed was admitted by German officers to some of their British prisoners—and from one cause and another they were disinclined to take risks.   That the isolation of these British detachments was undesigned in no way detracts from the merit of their achievement.[1]

The Retreat from the Battlefield

While this handful of men was thus mystifying the Sketch 4. German leaders, the main body of General Smith-Dorrien's Maps 3 & 13.

[1] Hauptmann Heubner, in his book " Unter Emmich vor Lüttich : Unter Kluck vor Paris," p. 87, confirms the view stated of the effect of the parties left behind.   His battalion of the *20th Regiment, 6th Division, III. Corps,* came on to the field late.   He says, " in front of us there " still swarmed a number of scattered English troops, who were easily " able to hide in the large woods of the district, and again and again forced " us to waste time in deployments, as we could not tell what their strength " might be."

force was in full retreat. The 5th Division train had started down the Roman road very early in the day, and two staff officers had accompanied it to keep it moving all night ; for there was fear of being overtaken by German cavalry. The 3rd Division train had followed it, cutting in on the Roman road from the north. Thus one serious encumbrance was removed, but the highway was, nevertheless, choked for miles with an interminable column of transport, with the inevitable consequence of long stoppages and frequent short checks. The bulk of the 5th Division and of the 19th Brigade reached Estrées (15 miles from Le Cateau) between 9 P.M. and midnight, where, wet, weary, hungry and longing for sleep, they were directed on to the cross roads, two miles beyond. There the sorting of the troops was taken in hand, a simple process on paper, but difficult enough in practice on a dark and dismal night : staff officers stood at the cross roads, shouting continuously, " Transport and mounted troops straight on, 3rd Division " infantry to right, 5th Division infantry to left." Then, when the men turned as directed, they were sorted by other officers according to brigades and battalions. By 2 A.M. on the 27th sorting was completed, and orders were issued for a start at 4 A.M., at which time all units of the 5th Division and the detachments from other formations marched off in good order ; some units, of course, were very weak in numbers, as many men had not come in. The transport and mounted troops were sorted out south of St. Quentin, and there, well after sunrise, a rearrangement of the column of the 5th Division was also made ; but this was a matter of reorganizing units, not individual soldiers as had been the case near Estrées.

About midnight, the 3rd Division, having marched by Elincourt and Malincourt, came into Beaurevoir, north of the 5th Division. The 3rd Cavalry Brigade with the Bays (1st Cavalry Brigade) and 4th Dragoon Guards (2nd Cavalry Brigade), seeing the crowd on the Roman road, retired east of Estrées to Brancourt, Montbrehain and Ramicourt. The 11th Hussars (1st Cavalry Brigade) came very late into Estrées. Half of the 9th Lancers (2nd Cavalry Brigade) withdrew a little to the south of the 3rd Cavalry Brigade to Fresnoy, the remainder having marched with the headquarters of the 2nd Cavalry Brigade right across the rear of the Army from Bohain, through Beaurevoir to Marquaix (11 miles north-west of St. Quentin). Of the 4th Division, the 10th and 12th Brigades, with the divisional artillery, retreated, 2½ miles west of the 3rd Division, by Malincourt and Villers Outréaux to Le Catelet and Vendhuille, which were reached between 11 P.M. and midnight. The 11th Brigade, finding its way blocked by the 3rd Division at Elincourt, remained there for the night.

Everywhere, when the order to halt was given, the men dropped down on the road, and were asleep almost before they reached the ground. The only precautions possible at the late hour were to push small piquets out a few hundred yards on each side of the road. Officers of the cavalry and artillery, themselves half dead with fatigue, had to rouse their men from a semi-comatose state to water and feed the horses, then to rouse them once more to take the nose-bags off, taking care lest they should fall asleep in the very act. And all this had to be done in inky darkness under drizzling rain. After three or four hours' halt, the order was given to resume the march. The officers roused the sergeants, and the men were hunted out, hustled on to their feet, hardly conscious of what they were doing, and by some means or other formed into a column. Then the column got under way, drivers and troopers drowsing in their saddles, infantry staggering half-asleep as they marched, every man stiff with cold and weak with hunger, but, under the miraculous power of discipline, plodding on.

Sir Horace Smith-Dorrien on arrival at St. Quentin on the evening of the 26th found that G.H.Q. had left for Noyon. After sending off a report of the situation in writing,[1] he proceeded there himself by motor car, to give personally to the Commander-in-Chief an account of the action and its successful breaking off. He arrived shortly after midnight and was informed that the orders, issued by G.H.Q. in the afternoon of the 26th, for the retirement to the St. Quentin (Crozat) canal—Somme line (La Fère—Ham) still held good. Earlier in the day, before Sir John French had quitted St. Quentin, General Joffre and General Lanrezac had visited him for a conference. Sir John pointed out the isolated position of the British Army, as he conceived it, and the French Commander-in-Chief had confirmed a " directive " already sent to British G.H.Q. In this he had stated his intention of withdrawing to the Laon—La Fère—Ham—Bray sur

---

[1] He had sent reports to G.H.Q. at 10.28 A.M., 12.10 P.M. and 3.47 P.M., in the last reporting the beginning of the retirement.

Somme position, and subsequently retaking the offensive, as soon as a new Army, the Sixth, could be formed on the left of the British. His main interest was that, in spite of the heavy losses they had suffered, the British should not fall out of the line. The Field-Marshal agreed to make his retirement as deliberate as possible.

Thus posted in the general situation, General Smith-Dorrien returned to his headquarters at St. Quentin. Under his instructions, the 5th Division and the 19th Brigade were intercepted at Bellenglise and turned south-eastward upon St. Quentin, where supplies awaited them, with directions to march thence upon Ollezy (4 miles east of Ham). The 3rd Division was to continue its march from Bellicourt and Hargicourt upon Vermand, heading for Ham. Unfortunately its supply column had missed it and it was without rations from the 25th until the afternoon of the 27th. The 4th Division was to proceed via Roisel, Hancourt, Monchy Lagache to Voyennes (4 miles west of Ham), picking up supplies *en route*.

THE I. CORPS ON THE 26TH AUGUST

Sketches A, 4 & 6. Maps 3, 9 & 13.

It is now time to return to the I. Corps and see what it was doing on the morning of the 26th whilst the II. Corps was engaged at the Battle of Le Cateau.

Whatever loss the Germans might have suffered in their repulse by the Guards at Landrecies, they had succeeded in disturbing the repose of the I. Corps and in keeping it on the alert all night in expectation of an attack. Its strategic position, besides, was far from satisfactory; for the enemy appeared to be about to break in between it and the II. Corps, and to be threatening the flank of its retreat from the west. Soon after midnight, from his headquarters at Le Grand Fayt, five miles from Landrecies, Sir Douglas Haig took measures to meet the situation, and to occupy a position facing north and north-west, preparatory to retiring southward. The trains, after dumping supplies, were ordered to Étreux, carrying the men's packs in the empty lorries. The 1st Division was to take position near Favril, a mile and a half S.S.E. of Landrecies, to cover the withdrawal of the 2nd Division on its right. The 2nd Division was divided, part retiring to the right and part to the left rear of the 1st Division, as follows :—

The 5th and 6th Brigades to close in from Noyelles and 26 Aug.
Maroilles upon Le Grand Fayt ;   1914.
The 4th (Guards) Brigade to retire as soon as possible from
Landrecies on La Groise, 7 miles to the south ;
The 5th Cavalry Brigade to cover the western flank of the
corps between Ors and Catillon on the Sambre canal.

Sir John French appears to have become uneasy about
the prospect of the I. Corps retiring due south ; for about
6 A.M., whilst General Haig was still at Le Grand Fayt, a
staff officer from G.H.Q. brought him instructions giving
him the alternatives of retiring south-westward on St.
Quentin, that is towards the II. Corps, or in a south-
easterly direction to seek shelter with the French,[1] in
which case his troops would have to rejoin the Expeditionary Force by train. The G.O.C. I. Corps considered it
best to allow the movements already ordered to proceed,
as he could do no more than he had done to comply with
the spirit of the instructions. He confirmed the fact that
he was retiring southward by a message at 10 A.M. Unfortunately, by this decision direct touch with the II. Corps
was broken, and not regained until the 1st September.[2]
The French Reserve divisions on the right of the I.
Corps were warned of the retirement, and a brigade, sent by
General Valabrègue to gain touch with the right of the
2nd Division, occupied first the line Marbaix—Maroilles,

[1] He informed General Lanrezac of this possibility. See page 136.
[2] There was no direct connection or communication between the I.
and II. Corps during the fighting on the 26th ; they were both, however,
in signal communication with G.H.Q. No information was sent by G.H.Q.
to either corps as regards the situation of the other after the message in
the early morning to the II. Corps informing General Smith-Dorrien that
the I. Corps had asked for assistance, and the subsequent message telling
him that the news from the I. Corps was reassuring. At 1 P.M. G.H.Q.
telegraphed to both corps and the Cavalry Division, " In case of retreat
" direct your movement on St. Quentin and then Noyon." There is then
a pause in the liaison. At 8.30 P.M. General Haig despatched an enquiry
to G.H.Q., " No news of II. Corps except sound of guns from direction of
" Le Cateau and Beaumont. Can I. Corps be of any assistance." To this
enquiry no answer was vouchsafed. At this hour G.H.Q. seems to have
given up the II. Corps as lost ; for from Noyon at 8.15 P.M. Colonel Huguet
telegraphed in cipher to G.Q.G. :
    " Bataille perdue par armée anglaise qui paraît avoir perdu cohésion.
" Elle demandera, pour être reconstituée, d'être sérieusement protégée.
" Quartier général ce soir Noyon. Plus amples détails suivront." [F.O.A.,
i. (ii.), Annexe (i.) p. 429.]
    Receiving no reply from G.H.Q., at 11 P.M. General Haig sent a message
(probably drafted earlier) to the II. Corps, via G.H.Q. : " Please let me know
" your situation and news. We are well able to co-operate with you to-day,
" we could hear the sound of your battle, but could get no information as
" to its progress, and could form no idea of how we could assist you."

and subsequently the high ground between Le Grand Fayt and Maroilles.

As matters turned out, the Germans made no attempt to renew their attacks.[1] The 3rd Brigade entrenched at Favril, and the 4th had passed it, totally unmolested, by 4.15 A.M. The 3rd Brigade was slightly engaged later in the day, but would probably have been left in absolute peace had not a section of British guns, by firing at a distant column of German infantry marching west,[2] provoked retaliation and a sharp attack by some dismounted cavalry, which resulted in a few casualties to the 1/Gloucestershire. At noon the 1st (Guards) Brigade relieved the 6th Brigade near Le Grand Fayt, enabling the latter to strike southward through Étreux, where the 4th (Guards) Brigade had secured the bridge leading across the Sambre to Venerolles. The retirement of the 1st Division then began ; between 1 P.M. and 2 P.M. the 1st (Guards) and 2nd Brigades left Favril for Fesmy and Oisy, both to the north of Étreux. Not one of these brigades reached its destination before 10 P.M., and the men were greatly fatigued. The 3rd Brigade remained at Favril till 5 P.M., and then marched straight to Oisy.

The progress of the 5th Brigade from Noyelles to Le Grand Fayt was arrested for several hours by the movement across its line of march south-westwards on Guise of General Valabrègue's divisions. About half a mile to the south-west of Marbaix towards 1 P.M. the transport of the main body was blocked ; the 2/Connaught Rangers, which formed the rear guard, came perforce to a halt. One company remained in rear of the transport, and the rest of the battalion halted on the road from Maroilles to Marbaix, a mile south of Taisnières. At this point French infantry was entrenching a position, whilst French cavalry patrols guarded the roads in all directions. From these it was understood that there was no enemy in the vicinity. After taking due precaution, therefore, to watch the approaches, the commanding officer, Lieut.-Colonel A. W. Abercrombie, allowed the Connaught Rangers to rest, sending word to

---

[1] The Germans expected to be attacked across the Sambre, and as their *7th, 5th* and *6th Divisions* were marching to the field of Le Cateau, they left the bridges guarded. Thus a battalion of the *165th Regiment* was for a time opposite Landrecies, being relieved by one of the *48th Regiment* and one of the *35th Regiment* ; the *12th Brigade (24th* and *64th Regiments*) arranged to guard the other bridges from Berlaimont upwards.
[2] Part of the *III. Corps* moving from Landrecies on Le Cateau. See " Regt. No. 48," pp. 16, 17.

LE GRAND FAYT 203

Br.-General Haking that he would move on to Le Grand 26 Aug.
Fayt at 3 P.M. unless otherwise ordered. At 3.15 P.M. 1914.
French patrols came in with the news that some two
hundred Germans, with a machine gun, were close at hand.
Colonel Abercrombie at once set out with two platoons
towards Marbaix, and, after advancing some six hundred
yards, was met by fire from artillery and a machine gun.
Calling up the rest of the battalion, he deployed it south
of the road. The companies then advanced over difficult
country, of high hedges and small enclosures, under rifle
fire, which however ceased after about an hour. A messenger sent to brigade headquarters to report the situation
was unable to find them ; and between 5 and 6 P.M. the
company commanders, being out of touch with Colonel
Abercrombie, began to withdraw independently through
Le Grand Fayt south-westwards upon Barzy with such men
as they could collect. At 6 P.M. Colonel Abercrombie
followed with about a hundred men, being assured by an
inhabitant that no enemy was in Le Grand Fayt ; but,
while passing through the village, his detachment was fired
upon by Germans concealed in the houses, and comparatively few escaped. Other parties were also cut off, and
altogether nearly three hundred officers and men of the
Connaught Rangers were missing.[1]

The 5th Brigade finally went into billets at Barzy, 5
miles north-east of the bulk of the 2nd Division. The 5th
Cavalry Brigade, which was little molested in its duty of
covering the left flank except by occasional shells, fell back
with trifling loss eight miles further to Hannapes, on the
Oise, about two miles south-west of Étreux, not reaching its
billets until far into the night.

The position of the I. Corps on the night of the 26th
was in and around Étreux ; in detail as follows :—

1st Division : Fesmy, Petit Cambresis, Oisy.
2nd Division : Étreux, Venerolles.
5th Cavalry Brigade : Hannapes.
Corps H.Q. : 1½ miles east of Hannapes.

[1] Vogel gives a full account of this fight. The attackers were the *1st
Guard Cavalry Brigade* and the *Garde-Schützenbataillon*. He states that
French troops also took part, and about 100 of them were taken prisoners,
as well as 93 English. According to him, it was the German cavalry
which was surprised, and the Divisional Staff, which was close up to the
vanguard, was under fire. He mentions that the German cavalry fought on
foot on this day for the first time in the war. His division billeted at Marbaix.

The German official list of battles shows that the *2nd Guard Reserve
Division* of the *X. Reserve Corps* was also engaged at Marbaix on the 26th
August.

The II. Corps and 4th Division and remaining cavalry brigades were 18 miles to the west, in retreat south-westward to the Oise, on the front of St. Quentin—Le Catelet. The French 53rd and 69th Reserve Divisions were to the south-east of the I. Corps at Iron and Lavaqueresse.

NOTE I

GERMAN ACCOUNTS OF LE CATEAU

Sketch 7.   Very little has been published in Germany about Le Cateau ;
Maps 3, 9, there is no official monograph on the battle, as there is on Mons
& 11.   and Ypres. The fighting on the 26th August was at first almost concealed by being included in the so-called " Battle of St. Quentin." There is no doubt that the enemy not only suffered heavy casualties and wasted a whole day in time, but, owing to misconception of the situation and indifferent staff work, lost a great opportunity of enveloping three British divisions. It is for these reasons perhaps that he has said little about it.

In the official list of battles issued at the end of 1919, it is called " the Battle of Solesmes—Le Cateau (25th-27th August 1914)," and the troops present are given as *III. Corps* (*5th* and *6th Divisions*), *IV. Corps* (*7th* and *8th Divisions*), *IV. Reserve Corps* (*7th Reserve* and *22nd Reserve Divisions*) and *II. Cavalry Corps* (*2nd, 4th* and *9th Cavalry Divisions*), whilst the *3rd Division* of the *II. Corps* is shown as engaged on the 26th at " Cambrai."

The official bulletin, issued by the Supreme Command on the 28th August, runs as follows :

" Defeat of the English at St. Quentin. The English Army,[1] to " which three French Territorial divisions [2] had attached themselves, " has been completely defeated north of St. Quentin, and is in full " retreat through St. Quentin.[3] Several thousand prisoners, seven " field batteries and a heavy battery fell into our hands." [4]

The troops were told that 12,000 prisoners had been taken.[5]

As already noticed,[6] Kluck's operation orders for the 26th, issued at Haussy, three miles north of Solesmes, at 10.50 P.M. on the 25th, merely gave instructions for a long march in pursuit, mainly in a direction in which there was not much to pursue. His summary of them runs :—

" The *First Army*, from parts of which severe marches are " demanded, will continue the pursuit of the beaten enemy.

" The *II. Corps* [commencing on the west] will march via Cambrai " on Bapaume, west of the road Valenciennes—Vendegies—Villers

---

[1] Only three out of five divisions were present at Le Cateau.
[2] Only one Territorial division—the 84th—was present. The 61st and 62nd Reserve Divisions were west of Cambrai, but not engaged (see page 210).
[3] Only the 5th Division, part of the cavalry, and some stragglers came through St. Quentin.
[4] See page 191, f.n. 1, for the correct figures.
[5] Bloem, p. 183.
[6] See page 169.

" en Cauchies—Cattenlères, till it is abreast of Graincourt [5 miles
" S.W. of Cambrai].
" The *IV. Reserve Corps*, starting early, via Vendegies—Villers
" en Cauchies to Cattenières.
" The *IV. Corps* from Solesmes and Landrecies, by two routes :
" via Caudry, and via Montay—Caullery—Walincourt, to Vendhuille;
" the road Landrecies—Le Cateau is allotted to the *III. Corps.*
" The *III. Corps* by the Landrecies—Le Cateau road to Maretz.
" Orders will be issued at Solesmes at 11 A.M.
" The *IX. Corps* will cover the flank march of the Army from
" the west and south-west fronts of Maubeuge, and will send any
" troops not required to follow the *III. Corps* via Berlaimont—
" Maroilles to Landrecies."

26 Aug.
1914.

Although General von Kluck before he wrote had read Sir John
French's despatch, from which he quotes at length, he was evidently
still labouring under considerable misapprehension as to the dispositions of the B.E.F. and its movements. It is best to quote his
narrative :—
" In the early morning Marwitz's cavalry corps, moving via
" Wambaix—Beauvois—Quiévy, attacked the enemy, who was
" withdrawing in a westerly (*sic*) direction, drove him partly back
" towards the south, and held him fast until the heads of the army
" corps came up." This account hardly corresponds with the long
pause in the fighting and Captain Wirth's story of finding regiments
of the cavalry corps cowering behind the shelter of houses.[1]
" The *IV. Corps* about 8 A.M. attacked strong British forces at
" Caudry—Troisvilles—Reumont, and encountered stout resistance
" from the enemy, who was well-established in his position. The
" *IV. Reserve Corps* was to envelop the northern [*sic*] and the *III.*
" *Corps* the southern [*sic*] flank of the position. The former, how-
" ever, struck against the French at Cattenières ; the *III. Corps*,
" moving on Maretz, did not get further than Honnechy on the
" 26th. By evening the *IV. Reserve Corps* succeeded in driving its
" opponents back in a southerly direction whilst the *IV. Corps*
" overthrew the right wing of the British. The *II. Corps* defeated
" stronger French forces at Cambrai." [2]
Apparently Kluck really thought that the B.E.F. was facing east,
and that if the *IV. Reserve Corps* drove it southwards, *i.e.*, off its
line of retreat to Calais—Boulogne, it would endeavour to get away
to the west. This is confirmed by the fact that when the *IV. Reserve
Corps* relieved Marwitz's cavalry corps, the latter moved west of
Cambrai, and on the 27th marched down the Cambrai—Bapaume
road to intercept any movement of the B.E.F. westwards. The *II.
Corps* also pushed on west-south-west of Cambrai on the 26th, and
its *4th Division* reached Hermies, half-way to Bapaume, where it
blocked any escape to the west.
Kluck's narrative of the battle ends with a statement, which
shows that he thought the British I. Corps and also the 6th Division,
still in England, were present. " The whole British Expeditionary
" Corps, six divisions, a cavalry division and several French Territorial
" divisions opposed the *First Army*. . . . If the English stand on the
" 27th, the double envelopment may yet bring a great success."

[1] See page 184, f.n. 1.
[2] This is hardly the case. See the action of the French 84th Territorial
Division at Cambrai, page 210.

206   LE CATEAU

He reported to the Supreme Command that he had won a victory, and not over three divisions but nine, and thereby, it is claimed by German writers, helped to mislead Moltke as to the real situation.[1]
Relying on the retreat of the British westward being intercepted by Marwitz's cavalry and the *II. Corps*, which was to march at 1 A.M., both directed on Combles (20 miles south-west of Cambrai), " so as to prevent the British escaping westwards," [2] he gave the remainder of his force a night's rest. His operation orders, issued at 8.13 P.M., directed the *IV. Reserve, IV.* and *III. Corps* " to cross " the line roughly Esnes—Caudry—Reumont at 4 A.M." This was the British battle front of the previous evening, and as the action was broken off by Sir H. Smith-Dorrien at 3.30 P.M. and all his three divisions were on the move by 5 P.M., they had nearly twelve hours' start of the enemy. Thus it was, the German cavalry having been given a wrong direction, that there was no pursuit.
The German Official Account [3] devotes only five and a half pages to the battle. According to it, the *II. Cavalry Corps* started from the neighbourhood of Avesnes (6 miles north-west of Solesmes) at 3.30 A.M. with its three divisions abreast, and " after a short march " ran into strong British forces of all arms in the villages north of " the Warnelle. Around these villages arose a stubborn conflict " which the cavalry corps had to maintain without assistance for " many hours." The attack of the *2nd Cavalry Division*, the westernmost, was brought to a stop by artillery fire from the Esnes direction ; only when the British retired could the *Jäger* battalions of the division take possession of the British position. From 5 A.M. onwards the *9th Cavalry Division* attacked Beauvois, and the *4th*, Béthencourt, and towards noon (when the 11th Brigade retired) the *Jäger* battalion of the *9th* " stormed the position south of Fontaine " au Pire and eastwards," the *4th Cavalry Division* being still held up at Béthencourt.
The *First Army* headquarters received the first news of these encounters at 9 A.M. by wireless. The message ran as follows : " *II. Cavalry Corps* in very serious engagement with enemy at " Solesmes and Le Cateau, who in places is advancing to attack. " Support requested." From this message it was supposed that the cavalry had caught up the British and forced them to battle. " This picture of the situation was emphasized by a message which " arrived soon after from the *2nd Cavalry Division*, saying that it " had attacked strong British columns marching westwards." General von Kluck did not consider any further orders need be issued, as the double envelopment of the British seemed to be going according to plan ; he was confirmed in his view by a further message from the *II. Cavalry Corps* which said that the *II.* (really the *IV.*) *Corps* had attacked at 8.10 A.M. from the direction of Solesmes.
In the *IV. Corps* (General Sixt von Armin), the *8th Division* had advanced early through Solesmes, without meeting resistance, the main body marching towards Viesly and the *72nd Regiment* towards Le Cateau. On reports that the enemy was standing on

[1] Tappen, p. 21. Kuhl's " Marne," p. 82. The latter writer, Kluck's Chief of the Staff, comments (pp. 81-2), now that the truth is known : " Where was [British] G.H.Q. that day ? One corps marches off, the other " remains contrary to orders and accepts an unequal battle."
[2] Poseck, p. 64. The hour at which the cavalry started is not stated.
[3] i. pp. 522-7.

the Cambrai—Le Cateau main road, the division deployed against Béthencourt and Beaumont.   As the British evacuated both these places after a short resistance, by advanced troops, the *8th Division* took possession of them about 11 A.M.   Meantime the *72nd Regiment* had pushed through Le Cateau and become engaged with the British on the heights beyond.   The situation of this isolated regiment became somewhat alarming, especially when it became known that troops were advancing on Le Cateau from the north-east.   " The " new enemy, however, turned out to be German troops." [1]   The *7th Division*, which was marching on Le Cateau via Montay and had deployed in front of Forest about 8 A.M., now arrived, and a large portion of the division (one brigade) was sent to envelop the British right flank ; but, after carrying the forward position south-west of Montay (*sic*), it could make no progress against the main position.

" The quick eye of General Sixt von Armin very soon detected " that he had to do with more than a mere pursuit action.   By a " corps order, issued at 11.15 A.M., he organized the hitherto dis-" jointed attack of his divisions into a combined operation."   He ordered the *8th Division* to attack west of the line Neuvilly—Trois-villes, and the *7th Division* to attack with the *13th Brigade* and the *72nd Regiment* between this line and the line Le Cateau—Reumont, whilst the *14th Brigade* enveloped the enemy right via Le Cateau railway station.

The commander of the *8th Division* at 1 P.M., after a long artillery preparation, ordered the attack against Caudry and Audencourt, and it is claimed that Caudry was taken and held,[2] but that Auden-court, though in flames, could not be captured.

The battle " went more favourably " for the *7th Division*, on whose front the superiority of the German artillery made itself felt. " The British right wing was beaten," the reinforcements put in " only added to the confusion " and the envelopment also began to become effective.

The presence of the *III. Corps* (General von Lochow) from the east now began to make itself felt.   Parts of the *5th Division* marching from Pommereuil came up gradually level with the *7th Division*, the remainder of the *5th Division* turning southward on Bazuel.

The histories of the four infantry regiments of the *5th Division* do not quite bear out this statement of the official historian.   The *8th Leib Grenadiers* (pp. 61-2), which was leading, says the division marched from Landrecies via Pommereuil.   " The participation of " the regiment was limited to the opening out of *II. Battalion* under " enemy artillery fire and the deployment of the machine-gun com-" pany against an enemy battery. . . . The disappearance of this " battery brought an end to the company waging war on its own " account " ;   towards midnight the regiment reached Honnechy and Maurois and billeted there.   The *52nd Regiment* followed the *8th* from Locquignol and bivouacked without incident at St. Benin ; the *48th* got no further than Bazuel ; the *12th Grenadiers* marched at the tail, and its history does not mention where it halted.   The total distance covered by the head of the division was thus only

---

[1] Lohrisch, pp. 102-3, states that troops of the two sister divisions, *7th* and *8th*, fired on each other at this time.

[2] It has been pointed out (page 181) that the *8th Division* does not agree about this.

eleven miles between dawn and midnight, for which there is no explanation

To return to the main narrative. Before the great envelopment movement could take effect, "the British resistance had broken. . . . " When the *7th Division* assaulted at 2.30 P.M. only a few machine " guns were firing. . . . The retreat of the beaten right wing was " carried out so quickly that the order for pursuit issued by General " Sixt von Armin at 1.15 P.M. could not take effect. Precious time " was lost in reorganizing on the Le Cateau—Honnechy road, the units " having become mixed up. In the evening [thus nothing was done " for several hours] the *7th Division* was drawn westwards to make " room for the *III. Corps*, the head of whose *5th Division* reached " Honnechy, whilst that of the *6th* came up to Forest." Information kindly supplied by the *Reichsarchiv* is to the effect that the *6th Division* on the night of the 25th/26th was in the Forest of Mormal, with its head outside the eastern exit near Aulnoye and its tail on the Roman road. Its orders were to march via Landrecies and Le Cateau on Maretz. At some time on the 26th these were counter-manded ; for the leading brigade was marched back north-westwards through the Forest of Mormal, whilst the second brigade, starting late, marched straight on down the Roman road, and the whole division, without going into action, went into billets in the area Forest—Bousies—Engelfontaine—Vendegies, which had been occu-pied by the *7th Division* on the previous night. The long marches of the *6th Division* therefore brought it little nearer the battle.

Of the infantry regiments of the *6th Division*, the history of the *24th*, the leading one, says it started at 3 A.M., " was drawn hither " and thither, and with few pauses it marched until late evening, " dropping a battalion to take and guard Berlaimont bridge." The *64th Regiment* had lain down to rest on the road at 12.30 A.M., started again at 3 A.M. eastward, and at 5 A.M. dropped two com-panies to guard the Sambre bridges in the sector Landrecies—Leval. About 8 A.M. it turned back through the forest, now ahead of the *24th Regiment*, and proceeded via Engelfontaine on Robersart, but at 7.15 P.M. went into bivouac " dead tired " round Engelfontaine. The *35th Fusiliers*, " at the tail of the division," starting at 9.30 A.M., following the other regiment of the brigade, the *20th*, marched straight down the Roman road to Engelfontaine, where it was told to send a battalion, with a battery, to Landrecies. The brigade then took up a position of readiness to support the *IV. Corps* near Bousies, one battalion of the *35th Fusiliers* being sent forward as artillery escort, but " the brigade did not come into action, as the " enemy had meantime disappeared."

The German Official Account continues that in the late afternoon the *18th Division* of the *IX. Corps* (Lieut.-General von Quast) reached Landrecies, the *17th* remaining before Maubeuge.

In the centre of the battlefield, after the *8th Division* had made towards evening " an unsuccessful thrust " against Audencourt, the G.O.C., at 5.30 P.M., ordered it to stand fast and await the effect of the enveloping attack of the *IV. Reserve Corps* next day.

The regimental histories of the *8th Division* give the following accounts. The three infantry regiments (the fourth, the *72nd*, the ad-vanced guard, was in Le Cateau) were deployed off the Solesmes—Le Cateau road for the attack against the 3rd Division. The *36th Fusiliers* advanced from Neuvilly against " Inchy and east of that village,"

the *93rd* from Viesly against Beaumont, and the *153rd* from Viesly
against Bethencourt. The *36th Fusiliers* did not move to the attack
until " about 12 noon," and then " without sufficient artillery
" preparation." The objective was the road Le Cateau—Beaumont,
but the regiment made no progress at first. " When at 4.30 P.M.
" the enemy evacuated his position, the regiment gained its objective
" and entered on pursuit towards Troisvilles " ; there it assembled
and then returned to Audencourt to billet. It had just 400 casualties
(51 dead). (" Fus. Regt. No. 36," pp. 9-11.) The *93rd Regiment*
(pp. 41-7 of its history) was ordered at 9.15 A.M. to attack Beaumont.
It got into the village after " considerable losses," about 11 A.M. ;
but " a further advance beyond the edge of the village proved im-
" possible "—all attempts to do so broke down under artillery and
rifle fire. The British remained in position until night, it is stated,
and then slipped away unseen. " The victory was dearly bought,"
there being 433 casualties (118 dead). The *153rd Regiment* (pp. 54-6)
came under artillery fire directly it left Viesly shortly before 9 A.M.,
in attack formation. By 10 A.M. British posts in Béthencourt had
been driven out, and the battalions then waited whilst the 5·9-inch
howitzers of *1/4th Field Artillery Regiment* fired on Caudry and farms
near. At noon a formal attack on Caudry was ordered for " early
" in the afternoon." Little progress was made and heavy losses were
incurred, and only at the " beginning of darkness " did the front
line reach assaulting distance. Then, " in view of the strength of
" the enemy position," the troops were ordered to hold on till next
day, when the enveloping attack of the *IV. Reserve Corps* would
have taken effect. The casualties of the *153rd Regiment* were 291
(51 dead).

On the western flank, the *IV. Reserve Corps* about 9 A.M. received
a summons from General von Kluck " to cut off the British, who
" were in full flight westwards," and, as we have seen, General von
Gronau at once sent forward the artillery of both divisions, with a
cavalry escort. Later the *First Army* ordered him to make a wider
sweep towards Crèvecœur, and then carry out an enveloping attack
against the enemy position at Caudry, but, as his infantry approached
the battlefield, the British " had already been thrown back by the
" cavalry corps on to their position south of the Warnelle stream.
" Without knowledge of this, at 1.30 P.M. General von Gronau ordered
" his corps to attack in the general direction of Haucourt." The
7th Reserve Division, as it advanced, was, however, attacked in flank
by a strong body of French cavalry (Sordet), and when this retired
the Germans followed it up to Crèvecœur. Thence the division tried
to get back to its original direction, crossed and became mixed up
with the *22nd Reserve Division*, and reached the heights north-west
of Haucourt in the night, when it was considered too dark to attack.
The *22nd Reserve Division* was not in action at all ; its leading units
reached Crèvecœur and spent the night in that neighbourhood.

The *II. Corps* (General von Linsingen), marching from Denain
on Cambrai, was " held up by weak French cavalry bodies and
" Territorial troops," and at night its leading units reached the
billets assigned to them south-west of Cambrai.

Marwitz's cavalry corps was assembled east of Cambrai after
the *IV. Reserve Corps* came up, and " did not participate further in
" the battle, and did not take up the pursuit of the British." At
dusk it concentrated around Naves and Cauroir, two villages a

couple of miles north-east and east of Cambrai. Of its losses, we are only told they were " relatively small." (Poseck, p. 63.) The German Official Account ends with the words : " the result " of the battle of Le Cateau was an uncontestable success for the " *First Army.*" An analysis of the day hardly confirms this claim. Of the 4½ German corps (the *III., IV., IV. Reserve, II.* and half of the *IX.*), that is nine divisions, within reach of the battlefield at dawn, we now know that General von Kluck managed to bring only two divisions (the *7th* and *8th*), with three cavalry divisions against General Smith-Dorrien's three. When the British general decided to stand, he fully expected to have to face the divisions of the German *First Army* which had been his opponents at Mons. It was the great concentration of German guns—the artillery of five divisions (*5th, 7th, 8th, 7th Reserve* and *22nd Reserve*) and three cavalry divisions, and sixteen 5·9-inch howitzers of the *IV. Corps,* against the artillery of three British divisions (the 4th Division without its 60-pdr. battery) and some of the guns of the Cavalry Division—which alone made the British stand difficult. Only on the right (east), however, where the German guns could enfilade the British line, was any impression made. Kluck's strong right wing of two corps (*IV. Reserve* and *II.*) was fortunately held up by the demonstrations of Sordet's cavalry corps and the 84th Territorial Division, and of his left (*III. Corps*), one division merely counter-marched outside the battlefield and the other marked time, its head covering only eleven miles between dawn and night.

NOTE II

GENERAL D'AMADE'S FORCE ON THE BRITISH LEFT
26TH AUGUST

Sketch 6.
Maps 3
& 10.

The part played on the left of the British during the battle of Le Cateau by one of General d'Amade's divisions has been generally overlooked in English accounts, and receives only one line and a half in the French Official Account (i. (ii.) p. 50) : " in the afternoon " the enemy attacked Cambrai and drove back the 84th Territorial " Division, which retired on Marquion." The full story of its operations has yet to be written, but sufficient is known to make it certain that this division accounted for the absence of the German *II. Corps.*[1] This corps had been ordered, on the evening of the 24th, to make a wide sweep to envelop the British left[2] and, on the 25th, as we have seen,[3] swung westwards through Denain, and arrived at night with the heads of its columns about nine miles north of Cambrai and little more than that distance from the British left ; it was, in fact, eight miles nearer to it than the *IV. Reserve Corps* at Valenciennes, which attacked the British 4th Division about 2 P.M. on the 26th.

The French 84th Territorial Division, which had been on the left of the British at Mons, retreated with them, and on the night of the 25th/26th its rear guards were opposing the passage of the Sensée canal by the western columns of the German *II. Corps,* at

---

[1] General d'Amade's 82nd Territorial Division was holding the Haute Deule canal and the other two the line Lens—Bethune.
[2] Kluck, p. 53.   [3] Page 209.

THE FRENCH 84TH TERRITORIAL DIVISION 211

Bassin Rond and Paillencourt, just south of Bouchain and some six 26 Aug.
miles north of Cambrai.   1914.
During the 26th August the division was gradually pushed back
to Cambrai, and then westwards through the town. To quote the
words of the best available account : [1]—
" The defence of Cambrai was organized along its north-western
" front from the Pont d'Aire to Tilloy (both 1½ miles north of
" Cambrai). . . . The attack developed on the morning of the 26th
" at Escadœuvres (1½ miles north-east of Cambrai on the Solesmes
" road). The outpost battalion of the 27th Territorial Regiment fell
" back to the 'Pont Rouge ' and the railway ; the 25th Territorial
" Regiment took up a position by the Schelde canal bridge. The
" final stand was made in the suburb Saint Olle (on the western side
" of Cambrai), which the staff of the 84th Territorial Division left
" at 12.30 P.M. Captain Saglier, of the 27th, defended the barricade
" near the church till about 2.15 P.M."
The French 61st and 62nd Reserve Divisions were available to
cover a retreat, but were not near enough to take part in the battle.[2]
These divisions were railed to the front from Paris, and, on the 25th
August, detrained at Arras, twenty miles from Cambrai. General
d'Amade, whose headquarters were in Arras, having received reports
that columns of German troops were marching southwards through
Orchies towards Bouchain, ordered the two divisions south-east
towards Cambrai, part of them by train. They got as near as
Marquion,[3] six miles from Cambrai, on the afternoon of the 26th,
when they received a special order from General Joffre ordering
them back to Combles and Péronne with a view to the formation
of the Sixth Army. They therefore turned westwards again, followed
by the 84th Territorial Division, which was later in action at Marquion
with the *14th Pomeranian Regiment (4th Division of II. Corps).*
Kluck's account claims that the *II. Corps* drove back strong
French hostile forces on the 26th. But for the presence of the 84th
Territorial Division there seems no doubt that the *II. Corps* would
have taken part at Le Cateau with both its divisions.

[1] An article in " La Renaissance " of 25th November 1916, quoted by
Colonel Bujac in his book " La Belgique envahie " (Fournier, Paris 1916).
[2] See F.O.A., i. (ii.) p. 119 ; Hanotaux, vii. p. 298 ; and Palat, v.
p. 134.
[3] Ouy-Venazobres, " Journal d'un officier de cavalerie," p. 23.

CHAPTER X

THE RETREAT (*continued*)

27TH–28TH AUGUST

(Sketches A, 4, 10 & 12A ; Maps 3, 4, 12, 13, 14 & 15)

SMITH-DORRIEN'S FORCE

Sketches
A & 4.
Maps 3,
& 13.

VERY soon after daylight on the 27th August, British troops began to pour into St. Quentin. The 1st Cavalry Brigade and most of the 2nd were fed and sent a few miles south to Grand Seraucourt, where they arrived, men and horses completely exhausted. The duty of forming a covering screen to the north of the town was therefore assigned to the 3rd Cavalry Brigade (Br.-General H. de la P. Gough), which, together with the Composite Regiment of Household Cavalry, had reached a position at Hombliéres just to the east of St. Quentin at 4 A.M.

At 5 A.M. the 14th Brigade trudged into the town, received its rations and re-formed its battalions. Trains had already been ordered on the railway, as well as carts and wagons on the roads, for the conveyance of men who could march no further. The remainder of the 5th Division came in later, when the sun of a scorching day was already high in the heavens. Stragglers from the 3rd and 4th Divisions who had drifted eastward—no doubt because the retirement had been commenced on the right—contributed to an appearance of confusion which was completely absent on the routes of those divisions themselves and of the battalions of the 5th Division, which marched into the town as properly formed bodies.[1] After a halt of an hour

[1] An extract from the war diary of a unit of the French 1st Cavalry Division of this date deserves quotation :
" We crossed the route of an English battalion retiring after having " suffered very heavy losses. It moved in touching order : at the head, " imperturbable, a party of wounded. I ordered a salute to be given to " these brave men."

or two for rest and food, the men recovered in an astonish- 27 Aug.
ing fashion ; when they resumed their march, they were 1914.
no longer silent and dogged, but cheerfully whistling and
singing. The 5th Division then pursued its way, after a halt
for the re-arrangement of the column, without any interference from the enemy, and before dark was in position south
of the Somme about Ollezy, with its ranks and batteries
sadly thinned, but ready again to meet the enemy.

The 3rd Cavalry Brigade, acting as rear guard, was
equally unmolested. It was joined at 10 A.M. by that part
of the 2nd Cavalry Brigade (Br.-General H. de B. de Lisle)
which had marched westward across the rear of the II. Corps
on the 26th and retraced its steps eastward at dawn on the
27th. Not until 2.30 P.M. was there any sign of the enemy
advancing southwards in this quarter,[1] and then the 3rd
Cavalry Brigade fell back deliberately to Itancourt (4 miles
south-east of St. Quentin), E Battery exchanging a few
rounds with the German guns before it retired. West of
St. Quentin, the 9th Lancers (2nd Cavalry Brigade) found
contact with the enemy near Fresnoy, but did not withdraw from that place until 6 P.M. and then only to Savy
(south-west of St. Quentin). There they and the greater
part of the 2nd Cavalry Brigade took up their billets for the
night, the 3rd Cavalry Brigade being on their right at Itancourt, and the 1st in support at Grand Seraucourt.

Further to the west, the 3rd Division was hardly more
molested than the 5th. After turning west from Bellicourt
(8 miles north by west of St. Quentin), it halted from 9 A.M.
until 1 P.M. at Hargicourt, and then continued its way south
to Villeret (2 miles south-west of Bellicourt). There a small
party of German cavalry, accompanied by guns, made some
demonstration of pursuit, but, having no wish to engage what
seemed to be British infantry, speedily retired when greeted
by a few rifle bullets from the men of the 109th Battery.
The division next marched to Vermand, where supplies
were issued about 4 P.M., and at 10 P.M. it resumed its march
to Ham. The 9th Brigade acted as rear guard throughout,
having suffered little in the battle of Le Cateau.

The 4th Division on the left was followed up rather
more closely by the German cavalry. The 11th Brigade,
from Serain, moved across country to Nauroy, just to the
south-east of Bellicourt, on the morning of the 27th, and
halted there at 8.30 A.M. to allow the 3rd Division to pass.

---

[1] The enemy seen, according to Bülow's Sketch Map 2, was divisional
cavalry of the *VII. Corps*, the right of his Army.

Rather more than an hour later the cavalry squadron of the 3rd Division reported the enemy's presence in the adjacent villages, and, before the brigade had left its billets, German guns opened on Nauroy at a range of a thousand yards. To cover the retirement of the brigade, Br.-General Hunter-Weston ordered Colonel S. C. F. Jackson of the Hampshire to engage the guns. Acting on these orders, the latter sent two parties to take up a position to the east of Nauroy and open fire on them. After an engagement with enemy's dismounted cavalry and cyclists, Colonel Jackson was wounded and taken prisoner, but his men stood fast until the retiring brigade was out of sight, and then withdrew, eventually rejoining the brigade on the high ground beyond the canal. The main body meanwhile had moved south-west to Villeret, picking up *en route* Major Prowse's party of the Somerset L.I. from Ligny, a party of the 1/Rifle Brigade under Captain Hon. H. C. Prittie, and other men who had stayed late on the battlefield. Thence the 11th Brigade, " fairly all right " as Br.-General Hunter-Weston reported, marched through Tertry, where it struck the divisional route to Voyennes.

The 10th Brigade and 4th Cavalry Brigade (in touch with General Sordet's cavalry on the left) had meanwhile passed on to Roisel (8 miles south-west of Le Catelet), where both made a short halt ; the 12th Brigade, which had gone on with the artillery, deployed at Ronssoy (4 miles south-west of Le Catelet), with the Carabiniers, borrowed from the 4th Cavalry Brigade, at Lempire to cover it, as several German aeroplanes flying over the division and the appearance of a few cavalry scouts were indications that the enemy might be in close pursuit. Nothing, however, happened. The 10th Brigade then pursued its way to Hancourt, where it arrived at 4 P.M. The 12th Brigade retired from Ronssoy at 11 A.M., and reached Hancourt between 5.30 and 6 P.M., where Major Parker's party of the King's Own overtook it. At Hancourt, by divisional orders, these two brigades entrenched and rested, awaiting the enemy ; but none appeared. At 9.30 P.M. (all wounded and transport, which included many requisitioned and country wagons, having been sent off two hours earlier) the march of the 4th Division was resumed in inky darkness by Vraignes, Monchy Lagache and Matigny upon Voyennes. There was not the slightest hindrance from the enemy, but men and horses were so utterly weary that the usual hourly halts were omitted for fear that if the whole division were once halted

and the men sat or lay down, they would never be got
moving again.

The stoppages and checks inseparable from the march
of a long column in the dark were doubly nerve-racking to
the Staff during this period ; for not only might they mean
that the division would be delayed and have incredible
difficulty in restarting—as men were lying on the roads
careless of whether wheels went over them or not—but also
that enemy cavalry had cut in ahead or on the flank of the
column. With strained ears the officers listened for firing,
and only breathed again when the tremor of movement
crept down the column and they heard the glad sound of
the crunch of wheels on the road. Such was the discipline,
however, that not a single shot was fired in alarm during
this and the many other nights of marching in August and
September 1914. Under direction of the divisional staffs,
parties sent on ahead blocked all side and cross roads, so
that units, even if gaps in the column occurred, could not
go astray. Measures were taken by the interpreters [1] in
all the villages passed through to detect the presence of
spies, generally by the simple process of a language test.
But for this precaution and the difficulties of adjusting the
foreign harness of the requisitioned vehicles, officers and
men might have dreamed, and many did dream, as they
mechanically moved on that they were back at autumn
manœuvres.

The Carabiniers remained in position about Lempire till
noon, by which time German infantry came into sight ;
but, though heavily shelled, the 4th Cavalry Brigade withdrew unharmed to Hesbecourt, and after waiting there till
2.30 P.M. fell back westwards in rear of the 4th Division by
Bernes, Hancourt and Cartigny to Le Mesnil, thence going
south, finally crossing the Somme after nightfall and reaching Rouy, near Voyennes, at 1 A.M. on the 28th. The 4th
Division, three hours later—at 4 A.M.—began passing the
Somme valley into Voyennes, at the very spot where Henry
V. had crossed the river in his retreat northwards on Agin-
court. At Voyennes Br.-General Hunter-Weston with the
main body of the 11th Brigade rejoined.

Thus by dawn on the 28th, Sir Horace Smith-Dorrien
had practically brought the whole of his force to the south
of the Somme, thirty-five miles from the battlefield of the
26th.

[1] A French officer or soldier was allotted to each Staff and unit as
interpreter and go-between in business with the local officials.

The position of the various formations was approximately as follows :—

1st, 2nd and 3rd Cavalry Brigades :
In a semi-circle, four miles south of St. Quentin, from Itancourt, through Urvillers and Grand Seraucourt to Savy.
The remainder of the force was south of the Somme, with rear guards on the northern bank.
5th Division and 19th Brigade :
South-west of the cavalry brigades, at Ollezy and Eaucourt, near where the Crozat canal meets the Somme.
3rd Division :
On the left of the 5th :
7th Brigade—Ham, on the Somme.
8th Brigade—On march to Ham from Vermand.
9th Brigade—Ham.
4th Division :
On the left of the 3rd, at Voyennes on the Somme.
4th Cavalry Brigade :
On the left of the 4th Division, at Rouy.

It was tolerably evident that the German pursuit, if it can be said ever to have been seriously begun, had been shaken off. There were, as a matter of fact, already some indications that General von Kluck was pressing south-westward rather than southward. General Sordet's cavalry corps and the 61st and 62nd Reserve Divisions had been in conflict with German troops about Péronne on the afternoon of the 27th, but British cavalry re-entering St. Quentin at dawn on the 28th found no sign of the enemy. These indications, however, came too late to be of any help to the British Commander-in-Chief on the 27th. As regards the German *II. Corps*, the most westerly of Kluck's Army, the reports of air reconnaissances in the early morning, taken in conjunction with General Smith-Dorrien's verbal report at midnight on the 26th/27th after the battle of Le Cateau, were reassuring. The road from Le Cateau was absolutely clear; there were neither British rear guards to be seen north, nor German advanced guards south of a line drawn east and west through Péronne. But, near Guise, a heavy column [1] had been observed moving southward on the road between La Groise and Étreux (12 and 6 miles, respectively, north of Guise), besides other troops at Le Nouvion (10 miles north-east of Guise) ; and Sir John French had as yet no clear information to show whether

[1] Bülow's *X. Reserve Corps.*

these were friendly or hostile.   Soon after 7 A.M. he received, 27 Aug,
through the French Mission, an encouraging telephone 1914.
message from French G.Q.G., that the Fifth Army had been
ordered to make a vigorous attack abreast of Vervins—
Guise against the enemy forces (*Second Army*) which were
following it, and that Sordet's cavalry corps would protect
the B.E.F. against an enveloping attack on the left.   The
enemy forces on the British front, it continued, appeared
to be worn out and not in a state to pursue : in these circumstances the B.E.F. could retire methodically, regulating
its pace by that of the Fifth Army, so as not to uncover the
flank of the latter.   At 11 A.M. General Joffre visited Sir
John French at Noyon to impress on him that he was
already preparing his counter-stroke, but, in order to effect
it, needed to fall back further than he had first intended to
a line from Reims to Amiens, of which he proposed that
the British should occupy the section between Noyon and
Roye (12 miles north-west of Noyon).   In furtherance of Sketch
this plan, Sir John French, in a message timed 8.30 P.M., 12A.
directed the II. Corps, with the 19th Brigade, to be clear Maps 3
of Ham by daylight on the 28th, to march to Noyon and & 4.
cross to the left bank of the Oise ; the 4th Division to cover
the retirement from ground north of the Somme ; and the
Cavalry Division to cover both the II. Corps and the 4th
Division.   He added an order that all unnecessary impedimenta and all ammunition not absolutely required should
be thrown away, so that vehicles might be available to
carry exhausted men.[1]
    On the 27th, although clouds made air observation
difficult, the Flying Corps was asked by G.H.Q. to ascertain enemy movement from the line Cambrai—Landrecies
southward, also any movement of enemy cavalry on the
western flank, and to obtain news of the I. Corps.   Communication was established with the latter, and a message brought
from General Haig ; but, as the German *First Army* was
leaving the area which was to be reconnoitred, and the
Second Army only just reaching it, little was seen of the
enemy : the march of the German *7th Division* from Le
Cateau to Le Catelet was, however, correctly reported.
Most of the troops seen on the roads were British, and one
airman, who came down so low that he could distinguish
khaki, was heavily fired on.   A report stating that there
were three battalions in Bernes (9 miles north-west of St.
Quentin), on the eastern flank of the line of march of the

[1] Appendix 17.

4th Division, was forwarded to Major-General Snow by
G.H.Q., with the addition that they were probably Germans. The officer despatched to reconnoitre soon established that they were units of the 3rd Division. Troops
were also reported marching westwards from Péronne ;
these are now known to have been French.

A spirit of pessimism, entirely absent from the three
divisions which had fought at Le Cateau, seems to have
prevailed at G.H.Q. in the evening ; for Colonel Huguet
telephoned, for the information of General Joffre, that he
had gathered the British Army would not be in a state to
take part in the campaign again until after a long rest and
complete reorganization : this for three out of the five
divisions would require a period of several days, even
several weeks, and under conditions which it was not yet
possible to determine : the British Government might
even insist that the whole force should return to its base
at Havre in order to recuperate.[1]

Sketches A & 4. Maps 3, 13 & 15.   After the very strenuous efforts of the previous days, a
further retreat with hardly a moment's rest was a very
serious trial to the II. Corps, for many of its units were still
on the march when the orders to continue reached them.
At 4 A.M. on the 28th the 5th Division marched from Ollezy
for Noyon, with frequent halts, since the day was oppressively
hot. As many men as possible were carried on vehicles
of one kind or another. The 52nd Battery of the XV.
Brigade, far from being demoralized by the loss of all its
guns, had already been formed into a corps of mounted
rifles ; on its way it passed Sir John French himself, who
praised its good work and assured it that this had not
been done in vain, since the battle of Le Cateau had saved
the left flank of the French Army.[2] After a short halt at
Noyon, the 5th Division moved on to Pontoise, and there
at last went into billets. The 3rd Division followed, halting
at Crissolles and Genvry, just short of Noyon, between 6
and 7 P.M. Physically it was nearly worn out after marching sixty-eight miles in fifty hours, but morally its spirit
was unbroken. Last came the 4th Division, not less
exhausted than the rest. At 4 A.M. this division had
received, by motor cyclist, G.H.Q. orders, issued at 8.30
P.M. on the previous evening, to occupy a position north of
the Somme ; but whilst preparations to do so were being
made, later orders arrived about 6 A.M. directing it to be

[1] F.O.A., i. (ii.) p. 56.
[2] See General Joffre's message in Note III. at end of Chapter.

ready to continue the retirement at 8 A.M. Leaving the 28 Aug.
12th Brigade for a time on the northern bank to work in 1914.
combination with the rear guard of the 3rd Division, the
remainder of the division, which still consisted of artillery
and infantry only, took up positions on the south bank of
the Somme. The retirement was continued at 1.30 P.M.,
the 3rd Division having withdrawn its rear guard from
Ham about an hour earlier. The 4th Division reached its
halting-places, Bussy, Freniches and Campagne, just north
of those of the 3rd Division, shortly before midnight.

Meanwhile, of the Cavalry Division, the 3rd Brigade
had extended eastward, seeking touch with the I. Corps,
and its movements will be related in due course with those
of that corps. The 1st Cavalry Brigade, after completing
its reconnaissance at St. Quentin, fell back with great
deliberation to the Somme at Ham, whence, having crossed
the river, it moved southwards to Berlancourt. The 2nd
Cavalry Brigade likewise fell back by Douilly upon Ham,
and halted just north-east of the 4th Division at Le Plessis
and Flavy le Meldeux. Patrols of German cavalry had
been seen at Douilly, but no force of greater importance.
The 4th Cavalry Brigade, on the extreme left, withdrew
shortly before noon to Cressy, a short distance south of
Nesle and four miles north of the 4th Division, leaving
French cavalry and guns, with which it had been in touch,
to deal with enemy troops reported to be at Mesnil, just
north of Nesle.

The worst trials of General Smith-Dorrien's force were
now over. Since the 23rd August, the II. Corps had
fought two general actions, besides several minor affairs,
and had marched just over a hundred miles, measured on
the map by the route taken by the 3rd Division.

HAIG'S I. CORPS

At 1 A.M. on the 27th the Staff of the French Fifth Sketches
Army arranged with General Haig that the road through A & 4.
Guise should be left to the British ;[1] and, since there was Maps 3,
                                                            12 & 13.
no choice but for the whole of the I. Corps to march by
this single highway, unless part were sent by less direct
roads on the west side of the Oise, all vehicles were " double-
banked," and staff officers were sent forward to Guise to
provide for the passage of two distinct streams of traffic
through the town. The operation promised to be critical,

[1] The Reserve divisions crossed the Oise by bridges above Guise.

in view of the gap between the I. and II. Corps having widened rather than decreased on the 26th, while to the north and north-east the enemy was reported to be in considerable strength. The situation was not rendered less anxious by a false report, which was current early in the afternoon, that the Germans were also in great force just to the north of St. Quentin. General Maxse's (the 1st, Guards) Brigade was detailed as rear guard to both divisions ; General Bulfin's (2nd) Brigade as a western flank guard ; and the 2/Welch, with the 46th Battery R.F.A., as eastern flank guard. Great stress was laid on the importance of holding the enemy at a distance from the high ground on the north-west between Fesmy and Wassigny, so that he should be unable to bombard Étreux, where supplies were to be issued to the troops as they passed through. The 5th Cavalry Brigade was sent well to the west on the other side of the Oise, with instructions to follow a route, parallel to the divisions, by Grougis, Aisonville, Noyales and Hauteville. Meanwhile, Br.-General Chetwode, its commander, led it to a central position five miles to the west of Étreux, between Mennevret and Le Petit Verly, and pushed out patrols to the north and north-west.

The corps was under way by 4 A.M., the 1st Division remaining in a covering position until the 2nd Division had all moved off. The latter reached its billets without the slightest molestation, but the march for the 5th Brigade from Barzy to Neuvillette (8 miles south-west of Guise) was long ; the 2/Highland Light Infantry, in particular, having been employed in repairing the roads at dawn, did not arrive at its halting-place until 10 P.M., after a tramp of thirty miles. The false alarm of the enemy's presence at St. Quentin kept the entire division in movement longer than would otherwise have been necessary, for the 4th (Guards) Brigade was sent out westward as a flank guard, and the 6th Brigade spent the night entrenching itself just east of the 5th, about Mont d'Origny.

The 1st Division remained in position until late in the afternoon, with rear and flank guards out, waiting for the road to be clear ; but there was no sign of serious pressure upon the line north-west of Étreux, to which so much Map 12. importance was attached. In Br.-General Maxse's rear guard, the 1/Coldstream were about Oisy (2 miles north of Étreux), beyond the canal, and the 1/Black Watch and 1/Scots Guards just to the west of them, in touch with the western flank guard at Wassigny ; the R. Munster Fusiliers, with two troops of the 15th Hussars and a section of the 118th Battery R.F.A., all under Major P. A. Charrier of the Munsters, formed the rear party east of the Sambre canal, and had been under arms, facing north-east, since dawn. The general position of this party was four miles from Étreux, and extended for two miles, from Bergues through Fesmy to Chapeau Rouge, where it struck the north—south road from Landrecies to Étreux. The eastern flank guard was in position to the south-east, on the hill south of Bergues. The ground here falls gently westwards to the Sambre canal, which flows first on one side, then on the other, of the Landrecies road. The country lent itself to defence, being divided into small enclosures by thick hedges, which were passable at certain gaps only. During the morning a thick white mist lay upon the ground, and later there was a thunder-storm, so that visibility was never good.

Two companies of the Munsters were about Chapeau Rouge as screen, watching the roads that run north-westwards and northwards to Catillon and La Groise, and the remainder of the rear party were half a mile to the south-east in front of Fesmy. Later, half a company, and one troop of the 15th Hussars, were pushed south-eastwards to Bergues. No sign of the enemy was seen until 9 A.M., when a German cavalry patrol came down the road to Chapeau Rouge from the north, halted within five hundred yards, and fired a few shots. The Munsters made no reply, but the Germans did not come closer. There were indications of another column of the enemy to the north-east, moving south-westwards from Prisches upon Le Sart, straight at the centre of Major Charrier's force ; but its advanced party had galloped back on the appearance of a corporal of the 15th Hussars. By 9.30 A.M. all was again quiet, and Lieut.-Colonel C. B. Morland of the 2/Welch informed Major Charrier that he was going to withdraw the eastern flank guard to Boué (2 miles north-east of Étreux). Br.-General Maxse directed the Munsters to hold on to their position until ordered or forced to retire, and Major Charrier sent back word that, the choice of the route being left to him, he also should fall back by the road to Boué. The best part of an hour passed away, when, towards 10.30 A.M., German infantry came down again from the north-east and opened an attack on Bergues, which a little later was extended also to Chapeau

Rouge. The Munsters being by this time entrenched, held their own with little difficulty ; the two guns found a target in a German column to the north-west, and all went well.

At 11 A.M., whilst this action was in progress, the 3rd Brigade was at last able to start southward from Oisy ; at the same time Colonel Morland's flank guard also moved south upon Boué. The firing died away, and at noon Br.-General Maxse confirmed Major Charrier's choice of the road for his retreat, at the same time sending to all units of the rear guard their final instructions for retirement, the hour only being left blank. By 12.20 P.M. the road at Étreux was reported clear of all transport ; and a little later Br.-General Maxse despatched orders (time 1 P.M.) to every unit of the rear guard, " Retire at once." This message, though sent by two routes, failed to reach the Munster Fusiliers.

Meanwhile, at 12.30 P.M. or thereabouts, German infantry developed its attack in greater strength on both flanks, at Bergues and at Chapeau Rouge, though, as yet, without the support of artillery. As the pressure became heavier, in accordance with Major Charrier's orders the two companies at Chapeau Rouge gradually withdrew south-eastwards towards Fesmy. The men, finding good shelter in the ditches by the side of the road, worked their way back with very slight loss, and by shooting down the Germans as they showed themselves at the gaps in the hedges, forbade any close pursuit. The guns also opened fire, first towards the north, and later to the north-east, in which quarter the enemy was now observed to be in greatest force. Following up the Munsters slowly, the Germans delivered a strong attack upon Fesmy, their guns now coming into action for the first time ; but they made little progress. The Munsters' machine guns did very deadly work, firing down the road from Fesmy to Le Sart ; the Germans tried to mask their advance by driving cattle down on the defenders, but to no purpose. At 1.15 P.M. Major Charrier sent to Br.-General Maxse this short message : " Am holding on to position north of Fesmy " village, being attacked by force of all arms. Getting " on well. The Germans are driving cattle in front of " them up to us for cover. We are killing plenty of them."

Thus holding his own, Major Charrier's chief anxiety was for his detachment at Bergues. He pushed out a platoon to the eastward, in the hope of gaining touch with it, but the platoon was driven back by superior numbers. 27 Aug. The troops at Bergues were, in fact, about this time forced 1914. out of the village and compelled to retreat southward to a farm ; here, after checking German pursuit by fire and then counter-attacking, the detachment retired westward to the Sambre canal, and thence down the road to Oisy.

Meanwhile, Major Charrier continued his defence of Fesmy with great spirit ; he had now the whole of his battalion, except the half-company at Bergues, under his hand ; and he had need of them. So resolute was the onset of the Germans that, in places, they approached to within a hundred and fifty yards of the village ; a few actually broke into it and shot down two of the artillery wagon teams. Every one of these bold men was killed or captured, and at 1.50 P.M. Major Charrier sent off the last message which came through from him to Br.-General Maxse : " We have German wounded prisoners, who say " that about two regiments are opposing us and some guns. " They belong to the *15th Regiment.*" [1]

About this time—1.45 to 2 P.M.—the 2nd Brigade, the western flank guard, marched away from Wassigny for Hannapes, south of Étreux, with little hindrance ; the Northamptonshire, who brought up the rear, lost only four men, and claimed on their side from forty to fifty German troopers killed, wounded or taken prisoner.[2] Thus the greater part of the 1st Division was now in motion to the south ; the 3rd Brigade was within an hour's march of Guise ; and there remained only the rear guard to bring off. Major Charrier, having struck the enemy hard, with little loss to himself, at 2.30 P.M. threw out flank guards wide upon each side and began his retreat upon Oisy. The movement was necessarily slow, the flanking parties being impeded by hedges, and it was some time before the rearmost of the Munsters and the two guns left Fesmy. At 3 P.M. the cyclist, who had failed to deliver the copy of Br.-General Maxse's final order to Major Charrier, reached the Coldstream Guards near Oisy, and gave them their instructions to retire

[1] They really belonged to the *15th Reserve Regiment,* of the *2nd Guard Reserve Division (X. Reserve Corps)* of the *Second Army.* The history of this regiment (p. 65) speaks of "receiving fire at every turn of the road, " whilst marching off it was impossible owing to the 2-metre high hedges, " threaded with wire and almost impenetrable. . . . 'Everywhere thick " hedges ! We are always getting fired on, we can't tell from where,' cursed " the field-greys. The only course was to plaster the hedges with lead."

[2] They belonged to the *16th Uhlans,* the corps cavalry of the *VII. Corps,* the right of the *Second Army* (" Geschichte des Ulanenregiments Nr. 16," p. 106).

forthwith.   Simultaneously, the detachment of the 15th Hussars and Munster Fusiliers from Bergues came into Oisy
Map 3. and took over the guard of the bridge there.   But it was now evident that the gap between the rear guard and the corps was increasing rapidly, the 3rd Brigade being by this time at Guise, the 2nd Brigade closing in upon Hannapes, some five miles in rear, whilst the 1st, at another five miles distance, was still in position at Oisy.   The 3rd Brigade was therefore halted at Guise, and the 1/South Wales Borderers and the XXVI. Brigade R.F.A. were sent back north about three miles to Maison Rouge, where at 3.30 P.M. they took up a position to cover the retreat of the 1st (Guards) Brigade.

By that hour the Coldstream Guards, Scots Guards and Black Watch had begun to withdraw ; but neither the permanent bridge over the canal near Oisy nor the temporary timber structure south of it (made by the 23rd Field Company R.E. by felling trees, as the permanent bridge was in full view of the high ground adjacent) was blown up or destroyed, although prepared for demolition, as at the last moment the instructions to do so were cancelled by triplicate orders sent by the 1st Division, 1st Brigade and C.R.E.   Shortly after 4 P.M. the rear-guard cavalry reported strong hostile columns moving south upon La Vallée Mulâtre, immediately to the west of Wassigny, and the three battalions of the 1st (Guards) Brigade, upon reaching the level plateau to the south of Étreux, found themselves threatened from the north and west by a German cavalry division [1] and two batteries.   There was a good deal of firing as they retired over the next three miles of ground to the southward, but it was confined chiefly to the artillery; for the enemy was held at a distance without much difficulty by the British batteries at Maison Rouge.   Thus the three battalions reached Guise with trifling loss, the 5th Cavalry Brigade retiring parallel to them on the west.   At dusk the firing died down, and the 1st Division went into bivouac, the 3rd Brigade at Bernot, just north of the 2nd Division at Mont d'Origny, at 9 P.M., and the 2nd and 1st Brigades at Hauteville and Jonqueuse, north-east and east of Bernot, at 11 P.M.   The 2/Welch of the eastern flank guard also reached Bernot at this hour : it had been much impeded by refugees, but, beyond a few rifle shots, had not been interfered with by the enemy.   The 5th Cavalry Brigade also came into the same area for the night ; the

[1] The *Guard Cavalry Division* of Richthofen's corps.

detachment of 15th Hussars at Oisy marched southward 27 Aug.
on to Mont d'Origny, which it reached at midnight. The 1914.
men were greatly fatigued by their long and trying day, but
they had been little pressed by the Germans. A cavalry
division had, indeed, appeared very late from the north-
westward, but no infantry had threatened them from the
north, and the reason for this must now be told.

As it left Fesmy the rearmost company of the Munsters Map 12.
had become engaged with German infantry, but was able
to disengage and rejoin the main body of the battalion,
then, about 5.45 P.M., half-way to Étreux, and continue its
retreat. But as it approached the village, Germans were
seen crossing the road ahead, and fire was opened not only
by German infantry from the houses on the northern outskirts, but from a battery not more than fifteen hundred
yards away to the eastward. Then for the first time the
Munsters began to fall fast. One of the two guns of the
section of the 118th Battery was disabled, a single shell
destroying the whole team. The other gun was promptly
brought into action against the German artillery, but over
three hundred rounds had already been fired, and ammunition was very nearly exhausted. Still undaunted, Major
Charrier pushed forward two companies to clear the way
through Étreux ; but the Germans had installed themselves in the trenches dug during the forenoon by the Black
Watch, and also occupied a house, which they had loopholed, west of the road. A house east of the road now
burst into flames, evidently giving the signal for a converging attack from all sides upon the Munsters. Major Charrier
ordered the remaining gun to be brought up to demolish the
loopholed house, but the range was so short that the team
and detachment were instantly shot down. A third company, which was supporting the advance of the two companies, was then sent to make an attack on the railway-
cutting to the east of Étreux station. In spite of enfilade
fire, both of infantry and artillery, the company worked up
to within seventy yards of the cutting and charged. The
men were mowed down on all sides, and only one officer
reached the hedge, with one man, who was then killed by
his side.

Meanwhile Major Charrier had led three charges against
the loopholed house, in one of which his adjutant actually
reached the building, and fired his revolver through a loop-
hole, only to drop stunned by a blow from falling brick-
work. These gallant efforts were all in vain. It was now

7 P.M.   The Germans attacked from south, east and west, and, though temporarily driven back at one point by a bayonet charge, continued to advance. Major Charrier was shot dead alongside the deserted gun on the road, and so many officers had by this time fallen, that the command devolved upon Lieutenant E. W. Gower. Collecting such men as were left, he formed them in an orchard, facing to all points of the compass, and continued to resist. Gradually the Germans crowded in on them from three sides, bringing fresh machine guns into position, and at 9.15 P.M. they closed in also from the north, and the little band of not more than two hundred and fifty of all ranks with ammunition almost spent, was overpowered. The Munsters had been fighting against overwhelming odds for nearly twelve hours, and discovered at the end that they had been matched against at least six battalions of the *73rd* and *77th Reserve Regiments*, of the *19th Reserve Division*, besides three of the *15th Reserve Regiment* of the *2nd Guard Reserve Division*, all forming part of the *X. Reserve Corps*. Beyond question, they had arrested the enemy's pursuit in this quarter for fully six hours, so that their sacrifice was not in vain.

The situation at midnight of the 27th/28th August was :

Sketches I. Corps (less a brigade).
A & 4.
Maps 3,
13 & 14.   5th Cavalry Brigade and 4th
(Guards) Brigade.

On the high ground southwards of Guise from Longchamps to Mont d'Origny.

West of the river Oise about Hauteville and Bernot.

At dawn on the 28th, although the weather was still extremely hot, the retreat of the I. Corps on La Fère was resumed under more favourable conditions ; for, although two German divisions were reported from eight to twelve miles north of St. Quentin, the rumour that they were actually in that town turned out to be false ;[1] moreover, the French XVIII. Corps was now in touch with the British on the east. The transport had begun to move off at 2 A.M. In addition to a rear guard, a flank guard (under Br.-General Horne) consisting of the 5th Cavalry Brigade, 5th Brigade and XXXVI. Brigade R.F.A., was thrown out to the west ; and the rear guard, the 2nd Brigade with a brigade of artillery and a squadron, held the heights of Mont d'Origny during the passage of the main body through

[1] On the night of the 27th/28th, the German *III.*, *IV.* and *IV. Reserve Corps* of the *First Army* were 6 miles north-west of St. Quentin on a front facing south and south-west.

Origny. Nothing was seen of the enemy until shortly after noon, when a German column of all arms appeared, working round towards the right rear of the 2nd Brigade; about 12.30 P.M. its guns opened fire, but with little effect.[1] The infantry then made some semblance of attack, but was easily held at a distance, and at 2 P.M. the last of the British battalions marched off, covered by infantry of Valabrègue's Reserve divisions, which occupied the position as they vacated it. The I. Corps then made its way, always by a single highroad, towards La Fère. The march was again most trying, for on the greater part of the way battalions, as well as transport, were " double-banked," and a swarm of refugees added to the congestion. Thus, choked with dust, on an airless, oppressive day, the I. Corps at last reached La Fère, crossed the Oise southwards, and, in the course of the afternoon, reached its billets :— the 1st Division just south of La Fère at Fressancourt, Bertaucourt and St. Gobain ; the 2nd Division further to the westward at Andelain, Servais and Amigny.

It remained to be seen whether the German cavalry would press into the gap between the I. and II. Corps, which was still some fifteen miles wide. On this day the 3rd Cavalry Brigade had been pushed eastwards by Major-General Allenby to gain touch with the I. Corps.[2] Early in the forenoon the brigade was in position six or seven miles south of St. Quentin, between Cérizy and Essigny, when at 10 A.M. firing was heard to the north, and this was followed shortly afterwards by the appearance of French (84th Division) Territorial infantrymen retiring south from St. Quentin through Essigny.[3] Learning from them that they had been surprised by German cavalry and artillery at Bellenglise, Br.-General Gough withdrew his right, the 4th Hussars, southwards from near Essigny to Benay, to cover their retreat. After a time, his patrols reported a brigade of Uhlans to be advancing on Essigny and a second column of all arms further to the east, moving on Cérizy. About 1 P.M. an advanced party of Uhlans was caught in ambush by the 4th Hussars about Benay and dispersed with loss, their killed being identified as of the *Guard Cavalry Division*. The column in rear of them thereupon attempted

28 Aug. 1914.

---

[1] From Bülow's map, the column would appear to belong to the X. *Corps* then, with the rest of the *Second Army*, moving south-westward. Later in the day, that Army turned south.
[2] See page 219.
[3] The bulk of the division retired from Cambrai on the 26th via Doullens, Amiens and Poix, where it remained until the 11th September.

to work round Br.-General Gough's eastern flank, but was stopped by the guns of E Battery R.H.A. Thus what seems to have been the western column of the *Guard Cavalry Division* was brought, with comparative ease, to a standstill.

The eastern column of the German cavalry was more enterprising, but no more successful. As commander of the left flank guard of the I. Corps, Br.-General Horne had sent the whole of the 5th Cavalry Brigade to the western bank of the Oise, and, at 10.30 A.M., Sir Philip Chetwode moved it to Moy, a village nearly abreast and 2 miles east of Cérizy, where he halted in the Oise valley. Leaving the Scots Greys on outpost, with the 20th Hussars in close support, on the high ground to the north-west by La Guinguette Farm, he rested the remainder of the brigade in Moy. About noon the enemy came into sight, advancing south along the main road from St. Quentin. Upon this a squadron of the Scots Greys, with a machine gun, was sent to occupy a copse on the eastern side of the road a little to the north of La Guinguette Farm (on the St. Quentin—La Fère road, ½ mile east of Cérizy), with one troop pushed forward to a building near the road about half a mile ahead, and a section of J Battery R.H.A. was unlimbered about half a mile to the south-east of the copse. The advanced troop of the Greys was driven back by superior numbers, but all attempts of hostile patrols to penetrate to La Guinguette were foiled by the fire of the remainder of the squadron. At length, at 2 P.M., two squadrons of the enemy advanced in close formation on the eastern side of the road, and, being fired on both by the Greys and by the two guns, there dismounted. Most of their horses, terrified by the bursting shells, galloped away, and the troopers, after discharging a few rounds, also turned tail. Br.-General Chetwode at once ordered the rest of J Battery into action and directed the 12th Lancers, with two squadrons of the Greys in support, to move round the enemy's eastern flank, and the 20th Hussars to advance along the St. Quentin road and turn him from the west. The dismounted Germans meanwhile made off in all haste, but the leading squadron, C, and the machine-gun section of the 12th Lancers, hurrying northward, caught sight of a body mounted about eight hundred yards away moving in close formation towards Moy. Attacking it with fire, the 12th Lancers compelled the Germans to dismount, and then stampeded their horses. The two other squadrons and J

Battery now coming into action, C squadron mounted and, 28 Aug.
led by Lieut.-Colonel F. Wormald, approaching over dead ^{1914.}
ground, got within fifty yards of the enemy and charged.
Some seventy or eighty of the Germans, who proved to be of
the *2nd Guard Dragoon Regiment,* were speared. The 12th
Lancers lost one officer and four men killed, and their
lieutenant-colonel and four men wounded. Further pursuit would obviously have been imprudent, but Br.-General
Chetwode remained on the ground long enough to collect
all his wounded—his casualties did not exceed thirty—and
to ascertain that his guns had played such havoc with the
German reserves that their total losses might fairly be
reckoned at three hundred killed and wounded. Finally
towards evening, he and Br.-General Gough fell back independently, the former to the left of the I. Corps, to Sinceny
and Autreville, the latter to rejoin the Cavalry Division,
west of the Oise canal at Frières (6 miles W.N.W. of La
Fère) and Jussy (just north of Frières). Though the action
of Cérizy had been comparatively insignificant, it very
effectually damped the ardour of the German cavalry.[1]

GENERAL SITUATION ON NIGHT OF 28TH/29TH AUGUST

When all movements had been completed on the night Sketches
of the 28th/29th August, the I. Corps was south of the $\substack{A \& 4. \\ Maps 13}$
Oise and of La Fère ; the II. Corps, with the 4th Division, & 15.

[1] The Chaplain of the *Guard Cavalry Division,* Dr. Vogel, gives the Map 3.
following account of this action. After relating the march of the division
on the 28th August from La Groise via Wassigny and Bohain to Homblières
(3 miles east of St. Quentin), which it reached at 1 P.M., and a fight around
St. Quentin with two battalions of the French 10th Territorial Infantry
Regiment (Kluck says that his *III. Corps* was also engaged there) which
lasted until 7 P.M., he states that " a report came from the Dragoon
" Brigade that it was in a severe action east of Urvillers [4 miles north-
" west of Moy whence the British 5th Cavalry Brigade had moved].
" It had stumbled on what appeared to be weak enemy infantry in
" the wood south-west of the village, and had attacked with three
" squadrons dismounted, intending to charge with the other three.
" It turned out, however, that the brigade had to deal, not with dis-
" organized fugitives, but with a strong detachment of the intact Franco-
" British Army which had advanced from La Fère. This was evident from
" the lively infantry fusillade which they received as they approached
" mounted. It was not easy to get clear, but with the assistance of a
" battery, the brigade succeeded in withdrawing behind the hill north of
" the wood, which was held by the *Guard Schützenbataillon.* Some British
" squadrons also which had deployed to charge were driven back by our
" guns, which opened at just the right moment. The *3rd Guard Uhlans*
" now reinforced the troops holding the hill. A troop of the Dragoons,
" under Lieutenant Graf Schwerin, was ridden over by British Hussars.
" The wounded, amongst whom were men with six or seven lance wounds,
" and several bullet wounds, were taken prisoner by the enemy."

was north and east of Noyon, with one division south of the Oise. Thus, the two wings of the Army were still 11 miles apart, the gap between them being more or less covered by cavalry on a curve from the left of the I. Corps to the northern end of the II. Corps. On the right, the British were 6 miles in rear of the left of the French Fifth Army, but on the left in touch with Sordet's cavalry.

Map 3. In detail, the positions of the British were :

I. Corps :
 On the northern edge of the Forest of St. Gobain and Coucy, from Fressancourt to Amigny.
5th Cavalry Brigade : Sinceny.
II. Corps (including 4th Division, 19th Brigade and Cavalry Division) :
 1st, 2nd and 3rd Cavalry Brigades :
  At Berlancourt, Flavy le Meldeux—Plessis, and Jussy, respectively.
 3rd, 4th (with 19th Brigade) and 5th Divisions :
  From Freniches, south and east, through Genvry to Pontoise.
 4th Cavalry Brigade :
  Cressy (3 miles south of Nesle) north-west of the 4th Division.

From the 28th onward every day was to bring the two wings closer to each other. Sir John French, after meeting some of the 5th Division on the march, as has already been told, had motored on to La Fère to see the I. Corps, and had satisfied himself as to the good spirit of the troops. He had also received the promise of the 6th Division from England about the middle of September and of a complete corps from India at a later date. Other important intelligence also reached him. The troops of General d'Amade, together with General Sordet's cavalry corps, had been seen in action between Péronne and Bray sur Somme, but by evening it appeared that they had been pressed back. There was good reason to believe that the German Supreme Command judged the British Army to be beaten beyond hope of speedy recovery, and were intent upon extending their enveloping movement westwards until they could sweep all opposing forces into their net.

On the 28th at 7.55 A.M., G.H.Q. asked for air reconnaissance of the area Péronne—Montdidier—Compiègne " to locate hostile cavalry, possibly believed to be about

" Péronne to-night," and of the area La Fère—Péronne—
Guise, to locate hostile columns. The first-named area
actually contained only a few French troops, and nothing
was seen of the German *II. Cavalry Corps* which, late in
the day, reached an area just north-west of Péronne. In
the second area a number of columns (now known to be
the *6th* and *7th Divisions* of the *First Army* and the *VII.*
and *X. Reserve Corps* of the *Second Army*) were seen and
all reported moving west between St. Quentin and Le
Catelet. The positions of the I. and II. Corps were also
discovered and reported.

General Joffre, during his visit to Sir John French Sketch
on the 27th, had mentioned the preparation of a counter- 12A.
stroke and the formation of a new Army on his left. The
first sign of it was seen on this day in the arrival of units
between Amiens and Ham. This Army, the Sixth, under
General Maunoury, was to be formed between the British
and General d'Amade. As a beginning, the VII. Corps,[1]
brought from Belfort, was detraining at Villers Bretonneux,
to the east of Amiens, and a Moroccan brigade was already
assembled further to the east.[2] On the same day General
Joffre—his Western Armies being on the general line
Reims—Amiens—ordered the French Fifth Army to take
the offensive towards St. Quentin along a line parallel
to the Oise from Guise to La Fère, hoping at best to strike
an effective blow which might check the German advance,
and at least relieve the British Army from all further
pressure.

On the evening of the 28th August, two corps (XVIII.
and III.) of the French Fifth Army proceeding westwards
were halted, in echelon, south of the Oise, east of Guise,
under cover of the X. Corps, the I. Corps being in reserve
to the south-east. General Lanrezac's troops were thus
in touch with, but in advance of, the British Army. During
the day, General Valabrègue's Reserve divisions, which
since the night of the 25th/26th, as already described, had
marched so close to the I. Corps as sometimes to share its
roads, had had hard fighting at the Oise bridges near Guise,

---

[1] 14th Division and 63rd Reserve Division. The 13th Division remained
in Alsace.
[2] According to Kluck, Marwitz's cavalry corps " was surprised in its
" billets [near Péronne] by the French 61st and 62nd Reserve Divisions
" (of d'Amade's force) on the morning of the 28th. The French, however,
" were driven from the field at Manancourt (7 miles S.W. of Bapaume)
" by parts of the *II. Corps* and *IV. Reserve Corps*." This was the action
of Mesnil.

had lost the bridges and withdrawn at nightfall to the left of the line of the Fifth Army.[1]

Sir John French issued orders at 11.30 P.M.[2] for the British to halt and rest on the 29th, but with the condition that all formations should be withdrawn to the south of a line practically east and west through Nesle and Ham, connecting with the French at Vendeuil. During the evening of the 28th, Sir Douglas Haig was asked by General Lanrezac to co-operate in his coming offensive. He agreed to do so, but, on informing G.H.Q. of the request, he received instructions that he was not to take part. The Field-Marshal, who seems to have continued to take a gloomy view of the state of his troops, was anxious to withdraw them from the line of battle for eight or ten days to some locality where they might rest and be re-equipped, and he accordingly arranged with General Joffre that they should fall back to a line a little to the south of the Aisne between Soissons and Compiègne. The situation was complicated by the fact that Kluck's sweep westwards had compelled the evacuation of the British advanced base at Amiens. On this day the suggestion was first made that St. Nazaire, at the mouth of the Loire, should take the place of Havre as the principal sea base of the British force in France.

Map 2.	It may be mentioned here that, with the view of creating a diversion on the western flank to assist the British Expeditionary Force and of supporting the Belgians, one battalion of R. Marine Artillery and three battalions of R. Marine Light Infantry, under command of Br.-General Sir George Aston, were landed at Ostend on the 27th and 28th August. They were re-embarked on the 31st.[3] News of this landing appears to have reached the German Supreme Command on the 30th.[4]

[1] See Note II. " The Battle of Guise," at end of Chapter XI.
[2] Appendix 18.
[3] For details see Sir Julian Corbett's " Naval Operations," i. pp. 92-4 and 123-4. The so-called brigade was without a signal section or office staff ; the battalions were in blue serge, had no horses, no transport, not even 1st-line ; no machine guns ; and the rifle ammunition was not charger-loaded.
[4] With regard to it the head of the Operations Branch of the German General Staff has written :—
" At this time there was, as may be imagined, no lack of alarming " reports at General Headquarters. Ostend and Antwerp took a prominent " part in them. One day countless British troops were said to have landed " at Ostend and to be marching on Antwerp ; on another that there were " about to be great sorties from Antwerp. Even landings of Russian " troops, 80,000 men, at Ostend were mentioned. At Ostend a great

NOTE I

MOVEMENTS OF THE GERMAN *FIRST* AND *SECOND ARMIES*
AFTER LE CATEAU

What became of the German *First* and *Second Armies* after the 27 Aug. battle of Le Cateau will now be related. 1914.
On the 26th August, Bülow [1] had issued orders for the continu- Sketch 10. ation of the pursuit in a " sharp south-westerly direction . . . as Map 3. " sufficient elbow room had to be obtained for the great wheel of the " *Third, Fourth* and *Fifth Armies* round Verdun." "After con- " tinuous fighting with French rear guards," the *I. Cavalry Corps* and three and a half corps of the *Second Army* [2] reached an approxi- mate S.E. and N.W. line a little in front of Avesnes, the cavalry and *X. Reserve Corps* moving to Marbaix, where they had the fight, already related,[3] with the Connaught Rangers ; but the *Second Army* took no part in the battle of Le Cateau.
On the 27th, after Le Cateau, Kluck, making a late start, in the belief that the British " would endeavour to escape south-westwards " in order not to lose communication with their ports " (G.O.A., i. p. 528), moved his troops about twelve miles in a south-westerly direction :—*III. Corps* via Maretz to Nauroy, *IV. Corps* to Belli- court—Vendhuille, *II. Corps*, with *II. Cavalry Corps* in front, to Sailly Saillisel—Fins (5 miles south-east of Bapaume) ; the *IV. Reserve Corps* followed between the *II.* and *IV. Corps* to Roisel— —Liéramont. The *IX. Corps* (less the *17th Division*) marched from Maubeuge via Le Cateau some five hours later than the rest of the Army, and billeted in and about Busigny. Except for en- counters with the Gordons and parties of stragglers on the night of the 26th/27th, he had no information of the whereabouts of the British beyond "that they were in full retreat" (G.O.A., i. p. 529). Even on the night of the 27th he was " by no means clear of the " direction taken by the British in their retreat. . . . Aviators " during the night of the 26th/27th had reported the retreat of " strong enemy columns from Landrecies on Guise [I. Corps] and " from Avesnes on Vervins [French] ; it was probable that the enemy " in his further retreat would try to turn more to the west or south- " west. The retreat to the west was, however, denied to him on " the evening of the 27th by the *II. Corps*." (G.O.A., i. p. 531.) There is no mention of any air reports on the 27th. The only fighting that Kluck records is isolated encounters of the *II. Corps* and cavalry with General d'Amade's forces on the British left, at Heude- court and westwards ; the identifications obtained thereby added to

---

" entrenched camp for the English was in preparation. [Aston's men did " commence digging.] . . . Though, of course, the security of the rear and " right flank of the army required constant attention, such, and even worse " information, could not stop the advance of the troops." (Tappen, p. 22.)
  [1] Bülow, p. 29.
  [2] The *13th Division* was left behind at Maubeuge, where General von Zwehl took charge of the investment with the *VII. Reserve Corps* (less *13th Reserve Division* on march from Namur), and the *17th Division* of the *IX. Corps*. The *13th Division* rejoined the *Second Army* in the nick of time to take part in the battle of Guise.
  [3] See page 203.

the obscurity of the situation. Regardless of any danger threatening his right flank, he determined to push on at all speed for the passages of the Somme.

The *Second Army* (still without the *13th Division*) reàched a S.E. and N.W. line through Étreux, where, as already narrated, the *X. Reserve Corps*, on its western flank, ran into the Munster Fusiliers.[1] The German Official Account (i. p. 532) speaks of the 27th August as being " a day of pure marching, in general, without contact with " the enemy."

During the day, Kluck was released from Bülow's command ; he was therefore free to make a wide turning movement to the west, instead of being tied to the *Second Army* in order to assist it to tactical successes.

On the 28th, therefore, the *First Army* sent on cavalry and field batteries in pursuit of d'Amade's forces, and there was rear-guard fighting ; the remainder of the Army moved south-west across the British front. The *III. Corps* got no further than Bellenglise— outskirts of St. Quentin, owing to the opposition met with from French Territorials, British cavalry and stragglers ; the heads of the three corps on the right just reached the Somme, on a front six miles on either side of Péronne ; the *IX. Corps* was still a march behind on the left.

In the *Second Army*, Bülow ordered the *Guard* and *X. Corps* on his left (east) to stand fast and reconnoitre, since the French Fifth Army was on their front behind the Oise, whilst his right swung round in touch with the *First Army*. " *I. Cavalry Corps*," he ordered, " will endeavour to attack the British in the rear, moving " round the south of St. Quentin " ; the *VII. Corps* (less *13th Division*) was to march early to St. Quentin ; the *X. Reserve Corps* was to make a short march of about six miles south-west from Étreux. Except for the cavalry fight at Cérizy[2] and the right of the *X. Reserve Corps* brushing against the rear guard at Mont d'Origny,[3] all touch with the British was lost. Bülow does not say what places the above-named corps reached by evening, but he records that in the afternoon of the 28th he received a message from Kluck asking him to deal with the disorganized English forces, which appeared to be falling back on La Fère. He therefore ordered the *X. Reserve* and *VII. Corps* (less *13th Division*) to push on westwards, towards the passages of the Somme and the Crozat canal near Ham and St. Simon (4 miles east of Ham), which they reached on the 29th.

Thus the B.E.F., though at first followed by the right of the *Second Army* and the left of the *First*, escaped from pressure on the 28th owing to the gap between these Armies steadily increasing to some fourteen miles.

During the evening of the 28th an officer from O.H.L. brought to Bülow and Kluck " General Directions for the Further Conduct of " Operations."[4] These directions foreshadowed a wheel inwards of the two great wings of the German forces, the right wing in accord-ance with the original plan, and the left wing by an advance through the French eastern fortresses, so as to bring about a surrender of the French Armies in the open field. They seem of sufficient im-portance to translate in full, and are as follows :—

" It is most important by a rapid march of the German forces on

---

[1] See page 221.   [2] See page 228.   [3] See page 226.
[4] G.O.A., iii. pp. 7-10.

" Paris to prevent the French Army from coming to rest, to stop
" the assembly of fresh bodies of troops, and to take from the country
" as much as possible of its means of defence.
" Belgium is placed under a German Governor-General and a
" German Administration. It is to serve as the hinterland for supply
" of the *First, Second* and *Third Armies*, and thus shorten the lines
" of communication of the German right wing.
" His Majesty orders the advance of the German forces in the
" direction of Paris.
" The *First Army*, with the *II. Cavalry Corps* attached, will
" march west of the Oise towards the lower Seine. It must be pre-
" pared to co-operate in the fighting of the *Second Army*. It will
" also be responsible for the protection of the right flank of the forces,
" and will take steps to prevent the enemy from assembling fresh
" bodies of troops in its zone of operation. The detachments
" (*III. Reserve* and *IX. Reserve Corps*) left behind for the investment
" of Antwerp are placed immediately under O.H.L. The *IV.*
" *Reserve Corps* is again put at the disposal of the *First Army*.
" The *Second Army*, with the *I. Cavalry Corps* attached, will
" advance via the line La Fère—Laon on Paris. It will also invest
" and capture Maubeuge, and later La Fère ; also Laon in co-
" operation with the *Third Army*. The *I. Cavalry Corps* will recon-
" noitre on the fronts of both the *Second* and *Third Armies*, and will
" send any information obtained to the *Third Army*.
" The *Third Army* will continue its march via the line Laon—
" Guignicourt, west of Neufchâtel, on Château Thierry. Hirson will
" be captured, also Laon with Fort Condé in co-operation with
" the *Second Army*. The *I. Cavalry Corps*, on the front of the
" *Second* and *Third Armies*, will provide the *Third Army* with in-
" formation.
" The *Fourth Army* will march via Reims on Epernay. The
" *IV. Cavalry Corps*, attached to the *Fifth Army*, will also send
" reports to the *Fourth Army*. Any siege material required for the
" capture of Reims will be provided. The *VI. Corps* is transferred
" to the *Fifth Army*.
" The *Fifth Army*, to which the *VI. Corps* is transferred, will
" advance against the line Châlons sur Marne—Vitry le François.
" It will be responsible for the flank protection of the forces, by
" echelonning back its left wing, until the *Sixth Army* can take
" over this task west of the Meuse. The *IV. Cavalry Corps* remains
" attached to the *Fifth Army*, but will reconnoitre on the fronts of
" the *Fourth* and *Fifth Armies*, and send reports to the *Fourth Army*.
" Verdun will be invested. Besides the five *Landwehr* brigades from
" the Nied position, the *10th* and *8th Ersatz Divisions* are also
" assigned to it, as soon as they can be spared by the *Sixth Army*.
" The *Sixth Army*, with the *Seventh Army* and the *III. Cavalry
" Corps*, in touch with Metz, has first to prevent an advance of the
" enemy into Lorraine and Upper Alsace. The fortress of Metz is
" placed under the *Sixth Army*. If the enemy retires, the *Sixth
" Army*, with the *III. Cavalry Corps*, will cross the Moselle between
" Toul and Epinal, and take the general direction of Neufchâteau.
" This Army will then be responsible for the protection of the left
" flank of the forces. Nancy and Toul are to be invested ; Epinal
" is to be masked with sufficient troops. In this case the *Sixth Army*
" will be reinforced by portions of the *Seventh Army* (*XIV.* and *XV.*

" *Corps* and one *Ersatz* division) ; but the *10th* and *8th Ersatz*
" *Divisions* will be handed over to the *Fifth Army*. The *Seventh*
" *Army* will then become independent.
  " The *Seventh Army* will at first remain under the *Sixth Army*.
" If the latter crosses the Moselle, the *Seventh Army* will become
" independent. The fortress of Strasbourg and the Upper Rhine
" fortifications, with the troops in them, will remain under it. The
" *Seventh Army* will prevent an enemy break-through between Epinal
" and the Swiss frontier. It is recommended that strong defences
" should be constructed opposite Epinal, and from there to the
" mountains, also in the Rhine valley in connection with Neubrei-
" sach, and that the main strength should be kept behind the right
" wing. The *XIV.* and *XV. Corps*, as well as one of the *Ersatz*
" divisions, will then be transferred to the *Sixth Army*.
  [The lines of demarcation between the Armies follow.]
  " All Armies will mutually co-operate with one another, and
" support each other in fighting for the various lines which are to
" be gained. The strong resistance which may be expected on the
" Aisne and, later, on the Marne, may necessitate a wheel of the
" Armies from a south-westerly to a southerly direction.
  " A rapid advance is urgently desirable in order to leave the
" French no time to re-organize and offer serious resistance. The
" Armies will therefore report when they can begin the advance.
" The Armies on the wings are recommended to attach infantry,
" in addition to *Jäger* battalions, to their cavalry divisions as
" required, in order to break any resistance of *franc-tireurs* and
" civilian inhabitants as quickly as possible. Only by severe
" measures against the population can a national rising be nipped
" in the bud."
  A completely erroneous appreciation of the situation appears
to have been current at O.H.L. at this time. It furnishes a clue to
the apparently haphazard way in which the German Armies moved,
and is so extraordinary that it is best, perhaps, to quote the words
of the Chief of the Operations Section [1] :—
  " The French, as expected, had offered battle to prevent us
" from penetrating into France. The highly favourable reports that
" came in daily, as late as the 25th August, in conjunction with the
" great victory of the *Sixth* and *Seventh Armies* in Lorraine on the
" 20th and 25th, aroused in Great Headquarters the belief that
" the great decisive battle in the West ḷad been fought and con-
" cluded in our favour. Under the impression that there had been
" a ' decisive victory,' the Chief of the General Staff resolved on the
" 25th, in spite of arguments to the contrary, to detach forces to the
" East. He believed the moment had come when, in conformity
" with the great operations plan, a decisive victory in the West
" having been won, considerable forces could be sent to the East to
" obtain a decision there also. For this purpose six corps were
" detailed, among them the *XI. Corps* and *Guard Reserve Corps*
" (besieging Namur). . . . Only after the whole extent of the victory
" at Tannenberg became known was the order cancelled as regards
" the four corps to be taken from the centre and left ; one of these,
" the *V. Corps* of the *Fifth Army*, was actually awaiting entrainment
" at Thionville. On the subsequent days further reports of suc-

SKETCH 8

THE BATTLE OF GUISE
29TH AUGUST 1914.

GERMANS .... GREEN
FRENCH .... BLUE
B.E.F. .... RED

N.

Movements on the 28th. {- - - - - -}
Movements during 29th. {———}

SCALE

MILES 5   0   5   10 MILES

" cesses came in. After O.H.L. had issued instructions on the 26th 28 Aug.
" and 27th for the continuation of the operations on the basis that 1914.
" great victories had been gained, the *First Army* reported on the
" 28th August that it had defeated the British Army, and that it
" was already half-way between the Belgian frontier and Paris. . . .
" The idea that the French retirement was according to plan was
" only expressed by a few solitary individuals."

This statement may be partly designed to throw some of the
blame on the Army commanders, for forwarding misleading reports
of victories, but the despatch of the two army corps to Russia and
the bringing of the *V. Corps* out of the line are established facts.
There was certainly good reason for sending reinforcements to the
Eastern theatre. On the 19th/20th the German *Eighth Army* had
fought the unsuccessful battle of Gumbinnen, the Russians had
invaded East Prussia, and, although Generals von Hindenburg and
Ludendorff had been sent to supersede Generals von Prittwitz and
von Waldersee and retrieve the situation, the result of the battle of
Tannenberg, begun on the 23rd August, was still in doubt. In both
the Austrian theatres Germany's Ally had been defeated. In the
southern, the invasion of Serbia had failed, and by the 25th August
all Austrian forces had recrossed the frontier, beaten. In the
Galician theatre, although the opening fighting had seemed to be in
Austria's favour, the First Battle of Lemberg, begun on the 26th,
was going against her, largely owing to her *Second Army*, recalled
from Serbia, not having reached the field. If she were not to be
overwhelmed, she would require substantial help before the date 6th
to 10th September (36th to 40th day of mobilization), for which it
had been promised by the German Chief of the General Staff.

NOTE II

MOVEMENTS OF THE FRENCH FIFTH ARMY FROM
CHARLEROI TO GUISE

The general line of retirement of the French Fifth Army after Map 3.
Charleroi was south-westwards, its orders being to reach the line
Laon—La Fère. The movements of General Valabrègue's two
Reserve divisions in contact with the British I. Corps have been
mentioned. The XVIII. Corps (35th, 26th and 38th (African)
Divisions), on their right, retired via Avesnes, and crossed the Oise
at Romery (4 miles east of Guise). The III. Corps, next on the
right (5th, 6th and 37th (African) Divisions), followed in echelon
behind the XVIII. ; it passed the French frontier on the 25th and
marched through Fourmies (10 miles south-east of Avesnes), and
crossed the Oise between Etreaupont and Ohis. The X. Corps
marched via La Capelle to Hirson, first south and then south-east,
to keep in touch with the Fourth Army, and thence to Vervins.
The I. Corps, from the right of the Army, after reaching Tavaux
(7 miles south of Vervins), was brought north-west into second line
between the III. and X. Corps.

Thus, by the evening of the 28th August, the Fifth Army was
drawn up facing north and north-west behind the Oise from Vervins
practically to La Fère, in the following order : 4th Cavalry Division,
51st Reserve Division, X. Corps, III. Corps, XVIII. Corps, Vala-

brègue's Reserve divisions, with the I. Corps coming up into second line. The German *Second Army* was in contact with the whole front of the Fifth Army, and had secured a bridgehead at Guise.

NOTE III

GENERAL JOFFRE'S CONGRATULATORY TELEGRAM

Dated 27th August 1914.

Commandant en Chef des Armées Françaises à Commandant en Chef Armée Anglaise Noyon Oise. No. 2425.

L'Armée anglaise en n'hésitant pas à s'engager tout entière contre des forces très supérieures en nombre a puissamment contribué à assurer la sécurité du flanc gauche de l'Armée Française. Elle l'a fait avec un dévouement, une énergie et une persévérance auxquels je tiens dès maintenant à rendre hommage et qui se retrouveront demain pour assurer le triomphe final de la cause commune. L'Armée Française n'oubliera pas le service rendu ; animée du même esprit de sacrifice et de la même volonté de vaincre que l'Armée Anglaise, elle lui affirmera sa reconnaissance, dans les prochains combats. JOFFRE.

NOTE IV

BRITISH LOSSES 23RD TO 27TH AUGUST 1914
(EXCLUDING MISSING WHO RETURNED TO THEIR UNITS)

	23rd.	24th. (Mons.)	25th.	26th. (Le Cateau.)	27th.
Cavalry Division	6	252	123	15	14
I. Corps :					
1st Division	9	42	32	61	826
2nd Division	35	59	230	344	48
II. Corps :					
3rd Division	1,185	557	357	1,796	50
5th Division	386	1,656	62	2,631	76
4th Division	..	..	65	3,158	58
19th Infantry Brigade	17	40	36	477	108
	1,638	2,606	905	8,482	1,180

The British losses at Waterloo were 8,458 (Wellington Despatches, vol. xii.).

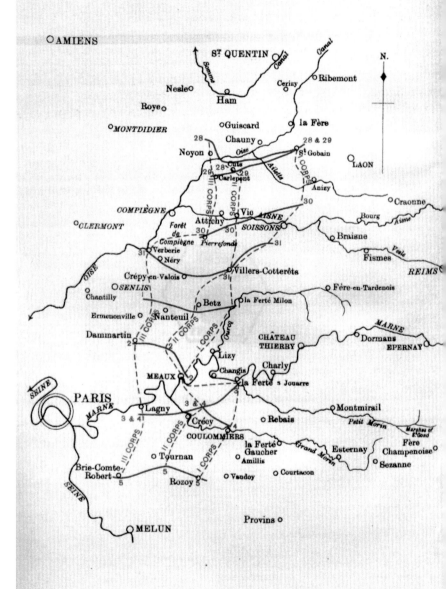

SKETCH

OPERATIONS, 28 AUGUST – 5 SEPTEMBER, 1914.
Retreat of B.E.F.
Positions at night are shown by dates.

SCALE

MILES 5 4 3 2 1 0   10   20 MILES

Ordnance Survey, 1920

CHAPTER XI

THE RETREAT (*continued*)

29TH–31ST AUGUST

(Sketches A, 8, 9, 10 & 11 ; Maps 3, 4, 14, 16, 17 & 18)

29TH AUGUST

EXCEPT for some minor adjustments to secure the best
ground possible, in the course of which the 4th Division
had moved back a little to the area Bussy—Sermaize—
Chevilly, the morning of the 29th August found the B.E.F.
halted in its over-night positions on the Oise. To the right
front of the British was the French Fifth Army, and to
their left front the newly-formed French Sixth Army,
General Maunoury's headquarters being at Montdidier.[1]
In pursuance of General Joffre's directions, the Fifth Army
began the battle of Guise by attacking towards St. Quentin
against the German *Second Army* ;[2] at the same time the
outer wing of the German *First Army*, swinging south-
westwards, was engaged with General Maunoury's Army,
and there was fighting at Proyart (10 miles south-west of
Péronne) and Rosières (6 miles south of Proyart).

For the British, except the cavalry, much of the 29th
was a day of rest, devoted to repairing the wear and tear
of the strenuous days through which they had passed.

The enemy was by no means wholly inactive on the
British front. At 5 A.M. the 16th Lancers were driven out
of Jussy (10 miles south of St. Quentin) on the Crozat canal

Sketches
A, 9 & 10.
Maps 3 &
16.

---

[1] At this time, General Maunoury's Army consisted of the VII. Corps
(14th Division and 63rd Reserve Division), 55th Reserve Division (just
arrived from the Army of Lorraine), the 61st and 62nd Reserve Divisions,
a Moroccan infantry brigade, two battalions of Chasseurs Alpins and a
Provisional Cavalry Division (General Cornulier-Lucinière) formed from
Sordet's cavalry corps, the rest of this corps having gone back to Versailles
to refit. The 56th Reserve Division arrived during the evening of the
29th August.
[2] See Note II. " The Battle of Guise," at end of Chapter.

by *Jäger* and machine guns,[1] but they held their own until
the bridge over the canal had been destroyed, when they
and the rest of the 3rd Cavalry Brigade fell back slowly
to Chauny (6½ miles W.S.W. of La Fère).   Before 8 A.M.
reports came in that German infantry and guns were
crossing the Somme at Pargny and Béthencourt well away
to the north,[2] and soon after the 2nd Cavalry Brigade
lying north of Smith-Dorrien's divisions was engaged with a
force of all arms[3] advancing from the direction of Ham.
The brigade retired with deliberation to Guiscard, which it
reached at 11 A.M., and thence went southward.   To support it, the 9th Brigade of the 3rd Division took position
at Crissolles (3 miles north of Noyon), and the 4th Division
sent a battalion to Muirancourt (2 miles north of Crissolles).
By 1 P.M. it was apparent that nothing serious was going
forward : the general trend of Kluck's Army was still
decidedly to the west of south, clear of the British, and
Bülow's was engaged with the French.   At 4.15 P.M., in
accordance with   G.H.Q. instructions, General Smith-
Dorrien issued orders for a short withdrawal of his force,
to bring the whole of it south of the Oise and nearer to the
Map 16. I. Corps.   At 6 P.M. the troops began their march :—the
3rd Division to Cuts, the 5th to Carlepont, and the 4th to
the north of Carlepont, leaving a rear guard of the 10th
Brigade north of the Oise.   The main bodies of all three
divisions reached their destinations between 9 P.M. and
midnight.   The 1st and 2nd Cavalry Brigades followed
them.   Thus by midnight practically the whole of General
Smith-Dorrien's force, except the rear guard, had crossed
to the south of the Oise, and during the night the engineers
of the 5th Division blew up behind it the bridges over the
Oise and Oise canal.   The 3rd Cavalry Brigade, on its right
front, billeted for the night at Chauny, and the 4th Cavalry
Brigade five miles west of Noyon, at Dives.   This south-
eastward movement of the II. Corps reduced the gap
between it and the I. Corps to seven miles.

   Throughout this day the I. Corps enjoyed undisturbed
repose.   During the afternoon General Joffre visited Sir
John French at Compiègne, whither G.H.Q. had moved
from Noyon on the 28th.   In view of the general situation,

---

   [1] The *5th Cavalry Division* is said to have driven off a British brigade
supported by artillery (Poseck, p. 74).
   [2] The *18th Division* according to Kluck's map.
   [3] This according to Vogel was part of the *Guard Cavalry Division* of
the *I. Cavalry Corps* which was filling the gap between the *First* and
Second Armies.

he was most anxious that the B.E.F. should remain in line with the French Armies on either flank, so that he could hold the Reims—Amiens line, which passed through La Fère, and attack from it.[1]

Sir John French, however, in view of the exertions of the British Army, and its losses in officers and men, and even more in material, was equally anxious to withdraw and rest it for a few days, in order to make good defects. He did not consider that it was in condition to attack ; but it was not until 9 P.M.,[2] when it became known that the left of the French Fifth Army was unable to make progress against the Germans, that he issued orders for further retreat to the line Soissons—Compiègne, behind the Aisne. He also warned Major-General F. S. Robb, the Inspector-General of Communications, that he had decided to make " a definite and prolonged retreat due south, passing Paris " to the east or west." Sketch A. Maps 3 & 16.

Air reconnaissances made during the day showed German columns sweeping southwards over the Somme between Ham and Péronne, coming down on the French Sixth Army, and between the Oise and Somme west of Guise ; the airmen reported many villages behind the German front in flames. From the French came the information that the forces engaged with the right of the Fifth Army were the *Guard, X.* and *X. Reserve Corps*[3] and that the rest of Bülow's Army and part of Kluck's were closing on its left. Without the B.E.F. to fill the gap between his Fifth and Sixth Armies, even if their initial operations had been successful, General Joffre felt that he could not, in view of the general situation, risk fighting on the Reims—Amiens line. His orders for the retirement of the Fifth Army were issued during the night of the

---

[1] See page 217.
[2] Appendix 19.
[3] The German situation at that time was roughly as follows. The *Second* and *First Armies* formed a gigantic wedge, of which the apex lay a little south of Ham : the *Second Army*, under General von Bülow, extending from Etreaupont on the Oise nearly to Ham, with its front towards south and south-east ; the *First Army*, under General von Kluck, from Ham to Albert, with its front to the south-west. Both of these Armies were already weaker than the German Supreme Command had originally intended. The *First Army* had been obliged to leave the *III. Reserve* and *IX. Reserve Corps* to invest Antwerp ; and upon this day the *Guard Reserve Corps* of the *Second Army*, as well as the *XI. Corps* of the *Third Army* (relieved by the fall of Namur), after marching back to Aix la Chapelle, began to move by rail to the Russian front. Further, the *Second Army* had to leave the *VII. Reserve Corps* and part of the *VII. Corps* to invest Maubeuge.

29th/30th, but " owing to an error in transmission," [1] they did not reach General Lanrezac until 6 A.M. on the 30th, and did not begin to take effect until about 8.30 A.M., when, without let or hindrance, the French I. and X. Corps began to withdraw.

30TH AUGUST

Sketches A, 9 & 11. Maps 3, 4 & 17.

Sir John French had left the time of starting to be settled by his corps commanders. The I. Corps began its march southwards at 3 A.M., covered on the eastern flank by the 5th Cavalry Brigade, and on the western by the 3rd. The day was intensely hot, and in the Forest of St. Gobain the air was stifling. Since crossing the Somme, the British had passed into a rugged country of deep woodlands, steep hills, narrow valleys and dusty roads. Severe gradients and crowds of refugees multiplied checks on the way. Such was the exhaustion of the men that it was necessary to curtail the march, and the 1st Division was halted for the night some eight miles north of Soissons, with its head at Allemant, with the 2nd Division a little to the south-west of it about Pasly. In the evening alarming reports were received by General Haig from the French Fifth Army, by telephone from Laon, stating that a large force of German cavalry was advancing in the direction of Noyon towards the south-west of Laon, that is, between Laon and Soissons. General Lanrezac made repeated appeals to the I. Corps to move out north-eastwards from Soissons to fill the gap and protect the left of his Army. As neither the Cavalry Division nor the I. Corps rear guards had seen or heard of any enemy cavalry in the area mentioned, or east of the Oise, until the evening, when enemy parties were seen on the heights west of Soissons, no attention was paid to the appeals.[2] There was practically no interference from the enemy on this day. The rear guard of the Cavalry Division was slightly engaged by Uhlans at 8 A.M., and two parties of engineers were fired on whilst engaged in destroying the bridges over the Oise, with the result that the bridge at Bailly was left undemolished.[3]

[1] F.O.A., i. (ii.), p. 517.
[2] " Poseck " shows that the German *I. Cavalry Corps* reached Noyon on the night of the 30th ; the bridges were down and its two divisions did no more than secure a bridgehead. The *II. Cavalry Corps* was well west of the *I.*
[3] A second attempt was made to destroy this bridge after dark ; but Major J. B. Barstow and the men of his party were killed by a volley at about fifteen yards' range, fired, according to Vogel, by the cyclists of the

The II. Corps, together with the 4th Division and the 30 Aug.
19th Brigade—the two latter from this day constituted 1914.
the III. Corps under Lieut.-General W. P. Pulteney—after
a few hours' rest on conclusion of its night march, continued its movement south-east, and halted on the Aisne
about Attichy, the 10th Brigade having been skilfully withdrawn without mishap by Br.-General Haldane from its
rear-guard position beyond the Oise. The 5th and 3rd
Cavalry Brigades lay for the night at Vauxaillon, between
the 1st and 2nd Divisions, and at Fontenoy on the Aisne,
between the I. and II. Corps, respectively ; the 1st, 2nd and
4th Cavalry Brigades were reunited under the hand of the
divisional commander, on the left of the Army, round
Compiègne.[1] The gap between the two wings of the B.E.F.
was now reduced to six miles.

General Lanrezac had little difficulty in carrying out his
retirement, though the Germans, apparently emboldened
by news from their aviators that the French were withdrawing, looked for a time as if they meant to continue

Guard Jäger. The suspension bridge over the Oise at Pontoise (3 miles
south-east of Noyon) in the II. Corps area was not rendered unserviceable at the first attempt to destroy it. About 8 A.M. on the 30th a motor
cyclist, Lieut. R. R. F. West (Intelligence Corps), brought the officer
commanding 59th Field Company R.E. (5th Division) a private note from
Major M. P. Buckle, D.S.O., second in command of 1/R. West Kent (13th
Brigade)—killed in action 27th Oct. 1914—informing him that the bridge
was still passable, and asking if anything could be done. Lieut. J. A. C.
Pennycuick, R.E., immediately volunteered to return with Lieut. West.
The motor bicycle was loaded up with a box of 14 guncotton slabs, and
Lieut. Pennycuick sat on top, his pockets filled with fuze, detonators and
primers. The two officers then rode back the eight miles, passing first
infantry and then through the cavalry rear guard. They climbed up one
of the suspension-cables and placed 13 slabs on the cables on top of the
pier, the fourteenth falling into the river. The first detonator failed, only
powdering the primer ; a second attempt was made and was successful :
the top of the pier was blown off and the cables cut, and the bridge
crashed down into the river. No enemy appeared during the operation,
and the two officers returned safely, after breakfasting at a farm *en route.*
They both received the Distinguished Service Order.

Throughout the retreat there was considerable confusion with regard
to the responsibility for the demolition of bridges, the full story of which
will be found in Major-General Sir R. U. H. Buckland's articles in the
" Royal Engineers Journal " 1932, " Demolitions at Mons and during the
Retreat 1914." Thus, near Guise a French officer had orders to destroy
all the bridges, whilst the 3rd Brigade was instructed to allow no one to
touch them ; near St. Simon the divisional field engineers prepared the
bridges for demolition, handed them over to the cavalry, who transferred
them to the French. See Chapter XIII with regard to difficulties at
Lagny. So far as British responsibility was concerned, each sector of
river was divided between the two, and later three, corps. In addition to
damaging bridges the R.E. made blocks across the roads at suitable places.

[1] See page 247.

the attack, particularly on his left wing ; but by noon the movement was well under way, and the Germans seemed content to let him go.[1]

General Maunoury's Army had also received orders to retire, and had fallen back, after sharp fighting, from the Avre south-westward to a line from Estrées St. Denis (where his right was within five miles of the British at Compiègne) to Quiry.   Kluck had shown signs of a change of direction, for his left or inner wing had wheeled nearly due south, though his right was still, for the present, moving south-west upon Amiens.   From the air nothing could be seen of the *VII. Corps* to the south of Ham, where it was expected (it is now known it was near St. Quentin, the *14th Division* having been sent back to help the *X. Reserve Corps*), and it was surmised that it was concealed ; but the columns of the *6th* and *5th Divisions* marching *south* on Roye, and the *7th* on Rozières, were observed and reported. This seemed to indicate, though as yet the movement was too imperfectly developed to make it certain, that Kluck either considered Maunoury's force to be for the moment powerless for any offensive action, or that he believed himself to have gained the position that he desired for the envelopment of the western flank of the Allied Army. The British Army he reckoned, as the German official bulletins testify, to have been thoroughly beaten on the 26th and following days ; and, as from a captured letter he heard of Sir John French's anxiety to give it rest,[2] his appreciation in this respect was less faulty than it may since have seemed.   If Maunoury's force could also be dismissed as negligible, there was nothing to hinder Kluck from wheeling south-east against the open left flank of the French Fifth Army, annihilating it in conjunction with Bülow, and then rolling up the French line from west to east.[3]

On the morning of the 30th General Joffre, considering that the defence of Amiens and the line of the Somme had ceased to be of any utility in view of the retirement of the left wing, ordered General d'Amade to withdraw his Territorial divisions on Rouen and reconstitute them on the left bank of the Seine.   To General Maunoury's enquiry, what would now be his mission and the direction of his retreat, the

---

[1] The *Second Army* was given a rest day on the 31st (Bülow, p. 44, Kluck, p. 76).
[2] Kluck, p. 81.
[3] Bülow had called upon Kluck for this very purpose. See page 250.

French Commander-in-Chief replied : " Your general direc- 30 Aug. " tion of retreat is on Paris. Do not let yourself be caught 1914. " and held. Take as your first position of retirement the " one which you propose," which was Compiègne—St. Just. He placed Sordet's cavalry corps under the Sixth Army. Later in the day General Maunoury reported that on the 31st he proposed to fall back to the line Verberie (on the Oise)—Clermont—Beauvais (35 miles west of Compiègne), which was approved of by G.Q.G.[1]

On a telephone request from General Joffre, conveyed to him before 7 A.M. on the 30th by the French Mission, Sir John French agreed to stay the retreat of his troops and continue to fill the gap between the Fifth and Sixth Armies, of which the B.E.F. was a day's march ahead. In thanking the British Commander-in-Chief for this assistance, General Joffre informed him of the order for retirement behind the Serre (which flows into the Oise at La Fère) which he had given to the Fifth Army, and told him of his further intentions in these terms :—

" I have in view the general retirement of the forces, " avoiding any decisive action, so as to hold out (*durer*) as " long as possible. But in the course of these movements, " it will be of the greatest importance that the British Army " keeps in constant liaison with the Fifth Army, so as to be " able to profit by favourable opportunities and administer " to the enemy another severe lesson like that of yesterday."

At noon, however, Sir John French gave Colonel Huguet a message, written by his own hand, to be telegraphed to General Joffre. In this he said that " the new plan of " retreat having been explained to me, I consider it ab- " solutely necessary to inform you that the British Army " will not be in a state to take its place in the line for ten " days. I am short of men and guns to replace losses " which I have not been able to ascertain exactly owing " to the uninterrupted retreat under the protection of " fighting rear guards. You will understand in these " circumstances that I cannot comply with your request " to fill the gap between the Fifth and Sixth Armies, that " is to say, on the line Soissons—Compiègne." [2]

---

[1] F.O.A., i. (ii.) pp. 516-7.
[2] Neither the Field-Marshal nor any of his chief advisers had been near the fighting troops since the 27th, and he seems to have been unaware of the complete recovery of the 3rd, 4th and 5th Divisions from the hard day of Le Cateau. Only the 5th Division had suffered any important loss of guns ; the I. Corps had hardly been engaged, and General Haig had indicated its state by his readiness to co-operate with the French at Guise.

Sir John French proposed to retire " westwards " behind the Seine, to an area just west of Paris ; [1] but it was pointed out to him by the French General Staff that such a march would cross the communications of the Sixth Army. He therefore agreed, at General Joffre's suggestion, to retire in the first instance by the east of Paris, behind the Marne between Meaux and Neuilly, so that, if necessary, he could pursue his retirement westwards by the south of the capital. At the same time, the French Commander-in-Chief informed his Government of Sir John French's state of mind.

At 5.15 P.M. G.H.Q. issued amended orders [2] for the B.E.F. to move south, the I. Corps and 5th Cavalry Brigade to the area about Villers Cottérêts ; the II. Corps, on the west of the I. Corps, to the area Feigneux—Béthisy St. Martin—Crépy en Valois ; the III. Corps further to the north-west, to the area St. Sauveur—Verberie; and the Cavalry Division, most westerly of all, to the line of the Oise beyond Verberie. General Allenby was subsequently informed that, as the French had closed in on the British left, he could use the area between the III. Corps and the river.

31ST AUGUST

Sketches A & 11. Maps 3, 4 & 18.

On the 31st, which saw the completion of the German victory at Tannenberg, the British accordingly resumed their march under the same trying conditions of dust, heat and thirst as on the previous day. The I. Corps opened the operations with the passage of the Aisne in two columns, at Soissons and just west of it. The transport was often in difficulties, owing to the steep gradients of the roads to the south of the river, and the scarcity of water everywhere was a great trial to both men and horses. Once again the infantry was wholly untroubled by the enemy— the men of the 6th Brigade actually had time for a bathe in the Aisne—and the cavalry rear guards, which covered the march, were never really pressed. The 3rd Cavalry Brigade had to keep some Uhlans at a distance when crossing the Aisne 6 miles west of Soissons at Fontenoy ; and heads of German columns were reported at Noyon

---

[1] Maps of the area from Paris westward to St. Nazaire were ordered by the Sub-Chief of the General Staff to be procured for issue to the troops. See also " Annals of an Active Life " (p. 206), by General Sir Nevil Macready, who was at the time Adjutant-General to the B.E.F.

[2] Appendix 20.

and south of it on the road to Compiègne.[1]   In this quarter, 31 Aug. west of the Oise, the 3rd Hussars (4th Cavalry Brigade) 1914. were in touch with hostile patrols from daybreak onward, the enemy's force gradually increasing until it drew the whole regiment into action.   The fight was, however, broken off without difficulty, and at noon, the 3rd Hussars retired, having suffered trifling loss and killed a good many troopers of the German *3rd Hussars*—divisional cavalry of the German *III. Corps*—which, by a curious coincidence, were opposed to them.

The heat of the day, the difficulty of the country and the exhaustion of the troops, however, compelled the greater part of the Army to stop short of their intended destinations.   The I. Corps halted for the night on the Map 18. northern, instead of on the western side, of the Forest of Villers Cottérêts, midway between it and the river Aisne :   1st Division around Missy, 2nd Division around Laversine.   The left of the French Fifth Army, which was continuing its retreat, was near Vauxaillon, 12 miles to the north.

The II. Corps halted at Coyolles, south-west of Villers Cottérêts, and at Crépy en Valois :   5th Division on the east, 3rd Division on the west.

The III. Corps, after a flank march through the Forest of Compiègne, reached its allotted area, at the south-western corner of the forest about Verberie, but at a late hour, some units not taking up their billets before 10 P.M.   The corps was separated by a gap of some five miles from the nearest troops of the II. Corps at Crépy, but in touch with the French on its left, some of the Sixth Army troops actually being in Verberie.

The 5th and 3rd Cavalry Brigades halted in the same area as the I. Corps.   Of the other brigades, the 4th was with the III. Corps at Verberie, and the 2nd west of it at Chevrières, in touch with the French Sixth Army, which, on this evening, reached the Chevrières—Beauvais line. The 1st Cavalry Brigade and L Battery R.H.A. on the western flank of the Army had moved out soon after dawn on the 31st from Compiègne on the road towards Amiens, and had remained halted for a considerable time, on the watch for German troops advancing in that quarter. Seeing no sign of any, the brigade, after a wide sweep

---

[1] The German *III. Corps* crossed the Oise in two columns at Noyon and Ribécourt, and Marwitz's cavalry crossed near Compiègne (see Kluck's map).

westward, recrossed the Oise to Verberie, and made its
way to Néry, there to form a link—though it could not fill
up the gap—between the II. and III. Corps. It did not
reach its destination until dusk, and L Battery did not
join it until half an hour later.

Aerial reconnaissance upon this day confirmed the fact
that Kluck had reached the limit of his western advance,
and was wheeling south-eastward, covering his southern
flank with his cavalry.[1] The columns of the *18th, 6th, 5th,
7th, 8th, 3rd* and *4th Divisions* marching towards the Oise
were reported, the heads of the first three close to it, and
at 1 P.M. it was noticed that cavalry was moving south-
east from the river at Thourotte, and that the road and
railway bridges at Compiègne were blown up. At least
two cavalry divisions were known to have reached the
Oise during the afternoon of the 31st ; and it appeared
that three actually crossed the river between Noyon and
Compiègne, two of which were reported to be moving east
upon Vauxaillon, while the third was passing through
Bailly (8 miles north-east of Compiègne) at 2.30 P.M.[2] The
capture of a trooper of the German *8th Hussars*, by the
2/Royal Welch Fusiliers after a brush with a German patrol
towards dusk to the north-west of Verberie, seemed to
indicate the presence of the German *4th Cavalry Division*
in this quarter. A heavy German column, reckoned to be
ten thousand strong, was also reported to have reached
Gournay (about eight miles north-west of Compiègne) at
3 P.M., and to be moving south.[3] A captured order issued
to the *8th Division* of the German *IV. Corps* from Beau-
court (14 miles south-east of Amiens) at 6.45 A.M. on the
31st, also revealed the project which was in Kluck's mind
at the time. The order gave the information that the
French troops (Maunoury's) on the Avre had been defeated
on the 29th and had withdrawn ; that the British were
retreating south-eastward (*sic*) ; and that Bülow had

[1] For the German movements see Note I. at end of Chapter.
[2] According to Kluck, on the 31st Marwitz's three cavalry divisions
(*2nd, 4th* and *9th*) crossed the Oise at Thourotte, and thence marched
through the Forest of Laigue to Attichy on the Aisne, but Poseck (p. 76
and map) puts them at night about six miles south of Compiègne.
Richthofen's two divisions (*Guard* and *5th*) reached Noyon on the 30th,
and moved on the 31st across the British front via Bailly and Ribécourt
to Vauxaillon, actually between the British and the left of the French
Fifth Army. General Lanrezac's fears of the previous day had materialized,
but the German cavalry did not persevere. The two divisions (*Guard* and
5th) passed the night north of Soissons, and next day remained just north
of the town.
[3] These are now known to have been French troops.

defeated at Guise the French Fifth Army, large bodies of 31 Aug. which were retiring through La Fère; and it set forth 1914. that the task of the German *First Army* was to cut off the retreat of that Army. It concluded: "Again, therefore, " we must call upon the troops for forced marches." [1]

However, at the moment, the one thing clear to Sir John French was that the German *First Army*, which had prac-tically left the British Army alone since the 26th, was again closing in upon it in great force. During the day several telegrams passed between him and the Secretary of State for War and between G.Q.G. and G.H.Q. Lord Kitchener's communications clearly showed the surprise and consterna-tion of the Government at the course which the British Commander-in-Chief was taking in withdrawing the B.E.F. from the fighting line, and their fear of its effect on the French. The latter had replied that he had already been left several times in the lurch by his Allies, that if there was a gap in the line it was their affair, and that the force under his command in its present condition could hardly withstand a strong attack from even one German corps : General Joffre had informed him in writing that, according to reports received, the Germans were withdrawing numer-ous troops (*XI.* and *Guard Reserve Corps*) from France for transfer to the Eastern Front, and that General Lanrezac's attack at Guise on the 29th had been a real check for the German *Second Army*, as Bülow's delay in the resumption of his advance was demonstrating. General Joffre had further stated that the Fifth and Sixth Armies now had instructions not to yield ground except under pressure ; but that they could not of course be expected to stand if there was a gap between them. " I earnestly request " Field-Marshal French," he wrote, " not to withdraw the " British Army until we are compelled to give ground, and " at least to leave rear guards, so as not to give the enemy " the clear impression of a retreat and of a gap between the " Fifth and Sixth Armies."

In spite of these suggestions and requests, at 8.50 P.M. Sir John French issued orders for the retreat to be con-tinued on the morrow.[2]

---

[1] Hauptmann Bloem relates that the three battalion commanders of his regiment made a protest to the regimental commander with regard to the excessive marching and were met by the brief reply "Sweat saves blood."

[2] Appendix 21.

NOTE I

MOVEMENTS OF THE GERMAN *FIRST* AND *SECOND ARMIES*
29TH TO 31ST AUGUST

Sketch 10.
Maps 16,
17 & 18.

The movements of the German right wing on the 30th and 31st August had a decisive effect on the campaign. Instead of pursuing his march towards the lower Seine, as ordered by O.H.L. on the 28th, and making a wide sweep which might have caught in it General Maunoury's Army and the B.E.F., Kluck wheeled his Army south-eastwards towards the Oise, in response to Bülow's request that he should help him to exploit the supposed success in the Battle of Guise and finish off the French Fifth Army. The messages are of interest.

Kluck says : " At 5.55 P.M. on 30th a wireless message (which was " also read at O.H.L.) was received from *Second Army* Headquarters : " ' Enemy decisively beaten to-day ; strong forces retiring on La " ' Fère. The British, who were barring the Oise south-west of La " ' Fère, are also retreating, some in a southerly, some in a south- " ' easterly direction.' This was followed by a second message at " 6.30 P.M. ' To gain the full advantages of the victory a wheel " ' inwards of the *First Army*, pivoted on Chauny, towards the line " ' La Fère—Laon is highly desirable.' "

Bülow does not give these messages, but says that on the 29th " The *First Army* was asked by wireless to support the *Second Army* " on the 30th, and at 7.5 P.M. on the 30th the following information " was received from the *First Army* : ' Right wing of *First Army* " ' has thrown the enemy over the Avre. Will advance to-morrow " ' against the Oise section Compiègne—Chauny.' " Kluck likewise does not give this message, but admits that " during the evening of " the 30th August O.H.L. was informed that the *First Army* had " wheeled round towards the Oise and would advance on the 31st " by Compiègne and Noyon to exploit the success of the *Second* " *Army*." [1]

The German Supreme Command concurred in the proposed moves, and at 9.10 despatched to the *First* and *Second Armies* the following message : " *Third Army* is wheeling south towards the Aisne, " attacking against Rethel—Semuy, and will pursue in a southerly " direction. The movements begun by the *First* and *Second Armies* " are in accordance with the intention of O.H.L." The lower Seine ceased therefore to be the objective of the *First* Army.[2] All appeared to be going well, except that the *Sixth* and *Seventh Armies* were not making much progress towards the Moselle, as instructed in the " General Directions " issued by O.H.L. on the 28th. Crown Prince Rupprecht reported " that there were still opposite him " strong French forces, of whom reports came in at one moment " that they were retiring, at another that they were attacking." [3] A deadlock on the eastern frontier, provided the *Sixth* and *Seventh*

[1] German critics consider that instead of taking his whole Army to exploit Bülow's supposed success, Kluck should have at least sent one corps and some cavalry to follow up and keep touch with the British, if not with the French whom he had " thrown over the Avre."

[2] G.O.A., iii. p. 187.

[3] G.O.A., iii. p. 188.

THE GERMAN ADVANCE, 17 AUGUST – 5 SEPTEMBER, 1914.

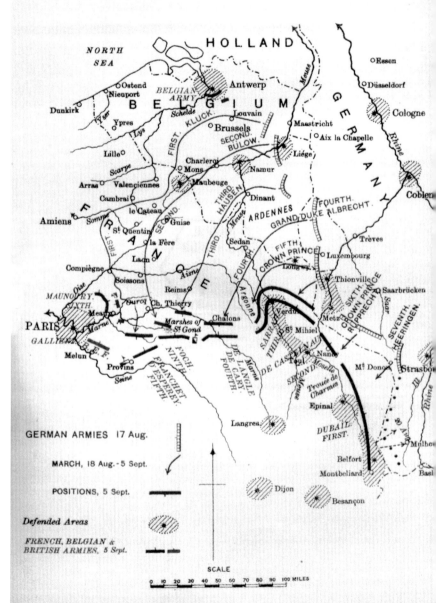

NORTH SEA

HOLLAND

BELGIUM

GERMANY

FRANCE

Essen
Düsseldorf
Cologne
Maastricht
Aix la Chapelle
Liége
Coblen
Trèves
Luxembourg
Longwy
Thionville
Saarbrücken
Metz
Mt Donon
Strasbo
Mulhou
Basl

Ostend
Nieuport
Dunkirk
Ypres
Lille
Arras
Valenciennes
Cambrai
Amiens
le Cateau
St Quentin
la Fère
Laon
Compiègne
Soissons
Ourcq
Meaux
PARIS
GALLIENI.
Melun
Provins

Antwerp
BELGIAN ARMY
Louvain
Brussels
Charleroi
Mons
Maubeuge
Namur
Dinant
Sedan

FIRST. KLUCK.
SECOND. BÜLOW.
THIRD HAUSEN.
FOURTH. GRAND DUKE ALBRECHT.
FIFTH. CROWN PRINCE.
SIXTH CROWN PRINCE RUPPRECHT.
SEVENTH. HEERINGEN.

Schelde
Lys
Scarpe
Somme
Oise
Aisne
Reims
Ch. Thierry
Marne
Marshes of St Gond
Chalons
Verdun
St Mihiel
Nancy
Toul
Epinal
Langres
DUBAIL FIRST.
Belfort
Montbeliard
Dijon
Besançon

ARDENNES

MAUNOURY. SIXTH.
B.E.F.
FOCH. NINTH.
FRANCHET D'ESPEREY. FIFTH.
FOURTH.
DE LANGLE DE CARY.
DE CASTELNAU. SECOND.
SARRAIL. THIRD.

Meuse
Moselle
Argonne
Seine

Trouée de Charmes

GERMAN ARMIES 17 Aug.

MARCH, 18 Aug. - 5 Sept.

POSITIONS, 5 Sept.

Defended Areas

FRENCH, BELGIAN &
BRITISH ARMIES, 5 Sept.

SCALE

0 10 20 30 40 50 60 70 80 90 100 MILES

Armies held an equal number of French there, did not, however, 29-31 Aug.
endanger, indeed it might actually favour, the accomplishment of the 1914.
main aim of the Schlieffen Plan without the First Army having to
pass west and south of the capital. But the Supreme Command
continued to believe that the time for the final stage of the Schlieffen
Plan, a complete " Cannæ " in the open field, had arrived, and on
the 30th August their representative, Major Bauer, informed Crown
Prince Rupprecht of the rapid progress of the right wing, but that
" serious resistance might still be anticipated between Paris and
" the eastern fortresses : of the *Sixth Army* it was therefore expected
" that it would fall on the enemy's flank in the gap between Epinal
" and Toul, and so bring about a decision." [1]
    Fortunately Kluck had wasted time by his thrust in the air west-
wards after Le Cateau, and his assistance to Bülow came too late.
The leading corps of the German *First Army*, the *IX.* and *III.*,
managed to cross the Oise between Chauny and Bailly on the 31st
and reached the line Vezaponin—Vic—Attichy, 12 miles beyond,
with the *II. Cavalry Corps* on their right front ; the *IV.* and *II.*
swung round behind them to the line Mareuil—Tricot—Maignelay,
west and abreast of Noyon, with the *IV. Reserve* still further in
rear, in and south of Amiens. Thus, on that day, German corps
were moving south-eastwards north of the Aisne, whilst the B.E.F.
was marching more or less south-westwards on the other side of
that river. Kluck, therefore, thinking by " extraordinary forced
" marches " to outflank the Allies,[2] was actually advancing into the
net that Joffre had in preparation for him.[3]
    The German *Second Army* rested on the 31st after its battle at
Guise on the previous two days, as already related.[4]

    [1] Bavarian O.A., ii. p. 584. G.O.A., iii. p. 285.
    [2] Kuhl's " Marne," p. 104.
    [3] The following description of General Kluck at Lassigny (12 miles
north of Compiègne) on the 30th August 1914, by M. Albert Fabre,
Conseiller à la Cour d'appel de Paris (given in M. Hanotaux's " Histoire
illustrée de la Guerre de 1914," viii. p. 158), seems worthy of quotation.
The general had déjeuner at M. Fabre's villa and gave him a " safeguard "
for the house signed by his own hand.
    " Bientôt, un mouvement se produisit parmi les officiers qui se rangèrent
" devant la porte de la propriété. Une automobile s'arrêta. Un officier
" d'allure impressionnante et arrogante en descendit. Il s'avança seul
" jusqu'au milieu du terre-plein de la villa. Il était grand, majestueux, il
" avait le visage rasé et ravagé, les traits durs, le regard effrayant. Il tenait,
" à la main droite, un fusil de soldat ; sa main gauche était appuyée sur la
" crosse d'un revolver d'ordonnance. Il fit plusieurs tours sur lui-même
" en frappant le sol de la crosse de son fusil et s'arrêta dans une pose
" théâtrale. Personne ne semblait oser l'approcher. Le personnage avait
" l'air véritablement terrible. J'eus la vision d'Attila. C'était le trop
" fameux von Kluck."
    [4] Hauptmann Brinckmann of the *Second Army* staff came over and
reported to the *First Army* that the *Second Army* " was exhausted by the
" Battle of Guise and unable to pursue " (Kuhl's " Marne," p. 109). Bülow
says : " On the 31st the troops of the *Second Army* were placed in positions
" of readiness for the attack on La Fère " (p. 44).

NOTE II

THE BATTLE OF GUISE [1]

(Called by the Germans, St. Quentin)

29TH–30TH AUGUST 1914

As early as the 24th August, after the French defeats in the Battles of the Frontier, General Joffre had proposed to make a counter-attack " in the centre " with the Fifth Army,[2] which, owing to the skilful leading of General Lanrezac, was still intact and unshaken. On the night of the 25th/26th, he postponed any action until he " had constituted on the left by the junction of the Fourth, " Fifth and British Armies, and forces drawn from the east, a mass " capable of resuming the offensive." [3] It was the intention of General Lanrezac himself to order a counter-attack directly he was clear of the enclosed and broken country of the Avesnes region, in which " his intact artillery could not effectively support his infantry."

Map 14. During the 27th his four corps, in line, crossed the Oise and its tributary, the Thon, his right being 25 miles east of Guise, and Valabrègue's group of two Reserve divisions, on his left, covering the passages near Guise. General Joffre, by telephone message, now urged the Fifth Army to take action, as the ground was suitable, adding, " you need not pay attention to what the British do on your " left."

Map 15. For the 28th, therefore, General Lanrezac ordered his corps " to " close on the left, so as to face north-west and be in position to " attack any enemy columns which cross the Oise." No sooner had these instructions been issued than he received from G.Q.G. (timed 10.10 P.M., date of receipt not stated), the following order :
" From information received, it appears that parts of the " German VII. and IX. Corps, forming part of the Second Army, " opposed to you, have been left before Maubeuge. [Actually these " corps had just been relieved by the VII. Reserve Corps.] It is " therefore possible to come to the help of the British Army by acting " against the enemy forces [X. Reserve, VII. and half IX. Corps] " which are advancing against it west of the Oise. You will in " consequence send your left to-morrow between the Oise and St. " Quentin to attack any enemy force marching against the British " Army."

At 9 A.M. on the 28th General Joffre himself visited General Lanrezac's advanced headquarters at Marle (13 miles south-east of Guise), and gave him the following written order :
" The Fifth Army will attack as soon as possible the enemy " forces which advanced yesterday against the British Army. It " will cover its right with the minimum of forces, sending recon- " naissances to a great distance on that flank."

---

[1] See the French and German Official Accounts, the two official monographs, " Schlacht bei St. Quentin," I. and II., General Lanrezac's " Le Plan de Campagne française," and General Rouquerol's " Bataille de Guise."

[2] " Joffre et la Marne," p. 64, by Commandant Muller (General Joffre's officier d'ordonnance).

[3] F.O.A., i. (ii.) p. 21 *et seq.*

The Fifth Army, therefore, made some modifications in the des- 29-30 Aug.
tinations allotted to its corps.   1014.
Near Guise the Oise, running in a large valley cut into the general Sketch 8.
plain of northern France, makes a nearly right-angled bend : by
Lanrezac's orders, under cover of the X. Corps facing northwards
behind the east and west course of the Oise, the III. and XVIII.
Corps were to continue the march westwards on the 29th, and,
with Valabrègue's Reserve divisions, cross the lower, north and
south, reach of the river towards St. Quentin to fall on the flank of
the German forces moving west of the river.   The I. Corps and 4th
Cavalry Division were to follow in reserve, the former well to the
south.
     On the evening of the 28th the advanced guards of the left wing
of the German *Second Army* (the *Guard* and *X. Corps*) gained possession of the bridges of the upper reach of the Oise, General von
Bülow being under the impression that he had in front of him there
only weak French and British rear guards. His right wing (*X.
Reserve* and *VII. Corps*) was nearly twenty miles ahead of his left,
south of St. Quentin, and aligned facing south-west, abreast of
Kluck's Army.   Thus there were two distinct battles on the 29th
August, fought on different sides of the Oise.
     In the thick mist of the early morning of that day the columns
of the French X. Corps, moving westwards as covering force, came
into collision with the heads of the two German corps pushing southwards uphill from the river to the plateau above, combats taking
place in the various villages where the roads, on which both sides
were marching, crossed.   Thus what had occurred in the original
advance of the French Third and Fourth Armies ten days earlier
was now reversed, the German columns blundering head-on into the
broadside of French columns crossing their front.
     The X. Corps, supported as the day went on by the artillery and
part of the 5th Division of the III. Corps, and later by the I. Corps,
though at first in some difficulty, eventually held its own, and at
night the French made a slight general advance, which sent the
German *Guard* and *X. Corps* back towards the Oise, and some
portions of them over it : the commander of the *Guard Corps* being
authorized, " after long and earnest discussion, to withdraw behind
" the Oise."   Actually, only Hutier's *1st Guard Division* on the
eastern flank appears to have recrossed.
     On the western wing, on the other battlefield, the advance of
the heads of the French III. and XVIII. Corps and Valabrègue's
Group equally came as a complete surprise to Bülow's scattered
right wing, their camp fires of the previous night having been mistaken by the Germans for those of their own left wing.   The G.O.C.
X. Reserve Corps and five of his staff actually motored up to a village
occupied by the French, and were all wounded.   Had the British
I. Corps been permitted by Sir John French to take part in the
battle, if only by fire on the German front whilst the French continued their flank attack, an important defeat might have been
administered to the *Second Army*.   In view, however, of the German
advance against the French right wing, and the inaction of the British,
the movement of the left wing could not be persisted in.   At 11 A.M.
the G.O.C. III. Corps reported that, his 5th Division having faced
north to assist the X. Corps in warding off the flank attack, he had
suspended the passage of any more of the 6th Division across the

lower reach of the Oise ; and the G.O.C. XVIII. Corps thereupon halted his division, which, after holding on all day, recrossed the Map 16. river at night, the Reserve divisions having retired a little earlier.

For the 30th, General Lanrezac ordered his left wing to hold the line of the Oise, whilst the III., I. and X. Corps drove into the river what Germans remained south of the upper reach.   In view, however, of the dangerous position of his Army, with both its flanks exposed and no hope of assistance on either side, General Lanrezac telephoned to G.Q.G. for further instructions, pointing out that if he delayed withdrawal his troops ran the risk of being surrounded. In the absence of General Joffre, General Belin, his Chief of the Staff, would give no orders ; but at 10 P.M. a ciphered telegram was despatched to General Lanrezac :—

" The effect of the attack of the Fifth Army having made itself " felt and disengaged in part the Sixth Army [in action that day " with Kluck], the Fifth Army will take measures to break off the " battle and retire behind the Serre.   The breaking-off should take " place before daylight."   Unfortunately, according to the French Official Account, this telegram went astray, and the first General Lanrezac heard of its contents was at 7 A.M. on the 30th, when it was sent to him over the telephone.

Fortunately the Germans had received too severe a blow for this curious delay to be of any consequence.   Bülow ordered the X. and *Guard Corps* to renew the attack on the 30th, but General von Emmich, commanding the former, refused to advance, fearing that the French were about to fall upon him : it was not until about 2 P.M. that his *19th Division* moved, and 4.30 P.M. before the *20th Division* did so.   It is not clear from German accounts what the *Guard Corps* did ; but it did not renew the attack, and seems to have taken up a flank position alarmed by the appearance of the French 51st Reserve Division, which had come up from the east to Voulpaix on the right of the Fifth Army.

Map 17.   The corps of the Fifth Army therefore retired practically unnoticed and unhindered.   About 1.50 P.M. a German aeroplane discovered that French columns were streaming away.   At 3.45 Bülow informed his Army of its victory, and ordered that the enemy should be pursued by " artillery fire and infantry detachments," but that on the 31st the Army would " halt and rest."   In commenting on the order for a rest day instead of a general pursuit, the German official monograph defends Bülow's consideration for his troops, recalling that after the Battle of St. Quentin in January 1871 General von Goeben had not ordered a pursuit.   The weather conditions and length of daylight were, however, somewhat dissimilar on the two occasions.

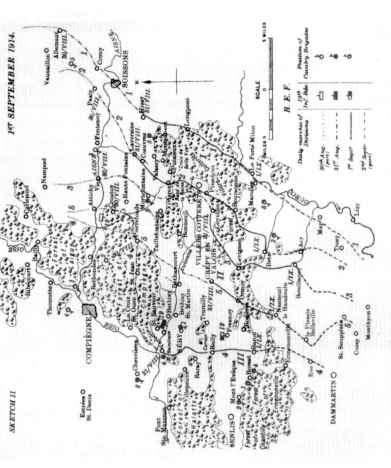

SKETCH 11.

1ST SEPTEMBER 1914.

B.E.F.

Daily marches of Divisions

30th Aug. (part)

31st Aug.

1st Septr.

2nd Septr. (part)

In./ Bde.

Position of Cavalry Brigades

SCALE

5 MILES

Ordnance Survey, 1924.

CHAPTER XII

THE RETREAT (*continued*)

1ST SEPTEMBER

NÉRY, CRÉPY EN VALOIS AND VILLERS COTTÉRÊTS

(Sketches A, 9, 10 & 11 ; Maps 4, 19 & 20)

THE FIGHT AT NÉRY

G.H.Q. operation orders [1] sent out at 8.50 P.M. on the Sketches 31st August from Dammartin en Goele gave the information 9 & 11. that the enemy appeared to have completed his westerly Maps 4 movement and to be wheeling to the south, and that large & 19. columns were advancing in a general south or south-easterly direction on Noyon—Compiègne, covered by at least two cavalry divisions which had reached the Oise that afternoon. The following movements towards the south-west, marches of some ten to fourteen miles, if all divisions reached their destinations on the 31st, were ordered to be carried out next day :

The I. Corps to move to the area La Ferté Milon—Betz.
The II. Corps to Betz—Nanteuil.
The III. Corps to Nanteuil—Baron.
The Cavalry Division to Baron—Mont l'Évêque.

Special instructions were given that the rear guard of the III. Corps was to reach a line drawn east and west through Néry by 6 A.M. ; but, owing to the lateness of the hour at which many units arrived at their billets, General Pulteney was obliged to represent that this was impossible. In obedience to the spirit of the order, however, he reported that the transport of his corps would move off at 1 A.M.

The night passed quietly, with rather less than the usual disturbances and alarms, except those occasioned by the French in and near Verberie disappearing about mid-

---

[1] Appendix 21.

night without a word of explanation. There was no indication that there would be contact with the enemy in the early morning. Several small actions, however, took place on the 1st September. They might be dismissed in a few words, were it not that they show that the British were more than able to hold their own when fortune brought them to grips with the enemy ; whilst the practical destruction, with loss of its guns, of the German *4th Cavalry Division* had important results on the conditions under which the Battle of the Marne opened a week later.

Dawn broke with dense mist, presaging another day of excessive heat. The 1st Cavalry Brigade and L Battery at Néry, bivouacking between the widely separated 5th and 4th Divisions, had been ordered to be ready to resume their march at 4.30 A.M., but, since it was impossible to see anything two hundred yards away, this was countermanded. The men were busy preparing their breakfasts and watering their horses when, at 5.30 A.M., the mist being as thick as ever, a patrol of the 11th Hussars returned with the report that it had ridden into a body of German cavalry in the fog, and had been hunted back to Néry. Immediately afterwards high-explosive shells burst over the village, and there was a roar of guns, machine guns and rifle fire from the ground, little more than six hundred yards distant, which overlooks the eastern side of the village. The horses of the Bays took fright and galloped down the road to the north. The battery was in mass, with the horses hooked in and poles down ; men and horses began to fall at once under German fire, and the battery commander was knocked over and temporarily disabled whilst hurrying back from brigade headquarters. In his absence, Captain E. K. Bradbury, with the help of the other officers and of such men as were not busy with the horses, unlimbered three guns and man-handled them round to reply to the German batteries which were taking them in flank. One gun was almost instantly put out of action by a direct hit. The other two opened fire, but had hardly done so before the gun under Lieut. J. Giffard was silenced, he and every man of his detachment being killed or wounded.

The remaining two subalterns now joined Captain Bradbury at the third gun, and immediately afterwards Lieut. J. D. Campbell was killed, but the one gun remained in action against the German twelve with good effect. In vain the enemy concentrated his fire on it ; he could not silence it. Meantime, the three cavalry regiments had manned the eastern face of the village, secured the northern and southern exits and opened fire, particularly with their machine guns. The German cavalrymen pushed their way dismounted to within five hundred yards of the village, but no nearer. Towards 6 A.M. Br.-General Briggs, after strengthening his own right, ordered two squadrons of the 5th Dragoon Guards, his last remaining reserve, to attack the enemy's right flank. They accordingly galloped northwards and then wheeling to the east, dismounted and pushed in to close range. Whilst the 1st Cavalry Brigade was thus holding the German *4th Cavalry Division*, there came a response to Br.-General Briggs's call for assistance. Just as the mist began to thin in the morning sun, the 4th Cavalry Brigade and I Battery arrived on the scene from St. Vaast on the north-west, followed by a composite battalion of the Warwickshire and Dublin Fusiliers of the 10th Brigade from Verberie in the same direction, and the 1/Middlesex from Saintines in the north. Four guns of I Battery unlimbered two thousand yards south-west of the German position. As they did so, the fire of L Battery ceased ; and for good reason. For some time its fire had been desultory ; Lieut. L. F. H. Mundy had been several times wounded, and man after man was struck down until there only remained Captain Bradbury, who was still untouched, and Sergt. D. Nelson, who had been wounded. Battery-Sergeant-Major G. T. Dorrell then joined them, and at that instant Captain Bradbury, whilst fetching ammunition from a wagon twenty yards off, fell mortally wounded. The survivors continued to fire until the last round was expended, and then—but not till then—L Battery was silent.

I Battery opened fire about 8 A.M. and speedily silenced the German artillery, and the enemy began to draw off. He made an attempt to save his guns, but the teams were caught by I Battery, and the men trying to man-handle the guns back were shot down by machine-gun fire ; nevertheless, four out of the twelve were carried off, only, as will be seen, to fall into British hands next day. The 1/Middlesex under Major F. G. M. Rowley followed by a squadron of the 11th Hussars charged into the batteries, to find that there was not a live German left near them. The Hussars thereupon pressed on in pursuit for a mile until they were recalled, capturing seventy-eight prisoners belonging to every regiment of the *4th Cavalry Division*. By 8.45 A.M. the action was over.

On the western flank of the force, on the heights near St. Sauveur (3½ miles E.N.E. of Verberie), the 1/East Lancashire and 1/Hampshire of the 11th Brigade had also been sharply engaged since dawn with German cavalry (*2nd Cavalry Division*).[1] When the fighting at Néry was over, there was no object in leaving the battalions in an exposed position and they were withdrawn across the ravine of the Autonne through the 1/Somerset L.I. and the 1/Rifle Brigade, the other battalions of the brigade, which were occupying a position on the high ground at Saintines (2 miles east of Verberie).

There can be no doubt that the 1st Cavalry Brigade was taken by surprise ; but it is not less certain that the German *4th Cavalry Division* was equally unaware of the near presence of a British force. Indeed, in an intercepted German wireless message, it was reported that the division had been surprised in its bivouac at Néry and surrounded by considerable hostile forces.[2] Captain Bradbury died very shortly after he was hit, and never received the Victoria Cross which was awarded to him, to his gallant companion, Sergeant Nelson, and to Battery-Sergeant-Major Dorrell. The casualties of the 1st Cavalry Brigade did not exceed one hundred and thirty-five officers and men killed and wounded; of these, five officers and forty-nine men belonged to L Battery. Among the killed was Lieut.-Colonel G. K. Ansell of the 5th Dragoon Guards, who had already distinguished himself at Elouges. The German casualties are unknown. They can hardly have been fewer, and were probably more numerous, than the British.

This was the first encounter with the enemy on the 1st September.[3]

[1] Poseck, p. 77. See also page 248, f.n. 2.
[2] For German movements see Note I. at end of Chapter.
[3] A German account of Néry by an officer of the *18th Dragoon Regiment* (of the *4th Cavalry Division*) has appeared in " Mecklenburgs Söhne im Weltkriege," Heft 13. He states that the three divisions of Marwitz's cavalry corps were sent forward at 4 A.M. on the 31st to reconnoitre towards Paris, and that his division marched without any halt worth mentioning ; this agrees with the statements of prisoners, who said that they had made a forced march of 26 hours to get to Néry. At dawn the advanced guard reported a British bivouac at Néry, and General von Garnier at first ordered the division to deploy and charge, but, the ground being found unsuitable, this was changed to an attack on foot, which progressed to within 500 yards of the village. British reinforcements then came up and " we held our ground against greatly superior numbers until " 2 P.M. (*sic*). We then had to withdraw or be destroyed. The brigades " were therefore directed to get through independently as best they could." Nothing is said about the guns. The Dragoon brigade apparently fled

The Rear-guard Action of Crépy en Valois

Further east, about Mermont and the ground north 1 Sept. of Crépy en Valois, the outpost line of the 5th Division, 1914. held by the 13th Brigade, was attacked at 6 A.M. by Sketch 11. mounted troops of the *IV. Corps* and by *Jäger*.[1] The Maps 4 pressure did not become serious until 10 A.M., when the & 19. 5th Division, which had delayed its march in consequence of the fighting at Néry, began to retire ; it then chiefly affected the West Kent on the left of the line, where the Germans delivered an infantry attack from Béthancourt (4 miles due north of Crépy). The West Kent were supported by a section of the 119th Battery, which came into action within one hundred yards of the firing line, opened at fourteen hundred yards' range and, firing one hundred and fifty rounds in five minutes, brought the Germans to a standstill. By noon the outposts having become rear guard had fallen back to the south of Crépy ; the Germans did not follow except with cavalry patrols, and all trouble ceased on this part of the line. On the right flank, the 2/Duke of Wellington's holding the cross roads

---

back into the forest of Compiègne. After dark it marched to the south-west (through Baron, according to inhabitants) and hid in the woods 15 miles south-west of Néry for 30 hours. On the 3rd September it escaped via Ermenonville back to Nanteuil. The traces found by the B.E.F. are noticed in the next chapter.

According to Poseck, pp. 78, 79, the *4th Cavalry Division* at first withdrew eastward, but, hearing the sound of firing at St. Sauveur in the north and at Crépy en Valois to the east (in actions described later in the text), decided that the path to safety lay to the south, and the brigades moved independently in that direction with the hope of concealing themselves in the forest and of doubling back north when the Allies had passed. This they actually accomplished, though at the cost of their remaining guns and of a considerable amount of transport and equipment. The brigades hid, without food or ammunition, in the great woods on either side of Rozières (just north-east of Baron) and saw the British columns march down the main road through Baron. " On account of want of " ammunition, an attack of the isolated brigades on the numerically " superior infantry columns was not possible." They remained in hiding until the afternoon of the 2nd September.

Kluck merely states that after a successful surprise the *4th Cavalry Division* became seriously engaged with superior forces, and incurred heavy losses. Kuhl (" Marne," p. 121) says that it suffered so heavily that on the 3rd September it was not reassembled and was not able to advance on the 4th with the rest of the corps. Altogether, the 1st September was decidedly to the disadvantage of the German cavalry, for, as will be seen, the *2nd* and *9th Cavalry Divisions* were unable to advance, far less pursue as ordered (see page 266).

[1] According to Kluck, the *IV. Corps* was in action north of Crépy en Valois later in the afternoon, and the first contact was with the five *Jäger* battalions of Marwitz's cavalry corps (Poseck, p. 77).

at " Raperie " (1 mile N.N.E. of Crépy) were supported by the two remaining batteries of the XXVII. Brigade R.F.A. ; and under cover of these guns Br.-General Cuthbert was able to withdraw his battalions with little difficulty.

THE REAR-GUARD ACTIONS OF VILLERS COTTÉRÊTS

Sketch 11.
Maps 4
& 19.

Still further to the east, the I. Corps marched at 4 A.M. by two roads through the forest of Villers Cottérêts, a large area closely planted with trees, in which there was no view or field of fire except on the roads and rides which cross it. The 1st Division from Missy took the Soissons road, which skirts the eastern side of Villers Cottérêts, and turns thence south-eastward on La Ferté Milon.

The 2nd Division, on the west of the 1st, moved by the road which passes through Vivières [1] and Rond de la Reine and the western side of Villers Cottérêts, south-west upon Pisseleux and Boursonne.

The 5th Cavalry Brigade covered the right rear from the region of Montgobert, and the 3rd Cavalry Brigade the left rear from Mortefontaine and Taillefontaine, both outside the forest.

Here again it was the western flank that was first engaged, the 3rd Cavalry Brigade being attacked on reaching Taillefontaine (5 miles N.N.W. of Villers Cottérêts) by a force of all arms advancing from the north.[2] As the brigade drew back to the north-western corner of the Forest of Villers Cottérêts, the 4th Hussars were continuously engaged until past noon, and lost their commanding officer, Lieut.-Colonel I. G. Hogg, in the sharp fighting in the woodlands.

A little to the east of Taillefontaine the 4th (Guards) Brigade was covering the retirement of the 2nd Division, with the Irish Guards and 2/Coldstream, under Lieut.-Colonel Hon. George Morris of the former regiment, in position between Vivières and Puisieux, and the 2/Grenadiers and 3/Coldstream in second line at Rond de la Reine. About 10 A.M. Colonel Morris's troops were attacked by a force of all arms moving from north-west to south-east. The 9th Battery replied effectively to the German guns, and the firing so far died away that Colonel Morris sent back the 2/Coldstream with orders to retire to the railway north of Villers Cottérêts, and prepared to follow them with the

---

[1] Spelt Viviers on some maps.
[2] The advanced guard of the *6th Division*.

Irish Guards. Just then, however, he received a verbal
order from the brigadier not to fall back too quickly, since
it was intended to give the main body of the division a long
halt, from 10 A.M. till 1 P.M.   The 2/Coldstream, owing to the
density of the forest, were already gone past recall, but the
Irish Guards stood fast, and, about 10.45 A.M., were again
and more seriously attacked.   A company of the Grenadiers
was sent forward to reinforce them, but before the Irish
Guards could be extricated, the Germans opened a direct
attack upon the western flank and front of the second line.
This line was drawn up along a grass ride which followed
the highest ridge in the forest, and passes from west to east
through the open space called Rond de la Reine to another
open space, about a mile distant, named Croix de Belle Vue.
The 3/Coldstream were on the west of Rond de la Reine,
being widely extended so as to block the numerous rides
that run from north to south towards Haramont, and
therefore had wide intervals between companies.   The
2/Grenadiers were on the right.   The Germans soon detected the gaps between the companies of the Coldstream
and penetrated between them ; but the battalion, though
compelled to fall back, did so very slowly, each isolated
party fighting vigorously as best it could.   The Grenadiers
were in like case, and behaved in like manner, and both
battalions were still close to their original positions when
company by company the Irish Guards at last joined
them.   Colonel Morris was killed early in this the first serious
engagement of his regiment ;   Br.-General R. Scott-Kerr
was severely wounded while leaving Rond de la Reine,
the Germans having brought up a machine gun which
raked the broad main ride.   Thus there was for a time no
one in general command ; but the three British battalions
were so much intermixed and the fighting in the woods
was unavoidably so confused, that little or no control
was possible.   However, Grenadiers, Coldstream and Irish
fought their way back, contesting every inch of ground, to
Villers Cottérêts, the 3/Coldstream retiring on their second
battalion, which was now on the railway line just to the
north of the town, and the remainder further to the east.
The 17th Battery was in position north of Villers Cottérêts
to support them, but did not fire, the Guards having beaten
off their assailants for the present.   It was by then about
2 P.M.
   Meanwhile the 6th Brigade had been halted about a mile
south of Pisseleux, immediately south of Villers Cottérêts,

to cover the retreat of the Guards, two companies of the Royal Berkshire being deployed upon either flank of the 9th Battery. The 5th Brigade had been ordered by 2nd Division headquarters to entrench in echelon a little further to the south-west, to serve as a rallying point for both brigades. Through the 5th Brigade the Guards retired, with the 2/Coldstream as rear guard ; the 17th Battery moved with them and unlimbered on the right of the 9th. Towards 4 P.M. the Germans, having apparently moved south-west from Villers Cottérêts, opened heavy rifle fire from the west of the railway, while their artillery engaged the British batteries. These last, after a sharp duel, were ordered to retire ; but the teams of the 17th Battery could not come up until the 1/King's had pushed forward to the western side of the railway and effectually checked the advance of the German infantry and artillery. Fighting lasted until 6 P.M., when the King's withdrew, under cover of the 2/Coldstream, and the action came to an end. The number of the enemy engaged was very superior to the British. The fight cost the 4th (Guards) Brigade over three hundred officers and men, and the 6th Brigade one hundred and sixty. Two platoons of the Grenadiers were surrounded and killed at Rond de la Reine, fighting to the last man. Some weeks later it was ascertained from prisoners that the Germans had suffered very heavily in this affair, having lost all sense of direction and fired on each other.

Sketches A & 11. Map 20.   During these clashes of the rear guards, the main body of the British Army tramped on through intense heat until far into the evening. The 1st Division reached its halting place about La Ferté Milon, 16 miles from its starting point, between 7 and 9 P.M. The 2nd Division and the 3rd and 5th Cavalry Brigades arrived at Betz (8 miles west of La Ferté Milon), and the villages to the east of it, after a nineteen-mile march, from one to two hours later. Of the II. Corps, the 3rd Division marched quite untroubled to the villages south-west of Betz, while the 5th Division, with greater precautions, but equally unhindered after the first bickering of the morning, came into Nanteuil (7 miles west of Betz) between 7.30 and 9 P.M.

Map 4.   On the extreme west, after the fight at Néry, the 11th Brigade as we have seen began to withdraw from St. Sauveur, the 12th Brigade at 9.30 A.M. being already in position 6 miles south of St. Sauveur between Mont Cornon and

Chamicy. At 10 A.M. the Germans [1] attacked the 1/Somerset 1 Sept. L.I. and 1/Rifle Brigade, which were covering the retire- 1914. ment of the 11th Brigade, but were beaten off with considerable loss, and this ended the British fighting in this quarter for the day. At 11 A.M. the 2nd and 4th Cavalry Brigades were sent to take up a line from Mont Cornon north-westwards to Villeneuve, and shortly after noon the 4th Division, passing through them, continued its march southward to Fresnoy, Rozières and Baron, to the west of the 5th Division. The Cavalry Division took up its billets Map 20. to the west of the 4th Division along the northern edge of the Forest of Ermenonville from Fontaine to Mont l'Évêque. The march, though absolutely unhindered by the enemy, was an anxious one, for there were persistent rumours that German cavalry was in the Forest of Ermenonville [2] to the south of the British Cavalry Division. When the 1/Rifle Brigade entered Rozières at 7 P.M., they found that three hundred Uhlans had just quitted the village in great haste, leaving a machine gun and sundry articles of equipment behind them.[3]

During the 31st August, as already mentioned, several telegrams had passed between the Secretary of State for War and the British Commander-in-Chief. It appeared to the Cabinet that Sir John French had determined to retire so far out of the Allied line that he would frustrate their policy of co-operating closely with the French and rendering them continuous support. The French President and General Joffre also seemed to be under this impression.[4]

---

[1] The advanced guard of the *II. Corps*. Kluck says that " the *II. Corps*, " supported by the *Cavalry Corps*, became involved in heavy fighting for " the possession of the important Oise crossings at Verberie and St. " Sauveur." The Provisional Division of Sordet's cavalry corps and some battalions of Chasseurs Alpins, the right of General Maunoury's Army which was also falling back, were engaged near Verberie.

[2] Fugitives of the *4th Cavalry Division* were hiding there, as we have seen.

[3] These troops are now known to have been survivors of Néry. Kluck says that the *4th Cavalry Division* " incurred heavy losses at Rozières."

[4] According to M. Poincaré's preface to the French edition of Sir George Arthur's " Life of Lord Kitchener," p. ix :—

" Field-Marshal French operated with excessive independence, and " strove, above all, to maintain his divisions intact.

" On Sunday, 30th August, General Joffre, uneasy at seeing French " hold himself thus aloof, telephoned to M. Millerand, the Minister of " War, that he feared the British were not for the moment disposed to " fight. . . . Next day, Monday, the Commander-in-Chief of our Armies " sent me a liaison officer to beg me to intervene and ensure that Field- " Marshal French should not carry out his retreat too rapidly, and should " make up his mind to contain the enemy who was on the British front."

The President then imparted his fears and the request of General Joffre

As it was difficult to judge of the situation in London, it was decided that Lord Kitchener should himself proceed to France and discuss it verbally with the Commander-in-Chief, so as to ensure that there would be no break-down in the relations between the chiefs of the French and British Armies. Leaving the choice of the meeting place to Sir John French—who fixed the British Embassy at Paris— Lord Kitchener left London at 2 A.M. on the 1st September, crossed the Channel to Havre in a destroyer, arrived in Paris about 3 P.M., met Sir John shortly after, and spent nearly three hours with him.

The result of the interview was recorded in a telegram sent by Lord Kitchener to the Government at 7.30 P.M., before he started on his return journey. It is as follows :

" French's troops are now engaged in the fighting line, where " he will remain conforming to the movements of the French " army, though at the same time acting with caution to avoid " being in any way unsupported on his flanks."

In forwarding a copy of this telegram to Sir John French, Lord Kitchener added :

" I feel sure you will agree that the above represents the " conclusions we came to ; but, in any case, until I can com- " municate with you further in answer to anything you may " wish to tell me, please consider it as an instruction.

" By being ' in the fighting line ' you of course understand " I mean dispositions of your troops in contact with, though " possibly behind, the French as they were to-day ; of course " you will judge as regards their position in this respect."

To this communication Sir John French replied on the 3rd September :

" I fully understand your instructions. . . . I am in full " accord with Joffre and the French."

The British Commander-in-Chief, on returning to his headquarters at Dammartin, 20 miles from Paris, at 6.45 P.M., after the interview with Lord Kitchener, found that the day's work had not been unsatisfactory : the enemy had been shaken off after several sharp actions, and the march, though long and exhausting to the men, had finally

to the British Ambassador, Sir Francis Bertie. About 10 P.M. Sir Francis came to the Élysée with an officer bearing a written answer from the British Commander-in-Chief to Joffre's request—" An answer, unfortunately, not very conclusive." (This letter cannot be found in the British records. Sir John French in his " 1914," p. 95, merely says, " I refused.")

reunited the British Army for the first time since the I. and 1 Sept.
II. Corps had been separated on the 25th August. The 1914.
Cavalry Division was in touch with the French cavalry
about Senlis, westwards of which, to a line from Creil to
the vicinity of Beauvais, General Maunoury had successfully brought back the French Sixth Army. The left of the
French Fifth Army was at Soissons ; as it had retired due
south from Guise and the British Expeditionary Force had
marched south-west a day ahead, the gap between the two
was widening. Owing to the mist, aerial reconnaissance Sketch 10.
had been difficult until the afternoon, but from 3 P.M. Map 20.
onward the Flying Corps sent in a series of valuable observations, all tending to confirm the previous reports of a general
wheel of Kluck's army to the south-east. German troops
were thick upon both banks of the Oise from Noyon southward to Verberie ; the greater number were already on the
eastern side of the river, and the heads of heavy columns
had reached Villers Cottérêts and Crépy en Valois. These
seemed to be wheeling to the south. It might be that this
was due to the direction taken by the roads at these two
points, but it was judged most important to withdraw the
British Army out of reach of a night attack.

Soon after midday the corps commanders had been
warned by the Chief of the General Staff that the retirement would be continued on the morrow towards the Marne,
and roads had been allotted ; but at 7 P.M., on realizing that
the enemy was so near and in such force, and that some of
his cavalry were actually behind the British front, Sir John
French decided to continue the retreat earlier than he had
intended and all the corps were ordered to get clear by a
night march.[1] At the same time, G.H.Q., to which German
cavalry escaping from Néry had passed quite close, commenced moving back from Dammartin to Lagny.[2]

NOTE I

GERMAN MOVEMENTS ON 1ST SEPTEMBER

General von Kluck, whose Army was now again in contact Sketch 10.
with the British, states that he made another effort on the 1st Sep- Maps 4
tember to catch them up. Their presence on his flank had com- & 20.
pelled him to desist from his attempt to reach and roll up the left
flank of the French Fifth Army, which had been noticed by and had

---

[1] Appendix 22.
[2] Further details of the fight at Néry and the move of G.H.Q. will be
found in the " Journal of the Royal Artillery," October 1927, pp. 307-68.

so alarmed General Lanrezac. He therefore ordered his corps to turn south to settle with the British. His *IX. Corps* (less the *17th Division*, which was still in rear, as it had stayed to co-operate with the right wing of the *Second Army* in the Battle of Guise), *III. Corps* and *IV. Corps* having crossed the Aisne between Ambleny and Compiègne were to press southward; the *II. Corps* was to reach the Oise at Verberie; the *II. Cavalry Corps*, from near Compiègne, was to move eastwards to attack the French in flank via Villers Cottérêts.

As a result of the day's operations, the *18th Division* of the *IX. Corps* reached Longpont (6 miles east of Villers Cottérêts), without anywhere meeting with foes.

The *III. Corps*, marching on two roads via Vivières and Taillefontaine, came in contact with the rear guard of the British I. Corps near Villers Cottérêts, as already related, and halted there for the night.

The *IV. Corps*, also moving by two roads, Compiègne—Crépy and Choisy—Pierrefonds, after a terrific march of over thirty miles, and its fight with the 5th Division north of Crépy, halted on the line on which the action had been fought.[1]

The *II. Corps*, after its action at St. Sauveur with the 4th Division and later at Verberie with the French, halted at the latter place for the night.

The *IV. Reserve Corps*, protecting the right flank, reached Quinquempoix, about twenty-five miles south of Amiens.

The general southward advance made by the German *First Army* on the 1st September, owing to the opposition with which it met, was under ten miles,[2] and Kluck had not struck to any purpose either the French Fifth Army or the B.E.F.

The *II. Cavalry Corps* had " varying fortunes, and part of it " very costly fights." (G.O.A., iii. p. 199.)

In consequence of an air report that the enemy had already reached Villers Cottérêts, General von der Marwitz decided not to continue the march of his corps eastwards, but to strike south (G.O.A., iii. p. 194). At 4 P.M. on the 31st, his corps then being on the eastern side of the Forest of Laigue (10 miles south of Noyon), he ordered " a relentless pursuit " that same night in the direction Nanteuil le Haudouin (Poseck, p. 76), that is nearly due south. Led horses, bridging train and telegraph vehicles were to be left behind. The *9th Cavalry Division*, followed by the *2nd*, marching on the main road Compiègne—Verberie, was, however, held up at the latter place and St. Sauveur east of it, and got no further on the 1st September. The *4th Cavalry Division* moved east of the others and came to Néry, as we have seen. The five *Jäger* battalions of the corps were sent to Crépy en Valois and fought there.

The German Official Account admits the loss of only one battery by the *4th Cavalry Division* at Néry ; it adds that, after the fight " the division found itself in the middle of the area through which " the British Army was retiring, but had lost all connection with the " corps commander. As it was extremely exhausted, had suffered " heavy losses, and no command of it as a whole existed, it was not " in a position to do the foe serious harm."

---

[1] G.O.A., iii. p. 199, says that the " *IV. Corps* was nowhere in contact " with the enemy " on 1st September, but Kluck, p. 80, mentions the action.

[2] See Kluck's map.

The *Second Army*, after its rest day on the 31st, got on the move 1 Sept. southwards again, with the bombardment of the old fortresses of 1914. La Fère and Laon in view. The Army was entirely out of touch with the French and a march behind the Armies on its flanks. It proved that both fortresses had been evacuated, but some time was lost over reconnaissance, and about 1.30 P.M. General von Bülow heard by wireless from the Supreme Command that the " Third, Fourth and " Fifth Armies were seriously engaged against superior forces." He therefore wheeled the two corps of his left wing south-eastwards to bring assistance to the Third Army, only to hear at 5.45 P.M. that the French in front of it were retiring. An aeroplane reconnaissance towards evening confirmed that the retreat of the French was continuing. The general southward advance of the *Second Army* was under ten miles.

NOTE II

THE ARMY OF PARIS [1]

On the 25th August the Minister of War had given General Joffre an order that, should his forces be compelled to retreat, he should direct an Army of at least three corps on Paris to ensure its protection. On the 1st September the French Commander-in-Chief began to take measures to comply with this order and to reinforce the garrison. Being unable to detail a corps of the Fifth Army, as he first proposed, owing to its being nearest the enemy, he directed the Third Army to supply one, and General Sarrail nominated the IV. Corps, which had been heavily engaged in the Ardennes, where its two divisions had suffered disastrous losses in the Battles of Ethe and Virton, respectively. To make up the balance, on the same day Joffre decided to incorporate the Sixth Army (then consisting of the 14th and the 63rd Reserve Divisions, called the VII. Corps, and Lamaze's Group cf the 55th and 56th Reserve Divisions) in the Garrison of Paris. " He considered that the Reserve divisions " which it comprised would be very good behind entrenchments, " and might constitute the garrison of the works, whilst the Active " corps [actually containing only one Active division !] would furnish " the mobile defence and might be called upon to take part in " operations." General Galliéni, the Military Governor of Paris, was informed of this increase of his forces by telephone at 6.35 P.M., General Joffre having earlier in the day advised the Government to leave Paris, which they did on the 2nd September.

[1] F.O.A., i. (ii.) pp. 529-31.

CHAPTER XIII

THE LAST STAGES OF THE RETREAT

2ND–5TH SEPTEMBER

(Sketches A, 1, 9, 10, 11 & 12 ; Maps 2, 4, 21, 22, 23 & 24)

Sketches
9 & 10.
Maps 4
& 21.
THE Army was growing hardened to continued retirements ; but in the I. Corps, to make the conditions easier for the men, General Haig on the 1st September decided to send off by train from Villers Cottérêts about half of the ammunition carried by his divisional ammunition columns, and to use the fifty wagons thus released to carry kits and exhausted soldiers. This was an extreme measure, taken only after mature deliberation, but it was more than justified by the result.

The next day in pursuance of Sir John French's orders, the divisions began moving back between 1 A.M. and 3 A.M. from their billets between La Ferté Milon and Senlis to the line of villages between Meaux and Dammartin, a march of some twelve miles. The I. Corps was on the right or east, the II. Corps in the centre and the III. Corps on the left, with the cavalry on either flank of the force. It was practically unmolested during this move. The 5th Cavalry Brigade, on the eastern flank, heard news of a German squadron moving from Villers Cottérêts upon La Ferté Milon, but saw nothing. The 3rd Cavalry Brigade, on the west of the 5th, had been in motion for fully six hours and was well south of Betz before German shells began to burst over the extreme tail of the rear guard. An hour or so later six or eight German squadrons were seen approaching Bouillancy, the next village south of Betz, but were driven off by the fire of D and E Batteries. The brigade, being no further troubled, then retired slowly to Isles les Villenoy behind the right of the I. Corps, where it arrived late in the evening.

The three brigades of the Cavalry Division on the left had been disturbed on the night of the 1st/2nd September by more than one report that the whole or parts of the German *4th Cavalry Division* were moving south through the Forest of Ermenonville behind the British left flank ; and at 2 A.M. the 2nd Cavalry Brigade, on the extreme left, had been ordered to march at once from Mont l'Évêque to clear the defile through the forest for the division. The brigade moved off at 2.30 A.M., taking the road through the forest towards Ermenonville. On debouching from the south-eastern edge it found the road littered with saddles, equipment and clothing. Some enemy force had evidently been in bivouac there and had hastily decamped. Reports came in from inhabitants that two squadrons of Uhlans were at Ermenonville and the next village east of it ; but the British were too late to intercept them. The enemy had withdrawn rapidly, and in the wooded country it was useless to pursue him. Before reaching Ermenonville the brigade came across some motor lorries of the 4th Division Ammunition Column, which had run into a party of German cavalry during the night, and also four abandoned German guns, the marks upon which proved that they were part of the batteries that had been in action at Néry.[1] It may be stated here that, except for skirmishes of cavalry patrols, there was no further contact with the enemy during the rest of the retreat.

Though the march of the British force this day was only a short one, averaging about twelve miles, and the leading units got in early, it was evening before all were in their billets. The heat of the day was intense and suffocating, and made marching so exhausting that several long halts were ordered. In spite of these, there were some cases of heat-stroke.

The march of the I. Corps proved specially trying, since the valley of the Ourcq, for the first half of the way, formed an almost continuous defile. During the passage of this region, the divisions were directed to piquet the high ground as in mountain warfare. The movement presented a fine opportunity to a really active and enterprising enemy, but no such enemy appeared.

An inhabitant of the district has put on record the appearance of the British during this period of the retreat :

" The soldiers, phlegmatic and stolid, march without appear-
" ing to hurry themselves ; their calm is in striking contrast

---

[1] The guns were destroyed by gun-cotton charges.

" to the confusion of the refugees. They pass a night in the
" villages of the Ourcq. It is a pacific invasion . . . as sports-
" men who have just returned from a successful raid, our brave
" English eat with good appetite, drink solidly, and pay royally
" those who present their bills ; . . . and depart at daybreak,
" silently like ghosts, on the whistle of the officer in charge." [1]

Sketches   The position of the Army at nightfall on the 2nd
A & 9.   September was as follows :
Map 21.

5th Cavalry Brigade . I. Corps	In the villages just north of Meaux.
3rd Cavalry Brigade .	Isles les Villenoy, S.S.W. of Meaux.
II. Corps . . .	In the area Monthyon—Montgé—Villeroy.
III. Corps . . .	Eve—Dammartin.
Cavalry Division .	In the area Thieux—Moussy le Vieux—Le Mesnil Amelot.

Roughly speaking, therefore, its front extended from
Meaux north-west to Dammartin. From Dammartin the
French Provisional Cavalry Division [2] prolonged the line
to Senlis, from which point north-westward through Creil
to Mouy and beyond it lay General Maunoury's Sixth
Army, which had been able to withdraw without serious
interference by the enemy. On the right of the British
the French Fifth Army was still a good march north
of them, with the left of its infantry south-west of Fère
en Tardenois, some twenty-five miles away; but General
Joffre had issued orders for Conneau's newly formed
cavalry corps (8th and 10th Cavalry Divisions and an
infantry regiment), which was a few miles nearer, to get in
touch with the British next day, and fill the gap between
them and the Fifth Army.

Map 4.   The 2nd September had thus passed more or less un-
eventfully for the troops, but aerial reconnaissance confirmed interesting changes on the side of the enemy, which
had been suspected on the previous day. His general
march south-eastward seemed for the time to have come
to an end, and to have given place to a southerly movement. The general front of Kluck's Army was covered by
cavalry from Villers Cottérêts through Crépy en Valois and
Villeneuve to Clermont.[3] Behind it from east to west

[1] " Les Champs de l'Ourcq, September 1914." By J. Roussel-Lépine.
[2] Formed temporarily from the fittest units of Sordet's cavalry corps.
[3] The II. Cavalry Corps was, according to Kluck, in line between the
IV. and II. Corps, so part of the covering cavalry was divisional.

opposite the British were the *III.*, *IV.* and *II. Corps*, and 2 Sept.
there were indications that the heads of the columns were 1914.
halting to allow the rear to close up, as if apprehensive of
danger from the south. The *IV. Reserve Corps* was to the
right rear north-west of Clermont about St. Just, and the
IX. Corps was east of Villers Cottérêts, on the same alignment as the cavalry. Up to 4 P.M. no hostile troops of any
kind had passed a line, about ten to twelve miles away,
drawn from Mareuil (at the junction of the Clignon with
the Ourcq) westward through Betz to Nanteuil le Haudouin.
In fact, it seemed as though Kluck had not foreseen any
such collision with the British as had taken place on the 1st.
Possibly he believed them to have moved south-eastward,
and such, indeed, had been their direction on the 30th,
though on the 31st it had been changed to south-west to
leave more space for the retreat of the French Fifth Army.
Moreover, but for the exhaustion which prevented the right
and centre of the British Army from reaching the halting-
places ordered for the evening of the 31st, it is probable
that there would have been no serious collision at all
between the British and the Germans on the 1st September,
but that the Germans would have merely brushed against
the British rear guards, reported the main body to be still
in retreat, and continued their south-easterly march to take
the French Fifth Army in flank. Events, however, having Sketch 10.
fallen out as they did, Kluck had made one further attempt Map 21.
to cut off the British. Meanwhile on his left Bülow was
pressing forward against the French Fifth Army and had,
with his main body, reached the line of the Aisne from
Pontavert (14 miles north-west of Reims) to Soissons, the
head of his advance being on the Vesle. On his front, the
Fifth Army had fallen back to the line Reims—Fère en
Tardenois.

Whilst in Paris on the 1st September, Sir John French Map 4.
made a proposal to the French Minister of War to organize
a line of defence on the Marne and there stand the attack
of the enemy. This was rejected on the 2nd by General
Joffre, mainly, apparently, on account of the position of
the Fifth Army, which on that date was close to the Marne
with the enemy near at hand. He added : " I consider
" that the co-operation of the British Army in the defence
" of Paris is the only co-operation which can give useful
" results," and suggested that it " should first hold the line
" of the Marne, and then retire to the left bank of the
" Seine, which it should hold from Melun to Juvisy [20

" miles below Melun and just outside the perimeter of the
" entrenched camp of Paris]."   Late in the evening, his
" Instruction Générale No. 4," which forecast a retreat

Sketch behind the Seine, reached Sir John French.[1]   Issued at
12A. 2 P.M. on the 1st September, it fixed as the limit of the
retirement the line " north of Bar le Duc—behind the
" Ornain, east of Vitry le François "—" behind the Aube,
" south of Arcis sur Aube, behind the Seine south of Nogent
" sur Seine."   The Field-Marshal therefore gave orders [2]
for the Marne to be crossed on the 3rd—as did General
Lanrezac also to his Army—and for the retreat of the
British Army to be resumed in a south-easterly direction ;
for its continuance in a south-westerly direction would have
brought it inside the perimeter of the entrenched camp of
Paris, besides tending to increase the gap between its right
and the left of the Fifth Army.   Since this movement was
in the nature of a flank march across the enemy's front—
although it turned out that his columns were marching
practically parallel to the British—it was necessary to
make arrangements to keep the Germans off the high
ground on the north bank of the Marne during its execution.

Early in the morning of the 3rd September, therefore,
the 5th and 3rd Cavalry Brigades were thrown out to an
east and west line north-eastwards of Meaux ; the former,
which was supported by a battalion and a battery, covering the loop of the Marne from St. Aulde westwards to
Lizy sur Ourcq, and the latter the ground thence westwards to Barcy.   German cavalry patrols appeared on the
front of the 3rd Cavalry Brigade between 8 and 9 A.M., but
did not approach closely, and at 10.30 A.M. the brigade
crossed the Marne at Germigny, behind the centre of its
sector, and then moving south-eastwards behind its sister
brigade, fell into the main road at La Ferté sous Jouarre
at noon.   The 5th Cavalry Brigade was not troubled until
4 P.M., when a hostile column, which included four batteries,
appeared at May en Multien, due north of Lizy on the
western bank of the Ourcq.   There was some exchange
of rifle and artillery fire as Br.-General Chetwode slowly
withdrew eastwards, but the Germans were evidently
content to see him go, for they did not follow, but took up
billets quietly on the western bank of the Ourcq from Lizy
northwards.   The 5th Cavalry Brigade then crossed the
Marne at La Ferté sous Jouarre and reached its billets at
7 P.M., having had no more than five casualties.

[1] Appendix 23.   See Sketch 9.   [2] Appendix 24.

Meanwhile, having started between 3 and 4 A M., the 3 Sept.
1st Division had crossed the Marne at Trilport, the 2nd and 1914.
3rd at Meaux, the 5th at Isles les Villenoy, the 4th at Sketch 9.
Lagny and the Cavalry Division at Gournay. Under Map 22.
authority from General Joffre, they or the French blew
up all the bridges behind them as they moved south-east,[1]
and by evening the B.E.F. was distributed along a line south
of the Marne from Jouarre westward to Nogent, I. Corps
patrols being again in touch with troops of the French Fifth
Army which was also south of the Marne. The Sixth Army,
north of the Marne, slightly overlapped the British left.

This march too had proved a trying one ; it was long
in point of time as well as distance, for the roads were
crowded with vehicles of refugees, and some units were
as much as eighteen hours on the road.

During the morning Sir John French learnt from a
Note issued by G.Q.G. at 9.30 P.M. on the 2nd, but which
did not reach British G.H.Q. and other recipients until the
3rd, that General Joffre had slightly changed his plans
from those announced in " Instruction Générale No. 4." Sketch
He now proposed to establish the whole of his forces on 12A.
a general line marked by Pont sur Yonne—Nogent sur
Seine—Arcis sur Aube—Brienne le Chateau—Joinville,
that is to withdraw his flanks further than originally stated,
and then pass to the offensive, whilst simultaneously the
garrison of Paris acted in the direction of Meaux.

Aerial reconnaissance on this day established the fact
that Kluck had resumed his south-eastward movement
with rapidity and vigour : the German columns which
had been following the British southwards had turned off
and were now making their way eastwards and south-
eastwards to the passages of the Ourcq. Unfortunately
there are no British air reports after 2.50 P.M. to be found ;
but at 5 P.M. G.H.Q. informed General Joffre and General
Lanrezac that there did not appear to be any enemy forces
left on the British front, and that the whole of the German
First Army was about to cross the Marne between Chateau
Thierry and La Ferté sous Jouarre to attack the left of the
Fifth Army. Between 8.20 and 8.40 P.M. a more detailed
message was telephoned by Colonel Huguet, on behalf of
G.H.Q., to G.Q.G., the Fifth Army and the Military
Governor of Paris :—

[1] The first troops of the 4th Division which arrived at Lagny found
French engineers about to blow up the bridges there ; only with difficulty
was a postponement obtained.

" It results from very reliable reports from British air-
" men, all of which agree, that the whole of the German
" *First Army* except the *IV. Reserve Corps* [that is to say,
" the *II., III.* and *IV. Corps* and *18th Division*] are
" moving south-east to cross the Marne between Chateau
" Thierry and La Ferté sous Jouarre, and attack the left
" of the Fifth Army. The heads of the columns will with-
" out doubt reach the Marne this evening."

At the same time an officer was sent to General
Lanrezac's headquarters at Sézanne with a map exactly
showing the situation.

The British air reports were confirmed by those of an
aviator sent out by the French Sixth Army, who reported,
between 7.30 and 8.30 P.M.,[1] the movements of columns
(*II. Corps*) from Senlis south - eastwards on the Sixth
Army front, and a very long column (*8th Division*) moving
south-east with its head at 6 P.M. at Etrepilly (close to
Lizy on the Ourcq). Nothing could be seen of the *IV.
Reserve Corps*, which had been marked down near Clermont
on the previous evening.

Opposite the Fifth Army the German columns were
still marching southwards. By 11 A.M. the head of the
German *IX. Corps* had already passed the Marne and
had a sharp engagement with the French at Chateau
Thierry, 15 miles north-east of the British right. Later
another column of this corps crossed at Chézy (below
Chateau Thierry), and at 6 P.M. the head of a column
(*13th Division*) was reported at Mézy (6 miles above
Chateau Thierry).

There are no reports, from either French or British
sources, of the Germans on the 3rd reaching the Marne
between Chézy and La Ferté sous Jouarre (exclusive).
The gap there between the French Fifth Army and British
does not appear to have been watched except by a party of
French cavalry at the bridge of Nogent, which cleared off
on the approach of German cyclists.[2] It is now known
from German sources that Kluck's divisions, by making
marches of 25-28 miles, secured all the bridges in this
sector by midnight.[3] Fortunately one and all arrived too

---

[1] The British reports reached the Sixth Army "early in the afternoon"
and were confirmed "several hours later." (F.O.A., i. (ii.) p. 618.)
[2] " Regt. No. 24," p. 47.
[3] The heads of the divisions of the *III. Corps* reached the bridges at
Nogent, Saulchery, Charly and Nanteuil between 8 and 9 P.M., and established outposts on the heights beyond them. Of the *IV. Corps* on the
night of the 3rd/4th the German Official Account (iii. p. 236) states that

latc at thc river, for the whole of the French Fifth Army was by that time safely across the Marne, and its left had fallen back after a fight at Chateau Thierry, and was now in line with the British though still separated by a gap of about ten miles.

At 4.35 P.M. the British Commander-in-Chief, certain from the air information that Kluck was moving from west to east and intended no immediate action against him, warned his corps commanders that, unless the situation changed, the troops would remain in their present billets, and would probably have complete rest next day.   During the evening, however, Sir John became alarmed by possibilities of the situation should the Germans press into the gap between the B.E.F. and the Fifth Army, and at 11.50 P.M. he issued orders [1] for the remaining bridges over the Marne in the British area to be destroyed and for the Force to be prepared on receipt of a further order to continue its retreat southward.   If he fell back it was his intention to bring the whole B.E.F. behind the Grand Morin, and, as a preliminary, to swing back the right or eastern flank.   The I. Corps, therefore, was to move first, through Coulommiers, with the 3rd and 5th Cavalry Brigades pushed out to the east, in order to protect its flank and to gain contact with Conneau's cavalry corps, which was reported to be at Rebais, 7 miles away.   The II. and III. Corps and Cavalry Division were to stand fast until the I. Corps had reached the Grand Morin, and then fall back in line with it.   Every precaution was to be taken to conceal the billets of the troops from aircraft. The movements of the British Army during the past few days had already misled the enemy once and, if its whereabouts could now be hidden, might mislead him again. [2]

---

it " reached the region of Crouy " (10 miles north of Lizy) ; Kluck's map, on the other hand, shows its line established south of the Marne.   Neither location is correct.   An examination of the histories of the eight infantry regiments of the corps reveals that only one of them, the *66th* (*7th Division*) crossed the Marne on the 3rd, at Saacy, arriving at midnight, and billeting there and in the adjoining village of Citry.   All the others in this division marched until midnight in clear moonlight, halting, the *26th* at Méry (on the north bank of the Marne opposite Saacy), the *27th* and *165th* at Dhuisy (6 miles N.N.W. of Saacy).   In the *8th Division*, the *93rd* and *153rd* reached St. Aulde (on the Marne N.N.E. of La Ferté) at 2 A.M. and midnight, respectively ; and the *36th* and *72nd* halted at two small villages, Rouget and Avernes (both 3 miles to the northward of La Ferté) at 2 A.M. and 10 P.M., respectively.

[1] Appendix 25.

[2] In this, according to Kluck, the II. and III. Corps were successful ; the march and bivouacs of the I. Corps only were observed.

Map 4. Accordingly, on the 4th, soon after daybreak, the 5th Cavalry Brigade, with the 3rd in support, advanced eastward to Doue, midway between the two Morins, and sent patrols forward along both banks of the Petit Morin. At the same time it despatched the Scots Greys to the east towards Rebais there to meet the French cavalry. At 8 A.M. the patrols reported a hostile column of all arms moving south-east along the main road north of the Petit Morin from La Ferté sous Jouarre to Montmirail, but evidently there were parties of the enemy south of the valley, for a troop of the Greys found Germans at Rebais, and had such sharp fighting that only five of its men escaped. At 11.45 A.M. a column of cavalry with guns and three battalions of infantry—evidently a flank guard— were seen moving south-east on the heights between the Montmirail road and the Petit Morin, from Boitron upon Sablonnières; some of them, crossing the stream, attacked an advanced party of the 5th Cavalry Brigade about a mile east of Doue, but without success. The enemy seems then to have decided that it was time to thrust back this prying English cavalry, and manœuvred to turn Br.- General Chetwode's position from the south; but when he fell back under cover of the 3rd Cavalry Brigade and the Germans occupied his ground about Doue, they were at once engaged by E Battery, which disabled one of the German guns and did considerable damage among the gun teams. At 6 P.M. Br.-General Gough in turn withdrew the 3rd Cavalry Brigade, protected by the fire of the 113th and 114th Batteries, and by the 2nd Brigade, which was in position about Aulnoy. He then crossed the Grand Morin at Coulommiers, and made for Chailly, a little to the south-east.

Meanwhile, by General Haig's orders, the 1st Division had at 4 A.M. been withdrawn into reserve and relieved in the duty of observation over the front from La Ferté to Sammeron (3 miles west of La Ferté) by the 2nd Division. There was some expectation of fighting; for, although the bridges at Sammeron and St. Jean had been blown up, one of the two bridges at La Ferté sous Jouarre owing to lack of time had not been thoroughly destroyed.[1] About

---

[1] The four bridges had been dealt with by the 23rd and 26th Field Companies R.E. The demolition of the stone-arched bridge at La Ferté was successful; the second was a six-arched steel girder bridge, and the girders were cut through; but the ends remained as cantilevers, and the gaps could be crossed by laying a few planks. There was no time to place heavy charges to complete the demolition.

8 A.M. indeed a German battalion crossed the river by this
bridge,[1] but it did not immediately press on, and the 1st
Division, pursuing its march methodically, halted at
Aulnoy and Coulommiers.   During the afternoon Sir John Map 23.
French visited I. Corps headquarters and gave General
Haig orders to withdraw—thus for the second time preventing him from fighting.   The 2nd Division, which at
4 P.M. began to fall back by brigades in succession to the
west of the 1st Division, upon Mouroux and Giremoutiers,
was followed only by a few cavalry patrols.   The II. and
III. Corps and Cavalry Division actually enjoyed a day of
rest on the 4th until after dark, when they too moved
off south through the night, as will be related.   For the
moment the Army was concentrated on the Grand Morin.
    The information obtained by the Flying Corps on this
day was particularly full and complete.   The early (6 to
7 A.M.) reports gave the bivouacs of all the corps of the
German *First Army* except the *IV. Reserve*.   The later
reports established the continued march, from the front
Chateau Thierry—La Ferté sous Jouarre south-eastwards
across the Marne towards the left of the French Fifth Army
and Conneau's cavalry corps, of the *IX., III.* and *IV.
Corps*.   About 4.30 P.M. two columns of cavalry were seen
moving southwards towards the 1st Division at Aulnoy
and Coulommiers, and some shelling was observed.[2]   From
the Governor of Paris came information that the *II. Corps*
was moving on Meaux and the *IV. Reserve Corps* on Betz
and Nanteuil.   General Franchet d'Espèrey, who had
taken over command of the Fifth Army from General
Lanrezac [3] the previous day, continued the withdrawal of
his troops, swinging back his left to meet the German
threat against his flank.
    It may be noted that on this day the French Ninth
Army, under General Foch, came into existence between
the Fourth and Fifth Armies.   It was organized, merely
for convenience of command, from the left of the Fourth
Army, and its formation did not, therefore, affect the
general situation.[4]

---

[1] The German *IV. Corps* and *II. Cavalry Corps* crossed at La Ferté
sous Jouarre.
[2] This was the action of the 3rd and 5th Cavalry Brigades.
[3] For an account of his sudden removal, see his book, " Le Plan de
Campagne français et le premier mois de la Guerre," p. 276 *et seq.*
[4] The French Ninth Army came officially into existence as an independent command at 11 P.M. on the 4th September.   It had actually been
formed on the 29th August as a " Détachement d'Armée."   It consisted

Sketch   During the afternoon of the 4th September, also,
12 A.   General Galliéni, the recently appointed Military Governor
of Paris, under whose direct orders the French Sixth Army
had been acting since the 1st September "in the interests
of the defence of Paris," came with General Maunoury to
British headquarters at Melun.[1] Sir John French was
absent, as we have seen, visiting the I. Corps, about whose
position he was alarmed, but to his Chief of the General
Staff, Lieut.-General Murray, General Galliéni pointed out
that advantage ought to be taken at once of the opportunity the German *First Army* had given by offering its
right flank.   He added that he had ordered the Army of
Paris, as he called his combined forces of the Sixth Army
and Paris garrison, to move eastwards that afternoon, and
that he proposed, with the concurrence of General Joffre
whom he had informed, to attack the German *IV. Reserve
Corps*, which was covering the movement of the *First
Army*.   This corps had been reported that morning marching in two columns towards Trilport and Lizy sur Ourcq.
Galliéni suggested that the British Army should cease to
Sketch retreat, and take the offensive next day in co-operation
12A.   with his forces.   In the absence of the British Commander-
Map 4. in-Chief, nothing could be decided, but it was settled provisionally that on the 5th the B.E.F. should change front
so as to occupy a general line behind the Grand Morin
from Coulommiers westwards (actually Faremoutiers—
Tigeaux—Chantéloup), " so as to leave the Sixth Army the
" space which was necessary for it." [2]   After waiting three
hours for Sir John French, but all in vain, at 5 P.M. General
Galliéni departed.   Whilst this interview between General
Galliéni and Lieut.-General Murray with regard to co-
operation was taking place at G.H.Q., another was in
progress at Fifth Army headquarters between other French
and British representatives.   On the morning of the 4th
General Franchet d'Espèrey had expressed a wish to meet
Sir John French, and it had eventually been arranged, as
the Commander-in-Chief wished to go to the I. Corps, that
the Sub-Chief of the General Staff, Major-General Wilson,

---

of the IX. and XI. Corps, 52nd and 60th Reserve Divisions and 9th Cavalry
Division from the left of the Fourth Army, and the 42nd Division from the
Third Army.   Its formation merely reduced the size of the Fourth Army,
and put the Fourth and Ninth Armies where the Fourth had been.
    [1] See " Mémoires du Général Galliéni.   Défense de Paris," p. 121, for
an account of this visit.   For the genesis of the orders for the Battle of
the Marne, see Note II. at end of Chapter.
    [2] F.O.A., i. (ii.) p. 789.

THE PROJECTED OFFENSIVE 279

with the head of the Intelligence Section, Colonel Mac- 4 Sept.
donogh, should be at Fifth Army headquarters at Bray sur 1914.
Seine at 3 P.M. On arrival there these officers found that
General Franchet d'Espèrey had a quarter of an hour earlier
received a telegram from General Joffre to the effect [1] that
it might be of advantage to deliver battle next day or the
day after with the Fifth Army, the B.E.F and the mobile
forces of Paris, and enquiring whether the Fifth Army was
in a fit state to fight. After comparing information as to
the movements of the enemy, and discussing the general
situation as far as they knew it, General Franchet d'Espèrey,
after agreement with Major-General Wilson, despatched the
following reply to General Joffre :

" I. The battle cannot take place until the day after to-
" morrow 6th (sixth) September.
" II. To-morrow, 5th Sept. the V. (Fifth) Army will con-
" tinue its retrograde movement to the line Sézanne—Provins
" [that is facing north-west, with a view to guarding the left
" flank of the French main Army rather than to an offensive].
" The British Army will make a change of direction, so as
" to face east on the line Coulommiers and southward—Changis
" [6 miles east of Meaux] provided that its left flank is supported
" by the Sixth Army, which should advance to the line of the
" Ourcq to the north of Lizy sur Ourcq [8 miles north-east of
" Meaux] to-morrow 5th (fifth) September.
" III. On the 6th (sixth) the general direction of the British
" offensive should be Montmirail ; that of the Sixth Army
" should be Chateau Thierry ; that of the V. (Fifth) Army
" should be Montmirail."

Thus it was suggested that the Fifth Army should
advance northwards, and the B.E.F. and Sixth Army eastwards.
To this message, which was timed 4 P.M., General
Franchet d'Espèrey added in his own handwriting :

" The conditions for the success of the operation are :
" 1. The close and absolute co-operation of the Sixth Army,
" which must debouch on the left bank of the Ourcq to the
" north-east of Meaux on the morning of the 6th.
" It must be up to the Ourcq to-morrow the 5th September.
" If not the British won't march.
" 2. My Army can fight on the 6th, but is not in a brilliant
" state, the three Reserve divisions cannot be counted on.
" In addition, it would be as well that the Detachment

[1] See Note II. at end of Chapter.

" Foch should take an energetic part in the action, direction
" Montmort [11 miles south-west of Epernay]."

With a note of these messages, Major-General Wilson
and Colonel Macdonogh returned to G.H.Q.

General Joffre had written to Sir John French earlier
in the day confirming his intention to adhere to the plan of
retirement already communicated to him.[1] He added :

" In case the German Armies should continue the movement
" south-south-east, thus moving away from the Seine and Paris,
" perhaps you will consider, as I do, that your action will be
" most effective on the right bank of that river between Marne
" and Seine.

" Your left resting on the Marne, supported by the en-
" trenched camp of Paris, will be covered by the mobile garrison
" of the capital, which will attack eastwards on the left bank
" of the Marne."

On his return from visiting General Haig, the British
Commander-in-Chief, after reading this letter, found that
his Chief and Sub-Chief of the General Staff had come to
two entirely different arrangements with the Governor of
Paris and the Commander of the French Fifth Army : one
that the British should be drawn up behind the Grand Morin,
facing more or less northward, and the other that it should
be north of the Grand Morin, facing east.   General Galliéni's
communication appeared to be authorized by General
Joffre, and to be in agreement with the latter's last letter,
whilst Franchet d'Espèrey's plan might land the B.E.F.,
with its left completely exposed, in the midst of Kluck's
Army.[2]   The Field-Marshal was much troubled by what
appeared to him to be constant changes of plan ; but there
seemed no doubt that the Generalissimo wished the B.E.F.
to be withdrawn further to make room for the Army of
Paris south of the Marne,[3] and in view of the gap which
existed between the B.E.F. and the Fifth Army, and
" because the Germans were exercising some pressure on
" Haig on this night [4th Sept.],"[4] Sir John French decided
to retire " a few miles further south."

At 6.35 P.M., therefore, orders [5] were issued from British

[1] See Appendix 26 for the original French.
[2] The German *II. Corps* on the 5th exactly covered the ground
Coulommiers—Changis which Generals Franchet d'Espèrey and Wilson
had agreed should be the starting line of the B.E.F.
[3] See Sir John French's letter to Earl Kitchener.   Appendix 27.
[4] Lord French's " 1914," p. 109.
[5] Appendix 28.

SKETCH 12.

THE MARNE

SITUATION: NOON, 5TH SEPT. 1914.

SIXTH
(CR. PR. RUPPRECHT)

SECOND
(DE CASTELNAU)

FIFTH
(CROWN PRINCE)

THIRD
(SARRAIL)

FOURTH
(GD DUKE ALBRECHT)

FOURTH
(DE LANGLE DE CARY)

THIRD
(HAUSEN)

SECOND
(BÜLOW)

NINTH
(FOCH)

FIFTH
(D'ESPEREY)

FIRST
(KLUCK)

SIXTH
(MAUNOURY)

B.E.F.

IV CAV. CORPS

IV CAV. CORPS

Argonne

REIMS
ÉPERNAY
PARIS

MOSELLE
METZ
MOSELLE
MEUSE
MARNE
AISNE
OISE
SEINE

Briey
St. Mihiel
VERDUN
Bar le Duc
Vouziers
Ste Menehould
Vitry le François
Châlons
Sézanne
Provins
Nogent
Toul
Nancy
Lunéville
MEURTHE
Charmes
Joinville

Thionville

Château Thierry
la Ferté Milon
Crépy en Valois
Senlis
Nanteuil
Compiègne
Verberie
Nery
Soissons
Villers Cotterets
Betz
Dammartin
Meaux
Coulommiers
Esternay
Sommesous

Chaumont

SCALE

Ordnance Survey, 1924.

G.H.Q. at Melun, for the Army to move south-west on the 5th, pivoting on its left, so that its rear guards would reach, roughly a line drawn east and west through Tournan. The times of starting were left to the corps commanders. The Cavalry Division was further warned to be ready to move from the western to the eastern flank of the Army early on the 6th. A message informing General Galliéni of the movements ordered was sent through the French Mission at British headquarters. 5 Sept. 1914.

Accordingly before dawn on the 5th, the I. Corps was again on the march southwards with the 3rd Cavalry Brigade as rear guard and the 5th as eastern flank guard. The latter had a skirmish at Chailly early in the morning, but otherwise the march was uneventful, and was indeed compared by the 3rd Cavalry Brigade to a march in peace time. The fighting troops of the III. Corps started at 4 A.M., but the II. Corps moved off several hours earlier, at 10 P.M., in order to avoid the heat of the day. Both corps were unmolested. During the 5th, definite orders for the Cavalry Division to move to the right flank were issued, and in the course of the afternoon it started eastwards across the rear of the Army. Map 4.

Thus by nightfall, or a little later, the British force had reached its halting-places south-south-east of Paris, and faced somewhat east of north : the I. Corps in and west of Rozoy, the Cavalry Division to its right rear in Mormant and the villages north of it, the II. Corps on the left of the I., in and east of Tournan, and the III. Corps on the left of the II., from Ozoir la Ferrière southwards to Brie Comte Robert, touching the defences of Paris. Sketch 9. Map 24.

The air reports showed during the day the advance of the German *First Army* across the Grand Morin, and at night the bivouacs of large forces south of that river ; two or three corps (the *III., II. Cavalry* and *IV.*) were between the Grand Morin and the Aubetin, and another corps (*II.*) between them and Crécy. South of a line through Béton Bezoches and west of a meridian through Crécy there were reported to be no Germans ; but the G.H.Q. situation tracing for the 5th September has " fighting at 2.45 P.M." marked on it in a circle around St. Soupplets, so the collision of Maunoury's Army with the German *IV. Reserve Corps* was known. The left of the French Fifth Army was during the afternoon reported to be around Provins, that is 15 miles to the right rear of the B.E.F.

General Franchet d'Espèrey, before the conference at

his headquarters on the 4th, had issued orders for the retirement to the Seine of the French Fifth Army on the 5th
and 6th " as quickly as possible and with the least possible
" losses " ; strong echelons of artillery were to be used in
successive positions and the enemy fought by guns without
being given a chance of holding on to the infantry. No
modification was made in these orders in consequence of
the question asked by General Joffre, as to when the Fifth
Army could fight ; so the XVIII. Corps and Reserve
divisions marched off at midnight of the 4th/5th, and the
other formations of the Fifth Army at 1 A.M.[1] Thus during
the early hours of the 5th both Franchet d'Espèrey and Sir
John French wheeled their forces back as if opening the
two halves of a double door, increasing the gap between
them, and presenting an entry into the Allied line to the
enemy.

Meanwhile, during the 5th September, north-east of the
capital, General Maunoury's Sixth Army had by General
Galliéni's orders advanced north of the Marne towards the
Ourcq, and in the afternoon had come into contact with
the German *IV. Reserve Corps* between Meaux and St.
Soupplets. This Army was steadily increasing in numbers
as divisions reached it from the east.[2] On the right of the
British, and slightly to the south of them, General Conneau's cavalry corps (4th, 8th and 10th Cavalry Divisions)
was near Provins, on the extreme left of the Fifth Army,
which had continued to retire during the 5th, and was now
extended north-eastwards from Provins to Sézanne. Thus
the gap in the Allied line on this side was some fifteen miles,
with four French and British cavalry divisions at hand to
fill it.

Sketches   Opposite the French Fifth Army and the right of the
10 & 12. B.E.F., Kluck's Army had continued its south-eastward
Map 24. movement. As aeroplane reconnaissance clearly showed,
the whole of it (except the *IV. Reserve Corps* and *4th
Cavalry Division*, which were observing Paris) had passed
the lines of the Ourcq and the Marne and had wheeled to

[1] F.O.A., i. (ii.) pp. 671-3, and Annexe No. 2394.
[2] It consisted on the 5th September of the VII. Corps (14th and 63rd
Reserve Divisions), 45th Division, 55th and 56th Reserve Divisions, the
Moroccan Brigade, and Gillet's cavalry brigade—some 70,000 men, with
Sordet's cavalry corps attached. Behind it were a group of Territorial
brigades under General Mercier-Milon, Ebener's Group of Reserve divisions
(61st and 62nd), and the actual garrison of Paris—four divisions and a
brigade of Territorial troops, with a brigade of Fusiliers Marins sent for
police duties. The IV. Corps was just arriving, so General Galliéni reckoned
he had about 150,000 men available for action as the Army of Paris.

the south, its front stretching along the line of the Grand 5 Sept.
Morin, which its advanced troops had crossed, from 1914.
Esternay (near Sézanne) to Crécy (south of Meaux). On
Kluck's left, the *Second Army* was a day's march behind
him, its right slightly overlapped by the *IX. Corps*, so that
for a time there was an impression that he had been reinforced. The moment for which General Joffre had waited
was come at last. Kluck, in his headlong rush eastwards,
had, it appeared, ignored not only the fortress of Paris, but
the Sixth Army which, with the British, was now in position,
as a glance at the map will show, to fall in strength upon
his right flank and rear.

Similarly, further east, parts of the German *Fifth Army*
and the *Fourth Army* had swept past the western side of
Verdun, with which fortress General Sarrail's Third Army,
facing almost due west, was still in touch. Thus, whilst the
German *Sixth* and *Seventh Armies* were held up by the
eastern fortresses, the *Fifth, Fourth, Third, Second* and
First Armies had penetrated into a vast bag or " pocket "
between the fortresses of Verdun and Paris, the sides of
which were held by unbeaten troops, ready to turn on the
enemy directly the command should come to do so. Credit
has been claimed for General Galliéni that he first discovered the eastward march of Kluck and brought its
significance to the notice of General Joffre, and that he
immediately took appropriate action with the troops under
his command, and prevailed upon the Commander-in-Chief
to change his plan for retiring behind the Seine. Be this
as it may, the decision to resume the offensive rested with
General Joffre.

The retreat of the B.E.F. had continued, with only one
halt, for thirteen days over a distance, as the crow flies, of
one hundred and thirty-six miles, or, as the men marched,
at least two hundred miles, and that after two days' strenuous marching in advance to the Mons canal. The mere
statement of the distance gives no measure of the demands
made upon the physical and moral endurance of the men,
and but little idea of the stoutness with which they had
responded to these demands. The misery that all ranks
suffered is well summed up in the phrase of an officer : " I
" would never have believed that men could be so tired
" and so hungry and yet live." An artillery officer whose
brigade marched and fought throughout the retreat with
the same infantry brigade has noted in his diary that, on
the average, mounted men had three hours', and infantry

four hours' rest per day. The late General Sir Stanley
Maude, who was on the III. Corps Staff, has put it on record
that he did not average three hours' sleep out of the twenty-
four ; [1] officers of the lower staffs had less. But all these
trials were now behind them : the Retreat from Mons was
over.

There have been three other notable retreats in the
history of the British Army. All three, that of Sir John
Moore to Corunna in the winter of 1808–9, of Sir Arthur
Wellesley after the battle of Talavera in 1809, and again
from Burgos to Ciudad Rodrigo in 1812, were marred
by serious lack of discipline, though the first was re-
deemed by its results and the success of the final action at
Corunna, while the last was reckoned by critics to be the
greatest of Wellington's achievements. The Retreat from
Mons, on the other hand, was in every way honourable to
the Army. The troops suffered under every disadvantage.
The number of reservists in the ranks was on an average
over one-half of the full strength, and owing to the force
of circumstances the units were hurried away to the area
of concentration before all ranks could resume acquaintance
with their officers and comrades, and re-learn their business
as soldiers. Arrived there, they were hastened forward
by forced marches to battle, confronted with greatly
superior numbers of the most renowned army in Europe,
and condemned at the very outset to undergo the severest
ordeal which can be imposed upon an army. They were
short of food and sleep when they began their retreat, they
continued it, always short of food and sleep, for thirteen
days ; and at the end of the retreat they were still an
army, and a formidable army. They were never demoralized, for they rightly judged that they had never
been beaten.[2]

The B.E.F., forming as it did only a very small portion
of the line of the French Armies commanded by General
Joffre, had no independent strategical rôle in the opening
phases of the war. When the Germans turned the Allied
left by an unexpectedly wide movement through Belgium,
the Generalissimo decided that his only chance of stopping
them was " by abandoning ground and mounting a new
operation " ; [3] to this Sir John French had naturally to
conform. The operation, which involved the assembly of a

---

[1] Callwell's " Sir Stanley Maude," p. 120.
[2] A table of the length of the daily marches will be found in Appendix 29.
[3] Rapport du Général Joffre au Ministre de la Guerre, 25th Aug. 1914.

new Army in the west to outflank the enemy, required time 5 Sept.
to prepare. General Joffre at first hoped, whilst his First 1914.
and Second Armies held Lorraine, to be able to stand on Sketch
the line Verdun—river Aisne (Vouziers—Berry au Bac)— 12A.
Craonne—Laon—La Fère—Ham, and thence along the Maps 2, 3
Somme. This line he intended to entrench.[1] The Ger- & 4.
mans, however, pressed on too closely to permit it, and
widened their turning movement. There was no alternative to fighting at a strategical and tactical disadvantage
but a further general retirement—" hanging on as long as
possible, avoiding any decisive action," but giving the
enemy severe lessons as opportunities occurred.[2]

Instead of being beaten piecemeal by superior forces
as in 1870, the French, after the initial failure of their
offensive, withdrew in good time. Such fights as took
place, and there were many all along the front besides
Guise,[3] resulted not in a Woerth or a Spicheren, but in
the Allies slipping away after inflicting severe losses on
the enemy.[4] In such operations, the B.E.F., at Mons and
Le Cateau and in smaller actions, was eminently successful :
it had no difficulty in more than holding its own whenever
contact occurred, hitting hard and then marching off unmolested. Only those who have commanded British troops
are able to conceive what they can accomplish.

By some it has been thought that the B.E.F. could
have done more ; in particular it might have assisted the
French at Guise. It has been shown in the narrative [5]
that one of the reasons that General Joffre ordered General
Lanrezac to take the offensive was to relieve the pressure
on the British, and Sir John French might at least have
allowed the I. Corps to assist. On the other hand, in his
dangerous position on the outer flank of the Allied Armies
for many days, he had not only to bear in mind General
Joffre's general instructions to avoid decisive action and
the necessity of husbanding his force for the coming battle
when the Armies should turn, but to recall that he commanded nearly all the available trained staff officers,

---

[1] Directive of 25th August, 10 P.M.
[2] General Joffre's letter to G.H.Q. of 30th August.
[3] Beaufort, La Marfée, Murtin, Tremblois, Chilly, Launais, besides the
Battles of Signy l'Abbaye and Réthel.
[4] General Graf Stürgkh, head of the Austrian Mission at German
G.H.Q., gives the heavy losses suffered by the Germans in the preliminary
engagements as one of the principal reasons for the defeat at the Marne
(" Im Deutschen Grossen Hauptquartier," p. 88). The extent of these
losses has not yet been revealed.
[5] See pages 231-2.

officers and men of the British Empire, the nucleus on which the New Armies were to be trained and initiated in war; above all, he had to remember the instructions of the Government, that "the greatest care must be exercised towards a minimum of losses and wastage."

On the 5th September there were some twenty thousand men absent of the original numbers of the B.E.F.; but, as in all great retreats, a fair proportion of these rejoined later; the official returns show a figure of a little over fifteen thousand killed, wounded and missing. The loss of war material is difficult to set down exactly. Some transport was abandoned, as is inevitable at such times; many of the valises and greatcoats were discarded or burnt, and a very large proportion of the entrenching tools left behind. As to guns, forty-two fell into the enemy's hands as the result of active combat, and two or three more, through one mishap or another, were left behind. Such a casualty list can, in the circumstances, be only considered as astonishingly light. Its seriousness lay in the fact that, whether in guns or men, the loss had fallen almost wholly upon the left wing: the II. and III. Corps, and above all upon the II. Corps, which had borne the brunt of the fighting.

Sketch 1.
Map 2.

It was impossible to expect that the deficiencies in men and material could be immediately made good. Practically all units received their first reinforcements—the "ten per cent reinforcements"—on the 4th and 5th September, and these, added to the replacement of the Munsters in the 1st (Guards) Brigade by the Cameron Highlanders (hitherto Army troops), brought the I. Corps more or less up to strength. But the far graver losses of the II. Corps, especially in guns and vehicles, could not be so quickly repaired. The rapid advance of the Germans to the west had made the bases at Boulogne and Havre unsafe, and had actually dispossessed the British of their advanced base at Amiens. The advisability of a change of base was foreseen by the Q.M.G., Major-General Sir William Robertson, as early as the 24th August, and from that date all further movement of men or stores to Havre or Boulogne was stopped. By the 27th, Boulogne had been cleared of stores and closed as a port of disembarkation; and on the 29th St. Nazaire on the Loire was selected as the new base.[1] At that time there

---

[1] The L. of C. ran from St. Nazaire by two railway routes—one via Saumur and the other by Le Mans—to Villeneuve St. Georges, just southeast of Paris, whence there was one route to a varying railhead.

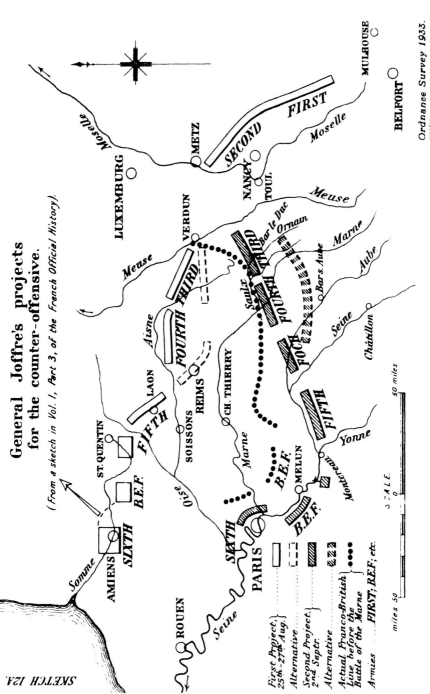

SKETCH 124.

General Joffre's projects
for the counter-offensive.

(From a sketch in Vol. I, Part 3, of the French Official History).

Ordnance Survey 1933.

3073/33.

SCALE.

miles 50   0   50 miles

First Project, } ⎯⎯⎯⎯
25th-27th Aug. }
Alternative ⎯ ⎯ ⎯ ⎯
Second Project, ▨▨▨▨
2nd Septr.
Alternative ⟋⟋⟋⟋
Actual Franco-British ●●●●
Line before the
Battle of the Marne
Armies ⎯⎯⎯⎯ FIRST, B.E.F.; etc.

ROUEN

Somme

AMIENS

SIXTH

ST. QUENTIN

B.E.F.

FIFTH

LAON

Oise

SOISSONS

REIMS

Aisne

FOURTH THIRD

VERDUN

Meuse

LUXEMBURG

Moselle

METZ

SECOND

FIRST

NANCY

TOUL

Moselle

MULHOUSE

BELFORT

Meuse

Bar le Duc

THIRD

Ornain

Marne

Saulx

FOURTH

Bar s.Aube

FOCH

Seine

Aube

Châtillon

CH. THIERRY

Marne

B.E.F.

MELUN

FIFTH

Yonne

B.E.F.

Montereau

PARIS

SIXTH

B.E.F.

Seine

were sixty thousand tons of stores at Havre ; also fifteen 1-5 Sept. thousand men and fifteen hundred horses, besides eight 1914. hundred tons of hay at Rouen, all awaiting transfer to St. Nazaire. By the 30th of August the Inspector-General of Communications, Major-General F. S. Robb, had telegraphed his requirements in tonnage to Southampton ; and on the 1st September the transports for the troops were ordered to Havre. By the 3rd September all stores had been cleared from Rouen, and all troops from Havre ; and by the 5th every pound of stores had been removed from Havre. In fact, in these four days twenty thousand officers and men, seven thousand horses and sixty thousand tons of stores had been shipped from Havre to St. Nazaire, a considerable feat of organization.

A mere comparison of dates, however, will show that, despite this great effort, some days were bound to elapse before the gigantic mass of stores could be landed, the new base thoroughly organized, and all arrangements working smoothly for the despatch of what was needed to the front by a longer line of communication. The arrival of the first reinforcements on the 4th and 5th September was only secured by most strenuous exertions. It was obvious that the II. Corps must enter upon the new operations with its ranks still much depleted, and lacking one-third of its divisional artillery.

NOTE I

OPERATIONS OF THE GERMAN *FIRST* AND *SECOND ARMIES*
2ND–5TH SEPTEMBER 1914

The apprehensions of the British Commander-in-Chief that on Sketch 10. the night of the 1st/2nd September General von Kluck was making Maps 2, 4, preparations to attack him turn out to have been fully justified.[1] 21, 22, From a captured document,[2] the German general had learnt that 23 & 24. " the British Army intended to go into rest billets midday on the " 1st September south of the line Verberie—Crépy en Valois—La " Ferté Milon. It, therefore, seemed still possible to reach it." At 10.15 P.M. on the 1st September he issued orders for the *First Army* to attack the British next day : " the *III.* and *IV. Corps* " against their front, crossing the line Verberie—Crépy at 7 A.M. ; " the *IX. Corps*, starting at 2 A.M., to envelop their right ; and the " *II.* with *IV. Reserve* in rear of it, to envelop their left, whilst " keeping a lookout towards Paris. The *II. Cavalry Corps* was to " connect the *IV.* and *II. Corps*.

---

[1] See page 265 and Kluck, p. 81.
[2] Captured on a cyclist. (Kuhl's " Marne," p. 110.) G.O.A., iii. p. 203, adds that it was a I. Corps operation order captured by the German *III. Corps.*

" These arrangements were in vain, the British Army escaped " envelopment by a timely withdrawal," for it slipped away in the night, as already related. The only collision that took place was near Senlis between the German *II. Corps* and French cavalry and infantry, where the latter offered a stubborn resistance. " The " possibility of dealing a decisive blow against the British could no " longer be reckoned on." Kluck, therefore, after another half day had been wasted, determined to wheel his two eastern corps south-east against the flank of the French Fifth Army in order to assist Bülow. The rest of the *First Army* was to continue its advance on Paris. Orders to this effect were issued at 12.15 P.M. and 1 P.M. on the 2nd. In spite of von Kluck's zigzag movements subsequent to the battle of Le Cateau, his Army was by this time a clear day's march ahead of the *Second*, and on the night of the 2nd his general front curved forward from near La Ferté Milon to Senlis.

On the 28th August, it will be recalled,[1] the German Supreme Command (O.H.L.) in pursuance of the Schlieffen plan had ordered the *Second Army* to march on Paris, and the *First Army* on the lower Seine, assuming that at least the French centre and left were in full retreat on the capital. After the battle of Guise (29th-30th August) both Kluck and Bülow had departed from these orders : the former turned south-eastwards to help Bülow who, instead of marching on Paris, was preparing to follow the French Fifth Army due south.

Approval of this change had been given by O.H.L. late on the 30th, but it was not until the night of the 2nd/3rd September that further orders, embodying a new plan, evidently founded on the optimistic reports received from the Armies, were issued by O.H.L. in the form of a message to the *First* and *Second Armies*. This ran :

" The French are to be forced away from Paris in a south-easterly " direction.

" The *First Army* will follow in echelon behind the *Second Army*, " and will be responsible henceforward for the flank protection of " the force.

" The appearance of some of our cavalry before Paris, as well as " the destruction of all railways leading to Paris is desirable."

These orders placed Kluck in an unpleasant dilemma :[2] the *Second Army* was " a heavy day's march behind the mass of the " *First Army*." To march back a day in order to get into the echelon position desired would have made it impossible to drive the French south-eastwards, an operation which the *First Army* had initiated and alone was at the moment in a position to attempt. For it to mark time for two days was even further out of the question ; the success for which O.H.L. hoped could not be achieved if the *First Army* stood still. Kluck, therefore, considered that he could best carry out the spirit of the orders if he detailed the *IV. Reserve Corps* and a cavalry division for the flank protection against Paris, and moved forward with the rest of his Army across the Marne to drive the French south-eastwards. He kept a second corps, the *II.*, in echelon behind his right as further cover against Paris, and informed O.H.L. that " the proposed driving of the enemy from Paris " in a south-easterly direction could only be carried out by the " advance of the *First Army*." On the evening of the 3rd he issued orders to his corps in accordance with his own views. They began :

[1] See page 235.   [2] See Kluck, p. 85 *et seq.*

" The *First Army* will continue its advance over the Marne 4 Sept.
" to-morrow in order to drive the French south-eastwards. 1914.
" If any British are met with, they are to be driven back."
The importance attached to the flank guard is indicated by the
fact that it was formed only of a Reserve corps, short of a brigade
left behind at Brussels, and the *4th Cavalry Division*, which had been
cut up at Néry. Further, no aeroplanes were allotted to the flank
guard, and air reconnaissance was ordered to the south and south-
east, not westwards.

On the 4th September, therefore, Kluck continued his march
south-south-east between the Marne and the Petit Morin, whilst
Bülow crossed the Marne and advanced a short way south of it
" without important fighting." At 7.30 P.M. Kluck, still under the
impression that his principal task was to drive the Allies south-
eastwards from Paris, and as usual quite in the dark as to the whereabouts of the B.E.F., issued the following orders for next day :—

" The *First Army* will continue its advance against the Seine
" with protection towards Paris. Should the British be caught
" up anywhere they will be attacked."
His corps were directed to cross the Grand Morin, and reach : the
IX., Esternay.; the *III.*, Sancy ; the *IV.*, Choisy ; even the *II. Corps*
was to cross the Marne and reach the Grand Morin below Coulommiers ; the *IV. Reserve Corps* with the *4th Cavalry Division* was to
come further southwards, to the north of Meaux, and the *II. Cavalry
Corps* to go forward to Provins ; that is the *First Army* was sent
southwards against the front of the Fifth Army and the gap between
it and the B.E.F. which grew wider again on this day.

In consequence of the *Third Army* being somewhat in rear of its
place in the line south and south-east of Reims, Bülow ordered for the
5th only a short march to Montmirail—Vertus for the *Second Army*,
thus increasing the start which the *First Army* already had.

During the afternoon of the 4th September, the true situation—
that the Allies were by no means beaten and that the French were
preparing to envelop the German right instead of submitting to
being enveloped—dawned on O.H.L.

How Moltke felt is recorded by Herr Helfferich, the Foreign
Secretary. On the evening of the 4th September, he says :—

" I found Generaloberst von Moltke by no means in a cheerful
" mood inspired by victory, he was serious and depressed. He
" confirmed that our advanced troops were only thirty miles from
" Paris [the Kaiser had just announced this triumphantly to
" Helfferich], ' but,' he added, ' we've hardly a horse in the army
" ' which can go out of a walk.' After a short pause, he continued :
" ' We must not deceive ourselves. We have had successes, but
" ' we have not yet had victory. Victory means annihilation of the
" ' enemy's power of resistance. When armies of millions of men are
" ' opposed, the victor has prisoners. Where are ours ? There were
" ' some 20,000 taken in the Lorraine fighting, another 10,000 here
" ' and perhaps another 10,000 there. Besides, the relatively small
" ' number of captured guns shows me that the French have with-
" ' drawn in good order and according to plan. The hardest work is
" ' still to be done.' " [1]
At 6.45 P.M. the Supreme Command issued the following memo-

[1] " Der Weltkrieg," ii. pp. 17, 18.

randum and orders to all Armies. They appear of sufficient importance to quote *in extenso*.[1] The substance was sent out in cipher by wireless, and was deciphered by the *First* and *Second Armies* about 6 A.M. on the 5th ; the originals were carried by officers in motor cars, who did not arrive until " evening."

" 4th September—7.45 P.M. [German time]

" To all Armies

" The enemy has evaded the enveloping attack of the *First* and " *Second Armies*, and a part of his forces has joined up with those " about Paris. From reports and other information, it appears " that the enemy is moving troops westwards from the front Toul— " Belfort, and is also taking them from the fronts of the *Third, Fourth* " and *Fifth Armies*. The attempt to force the whole French Army " back in a south-easterly direction towards the Swiss frontier is thus " rendered impracticable. It is far more probable that the enemy is " bringing up new formations and concentrating superior forces in " the neighbourhood of Paris, to protect the capital and threaten " the right flank of the German Army.

" The *First* and *Second Armies* must therefore remain facing " the eastern front of Paris. Their task is to act against any opera- " tions of the enemy from the neighbourhood of Paris and to give " each other mutual support to this end.

" The *Fourth* and *Fifth Armies* are still operating against " superior forces. They must maintain constant pressure to drive " them south-eastwards, and by this means open a passage for the " *Sixth Army* over the Moselle between Toul and Epinal. Whether " by co-operating with the *Sixth* and *Seventh Armies* they will then " succeed in driving any considerable part of the enemy's forces " towards Swiss territory cannot yet be foreseen.

" The *Sixth* and *Seventh Armies* will continue to hold the enemy " in position on their front, but will take the offensive as soon as " possible against the line of the Moselle between Toul and Epinal, " securing their flanks against these fortresses.

" The *Third Army* will march in the direction Troyes—Vendeuvre " [that is south]. It will be employed, as the situation demands, " either to the west to support the crossing of the *First* and *Second* " *Armies* over the Seine, or to the south and south-east to co-operate " in the fighting of our armies on the left wing.

" His Majesty therefore orders :

" (1) The *First* and *Second Armies* will remain facing the eastern " front of Paris, to act offensively against any operations of the " enemy from Paris. The *First Army* will be between the Oise " and the Marne, the *Second Army* between the Marne and the Seine. " *II. Cavalry Corps* will be with the *First Army*, *I. Cavalry Corps* with " the *Second Army*.

" (2) The *Third Army* will advance on Troyes—Vendeuvre.

" (3) The *Fourth* and *Fifth Armies*, by a determined advance in a " south-easterly direction, will open a passage across the Upper

[1] Translated from Baumgarten-Crusius' " Die Marneschlacht 1914," pp. 73-4. G.O.A., iii. pp. 311-12, gives not these written omnibus orders, but three separate wireless messages, to the same effect, sent at 7.20, 7.30 and 7.30 P.M. to the *First* and *Second Armies*, the *Third Army*, and the *Fourth* and *Fifth Armies*, respectively.

" Moselle for the *Sixth* and *Seventh Armies*. The right wing of the 4 Sept.
" *Fourth Army* will move through Vitry [on the Marne, 15 miles 1914.
" south-east of Reims], and the right wing of the *Fifth Army* will
" move through Revigny [20 miles E.N.E. of Vitry]. The *IV.*
" *Cavalry Corps* will operate in front of the *Fourth* and *Fifth Armies*.
" (4) The task of the *Sixth* and *Seventh Armies* remains un-
" changed.[1]   VON MOLTKE."

The German Chief of the General Staff, in view of the situation,
had first considered ordering a general halt and a rearrangement of
the forces for a new operation, but finally had decided to carry on
with the original plan in a modified form.[2]
    The orders to the *First* and *Second Armies*, it will be observed,
clearly intended emphasis to be laid on their remaining facing Paris
and not attacking unless the enemy moved against them ; for, in
accordance with German principles, every commander would act
offensively if within reach of the enemy.
    Bülow took immediate steps to obey O.H.L. orders literally.
He stopped the advance of his Army, and wheeled the left wing
slightly forward, so as to begin changing the front gradually from
south to west, in expectation that the *First Army* would conform.[3]
    The staff of the *First Army*, however, was puzzled by the orders
—for the position of the troops in detail had been reported by wireless to O.H.L. The Army could not " remain " between Oise and
Marne, for the greater part of it had crossed the Marne. If there
was danger brewing for the right flank in consequence of further
transfers of troops to Maunoury, Kluck considered the best method
of countering it was to attack all along the line. After receipt of the
wireless summary of the orders, he therefore sent the following
message to O.H.L. : [4]
    " *First Army* in compliance with previous instructions of O.H.L.
" is advancing via Rebais—Montmirail against the Seine. Two
" corps cover it towards Paris, on either side of the Marne. At
" Coulommiers there is contact with about three English divisions,
" at Montmirail with the west flank of the French. The latter are
" offering lively resistance with rear guards, and should suffer very
" considerably if pursuit is continued to the Seine. They have
" hitherto only been driven back frontally and are noways beaten
" out of the field. Their retreat is directed on Nogent sur Seine.
" If the investment of Paris which has been ordered is carried out,
" the enemy would be free to manœuvre towards Troyes. The strong
" forces suspected in Paris are only in the act of assembly. Parts
" of the Field Army will no doubt be sent there, but this will require
" time. Consider breaking contact with the thoroughly battle-fit
" Field Army and shifting of the *First* and *Second Armies* is undesir-
" able. I propose instead :—pursuit to be continued to the Seine
" and then investment of Paris."
    The *First Army*, notwithstanding this proposal, began to make
preparations to obey O.H.L. orders, but it was practically impossible

---

[1] Next day, it may be added, Moltke began withdrawing the *XV. Corps*
and *7th Cavalry Division* from the left, to be railed through Belgium to
reinforce the right.
[2] See page 234.
[3] Bülow, p. 52.
[4] Kuhl's " Marne," p. 128 *et seq.* The time is not given.

at 6 A.M. to get new instructions to the corps in time to stop the marches in progress. The *IV. Reserve Corps*, close at hand, was directed to halt where it happened to be on receipt of the message ; as this order did not reach it until 11 A.M., it had already completed its march for the day. To the *II. Cavalry Corps* instructions were sent by wireless not to get out of touch of the Army Headquarters by advancing further south. As there was no signal communication with the other corps and the officers detailed by them to receive orders were due at 11 A.M. in Rebais, no instructions were sent out to them. It was decided that orders for the new situation should be issued in the evening.

During the day reports showed that the Allies were retreating on the whole front from Montmirail to Coulommiers and " there was no sign of danger to the right flank north of the Marne." Towards evening Lieut.-Colonel Hentsch [1] arrived from O.H.L. to explain the situation, and another officer brought the written copy of the earlier wireless orders. Lieut.-Colonel Hentsch stated that the general situation was dubious (*misslich*). The left wing was held up before Nancy—Epinal, and, in spite of heavy losses, could not get on. The *Fourth* and *Fifth Armies* were only making slow progress. Apparently transfers of troops were being made from the French right wing in the direction of Paris. " It was reported that further " British troops were about to land, perhaps at Ostend. Assistance " to Antwerp by the British was probable." When Lieut.-Colonel Hentsch was informed of the preparations that had been made to stop the advance, he said " that they corresponded to the wishes of " O.H.L., and that the movement could be made at leisure ; no " special haste was necessary." [2]

Sketch 5B.   Thus, on the afternoon of the 5th September, four corps of the German *First Army* were across the Grand Morin with two cavalry divisions ahead of them, but with only a weak flank guard behind the western flank. The Army was thus well inside the angle formed by the fronts of the French Fifth Army and the British Expeditionary Force with that of the French Sixth Army. Kluck's orders for the 6th were not issued from Rebais until 10 P.M. They will be given after the British operations for that day have been described. There was a collision between the flank guard and the French Sixth Army near St. Soupplets (7 miles N.N.W. of Meaux) on the afternoon of the 5th ; but news of this did not reach Kluck until " late at night long after his orders had gone out," [3] and did not therefore affect his decision.

---

[1] He was the General Staff officer in charge of the Intelligence Section at O.H.L.

[2] Kuhl's " Marne," p. 128. These remarks, it is stated by Kuhl, were made in the presence of a witness, Lieut.-Colonel Grautoff, the senior General Staff officer of the *First Army*. In judging of the proceedings, Kuhl points out that it should be borne in mind that " Neither O.H.L. nor " the *First Army* staff had the remotest idea that an immediate offensive " of the whole French army was imminent. The continuation of the " French retreat was accepted as certain. . . . Not a sign, not a word " from prisoners, not a newspaper paragraph gave warning."

[3] Kuhl's " Marne," p. 133. According to Kluck, p. 98, hostile forces had been reported near Dammartin and St. Mard on the 4th September.

NOTE II

THE GENESIS OF THE BATTLE OF THE MARNE
SEQUENCE OF EVENTS ON THE 4TH SEPTEMBER 1914

At 9 A.M. General Galliéni, in order to be prepared to take ad- 4 Sept.
vantage of the march of the German *First Army* south-eastwards 1914.
past Paris, issued a warning order to General Maunoury (Sixth Map 4.
Army) :—
    " It is my intention to send your Army forward against their
" [the German] flank, that is in an eastward direction, in liaison
" with the British troops.
    " I will indicate your direction of march as soon as I know that
" of the British Army.   But take measures at once, so that this
" afternoon your troops will be ready to march, and to-morrow can
" begin a general movement east of the entrenched camp of Paris.
    " Send cavalry reconnaissances immediately into the sector
" between the Chantilly road [which runs northward from Paris]
" and the Marne." [1]
    This plan was telephoned to G.Q.G. about 11 A.M. (possibly as
early as 10 A.M.), with the suggestion that " an order should be
" issued from G.Q.G. that the Army of Paris should get on the
" march in the evening, towards the east, this Army being able to
" operate, according to circumstances, either north or south of the
" Marne."
    General Galliéni subsequently set out to visit British G.H.Q. as
related in the text.
    On his return he found the following cipher telegram from the
Commander-in-Chief (sent off at 12.20 P.M., received in Paris 2.50
P.M.) :
    " Of the two proposals which you have made to me relative to
" the employment of the troops of General Maunoury, I consider
" the more advantageous one is to send the Sixth Army on the
" left [south] bank of the Marne, south of Lagny.
    " Please arrange with the Field-Marshal Commanding-in-Chief
" of the British Army for the execution of the movement." [2]
    Immediately after the despatch of this message General Joffre
telegraphed to the commander of the Fifth Army :
    " Circumstances are such that it might be advantageous to
" deliver battle to-morrow or the day after to-morrow with all the
" forces of the Fifth Army, in co-operation with the British Army
" and the mobile forces of Paris, against German *First* and *Second*
" *Armies*.
    " Please inform me if you consider that your Army is in a state
" to do so with any chance of success.   Reply at once." [3]
    What happened at G.Q.G. at Bar sur Aube has been related at

    [1] " Mémoires du Général Galliéni," p. 114 ;   General Clergérie's
(Galliéni's Chief of the Staff) " Le rôle du Gouvernement de Paris du 1
" au 12 septembre 1914," p. 75.
    [2] F.O.A., i. (ii.), Annexe No. 2326, where it is stated that this answer
is in the records, but not the telephone message which occasioned it.
    [3] Idem, No. 2327. He also asked the same question of General Foch,
who replied at once that he " would be ready to take part in the battle
" proposed for the 6th."

length by Commandant Muller, General Joffre's officier d'ordonnance.[1] The Operations Staff was divided in opinion, some of the officers being in favour of allowing the Germans to penetrate further into the space between Verdun and Paris before striking ; the others advocated seizing the opportunity, " essentially fleeting," which had presented itself. The Commander-in-Chief had not yet made up his mind. " The heat was stifling. Seated in the shade of a large " weeping ash, in the yard of the school of Bar sur Aube, or astride " a straw-bottomed chair, in front of his maps hung on the wall, " he turned over in his mind the arguments for and against. Silently, " as the afternoon passed, his decision ripened. . . . He came to the " idea of extending the local action proposed for the Paris garrison " to all the Allied forces of the left wing. Towards 6 P.M., without " waiting for the information he had requested, he ordered the " draft of an Instruction in this sense to be prepared."

During dinner the answer from General Franchet d'Espèrey arrived, which stated that the battle could not take place before the 6th, and towards 8 P.M., as General Joffre was making himself acquainted with it, he was called to the telephone by the Governor of Paris with reference to the telegram he had received in which General Joffre had stated that it would be more advantageous to use the Sixth Army south of the Marne.

" General Galliéni reported to General Joffre that the Sixth Army " had made arrangements to attack north of the Marne (right bank) " and it appeared to him to be impossible to modify the general " direction to which the Army was already committed, and he " insisted that the attack should be launched without any change " in the conditions of time and place already laid down. Very " quickly, the General-in-Chief accepted the suggestion, which, " for that matter, fitted in with the combined operation of which he " had already admitted the eventuality, and on which, at this " moment, considering himself sufficiently enlightened, he irre- " vocably decided."

General Joffre gave his decision to General Galliéni on the telephone, and the latter was thus able to issue his definite order to the Army of Paris at 8.30 P.M. on the 4th for its movement eastwards on the north bank of the Marne, so as to be abreast of Meaux on the morning of the 6th, ready to attack in liaison with the British.

For the B.E.F. and the other French Armies orders had to be prepared, enciphered and despatched, and this, as will be seen in the next chapter, took many hours, so that none of the commanders, except Galliéni, received instructions for the battle until the morning of the 5th.

---

[1] " Joffre et la Marne," pp. 81 *et seq.*

OPERATIONS, 6 - 13 SEPTEMBER, 1914.
Advance of B.E.F.
Positions at night are shown by dates.

CHAPTER XIV

THE BATTLE OF THE MARNE

6TH SEPTEMBER : THE RETURN TO THE OFFENSIVE

(Sketches B, 10, 12, 13 & 14; Maps 2, 4, 24, 25 & 26)

IN the early morning of the 5th, a little after 3 A.M., a Sketches copy of General Joffre's Instruction No. 6 for an offensive 10, 12, on the 6th was brought to British G.H.Q. by Colonel 13 & 14. Maps 4, Huguet of the French Mission.[1] It was significant that 24, 25, 26. the orders dealt first with the Armies of the left. Their general purport was that the two Armies of the centre (Fourth and Ninth) should hold on whilst the three Armies of the left (including the British Army), and the Third Army on the right, attacked the flanks of the German forces which were endeavouring to push forward between Verdun and Paris. On the extreme left, the Sixth Army, with the I. Cavalry Corps, was to cross the Ourcq north-east of Meaux, between Lizy sur Ourcq and May en Multien (4 miles north of Lizy), and attack eastwards in the direction of Chateau Thierry. Owing to the progress of the enemy, this latter order was subsequently altered to an advance on Meaux. The British Army, facing east, was to attack from the front Changis (7 miles east of Meaux)—Coulommiers in the general direction of Mont-mirail, the French II. Cavalry Corps ensuring connection between it and the Fifth Army. The Fifth Army (General Franchet d'Espèrey) was to attack northwards from the front Sézanne—Courtacon (6 miles south of La Ferté Gaucher), and not north-westwards from Sézanne—Provins, as its commander had proposed. In the centre, the Ninth Army (General Foch) was to cover the right of the Fifth Army, by holding the southern exits of the passages over

---

[1] See Appendix 30. For an explanation of the delay in the receipt of the orders, see Note II. at end of Chapter.

the St. Gond marshes (the gathering ground of the Petit Morin), but with part of its forces on the plateau west of the marshes. On the right, the Fourth (de Langle de Cary) and Third (Sarrail) Armies were to act in conjunction, the former holding the enemy whilst the latter was to attack westwards against the flank of the Germans advancing along the eastern edge of the Argonne.

Fortunately or unfortunately, these orders not having reached Sir John French until the early morning of the 5th, it was too late, without causing confusion, to stop the British columns, which had started early, the II. Corps before midnight and the I. and III. Corps before daybreak. They were therefore allowed to complete their marches southward on this day, and then rest, as already related ; for they were too weary to be called on to retrace their steps. Thus on the night of the 5th/6th, the B.E.F. was, on the right, 10 miles, and on the left, 20 miles in rear of the position, actually in occupation of the Germans, in which the French Commander-in-Chief expected it to be.

General Franchet d'Espèrey, on receipt of Instruction No. 6 at 4 A.M., was also unable to stop the march of his troops ; but at 6 A.M. he issued an order slightly modifying the halt areas of his eastern corps, so that they were given greater depth ; the area of the XVIII. Corps, however, on the left near Provins was not changed, and " in the evening the Fifth Army was established north of " the Seine on the general line Sézanne—Provins," [1] facing north-west, and not on the line Sézanne—Courtacon facing north, as ordered by General Joffre. Thus, although the right was in its proper position, the left was 9 miles in rear of where it should have been, and 12 miles in rear of the British right.

At 9 A.M., soon after Sir John French had decided to take part in the French offensive, General Maunoury arrived at his headquarters and explained fully the course which the Sixth Army would take, stating that it would be west of the Ourcq at 9 A.M. on the 6th ready to attack " à fond." The Field-Marshal promised his support. At 2 P.M. General Joffre, who this day shifted G.Q.G. to Chatillon sur Seine (75 miles south-east of Provins), also arrived at British G.H.Q. " to beg in the name of France " the intervention of the British Army in a battle into

---

[1] F.O.A., i. (ii.) p. 677.

" which he had decided to throw his last man " [1]   Visibly 5 Sept.
moved by the appeal of the French Commander-in-Chief, 1914.
Sir John French gave his word that his Army would do all
that it was possible for men to do.

The ground over which the British Army was about to
advance forms part of the great plateau, east and north-
east of Paris, whose eastern edge, roughly indicated by
Craonne—Reims—Epernay—Nogent sur Seine, is 400 to
500 feet above the plain of Champagne.   It is a country of
great open spaces, highly cultivated, dotted with woods and
villages, but with no great forests except those of Crécy,
Armainvilliers and Malvoisine, all south of Coulommiers.
It is cut into from east to west by the deep valleys, almost
ravines, of the Grand Morin, the Petit Morin, the Marne,
the upper course of the Ourcq, the Vesle, the Aisne and the
Ailette.   These rivers are passable only at the bridges or by
bridging, and form ideal lines on which to fight delaying
actions.   Otherwise, the region on the east of the line
Soissons—Meaux presents no definite positions.

Sir John French's operation orders issued at 5.15 P.M.
on the 5th September directed the Army to advance eastward with a view to attacking, and, as a preliminary, to
wheel to the east pivoting on its right, so that it would come
on to the line—facing north-east, with the right thrown
back and roughly parallel to the Aubetin and lower course
of the Grand Morin, and 5 miles from them—marked by
La Chapelle Iger (south-east of Rozoy)—Villeneuve le
Comte—Bailly (5 miles south-west of Crécy).[2]   This movement was to be completed by the right wing by 9 A.M.
and by the left by 10 A.M.   The Cavalry Division (Major-
General Allenby) and the 3rd and 5th Cavalry Brigades
(acting together under Br.-General Gough)[3] were to cover

---

[1] The scene is described at length in the books of Commandant Muller
(" Joffre et la Marne," pp. 105-7) and Br.-General J. L. Spears (" Liaison,"
pp. 115-18), who were both present.

[2] Sir John French's operation orders and the operation orders of the
Cavalry Division and the I., II. and III. Corps will be found in Appendices
31 to 35.

General Franchet d'Espèrey issued his orders at 6.30 P.M. (F.O.A., i.
(ii.) pp. 679-80).   He informed the Fifth Army that it would attack the
German *First Army* in front, whilst the B.E.F. and Sixth Army attacked
it in flank and threatened its retreat.   The Fifth Army was to advance
in echelon northwards at 6 A.M. on the 6th, the right in front, in the general
direction of Montmirail.   From right to left the corps were X., I., III.,
XVIII. and II. Cavalry, with the group of Reserve divisions following in
second line between the III. and XVIII. Corps.   The cavalry corps was
to keep constantly in liaison with the British.

[3] Henceforward, until officially designated the 2nd Cavalry Division
on the 16th September, the 3rd and 5th Cavalry Brigades acted together

the front and flanks of the force, and connect with the French Armies between which the British were moving. Pezarches, 5 miles to the north of Rozoy, was reached about 7 A.M. by the 3rd Cavalry Brigade without opposition, and thence patrols were pushed out northwards towards the Forest of Malvoisine, north-eastwards upon Mauperthuis and eastwards upon Touquin. At all these points and also in the Forest of Crécy touch was gained with the enemy. The advanced parties of the 2nd Cavalry Brigade on the right flank, reconnoitring towards Pécy (5 miles east by south of Rozoy), in order to get in touch with the French, found themselves in the presence of formidable forces. Large masses of German cavalry could be seen moving southwards upon Jouy le Chatel (east of Pécy),[1] but heavy hostile columns observed on the road north of Pécy, suddenly and without assignable cause, turned about while still two miles distant, and counter-marched to the north.[2]

This was noticed between 8 and 9 A.M.; but immediately afterwards the German cavalry and artillery became aggressive against the right flank. The 2nd Cavalry Brigade was shelled out of Pécy and compelled to retire for a short distance until the rest of the division could come up. The leading regiment of the 3rd Cavalry Brigade, somewhat later, was forced back from Touquin, then shelled out of Pezarches and finally, having no guns in support, was driven back to Rigny (1 mile south-west of Pezarches). As it retired German battalions [3] were seen moving westward from Vaudoy towards Rozoy; this column, which had been sighted by the Flying Corps earlier in the morning, was described by the observers as being of the strength of a brigade, with a brigade of artillery attached to it. The I. Corps, which was to face practically east with its centre about Rozoy, was moving into position, when, about 9 A.M.,

Sketch 14.
Maps 25
& 26.

---

under the command of Br.-General Hubert Gough, and the Cavalry Division contained the 1st, 2nd and 4th Cavalry Brigades. Br.-General J. Vaughan succeeded Br.-General Gough in command of the 3rd Cavalry Brigade.

[1] The German *II. Cavalry Corps* had orders to demonstrate towards Lumigny—Rozoy to cover the withdrawal of the left of the German *First Army*.

[2] The advance of Marwitz's cavalry corps, according to Poseck (p. 92), was not stopped until " about 11 A.M. "; it would appear that the columns seen to retire were ammunition or baggage columns.

[3] If Kluck's map is correct, these must have been *Jäger*. There were four battalions, *Nos. 3, 4, 9, 10*, with the *2nd* and *9th Cavalry Divisions*. According to Kluck, pp. 152-3, the *3rd* and *4th Jäger* were carried in motor lorries.

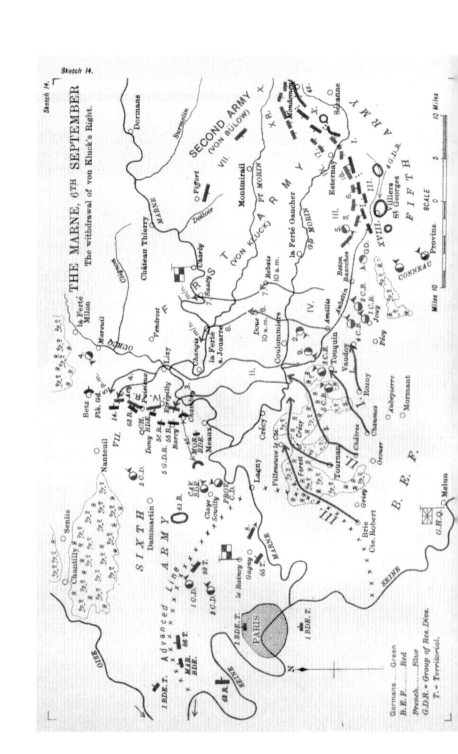

Sketch 14.

THE MARNE, 6TH SEPTEMBER

The withdrawal of von Kluck's Right.

SECOND ARMY
(VON BÜLOW)

FIRST ARMY (VON KLUCK)

FIFTH ARMY

SIXTH ARMY

B. E. F.

PARIS

Germans........Green
B.E.F.........Red
French.......Blue
G.D.R. = Group of Res. Divs.
T. = Territorial.

SCALE
Miles 10   0   5   10 Miles

its leading troops, the advanced guard of the 1st (Guards)
Brigade, found themselves checked when no more than two
miles east of Rozoy by this party of the enemy ; the II.
Corps being, as ordered, near La Houssaye (6 miles north-
west of Rozoy), 5 miles from the left of the I., General Haig
felt uneasy about his left, overshadowed as it was by the
great forests of Crécy and Malvoisine, which could easily
conceal large numbers of the enemy.   He therefore directed
the I. Corps to halt, and its advanced guards to take up a
covering position.   On receiving Haig's report of this action,
the Commander-in-Chief sent orders to the II. Corps to
close in on the I. to Lumigny (4 miles north of Rozoy).
     West of the I. Corps, the II. and III. Corps had marched
north-eastward at 5 A.M. and 3 A.M., respectively, to a line
running from La Houssaye, through Villeneuve le Comte
to Bailly, as ordered.   Both corps reached this destination
in the forenoon, without molestation ; for, though hostile
patrols were encountered as the columns moved through
the Forest of Crécy, the main body of the Germans, estimated at a cavalry division, retired at once.   Shortly after
11 A.M., however, the II. Corps as already mentioned, and
also the III. Corps, received the Commander-in-Chief's
orders to close in to the left of the I. Corps ; and between
1 and 1.30 P.M. they resumed their march in the new direction.   By 3 P.M. their approach had cleared the enemy from
the left flank of the I. Corps ; and shortly afterwards the
1st Division, again advancing eastward upon Vaudoy,
found that the Germans had evacuated their positions and
retreated northward.[1]
     On this day the Commander-in-Chief allotted three
aeroplanes each to the I. and II. Corps for tactical reconnaissance ; many flights were made by the R.F.C., but the
information obtained, except of small bodies moving in
various directions, was chiefly negative, although it revealed the retirement of the German *II. Cavalry Corps* on
Coulommiers, and established that the French Fifth and
Sixth Armies were engaged in battle.   The area in front of
the British, except on the right flank, where the German *IV*.

---

[1] The Germans in question, who had advanced to Vaudoy and Pécy,
were the *2nd* and *9th Cavalry Divisions* and a cyclist battalion ; the *Jäger*
of the *II. Cavalry Corps* were holding the passages of the Grand Morin
near Coulommiers.   Towards 11 A.M., in consequence of the increasing
British artillery fire and the obvious advance of infantry, General von der
Marwitz ordered that the advance should be stopped, and at 1 P.M. that
the fight should be broken off and a retirement made to a position just
south of Coulommiers.

and *II. Corps* had been on the previous day, was reported clear of troops.[1] It was not until 5.15 P.M. that bivouacs and large assemblies of troops were reported at Rebais, mostly north of the town, and at Doue, and correctly identified by the Intelligence Section as the *IV. Corps* ; a little later General Galliéni reported that German troops from the south were recrossing the Marne above Meaux and reaching the Ourcq battlefield. As it had been established that the units of the *II. Corps* which had been engaged with the British left earlier in the day had withdrawn across the Grand Morin, it was assumed that the greater part of the *II. Corps* was already north of the Marne, and that there were no important bodies of the enemy immediately opposite to the British except parts of the *II.* and *IV. Corps* and several cavalry divisions.

At 3.30 P.M. Sir John French issued orders by telegraph for the I. Corps to advance to a line just short of the Grand Morin, from Marolles (4 miles E.S.E. of Coulommiers) to Les Parichets (1 mile south-west of Coulommiers) ; for the II. Corps to come up to west of it from Les Parichets to Mortcerf (5 miles south of Crécy) ; and for the III. Corps to move up into the loop of the Grand Morin south-west-ward of Crécy, between Tigeaux (2½ miles south of Crécy) and Villiers sur Morin (2½ miles north-west of Tigeaux). The Cavalry Division was to advance north-east to the line Choisy—Chevru (4 miles and 6 miles south-west of La Ferté Gaucher), and cover the right flank ; and Gough's cavalry brigades were sent in rear of the left of the I. Corps. But by the time that these orders reached the I. Corps, it was too late for it to make more than a short move to the line Vaudoy—Touquin—Pezarches, 8 miles short of its intended destination, where it halted at 6.30 P.M. In the II. Corps, however, the head of the 3rd Division reached Faremoutiers: whence, after a few skirmishes with the German piquets, the 1/Wiltshire of the 7th Brigade, at 11 P.M., forced the passage of the Grand Morin and seized the heights of Le Charnois, about a mile north of the river. The other divisions of the II. and III. Corps also got to their places. The final positions taken up for the night were as follows, the heads of the II. and III. Corps being up to the Grand

---

[1] The *II. Corps* had marched northwards at 3 A.M., and the *IV. Corps* at 4.30 A.M., leaving weak rear guards on the Grand Morin, and the recon-naissances were not sent far enough afield to discover these movements until the afternoon. It was not until 1.45 P.M. that G.H.Q. asked that an area bounded on the north by Rebais should be reconnoitred.

Morin and the I. Corps and cavalry echeloned to the right
rear :—

Cavalry Division . . .	Jouy le Chatel.
I. Corps	Vaudoy—Touquin—Pezarches.
Gough's Cavalry Brigades	Pezarches—Lumigny.
II. Corps :	
3rd Division	Lumigny northward to Faremoutiers.
5th Division	Mortcerf northward to La Celle sur Morin (1½ miles west of Faremoutiers).
III. Corps	Villiers sur Morin southward to Villeneuve le Comte and Villeneuve St. Denis.

margin: 6 Sept. 1014. Sketches B, 13 & 14. Maps 4 & 26.

The intelligence gathered during the day by the French and British was thus summed up at night, correctly except as regards the *II.* and *IV. Corps* : the *III.* and *IX. German Corps*, with the *Guard Cavalry Division* on their western flank, were opposing the French Fifth Army south of the Grand Morin on the line Esternay—Montceaux—Couperdriz (5 miles W.S.W. of Montceaux): echeloned to the west in second line between the Grand and Petit Morin were part of the German *IV. Corps* at Rebais, with the *5th Cavalry Division* in front of it north of Marolles, the greater part of the *II. Corps* near Meaux, and the *X. Reserve Corps* (as was conjectured) west of Montmirail: the *2nd* and *9th Cavalry Divisions* were opposite the British, and the remainder of the *IV. Corps*, the *IV. Reserve Corps* and the *4th Cavalry Division* opposite the French Sixth Army. Both the Fifth and Sixth French Armies were reported to have pressed the enemy back ; but of their position G.H.Q. had no more information than was derived from British air reports. One of these stated that at 4 P.M. the Fifth Army was fighting south of Esternay and north of Villers St. Georges, and another that at 5 P.M. the Sixth Army was still west of the Ourcq, where on the northern flank, May—Marcilly, a good deal of movement was going on and many shells were bursting. Sir John French therefore issued no orders on the night of the 6th September except a Special Order of the Day [1] and a warning that all the troops should be ready to move at short notice any time after 8 A.M. By evening practically all the " first reinforcements " for the British Army had arrived from the Base.

[1] Appendix 36.

Sketch 14.
Maps 25
& 26.

There had been a collision, the beginning of " the Battle of the Ourcq," as we have seen, on the afternoon of the 5th, between the leading troops of General Maunoury's Sixth Army and the flank guard of the German *First Army*, under General von Gronau, consisting of his *IV. Reserve Corps* and the remains of the *4th Cavalry Division* (cut up at Néry). The German force, " driven into a semi-" circle of 2½ miles' radius, and under fire of superior artillery," had, during the night, fallen back and broken contact. During the 6th—a day of taking contact all along the front—the Moroccan Brigade, 45th, 55th Reserve, 56th Reserve, 63rd Reserve and 14th Divisions had moved forward, getting touch with the German infantry from 10.30 A.M. onwards, and driving it in, so that at night, after Gronau had been reinforced, the two opponents were facing each other west of the Ourcq on a nearly north and south line, Varreddes (north-east of Meaux)—Etrepilly—Acy. There, with little change except extension northwards, they were to remain until the last day of the battle. Between the right of Maunoury's Army and the left of the B.E.F. there was a gap of eight miles, in which, tending to increase the separation, lay both the Marne and its tributary the Grand Morin. At 4.30 P.M., however, G.Q.G. telephoned to G.H.Q. stating that a division and a cavalry brigade would arrive early on the 7th on the left of the B.E.F. to fill the gap and furnish support to the British left flank.

The French Fifth Army also made little progress on the 6th. Having on the previous day, like the B.E.F., continued the retreat, it had not, on the night of the 6th/7th, except on the right and a single point in the centre (Montceaux at 10 P.M.), reached the line, the great highway Sézanne—Esternay—Sancy—Courtacon, fixed by General Joffre as its starting line at the opening of the battle in the morning. It did not move on the 6th until 6 A.M. and its average advance was only four or five miles, as it proceeded with the utmost caution.

In his orders issued at 6.30 P.M. on the 5th, General Franchet d'Espèrey ordered his corps to march northwards to the attack, in echelon, the right leading, adding, " the corps commanders will take " great care not to engage all their infantry at once, as the operation " will probably last several days."

Conneau's cavalry corps at noon found that there was no enemy within nine miles ; but it did not push on to the great highway. Towards evening, going forward again at 4.30 P.M., it had an exchange of artillery fire with Germans established in Courtacon, and then, as the day had been hot and water was scarce, the whole corps except one division was sent back to Provins, the starting place of the morning.

Until midday the XVIII. Corps, the left corps of the Fifth Army, did nothing but reconnoitre and push forward advanced guards, which were " not to engage any important element of the enemy " beyond the Aubetin," which runs 2½ miles south of the great highway. The III. Corps, its 5th and 6th Divisions commanded by Generals Mangin and Pétain, advanced at first without difficulty, then received artillery fire from heavy guns, and, about noon, being

[1] Summarized from the French Official Account.

two miles south of the great highway, was getting ready to attack 6 Sept. the Germans reported on it. The I. and X. Corps drifted north- 1914. eastwards, for, as early as 9 A.M., the left of Foch's Army was calling for help ; at noon, the 1st Division, the left of the I. Corps, was held up two miles south of Esternay by machine-gun fire ; the 2nd Division and X. Corps had seen nothing of the enemy.

At 1.30 P.M. General Franchet d'Espèrey issued the following order :

" In order that the co-operation of the neighbouring Armies may " make itself effectively felt, the Fifth Army will not this evening " cross the line [left to right] Couperdrix [2 miles south of the great " highway]—Montceaux [on the highway]—Courgivaux—Esternay " [both on the highway]—Clos le Roi—Charleville [5 miles north of " the highway].

" On this front, all the corps and the Group of Reserve divisions " will very solidly entrench, so that they can resist coûte que coûte " any enemy counter-attack."

Except in the centre, the line defined, facing north-west, was reached, after some fighting with German rear guards, the III. Corps losing Courgivaux after it had reached the village, and the X. Corps being driven back a little.

At night the Fifth Army ordered for the 7th : " continuation of " the offensive manœuvre under the same conditions of economy " of force." The X. Corps, then ahead, was to start at 7.30 A.M., the other corps at 6 A.M.

The operations of the French Ninth Army, on the right of the Fifth, must receive some notice, as they had a most important influence on the battle.

The Ninth Army had been ordered " to cover the right of the " Fifth Army," by " holding the southern exits of the Marshes of St. " Gond," and " sending part of its forces to the plateau north of " Sézanne." It would seem that General Foch determined to take a share in the offensive with his left and centre, leaving the protection of the flank of the Allied attack to his right wing alone. He put his XI. Corps (2 divisions) behind the upper course of the Somme (which, running north-west, almost touches the Marshes of St. Gond before turning north-east), and the IX. Corps (3 divisions) behind the marshes, but directed it on the 5th to push strong advanced guards over them and be prepared to advance on the 6th. The left, the 42nd Division (not attached to a corps), was sent to the plateau north of Sézanne, but definitely ordered to attack with the Fifth Army on its left.

On the 6th, the advanced guards of the IX. Corps were driven back across the marshes, which could only be crossed on a few causeways ; the XI. Corps lost the line of the Somme, its left falling back about one and a half miles, and Foch reinforced it with the one division in his reserve. The 42nd Division left the plateau and attempted to advance northwards, but, meeting the German *19th Division (X. Corps)*, was driven back and appealed to the X. Corps (Fifth Army) on its left for help.

Of the rest of the French forces on the eastern wing, it need only be said that the First Army (General Dubail) and Second Army (General de Castelnau) successfully resisted the attacks of the German *Seventh* and *Sixth Armies* under Crown Prince Rupprecht of Bavaria, although the XV. Corps had been taken from de Castelnau and the

XXI. Corps from Dubail and sent to fill the gaps on either flank of the Fourth Army, near Revigny and Mailly. So stout was the French defence that on the 8th September Moltke decided to " abandon the " Lorraine enterprise completely, as it had no hope of success." The Third Army (General Sarrail) and Fourth Army (Gen. de Langle de Cary) also practically held their ground, with some vicissitudes, against the German *Fifth* and *Fourth Armies* and the left half of the *Third Army*; their success was mainly due to the field artillery, which pinned the Germans to the ground by day, and induced the German Crown Prince to attempt, without much success, a night attack.

NOTE I

THE GERMAN RIGHT WING ON THE 6TH SEPTEMBER

Sketch 14. Maps 25 & 26. On the evening of the 5th September, the German *First Army* had four corps (*IX.*, *III.*, *IV.* and *II.*) and two cavalry divisions (*2nd* and *9th*) south of the Marne, beyond the Grand Morin. Only the extreme left had been in contact with French rear guards, and it was assumed by General von Kluck that both British and French would continue their retreat next day. North of the Marne, and west of the Ourcq, was the flank guard, consisting of the *IV. Reserve Corps* and the *4th Cavalry Division*, in action with Maunoury's Army. During the evening an officer of the *II. Corps*, who came to Army Headquarters to receive orders, brought an air report that the flank guard was in action against an enemy from the direction of Paris ; but no special attention was paid to this " in no way alarm- ing " report. At 10 P.M. General von Kluck issued the following orders for the 6th : [1]
" After the *First Army*, in co-operation with the *Second Army*, " has driven the British and French opposite them over the Seine, " both Armies have been assigned by O.H.L. the task of remaining " opposite the east front of Paris in order to deal offensively with " hostile enterprises from Paris, the *First Army* between Marne and " Oise, the *Second Army* between Marne and Seine. Aviators report " strong hostile columns in retreat on Tournan and Rozoy, as well " as from Courtacon on Provins, and from Esternay on Nogent sur " Seine."
Summarizing the details, the three corps on the right were to make a retirement, short on the left (east) and some fifteen miles on the right (west), so as to face south-west, the *III.* going to La Ferté Gaucher, the *IV.* to Doue, and the *II.* to north-east of Meaux, whilst the *IX. Corps* (next to the *Second Army*) and the *IV. Reserve Corps* (the flank guard) halted, and the two cavalry divisions covered the march of the three left corps by advancing to the area around Rozoy—Lumigny—where they ran into the right of the B.E.F.
Nothing had been heard from the flank guard during the 5th, but towards midnight, after the issue of the above order, a telephone message was received from the *II. Corps* that the *IV. Reserve Corps* had run into an enemy of superior force, and, after dusk, had retired (6 miles) behind the Thérouanne stream. At 4.30 A.M. on the 6th it retired still further to a north and south line through Etrepilly. Later a staff officer, whose car had broken down, arrived from the

[1] Given in full in Kluck, pp. 106-8.

IV. Reserve Corps, and gave a clear account of the danger threatening 6 Sept. the flank of the Army. Kluck decided to support the *IV. Reserve* 1914. *Corps,* and at once ordered the *II. Corps* to its assistance. The corps started northward at 3 A.M., sending artillery ahead, and leaving only weak rear guards on the Grand Morin. It began to reach the Ourcq battlefield about 10 A.M., from which, about 3 P.M., one of its divisions, the *3rd,* on the southern flank, reported that it was in difficulties, being attacked by British forces ! This report as it happened misled O.H.L. (see Sketch 16). The *IV. Corps,* according to the original order, recrossed the Grand Morin at 4 A.M. without interference, and by 9 A.M. was assembled, the *7th Division* near Rebais and the *8th* near Doue, where they remained all day, just beyond the area reconnoitred by the British airmen until the late afternoon.

Owing to the critical state of affairs on the Ourcq, at 4.30 P.M. the *IV. Corps* was sent an order (received at 5.45 P.M.) to " march " to-day north of La Ferté sous Jouarre, in order to be ready to sup- " port the *IV. Reserve Corps* and *II. Corps.*" At 9.30 P.M. a further order was issued for it to continue its march during the night so as to be on the Ourcq battlefield by the grey of dawn. The divisions of the corps started off at 8 P.M. and marched all night, covering twenty-five to twenty-seven miles. After a short halt for coffee about 4 A.M. they reached the battlefield between 7 and 8 A.M. on the 7th.[1]

By the removal of the *II.* and *IV. Corps* the country north of the B.E.F. was entirely cleared of troops except weak rear guards on the Grand Morin, and the two cavalry divisions which, as we have seen, had fallen back on Coulommiers. When the *IV. Corps* marched back, General von der Marwitz was directed to cover the front vacated by it and the *II. Corps.* To assist in this Richthofen's cavalry corps was also available, as it had moved during the 6th to the right of the *III. Corps,* now Kluck's right corps beyond the Marne. Owing to French artillery fire, the *III. Corps* had not been able to carry out its retirement to La Ferté Gaucher, and had taken up position to protect the right of the *IX. Corps,* which was surprised by fire and very soon seriously engaged with the French Fifth Army, around Courgivaux.

In the *Second Army,* in obedience to the O.H.L. instruction to face towards Paris, General von Bülow issued the following order on the evening of the 5th September, which, if it had been possible to carry it out, would have left the Army facing south-west with half its wheel towards Paris completed :

" The *I. Cavalry Corps* will observe the south front of Paris " between Marne and Seine. The *VII. Corps* [near Montmirail] " will remain in its quarters, ready to march. It will maintain con- " stant communication with the *First Army.*

" The *X. Reserve, X.* and *Guard Corps* will, with their advanced

---

[1] The maps both of the German Official Account and of the official monograph " Das Marnedrama " show the *7th* and *8th Divisions* still at Rebais and Doue at midnight on the 6th/7th, and neither account mentions the time of starting nor the night march ; but the histories of seven of the eight infantry regiments which are available all give the above times and speak of the hardships of the long night march, the men depressed by the knowledge that they were retiring by the roads by which they had advanced a few days earlier.

" guards, reach the line Montmirail—Marigny le Grand [7½ miles " south of Fère Champenoise]."

The attempted advance, as we have seen, brought the *Second Army*, supported on the left by half of the *Third Army*, and on the right by the *IX.* and *III. Corps* of the *First Army*, in contact with Foch's troops and Franchet d'Espèrey's right (X.) corps. But, as the German Official Account says, " in spite of every sacrifice, and in " spite of heavy losses, they could gain only a little ground towards " the south."

Thus, on the night of the 6th/7th, the *Second Army* was still facing south ; on its right the *IX.* and *III. Corps* of the *First Army* faced E.S.E., all except the western half of the *III. Corps* in contact with the French. On the Ourcq, facing west, the *II.* and *IV. Reserve Corps* were engaged with Maunoury's Army, with the *IV. Corps* hurrying to their assistance. To fill the gap between the two halves of the *First Army*, over thirty miles across, opposite the B.E.F., there were available only four cavalry divisions, with a few cyclist and *Jäger* battalions. A series of rivers, however, the Grand Morin, the Petit Morin and the Marne, gave the German troops excellent lines on which to stand and delay an enemy.

NOTE II

THE DESPATCH OF GENERAL JOFFRE'S ORDER FOR THE BATTLE OF THE MARNE

According to the French Official Account [i. (ii.) p. 785], ciphered telegraphic orders were despatched on the 4th September to the Fifth and Sixth Armies at 11.15 P.M. ; to the Ninth Army and the Military Government of Paris at 11.50 P.M. ; and to the French Mission at G.H.Q. at 12.10 A.M. on the 5th. Copies were also carried by officers in motor cars. The first copy, whether written or telegraphed is not stated, reached General Foch at 2.30 A.M. ; General Franchet d'Espèrey at 4 A.M. ; General Galliéni, at about the same time (he telephoned at 4.30 A.M. to G.H.Q. to say that he had " received definite orders, and am sending you a copy by a French " officer, who is leaving at once in a fast car," and this copy is marked 4 A.M.) ; and Colonel Huguet, about 3 A.M. (p. 95 of his book, English translation). At 10 P.M. Lieut.-Colonel Brécard, the liaison officer between G.Q.G. and the French Mission at G.H.Q., had telephoned to Colonel Huguet, " J'y ai trouvé une solution un peu différente " résultant de la conférence de Bray entre le général Wilson et le " général Franchet d'Espèrey, solution que le général Joffre avait " prise comme base de ses ordres. Copie de ces ordres vous est " envoyé en télégramme chiffré que je vous prie de transmettre au " maréchal French en lui demandant son assentiment." It was added that written confirmation of the telegram would be carried by an officer, Captain de Galbert. There is no note in the records of G.H.Q. or of the French Mission that this warning of fresh orders being on their way was delivered to G.H.Q. by Colonel Huguet. According to Commandant Muller, Joffre's officier d'ordonnance (" Joffre et le Marne," pp. 93-4), Captain de Galbert (later killed in action) left G.Q.G. (Bar sur Aube) at about 11 P.M. for Melun, 90 miles away, with special instructions to clear up any misunderstanding there might be as to which of the various plans that had been 6 Sept. discussed was to be executed.   He returned at 9 A.M. " without 1914. " having been able to take direct contact either with the Field- " Marshal or his staff."   The use of the word " direct " is no doubt intended to convey that he reached the French Mission, but was not allowed by Colonel Huguet to see any British officer.

In " 1914 " (p. 109), Sir John French states that Colonel Huguet, " with a staff officer from Joffre," visited him during the night and communicated to him the French Commander-in-Chief's proposals. On the other hand, Huguet in his book (p. 95) distinctly says that General Wilson took Joffre's orders to Sir John French soon after 3 A.M., and this is confirmed by the entry in Sir Henry Wilson's diary (" Field-Marshal Sir Henry Wilson," i. p. 174) :   " At 3 A.M. Huguet " brought me Joffre's orders."   It continues, " I went to see him " [*i.e.* Sir John French] at 7 A.M., and he has agreed to retrace his " steps and join in the offensive."

The officers on duty at G.H.Q. on the night of the 4th/5th saw nothing of Captain de Galbert.   Immediately after the latter's return, however, a telephone message was received at G.Q.G. notifying Sir John French's adhesion in principle to the operations ordered—no doubt as the result of General Wilson's 7 A.M. visit—so de Galbert's failure was of no consequence.

CHAPTER XV

THE BATTLE OF THE MARNE (*continued*)

7TH SEPTEMBER : THE MARCH TO THE GRAND MORIN

(Sketches B, 13 & 15 ; Maps 4, 25 & 27)

Sketch 15.
Maps 4,
25 & 27. OWING to delay in transit, the instructions from General Joffre to push on, not eastwards as first ordered, but northwards, echeloned left in front so as to be ready to fall on the right flank of the German forces if they offered battle to the Fifth Army, did not reach G.H.Q. at Melun till 11 A.M. on the 7th. But the British cavalry was early on the move ; the Cavalry Division on the right pushed eastward to the Grand Morin, upon Leudon (3½ miles south of La Ferté Gaucher) and Choisy, and the 3rd and 5th Cavalry Brigades on its left, northward upon Chailly and Coulommiers. The advanced parties of the 3rd Cavalry Brigade found that the Germans had left Mauperthuis (3 miles south of the Grand Morin) just as they themselves entered it. The enemy seemed to be withdrawing his covering troops northward. The 4th Cavalry Brigade, advancing further east, came upon cavalry, cyclists and guns south of Dagny (2 miles south-west of Choisy), and forced them back north and east across the front of the 2nd Cavalry Brigade. The 9th Lancers, who were at the head of the latter brigade, thereupon pushed on to the hamlet of Moncel, a mile and a half to the south-east of Dagny, which was held by the enemy. A German patrol was driven out of the latter, and it was then occupied by a squadron of the 9th. A troop of the 9th was sent northward to protect the left flank of this squadron ; another troop, with Lieut.-Colonel D. G. M. Campbell and the headquarters of the regiment, halted at the northern outskirts of the village ; and the machine-gun section was posted in an orchard to the west of it. A patrol presently reported the advance of a German

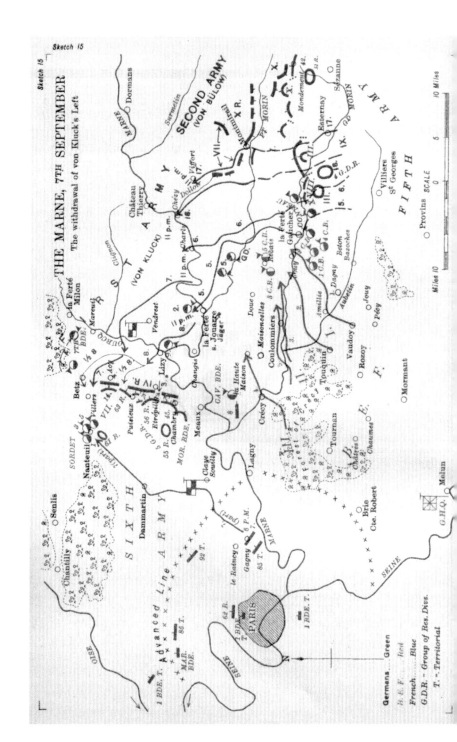

THE MARNE, 7TH SEPTEMBER

The withdrawal of von Kluck's Left

SECOND ARMY (VON BÜLOW)

FIFTH ARMY

SIXTH ARMY

A R M Y (VON KLUCK)

MARNE

Germans...Green
B.E.F. ...Red
French.....Blue
G.D.R. = Group of Res. Divs.
T. = Territorial

SCALE

Miles 10   5   0   5   10 Miles

PARIS

G.H.Q.

N

squadron, one hundred and twenty strong, which came up at a canter in one rank towards Colonel Campbell's party. Unfortunately the machine gun jammed immediately ; [1] but Colonel Campbell with about thirty men charged at once at top speed. The Germans did not increase their pace to meet the shock and were completely overwhelmed, as far as the narrow front of the 9th Lancers extended. Colonel Campbell was wounded, but the survivors were rallied and led back into Moncel ; the Germans, fearing a trap, did not follow. Further to the right, a squadron of the 18th Hussars working its way forward on foot was charged just beyond Faujus ($2\frac{1}{2}$ miles south of Choisy) by a weak German squadron,[2] which it practically annihilated by rapid fire at two hundred yards' range. Sixty-three of the *1st Guard Dragoons* were killed or wounded in this affair, and only three escaped ; the 18th Hussars had only two of their led horses slightly wounded.

To the west of the cavalry, the Wiltshire (3rd Division), in their advanced position across the Grand Morin near Le Charnois, were attacked at 6 A.M. by some two hundred dismounted men of the *Guard Cavalry Division*, whom they beat off without any difficulty. The 2/South Lancashire, making its way forward to cover the right of the Wiltshire, was engaged by the enemy in the woodlands and suffered some loss. Cyclist patrols of the III. Corps, however, ascertained that by 7 A.M. the ground within a radius of 3 miles north and north-west of Crécy on the Grand Morin was clear. Aerial reconnaissances confirmed the general impression that the enemy was withdrawing northward, though there were still considerable bodies both of cavalry and infantry just north of the Grand Morin beyond La Ferté Gaucher.

Acting upon this information the Field-Marshal issued orders at 8 A.M. for the Army to continue its advance northeastward across the river in the general direction of Rebais. The corps were to march north-eastwards upon as close a front as the roads would permit, and on reaching the line Dagny—Coulommiers—Maisoncelles, the heads of columns were to halt and await further orders. Meanwhile, the

---

[1] The German account in Vogel is that the gun was spotted, and that a sergeant and six men galloped up, drove off the gun crew and damaged the mechanism with a stone ; otherwise the two accounts agree. The attackers were Rittmeister von Gayling's (2nd) squadron, *1st Guard Dragoons*.

[2] Two-thirds of the 4th Squadron, *1st Guard Dragoons* (Poseck, p. 99).

Cavalry Division moved northward, making good the
course of the Grand Morin as far east as La Ferté Gaucher ;
it met nothing but a few patrols, but ascertained that
a German cavalry brigade and a battery had re-crossed
the Grand Morin at 3 A.M. The 5th and 3rd Cavalry
Brigades also pushed northward, the former on Rebais,
the latter on Coulommiers. The 3rd met with some
little resistance at the bridges over the Grand Morin
just east of Coulommiers, and its guns came into action to
silence some German artillery on the north bank of the
stream, and to shell retiring parties of the enemy. This
caused some delay, but the brigade was able to pursue
its way 4 miles towards Doue, where it was checked by
infantry and machine guns. The 5th Cavalry Brigade,
with little hindrance, between 5 and 6 P.M. reached Rebais,
whence the German rear parties retired leaving a few
prisoners in the hands of the British.

Behind the cavalry screen, the infantry continued its
march without serious incident ; the arrival of the " first
" reinforcements " had tended to raise the spirits of the
men, and there was cheering evidence of the enemy's demoralization. The country near the roads was littered
with empty bottles ; and the inhabitants reported much
drunkenness among the Germans. Indeed, some British
artillery drivers while cutting hay discovered German
soldiers, helplessly drunk, concealed under the topmost
layer of the stack.

Sir John French issued no orders for any advance beyond
the line Dagny—Maisoncelles, but General Haig, in order
to keep touch with the French, swung his right five miles
forward to the Grand Morin. Thus the general forward
movement on the 7th, although it brought the infantry
up to and across the Grand Morin and met General Joffre's
wishes, did not average more than seven or eight miles.

The positions taken up by the Army for the night
beyond and along the Grand Morin were as follows :—

Sketches
B, 13 &15.
Maps 25
& 27.

Cavalry Division	South of the Grand Morin at Choisy, Feraubry.
5th and 3rd Cavalry Brigades, and 4th (Guards) Brigade	North of the Grand Morin on the west side of Rebais.
I. Corps (less 3rd and 4th Brigades)	Along south bank of the Grand Morin from Jouy sur Morin to St. Siméon.
3rd Brigade	La Bochetière (9 miles south-east of Coulommiers).

II. Corps . . . . . Along north bank of the Grand 7 Sept.
Morin from Chauffry to 1914.
Coulommiers.

III. Corps . . . . . North of the Grand Morin in
front of Maisoncelles, facing
north-east, from Giremou-
tiers to La Haute Maison.

Throughout this day the Fifth and Sixth French Sketch 15.
Armies were reported to be making good progress. By Maps 4,
evening General Franchet d'Espèrey's XVIII. Corps—the 25 & 27.
cavalry on its left being in touch with the British—and
III. Corps, had reached the Grand Morin, the heads of the
5th and 6th Divisions getting across its upper course.
The I. and X. Corps were abreast of them. The position
of the Army was reported to be a line from Charleville (7
miles south-east of Montmirail) to La Ferté Gaucher.
General Maunoury, having advanced to the line Penchard
—Etrepilly—Betz, some five miles west of the Ourcq, was
able to report that German artillery was retiring to the
eastern bank of that river. There was still a gap of some
ten miles between his Army and the British, but there
were assembling in this gap, south of the Marne at Meaux,
the 8th Division of the IV. Corps and a cavalry brigade.[1]
Aerial reconnaissance indicated that Kluck was withdrawing two of his corps (*II. and I V.*)[2] with all haste northward ; and, from identifications by contact during the day
and the fact that two German cavalry divisions had been
seen between 5.15 and 6.30 P.M. moving into bivouac at
Orly (3½ miles north and a little west of Rebais), with yet
more cavalry passing northward to the east of them, to
Le Trétoire, Bellot and other passages of the Petit Morin,
it seemed as if the enemy was trusting to the *I. and II.
Cavalry Corps*[3] to hold the British in check at the Petit

---

[1] The IV. Corps had been brought from the Third Army to Paris ;
its 7th Division had been badly cut up at Ethe, and its 8th at Virton, on
22nd August. Of the latter, General de Lartigue, its commander, reported :
" full (bourrée) of reservists recently arrived at the depôts, and with in-
" sufficient officers and N.C.O.'s [most of whom had fallen], it had only
" a feeble offensive value, and to engage it too soon would be to risk
" disorganizing it."

[2] The Intelligence map shows the *II.* on the Ourcq and the *IV.* north
of the Marne, between Chateau Thierry and Charly (7 miles south-west of
Chateau Thierry). The divisions of the latter corps really crossed the
Marne on either side of La Ferté sous Jouarre, and on the 7th were in
action in the battle of the Ourcq.

[3] It is again recalled that these cavalry corps included eight infantry
(*Jäger*) battalions besides cyclist companies and machine-gun companies.
(See Appendix 7.)

Morin during a change of dispositions. The bridges over the Marne from Trilport (just above Meaux) to Trilbardou (below Meaux) and one at La Ferté sous Jouarre were reported destroyed, and the congestion at the remaining bridge at La Ferté was such as to offer good results from a rapid advance towards that point. It was also reported, however, that a considerable force of the enemy lay at Pierre Levée (5 miles south-west of the bridge) to guard against any such attempt.[1]   Indeed, the left of the British III. Corps had not been allowed to take up its position between Maisoncelles and La Haute Maison, some two or three miles only from Pierre Levée, without being shelled. The 8th September, therefore, promised to be an important day.

General Joffre's Instruction No. 7, issued at 3.45 P.M. on the 7th September, directed the Armies on the left to follow the enemy with the bulk of their forces, but in such a manner as always to retain the possibility of enveloping the German right wing.   For this purpose, the French Sixth Army was to gain ground gradually towards the north on the right bank of the Ourcq ; the British forces were to endeavour to get a footing " in succession (sic) across the " Petit Morin, the Grand Morin and the Marne " ; the Fifth Army was to accentuate the movement of its left wing, and with its right support the Ninth Army.   The road Sablonnières —Nogent l'Artaud—Chateau Thierry, allotted to the British, was made the boundary between them and the Fifth Army.

Accordingly, on the evening of the 7th September, the Field-Marshal issued orders [2] for the advance to be continued against the line of the Marne from Nogent l'Artaud to La Ferté sous Jouarre : the cavalry to push on in pursuit, keeping touch with the French Fifth Army on the right, and with the Sixth Army on the left.   The Grand Morin was already behind the British, but before the Marne could be reached, the Petit Morin had to be crossed : a canal-like stream, twenty feet wide, running through a narrow valley, with steep, wooded sides, approachable only through close, intricate country, studded with innumerable copses, villages and hamlets, and with only six bridges in the sector in question.   The Marne itself, from seventy to eighty yards wide with many windings, runs through a deeper, but wider and more open valley, so that from

---

[1] Four *Jäger* battalions and a cavalry brigade, according to Kuhl's " Marne," p. 207.   [2] Appendix 37.

either side the heights on the other appear to be command- 7 Sept.
ing ; most of the bridges had been destroyed by the Allies 1914.
during the retreat, and any repairs which had been done
by the Germans would no doubt be demolished.   Thus the
ground was all in favour of the enemy's rear guards.

THE FRENCH ON THE 7TH SEPTEMBER [1]

The summary of the operations of the Sixth Army on the Ourcq Sketch 15.
is as follows :—   Maps 25
" The success of the operations of the Sixth Army on the 7th & 27.
" September depended on the entry into line, on the left of the Army,
" of the 61st Division and Sordet's cavalry corps ; for on the right
" the 5th Group of Reserve Divisions (General Lamaze) was held up
" by the enemy ; its commander even began to consider the eventu-
" ality of a retirement and had organized a position behind his front.
" The 61st Division and the cavalry corps came into the line towards
" midday, but could make no progress against an enemy also re-
" inforced ; they even drifted back in the evening on Nanteuil les
" Haudouin."

The 8th Division, which, with a provisional cavalry brigade
under Colonel Brantes, formed from the 5th Cavalry Division,
was to fill the gap between the Sixth Army and the British, reached
Chessy (6 miles south-west of Meaux) about 5 A.M., the cavalry arriving at 6.40 A.M.   On receiving orders from General Maunoury to
act offensively in co-operation with the B.E.F., the commander of
the 8th Division, General de Lartigue, replied that his division " was
" in a state of extreme fatigue, as a result of the presence in its ranks
" of too great a number of reservists without cadres and without
" training, who had been sent to replace the casualties suffered in
" Belgium and on the Meuse." [2]   He gave his men a long rest until
1 P.M., after which they made a short advance.   As this division
took no part in the fighting, was in fact incapable of fighting, and
was withdrawn at 2.30 P.M. on the 9th to join Maunoury's Army on
the Ourcq, no further mention of it will be made, or of the provisional cavalry brigade, which did not obtain touch of the enemy.

In the Fifth Army, General Franchet d'Espèrey, between 7 and

[1] Summarized from the French Official Account.
[2] According to Commandant Grasset, in " Virton," pp. 178-9, the losses
of the four infantry regiments of the 8th Division, then in the Third Army,
in the battle of Virton on the 23rd August, had been :

130th : all the field officers and nearly all the other officers ; the débris
    formed a weak battalion ;
124th : the 3 battalion commanders and 770 other ranks ; it had
    hardly any officers left ;
115th : one battalion was reduced to two companies and its commander
    killed ;
117th : a battalion commander and 725 officers and men lost.

On the 30th-31st August, the division was engaged in the " combats vers
" Mont devant Sassy " and " Villers devant Dun," in defence of the
passages of the Meuse ; but its losses there have not been published.   It
was then drawn into reserve and was thus available to be transferred by
rail to the Sixth Army.

9 A.M., heard from his aviators that on his front numerous German columns were retreating northwards, leaving only weak detachments behind. " Between 10 and 11 A.M. the British Air Force reported, " the message being telephoned from G.H.Q. to the Sixth and Fifth " Armies, that all the German Army facing the Fifth Army was in " retreat northward." This was the case.

At 8 A.M. General Joffre by telephone told General Franchet d'Espèrey that " it would be of utility if he made the left of the Fifth " Army get up level with the British right." The latter duly informed the XVIII. Corps of the Commander-in-Chief's wishes, and all his corps of the reported retreat of the Germans. Nevertheless, their progress was very slow, being " hampered at least by rear " guards. . . . Towards the end of the morning these rear guards " slipped off . . . the march was resumed," again with great precaution ; for General d'Espèrey in instructions issued at 10 A.M. had " insisted on the necessity of acting methodically and, in particular, " of co-ordinating efforts." In view of German counter-attacks, which, he said, he considered possible at the end of the afternoon, he ordered " every position taken to be solidly organized immediately ; " this operation performed, the movement ahead will not be re- " sumed, until aid has been given, by every means, to facilitate the " progress of neighbouring corps." [1] The commander of the Fifth Army thereupon called on General Foch to cover his right during the attack on Montmirail. On this flank the X. Corps had only had an artillery fight to stop an attack on Foch's 42nd Division, which was retiring ; d'Espèrey had previously told the X. Corps that it was more important to support the left of the Ninth Army than to cut off the retreat of the Germans in front of the I. Corps from Montmirail. To the B.E.F., which had informed him that all the Germans in front of him were retiring, he telephoned at 10.15 A.M., " it is " extremely urgent that the British Army should act on the flank of " the retreating German columns."

In the afternoon Conneau's cavalry, then well behind the British, being ordered to pursue, advanced without gaining contact with the enemy and halted on the Grand Morin at 6.30 P.M. The XVIII. and III. Corps got up to the Grand Morin, 5 miles from the great highway, Sézanne—Sancy ; the 2nd Division of the I. and the X. Corps were abreast of them, the 1st Division alone pushing on somewhat further to within a couple of miles of Montmirail. The marches of the Fifth Army were accomplished without incident, except that between 5.30 and 6.30 P.M. one battery, on ahead with a cavalry regiment, fired on a German column marching on Montmirail, and was shelled in reply. " At 6.30 P.M. the detachment, judging its " mission terminated, went to its billets."

The Ninth Army, except the 42nd Division, which was driven in a little, had practically a quiet day, for the Germans opposite were side-slipping eastward so as to get clear of the Marshes of St. Gond before attacking. The result was that Foch informed Franchet d'Espèrey that the situation on his left, " without being " compromised, was serious. . . . Whereas the right was making " progress against the enemy, who was drawing back." Neverthe-

[1] He had forgotten the maxim :

" Il faut qu'il attaque, pousse et poursuive sans cesse.
Toutes les manœuvres sont bonnes alors, il n'y a que les sages qui ne valent rien." (Maurice Comte de Saxe.)

less he reinforced his right with his last and only reserve, the 18th 7 Sept. Division. In his 3.45 P.M. order [1] General Joffre only required of the 1014. Ninth Army that it should " hold on, on the front it occupied, until " the arrival of the reserves of the Fourth Army on its right would " enable it to participate in the forward movement."

NOTE

THE GERMAN RIGHT WING ON THE 7TH SEPTEMBER

On the evening of the 6th September the liaison officer of the Sketch 15. *First Army* brought to General von Bülow at his headquarters at Maps 25 Montmort (13 miles E.N.E. of Montmirail) a message from General & 27. von Kluck, taken down in a note book, confirming that the *II.* and *IV. Corps* had been moved to the Ourcq, and informing him that the gap left in the line by them was made secure by the *I.* and *II. Cavalry Corps*, ample for the purpose " as the repeatedly beaten British will " scarcely be quickly induced to come forward and make a powerful " offensive " : further, that the *IX. Corps* was placed under the *Second Army* to assist in the offensive against the French and that the *III. Corps* was to cover its right flank ; it was added, however, that Kluck might require the *III. Corps*, and if Bülow's *VII. Corps* could be used to cover the flank, so much the better, as the *III.* would then be free.

Bülow then proceeded to issue orders to the *Second Army* and to the *IX.* and *III. Corps* for the continuation of the offensive ; but he had no sooner done so than, " after 11 P.M.," his liaison officer brought him a copy of Kluck's orders, issued at 9 P.M., directing the *IX.* and *III. Corps* to fall back during the night behind the Petit Morin, from west of Montmirail to Boitron (north of Rebais). Confronted with this sudden change, Bülow, at 1.25 A.M. on the 7th, decided to conform to it by directing that only his left (eastern) wing, the *Guard* and *X. Corps*, should carry out the offensive ; his centre, the *X. Reserve Corps*, which had crossed the Petit Morin, was to go back behind the river in line with the *IX.* and *III.*, whilst the *VII.* would be to its right rear. Thus Bülow, instead of making the wheel to face Paris on his right as a pivot, set about making it on the centre point of his front.

There was some confusion as a result of the two sets of orders, and consequent counter-orders, but the *III. Corps* marched off, the *5th Division* at 3 A.M. without any interference, and the *6th* somewhat later, its rear guard shaking clear about 7 A.M., after a little firing " without loss and without the enemy infantry attempting to " follow." General von Quast of the *IX. Corps*, who seems to have obeyed Bülow's orders in preference to Kluck's, did not hear that the attack had been cancelled until 5 A.M. ; but, under cover of artillery fire, his corps retired in broad daylight ; only the rear guards of the *18th Division* had a little fighting, and they also got clear by 8.45 A.M. Thus the Germans in front of Franchet d'Espèrey's left swung back, and soon disappeared.

During the morning of the 7th, Kluck, informed by O.H.L. that it had been learnt from a captured order (see below) that the French were making a general offensive, seems to have become thoroughly alarmed by the situation on the Ourcq. He sent the

[1] See page 312.

following wireless messages to Bülow: At 10.10 A.M., "*II.*, *IV.* and " *IV. Reserve Corps* heavily engaged west of lower Ourcq. Where " are the *III.* and *IX* ? What is situation there ? Reply urgent " ; and at 11.15 A.M., " Participation of *III.* and *IX. Corps* on Ourcq " most urgent. Enemy considerably reinforced. Send corps in " direction of La Ferté Milon and Crouy (6 miles S. by W. of La " Ferté Milon) " ; that is the two corps were to make a march north- westward of some thirty-five miles. Kluck also shifted his head- quarters from Charly on the Marne, where he had moved on the 6th from Rebais, to Vendrest east of the Ourcq, behind the battle-front there.

Bülow passed on the *First Army* order to the *III. Corps*, but, in view of the danger to his right flank and the increase in the gap occasioned by Kluck's withdrawal of the remaining troops of the *First Army*, he directed the *IX. Corps*, which he conceived to be still at his disposal, to wheel back behind the Dolloir (a stream which flows a little west of north into the Marne about 5 miles below Chateau Thierry), and his *VII. Corps* to fill the space between the *IX.* and *X. Reserve*, whose right held Montmirail.

After its fifteen-mile march to the Petit Morin, the *III. Corps* was resting behind the river, when, at 4 P.M., it received Kluck's con- firmatory order to march to the Ourcq. It resumed its retirement at 5 P.M., and the *5th Division* reached La Ferté sous Jouarre " late at " night," and the *6th*, Charly " about 11 P.M." It was nearly mid- night, too, when the *IX. Corps* reached its position behind the Dolloir, and General von Quast received notification that he was again under the orders of the *First Army*, and instructions to march to its right flank without delay. He decided to continue the march after a short rest. Both the *III.* and *IX. Corps* resumed their march north- westward at 1 A.M. on the 8th.

The two cavalry corps, in the gap between the *First* and *Second Armies*, had also fallen back, Generals von Richthofen and von der Marwitz acting independently, no commander for both corps or for the troops in the gap ever being appointed. The *I. Cavalry Corps*, which had been covering the flank of the *III. Corps*, fell back with that corps before daylight, and, after some skirmishes with the British already mentioned, pursued also for a time by artillery fire, took position behind the Petit Morin around Orly, in front of the British right. Thus between Montmirail and Orly, some sixteen miles, opposite the French Fifth Army, there were no Germans whatever except the retiring *IX.* and *III. Corps* and *I. Cavalry Corps*.

The *II. Cavalry Corps*, which spent the night around Coulom- miers, also retired before daylight, its *9th Division* being summoned to the Ourcq, whilst the *2nd*, and the four *Jäger* battalions and infantry battalion with it, fell back on Pierre Levée just south of La Ferté sous Jouarre, where they were seen and fired on, as already noticed. At night, all except one cavalry brigade, the *Jäger*, the horse artillery and machine-gun troop, were sent north of the Marne.

On the Ourcq during the 7th the German situation had certainly given cause for anxiety, and at night both the right and left flanks of the *First Army* were swung back, the *7th Division* on the right retiring a couple of miles, leaving its wounded behind, in order to avoid envelopment.

On Bülow's left wing, around the Marshes of St. Gond, in spite of his order for attack, action was confined to artillery fire and nothing of importance happened owing to the difficulties of the terrain, the

Guard Corps taking ground to the east in order to get clear of the marshes.

No orders of any kind were issued by the Supreme Command either on the 6th or the 7th. On the evening of the 6th, the *Fourth Army* transmitted to it over the telephone [1] the text of General Joffre's Order of the Day issued on the morning of the 6th at 9 A.M., a copy of which had been found in the afternoon by the 30th Brigade at Frignicourt (immediately south of Vitry le François). This important news was at once communicated to the Armies, where it seems to have had the same depressing effect as at O.H.L. Moltke was confirmed in his view that a dreadful mistake had been made in believing that the French had been beaten : " the foe had " obviously retired according to plan and during the retreat had " regrouped his forces. . . . His plan of battle seemed clear.   Whilst " his front brought the German pursuit to a stop between Marne and " Seine, carefully concealed offensives from Paris and Verdun against " the momentarily unprotected German flanks would bring about the " decision." (G.O.A., iv. p. 137.)   Would the German troops, worn out by the superhuman efforts of the past week, their ranks reduced about 50 per cent by march and battle casualties, stand the shock. " The strategic plans and hopes of the Chief of the General Staff " seemed suddenly to collapse."   The news from the Armies which came in during the night and early morning were disquieting and brought no relief : three corps of the *First Army* were fighting on the Ourcq against the enemy from Paris, and Kluck judged that he must bring the *III.* and *IX. Corps* there ; the *Second Army* spoke of the gap in the line, and clamoured that the *III.* and *IX. Corps* should be left to guard its flank ; the *Third Army*, which ought to have thrust itself into a gap in the French front opposite it, had divided itself into two to help its neighbours, both of whom were calling for help.   Little definite news came from Armies during the day ; the evening reports of the *Fourth* and *Fifth* brought nothing new, only that fighting was continuing with undiminished violence without a decision anywhere ; the *Sixth* and *Seventh Armies* were at a deadlock ; good news came only from Hindenburg, who was chasing Rennenkampf's Army back into Russia in the Battle of the Masurian Lakes, begun on the 5th.   Moltke had no troops in reserve : the *XV. Corps* of the *Seventh Army* had been ordered round from Lorraine to Belgium on the 5th, but could not reach the front for several days.[2] He seems to have thought of shifting the Supreme Command Headquarters nearer to the battle, but he did nothing, did not send even an inspiriting message.   The Kaiser, who returned that evening, disappointed of his triumphal entry into Reims, on being informed of the situation, could, according to the statement of his personal staff, only suggest, " attack as long as we can—in no circumstances a step " backwards."

[1] O.H.L. was connected to the four Armies of the left wing by telephone, to the *Third, Second* and *First Armies* by wireless only. There was grave delay in the transmission of wireless messages, due to there being only one receiving station at O.H.L., and to interruptions by weather and by the French field stations, owing to the bluntness of the tuning curve. They arrived so mutilated that they had to be repeated three or four times before they could be read. (Kuhl's " Marne," p. 28.)

[2] Moltke had asked for a corps each from the *Sixth* and *Seventh Armies*, but Crown Prince Rupprecht could only spare one. The *XV. Corps* arrived on the Aisne on 14th September.

CHAPTER XVI

THE BATTLE OF THE MARNE (*continued*)

8TH SEPTEMBER : THE FORCING OF THE PETIT MORIN

(Sketches B, 13 & 16 ; Maps 4, 25 & 28)

Sketch 13. THE cavalry moved off at 4 A.M., covering the front of
Maps 4, the I. and II. Corps. In the Cavalry Division, the 1st and
25 & 28. 2nd Brigades made for the line of the Petit Morin from
Bellot (due north of La Ferté Gaucher) westward to La
Trétoire, with the 4th Cavalry Brigade in support. Gough's
5th and 3rd Cavalry Brigades on its left headed for the river
from La Trétoire to St. Cyr. The 5th Dragoon Guards, at
the head of the Cavalry Division, moved by La Ferté
Gaucher on Sablonnières, and the 4th Dragoon Guards on
the wooden bridge at La Forge, 2,000 yards lower down.
Driving scattered parties of German horsemen before them,
they plunged down into the wooded valley of the Petit Morin.
The two bridges at Sablonnières were reported to be lightly
held, but a direct advance upon them was found to be
impossible owing to the enemy's rifle fire ; an attempt to
turn the position from the east by way of Bellot was also
checked. At the La Forge bridge, to which the approach
lay over a railway bridge, a troop of the 4th Dragoon
Guards tried to carry both by a rush, and secured the first,
but were foiled at the river bridge which was barricaded.
On their left, 3 miles further westward, a reconnoitring
party of the Greys discovered just south of the river, near
Gibraltar (1¼ miles S.S.W. of Orly), half a battalion of
Jäger and a cavalry brigade comfortably eating their breakfasts. Stealing back unperceived they were able to indicate
this target to a section of J Battery at Boisbaudry, which
broke up the picnic abruptly with shrapnel, and sent the
enemy fleeing across the valley with considerable loss.
German artillery, however, forbade any further advance
of the 2nd Cavalry Brigade, and the 5th was likewise

brought to a standstill. On their left, the 5th Lancers of
the 3rd Cavalry Brigade penetrated into St. Cyr, and D
Battery did some execution among the Germans retreating
before them. But very soon the enemy counter-attacked,
drove the 5th Lancers out of St. Cyr, and stopped further
progress by a heavy cross-fire of artillery from the high
ground above Orly (opposite Gibraltar). D and E Batteries, being in an exposed position, were for the time out
of action, for their teams could not come up to shift them
and the detachments were obliged to leave their guns and
take cover. By about 8.30 A.M. the whole of the British
cavalry was at a standstill, the hostile rear guards being
too strong and too well posted to be dislodged from the line
of the Petit Morin until further forces arrived.

On the extreme left, infantry of the 4th Division ascertained between 3 and 4 A.M. that the enemy had evacuated
Pierre Levée, which defended the approaches to La Ferté
sous Jouarre ; so at 6 A.M. the 12th and 19th Brigades
advanced, the former against Jouarre, the latter on its left
against Signy Signets. Aerial reconnaissances about this
hour reported a great number of the enemy massed about
La Ferté sous Jouarre, waiting their turn to cross the river,
whilst the passage of infantry over the bridge was unceasing.[1] But the movement of the British was necessarily
slow, for there were many copses and coverts to be cleared
in front, and a large belt of wood—the Bois de Jouarre—on
the right flank. No serious opposition however was encountered until about 11 A.M., when the leading battalion
of the 19th Brigade had passed beyond Signy Signets and
reached the ridge overlooking the Marne, where it was
caught by artillery fire from the heights just north-west
of La Ferté sous Jouarre. No great damage was done, and
the German guns were soon silenced by two batteries of
the XXIX. Brigade R.F.A. But the brushing away of the
enemy's advanced troops revealed the German main body
holding the north bank of the Marne in strength, with a
bridgehead, well provided with machine guns, at La Ferté
sous Jouarre.[2] It was thus evident that the passage of

---

[1] The whole of the *5th Division* passed through La Ferté sous Jouarre
on the 8th.

[2] La Ferté was defended by the *2nd Cavalry Division*, the *5th* was at
Orly and the *Guard* at Boitron. The *9th* was at the battle of the Ourcq,
but returned in the evening to defend the Marne below La Ferté. With
the *5th Cavalry Division* were four *Jäger* battalions, with each of the
others, one. Each division had a machine-gun troop (6 guns) and each
Jäger battalion a machine-gun company (6 guns). Each cavalry corps
had formed a cyclist battalion. G.O.A., iv. p. 178, speaks of there being

the Marne would not be easily forced ; and there was nothing for the moment to be done but to bring the artillery forward to knock out the machine guns, and to seek a way round. This was exasperating, for heavy columns of the enemy were still crossing the river at La Ferté, and masses of troops were in sight on the slopes of the northern bank ranged like a gigantic amphitheatre around the town, but out of range.

On the right of the Force, shortly before 9 A.M., the advanced guard of the 1st (Guards) Brigade (the 1/Black Watch and the 117th Battery R.F.A.) reached the edge of the plateau above Bellot, and passed down a narrow defile into the valley of the Petit Morin, German shrapnel bursting over their heads as they marched. The 118th and 119th Batteries unlimbered near the crest of the hill, and soon silenced the German guns. By 9.30 A.M. the Black Watch reached Bellot, where they found French cavalry in possession but unable to advance, although the bridge was intact ; pushing through the village, they crossed the river and entered the woods on its north side. They then turned westward upon Sablonnières to facilitate the crossing there, but were stubbornly opposed by dismounted cavalry and the *Guard Jäger*, until the Cameron Highlanders, with dismounted troopers of the 4th Cavalry Brigade, came to their assistance. The advent of the Camerons was decisive ; for soon after 1 P.M. the British were masters of Sablonnières with over sixty German prisoners.[1]

While this was going forward, the 2nd Division, next on the left, headed by the 4th (Guards) Brigade and the XXXVI. and XLI. Brigades R.F.A., had come up to La Trétoire at the edge of the plateau overlooking the Petit Morin, and had been greeted, like the 1st Brigade, with continuous shrapnel fire from batteries on the heights opposite in the vicinity of Boitron. The British guns soon compelled the Germans to move ; but skilfully placed machine guns made the advance of infantry across the river valley a very difficult matter, and the vanguard (2 companies of the 3rd Coldstream) tried in vain to make its way down to the water. The Irish Guards was sent

an " infantry battalion " (now known to have been the II. Battalion of the *27th Regiment*) at La Ferté. The retirement north of the Marne of the detachment near Jouarre was ordered by General von der Marwitz at 9 A.M. (Poseck, p. 102).

[1] According to Vogel, the troops which defended Bellot and Sablonnières were the *Garde-du-Korps* and *Garde-Kürassier* regiments and part of the *Garde-Jäger* battalion.

to its help, but could make no progress ; the forward elements of both battalions were therefore slightly withdrawn whilst the valley was further searched by artillery ; for which purpose, owing to the steepness of the sides of the valley at this point, the XLIV. Brigade R.F.A. came into action, also the 35th Heavy Battery, well away on the flank.[1] About noon the six companies of the Coldstream and Irish Guards, urged on by Generals Haig and Monro, who were present, again advanced, whilst on their left the 2/Worcestershire, at the head of the 5th Brigade, moved down on Bécherelle (1¼ miles N.N.W. of La Trétoire), east of which was a bridge ; and on their right the 2/Grenadiers and 2/Coldstream on La Forge, where the 4th Dragoon Guards had secured both bridges. This attack on a front of nearly a mile and a half was pushed successfully as far as the road which runs parallel with the Petit Morin on its southern bank. The Worcestershire then carried the bridge near Bécherelle, capturing a few prisoners in the farm close to it ; and, with the approach of this battalion on his right flank and of the two battalions of Guards on his left, the enemy retired. Thus, before 2 P.M. the passage of the Petit Morin had been forced at the eastern extremity of the line, and the Cavalry Division was able to cross the valley and push northward.[2] The 2nd Cavalry Brigade pursued the hostile guns a short distance, taking some prisoners and inflicting appreciable losses ; whilst the 4th Cavalry Brigade, relieving it at 3.30 P.M., struck the flank of a German column seen on its left retiring northward from Orly and did some execution with its guns.

The I. Corps was now free to send help further to the west ; and not before it was needed. The 8th Brigade[3] had come up to the support of the 5th Cavalry Brigade about Gibraltar between 9 and 10 A.M., but could make no progress. The enemy was entrenched on the slopes on the north side of the Petit Morin about half a mile west of Orly, and his machine guns were so cunningly

---

[1] A single gun of the 16th Battery, XLI. Brigade, which had been sent forward in close support of the infantry, got a direct hit on and destroyed a German horse artillery gun and team, which were galloping for the safety of a reverse slope.

[2] In consequence of the renewal of the attack, the commander of the German *I. Cavalry Corps* " found himself obliged at 12.45 P.M. to order " a retirement. . . . The greater part of the *5th Cavalry Division* had " already withdrawn." (" Das Marnedrama 1914," ii.)

[3] Only about two thousand strong in spite of " first reinforcements," as a result of the heavy losses of the 2/Royal Irish and 4/Middlesex at Mons, and of the 1/Gordons at Le Cateau.

hidden that field guns could not find them. It was noon
before howitzers could be brought up, but even then the
machine guns could not be located, and they rendered a
frontal attack impossible. Further west the 13th Brigade
and the 121st Battery had joined the 3rd Cavalry Brigade
between 8 and 9 A.M. ; and two battalions were deployed
for attack on St. Cyr. But the fire from the enemy's concealed batteries was exceedingly trying, and little or no
progress was made. Soon after 9 A.M., therefore, the 14th
Brigade, which was halted at Doue, was sent forward
to the attack of St. Ouen, a mile east of St. Cyr. The
Duke of Cornwall's L.I. and the East Surrey led the way,
advancing in open formation for two miles under shrapnel
fire till they reached the valley, and plunged into the
dense wood which shrouded the descent to the river. So
steep was the declivity and so thickly tangled the undergrowth, that the Cornishmen, though little opposed, were
obliged to work down to the water man by man and re-
form by the railway at the foot of the slope. They found
before them two seemingly impassable streams, traversed
by a single continuous bridge which was swept by two
machine guns on the ridge beyond. After a time, however,
an undefended footbridge was found over one stream, also
a boat, and a ford through the other. Thus two companies of the D.C.L.I. were able gradually to effect a passage. By this time Lieut.-Colonel J. R. Longley of the
East Surrey had received a message from the brigade
headquarters giving the position of the enemy trenches,
and by arrangement his battalion crossed next. Pushing
on, the East Surrey attacked the Germans in flank and
turned them out, whilst the Duke of Cornwall's cleared St.
Ouen and occupied St. Cyr, the 5th Division cyclists going
through them, right-handed towards Bussières.

It was now nearly 3 P.M. The river had been crossed
on both sides of Orly (2½ miles east of St. Cyr), and the
enemy's situation at that place became perilous.[1] In the
2nd Division, the Oxfordshire and Buckinghamshire L.I.
and the Connaught Rangers of the 5th Brigade turned
westward from Bécherelle after they had crossed the
Petit Morin, and approached Orly from the east. The
4th (Guards) Brigade had pushed on 3 miles from the river
to the cross roads about Belle Idée on the Montmirail—
La Ferté sous Jouarre main road, almost behind the

[1] The order to retire had not reached the *11th Cavalry Brigade* and
Guard Schützen engaged there. (G.O.A., iv. p. 179.)

German position.   The 60th Howitzer Battery now began 8 Sept.
to search the woods with high-explosive shell, with the 1914.
result that German cavalry and infantry soon emerged
from their cover within close range of the Guards at La
Belle Idée and were heavily punished ; the few who remained in the woods were enveloped by the 2/Coldstream
and Irish Guards and shot down or captured.[1] Such
fugitives as made their escape were pursued so vigorously
by the shells of the British guns that the infantry could not
follow up its success.   Meanwhile the 8th Brigade began
again to press upon Orly itself from the south, and
the 9th Brigade did so from the east ; about 4 P.M. the
village was captured and one hundred and fifty prisoners[2]
with it.   Simultaneously, the Cyclist Company of the 5th
Division reached the main road, La Ferté sous Jouarre—
Montmirail, 3 miles west of the point where the 4th (Guards)
Brigade had struck it, and came upon the flank of two
hundred German *Guard Schützen,* and after five minutes'
fighting compelled them to lay down their arms.   Unfortunately, a battery of the 3rd Division which had been
pushed forward to north of Orly, peppered both captors and
captured so energetically with shrapnel that all but seventy
of the prisoners were able to escape.   Both divisions however of the II. Corps pressed northward from Orly and
St. Ouen as soon as they could, and by dusk the head
of the 3rd Division was at Les Feuchères (1½ miles east of
Rougeville), and the head of the 5th Division at Rougeville, where they were within less than a mile of the Marne.

The reaction of these operations on the right made
itself felt about La Ferté sous Jouarre between 3 and 4 P.M.
The guns of the 4th Division had come up about noon, and
had shelled the bridges at La Ferté and the ground in front
of Jouarre very heavily.[3]   The 108th Heavy Battery of
the 5th Division, unlimbering at Doue (4½ miles S.S.E. of
Jouarre) and firing by the map, silenced one troublesome
battery near Jouarre and another some distance further
east.   At 1 P.M. the German fire ceased opposite to the 4th
Division ; and soon after 2 P.M. orders were issued for the
11th and 19th Brigades to advance on the bridge at La
Ferté over the Petit Morin, and for the 12th Brigade to
move upon that of Courcelles about a mile and a half to

[1] The guns and some men of the *Guard Machine-Gun Abteilung* (with
the *Guard Cavalry Division*) were captured.
[2] *Guard Schützen* and men of the *11th Cavalry Brigade.*
[3] La Ferté sous Jouarre lies in the valley, on the Marne ; Jouarre is
on the heights above it, on the south side of the valley.

the eastward. Courcelles was quickly evacuated by the enemy at the approach of the 2/Essex and 2/Inniskilling Fusiliers, who thereupon moved on to La Ferté, where both bridges were found to have been blown up. These battalions were joined there by the King's Own, who had already cleared Jouarre, and by some of the Welch Fusiliers. The Germans firing from the houses made some show of resistance, but by dark the portion of the town that lies south of the Marne had been cleared of the enemy and was in full occupation of the British.

The day's operations now practically came to an end. Troops of the I. Corps did indeed advance as far as Basse-velle, midway between the Petit Morin and the Marne ; but at 6 P.M. a very sultry day ended in a violent thunder-storm with such torrents of rain as made it difficult either to see or to move. Nearly the whole of the 8th had been spent in forcing the passage of the Petit Morin. The ground was ideally suited to a rear-guard action, and the enemy's positions were well chosen, and most skilfully and gallantly defended. The total loss of the British was under six hundred killed and wounded, against which were to be set some five hundred Germans captured, at least the same number killed and wounded, and about a dozen machine guns taken in the trenches by the river.[1]

Sketches B & 13. Maps 25 & 28.

The troops halted for the night in the following posi-tions, all south of the Marne :—

Cavalry Division . . .	. Replonges.
I. Corps	. Bassevelle, Hondevillers (2½ miles south of last named), Boitron.
II. Corps	. Les Feuchères, Rougeville, Charnesseuil (1½ miles west of Bussières), Orly.
III. Corps . . . . 3rd Cavalry Brigade	. Grand Glairet (1 mile west of Jouarre), Venteuil Chateau (1 mile south of La Ferté sous Jouarre), Signy Signets.
5th Cavalry Brigade .	. Between Gibraltar and Rebais.

The air reports of the day referred, except for the passage of many troops through La Ferté, almost entirely to small enemy columns, and to the positions of the British

---

[1] Vogel speaks of " the celebrated heavy-in-losses and important fight " at Orly." The *Guard* and *5th Cavalry Divisions* were engaged ; " many " of the companies of the *Guard Jäger* and *Schützen* came out of action with " only 45 men."

and of the French Armies on either side of them. The 8 Sept.
lines of march of the German *IX.* and *III.* *Corps* were 1914.
beyond the areas reconnoitred except those of the *5th
Division* through La Ferté, and of a large detachment of
the *IX. Corps,* which, as we shall see, had been diverted
to the British front, which were duly reported. The
French stated that the *III. Corps* (or the *IX.*) was still on
the Fifth Army front next to the *VII. Corps*—where the
IX. Corps had been on the night of the 7th/8th. Thus the
general situation of the German forces near the British
was summed up by the Intelligence Section as follows : the
two divisions of the *I. Cavalry Corps* had fought on the
Petit Morin and had retired northwards ; the *III. Corps*
on Fifth Army front ; the *IX. Corps* north of the Marne,
part (actually a quarter) near Montreuil aux Lions (6
miles N.N.E. of La Ferté), part (actually the *5th Division*)
near Cocherel (5 miles N. by W. of La Ferté) and part
(actually the tail of the *18th Division*) near Chézy (5 miles
south of Chateau Thierry) ; and the *IV. Corps* was thought
to be divided, part being on the Ourcq, and part on the
northern bank of the Marne near Nanteuil (what was seen
must have been either the tail of the *6th Division* or the
retiring *5th Cavalry Division*). Thus it appeared that the
greater part of the *IV.* and *IX. Corps* (actually only one
division and one mixed brigade, and that division under
orders to continue its movement to the Ourcq) was opposite
the British on the north bank of the Marne, quite enough
to make Sir John French feel cautious when forcing the
passage of a wide river.

The news that came in at nightfall from the French Maps 4
Armies on the right and left was less satisfactory than on & 25.
the 7th. To the eastward the French Fifth Army was said to
have made good progress, encountering no very serious opposition ; on its extreme left Conneau's cavalry corps, however, was five miles behind Haig's corps. Next to it the
XVIII. Corps had crossed the Petit Morin to L'Épine aux
Bois (4 miles west of Montmirail), and the rest of the Army
was extended from Montmirail eastward to Champaubert,
beyond which General Foch's Ninth Army stretched from
St. Prix (3 miles south of Champaubert) to La Fère Champenoise. To the westward, the Germans, having been
strongly reinforced by the troops withdrawn by Kluck
from the south, were offering a determined resistance to
the French on the Ourcq, and General Maunoury, in spite
of all efforts, had failed to gain ground. Indeed, his centre

had actually been forced back, and he had been obliged to recall the French 8th Division, which should have linked his right to the British Army, from the east to the west bank of the Ourcq. From this information it became evident that the quicker the advance of the British upon the left flank and rear of Kluck, the speedier would be General Maunoury's deliverance, and the more telling the damage inflicted upon the Germans.

Instruction No. 19, issued by General Joffre at 8.7 P.M. on the 8th September, drew attention to the fact that the right wing of the German Army was now divided into two groups, connected only by some cavalry divisions, supported, in front of the British troops, by detachments of all arms. It was therefore important to defeat the German extreme right before it could be reinforced by other formations released by the fall of Maubeuge. This task was confided to the Sixth Army and the British. The Sixth Army was to hold the troops opposing it on the right bank of the Ourcq, whilst the British forces crossing the Marne between Nogent l'Artaud and La Ferté sous Jouarre were to advance against the left and rear of the enemy on the Ourcq; the Fifth Army was to cover the right flank of the British Army by sending a strong detachment against Chateau Thierry—Azy, which, as will be seen, it failed to do.

THE FRENCH ON THE 8TH SEPTEMBER [1]

Maps 25 & 28.   The Sixth Army on the Ourcq remained stationary on the 8th September. Its left was prolonged by the arrival of the IV. Corps (7th Division and 61st Reserve Division); General Bridoux, who had superseded General Sordet in command of the cavalry corps, despatched a (5th) provisional division, under General Cornulier-Lucinière, on a raid round the rear of the German *First Army*. " As " each of the other formations of the Army waited before moving " for the advance of the formation on its left, the Army as a whole " maintained the positions it occupied and entrenched them."

The Fifth Army closed up to, and on the left, crossed the Petit Morin. The orders for the 8th deflected its advance from north-south to " slightly north-north-east " so as to give support to the Ninth Army. They said that, in view of the large enemy forces reported north of Montmirail, resistance was to be expected on the Petit Morin, and measures were to be taken accordingly : the X. Corps was not to cross the Montmirail—Champaubert road without further orders, its business being to outflank, in co-operation with the 42nd Division (Ninth Army), the Germans attacking the left of the Ninth Army. The XVIII. Corps was to start at 6 A.M., other formations at 7 A.M.

[1] Summarized from the French Official Account.

The two left divisions, the 4th and 8th, of Conneau's cavalry
corps, found the Germans holding the Petit Morin, and halted, " but
" the entry into action of a British infantry brigade about 11 A.M.,
" at Bellot, where it crossed, drove the enemy detachment away,
" and brought about the abandonment of the heights." The 10th
Cavalry Division met with no opposition on the Petit Morin. The
three divisions, after watering horses, advanced a short distance.
General Conneau heard from air reports that many German columns
were retreating across the Marne ; but as soon as his three divisions
got abreast of Vieils Maisons about 5 P.M., they were ordered, as at
manœuvres, to return to the Petit Morin to bivouac. It so happened
that they slept under the protection of the British 1st Cavalry
Division, which that night pushed the 11th Hussars across the
Marne.

The XVIII. Corps advanced in four columns at 8 A.M., two hours
late, and then the right column was delayed by the left column of
the III. Corps being on the same road. The movement was covered
by advanced guards, " forming detachments of pursuit." By 10.30
A.M., after the Grand Morin had been passed without opposition,
General Maud'huy came to the conclusion that there were no
Germans between the two Morins, and, north of the Petit Morin,
none in front of his left, the 36th Division ; but, from information
given by the III. Corps, there were some batteries on the west of
Montmirail ahead of the 35th Division. He therefore ordered that
" the positions which might be occupied north of the Petit Morin
" should be approached with precaution, and that they should not
" be attacked without reconnaissance and until after a vigorous
" artillery preparation ; above all, he recommended waiting the
" effect of flank attacks executed by any troops which might have
" already crossed the stream."

The advanced guard of the 35th Division, " very late in conse-
" quence of the block on the road," on approaching the Petit Morin
about 3 P.M., came under gun fire for a short time, although the
divisional squadron and infantry detachments had reached the
bridges and sent reconnoitring parties on to the heights on the north
bank. The main body of the leading brigade crossed the river a little
before 5 P.M. and bivouacked on the heights about half a mile from
the river at 8 P.M. The 36th Division crossed the Petit Morin without
any opposition ; there appeared to be nothing in front of it, " but
" before pushing ahead General Jouannic waited [apparently from
" 12 noon to 2.15 P.M.] to make sure there was nothing on his left."
Germans were then discovered in the woods ahead, who stopped
further progress until night, when both regiments of the leading
brigade made a night advance and reached the Montmirail—Vieils
Maisons road and bivouacked north of and in front of the 35th Division. The 38th Division halted for the night in rear of the 35th.

The III. Corps did very little ; the two leading divisions advanced
about six miles to within two miles of Montmirail, where the aviators
reported " a lot of artillery, but little infantry, with the main bodies
" in retreat on Chateau Thierry." The divisions dug in there about
3 P.M., it being General Hache's intention " to form a barrier south
" of Montmirail to attract the enemy's artillery and thus permit the
" XVIII. Corps to cross the Petit Morin." In this position the
corps remained until 7 P.M., when the bivouac orders necessitated
a slight forward movement. The 6th Division billeted in rear of

the 5th and 37th, with the Group of Reserve Divisions behind it
again.

The I. Corps also did little during the day, the 1st Division advancing two miles eastward, and the 2nd, three miles north-eastward. It waited until noon for the III. Corps to come abreast of it
and attack Montmirail, and at that hour was ordered by the Army
to cross the Petit Morin. It moved about an hour later, and was
almost at once held up by fire from the villages on the stream.

Finding his corps stationary, General Deligny called for help
from his neighbours, which they apparently did not give. No
further progress was made except to get a footing in two of the
villages. The corps therefore bivouacked south of the Petit Morin,
and its commander in his evening report blamed the corps on his
right and left for not giving assistance, and stated that his troops
were very tired and would probably be more tired after another night
in bivouac.

In the X. Corps, at Foch's repeated requests for help by a flanking attack, the 51st Division was used in defence to assist the left
of the Ninth Army, and the 19th and 20th Divisions, after swinging
to the north-east a short distance, dug in.

The Ninth Army had a disastrous day. Foch overnight had
issued only a preparatory order for the troops " to be under arms
" at 5 A.M. ready to resume the offensive," but not until 3 A.M. on
the 8th did he send out an instruction directing reconnaissances to
be made " to determine the points still occupied by the enemy."
Before this could have reached the troops the Germans, by a dawn
attack (4.15 A.M.), drove back Foch's right wing. Its retreat,
besides increasing the gap between the Fourth and Ninth Armies,
which the XXI. Corps was moving up to fill, involved the retirement
of the centre from the southern exits of the Marshes of St. Gond,
which it had been ordered to guard.

Foch's opinion in the evening was that " the vigorous offensive
" which my Army has had to withstand for two days had the purpose
" of concealing the true design of the enemy, and had no other object
" except to cover the retreat of the German right wing (*First Army*
" and part of the *Second*), which since the 7th September has been
" retiring in the direction of the Marne." He therefore at 9 P.M.
ordered the IX. and XI. Corps to attack towards Champaubert,
secure the higher ground beyond it and dig in. At the same time
he begged the Fifth Army to take over the ground held by his 42nd
Division so as to free it as a reserve. General Franchet d'Espèrey
not only agreed to do this, but for the purpose placed the X. Corps
(2 divisions) at his disposal. Steady progress north-west by the
whole Fifth Army would probably have given the Ninth Army more
effective assistance. And the loan of the X. Corps was to be followed
by the diversion of the I. and III. Corps eastwards to help Foch.

NOTE

THE GERMAN RIGHT WING ON THE 8TH SEPTEMBER

Maps 25   At 6 A.M. on the 8th General von Kluck received a report from his
& 28.   left centre that a break-through was threatening near Trocy, and an
urgent request for assistance via Lizy. He had no reserve except

Sketch 16.

8TH SEPTEMBER 1914.

Situation as known at German G.H.Q.
before the despatch of Lieut.-Colonel Hentsch.

(From Map 5, German Official History, Vol. IV).

the *III.* and *IX. Corps*, then crossing the Marne in their march north-
westwards. Although any detachment from them would weaken
the decisive enveloping attack which he meant to make from his
northern flank, he ordered the *5th Division*—the westernmost column
whose head was about six miles north of La Ferté sous Jouarre when
the order took effect—to turn towards the Ourcq, and the *6th
Division*, next to it, to follow a route which would bring it behind
the centre of the battlefield. The Ourcq front, however, held fast,
and it was not necessary to engage the *5th Division*, which (except
for " parts of two regiments which went up to the firing line ")
remained in reserve behind the left flank, its move having been
observed by British aviators, as we have seen. Equilibrium having
been established on the Ourcq, Kluck might well look forward to a
success there when the rest of the *III. Corps* and the *IX. Corps*
arrived.

    The situation on the Petit Morin and the Marne, according to
the reports which had come in from General von der Marwitz during
the night, appeared to indicate that assistance should be sent there ;
at 8.15 A.M., therefore, Kluck ordered the *IX. Corps* to drop an infantry regiment and a field artillery brigade at Montreuil aux Lions
(6 miles north-east of La Ferté sous Jouarre). News soon came in of
the British attacks against the Petit Morin line, and air reports of the
advance of three (of the six) British columns. The success of Kluck's
plans depended on the line being held ; so at 10.20 A.M. he sent
another order to the IX. Corps to send two brigades and two regiments of field artillery to hold the Marne from Nogent (6 miles below
Chateau Thierry) to La Ferté, and to destroy all the bridges ; and
he released the detachment ordered to Montreuil. He then proceeded to La Ferté Milon, on his right wing, to organize the attack
for next day, and whilst there was nearly captured by Cornulier-
Lucinière's cavalry raid (Kluck, p. 118), which must have been an
unpleasant surprise to him, and may have influenced his action next
day.   General von Quast, no doubt disliking being deprived of half
his force, took upon himself the responsibility of sending only one
brigade and one artillery regiment, instead of two, under Major-
General von Kraewel, and he omitted to send an engineer company,
so there were no explosives available to destroy the bridges. The
remaining bridge at La Ferté had, however, been prepared for demolition by the engineers of the *8th Division* on the night of the 6th/7th.
Kraewel's composite brigade arrived at Montreuil by 5.45 P.M., and,
in view of the fatigue of the men, who had been continuously in
action or marching since the morning of the 6th, he did not move
them down to defend the Marne crossings. At La Ferté itself was
the *2nd Cavalry Division*, with one infantry and four *Jäger* battalions ;
but along the course of the Marne upwards from this town there were
no German troops, except stragglers of the *III.* and *IX. Corps*.
The *I. Cavalry Corps*, driven from the Petit Morin, had cleared away,
the *Guard Cavalry Division* to the right flank of the *Second Army*
behind the Dolloir, and the *5th Cavalry Division*, well north of the
Marne, broken into two parts, one part retiring to Marigny (9 miles
N.N.E. of La Ferté) and the other to Domptin (5½ miles south-west
of Chateau Thierry). From Chateau Thierry (inclusive) to La Ferté
(exclusive)—15 miles in an air line—opposite the left of Franchet
d'Espèrey's Army and the right and centre of the B.E.F., that is to
say in the gap between the right of the *Second Army* and the left of

THE MARNE

the *First Army*, the passages of the Marne were abandoned by the Germans. The German *Second Army* had a day of varied fortunes on the 8th, which resulted in its pivoting on its centre. East of the Marshes of St. Gond, the *Guard Corps*, with the right half of the *Third Army*, made a successful early morning attack, driving Foch's troops back, and entering Fère Champenoise ; but after this effort it halted. The centre, the *14th* and *20th Divisions*, pushed over the western end of the marshes ; the *19th Division* and *X. Reserve Corps* held their line hardly troubled ; but at night the *13th Division*, on the extreme right, fell back in panic, or was driven back, although the French make no claim to have done so. Summed up in Bülow's message to Kluck, the situation was " Right wing of *Second Army* " pulled back to Le Thoult [7½ miles east by south of Montmirail]— " Margny [6 miles north-east of Montmirail].[1] *Guard Cavalry* " *Division* held Dolloir until 7 P.M., is being driven back to area " around Condé en Brie [8 miles south-east of Chateau Thierry]. " *5th Cavalry Division* driven north of the Marne." The right wing had, in fact, been rallied on the line of the railway running north from Montmirail, and then withdrawn further east.

Sketch 16.   The critical state of the battle had impressed itself deeply on General von Moltke at O.H.L. on the morning of the 8th (see Sketch 16). More or less good news came from the *First Army* by wireless (received 3 A.M., but sent off at 4 P.M. the previous evening, a fact which exhibits the delays of the German communication system). In this Kluck said that he hoped to continue the attack next day " with prospects of success." At the same time Moltke heard that the *Second Army* had held its own on the 7th and would make a dawn attack with the bayonet, but Bülow had added " in conse- " quence of heavy losses, the *Second Army* has only the fighting " power of three corps." At 8 A.M. a wireless communication be- tween the *I.* and *II. Cavalry Corps* headquarters was overheard at O.H.L., in which the former said, " the Petit Morin position Biercy " Orly—Villeneuve broken through, *I. Cavalry Corps* goes slowly " behind the Dolloir." On hearing this, " it seemed to General von " Moltke that the danger of a break-through between the two " Armies of the right wing had come perilously nearer." He ordered all available troops of the *IX. Reserve Corps* (observing Antwerp) and of the *VII. Reserve Corps* (besieging Maubeuge) to be sent at once to St. Quentin, and portions of the *XV. Corps* (begin- ning to leave the *Seventh Army* in Alsace) to be sent along as they arrived ; but he issued no directions to the fighting Armies, except to the *Sixth* and *Seventh*, whose unsuccessful attempt to break through in Lorraine and cross the Moselle he stopped. He did not send a liaison officer to each Army of the right wing to find out exactly what was happening, or telephone to the *Fifth* and *Fourth Armies*, as he could have done. Instead he despatched Lieut.-Colonel Hentsch, whose previous visit to the Armies has been mentioned, to go to the *Fifth, Fourth, Third, Second* and *First Armies* in turn, in that order, a round trip of 400 miles ; and Colonel Hentsch proceeded not by aeroplane but by car, leaving Luxembourg about 10 A.M. He

---

[1] Lieut.-Colonel Hentsch said in his report on his trip (p. 1), that whilst he was at *Second Army* headquarters on the night of the 8th a report came in that " the right flank of the Army had been enveloped or " driven back, and must be withdrawn behind the Verdonelle."

reached the first four of the Armies on the 8th, and reported that the *Fifth* and *Fourth Armies* were in general holding their own, whilst the situation of the *Third Army*—divided into two distinct halves— was " thoroughly satisfactory." He spent the night at Bülow's headquarters.   As no action was taken as a result of his visit there until the 9th, the controversy about the instructions which he received, the way he carried them out, and the result, will be dealt with under that date.

CHAPTER XVII

THE BATTLE OF THE MARNE (concluded)

9TH SEPTEMBER 1914: THE PASSAGE OF THE MARNE
AND THE RETREAT OF THE GERMANS

(Sketches B, 13 & 17 ; Maps 4, 25, 29 & 30)

Sketches THE orders issued by the British Commander-in-Chief
13 & 17. on the evening of the 8th September directed the Army to
Maps 4, continue its advance northward at 5 A.M., attacking the
25 & 29. enemy rear guards wherever met, the cavalry maintaining
touch with the French Armies to right and left, as before.[1]
It had been expected that the Germans would offer stubborn
resistance on the line of the Marne ; the great width of the
river, the few bridges over it, the houses on its banks, and
excellent artillery positions and observation on the high
ground above presenting very favourable ground for a rear-
guard action. The array of troops on the British front
seemed to confirm that this was their intention. On the
other hand, the evening reports of the Flying Corps showed
that the idea might have been abandoned. Many columns
had been seen moving northward in haste, and the bridges
had not been destroyed, except those of La Ferté sous
Jouarre, Sammeron (2 miles west of La Ferté), and Changis
(3 miles west of Sammeron). The 11th Hussars, who had
reconnoitred towards the bridge at Charly and found it
occupied by the enemy on the evening of the 8th, ascertained during the night that the Germans had retired leaving
the passage clear, and had secured it.

Early on the 9th September therefore the 1st Cavalry
Brigade was pushed forward on Nogent and Charly, and by
5.30 A.M. it was in possession of the bridge at Nogent, whilst
the 4th Cavalry Brigade seized that at Azy further to the
east and 3 miles below Chateau Thierry. The two brigades

[1] Appendix 38.

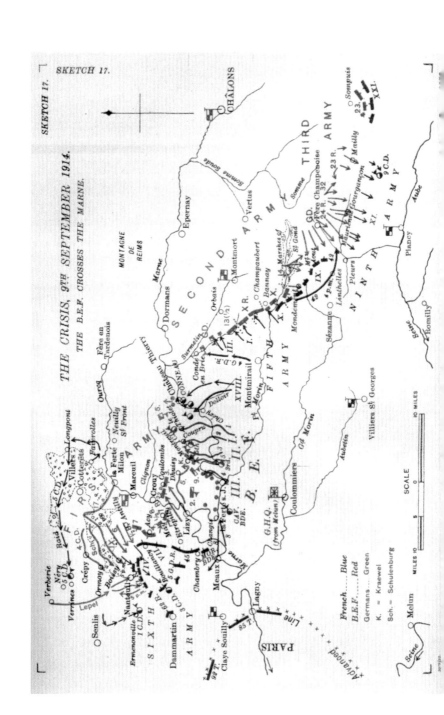

THE CRISIS, 9TH SEPTEMBER 1914.

THE B.E.F. CROSSES THE MARNE.

French ...... Blue
B.E.F. ...... Red
Germans .... Green
K. = Kraewel
Sch. = Schulenburg

SCALE

MILES 10   5   0   10 MILES

then moved about three miles northward from Nogent to 9 Sept.
Mont de Bonneil to cover the passage of the infantry. By 1914.
7.30 A.M. the Queen's, the leading battalion of the 3rd
Brigade, the advanced guard of the 1st Division, had passed
the Marne at Nogent and was crowning the heights north
of the river. The 6th Brigade, with the XXXIV. Brigade
R.F.A., the advanced guard of the 2nd Division, on reaching Charly, drove off a party of Germans who had evidently
returned to demolish the bridge, but found a barricade on
the bridge which took three-quarters of an hour to remove.
By 8.15 A.M., however, the brigade had secured the high
ground north of the river without fighting. By 10.15 A.M.
the 3rd Brigade had pushed on to Beaurepaire Farm (2½
miles north of Charly) without seeing a sign of the enemy.
The 1st Cavalry Brigade had already made good the next
ridge to the north, and the 3rd Brigade had advanced about
another mile to Les Aulnois Bontemps, before the advanced
guards received orders to stand fast. The Flying Corps had
reported " large hostile forces " at 8.30 A.M., both halted
and marching, north of Chateau Thierry, and the bridge
there intact. A further report at 12.30 P.M., however, put
the force halted about four miles north of the town at only
a division, with a long column going north, and further
small columns on roads to the east all going north.[1] About
1½ battalions were seen near Montreuil, where there was
" artillery activity." Most of the machines were, however,
employed to discover the position of the heads of the British
columns, and what was happening on the British right and
left. The nearest troops of the French Fifth Army were
seen at 7 A.M. near Viels Maisons (10 miles south of Chateau
Thierry), moving north-east, that is away from the B.E.F.
On the Ourcq, the air reports indicated that the situation
was much the same as on the previous day, with the French
8th Division on the immediate left of the British moving
away north-westwards.

In view of the supposed large hostile forces north of
Chateau Thierry, and the absence of support on the right
from the French, the whole of the I. Corps was ordered by
Sir Douglas Haig to halt until the situation could be cleared
up ; such of the artillery of the 2nd Division as had not
crossed the Marne was directed to remain in observation

[1] According to German accounts, there were no troops near Chateau
Thierry except the *5th Cavalry Division*, the two portions of which joined
up in the course of the day and retired on Beuvardes (7½ miles north-east
of Chateau Thierry). The columns seen must have been stragglers or
transport, but at the time they were thought to be the *III.* or *IX. Corps.*

on the south bank of the river, and the 5th Brigade to entrench there. The latter part of the order, sent verbally
by an officer, led to a misunderstanding ; for it was taken
by Major-General Monro to mean that his division was to
hold a position on the south bank, and he began withdrawing the troops who had crossed and sending back his baggage. Fortunately this was discovered by General Haig,
who saw the transport retiring, before much time had been
lost, and he directed the columns to close up on their heads
north of the river. The rest of the Cavalry Division joined
the 1st Cavalry Brigade to the left front of the 3rd Brigade
early in the afternoon, and a few men of the German rear
parties were cut off and captured. The remainder of the
1st Division crossed the river at Nogent, and in due time
the 2nd Division also, at Charly. But no further advance
was made by the I. Corps until 3 P.M., after two aeroplanes
sent to reconnoitre by General Haig had reported " all
clear " on the I. Corps front, when, preceded by the cavalry,
both divisions moved forward until their heads reached
the vicinity of the Chateau Thierry—Montreuil road at Le
Thiolet and Coupru respectively. Then, as no French
troops had come up on the right, only a few cavalrymen
had in fact crossed the Marne, and as the Sixth Army on
the left was making no progress and had withdrawn the
8th Division, the connecting link, north-westwards, Sir
John French, who had motored up to see General Haig,
instructed him to stop the advance. The 1st and 2nd
Divisions therefore halted and billeted in depth along the
roads on which they were marching, with the 1st and 2nd
Cavalry Brigades in front of them, and the rest of the
cavalry in rear.

Sketches
13 & 17.
Maps 4,
25 & 29. The II. Corps found the Marne bridges at Nanteuil and
Saacy intact ; the 3rd Division crossed by the former, the
5th Division by the latter. Before 8 A.M. the vanguard of
the 3rd Division, and about an hour later that of the 5th
Division, which met with strong opposition, had established
themselves on the heights of the northern bank, and the
9th Brigade, which with a brigade of artillery formed
the advanced guard of the 3rd Division, at once sent forward two battalions to Bezu les Guéry, two and a half
miles from the river. The vanguard (the Northumberland
Fusiliers), pushing on for another mile to Ventelet Farm,
found the ridge near it clear of the enemy. By 10.30 A.M.
Br.-General Shaw had fixed his headquarters at Bezu : all

seemed to be going well.   On the left of the 3rd Division also everything appeared at the outset to promise an easy advance for the 5th Division to Montreuil (2 miles north-west of Bezu, on the Chateau Thierry—La Ferté sous Jouarre main road), at which point it would cut off the Germans who were defending the passage of the Marne about La Ferté.   No sooner, however, did the vanguard (2/Manchester) of the 14th Brigade show itself about La Limon (1 mile north of Saacy) than it was greeted at various points by heavy shell fire from concealed batteries. Harassed by bursting shells on front and flank, the 14th Brigade now led by the 1/Duke of Cornwall's, with the 65th (Howitzer) and the 80th Batteries, began its advance upon Montreuil.   The direct road from Saacy along the bank of the northward bend of the Marne, via Méry, being too much exposed to the German fire, the brigade moved through the woods half a mile to the east, while the batteries unlimbered south of La Limon.   The growth of small trees was so dense that it was extremely difficult for the men to keep touch and maintain direction, and consequently pro-gress was slow.   In fact the 14th Brigade was swallowed up by the woods for more than an hour.

The advanced guard of the 3rd Division, to the east of this attack, had not met with opposition ; but the main body had come under persistent shrapnel fire from a German battery,[1] and Major-General Hamilton had moved it off the Nanteuil—Bezu road into the woods on its left. In order to deal with the German battery, which had been located in the Bois des Essertis west of Bezu, Br.-General Shaw sent two companies of the Lincolnshire through the woods to try and capture the guns.   The men crept up unseen to within a hundred and fifty yards of them, and in a few minutes shot down the German gunners literally almost to a man.   Dashing out of the thicket to secure the guns, however, they were fired upon first by the escort, that was on the opposite flank of the battery, with which they at once dealt, and then by the 65th (Howitzer) Battery.   They were compelled again to seek cover, with a loss of four officers and some thirty men killed or wounded, and the guns were not captured until next morning.   This unfortunate mistake arose from the 65th believing that

[1] *No. 6 Battery* of the *45th Field Artillery Regiment*, according to its diary, which says the battery was heavily shelled.   The other two batteries of the brigade had suffered so much from shell fire that they had already been withdrawn.

the German battery had been silenced by some other British artillery, and that the men of the Lincolnshire were German gunners returning to their abandoned guns.

Just about this time—11.30 A.M.—the Duke of Cornwall's at the head of the 14th Brigade at last emerged from the woods, and were fired upon by German infantry in position to the south of Montreuil. Thereupon, the brigade was ordered to attack towards the north, on a front of two battalions, with the left flank on the road from Méry to Montreuil; while the 15th Brigade was directed by 5th Division headquarters to move round further to the east, by Bezu and Bois des Essertis, and attack Hill 189 (immediately to south-east of Montreuil) from the flank. The 14th Brigade, with the 2/Manchester now on the right of the Duke of Cornwall's, meanwhile continued its advance, always slowly, owing to the density of the woods ; and, the Manchesters drifting to the right, the East Surrey were brought up to fill the gap. The leading companies of the D.C.L.I. now came under heavy fire from infantry entrenched on Hill 189, and from two batteries, which were still unsilenced, at La Sablonnière and Chamoust (south-west and north of Montreuil, respectively). Under this cross-fire of artillery, the Cornishmen, after struggling for a time to work forward, were counter-attacked and compelled to fall back, leaving a few prisoners behind them, and the 14th Brigade came to a dead stop. The Germans at 2 P.M. even launched a counter-attack against the left of its line, but the effort was at once smothered by British shrapnel. After more than an hour of deadlock, the Norfolk and Dorsetshire of the 15th Brigade between 3 and 4 P.M. came up to the western edge of the Bois des Essertis, on the flank of Hill 189, where they were abruptly checked by a violent fire from rifles and machine guns and from the battery at La Sablonnière. Unable to make progress, they stood fast, and engaged in a short-range fight with the German infantry, which was entrenched within a hundred and twenty yards of them. Forty-seven dead Germans were found next day in the trenches opposite to the Dorsetshire ; but the 15th Brigade needed the support of artillery, and the British batteries could find no positions from which to give it. Some time before—about 3 P.M.—two battalions of the 13th Infantry Brigade had been ordered to the left via Moitiébard (2 miles south of Montreuil) to discover and, if possible, destroy the battery at Chamoust ; but it was not until 6 P.M. that an officer of artillery, by a personal reconnaissance, at last found the exact position 9 Sept. of the German guns. They were silenced within ten 1914. minutes by the 37th (Howitzer) Battery ; but by that time the light was waning, and the best of the day was gone.[1] The 3rd Division, when it found that neither the I. Corps on its right nor the 5th Division on its left, was coming up in line with it, after helping the 5th Division as already related, remained from the morning onwards with its head at Ventelet Farm on the Chateau Thierry—Montreuil road, which thus marked the limit of British progress in this quarter.

Further to the west, the III. Corps was delayed by a Sketches most effective barrier. The enemy was holding the right 13 & 17. bank of the Marne at all likely points of passage, with 25 & 29. artillery near Caumont at the top of the big loop of the river enfilading the western reach of it nearly as far as La Ferté sous Jouarre, and with other guns north-west of the town. The only intact bridge was the railway viaduct half-way down the above-mentioned enfiladed reach of the river. The four service pontoons of the field companies of the one division at the disposal of the corps could only bridge 75 feet, and were obviously insufficient for crossing the Marne at any point in this section—for it was from 70 to 90 yards wide and very deep—without the help of additional material, and there was none to be found ready for use except at La Ferté sous Jouarre.

Pursuant to General Pulteney's orders, the 11th and 12th Brigades advanced at 4.45 A.M. in two columns, with the intention of repairing the bridges in front of them, and if possible of crossing the river and establishing a

---

[1] The enemy at Montreuil was at first Kraewel's *Composite Brigade*, hastily formed on the 8th of two infantry regiments and six batteries of artillery from the two divisions of the *IX. Corps* (see Note at end of previous Chapter). General Kraewel's instructions were to hold the line of the Marne from Nogent to La Ferté (actually the British front) and destroy the bridges (which he did not do), whilst the three cavalry divisions held the Petit Morin (which they had already abandoned). He slipped away at 8 P.M. on the 9th, leaving the guns of one battery behind him (" Militär Wochenblatt," Nos. 73 and 74 of 1920).

In the course of the fight, Kraewel's brigade " was supported by the " *9th Cavalry Division*, which attacked towards Montbertoin, and by the " leading troops of the Prussian *5th Division*, which had been sent by " [*First*] *Army Headquarters* to reinforce it, and had marched via Cocherel." (Lieut.-Colonel Müller Loebnitz, formerly of the Great General Staff, in " Der Wendepunkt des Weltkrieges," p. 35.)

Four *Jäger* battalions and " a detachment of the *3rd Division* from Mary " (6 miles to the west of Montreuil) were also present, according to Kuhl's " Marne," p. 207.

bridgehead north of La Ferté. They seized the high ground at Tarterel, immediately to the east of La Ferté, so that artillery could be brought up to deal with the German guns and the portion of the town south of the river. The broken bridges at La Ferté were, however, found by the 11th Brigade to be unapproachable, the buildings adjacent to them on the northern bank of the river being full of German snipers and machine guns. Attempts to cross by boat further down were also unsuccessful. It was extremely difficult to tell which houses were occupied, and impossible to deal effectively with them, except by howitzer fire ; the greater part of the forenoon was occupied with dropping shells on the most likely ones from Tarterel, and from Jouarre, south of La Ferté. The 12th Infantry Brigade, however, pushed two battalions up the left bank of the river into the loop between Chamigny and Luzancy, as there was a weir (actually a lock, barrage and weir nearly a hundred yards in total length) marked on the map near the former place. They found it, and succeeded by fire in silencing the defenders. Then the 2/Essex, led by Major F. W. Moffitt and followed by the 2/Lancashire Fusiliers, crossed by the weir, along which was a broken plank footway, in single file, only two men of the Essex being wounded by machine-gun fire during the passage. The Germans did not wait, and although the two battalions climbed up the slopes of the valley to the road which leads from La Ferté to Montreuil, the line of the enemy retreat, they reached it too late to intercept any German troops. Officers who took part in this extraordinary passage of a wide river in broad daylight in the face of an enemy can only explain it by the supposition that the *Jäger* defending the weir were too tired or dispirited to have heart to fight. The British were equally weary, and it was only that they were on the move forward which kept many of them from falling asleep.[1]

During this movement, shortly before noon, the British infantry was withdrawn from the southern half of La Ferté and the town was heavily bombarded, with the result that the Germans about 2.30 P.M. abandoned the direct defence of the bridges, which Royal Engineer officers were

[1] It may, however, be mentioned that Lieut.-Colonel Hentsch, the representative of O.H.L., who passed behind the front during the morning, found trains and wounded going back " in wild haste " fearing to be cut off by English cavalry, and in one place " complete panic." (Hentsch's report to the C.G.S., p. 3.)

thcn able to reconnoitre. But it was 4 P.M. or later before 9 Sept. any effectual repair work could be begun. However, the 1914. 1/Rifle Brigade followed the two battalions of the 12th Brigade across the weir, and the 2/Inniskilling Fusiliers crossed the river higher up by the railway viaduct which was still intact. They were shelled as they did so, but suffered no loss. The 1/East Lancashire and the 1/Hampshire were ferried across in boats below La Ferté, and this tedious operation on a broad and rapid river was not completed until 9 P.M., by which time the Engineers had collected sufficient barrel piers, boats and planks to supplement the pontoons and begin the construction of a floating bridge.[1] When darkness fell on the 9th, six of the twelve battalions of the 4th Division were still on the south side of the river : the 10th Brigade at Grand Mont Ménard (2 miles east of La Ferté), the King's Own (12th Brigade) at Luzancy, the Somerset Light Infantry (11th Brigade) at Les Abymes (just south of La Ferté). The 19th Brigade was between Jouarre and Signy Signets.

The other divisions and the cavalry (less a brigade) were Sketches across the Marne. The positions of the Army at the end B & 13. of the day were as follows, extending from Chateau Thierry Maps 25 (exclusive) through Bezu and La Ferté sous Jouarre to & 30. beyond Jouarre :

Cavalry Division . . .	Lucy le Bocage, Domptin.
5th Cavalry Brigade .	La Baudière (half a mile west of Domptin).
I. Corps	Le Thiolet, Mont de Bonneil, Domptin, Coupru.
II. Corps	Bezu, Crouttes, Caumont.
3rd Cavalry Brigade .	Grand Mont Ménard (south of the Marne).
III. Corps	Luzancy, Grand Mont Ménard, Jouarre, Chamigny.

At 1 P.M., on behalf of the British Commander-in-Chief, the French Mission at G.H.Q. had telephoned to General Joffre : " Our III. Corps is stopped in the environs of La " Ferté as the bridges are broken. The enemy is in force " on the line Chateau Thierry—Marigny. It is of the " utmost importance that the XVIII. Corps should come " to the help of our I. Corps in the environs of Chateau " Thierry."

This message G.Q.G. at once telephoned on to General

---

[1] It was formed of 2 trestles, 4 pontoons, 4 barrel piers, 1 barge and 2 boats, and completed at 7 A.M. on the 10th.

Franchet d'Espèrey, but the only result was that, towards 5 P.M., the French 4th Cavalry Division arrived on the right of the I. Corps, and later an infantry brigade crossed at Azy, and formed an outpost line behind the cavalry, whilst Chateau Thierry was occupied about 5 P.M. by the 10th Cavalry Division, subsequently joined by two infantry battalions.[1]

Sketches 13 & 17. Maps 4, 25, 29 & 30.

The 9th September, though we now know that the advance of the B.E.F. was the decisive factor in influencing the Germans to abandon the field of battle,[2] seemed at the time a disappointing day for the British, despite their passage of the Marne. The more so since General Maunoury, having been hard pressed on his left and left flank throughout the 8th, had asked for a brisk attack against the left flank and rear of Kluck. Had the entire British line been able to come up level with the 9th Brigade when it reached the road from Chateau Thierry through Montreuil to Lizy sur Ourcq at 9 A.M., great results might have followed; for Kluck's left was then well to the south of Lizy, and by a general advance Kraewel's force at Montreuil would have been swept away or surrounded. But the I. Corps, on the right, was halted for several hours on account of a misleading air report that there were large enemy forces north of Chateau Thierry, and the French on its right were too far in rear to give assistance in case of counter-attack; the III. Corps, on the left, was held up by the destruction of the bridges at La Ferté sous Jouarre.

That the German *First* and *Second Armies* were abandoning the field of battle did not become apparent until about 5.30 P.M. The British air reports of the earlier part of the day, consolidated on a map at 3 P.M., showed no sign of retrograde movements except north of Chateau Thierry. Observations made from the air from 3.55 P.M. onwards, however, discovered first a long column (*3rd Division*) marching northwards from Lizy at the back of the Ourcq battlefield, and then other columns of transport and troops retiring north-north-eastwards on Neuilly and La Ferté Milon. The ground on the left flank of the B.E.F., in the angle between the Marne and the Ourcq, was reported quite clear; but it had been noticed that two columns marching eastwards had halted on the British

[1] See page 345.
[2] See Note I at end of Chapter.

front at Dhuisy (6 miles N.N.E. of La Ferté Jouarre).[1] 9 Sept.
The R.F.C. general report, timed 5.20 P.M., which reached 1914.
G.H.Q. soon after, ended with the words, " General retire-
" ment N.N.E. on Soissons," which turned out to be correct;
but the situation map on information derived from the
French still showed incorrectly the German *III. Corps*
opposite the French north-east of Chateau Thierry, and
the *VII. Corps* behind it.

Information that the French were approaching Chateau
Thierry, and that there appeared to be a German rear
guard five miles north of that town, arrived at G.H.Q. very
soon after this air report ; also news from the other flank,
from General Maunoury, that Kluck was retiring north-
eastwards covering his retreat by his heavy artillery.
But it was too late to order a general and combined advance;
in fact, both men and horses of both French and British
were, after the continuous operations since the 20th August,
too worn out for further effort without some rest and re-
freshment. It was the physical exhaustion of the belligerents which prevented the local tactical advantages
gained by both sides on certain parts of the field from being
developed into decisive successes. As, however, the line
of retreat of the *First Army* appeared to lie more or less
across the British front, Sir John French still had some
hopes of intercepting the Germans. Acting in anticipation
of General Joffre's instructions, which did not arrive until
next day, at 8.15 P.M. he ordered his troops to continue
the pursuit northwards at 5 A.M. next morning.[2]

The gigantic struggle of the 6th to the 9th September,
known as the battle of the Marne, in which, between
Verdun and Paris, so far as can be ascertained, 49 Allied
divisions, with eight cavalry divisions, contended against
46 German divisions, with seven cavalry divisions,[3] was
over, and with it all the hopes of the rapid knock-out blow

---

[1] Now known to be part of the *5th Division* and *II. Cavalry Corps* sent
to stop the British advance.
[2] Appendix 39.
[3] As evidence of the failure of the German strategy, G.O.A. (iv. pp.
524-5) states that on the vital western wing, the Allies (Ninth, Fifth and
Sixth Armies and the B.E.F.) had a superiority of roughly 200 battalions
and 190 batteries over the Germans (*First, Second* and half the *Third
Armies*), whereas at Namur—Mons the Germans (*First, Second* and *Third
Armies*) had a superiority over the French Fifth Army and B.E.F. of
more than one hundred battalions and 175 batteries. In the centre there
were 321 German battalions opposed to 277 French, and on the eastern
wing 329 Germans opposed to 316 French, whilst 44 battalions and 53
batteries were on the move from Alsace to Belgium.

on which Germany had counted for winning the war against her unprepared opponents. Tactically it was not fought to a finish, but strategically its results were far-reaching, so that it must be regarded as one of the decisive battles of the world.[1] Its general result is well summarized in a proclamation issued by General Franchet d'Espèrey on the evening of the 9th September to the Fifth Army :

" Held on his flanks, his centre broken, the enemy is " now retreating towards the east and north by forced " marches."

In the area between Verdun and Paris the Armies of Generals Sarrail and de Langle de Cary on the right had more or less held their ground against the German *Fifth, Fourth* and part of the *Third Armies*, just as Maunoury had against the *First Army*. In the centre, the right and centre of General Foch's Army had been driven back by the left of the German *Second Army* and the right of the *Third*; he was about to attempt to restore the situation by the counter-attack of a division transferred from his left to his right, when the Germans retreated. General Franchet d'Espèrey, too, had contributed little towards the victory : he had lent his X. Corps to General Foch to succour the latter's right ; his I. and III. Corps had wheeled to the right, following cautiously, but not catching up, the right of Bülow's Army, which had swung back eastwards ; and his XVIII. Corps and Conneau's cavalry corps, with little or no opposition in front of them after the 6th September, had lost touch with the enemy and fallen gradually behind the British, the heads of their columns not coming up until the general retirement of the Germans was well under way.

On Franchet d'Espèrey's left, the B.E.F. had driven back a strong screen under Generals von Richthofen and von der Marwitz, formed of four cavalry divisions (including one infantry and eight *Jäger* battalions), a composite brigade of the *IX. Corps*, rear guards of the *II.* and *IV. Corps*, and a detachment of the *III. Corps*.[2] On ground eminently advantageous to the defence, it had forced the passage of the Grand Morin, the Petit Morin and the Marne,

---

[1] Falkenhayn (p. 1) tells us that the removal of Moltke from the post of Chief of the General Staff which followed (see page 426) was concealed so that the change of leadership should not give the enemy propaganda " further ostensible proof of the completeness of the victory obtained on the Marne."

[2] All these formations are definitely mentioned in different German accounts.

and had not only interposed itself between the German
First and *Second Armies*, but whilst the former was fully
engaged in front with Maunoury's Army, had turned its
left flank. The Germans had no choice, as Kluck's Chief of
Staff admits,[1] except between complete disaster to their
right wing and retreat in order to make good the 25 miles'
gap in their line of battle. This gap was certainly created
by their own action; and unfortunately it was exploited
only by the B.E.F.

The advance of the British has been adversely com-
mented upon as slow and hesitating by several French
writers.[2] It has been pointed out[3] that owing to the delay
in General Joffre's order reaching Sir John French, the
B.E.F. retired on the 5th, instead of advancing, and therefore started two marches behind where the French expected
it to be on the morning of the 6th. For the same reason,
also, the left of General Franchet d'Espèrey's Army was
to the south of where it should have been, to the right rear
of the British ; and it remained behind them practically
throughout the battle, and was behind them at the end.
The average advance on the 6th was eleven miles ; on the
7th under eight, with the passage of the Grand Morin ; on
the 8th, ten, with the forcing of the Petit Morin ; and on
the 9th, seven, with the crossing of the Marne. In view
of the previous labours of the B.E.F., the difficulties of the
ground, and the opposition of the enemy, little more could
be expected.

A greater effort might possibly have been made on the
9th, but no demand for it came from General Joffre, who
alone knew the situation as a whole. The French on either
flank of the B.E.F. were not making definite progress—
it is now known that Foch's right and Maunoury's left were
actually falling back—and until 5.30 P.M., for all the British
commander knew, if he pushed forward wildly north of
the Marne he might be thrusting his troops into a trap
prepared for them : a fear urged as excuse for the smaller
progress of the French Fifth Army.

[1] See Note I at end of Chapter.
[2] *E.g.* General Palat. He adds, however, " It seems likely that their
" confidence in themselves and particularly in us, had suffered in the
" first encounters, which were so little encouraging " (vi. p. 248).
[3] See page 296.

Sketch 17.
Maps 4,
25, 29
& 30.

General Joffre had now no hope of the Sixth Army enveloping the German right, and required no more of General Maunoury than that he should hold fast the enemy opposite to him. " He even directed " him to avoid all decisive action, withdrawing his left in the direc- " tion of the entrenched camp of Paris until the arrival of rein- " forcements enabled him to resume the offensive." As it happened, reinforcements for the Germans arrived first and advanced to attack the left of the Sixth Army ; and, on their appearance, it was swung back. On the other flank on the Ourcq, opposite Maunoury's right wing, the enemy withdrew, and thus by night all touch with the Germans had been lost. The French troops were very tired, but General Maunoury proposed to resume the offensive next day, as soon as he had been reinforced by the 8th Division.

In the Fifth Army sector the Germans seemed to have disappeared. " The Fifth Army marched towards the Marne and the Surmelin " [a tributary of the Marne on its southern side, running N.N.W.] " without encountering, as a whole, any resistance."

The Fifth Army orders for the 9th, issued at 8.15 P.M. on the previous evening, directed the corps to advance in echelon during the morning towards the Marne (further orders would be issued for the afternoon), the left leading, pushing on advanced guards to hold the passages of the Surmelin. Thus placed, the Army would be ready to engage either towards the north or north-east—but not north-west to help the B.E.F.

Half an hour after these orders had been issued, General Franchet d'Espèrey received General Joffre's Instruction No. 19,[2] in which the Commander-in-Chief announced that the German right wing now formed two distinct groups, and laid down that the " rôle of the " Fifth Army was to cover the right flank of the British Army by " directing a strong detachment on Chateau Thierry—Azy. Con- " neau's cavalry corps, crossing the Marne, if necessary behind this " detachment or behind the British columns, was to ensure effective " liaison between the British Army and the Fifth Army."

" General Franchet d'Espèrey did not in any way alter the orders " which he had just given ; " but at 9 P.M. he issued an addition to them " informing his corps that the enemy was in full retreat, and " directing that they should not let themselves be stopped by the " resistance of rear guards : these should be crushed by violent " artillery fire, turned by infantry and pursued by cavalry. Only " a vigorous pursuit, he added, will permit us to gather the full fruits " of the present situation." In spite of these most appropriate in- structions nothing of the nature of a pursuit took place.

As the Fifth Army became in the course of the day divided into three portions : the right (I. and III. Corps) which, with the X. Corps, went to General Foch's assistance ; the left, Conneau's cavalry corps, which came up on the right of the B.E.F. ; and the centre (XVIII. Corps and Group of Reserve Divisions), which hung back in reserve, its operations will be summarized in that order.

The III. Corps had passed the night in front of Montmirail in

---

[1] Summarized from the French Official Account.
[2] See page 326.

contact with the enemy.   General Hache, therefore, ordered his 9 Sept.
divisions on the 9th to pass right and left of the town.   But no 1914.
enemy was encountered ; only about noon did the corps cavalry
regiment receive a few rifle shots, probably from a party of cyclists,
and parties of German cavalry were seen retiring.   Less the 37th
Division, ordered at 9.15 A.M. to be transferred to the Sixth Army,
the corps (5th and 6th Divisions) went forward about six miles north-
eastward, and at 1 P.M., just as the right had come under artillery
fire, it received Army orders to halt, practically where it was, and
protect itself from the direction of the Surmelin, 2½ miles to the
front.   The reason given for this order was that Foch's Army had
been violently attacked, and the X. Corps had gone to its assistance,
and the I. Corps was preparing to do so.   The III. Corps subsequently moved up towards the Surmelin and went into bivouac.
The whole right wing (3 corps) of the Fifth Army had swung practically eastward.   The I. Corps advanced half-deployed in order to
deal with enemy rear guards.   At 8 A.M. it reached its first objective,
Vauchamps, without seeing anything of the enemy, although the
19th Division on its right (the third division of the X. Corps, not
handed on to Foch and now attached to the I. Corps) was fired on.
Continuing on, at 10.45 A.M. the corps was ordered to halt and be
ready to face east or north-east, as the Ninth Army was being
violently attacked.   Soon after 1 P.M. General Franchet d'Espèrey
arrived at corps headquarters, and announcing that he had halted
the III. Corps, ordered the I. " to throw the maximum of force
" towards Champaubert to disengage the left of the Ninth Army."
General Deligny detailed the 19th Division and half the 2nd, with
all the corps artillery, but at 3.10 P.M., before any offensive action
had been taken, new instructions were received from the Fifth
Army, ordering the I. Corps, whilst protecting itself from the north,
to turn back south-east (sic) to disengage the X. Corps by an immediate attack " à fond."   To array the formations of the corps on the
new alignment " required nearly three hours," and the attack was
about to be launched when information was received from General
Foch that he was going to resume the general offensive.   Direction
was therefore again altered to north-east, and the corps progressed
without difficulty, " for the enemy were retiring rapidly."   The total
day's advance north-eastwards was six miles by the 1st Division on
the left, and five miles by the 19th Division on the right.   The 1st
and 2nd Divisions throughout the day never had contact with the
enemy, but the advance eastward of the 19th Division had been
stopped by fire.
    Turning to the left of the Fifth Army, General Conneau sent for-
ward only the 4th and 10th Cavalry Divisions from the Petit Morin,
leaving the 8th resting.   The 4th began to cross the Marne at Azy
(7½ miles from its starting place) at 1 P.M., " behind the British
" cavalry," completing the passage at 2.30 P.M. ; the 10th went forward a short distance, and then " made a long halt, sending recon-
" noitring parties towards Chateau Thierry."
    At 1 P.M. the Cavalry Corps received General Franchet d'Espèrey's
orders to cross the Marne at Azy " during the day," supported by a
mixed brigade of the XVIII. Corps.   (The 72nd Brigade, 3 batteries
of artillery, some engineers and half a troop of cavalry were detailed,
and arrived at Azy about 5 P.M.)   General Conneau's task was " to
" act against the German columns in retreat north of the Marne,

" cover the right flank of the British, and assure the debouching of
" the XVIII. Corps on the right bank of the Marne."

The 4th Cavalry Division, on going forward, passed the rearmost
British cavalry brigade, the 4th, in bivouac. Its reconnoitring
parties reported the enemy " three to five miles ahead. At the end
" of the day the 4th Division billeted two miles south-west of
" Chateau Thierry," on the right of the British I. Corps.

The 10th Cavalry Division, after its long halt, continued on towards
Chateau Thierry at 2 P.M. Hearing that the town was occupied, two
squadrons were sent east and west to turn it. " At 4.30 P.M., the
" enemy, a few cavalry patrols it would appear, retired. The 10th
" Division entered the town and sent reconnoitring parties north
" and north-east. The halt order left the division in the town and
" its western suburbs." In the evening, two infantry battalions
attached to the division arrived to hold a bridgehead, and the 10th
Dragoon Brigade was sent on outpost ahead of them.

The 8th Cavalry Division was moved from its overnight billets
at 2 P.M. and brought up south of the river, south-west of Chateau
Thierry.

The XVIII. Corps (of Franchet d'Espèrey's centre) advanced
in two columns, preceded by the corps cavalry regiment, with the
intention of halting at Viffort, about six miles north of the Petit
Morin. The cavalry soon learnt from the inhabitants that the enemy
had gone, leaving only a few cavalry patrols, and the corps reached
its destination without difficulty, " at the end of the morning." At
12.30 P.M., in consequence of G.Q.G. instructions, General Franchet
d'Espèrey ordered the XVIII. Corps to send a mixed brigade, as
already mentioned, to support the cavalry corps ; but it was not
until 4.15 P.M. that he passed on the further G.Q.G. instructions,
telephoned at 2.10 P.M., that " the XVIII. Corps should try to pass
" the Marne this evening at Chateau Thierry in order to support
" effectively the right of the British Army [already over the Marne],
" which is marching from Charly on Domptin and the north."

The XVIII. Corps then got on the march again, and at 5.20 P.M.
General Maud'huy ordered his two leading divisions to halt for the
night on the south bank of the Marne, with the third division behind
them at Viffort. They were to be covered on the left by the mixed
brigade with the cavalry, and on the right by four battalions of
Zouaves. One of the latter crossed the river at 7 P.M. and bivouacked
with the outposts.

The Group of Reserve Divisions marched up one division behind
the other, and at night filled the gap between the XVIII. Corps and
the III.

Thus the five divisions of the centre gave assistance neither to the
main body of the Fifth Army on the right nor to the British on the
left, neither did they encounter any enemy, and no advantage was
taken of the complete gap in front of them.

On this, the last day of the battle, Foch suffered a greater set-
back than on the previous day. The Germans, having driven the
defenders from the southern exits of the Marshes of St. Gond on the
8th, " attacked the whole front of the Ninth Army except that of the
" [attached] X. Corps. On the left (the Moroccan Division) resist-
" ance was offered not without difficulty ; on the right (IX. and XI.
" Corps) a retirement of three or four miles was made." At noon
Foch issued " a supreme appeal to his troops." Then came a pause

and the beginning of a gradual German retirement.   The 42nd 9 Sept.
Division had marched at 7 A.M. from the left of the Army, where it 1914.
was relieved by the X. Corps, towards the centre to form a reserve. At
1.45 P.M. Foch gave its commander, General Grossetti, orders to
counter-attack at 4 P.M. from Pleurs north-eastward.   Its advance
was to be the signal for all the other divisions to go forward.   " But
" it was 6 P.M. when it reached the road Linthes—Pleurs [its starting
" base] and already [growing] dark, so General Grossetti decided to
" suspend the attack and let his troops bivouac on the positions they
" had reached."
    Of the other troops of the Ninth Army, only one brigade of the
XI. Corps, finding nothing in front of it, went forward, and continued
onwards till 11 P.M., when it was ordered back to its starting place.
Its sister brigade of the 22nd Division entrenched.   The 9th Cavalry
Division, guarding the right of the Army, came up abreast of the
infantry, its cyclist point reaching Mailly at 8 P.M., to learn that the
Germans had left two hours earlier.   " Night alone prevented a
pursuit."

NOTE I

THE GERMAN RIGHT WING ON THE 9TH SEPTEMBER

    The German Official Account (iv. p. 270) states, in italics : " The Sketch 17.
" mighty struggle on the Ourcq and Marne, one of the greatest Maps 4,
" events of world history, was broken off !   The German right wing 25, 29
" turned from its already-won victory to retreat."   No claim is, & 30.
however, made for success on the rest of the front or in the battle as
a whole.   On the left (east) there was, indeed, acknowledged failure :
" on the afternoon of the 8th September General von Moltke made
" the decision to abandon entirely the prospectless operations in
" Lorraine."   Crown Prince Rupprecht that evening ordered the
offensive to be stopped, and at 10 P.M. the retirement was begun ;
at 12.20 P.M. on the 9th the Supreme Command ordered : " prepara-
" tions for occupying a rearward defensive position to be made at
" once." [1]   As regards the German centre (*Fifth, Fourth Armies* and
part of the *Third*), Moltke reported to the Kaiser on the morning of
the 9th that " the Army [*Fifth*] of the Crown Prince was caught as
" in a sack " (G.O.A., iv. p. 318) ;   Colonel Tappen (head of the
Operations Section, O.H.L.) considered " the right wing of the *Fifth*
" *Army*, in places in very difficult ground, was liable to be pressed
" against the fortress of Verdun, and therefore was exposed to
" annihilation."   In any case, the *Fifth Army* was pinned to the
ground during daylight by French artillery fire.   The *Fourth Army*
had come to a standstill owing to the weariness of the men, the great
heat, and the " ever-increasing weight of French artillery fire."   On
the 8th, " as a whole, the attack of the *Fourth Army* had again been
" shattered by the superior French artillery."   For the 9th there
is the same story, the corps could not advance ; and at 8.30 A.M.
the Army ordered them to " hold their positions " (G.O.A., iv. pp.
166-71).
    The *Third Army* was divided in two, half sharing the fortunes of
the *Fourth Army* and half those of the *Second Army* on the right

[1] Bavarian Official Account, " Die Schlacht in Lothringen," ii. pp.
801-3.

wing ; the gap between the two portions amounted to some six miles ; fresh French troops (actually only the 6th Cavalry Division) were reported to be moving towards the gap, " and it could not be " doubtful that the *Third Army* in its present situation should not " be exposed to a renewed serious attack of the enemy " (Tappen, p. 27).

The claim to an already-won victory on the right wing (*First* and *Second Armies*, with part of the *Third*) reduces itself on examination to little more than local successes at the two extremities of its line : on the left wing of the *Second Army* and on the right wing of the *First Army*. The compilers of the German official monograph on the battle (" Marnedrama," iv. p. 343) do not go so far as those of the Official Account ; for they speak of no more than " the possibility " of the German victory, for which there were great prospects," but no more than for an Allied success. All that can be said for certain is that the centre of the German right wing held by Richthofen and Marwitz was broken, and the *Second Army* had wheeled back, increasing the gap between it and the *First* to nearly thirty miles.

The events leading to the German decision to retreat from the Marne are briefly as follows :—Lieut.-Colonel Hentsch arrived at *Second Army* headquarters at 7 P.M. on the 8th,[1] and had a long discussion with General von Bülow, his Chief of the Staff, and the Operations General Staff officer. As a result of this, he reported by wireless to O.H.L., " Situation of the *Second Army* serious, but not " without hope (*aursichtslos*)." Between Bülow and Hentsch " it was " finally agreed that the *Second Army* should go back only if the enemy " actually crossed the Marne in considerable strength and appeared " in rear of the First Army." (G.O.A., iv. p. 241.) At dinner, after the conference, the tone was " depressed," but between 10 and 11 P.M. Bülow issued orders that the attack should be continued next day by his left wing (*Guard Corps* and three Saxon divisions of the *Third Army*) astride the Fère Champenoise—Sézanne road, whilst his centre (the *14th Division* and *X. Corps*) stood fast, and his right wing (*X. Reserve Corps* and *13th Division*) retired on to the Le Thoult —Margny position, to which, as already mentioned, it was then retreating. There was no statement in the order as to Bülow's intentions, but it seems evident that he meant to align his Army facing Paris, as ordered by O.H.L. on the 5th September, regardless of the fact that by so doing he would place it at right angles to the general

---

[1] The instructions and the powers given by Moltke to Lieut.-Colonel Hentsch are in dispute ; they were, at any rate, verbal, not written. The matter is not of sufficient importance to the British Army to devote space here to the controversy. Those interested should consult the German official pamphlet, " Die Sendung des Oberstleutnants Hentsch " (Berlin, Mittler), in which are printed Hentsch's report of his mission, dated 15th September 1914 ; his further report, dated 14th May 1917, when General Ludendorff instituted an enquiry into the case ; and Ludendorff's review of it, which was circulated " down to divisional staffs." Ludendorff found that Hentsch had not exceeded his powers. The main factors of the case, and reference to other sources, are given in an article " The Scapegoat of the Battle of the Marne 1914 " in the " Army Quarterly " of January 1921. It may be added that Lieut.-Colonel Hentsch continued to be employed at O.H.L., and was sent by Falkenhayn on a similar important mission to the Eastern Front in November 1914 (G.O.A., vi. p. 55), and in September 1915 to organize the invasion of Serbia (G.O.A., lx. p. 200). He died in 1917 in Rumania, whilst on a mission there.

Frcnch front ; would expose his outer flank, when he knew his 9 Sept. inner flank was threatened by Franchet d'Espèrey's advance (3ce 1914. Sketch 16) ; and would widen the gaps (6 miles and 30 miles) already existing on his left and right.

On the morning of the 9th, Bülow's left wing made good progress, and it claimed that the resistance of the four divisions of Foch's right and two divisions of his centre (leaving only two divisions and two borrowed from Franchet d'Espèrey in position) " had been " broken or were about to be broken," when orders were received from Army headquarters by telephone at 10.45 A.M. to retire north-wards, beginning on the left at 12 noon, the centre going " not before " 1 P.M." and the right " not before 2 P.M."

Lieut.-Colonel Hentsch left Montmort at 6 A.M. on the 9th for the *First Army*, without seeing Bülow again ; but " shortly before 9 A.M." an aviator reported to Bülow five hostile columns (by their routes, all British), with their heads, between 8 and 8.15 A.M., on or across the Marne. Another aviator had already reported the ground in front of the British advance as clear of troops. This grave news was at 9.40 A.M. confirmed by an overheard wireless message from General von der Marwitz to the *First Army*. In this he said, " Strong in-" fantry columns advancing northwards via Charly and Nanteuil." At 10.2 A.M. Bülow informed the *First Army* by wireless : " aviators " report advance of four long columns [it would seem that it was " known that the fifth was a short cavalry column] over the Marne. " Heads at 8 A.M. at Nanteuil, Citry, Pavant and Nogent. *Second* " *Army* begins retirement right flank Damery [subsequently cor-" rected to Dormans]." This message is said to have been received at *First Army* headquarters " only shortly before noon," but not handed to the Chief of the Staff till 1.4 P.M. Having thus warned Kluck, Bülow issued orders by telephone for the retirement. Any further advance of his left wing might have led it into trouble, there were no reserves behind it, so it is doubtful whether " a far-reaching " victory was in sight." Recalling that at the battle of Guise, the fire of one horse artillery battery and the appearance of the head of a Reserve division on the outer flank of the *Guard Corps* had stopped the advance, it seems possible that the guns of the French 9th Cavalry Division, not to say the 13th, 23rd and 43rd Divisions (XXI. Corps sent to fill the gap between the Fourth and Ninth Armies), which were at hand on the flank of the advancing Germans, might equally have checked the Guards and Saxons.

It is stated that the *Second Army* had little difficulty in breaking off the action and getting clear " without any loss worth mentioning," and that the bridges over the Somme and the Marshes of St. Gond were held by rear guards without seeing a Frenchman until daylight on the 10th. By ordering a retirement Bülow claimed to have saved the rashly adventuresome *First Army* from being caught between the B.E.F. and the French Sixth Army and annihilated ; and the right wing of the German line as a whole from being enveloped and rolled up (Bülow, pp. 60-1). The Supreme Command seems to have taken this view, for next day it issued an order, which must have been bitter reading for General von Kluck : " *First Army* until " further orders is placed under commander of *Second Army*." [1]

---

[1] Bülow was promoted Field-Marshal on 27th January 1915, but two months later, being then 69 years of age, he had a stroke, and was not further employed ; he died in August 1921.

Lieut.-Colonel Hentsch, after leaving *Second Army* headquarters, " everywhere ran into the trains and baggage of the cavalry divisions " retiring in wild haste." Warned that the British cavalry was advancing and the roads blocked, he motored round by Neuilly ; repeatedly he " had to descend and use force in order to get through," and it was 11.30 A.M. before he reached *First Army* headquarters at Mareuil. There he found the situation dubious. General von Kluck had been made aware on the night of the 8th/9th, as we have seen, of the withdrawal eastwards of Bülow's right wing, and of the retirement of the *I.* and *II. Cavalry Corps* ; he had heard nothing from Kraewel ; but he was relying on the greater part of the *III.* and *IX. Corps* (the *5th Division* and Kraewel's composite brigade had been detached) on his northern flank at dawn, in combination with Lepel's brigade (4¾ battalions of the *IV. Reserve Corps* and two *Landwehr* batteries which opportunely reached Verberie from Brussels on the night of the 8th/9th), to envelop and roll up Maunoury's Army, and turn the scale in favour of the Germans. The state of the troops of the two corps, after two days' and two nights' practically incessant marching in hot weather, with little food,[1] may be summed up in the words of one company commander : " I will " come with the officers alone : there won't be any others." Beyond La Ferté sous Jouarre " only a confused mob of limping shadows " climbed the hill."[2]

The columns were late in arriving at the rendezvous,[3] and slow in advancing from it, so that, instead of attacking at dawn, Kluck's liaison officer with the *IX. Corps* reported at 9.15 A.M. (received 10 A.M.) that the infantry were still 5 miles north of Antilly on a north and south line ready to begin their wheel south-west to fall on the French flank. Lepel's brigade had marched at 4.30 A.M., had reached the high ground south of Rully by 7.45 A.M., and reported (message received about 9 A.M.) that it was in rear of the, supposed, French position. All seemed to be going well ; but now, between 9.28 and 10.11 A.M., Kluck received what the German Official Account calls " three bad Job's posts " :—an overheard wireless of the *Guard Cavalry Division*, which said " strong enemy infantry and artillery " [British 2nd Division] at Charly over Marne bridge " ; a report from Marwitz, " strong enemy infantry [British 2nd and 3rd Divisions] " advancing via Charly and Nanteuil " ; then another message from Marwitz, interrupted, the last words from the operator being, " I must " be off quickly."

" The condition on which the success of the operations was based, " the holding of the Marne line, seemed shattered." Immediate retreat and the sending of all available forces to drive back the British was considered, but the *First Army* finally decided to swing back the

---

[1] " Regt. No. 24," p. 63, says that on the night of the 8th/9th there had been no rations for 24 hours—half a loaf was shared by 14 men.

[2] See the description of the march in Bloem's " Vormarsch," pp. 244-72. The routes of the *6th*, *17th* and *18th Divisions* measure over fifty miles ; 36 miles is said to have been covered by the *IX. Corps* in 22 hours on the 8th. The strength of the infantry regiments on 6th September was under two-thirds establishment, and the *5th Division*, the strongest, marched on the 9th at about the strength of a composite brigade. ("Marnedrama," iv. pp. 347-50.)

[3] Colonel von der Schulenberg, who had a detachment of 12 companies of different regiments, combed out from the lines of communication, joined in the advance of the *17th Division*.

left wing (Linsingen's group) [1] as flank protection, and proceed with the attack of the *6th, 17th* and *18th Divisions* (Quast's Group). (G.O.A., iv. pp. 207-8.) Under the Chief of the Staff's (Kuhl's) instructions, a general staff officer telephoned the following message, which is recorded as arriving at Linsingen's headquarters at 10.40 A.M.:

9 Sept. 1914.

" *Second Army* has withdrawn its right wing considerably east-
" wards beyond Montmirail. In consequence the British are re-
" ported at 10 A.M. to-day crossing the Marne in strength at Charly
" and Nanteuil. General von Linsingen, including Group Lochow
" [left centre] under him, will go back at once in direction Crouy with
" flank protection via Coulombs in direction La Ferté Milon—Neuilly
" St. Front (*sic*). *II. Cavalry Corps*, with Kraewel's brigade, will
" receive orders to cover the flank. Group General Sixt von Armin
" [right centre] will receive orders to cover the withdrawal and then
" go back behind the line Mareuil—Antilly. Group General von
" Quast will cover movement with a thrust (*Vorstoss*) in direction
" of Nanteuil." (G.O.A., iv. pp. 208-9.)

The movements thus ordered and forecast were those which took place ; but General von Kuhl has since stated that the message " did " not correspond to his actual intentions." The formal operation order, however, issued " about 11 A.M." (the actual time typed on it is 11.30 A.M., 10.30 A.M. Allied time), differs from it but little. It runs, after giving the same information as to the enemy :—

" Left Army Wing (General von Linsingen with Group Lochow
" under him) will send *5th Division* to attack direction Dhuisy, and
" withdraw the rest at once to the region Crouy—Coulombs. *II.*
" *Cavalry Corps* with Kraewel's brigade has orders to protect flank.
" Group Sixt v. Armin has orders to protect the movement by attack
" in direction Villers St. Genest—Acy en Multien.

" Group General v. Quast will co-operate by thrust in direction
" Nanteuil le Haudouin."

This order meant in plain language that from facing west, the *First Army* was to face south, pivoting on its centre, ready, as the telephone order indicated, to retire northwards. The much-marched right wing (*6th, 17th* and *18th Divisions*), at first designed to roll up General Maunoury's line and achieve a decisive victory, was to do no more than make a thrust to facilitate a retirement.

Some half an hour after this order was issued, Lieut.-Colonel Hentsch arrived at *First Army* headquarters. His instructions were, according to his own account : " Should rearward movements have " already been initiated on the right wing, endeavour to direct them " so that the gap between the *First* and *Second Armies* is closed again. " *First Army*, if possible, direction Soissons." Whilst he was actu- ally discussing the situation with General von Kuhl, further reports came in of the progress of the British north of the Marne ; possibly he assumed that, by now, the *Second Army* was retiring—it has been hinted that Kuhl knew it for certain when he issued the first retire- ment order " about 11 A.M."—in any case Hentsch ordered the *First Army* to retire in the direction Fismes—Soissons. Lieut.-Colonel Hentsch has left on record the reasons which underlay his decision :—

" The situation of the *First Army* about midday was such that
" its left wing had *already* received the order to go back to the line

[1] Owing to the intermixing of the corps, Kluck had divided the front between four corps commanders, left to right, Linsingen, Lochow, Sixt von Armin, Quast.

" Crouy—Coulombs. The possibility of the *Second Army* holding
" the line of the Marne was therefore put out of the question : that
" Army must retire if its flank and rear were not to be enveloped by
" the British on the 10th at latest.

"Any question whether immediate assistance could not be afforded
" to the *Second Army* was answered in the negative, the situation
" of the left wing being given as the reason. . . . Just at this time
" a report came in from the *IV. Corps* (Sixt von Armin), that it could
" not carry out the attack ordered, being itself attacked by strong
" forces. . . . I asked General von Kuhl if the *First Army* would
" not be in a position to support the *Second* next day (10th) with the
" whole of its force, if it succeeded in defeating its own opponents on
" the 9th. This was answered in the negative in view of the con-
" dition of the Army." [1]

General von Kluck states (p. 104), " on the ground of the now
" fully changed condition of affairs, the Army commander [himself]
" —bearing in mind the seriousness of his decision—decided on an
" immediate commencement of the retirement in a northern direc-
" tion."

The representatives of the *First Army* have since claimed that
they had no intention of making a general retirement, and that
Hentsch decided on the retreat in spite of their protests. It is, however, undisputed that the Chief of the Staff did not demand that this
momentous order should be put in writing, nor did he write it down
and ask Hentsch to initial it, the usual course in all Armies when an
important, and unpleasant, order is given verbally ; [2] nor, most extraordinary fact of all, did he think it necessary to take the representative
of the Supreme Command to see the Army commander, General von
Kluck. Kuhl accepted the order, and the *First Army* acted on it,
which seems only explicable on the assumption that Kluck and Kuhl
had already decided to retreat.

Lieut.-Colonel Hentsch left the *First Army* about 1 P.M., and
immediately after this instructions were sent by telephone and
officers in motor cars for the beginning of the retreat. Thus, as the
German Official Account says, " the commanders of the *First* and
" *Second Armies* issued orders almost simultaneously for the breaking
" off of the battle." Kluck's orders, according to " Marnedrama "
(iv. p. 290), contained the following :—

" The situation of the *Second Army* demands its retirement

---

[1] Kluck, p. 123, confirms this conversation, giving as reasons for the
answer—it is not clear whether they are his own or Hentsch's—that " an
" exploitation of the success begun against Maunoury might certainly be
" expected in the course of the next few days ; but then the necessary
" shaking clear, reorganization of the corps [divisions, brigades, even
" regiments, were mixed up], replacement of ammunition and supplies,
" sending back the trains, arrangements for security of communications,
" all measures taking time, must bring the British temporarily held up at
" Montbertoin [immediately south of Montreuil], and their columns further
" east, as well as the left wing of the more mobile Army d'Espèrey, on to
" the flank and rear of the *First Army*, then at the limit of its extraordinary
" exertions."

[2] *E.g.*, when next day Lieut.-Colonel Hentsch, as representative of
O.H.L., directed the *Fifth Army* to retire northwards to the line St. Ménehould—Clermont, the Crown Prince and his Chief of the Staff declined to
do so without a clear written order of the Kaiser or the C.G.S. (G.O.A.,
iv. p. 307).

" behind the Marne on both sides of Epernay. By order of O.H.L., 9 Sept.
" the *First Army* will be withdrawn in the general direction of 1914.
" Soissons to protect the flank. A new German Army is to be
" assembled near St. Quentin. The movement of the *First Army*
" will be begun to-day. The left wing, under General von Lin-
" singen, including General von Lochow's group, will therefore be
" withdrawn at once behind the line Montigny l'Allier—Brumetz
" [10 miles N.N.E. of its position, facing south, east of the Ourcq].
" Group of General Sixt von Armin will conform to this movement
" as the battle situation permits until the line Antilly—Mareuil is
" reached [that is, until it is aligned alongside Linsingen's group,
" facing south, but west of the Ourcq]. The offensive movement of
" the group of General von Quast will not be carried further than is
" necessary to shake clear of the enemy, and in such a way that con-
" nection with the movement of the rest of the Army is possible."
Whilst this order was being prepared, the message from General
von Bülow, sent off at 10.2 A.M., informing the *First Army* of his
retirement, was handed to General von Kuhl (" Marnedrama," iv.
p. 290). The die had been cast, and it remains only to see what
happened on the different parts of the *First Army* front.
On the Marne front, Kraewel's brigade managed to hold its own
at first in an awkward position, owing to its original line having
faced south-west, and the reinforcements having to be put in on the
left facing east to protect its flank. When General von der Marwitz,
towards 9 A.M., discovered that the British had only a weak force
below La Ferté sous Jouarre (19th Brigade), and that their main forces
were further east, he left only a few troops on the Marne, and about
noon withdrew the *2nd* and *9th Cavalry Divisions* and the *Jäger* to the
heights near Cocherel (4½ miles west of Montreuil).[1] At 12.15 P.M.
Marwitz issued an order for the *II. Cavalry Corps*, with the 5th
Division and Kraewel's brigade placed under it, to attack the British
eastwards, whilst the *5th Cavalry Division* (which had moved away
towards the *Second Army*) was to delay their advance. Nothing
came of this order, which seems to have been only a gesture. It was
not until 2.30 P.M. that the head of the *5th Division* (6 battalions)
" neared " Dhuisy (2½ miles north-west of Montreuil).[2]

[1] Thus Poseck, p. 108. The history of the *9th Jäger* (the only one which
mentions the time) states the order to retire was received about 12 noon :
" it withdrew with difficulty in small parties " and at 3 P.M. was still a
couple of miles south of Cocherel. The map in " Marnedrama," iv., shows
the withdrawal of the *9th* and *10th Jäger* to Cocherel, the *3rd* and *4th* to
positions 4 and 2 miles south of the village, facing south-eastward towards
the railway bridge and the weir by which parties of the 4th Division
crossed. The text mentions they were sent there at 3 P.M. The withdrawal from La Ferté of the battalion of the *27th Regiment* and the cyclist
battalion is not marked or mentioned.
[2] An examination of the histories of the four regiments of the division
shows that the *12th Regiment* was left on the Ourcq with the *22nd Reserve
Division*, and two battalions of the *48th* with the *8th Division*. Five
companies of the *52nd* were also left behind. Thus less than six battalions
marched against the British. Of these, only *III./48th* was in action on
the right of Kraewel's brigade. It was the fire of this battalion which
struck the Duke of Cornwall's. The map in " Marnedrama," iv., shows
the *52nd Regiment* on the left of Kraewel. The history of the regiment
merely states that it was " in readiness " from 6 to 8 P.M. 1 km. north of
Dhuisy ; the *8th Grenadiers* are shown on the right of Kraewel's brigade,

It was not until 4 P.M. (" Marnedrama," iv. p. 268) that the *9th Cavalry Division* acted on the corps order to attack, when its dismounted men, with the *9th* and *10th Jäger*, moved south-eastwards ; they were at once fired on by artillery (there is no trace of this in the British records), halted until their own guns could give them support, and did not advance again.

It was near this time, " about the fourth hour in the afternoon," that General von der Marwitz received the general order to retreat. He at first thought of " solving his problem offensively " ; but, " on hearing at 5.30 P.M. of the advance of British columns from " Chateau Thierry on Torcy (5 miles north-west of Chateau Thierry) " [no Allied troops thus marched ; the columns reported were evi- " dently the Germans north of Chateau Thierry] which would " threaten his left," he thought better of it and ordered the cavalry divisions and *Jäger* to retire northwards on Coulombs, Kraewel's brigade to break off the fight and, with the *5th Division*, retreat on Gandelu. Such was the confusion, that Kraewel did not receive Marwitz's order for some hours, and the *5th Division* never got it at all. At 6.15 P.M., however, the division received an order from General Linsingen to withdraw via Coulombs on Brumetz, and at once did so. Kraewel noticed that the troops on either side of him were marching off, but determined to remain ; shortly afterwards Marwitz's orders reached him, and by 8 P.M. the whole of the *II. Cavalry Corps*, the *5th Division* and Kraewel's brigade were on the march northward.

For Sixt von Armin's group (Kluck's right centre), no success is claimed. It received the order to retire at 2.15 P.M. ; but as Linsingen's group was slow in starting, it waited until 9.30 P.M. before moving, and then retired without interference from the French.

It remains to relate what happened to Quast's group on the right, which we left at 9.15 A.M. reported as ready to deliver the blow that was to roll up Maunoury's Army. It had to traverse two belts of wood (southern part of the Forest of Villers Cottérêts and the Bois du Roi), each about 2½ miles across, with a clearing of much the same width between them, Nanteuil lying outside the south-western extremity of the Bois du Roi. The passage of the woods on narrow paths by tired men was slow. Quast reported that his Group would leave the southern edge of the first belt to attack the northern edge of the second between Antilly and Crepy at 10.45 A.M. (G.O.A., iv. p. 211).[1] Some artillery and sniping fire was encountered throughout the advance, but there was no infantry action. " The " attack certainly went slowly," and on the right, on which the pace of the wheel and the connection with the Lepel detachment depended, " there was a temporary halt." The next objective was the railway line in the second belt, where the *6th* and *18th Divisions* waited for the *17th*, on the outer wing, to come up. Then a move was made to the southern edge of the Bois du Roi, where the divisions were re-

but their history states that, although two battalions came under artillery fire, only *No. 5 Company* was about to go into action when the order to retire came. Thus the opposition to the British was less than that shown on the map and hinted at in the text. Only one battalion of the *5th Division* arrived in time to assist Kraewel's exposed brigade before the order to retreat northward arrived, and no part of the division attacked.

[1] Regimental accounts show that there was delay in the *6th* and *17th Divisions* in getting off, and make the time of starting 65 minutes later.

assembled, and the guns brought forward before proceeding further. 9 Sept. The next time mentioned is 5 P.M., about which hour the double 1014. village of Boissy Fresnoy, just south of the wood, was " taken by " storm " by the *17th Division*, and the French were seen in flight. With this success, the official account ends, but the regimental histories continue the story. Three regiments of the *17th Division* put the village in a state of defence ; " heavy artillery fire caused a " slight retirement, and after darkness fell the division dug in 550 " yards north of the village " (" Regt. No. 76 "). The *18th* and *6th Divisions* stopped short of Villers St. Genest, which was in flames, and went into bivouac at 7.50 P.M. The left of Quast's group was then some thousand yards from the French position, and its right over five miles.

Lepel's brigade had towards 4 P.M. reached Nanteuil, but it had suffered much from artillery fire, the two *Landwehr* batteries being useless in face of the French 75's, and, as General von Lepel had no reserves left, and heard that French cavalry (5th Cavalry Division) were in his rear at 5 P.M., at the same time that Quast's troops were entering Boissy Fresnoy, he gave the order to retire. By 5.30 P.M. his men were in full retreat.

There had been no battle, only an advance which never reached the French infantry line, and was finally stopped by gun fire, as happened elsewhere on the battlefield. There seems no justification for the further claim of the official account (iv. p. 219) :

" On the German right wing a battle success had been won " whose decisive strategic effect could only be a question of a few " hours."

Where this effect would be manifest we are not told ; the further advance of Quast's three weak and very tired divisions would only have brought them to the exterior line of fortifications of Paris, still fifteen miles ahead. It is not stated at what hour General von Quast received the orders for retirement, but we are told that he immediately protested against them, and was given permission by Kluck to go a little further, thus completing the " thrust " which he had been ordered to make, as this might be the best way of breaking off the battle. Orders for the retreat did not reach the divisions until about 11 P.M. and they began to move off, unmolested, three or four hours afterwards.

At 7.15 P.M. the *First Army* had issued a further operation order, in which General von Kluck thanked his troops and informed them that the right wing was in victorious advance, that the *5th Division* and *II. Cavalry Corps* had attacked the British who had crossed the Marne, and that the Army retired by order of O.H.L. It directed that the main bodies of Groups should reach the line of the Upper Ourcq—Ferté Milon—Crepy, two Groups east and two west of the Lower Ourcq. The *II. Cavalry Corps* and Kraewel's brigade were to protect the eastern flank ; parties were to be sent on to prepare the bridges of the Ourcq for demolition, and take possession of the Aisne bridges. The much mixed corps were to be reorganized next day—which must have been very necessary, for the history of the *24th Regiment* states that there were men of twenty different regiments in one company.

General Ludendorff said in his circular to the General Staff on the Hentsch incident :

" Whether the decision of *Second Army* headquarters and the

" order of Lieut.-Colonel Hentsch to *First Army* headquarters to
" retreat were from the situation actually necessary must be decided
" by historical research in later years."
      The verdict has been given by a Saxon general : [1] " The great
" attack in the West ran like a gigantic Kaiser manœuvre with extra-
" ordinary exertions on the part of the troops, unrivalled in military
" history, and with brilliant initial successes, only to puff out in the
" end like a wonderful set-piece in a firework display." To have
continued the battle on the strength of one success early in the day
of five divisions of Bülow's exposed left—whilst his inner right flank
was swinging back—and of the advance midday of three divisions
of Kluck's right, when the British and Franchet d'Espèrey's left had
interposed between Bülow and Kluck, would have been a gamble on
which no great captain would have risked the fate of an Empire.
German leadership had failed, the enemy had been underestimated
and the penalty had been defeat.   On the night of the 9th September
Moltke recognized this, and wrote with truth and vision to his wife :—
" Things are going badly, the battles east of Paris will not be
" decided in our favour. . . . The war which began with such good
" hopes will in the end go against us. . . . We must be crushed in the
" fight against East and against West. . . . And we shall have to pay
" for all the destruction which we have done." [2]
      He could find little consolation in the other theatres.   On the
5th September Hindenburg had begun the " Battle of the Masurian
" Lakes," and its results were still doubtful.   It did not end until
the retreat of the Russians on the 15th.   In the Galician theatre,
the Austrians had already lost the " First Battle of Lemberg "
(26th-30th August), and in the " Second Battle," begun on the 8th
September, they were already in difficulties, and further retreat was
imminent.   The battle closed on the 11th with their complete
discomfiture.

NOTE II [3]

THE SECOND BELGIAN SORTIE FROM ANTWERP:
9TH–13TH SEPTEMBER

Sketch 3.   After the first sortie from Antwerp [4] the Belgian Field Army was
Map 2.   employed for some days in assisting the fortress troops to improve
the defensive works between and in the forts ; the Germans also
spent the time in consolidating their defences, roughly on an east
and west line eight miles north of the centre of Brussels, and therefore
some four or five miles from the nearest forts of Antwerp.   From
the 1st September onwards there were indications of German movements towards the Belgian western flank on the Schelde at Termonde,
culminating in an attack on the 4th.   It was obvious, however,

      [1] " Die Marneschlacht, 1914. Nach der Kriegsakten bearbeitet." By
Major-General Baumgarten-Crusius, p. 187.
      [2] Moltke's " Erinnerungen. Briefe, Dokumente," p. 385.
      [3] Mainly from the translated official report, " Military Operations of
" Belgium, compiled by the Belgian General Staff for the period 31st July
" to 31st December 1914," and anniversary articles contributed to the
Press.
      [4] See page 151.

that this was only a feint to cover the withdrawal southwards of part 4-13 Sept. of the investing force ; for the Belgian General Staff had information 1914. that the *IX. Reserve Corps* and the *6th Division* of the *III. Reserve Corps* were to be moved to France and their places taken by the *Marine Division* and *Landwehr* formations. On the 5th definite news of the movement came in and it was confirmed on the 6th and 7th. The Belgian Army Command, therefore, considered that a favourable moment for the execution of another sortie had arrived, with the purpose of compelling the enemy to recall forces despatched to take part in the decisive battle in France, or, failing this, to defeat the weakened forces in front of Antwerp and to threaten the German communications.

The operations were planned to begin on the 9th September. In view of the strength of the German entrenchments, a frontal attack was out of the question ; two divisions therefore were detailed to cover Antwerp, whilst three divisions and the cavalry turned the enemy's right (eastern) flank towards Aerschot.

The sortie began successfully ; the passages of the Demer and Dyle were seized and Aerschot captured ; a troop of cavalry even entered Louvain on the 10th. The Germans meanwhile took counter measures ; they brought back the *6th Reserve Division* permanently, stopped the march of the *IX. Reserve Corps*, and detrained at Brussels, to assist in repelling the sortie, the leading division (the *30th*) of the *XV. Corps* which was on its way from Alsace to the extreme right flank of the German Armies. This division went into action and remained from the 10th to 13th in the neighbourhood of Brussels.[1] The Belgian advance was brought to a halt, and on the 13th the whole Army retired again to Antwerp. The delay of the *IX. Reserve Corps* and *30th Division* in reaching the front did not actually affect the battle of the Marne, as Kluck and Bülow retreated on the 9th before these reinforcements could have reached them ; but the three divisions might well have been in time to have prepared a position on the Aisne for the retreating Armies, or to have made a flank attack on the advancing Allies.

[1] " Schlachten und Gefechte," p. 14.

CHAPTER XVIII

Sketch 18.
Map 4.
As the line of retreat of the German *First Army* appeared to be more or less across the British front, there seemed some hope of intercepting it. Acting, therefore, in anticipation of General Joffre's written instructions, Sir John French, at 8.15 P.M. on the 9th September, had ordered his troops to continue the pursuit northwards at 5 A.M. the next morning.[1]

A telegram from French G.Q.G., giving a summary of the instructions for the 10th September, timed 11.59 P.M. on the 9th, reached G.H.Q. at 7.45 A.M. on the 10th. It said : " The Fifth and Sixth Armies and the B.E.F. will " take steps to attack the enemy's positions. The British " will try to reach the Clignon between Bouresches [4 " miles north-west of Chateau Thierry] and Hervilliers [just " east of Crouy on the Ourcq]. They will be supported on " the left by the 8th Division, and on the right by the " XVIII. Corps, which will organize a bridge-head at " Chateau Thierry." Joffre's Instruction No. 20 arrived later, brought by an officer ; it gave as information that the Germans were entrenching, and added to the summary of instructions given above : " the Fifth Army will sup- " port the movement of the XVIII. Corps by driving back " the enemy towards the north, without losing touch with " the Ninth Army [a somewhat difficult condition]. It " will endeavour to reach the line of the Marne between " Chateau Thierry and Dormans and prepare crossings. " Conneau's cavalry corps will gain touch with the enemy

[1] Appendix 39.

THE MARNE, 1914.
CONCLUDING PHASE,
& GERMAN RETREAT.

SKETCH 18.

POSITIONS ON
5TH SEPTEMBER.
GERMANS
FRENCH
B.E.F.

Flanks
of B.E.F.
during
Advance

SCALE
5   0   10   20   30 MILES

Ordnance Survey, 1924.

" and try to penetrate in the general direction of Oulchy 10 Sept.
" le Chateau. 1914.

" The Sixth Army, with its right on the Ourcq, will
" continue to gain ground towards the north and thus
" envelop the enemy's right ; Bridoux's cavalry corps will
" try to reach the flank and rear of the enemy."

Although it did not look as if much support could be
expected on the right except from Conneau's cavalry corps,
while on the left the French 8th Division had disappeared—
it had, indeed, gone to the left of the Sixth Army beyond
the Ourcq—Sir John French saw no reason to modify his
orders.

Low clouds and heavy mists made aerial reconnaissance Sketch 13.
almost impossible until late in the afternoon of the 10th Maps 4
September ; the pursuit ordered by Sir John French was & 31.
begun, and by 7.15 A.M. it was assumed that the Germans
were clear of the valleys of the Ourcq and Marne ; nothing
was visible from the air, except a small convoy and its
escort on an unimportant road 7 miles north-east of Lizy.

At 3 P.M., however, the R.F.C. was able to report—the
information was at once sent to G.Q.G.—that near Troësnes
(on the Ourcq above La Ferté Milon), German artillery and
cavalry were retreating at a rapid pace, and that Villers
Cottérêts was blocked with trains and all the sidings were
very full. Later at 5 P.M. it added that there were numerous bivouacs around Soissons, where troops coming from
the south were being assembled ; that the bridges of Vailly
and Vic on the Aisne were intact ; that no movements
could be seen north of the Aisne ; and that there were
numerous dumps of supplies piled at Anizy (10 miles north
of Vailly), south of the Oise canal. Meanwhile, the Cavalry
Division, under Major-General Allenby, on the extreme
right of the B.E.F., had marched at 5 A.M. to the high
ground north-west of Bonnes (7 miles north-west of Chateau
Thierry), where it came under heavy artillery fire from
Latilly, about two miles to the north, and suffered some
loss. The 5th Dragoon Guards pushed on to Latilly, but,
finding the village strongly occupied by German cyclists
and cavalry, awaited the arrival of the 1st Cavalry Brigade
and Z Battery R.H.A. ; [1] when they came up the Germans
decamped.

[1] Z Battery was formed on 1st September, of two sections of I, to
replace L Battery destroyed at Néry. On the 3rd, one section of I was
replaced by one of D, which on the 16th was exchanged for a section
of J Battery. When on 28th September H Battery joined the 1st Cavalry
Division, Z Battery was broken up.

Proceeding to the summit of a hill a little further north-east, the 1st Cavalry Brigade, between 11 A.M. and noon, caught sight of the main body of a German rear guard—five regiments of cavalry, two batteries, a couple of hundred cyclists, and five hundred wagons, moving from La Croix (2 miles north-east of Latilly) northwards upon Oulchy le Chateau. This party was not more than two miles away, but, as the ground had been soaked by heavy rain, Z Battery could not get into action until all but the wagons of the column had passed out of reach ; and when it did open fire, it was silenced by German guns of greater range. The other batteries of the Cavalry Division therefore advanced north-eastwards through La Croix, and at 1.30 P.M. again opened fire on the convoy. Then a French cavalry division of Conneau's corps, supported by infantry in motor lorries, came up from Rocourt (3 miles east of Latilly), fell on the flank of the column of wagons, and captured the greater part of it.

On the left of General Allenby's cavalry, the 1st Division advanced from Le Thiolet north-north-west upon Courchamps (8 miles north-west of Chateau Thierry), the 2nd Brigade leading. Soon after 8 A.M. the divisional cavalry brought intelligence that the enemy was in position beyond Priez, a couple of miles to the north of Courchamps on the northern side of the Alland, a small stream in a wide shallow valley. The Sussex and Loyal North Lancashire were therefore pushed through Priez, where they deployed and began to ascend the hill beyond it. They were met by heavy artillery and rifle fire at a range of less than a thousand yards, but continued to advance slowly until a British battery in rear, mistaking them for Germans, also shelled them severely and they fell back on Priez. Some of the men in retiring passed by the observing station of the 40th Battery and through the intervals between the howitzers, drawing the German fire upon both, so that Br.-General Findlay, who was reconnoitring a position for his guns, was killed by a shell. There then ensued a lull in the fighting during which the 1st (Guards) Brigade, heading for Latilly, came up on the right of the 2nd Brigade, and the 3rd Brigade, making for Monnes against slight opposition, appeared on its left. In face of this display of force, between 2 and 3 P.M., the Germans began to fall back slowly. The British batteries followed them up, but did not arrive within effective range until the German columns, after crossing the Ourcq, were filing out

of Chouy (5 miles north of Priez), when both field guns 10 Sept.
and howitzers opened fire on them, apparently with good 1914.
effect.

Further west, the two cavalry brigades under Br.-
General Gough, and the 2nd and 3rd Divisions were more
successful. The 5th Cavalry Brigade led the way, with
the 20th Hussars as advanced guard covering a front of
5 miles from Bussiares (1 mile west of Torcy) south-westwards to Germigny. At 6.30 a.m. a hostile column was
sighted moving north-eastward from Brumetz (3 miles
north of Germigny) upon Chézy, while another, composed
chiefly of wagons, was halted on the slopes between those
two villages. The brigade therefore moved westwards
to Prémont (a mile north-east of Germigny), whence J
Battery opened fire at long range ; as there was no reply
to this fire, Brigadier-General Chetwode at 9 a.m. advanced
for about another mile northward to the high ground south
of Gandelu (immediately south-east of Brumetz), whence
he sent two squadrons of the Scots Greys to clear that
village, and ordered the 12th Lancers to cross the Clignon
a little further to the west at Brumetz, and cut off the
enemy's retreat.

Meanwhile, the 6th Brigade and the XXXIV. Brigade
R.F.A., which formed the advanced guard of the 2nd
Division, were crossing the valley of the Clignon at Bussiares
to the right of Gough's cavalry ; and, when Hautevesnes,
2 miles further on, was reached soon after 9 a.m., a German
convoy could be seen a mile or more to the west toiling up
the road from Vinly in the valley of the Clignon north-
westwards towards Chézy. Four guns, which formed part
of its escort, unlimbered on the heights above Brumetz,
while infantry took up a position in a sunken road, facing
eastward, to meet the storm that threatened them from
Hautevesnes. The British batteries coming into action
soon forced the German guns to retire ; and shortly after
10 a.m. the 6th Brigade was ordered to attack. The
1/K.R.R.C. deployed and advanced over ground which offered
not an atom of cover. Nevertheless, the riflemen closed
to within seven hundred yards of the Germans, and at that
range pinned them to their cover, whilst the 1/R. Berkshire
on the right, and the 2/S. Staffordshire on the left worked
round both their flanks, when the whole line of Germans
surrendered, having lost about one hundred and fifty killed
and wounded out of a total of about five hundred present.
They were found to be men of the *4th Jäger*, the *2nd Cavalry*

Division, the *Guard Cavalry Division* and the *27th Regiment* of the *IV. Corps*.[1]

Meanwhile, in Gough's force the 12th Lancers had caught a party of nearly three hundred more, with thirty wagons and four machine guns, who had been driven from Gandelu by the Greys. Moreover, the 9th Brigade and the 107th Battery, the advanced guard of the 3rd Division, coming up between the 2nd Division and the cavalry, had struck into the woods near Veuilly (3 miles west of Torcy) north-westward upon Vinly whilst the 6th Brigade was attacking westward from Hautevesnes, and had taken another six hundred prisoners, a most variegated assortment, consisting of men of the *II.*, *III.* and *IV. Corps* and of five *Jäger* battalions of Marwitz's cavalry corps. These, with the exception of a party entrenched to north of Vinly, had offered no very serious resistance. The country was, however, so close that many Germans were left undiscovered in the valley of the Clignon, from which they continued to issue for some days to plunder the neighbouring villages and oppress the villagers, until they were gradually rounded up.

Throughout this little action, General Haig had been chafing to act on a message received about 9 A.M. from General Maud'huy of the French XVIII. Corps on his right, giving him intelligence that fifty-four German heavy guns were moving from Lizy sur Ourcq north-eastward upon Oulchy and offering to co-operate in capturing them. As the heads of both the 1st and 2nd Divisions were sharply engaged at the moment, he could give no immediate orders ; and the clouds were so low that later in the forenoon, when he asked for more exact indications from the Flying Corps, such observation as was possible gave no definite result. By 1 P.M. the German column was too far north to be intercepted.

West of the 3rd Division, the 5th Division and the III. Corps met with no opposition. The former advanced to Montreuil early, but Kraewel's brigade had slipped away, and it was too late to cut off any of it except a few wounded. The III. Corps, being occupied for the best part of the day with the completion of the passage of the Marne by a floating bridge at La Ferté sous Jouarre and the railway bridge at Le Saussoy, was obliged to content itself with occasionally shelling distant targets and with the collection of stragglers. The British casualties on this day did not

[1] Part of this regiment had defended La Ferté sous Jouarre.

exceed three hundred and fifty, two-thirds of which were
incurred by the 2nd Brigade in its check near Priez, and the
remainder by the 6th Brigade in its successful action near
Hautevesnes.[1] For these the capture of some eighteen
hundred Germans, including wounded, as well as the battery
taken by the Lincolnshire, offered some compensation ; and
the spirits of the troops rose high at the sight of so much
abandoned transport and of so many stragglers, all pointing
to the beginning of confusion on the enemy's side.   Nevertheless, it was a disappointment that the Germans had not
been more severely punished.   The general advance during
the day had been only about ten miles, and the *First Army*
seemed to be already out of reach ; for an aeroplane reconnaissance between 5 and 6 P.M. revealed columns crossing the Aisne between Vailly and Soissons, and a very large
number of bivouacs north of the latter town.   The Intelligence situation map, compiled at dusk, showed the
heads of the *III., IX.* ($\frac{1}{2}$) and *IV. Reserve Corps* approaching the Aisne, covered on the Upper Ourcq by three cavalry
divisions, with the *II. Corps* near Villers Cottérêts ; on the
right it left a gap from Vailly to south of Fismes, where
the *VII. Corps* was placed.   This was remarkably near
the mark, but in the west Quast's Group (*6th, 17th* and *18th
Divisions*) on Maunoury's front was not shown, as no news
of it had reached G.H.Q. from the French.

On the evening of the 10th September the four divisions Sketches B & 13. Maps 4 & 31.
of the I. and II. Corps were astride the river Alland, with
the cavalry in front astride the upper course of the Ourcq,
and the III. Corps behind the left flank.   In detail, the
positions were :—

Cavalry Division . .	Breny, Rozet.
3rd and 5th Cavalry Brigades	Macogny (1½ miles east of Passy), Marizy, Passy, Mosloy (2 miles west of Passy).
I. Corps	Latilly, westward through Rassy to Monnes.
II. Corps	Dammard, St. Quentin, Chézy.
III. Corps . . .	Vaux sous Coulombs, and south- ward through Coulombs to Chaton.

[1] The total British casualties from the 6th to the 10th September were :
I. Corps, 779 ; II. Corps, 654 ; III. Corps (4th Division and 19th Brigade),
133 ; Cavalry, 135 ; total, 1,701.

THE FRENCH ON THE 10TH SEPTEMBER

Sketch 18.
Maps 4
& 31.

The French pursuit, owing to the troops and horses being tired, and to bad weather which prevented air information being obtained, made the roads and ground muddy, and rendered the nights in bivouac a misery, " was relatively slow, six to seven miles a day " on the average," about half what the British did. It is not necessary here to mention more than the Fifth and Sixth Armies on the right and left of the B.E.F., adding something very brief about the Ninth, as the other French Armies, after a short advance, were held up, and the line except near St. Mihiel settled down where it was to remain for the greater part of the War.

" On the 10th September the [French] Fifth Army advanced to " the Marne without having to fight." The whole of the XVIII. Corps, next to the B.E.F., passed across the river, its advanced guard halting five miles north of Chateau Thierry. The other corps had only " their advanced guards solidly established north of the " Marne, their main bodies were south of it." Between the right of the Fifth Army and the left of Foch's, which was still around the Marshes of St. Gond, there was a gap of fifteen miles. Conneau's cavalry corps reached the line of the Ourcq, level with the British cavalry, without encountering anything but the tail of the enemy rear guards.

The French Sixth Army took some hours to realize the change in the situation. After its escape from the envelopment of its left on the afternoon of the 9th, " the night had been quiet. On the " morning of the 10th, patrols found the country empty, the enemy " had gone." Towards 10 A.M., when this event had been fully confirmed, General Maunoury gave orders for a general offensive at noon, left leading (the right actually led). A start was made between 2 and 4 P.M., and a short march was accomplished " without fighting, " without contact even with the enemy." Patrols of Bridoux's cavalry corps (he actually had only one division at his disposal, as Maunoury retained one, and the 5th, absent on a raid, did not return until this day) went 25 miles without seeing an enemy.

11TH SEPTEMBER : THE INCLINE TO THE NORTH-EAST

Sketches
13 & 18.
Maps 4
& 32.

By General Joffre's Instruction No. 21, dated 10th September, the British force had definite boundaries assigned to it between which it was to advance : the road Fère en Tardenois—Bazoches (3 miles west of Fismes) on the right and La Ferté Milon—Longpont—Soissons (but exclusive of this town) on the left ; these involved the B.E.F. inclining half right.[1] Accordingly operation

[1] In this Instruction General Joffre further said :
" To confirm and exploit this success, the advance must be pursued " energetically, leaving the enemy no respite : victory is now in the legs " of the infantry."
He gave the general direction as N.N.E., in the hope of dislodging the Germans who had not yet fallen back in front of the Fourth and Third Armies ; but Bridoux's cavalry corps was to gain ground on the outer wing in order to attack the German lines of communication and hinder the retreat.

orders for the Army on the 11th directed it to continue 11 Sept.
the pursuit north-eastward at 5 A.M., crossing the Ourcq 1914,
and making for a line from Bruyères (3 miles west of
Fère en Tardenois), north-westward through Cugny to
St. Rémy and thence 2½ miles westward to La Loge Farm.[1]
The march proved a troublesome one, for the front allotted
was so narrow that it was impossible to assign a separate
road to each division. The advance was covered by the
cavalry, General Allenby's division making good the ground
from Fère en Tardenois westward to within about a mile
of the road from Chateau Thierry to Soissons, and General
Gough's two brigades the space from that line for some
three miles further west. The advance of the cavalry
brought it to a line : Cuiry Housse (6½ miles north of
Fère en Tardenois) through Buzancy to Vierzy (9 miles
west of Cuiry Housse). No large parties of the enemy
were seen except a brigade of cavalry at Braisne on the
Vesle (3½ miles north-east of Cuiry Housse) and a party
of infantry throwing up entrenchments at Noyant (9 miles
west of Braisne). There were clear indications that hostile
cavalry had retired in two bodies upon Braisne and Soissons,
the former in good order, the latter in some confusion ;
but although wounded and stragglers were picked up
there was no encounter of any kind with the Germans.
  The march of the infantry, therefore, was wholly undisturbed, except for the congestion of the roads—the III.
Corps, in particular, was long delayed by a French column
—and by rain which came down heavily in the afternoon
and drenched the men to the skin. Owing to the bad weather,
no air reconnaissance was possible, but a wireless message of
Marwitz's cavalry corps was intercepted at 8.45 A.M. both by
G.H.Q. and G.Q.G., which said that the *4th* and *9th Cavalry
Divisions* were south-east and south-west of Soissons " in a
" terrible state of fatigue, without food for several days, and
" not able to move owing to the roads being blocked."
  The general advance on the 11th was again about ten Sketches
miles. At nightfall the three centre divisions were across B & 13.
the Ourcq with the cavalry in front 5 miles from the Vesle, Maps 4
and the 1st and 4th Divisions echeloned back on either & 32.
flank. In detail :—

Cavalry Division   . Loupeigne (3½ miles N.N.E. of Fère
                        en Tardenois), westward to Arcy
                        Ste. Restitue (4½ miles N.N.W. of
                        Fère).

[1] Appendix 40.

Gough's Cavalry Brigades	Parcy Tigny (6½ miles west of Arcy), north to Villemontoire.
I. Corps . . .	Beugneux (3 miles W.S.W. of Arcy), Bruyères, south-west to Rocourt, Oulchy le Chateau.
II. Corps . . .	Hartennes, south-east to Grand Rozoy (just west of Beugneux), Oulchy la Ville, Billy sur Ourcq, St. Rémy (all just north-west of Oulchy le Chateau).
III. Corps . .	La Loge Farm to Chouy.
G.H.Q. . . .	Coulommiers.

Owing to the wheel of the B.E.F., its right was now slightly behind the left of the French Fifth Army, but on the other flank it was abreast of the Sixth.

THE FRENCH ON THE 11TH SEPTEMBER

Maps 4 & 32.   In the Fifth Army, General Franchet d'Espèrey had already issued orders for an advance due north on the 11th, when at 11 P.M. on the 10th he received G.Q.G. Instruction No. 21 to go practically north-east. There was, in consequence, some delay and confusion next morning ; otherwise the marches " were executed without " difficulty, the enemy having retired " ; there was no contact except by Conneau's cavalry corps, which, towards 8 P.M., found the passages of the Vesle blocked, but the part of Fismes south of the river was occupied after a skirmish. In front of Foch's Army the enemy retired " without seeking to utilize the defensive positions " which offered themselves. . . . Its advanced guards reached the " Marne . . . but they did not, except on the left at Damery and " Epernay, occupy the bridges." The total advance was ten to fifteen miles.

The Sixth Army had " a day of marching, of very prudent " pursuit, without any contact with the enemy, except some skir- " mishes " ; it advanced, in fact, 7½ to 9 miles. Bridoux's cavalry corps, which was trying to pass to the west side of the Oise, was held up by the bridge at Verberie being damaged, and a crossing could not be made until 6 A.M. on the 12th ; but the French Official Account mentions that the bridge Croix St. Ouen, 2 miles north of Verberie, was " intact."

12TH SEPTEMBER : THE ADVANCE TO THE AISNE

Sketch 13.   Low clouds and rain made aerial reconnaissance so Maps 4 & 33.   difficult that the Flying Corps could furnish no reports of value on the 12th. News, however, came that Maubeuge had fallen on the 7th, an event which was most opportune for the enemy, since it released the *VII. Reserve Corps* and other German troops for work further south.

The German Armies were falling back, mostly in a north- easterly direction, along the whole front as far as the Argonne, with exhausted horses, deficient supplies, and signs of failing ammunition. It remained to be seen how much further the Allies could push their success. There was no sign yet of any movement of enemy reinforcements from the north, but there were some indications that the enemy might hold the line of the Aisne : it was impossible, however, to forecast in what strength, and whether as a mere rear-guard or as a battle position.

The situation with which the Allies were now confronted was by no means clear. If the retreat of the German Armies from the Marne had been followed by disorganization and loss of morale, as appeared probable from the numerous stragglers and the mix-up of units evident from the prisoners captured, the operation of converting confusion into disaster must be of the nature of a pursuit. If, on the other hand, their power of resistance, though diminished by heavy loss, was unbroken, as had been the case of the Allies in the retreat to the Seine, the problem of completing their discomfiture would involve bringing them to action again, and winning a fresh battle before pursuit, properly so called, could be resumed. Orders quite appropriate to the pursuit of a broken and disorganized enemy can be wholly unsuited to the very different problem of beating an unbroken foe. They may well lead to defeat, for the latter situation clearly demands that an organized battle should be delivered with all forces united and co-operating.

The enemy certainly appeared to be disorganized, and there were undoubtedly very weak spots in his front. In any case, it was of vital importance that no time should be lost, and no opportunity given to the Germans to reorganize and reinforce these vulnerable places. Unfortunately for the Allies, there was heavy rain on the 12th September, and only very few reconnaissance flights were made.

General Joffre's Instruction No. 22, received on the evening of the 11th, gave the intelligence that " on the " front of the Sixth Army and B.E.F., the enemy was retir- " ing behind the Aisne ; the German *VII. Corps*, originally " on the right of the *Second Army*, had been identified on " the Vesle between Fismes and Braisne, in front of the " left of the Fifth Army ; before the Ninth and Fourth " Armies the enemy is retiring north of the Marne and the

" Saulx." It directed the Sixth Army (reinforced by the XIII. Corps from the First Army), the British Army, and a portion of the Fifth Army specially detailed to support the British, to deal with the right wing of the German forces, endeavouring always to outflank it by the west. To the B.E.F. the boundaries Bazoches—Craonne on the east, and Soissons—Laon on the west were assigned.[1]

The French XVIII. Corps reported that the German retreat in front of it was nearly a rout ; otherwise there was no definite information.

Sketch 18.
Maps 4
& 33.

G.H.Q. orders for the 12th were that the pursuit should be continued, and that the crossing-places of the Aisne should be seized and the high ground on the northern side of the river secured.[2] The day was dark, with torrents of rain which turned the roads into seas of mud, so that observation and movement were both equally difficult. The cavalry was pushed forward early, and at Braisne came to the first obstacle that lay between it and its objective, the river Vesle, running from south-east to north-west down a broad valley to join the Aisne at Condé. On the right of the British, General Conneau's cavalry had already seized the bridge over this stream at Bazoches : and reconnaissance revealed that of the bridges on the British front, that of Courcelles, next below Bazoches, had been destroyed, also one of the two at Braisne[3] and that of La Grange Farm, a mile further down-stream. The second bridge at Braisne was, however, intact and defended by German cavalry and infantry. After clearing away parties of the enemy from La Folie (the ruins of a chateau, 1 mile south-west of Braisne) and Augy (1 mile west of Braisne), the 1st Cavalry Brigade about 11 A.M. attacked Braisne with all three of its regiments dismounted, the battery being unlimbered half a mile north-west of Augy to check the arrival of German reinforcements from the north.

For more than two hours there was sharp fighting, during which, on the right of the 1st Cavalry Brigade, the

---

[1] Instruction No. 22 continued : " the Ninth and Fourth Armies will " concentrate their efforts against the German centre group and left wing. " The Fifth Army, maintaining one detachment on the right of the British " Army and another on the left of the Ninth Army, will dispose the main " part of its forces so as to be able to act either against the north-western " enemy group or the north-eastern one, according to the situation."

[2] Appendix 41. It will be seen that there is no mention in the orders of the gap in the German front.

[3] This appears to have been a mistake, as both bridges were subsequently used.

1st Division marched down to the bridge at Bazoches, and the 2nd Division towards that of Courcelles, where the 5th Brigade, its advanced guard, by various expedients, contrived to effect a crossing, but the main body subsequently crossed by the easternmost of the two bridges at Braisne. The Worcestershire and some of the Oxfordshire L.I. at once pushed on to the Monthussart Farm (1 mile to the north-east of Braisne), reaching it about 1.30 P.M. Just at that time, the 9th Brigade at the head of the 3rd Division having previously cleared the outskirts of that village, the 1st Cavalry Brigade succeeded in driving the enemy out of the buildings of Braisne on to the hill beyond it, and then advanced on the road to Brenelle. The retreating Germans were thus caught first by the fire of the 5th Dragoon Guards from the west, and then by that of the Oxfordshire L.I. from the east. Such of them as survived, about one hundred and thirty in number, laid down their arms. A few of them were *Guard Uhlans*, but the majority were of the *13th Landwehr Regiment* of the *25th Landwehr Brigade*, which, though Line of Communication troops attached to the *Second Army*,[1] had been hurried to the front.

Meanwhile, further to the left, the 3rd and 5th Cavalry Brigades had proceeded to Serches (4 miles west of Braisne) and pushed out advanced parties northward to Ciry, and thence north-eastward to the bridge over the Vesle leading to the village of Chassemy. The bridge was not destroyed, and so lightly held that the 4th Hussars soon cleared it and pushed on towards Chassemy. Being shelled, however, when in column of route, they sought shelter in the woods to the eastward, and advanced, dismounted, against the chateau on the heights north of the village. The rest of the 3rd Cavalry Brigade then moved to the high ground north-east of Chassemy; and on reaching it the 4th Hussars, together with two guns, were sent down into the valley of the Aisne to seize the bridge of Vailly. It was now between 3 and 4 P.M. The British horse batteries were just picking up the range of the German guns which had been shelling the 4th Hussars, when two companies of German infantry were reported moving south from Brenelle. The 5th and 16th Lancers at once opened fire on both flanks of this column while the batteries and machine guns engaged it in front. About

---

[1] This brigade is now known to have been on the extreme right (west) of the German *Second Army*.

seventy Germans fell, and at 4.30 P.M. the remainder, about one hundred in all, surrendered. These also belonged to the *13th Landwehr Regiment*, and apparently had been sent westwards to reinforce Braisne, but were driven by the advance of the 5th Brigade into the jaws of the British cavalry. Meanwhile, the 4th Hussars sent to surprise the bridge of Vailly reported it destroyed ; and the bridge of Condé, a mile and a half below Vailly, though intact, was found to be strongly held. When darkness fell, therefore, the results had fallen far short of the object set forth in operation orders : not a single bridge over the Aisne was in British hands, and no information of value as regards the enemy's strength and capacity for resistance had been obtained.

The nature of the country—high open ground cut by a succession of streams flowing through deep valleys—was chiefly responsible for this, since it greatly favoured the delaying tactics of the enemy. Heavy rain, with its inevitable result of deep muddy roads, did not help matters for the Allies, and the I. and II. Corps were still 2 miles distant from the Aisne when they halted for the night. On the left the III. Corps had made a great stride forward ; hearing that the French 45th Division on its left had become engaged with the enemy holding a position covering Soissons, the corps advanced in a preparatory formation towards the river ; but it was 3 P.M. before the leading infantry brigade reached the heights of Septmonts (3 miles south-east of Soissons) overlooking the valley of the Aisne. The news then sent in by the divisional cavalry was interesting : the bridge over the Aisne at Venizel, some three miles north-east of Septmonts, had been damaged, but was still passable both by infantry and cavalry ; the ground to the north of it had been entrenched for defence, and a large column of Germans [1] was moving north-east from Soissons over the plateau, on the north side of the river. With great difficulty the 31st Heavy Battery was hauled to the top of the ridge of Septmonts to open fire on this column, and the XXIX. Brigade R.F.A. also unlimbered to support an advance of the infantry upon Venizel. But all this took time ; the light failed early, shut out by a canopy of rainclouds, and darkness had intervened before these preparations could lead to any result. Major C. A. Wilding (commanding the 2/Inniskilling Fusiliers), who, with two companies, was on outpost duty on the edge of the high

[1] *III. Corps* of the *First Army.*

ground overlooking Venizel, on his own initiative had earlier
sent down a party to the bridge. Its appearance was the
signal for the Germans to attempt the demolition of the
roadway. But of the charges laid all had not exploded and
the fuzes of these were found and removed by Captain
S. G. Roe by the light of an electric torch, within close range
of the Germans entrenched on the northern bank.[1]
    The situation at nightfall of the 12th September found Sketches
the B.E.F. across the Vesle and close up to the Aisne.   B & 13.
                                                           Maps 4

Cavalry Division   .   .   . Dhuisel, Villers en Prayère, & 33.
                                       Vaustin.
I. Corps   .   .   .   .   . Dhuisel—Vaucère—Bazoches
                                       Paars—Courcelles.
3rd and 5th Cavalry Brigades   Chassemy and north-west of
                                       Braisne.
II. Corps   .   .   .   .   . Brenelle, Braisne, Serches,
                                       Chacrise (3 miles south-
                                       west of Serches).
III. Corps .   .   .   .   . Septmonts, Buzancy.

    There were many indications that the enemy intended Map 35.
to make some kind of stand on the line of the Aisne, which
indeed offered great facilities for defence, so that there
was good reason for attempting an enveloping operation
round the German right flank, if only with Bridoux's cavalry
corps. The river, winding and sluggish except when in
flood, and some two hundred feet wide, is unfordable ; it
runs through a valley which has steep sides covered with
patches of wood, but with a gently sloping or level bottom
from a mile to two miles in breadth and over three hundred
feet below the level of the plateau through which the course
of the stream has been cut. As in the case of many other
valleys in the north of France, the sides form a series of
spurs and ravines, wooded on the toes of the spurs and sides
of the ravines, and in its winding course the stream passes
first close to one side and then to the other. There is little
cover on the low ground in the valley itself for infantry
seeking to force a passage from the south, and no position
for artillery to support it, except on the southern heights.
The German artillery could harass British troops in the
valley at a range of three thousand yards, and yet have no
British battery within closer range than five to six thousand
yards.
    In the section opposite the British from Bourg to Venizel

---

[1] Captain Roe, Inniskilling Fusiliers, was killed in action 20th October 1914.

(both inclusive) there were seven road bridges, an aqueduct carrying the Oise—Aisne canal over the river at Bourg, and a railway bridge east of Vailly, where a narrow-gauge railway which runs along the southern bank from the direction of Reims crosses the river to the northern bank on its way to Soissons. All these bridges, except that at Condé, were eventually found to be more or less unserviceable.

Whether the enemy was in a position to avail himself of the advantages afforded by the line of the Aisne remained to be seen. Though the weather had prevented air reconnaissance, reports from inhabitants and escaped prisoners seemed to show that large bodies of German troops had been moving eastward from Soissons on Neufchatel (15 miles north of Reims) during the previous three days, which indicated that the enemy feared his centre might be broken and was making efforts to concentrate more troops in front of the French Fifth Army and the British.

THE FRENCH ON THE 12TH SEPTEMBER

Maps 4 & 33.

On this day the French Armies on either side of the British were in close touch with them. General Franchet d'Espèrey informed the Fifth Army that its mission was to act, marching north-eastwards, left leading, against the eastern mass (*Second* and *Third Armies*) of the German host, whose columns were retreating before Foch's Army, whilst the B.E.F. and the Sixth Army would deal with the western mass (*First Army*) ; the corps of the left wing were, however, to be ready, in case of need, to act in the direction of Soissons and the B.E.F. General Franchet d'Espèrey most unfortunately considered the enemy in front of Foch was the more important, and moved north-east against him. At night, the Fifth Army was strung out along the course of the Vesle. Only on the left wing was resistance encountered : the right, the X. Corps (returned in the morning to the Fifth Army by Foch), the I. Corps and the right of the III. Corps, marching in the rain until a late hour, reached the Vesle west of Reims without any fighting; the left of the III. Corps and the leading division of the Group of Reserve Divisions reached and crossed the Vesle about 4.30 P.M. without any resistance ; the XVIII. Corps, sent to support the cavalry, drove the Germans away from Fismes and began crossing the Vesle at 4 P.M. ; Conneau's cavalry corps was unable to carry out even the reconnaissances ordered, and at night returned to the billets of the previous day.

Foch's Army at last crossed the Marne, " the enemy did not " defend the river line and had retired northwards." It closed up within six miles of the Fifth Army, facing north-east : only its extreme right reached the Vesle, the average march having been less than ten miles.

Although General Joffre had on the 11th urged the Sixth Army, " always keeping something on the left of the B.E.F., to send forces " to the right [west] bank of the Oise, in order to outflank the enemy,"

General Maunoury, being still uncertain of the whereabouts of the enemy, decided to send his whole Army against the Germans in his immediate neighbourhood, who were retiring across the Aisne, and ordered only the Cavalry Corps to go west of the Oise. General Bridoux crossed the Oise at Verberie towards 1 P.M., but was unable to obtain contact with any enemy. The rest of the Sixth Army closed up to the Aisne under some artillery fire from the northern bank. In the centre, the leading division (14th) of the VII. Corps, following up the retreating Germans closely, crossed the river at Vic from 5.30 P.M. onwards, while towards midnight its other division, the 63rd, got a small party across at Fontenoy over a damaged bridge, man by man, and then, having made a floating bridge, passed over a brigade. On the left, a battalion of the IV. Corps managed to cross at Attichy : but on the right next to the British, as the bridges in Soissons were down, the French were unable to pass the river.

12 Sept.
1914

NOTE

THE GERMAN RETIREMENT FROM THE BATTLE OF THE MARNE

The line on which the German *First Army* stood on the afternoon of the 9th September made its withdrawal northwards a compara- tively easy task, although it could not retire north-eastwards to join up with the *Second Army* : if it attempted to do so, it would cross the front of the B.E.F. Its right, in its endeavour to envelop the French, was already facing south, and its left centre and left (Linsingen), owing to the British advance, had already been ordered back to the line May en Multien—Crouy—Coulombs. Consequently all that had to be arranged further was that the right centre should conform, and then all the divisions of the Army could retire north- wards together. The movement of Linsingen's wing was completed early enough for the retirement to be begun before the B.E.F. could come up with him. Marwitz with the *2nd* and *9th Cavalry Divisions*, *5th Division* and Kraewel's brigade formed the general rear guard.

Sketch 18.
Maps 4,
30, 31,
32 & 33.

After the return at 2 P.M. on the 10th of Lieut.-Colonel Hentsch, who, on leaving Kluck's headquarters had visited *Third, Fourth* and *Fifth Army* headquarters to direct their retirement, the Supreme Command at 4.30 P.M. issued the following order : [1]

" His Majesty's orders :

" *Second Army* will go back behind the Vesle, left flank Thuizy " (10 miles south-east of Reims). *First Army* will receive instructions " from *Second Army.* *Third Army*, in touch with *Second Army*, will " hold the line Mourmelon le Petit—Francheville au Moivre. *Fourth* " *Army*, in touch with *Third*, north of the Rhine—Marne Canal as " far as Revigny area. *Fifth Army* will remain where it is. *V. Corps* " and *Metz Main Reserve* are attacking Forts Troyon—Les Paroches " —Camp des Romains. The positions reached by the Armies will " be entrenched and held. The first portions of the [new] *Seventh Army* " (*XV. Corps* and *VII. Reserve Corps*) reach about midday on the " 12th September area St. Quentin—Sissy, and make connexion " thence with *Second Army*."

[1] It reached General von Bülow at Reims at 4.45 (Bülow, p. 63).

On receipt of this, Bülow sent the following order to Kluck :
" The *First Army* on 11th September will retire behind the Aisne
" and, covered by the Aisne valley, will close on the right of the
" *Second Army.* The passages of the Vesle valley at Braisne and
" Fismes are being blocked by the *Second Army* with a mixed brigade
" at each place."

Map 31. By the night of the 10th September, the German rear guards were
on an east and west line beyond the upper Ourcq, opposite the front
of both the B.E.F.—just approaching that river—and the French
Sixth Army, from about eight miles east of Fère en Tardenois to
Map 32. Crépy en Valois. Next day Kluck made a short march to the Aisne ;
Map 33. and on the 12th he began sorting out his divisions into their proper
corps, and occupied a line on the heights north of the Aisne. This
line was in detail : Vailly (*II. Cavalry Corps*)—Vregny (*III. Corps*)
—Vauxrezis (*II. Corps*)—Nouvron (*IV. Corps*)—Autreches (*IV.
Reserve Corps*)—Tracy le Mont (*IX. Corps*). The condition of the
First Army may be judged from its own report to O.H.L. (G.O.A., iv.
p. 330): " Army after 5-day battle and the retreat ordered seriously
" mixed up and exhausted. Ready for offensive on the 12th at
" earliest." It had been shaken, but was not beaten.

 The German *Second Army* had lost heavily in its encounters with
the French Fifth Army at Charleroi and at Guise, and must also have
suffered severely at the Marne, as Lieut.-Colonel Hentsch reported
that it was "burnt out to a cinder (*Schlacke*)." It was withdrawn
Map 31. without the slightest interference from the French. By the evening
of the 10th September, it was, for the most part, across the Marne,
with its rear guards still south of the river from 10 miles west of
Chalons to Dormans, its right some 9 miles south of the left of
Kluck's Army, and with an actual gap of 16 miles between them.

 At 4 A.M. on the 11th September General von Moltke set forth to
visit the Armies of the centre and right. He found the *Fifth Army*,
which had got clear after a night attack on the 9th/10th, confident
and averse to retiring any further ; the *Fourth Army*, too, had broken
off the battle without difficulty, and was confident ; the *Third Army*
was greatly exhausted, its sector was too wide for its numbers, and
it was fearful of a break-through on its right ; this fear was confirmed
by General Bülow of the *Second Army*, who was in expectation of
attack on his left. Thus a new danger had arisen, and at 2.30 P.M.
Moltke ordered a further retirement of the *Fifth, Fourth*, and *Third
Armies* to a line St. Menéhould and eastward—Thuisy (9 miles E.S.E.
of Reims), which they were to entrench and hold. After further
discussion with Bülow, it was agreed that in order to join up together
the *Second* and *First Armies* must go behind the Aisne, and that they
must stand on the defensive until the *Seventh Army* could be assembled
on their right. Moltke had already placed the *First Army*, which
he did not visit, under Bülow ; he now put the *Seventh Army* also
under him.

Map 33. The condition and exposed situation of his right wing were such
a source of anxiety to Bülow on the evening of the 12th September,
that he evacuated Reims and swung back the right (*X. Reserve Corps*)
of his main line east of the town to form a defensive flank. He
ordered the *13th Division*, which, as right flank guard, had been holding the passages of the Vesle near Fismes and Braisne, to retire
eastwards on the X. *Reserve Corps*, its place being taken by the *25th
Landwehr Brigade*, which, we have seen, got into serious trouble, and

retired leaving many prisoners.   Thus by the night of the 12th/13th 12 Sept.
he had increased to some thirty miles the gap between the right of the 1914.
Second Army and the left of the *First Army*, which was at Vailly.
In this gap were only three cavalry divisions, the *Guard*, *2nd* and *9th*,
under Marwitz,[1] the disorganized remains of the *25th Landwehr
Brigade* and the *13th Division*, badly shaken on the 8th and 9th
September, which were making a night march out of the gap towards
the north of Reims.

The first and most insistent problem was how to fill the gap before
the Allies could reach it in force and pierce the German line of battle
by separating the *First* and *Second Armies*.   It is not too much to
say that the fate of the German Armies on the Western front turned
on the solution of this problem.   The retreat from the Marne had
already begun to have a demoralizing effect on the troops, exhausted
as they were by hard fighting following on the great physical strain
of the headlong rush through Belgium to the Marne.   If the gap could
not be filled, prudence dictated a continuance of the retreat ; but
that meant a further disintegration of units, and in their present condition was an alternative to be accepted only in the last resort.   The
Aisne was a good line to stand on, and there if possible a stand must
be made.   Moltke hoped to give his Armies eight days' rest, bring
up reinforcements, and replenish supplies and ammunition.   No one
could forecast what condition the German Army would be in if the
retreat was unduly prolonged, although Bülow was actually prepared
to go back to the La Fère line.   To give battle on the Aisne would
be fatal if the Allies could penetrate between the *First* and *Second
Armies*, and drive the former north-west and the latter north-east.
It might well be the beginning of the end in France, and, as the
Austrians were already falling back beaten from Lemberg, a
German defeat might lead to the complete collapse of the Central
Powers.

On the 12th September Bülow had ordered the *First Army* to close
on the right of the *Second* ; but, as the British were reported advancing on the gap between the Armies, he directed the *VII. Reserve* and
XV. Corps towards it, the former to march to Laon (12 miles north
of Bourg), and the latter to assemble at La Fère (20 miles north
of Soissons).[2]   Kluck, as usual, ignored the order, and replied at
7.50 P.M. :

" *First Army* heavily attacked on the front Soissons—Attichy,
" a battle is expected to-morrow.   It is holding north bank of the
" Aisne from Attichy (10 miles west of Soissons) to Condé.   Left wing
" can be further prolonged,[3] but any advance towards St. Thierry
" (5 miles north-west of Reims) is out of the question."

According to General von Zwehl, who commanded the *VII.
Reserve Corps*, which came up on the 13th on the left of the *III. Corps*,
the eastern flank of the *First Army* was then at Ostel, north of

---

[1] The *4th Cavalry Division* was on the extreme right of the *First Army*,
and the *5th* had been sent to the *Third Army*.

[2] On the evening of the 11th September, one division of the *XV. Corps*
(from Alsace), which had been detained before Antwerp, was detraining
at St. Quentin ; the *VII. Reserve Corps* (from Maubeuge) was near Guise ;
the *IX. Reserve Corps* (from Antwerp), near Tournai ; and the *7th Cavalry
Division* (from Alsace) near Cambrai.

[3] He had one division of the *III. Corps* in reserve north of Condé,
which he ordered to come up on his left and cover Vailly.

Chavonne. The gap between the *First* and *Second Armies* which was covered by the three cavalry divisions was therefore reduced to the 25 miles between Reims (exclusive) and Ostel. The Germans had begun entrenching, and Kluck goes so far as to say that trench warfare commenced on the 12th September 1914. There is no indication that any entrenchments had been prepared in anticipation of a retirement to the Aisne as was rumoured at the time.

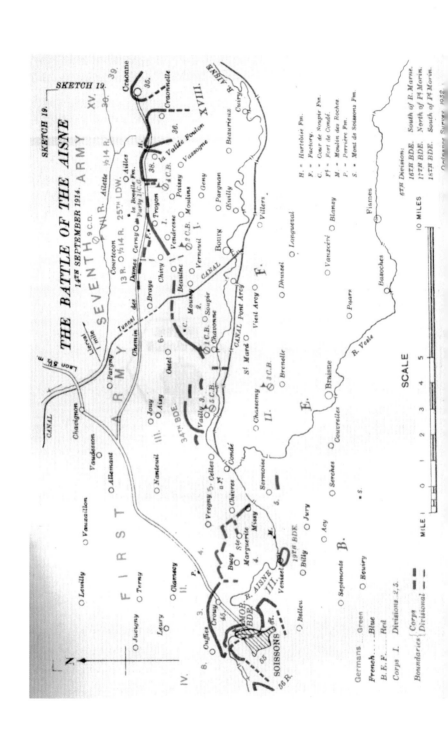

SKETCH 19.

THE BATTLE OF THE AISNE
14TH SEPTEMBER 1914.

6TH Division:
16TH BDE.   South of R. Marne.
17TH BDE.   North of Fᵗ Morin.
18TH BDE.   South of Fᵗ Morin.

H. = Hurtebise Fm.
F. = Factory.
C. = Cour de Soupir Fm.
Fᵗ = Fort de Condé.
M. = Moulin des Roches.
P. = Perrière Fm.
S. = Mont de Soissons Fm.

SCALE

Germans ..... Green
French .... Blue
B.E.F. .... Red
Corps I.   Divisions 2, 3.
Boundaries { Corps
           { Divisional

MILE

10 MILES

Ordnance Survey 1932

CHAPTER XIX

THE BATTLE OF THE AISNE

13TH SEPTEMBER 1914

THE PASSAGE OF THE AISNE

(See Sketches B, 13, 18 & 19 ; Maps 2, 3, 4, 33, 34 & 35)

IN order to make clear the narrative of the battle of the Sketches Aisne, it seems best, for once, to review the German situa- 18 & 19. tion before the British, although of course it was not at Maps 4, 33 & 35. the time thus fully known to the Allies. The night of the 12th/13th September marks the end of the retreat so far as the German *First* and *Second Armies* are concerned. During the closing hours of the 12th those of Kluck's troops (the *5th* and *3rd Divisions, IV. Corps* and half of the *IX. Corps*) which were still on the south side of the Aisne, entrenched on the line Billy (south of Venizel)— Cuise Lamotte (south-west of Attichy), covering Soissons, were withdrawn over the river. The re-sorting of his divisions into their original corps from the groups in which they had fought the battle of the Ourcq had meanwhile been carried out.

During the same night, Bülow, alarmed by the forcing of the line of the Vesle by the left of the Fifth and right of the British Armies, swung back his right wing east of Reims, as already described, placed his reserve, the *1st Guard* and *14th Divisions*, behind his right flank and brought back to this flank, from the Vesle, the *13th Division*. Thus, the fronts of the German *First* and *Second Armies* now formed a wide re-entrant angle, marked by the lines Prosnes (11 miles south-east of Reims)—Reims (exclusive) —Berry au Bac and Ostel (11 miles E.N.E. of Soissons)— Soissons—Compiègne, but with a gap of 25 miles, at least —Brimont (north of Reims) to Ostel—between their inner flanks. Towards the gap, held by the *Guard, 2nd* and *9th*

Cavalry Divisions, were advancing the left of the French Fifth Army (the XVIII. Corps, Valabrègue's Group of Reserve divisions and Conneau's cavalry corps), and the British I. Corps and Allenby's cavalry division.

Sketch 19.
Maps 4
& 34.
General Joffre's Instruction No. 23, issued on the 12th September and received at British G.H.Q. at 2 P.M.,[1] directed the Sixth Army after the passage of the Aisne, if the Germans continued to give way, to send the bulk of its forces gradually to the right bank of the Oise, so as to make sure of outflanking them, but, whatever happened, to detail a strong detachment to keep in close touch with the British Army. The latter force was to move north between Bourg and Soissons, its right boundary, previously Bazoches— Craonne, being thus, with the whole zone of its operations, shifted westwards. The Fifth Army, equally in close touch with the British, was to commence crossing the Aisne. There was no change in the orders to the other Armies.

Map 35.
G.H.Q. operation orders issued at 7.45 P.M. on the same evening,[2] fixed the starting time at 7 A.M., and directed that the heads of the three British corps should reach a line about five miles beyond the Aisne :—Lierval (7 miles north-east of Vailly)—Chavignon (5 miles north of Vailly)— Terny (4½ miles north of Soissons). The destination of the B.E.F. was thus roughly the top of the plateau, at this point little more than a ridge, which lies between the valleys of the Aisne and the Ailette and is traversed from east to west by the now well-known road, the Chemin des Dames. No specific duties were assigned to the two cavalry divisions, they were merely allotted roads. Major-General Allenby therefore continued to carry out the directions given him on the 9th September, to act in close association with the I. Corps and keep touch with the French Fifth Army, and Br.-General Gough remained with the II. Corps.[3]

The orders allotted the crossings of the Aisne as follows :

Cavalry Division and I. Corps : Bourg, Pont Arcy and Chavonne ;
Gough's cavalry and the II. Corps : Vailly, Condé and Missy.
III. Corps: Venizel and Soissons. The last place was later handed over to the French.

Map 33.
In the III. Corps sector a passage was actually effected on the night of the 12th/13th. About 9 P.M., Br.-General

---

[1] Appendix 42. [2] Appendix 43. [3] Appendix 39.

Hunter-Weston, commanding the 11th Brigade of the 13 Sept. 4th Division, then at Septmonts, 3 miles from the Aisne, 1914. after a conference at divisional headquarters, was instructed by Br.-General H. F. M. Wilson [1] to push forward and seize a crossing at Venizel bridge, with the assurance that he should have the support of the whole divisional artillery at daylight. Sending on two reconnoitring officers, Br.-General Hunter-Weston led the brigade at 11 P.M. through the outposts down into the valley. On his arrival at Venizel at 1 A.M. the engineer reconnoitring officer reported that one of the four large charges placed to destroy the bridge had failed to explode, and that, although the main girders on each side of the principal span were cut, the reinforced concrete of the roadway would probably be sufficiently strong to enable infantry to cross, if great care were taken : there was, however, considerable risk that the bridge might give way without warning. The infantry reconnoitring officer informed the general that there were fresh German trenches close to the bridge on the south bank, but that they did not appear to be occupied, and that a German patrol which had fired on him from the north bank had immediately retired. Br.-General Hunter-Weston, after inspecting the bridge himself, as there were still four hours of darkness, decided to cross and attempt to seize the heights beyond. Owing to the state of the bridge, the men were sent across in single file, and the ammunition carts were unloaded and with their contents passed over by hand.

By 3 A.M. on the 13th the passage was completed, and the brigade was then ordered to secure the heights above by a bayonet charge. This operation was entirely success-ful, and just as day was dawning the German outposts on the crest, completely surprised by the sudden appear-ance of the British, incontinently abandoned their trenches and fell back on their main line some hundreds of yards away. Then the 11th Brigade, the first British formation to cross the Aisne,—although the 4th Division cyclists by seiz-ing Missy bridge at 1 A.M. shared the honour of being the first unit,—occupied the edge of the plateau from the spur north of Ste. Marguerite westwards through a farm called La Montagne to within a mile of Crouy, 2 miles north-east of Soissons. It was a most satisfactory end to a trying march of some thirty miles through the pouring rain, in a

---

[1] Commanding the 4th Division in succession to Major-General Snow who had been disabled by an accident on the 9th near La Ferté Jouarre.

temperature more appropriate to November than early autumn, and with little or no food for more than twenty-four hours. Had other divisions been equally enterprising, —and their marches on the 12th had been shorter than those of the 4th Division,—the fighting on the 13th might have had a different result.

The morning was still wet and miserable, when on the extreme right of the British front, the advanced guard of the Cavalry Division rode out from its billets and pushed two reconnoitring patrols forward to the crossings of the Aisne at Villers and Bourg. In every case the road bridges over the river were found to have been destroyed, but not those over the Aisne canal, which lies south of it.[1] A sharp fire was opened on the British dragoons by Germans[2] sheltered in houses or entrenched along the bank of the branch canal which, starting close to Bourg, runs north-westwards from the Aisne canal to the Oise. The aqueduct which carries this branch canal across the river, however, had been only slightly damaged, and J Battery and the XXXII. Brigade R.F.A.[3] came into action to support the attack of the 2nd Cavalry Brigade upon it. But it was not until assistance arrived from the 1st Division that the cavalry was able to effect a crossing.

Sir Douglas Haig's orders for the 13th had directed the I. Corps to continue its advance and, in the first instance, to push forward patrols to the river crossings ; the divisions were to close up, well concealed and ready to act on the information obtained by the cavalry. In the event of the enemy seriously disputing the passage of the Aisne, attack orders would be issued ; in the event of his continuing his retirement, the 1st and 2nd Divisions were to occupy ground beyond the river at Bourg, and at Pont Arcy and Chavonne (3 miles below Pont Arcy), respectively, their advanced guards covering the crossings, and were to push reconnaissances towards the enemy.

The 2nd Brigade, the leading troops of the 1st Division, therefore, followed the Cavalry Division, after assisting its crossing at Bourg, and took up a covering position on the northern bank. The 1st Cavalry Brigade at once struck eastwards upon Pargnan to gain touch with the French, and Br.-General de Lisle took the 2nd Cavalry Brigade

---

[1] It finally enters the river lower down, near Vailly.
[2] The enemy in this area consisted of parts of the *Guard Cavalry Division* and *25th Landwehr Brigade*, of the *Second Army*.
[3] Temporarily attached to the Cavalry Division from the 4th Division.

northwards along the ridge immediately north of Bourg, 13 Sept. from which a German column could be seen moving north 1914. from Vendresse. I Battery opened fire upon this with shrapnel, but was answered with such vigour that the 2nd Cavalry Brigade was obliged to fall back to the south side of the ridge.

Further to the left, the divisional cavalry of the 2nd Division reported soon after dawn that the bridge at Chavonne had been destroyed and that the approaches to it were commanded by German snipers. At Pont Arcy itself, however, the demolition of the bridge was only partial, men on foot could use it, and it was feebly defended. The greater part of the 5th Brigade was able to cross there, practically unopposed, and thus enabled the engineers to begin the construction of a pontoon bridge further downstream. At noon the 2/Coldstream was sent to Chavonne to secure, if it could, the passage at that point.

Still further to the left, the II. Corps, in pursuance of G.H.Q. orders, pushed forward the 3rd Division against the bridges at Vailly (where both canal and river must be crossed), and the 5th Division against the bridge of Missy. These two passages are 4 miles apart. The bridge at Condé, midway between them, was intact ; it also was allotted to the 5th Division, but the approaches to it, over a wide flat stretch of water meadows, could be so easily commanded by machine guns that it had evidently been left open by the enemy as a trap.

The 8th Brigade, which led the advance of the 3rd Division upon Vailly, was checked when it reached Chassemy, on the edge of the plateau, 1½ miles from the river, by the fire of German howitzers on the promontory of Chivres, a large spur flanking the valley, and it could progress no further. The artillery of the division came into action above Brenelle, to the right rear of Chassemy ; but the 49th Battery, unlimbering in the open, was promptly silenced, the detachments being driven from their guns. At 10 A.M. the Royal Scots, working their way down through the woods on the slopes of the valley north of Chassemy, were able to reach the canal not far short of the two bridges ; but the outlook was not promising. The light railway bridge a mile above Vailly had been entirely destroyed, and the road bridge over the river was also broken, though the gap was spanned by a single-plank footway which the Germans, in their haste, had left behind them.

When the 4th Division cyclists had seized Missy bridge at 1 A.M., they had left a party to hold it for the II. Corps. But this party had been driven off by superior numbers of Germans at 4 A.M. and the condition of the bridge was now uncertain. An hour or two later two companies of the Royal West Kent, which was the leading battalion of the 13th Brigade, came down towards this bridge and engaged the hidden machine guns and riflemen on the northern bank and compelled them to retire, though themselves suffering several casualties. It was then possible for a party of the 59th Field Company R.E. to advance and examine the bridge more closely, when it was ascertained that the girders of the two most northern of the three spans had been destroyed, leaving gaps of some twenty feet. Heavy fire then compelled the party to withdraw, but the two companies entrenched to the east of the bridge.

Simultaneously with the movement of the 13th Brigade upon Missy, the 14th Brigade, with the 121st Battery, was sent down a side valley to Moulin des Roches, just upstream from Venizel, which had been selected by the engineers as the most suitable place for bridging, and there the brigade remained until past noon whilst the 17th Field Company was constructing a raft.

Still further to the west, in the III. Corps area, the 12th Brigade, soon after 6 A.M., had begun to defile across the damaged bridge at Venizel, which had by that time been made somewhat safer ; and, west of it again, a brigade of the French Sixth Army was steadily passing the river at Soissons. Both French and British were greeted by fire from German artillery, chiefly 8-inch and 5·9-inch howitzers, in action on the heights to the north. The most troublesome of these, so far as the British were concerned, were three batteries, already mentioned, on the spur of Chivres (just north of Missy), the commanding position in that section of the valley. One of these batteries seemed to be on the eastern branch of the spur, overlooking Condé, and the two others a mile or more further to the north about Les Carrières. The artillery of the 4th and 5th Divisions had by this time taken up position on the plateau, from Le Carrier (1½ miles east of Billy) to Mont de Belleu Farm, on both sides of the valley which cuts into it from Venizel. The 31st and 108th Heavy Batteries succeeded in silencing for a time the German guns which were impeding the advance of the Allies ; but they were soon forced by the fire of the German heavy howitzers either to 13 Sept. shift position or to withdraw their detachments. These 1914. howitzers, in fact, outranged all the British artillery, except the 60-pdr. batteries, and for the time being had complete mastery of the situation.

However, by 11 A.M., covered by the 11th Brigade on the edge of the heights, all the 12th Brigade (except the 2/Inniskilling, which had been left behind to bring the guns over the bridge) was across the Aisne at Venizel. In widely extended order, the three battalions made their way across the two miles of water-meadows to Bucy le Long at the foot of the heights, under a hail of shrapnel bullets, which did little damage.[1] The 68th Battery followed them, moving by sections, and escaped without casualties. The 10th Brigade meanwhile took up a position behind the railway embankment westwards from Venizel for 2 miles to Villeneuve St. Germain, to cover a retirement if it should be necessary. The 11th Brigade, holding the southern edge of the heights above Bucy le Long since early morning, was absolutely unmolested, though German troops were entrenched within eight hundred to fifteen hundred yards north of it, and in the valleys of Chivres and Vregny to its right and front. On the right of this brigade, indeed, the 1/Rifle Brigade had stolen through the woods on the western side of the Chivres valley and was effectively enfilading the German trenches on the eastern side.

Such, then, was the situation about noon. The passage of the Aisne had been forced at both extremities of the

---

[1] A translation of what Hauptmann Bloem saw of this advance from Chivres ridge is, apart from its vividness, of interest as showing the superior observation enjoyed by the Germans :

" Across the wide belt of meadow extending between our chain of " heights and the course of the river, stretched what seemed to be a dotted " line formed of longish and widely separated strokes. With field-glasses, " we could see that these strokes were advancing infantry, and unmistakably " English. . . .

" From the bushes bordering the river sprang up and advanced a second " line of skirmishers, with at least ten paces interval from man to man. " Our artillery flashed and hit—naturally, at most, a single man. And " the second line held on and pushed always nearer and nearer. Two " hundred yards behind it came a third wave, a fourth wave. Our artillery " fired like mad : all in vain, a fifth, a sixth line came on, all with good " distance, and with clear intervals between the men. Splendid, we are " all filled with admiration.

" The whole wide plain was now dotted with these funny khaki figures, " always coming nearer. The attack was directed on our neighbour corps " on the right [the II.]. And now infantry fire met the attackers, but " wave after wave flooded forward, and disappeared from our view behind " the hanging woods which framed the entrance to the Chivres valley."

British line; and it remained to be seen how far this success would assist the passage of the centre. From all the information furnished to General Haig the gap had not been closed which had existed between the German *First* and *Second Armies* ever since the battle of the Marne, and there was nothing in front of him but a strong force of cavalry—either a weak corps or a division at full strength —and five batteries entrenched on the Chemin des Dames. Against such a force, he naturally hoped to gain ground without making a formal attack.[1] There was news, too, that the 35th Division of the French XVIII. Corps had at 10.30 A.M. crossed the Aisne at Pontavert, 7 miles to his right, with the Germans only one hour ahead of it, and that this division and Conneau's cavalry corps were pressing on to the eastern end of the Chemin des Dames ridge and beyond. The prospects of a break-through never were brighter.

Sketch 19.
Map 35.
The ground facing the British I. Corps presented a series of high spurs projecting generally southwards from the Chemin des Dames ridge towards the Aisne. First, commencing from the east, are the Paissy—Pargnan and Bourg spurs, both extending nearly to the river, with the village of Moulins at the top of the valley between them. Next is the short Troyon spur, with Vendresse in the valley east of it, and Beaulne and Chivy west of it. Westwards of these again are the three spurs at the foot of which lie Moussy and Soupir and Chavonne, respectively; only the last of these comes close down to the river.

By 1 P.M. the 2nd Brigade, the advanced guard of the 1st Division, had reached the top of the spur north of Bourg, enabling the 2nd Cavalry Brigade to advance again some two miles, as far as Moulins, where it was checked by German forces on the ridge north of Troyon. Other German troops were seen moving towards Bourg from Chivy, about a mile west of Troyon, and the Flying Corps reported the concentration of yet more, a mile or two further to the north of Courtecon.[2] The 1st (Guards) and 3rd Brigades were therefore sent across the river in all haste, and by divisional orders were directed north-eastwards towards Paissy to the right of the 2nd Cavalry Brigade. About 4 P.M. the 2nd Brigade took up a position from Moulins

---

[1] This estimate of the German force was correct at the time : the *Guard* and *2nd Cavalry Divisions* had opposed the I. Corps, but reinforcements were approaching, as will be narrated later. See page 393.
[2] Part of the *VII. Reserve Corps.*

south-west towards Bourg, and released the 2nd Cavalry 13 Sept.
Brigade to withdraw to its billets east of Bourg. By 6 P.M. 1914.
the last infantryman of the 1st Division was on the north
bank of the Aisne. The artillery, as it came up to Bourg,
was pushed on to the next spur to the east, north of Pargnan, whence, towards evening, the XXV. Brigade R.F.A.
and 30th Battery engaged the Germans about Troyon at
long range. At dusk, the action, in which the artillery of
the French Fifth Army had shared, died down ; and the
1st Division and 2nd Cavalry Brigade settled down for
the night at Paissy, Moulins, Oeuilly and Bourg, the 1st
Cavalry Brigade re-crossing to the southern bank of the
river at Pont Arcy. The casualties of the 2nd Cavalry
Brigade had been slight ; fifty German prisoners had been
taken and all seemed to be going well. Had the enemy
intended to drive the I. Corps back across the Aisne, his
chance was gone.

On the left of the 1st Division, the pontoon bridge at
Pont Arcy was not completed until 4.30 P.M. ; meanwhile
the 2/Coldstream (4th (Guards) Brigade), with the help
of artillery, had driven the German sharpshooters from
Chavonne, crossed the river by the bridge there (the enemy
having left a temporary trestle construction over a broken
span) and advanced to the top of the ridge beyond it.
Here, however, the battalion came under heavy artillery
fire, against which the British guns were powerless to help,
for they were out-ranged. When, however, Colonel G. P. T.
Feilding reported to the 2nd Division that the 2/Coldstream
was across and he proposed to send another battalion over,
Major-General Monro, after personally examining the situation at the bridge, ordered him to withdraw the Coldstream,
leaving only one company to guard the bridgehead ; there
were no engineers available to make the bridge serviceable,
as both divisional field companies R.E. were employed in
throwing a pontoon bridge at Arcy, and until the passage
was improved it seemed inadvisable to leave many men on
the far side. Neither the 4th (Guards) nor the 6th Brigade,
therefore, crossed the Aisne. The 5th Brigade, the only
infantry of the 2nd Division on the northern bank,[1] after
enduring some hours' bombardment, moved under cover
of darkness towards the left of the 1st Division, between
Moussy and Verneuil and placed a line of outposts half a
mile further north, astride the Beaulne spur and the two
valleys which flank it to the east and west.

[1] See page 381.

Further to the left, in the II. Corps, Major-General Hubert Hamilton, commanding the 3rd Division, after personal inspection of the bridges at Vailly, at 1 P.M. ordered the 8th Brigade to advance upon them. As already stated, the railway bridge had been completely destroyed, and the road bridge had been broken ; but by the single plank spanning the breach in the latter, the Royal Scots and the Royal Irish began at 3 P.M. to cross the Aisne. They were steadily shelled as they did so, and a few men were wounded ; but by 4 P.M. the Royal Scots were established in Vauxelles Chateau (1 mile north-west of Vailly) and on the high ground north-west of it ; and before nightfall the rest of the 8th Brigade was in support at St. Pierre (just west of Vailly). The 9th Brigade followed by the same tedious way during the night ; while the engineers, under continued shell fire, began the construction of a pontoon bridge. For the best part of the night, however, the only communication in the 3rd Division between the 8th and 9th Brigades on the north bank of the river and the 7th Brigade at Braisne, was a single-plank footway.

Owing to a misunderstanding a demonstration which was to have been made at Condé bridge by General Gough's cavalry did not take place.

At Missy bridge, where the river was 70 feet wide and 12 feet deep, the R. West Kent (13th Brigade) were unable to move from their trenches [1] until nightfall, when under cover of darkness they began to dribble men across the Aisne : first in a boat which had been found under the north bank by a sapper who swam across, then on five small rafts, each capable of carrying five men, constructed by the 59th Field Company R.E. of planks, straw and wagon covers. The annihilation of a German patrol, which came down to the bank after about forty men had crossed the river, saved them from interruption by the enemy ; and though it was past midnight before the whole battalion had been transferred to the north bank the process was practically unhindered by the Germans. The 2/Scottish Borderers followed and were all across shortly after daylight. The two remaining battalions of the 13th Brigade were left for the moment at Ciry and Sermoise, a mile or more south of Missy bridge.

To the west again, at Moulin des Roches, above Venizel, a raft to carry 60 men had been completed by noon on the 13th, and the leading battalion of the 14th Brigade (the

[1] See page 382.

2/Manchester) began to cross the river, the men concealing 13 Sept. themselves as they landed behind a convenient wood on 1914. the northern bank. The East Surrey followed them, and by 3 P.M. both battalions, together with their pack animals, were on the German side of the Aisne, and beginning their advance without waiting for the rest of the brigade. As they left the cover of the trees, they came under heavy shrapnel fire from the promontory of Chivres, but pursued their way in extended order towards the eastern end of Ste. Marguerite (half a mile west of Missy) to support the 12th Brigade, which held the village. As they were approaching, they received a message from Lieut.-Colonel F. G. Anley, then commanding that brigade,[1] that he was attacking the Chivres spur from Ste. Marguerite, and begged the 14th Brigade to help him by striking in from the south. It was too late, however, to fall in with this suggestion, but the direction was changed so that the East Surrey should come in on the right of the 12th Brigade with the Manchester in echelon to its right rear. The Lancashire Fusiliers and the Essex of the 12th Brigade were in fact advancing, the former on the right, the latter on the left of the road which leads from Ste. Marguerite to Chivres, against a position of which they knew remarkably little. The ground was swampy and the undergrowth of the woods on the way was very thick, so that progress was slow ; but about 5 P.M. the Lancashire Fusiliers came under heavy fire on their front from trenches south of Chivres village, and on their right flank from the western slopes of the Chivres spur. Two companies engaged the enemy in front while a third drove back or silenced the enemy on the flank, the Essex giving such support as they could from the hill above Ste. Marguerite. But the Lancashire Fusiliers could advance no further ; and it so happened that just at this moment two guns of the 68th Battery opened fire from an exposed position near the head of the ravine of Le Moncel (half a mile north-west of Ste. Marguerite), drawing heavy retaliation on that area. The guns were compelled to retire, and some parties of the 1/Rifle Brigade (11th Brigade) which were pushing on were also driven back with considerable loss.

These incidents put a stop to the advance on Chivres. The two battalions of 14th Infantry Brigade had not been able to assist much, as having to change direction under shrapnel fire they did not come up until the moment for co-operation had passed, and then behind rather than on

[1] *Vice* Br.-General H. F. M. Wilson, now commanding the 4th Division.

the right of the 12th Brigade. The Lancashire Fusiliers clung to their ground until nightfall, when the Manchester came forward to relieve them. They had lost 6 officers and over 170 men, and were obliged to leave many of their wounded on the ground, as they were too near the German trenches to permit of removal. It was long before any troops of the Allies approached nearer than the Lancashire men had to the commanding promontory of Chivres. However, a passage at Moulin des Roches had been effected; and at 9 P.M. the 15th Brigade marched down to the raft which the 14th had used and began crossing the river, leaving behind their horses and vehicles to follow at daybreak. Thus before dawn of the 14th September a footing, albeit a precarious one, had been gained on the north bank of the Aisne at several points. The situation of the British Army was as follows :—

North Bank of Aisne.

Sketches B & 19. Maps 4, 34 & 35.

Cavalry Division		
1st Division.		Between Paissy and Verneuil.
5th Brigade		

Gap of 5 miles.

.8th and 9th Brigades   .   .   Vauxelles.

Gap of 3 miles.

1/West Kent and 2/K.O.S.B. of the 13th Brigade   .   .   .   Missy.

14th and 15th Brigades   .   . ⎫
4th Division   .   .   .   . ⎭ Ste. Marguerite to Crouy.

South Bank of Aisne.

4th (Guards) and 6th Brigades   Vieil Arcy, Dhuizel, St. Mard.

3rd and 5th Cavalry Brigades . ⎫
7th Brigade   .   .   .   . ⎭ Braisne and vicinity.

13th Brigade (less two battalions)   .   .   .   .   .   South of Missy.

19th Brigade (II. Corps reserve)   Septmonts.

Both flanks of the British Army were in close touch with the French. On the right the French Fifth Army, it was known, had met with varying fortune. On the left of the British the French Sixth Army had made little progress, General Maunoury's difficulties in this section of the line being exactly the same as our own. The German guns could shell his troops in the valley at comparatively short range, but could not be reached by the French guns except at long range. The 45th Division, next to the British, 13 Sept. crossed at Soissons, but, though supported by the 55th 1914. Division of Lamaze's Group, had been unable to get beyond Cuffies.

The Chemin des Dames ridge, which lay athwart the Map 35. advance of the British and of the French immediately on their flanks, rises out of the plain of Champagne near Craonne and extends thence, between the valleys of the Aisne and the Ailette, in a continuous unbroken line westward for some five and twenty miles until abreast of Soissons, where it bifurcates near the village of Juvigny, its south-western fork ending a mile or two beyond Nouvron. The XVIII. French Corps seemed to have good prospect of getting on to the eastern edge of the ridge at Craonne ; if, in conjunction with the British I. Corps, it could secure the eastern section of the Chemin des Dames from Craonne to Courtecon and then strike westward, it would ease the task of the II. and III. Corps and of General Maunoury's right. If the latter's VII. Corps could simultaneously gain Nouvron and thence strike eastward, it is obvious that there was very good prospect of completely sweeping the Germans from the ridge.

Reviewing the general position, Sir John French decided that he was justified in making a great effort to carry out General Joffre's instructions for an energetic pursuit by attacking along the whole front on the 14th. For all he knew, the Germans might still be in retreat, and there might be nothing before him except obstinate and skilfully posted rear guards. Captured documents proved that the retreat of the enemy was not a mere strategic movement, but had been forced on him as the result of an unsuccessful battle. The weather had been very unsettled on the 13th, though it improved in the afternoon, but aerial reconnaissance had revealed only one German cavalry division and about two infantry divisions between Cerny (8 miles S.S.W. of Laon) and Aizy (2 miles north of Vailly), and another division near Laon.[1] Appearances seemed to

---

[1] This report, as is now known, was correct. The two infantry divisions in the line were the *13th Reserve Division* (just arrived) and the *6th Division*. But on the east of the space reported on, Cerny—Aizy, the *14th Reserve Division* was coming up, and on the west, opposite the British, were the other division of the *III. Corps* and the whole of the *II. Corps*. The *Guard Cavalry Division* was still in line, but the *2nd* and *9th* were pulled out as the infantry came up.

Thus, there were six infantry divisions and a cavalry division in front of the British, with a corps, the *XV.*, behind. This corps went in next day against the French on the east of the *VII. Reserve Corps*.

indicate that, except for local counter-attacks, the whole German line was retiring in a north-easterly direction. By dawn on the 14th, the engineers would have laid a pontoon bridge and a trestle bridge near Vailly. At Missy the bridge had been so much damaged that it could not be repaired in a single night. But even without additional bridges much might be done.

Map 3. General Joffre also, in his Instruction No. 24 of the 13th, was of opinion that "the enemy was retreating on "the whole front without serious resistance on the Aisne "and the Marne." He ordered that the pursuit should be continued energetically in a general northerly direction, by the British between Athies (just east of Laon) and the Oise, and by the Sixth Army west of the Oise.

G.H.Q. operation orders for the 14th,[1] therefore, directed the Army to continue the pursuit and act vigorously against the retreating enemy, advancing northward to the line Laon—Fresnes (12 miles west of Laon), the Cavalry Division covering the right and Gough's cavalry brigades the left of the force.

Map 35. Sir Douglas Haig decided to make the Chemin des Dames ridge the first objective of the I. Corps and ordered the 1st Division to advance to the section from Cerny westward to Courtecon, and the 2nd Division from Courtecon, exclusive, westward to the tunnel through which the Oise canal pierces the hill from Pargny to Braye. Whether further progress could be made would depend on the movements of the II Corps. The Cavalry Division was directed to be prepared to push on to Laon. The orders entailed the 4th and 6th Brigades of the 2nd Division crossing the Aisne at daybreak.

In the II. Corps, both divisions were ordered to continue the pursuit northwards, Gough's cavalry following as soon as the bridges were clear.

In the III. Corps, similarly, the 4th Division was ordered to resume the offensive and gain first the northern edge of the high ground between Vregny—Braye, some two and a half miles from the southern edge of the plateau where the division was established. The divisional artillery and the 19th Brigade were still to remain on the south bank of the Aisne.

[1] Appendix 44.

THE FRENCH ON THE 13TH SEPTEMBER

By General Joffre's Instruction No. 23,[1] the left of the Fifth 13 Sept.
Army was to cross the Aisne, that is move N.N.W. into the gap in 1914.
the German line. As on a previous occasion, General Franchet Maps 4
d'Espèrey had already issued his orders, sending his troops north- & 34.
east, and drawing the Group of Reserve Divisions into reserve, when
he received the G.Q.G. Instruction. It increased his front eastward,
as we have seen, but he got over this difficulty by issuing a correction
to his orders at 9 P.M., which brought Valabrègue's Group again
into the line, between the III. and XVIII. Corps, only the latter
corps moving N.N.W. His Army, divided as on the 9th September,
fought two distinct actions during the day : whilst his right the X., I. and III. Corps,
not in contact with the enemy, his right the X., I. and III. Corps,
facing a little north of east, encountered Bülow's Army, and was
definitely held up on the line marked by the course of the Vesle
above Reims, the eastern and northern suburbs of that town, and
the Berry au Bac canal. On the left, the XVIII. Corps fought its
way " painfully " north-westwards, alongside the B.E.F., towards
the Chemin des Dames. The Group of Reserve Divisions and
Conneau's cavalry corps in the centre, were opposite the 10-mile gap
in the German line, into which they penetrated without difficulty.
But they did no more than this. The 10th Cavalry Division, crossing the Aisne at Pontavert at 8.30 A.M., reached Amifontaine, 7
miles to the north-east, at 2.30 P.M., and, after sending out patrols,
pushed on six miles northward to Sissonne, where it passed the night,
without any contact with the enemy. The 4th Cavalry Division,
finding that it was unable to move by the western route assigned
to it, via Corbeny, which was occupied by the enemy, followed the
10th towards Sissonne, but was brought back to bivouac at Amifontaine. The 8th Cavalry Division, being in reserve, did not do
more than reach the Aisne at Berry au Bac, where it billeted at 6
P.M. Without being aware of it, at Sissonne Conneau's cavalry corps
was some forty miles behind the general line of the German *Third
Army*, and fifteen miles north of the thrown-back flank of the *Second
Army*. It had only to move eastwards across the enemy lines of
communication to cause at least alarm and confusion.
     Of Valabrègue's Group, the left division, the 53rd, crossed the
Aisne at Berry au Bac at 11.30 A.M., intending to go northwards to
Amifontaine ; but, receiving some small fire from the direction of
Corbeny, it wandered eastward and settled down for the night with
its main body north of the Aisne at Guignicourt (3 miles above Berry
au Bac), and detachments to the north and south-west at Juvin-
court and Berry au Bac. Valabrègue's right division, the 69th,
directed on Guignicourt, was called on for assistance by the III.
Corps and sent a brigade with guns south-eastwards for this purpose. The detachment, after being in action, was at night halted
near Cormicy on the left of the III. Corps. The rest of the division,
continuing northwards, reached Guignicourt in the afternoon and
billeted there and in Prouvais, two miles to the northward.
     Foch's Army, on the right of the Fifth, facing now nearly due
north, was delayed by enemy rear guards and " by evening had
" advanced only some six miles."
     General Joffre's instructions to the Sixth Army were to the effect

─────────────
[1] Appendix 42.

that it should gradually transfer its forces west of the Oise, so as to outflank the German right, leaving only a strong detachment west of the Forest of St. Gobain area to ensure liaison with the British. To carry out this plan, General Maunoury ordered the 8th Division (IV. Corps) on the left to be shifted westwards to act in co-operation with the 37th Division (brought from the Fifth Army), which was moving up to Compiègne, and the XIII. Corps (from the Fourth Army) assembling behind it. The IV. Corps was, however, in the process of crossing the Aisne and pushing on, as Kluck had withdrawn his right flank, before the Army order arrived ; and, in spite of reiterated orders, General Boëlle, his corps being engaged, could do no more than detail one brigade to proceed westwards with orders to reconnoitre the passages of the Oise.

Next on the right, Ebener's Group of Reserve divisions having made floating bridges during the night, crossed the Aisne without resistance : but the passage took time and the leading division was unable to reach Nampcel, and push on to the Oise, as directed by the Army.

The VII. Corps, the greater part of which was already across the Aisne, prepared to march northwards in pursuit in much the same fashion as the B.E.F. ; but it soon encountered organized resistance, well supported by artillery, on the edge of the heights bordering the Aisne valley, and was unable to obtain a footing on them. Lamaze's Group of Reserve divisions, next on the right, owing to enemy fire, could not throw bridges, and did not cross the Aisne, except for a small party on the left next to the VII. Corps In the 45th Division, next to the British, all the 90th Brigade, except three companies, crossed the Aisne at Soissons during the night of the 12th/13th, mainly man by man, over the débris of a permanent bridge, and from 4.30 A.M. onwards by means of rafts. Towards 6 A.M. enemy gun fire stopped further movement. A battalion of the 89th Brigade managed to cross by a footbridge on the débris of another permanent bridge, but in the course of the day both bridges were destroyed and owing to the fierceness of the fire the engineers were unable to repair them or to construct others. The 90th Brigade, however, was not entirely cut off, as it established contact with the British 4th Division on its right.

There seemed little chance of the Sixth Army carrying out the rôle assigned to it by Joffre.

NOTE

THE 13TH SEPTEMBER ON THE GERMAN SIDE

Map 2.   With better management and more luck than at the Marne, the German Supreme Command at the Aisne had divisions available to fill the gap between the *First* and *Second Armies*. On the 7th September, as we have seen, the *XV. Corps (Seventh Army)* and the *7th Cavalry Division (Sixth Army)* had been ordered westward from the left in Alsace, with the intention of placing them, with the *IX. Reserve Corps* from Antwerp, as a new *Seventh Army*, on the extreme right of the German Force, so as to outflank Maunoury's Army, just as that Army had outflanked Kluck on the 6th September.

These troops became available too late to fulfil that purpose during the battle of the Marne, and were almost too late at the Aisne.

The *VII. Reserve Corps* released by the fall of Maubeuge arrived in 13 Sept.
the nick of time on the 13th to stop the gap on the Chemin des 1014.
Dames. It anticipated the British I. Corps by a couple of hours
only ; on this small margin of time did the stand of the Germans
on the Aisne depend. Next day the *XV. Corps* in a similar way
stopped the French advance on the British right.

It is therefore of some interest to examine the movements of the
German troops concerned. Maubeuge had surrendered on the
evening of the 7th September, with effect from noon on the 8th,[1]
and the *VII. Reserve Corps*, leaving two battalions as garrison and
three as escort to prisoners, was at first under orders to proceed
northwards against the British who had landed on the Flanders
coast.[2] The orders were subsequently cancelled and the corps left
Maubeuge on the 10th September to march to La Fère, where it was
to form the nucleus of the new *Seventh Army*, whose commander,
General von Heeringen, had arrived in Brussels. The necessity of
filling the gap between Bülow and Kluck and preventing a break-
through was deemed to be so urgent that for the moment all thought
of outflanking movements was abandoned. At 9.40 A.M. on the
12th the orders of the *VII. Reserve Corps* were again changed, and
General von Zwehl, its commander, was directed to march it with all
speed to Laon. Learning at 6.30 P.M. the situation on the Aisne
he gave his divisions a two-hour halt, and decided to continue the
march through the night to the high ground south of the town.
About 5 A.M. on the 13th the corps bivouacked in two groups 5 miles
south and south-east of Laon, after a march of 40 miles in twenty-
four hours ; from a fifth to a fourth of its infantry had fallen out.[3]

At 8 A.M. the *VII. Reserve Corps* was instructed by Bülow— Maps 34
under whose orders the *Seventh Army* and also the *First Army* had & 35.
been placed—to move up on the left (east) of the *First Army*, which
" was awaiting battle on the general line Vailly—Soissons—Attichy."
General von Zwehl ordered the march to be resumed at 9.30 A.M.
in a south-west direction towards Chavonne, so as to reach the
Chemin des Dames as soon as possible. He directed his *13th Reserve
Division* on Braye en Laonnais and the *14th Reserve Division* on
Cerny. He hoped thus, by being in a position to move either south-
east or south-west, to be able to hold the gap. Shortly before 11
A.M. a further order was received from Bülow, ordering the *VII.
Reserve Corps* to Berry au Bac, 15 miles east of Chavonne, where his
right was threatened by the French advance. Unfortunately for the
B.E.F., Zwehl considered his troops too far committed to the direc-
tion which he had given them, and he ignored Bülow's cry for help.
Had he moved his corps to the south-east, he would have left the way
clear for the British I. Corps to establish itself on the Chemin des
Dames ridge, and the flank of all the German forces west of it might
have been turned. As it was, by 2 P.M. on the 13th September the
entire *13th Reserve Division* was in position along the Chemin des
Dames, north of Braye, its foremost troops having reached it and

[1] A full account of the siege of Maubeuge will be found in Zwehl and in
Commandant P. Cassou's " La vérité sur le siège de Maubeuge." (Paris,
Berger-Levrault.)
[2] Zwehl, p. 54. Four battalions of Royal Marines had landed, but
had re-embarked (see page 232).
[3] Zwehl, p. 59 *et seq.*, from which the details of the operations of the
VII. Reserve Corps are taken.

relieved the cavalry considerably earlier. It was thus ready when the leading troops of the I. Corps approached. The *14th Reserve Division*, the other division of the corps, was divided into two portions :—one brigade, the *27th Reserve*, with three batteries, came up on the east of the *13th Reserve Division* at Cerny (north of Troyon) about 2 P.M. ; the *28th Brigade* marched further eastward against the French. Between these two brigades Marwitz's cavalry corps assembled.[1]

Thus, even by the afternoon of the 13th, the crisis of the battle was, for the Germans, practically past. Although there was still a space of 11½ miles opposite the French between the right of the *Second Army* and the left of the *VII. Reserve Corps*, with only an isolated brigade of the latter corps in it, other troops were close at hand, and the screen in the gap had been sufficiently strengthened to stop the British advanced guards, and by troops who had not borne the burden of the rapid advance to the Marne and the disheartening retreat to the Aisne. In front of the British there was now a continuous line from east to west :—part of the *II. Cavalry Corps, VII. Reserve Corps*, the *III. Corps* with the *34th Brigade* of the *IX. Corps* interpolated in its centre opposite Vailly, the *II. Corps*, and part of the *IV. Corps*.[2] Moreover, the German *First* and *Second Armies* had held their ground and gained time to improve their defences. Bülow was naturally much alarmed by the French advance across the Aisne towards Amifontaine, and used his reserves and the *13th Division* to extend his right flank northwards to the river. At 2 P.M. he decided that he must abandon temporarily his plan for employing the *Seventh Army* on the right of the *First*, and ordered the *XV. Corps* to march to Laon (which it reached in the evening). On being informed by Bülow of this action, O.H.L. made arrangements to withdraw one corps from each of the *Third, Fourth* and *Fifth Armies*—the *V., XII.* and *VIII. Reserve* were selected—in order to replace the *VII. Reserve Corps* and *XV. Corps* in the *Seventh Army* on the right of the line. At 8.30 P.M. orders were issued[3] by General von Heeringen that on the 14th the *XV. Corps* should advance down the Laon—Reims road and attack the enemy who had penetrated between the *Second* and *First Armies*, and throw him back over the Aisne. Marwitz's cavalry was requested to cover the arrival of the *XV. Corps*, and then secure its eastern flank. The *VII. Reserve Corps* and *6th Division* of the *III. Corps* were to participate in the attack.

The *First Army* did no more on this day than improve and hold its defences and swing back its right flank in view of the reported advance of strong French forces. As the *IX. Reserve Corps* from Antwerp and the *7th Cavalry Division* had been ordered to this flank, there seemed no reason for alarm.

The *Third* and *Fourth Armies* continued their retreat and reached on the 13th the new positions assigned to them ; but it was not until next day that the *Fifth Army* arrived there.

---

[1] It may be added that on the afternoon of the 13th, the remains of the *25th Landwehr Brigade* joined the *VII. Reserve Corps* ; on the 13th also, 1,200 reinforcements, intended for the *X. Corps*, were assigned to the *27th Reserve Brigade*, as also a Horse Artillery *Abteilung* of the *9th Cavalry Division*, and two 8-inch howitzer batteries were allotted to the corps ; on the 14th two battalions arrived from Maubeuge ; and on the 17th a complete brigade of the *XII. Corps* reinforced it.

[2] See Zwehl, Maps 3 and 4.   [3] The operation order is in Zwehl, p. 68.

CHAPTER XX

14TH SEPTEMBER

THE FIGHT FOR THE CHEMIN DES DAMES

(Sketch 19; Maps 4 & 35)

IN the description of the actions of the 14th September, Sketch 19.
although some sort of order may appear in the narrative, Maps 4
it must be borne in mind that in consequence of thick & 35.
weather, of the fighting being at close quarters, sometimes
even hand-to-hand, and of the heavy casualties, actually
very great confusion prevailed. It was most difficult
for divisional and brigade staffs, even for battalion commanders, to follow all the vicissitudes of the combat, and
impossible to record them in detail. Even could they have
done so, their accounts could scarcely have done justice
to the desperate character of the encounters on the
Chemin des Dames ridge and on the spurs and in the valleys
leading up to it, particularly near the Troyon factory,
Soupir and the Chivres spur. The fighting resembled that
of Waterloo or Inkerman, except that the combatants,
instead of being shoulder to shoulder, controlled by their
officers, advanced in open order and in small parties, and
fought usually behind cover or lying down ; there was
little of a spectacular nature, except when the enemy tried
to bear down all opposition by weight of numbers.

To epitomize the day's work—the British divisions in
a literally uphill contest, without much artillery support,
came piecemeal on to the battlefield to the assistance of the
advanced guards already across the Aisne. They found
the enemy not only in position, entrenched and supported
by 8-inch howitzers, but in such force that so far from
manifesting any intention of continuing his retreat, he
made every effort to drive the British back over the river.

Thus the 14th September passed in alternate attack and counter-attack, and ended in no decisive result. It was the first day of that " stabilization " of the battle line which was to last so many weary months—the beginning, for the British, of trench warfare.

Sketch 19.
Map 35. In the I. Corps, reconnaissances during the night had established the fact that parties of the enemy were established in a sugar factory a little north-west of Troyon and at some cross-roads just beyond. To protect the march of the 1st Division, therefore, the 2nd Brigade, with two batteries of the XXV. Brigade R.F.A., all under Br.-General Bulfin, was ordered to seize before daybreak the top of the Chemin des Dames ridge from Cerny to a road junction a mile westward. Under cover of, and through, this force, the advanced guard of the division—the 1st (Guards) Brigade, a battery, and a field company, under Br.-General Maxse—clearing Moulin by 7.30 A.M. was to march northward on Chamouille via Cerny. The main body of the division was then to follow, except two brigades of artillery and the heavy battery, which were to support the advance from Paissy spur.

At 3 A.M., amid heavy rain and dense mist, Br.-General Bulfin's force moved by Vendresse upon Troyon, the 2/K.R.R.C. leading, followed by the 2/R. Sussex. The commanding officer of the former, Lieut.-Colonel Pearce Serocold, had orders from Br.-General Bulfin to seize and secure the high ground above Troyon, whilst Lieut.-Colonel Montrésor of the Sussex was to keep his battalion in support at Vendresse until needed. The leading company of the K.R.R.C., with a party of the 9th Lancers, on reaching the top of the hill, surprised, about 4.45 A.M., a German piquet, but could not progress much further, so that Colonel Serocold sent up two more companies to extend his line. The din of rifle fire now gradually increased, although there was a marked absence of artillery fire, and by 5.30 it had become a roar. It was evident that the Germans were in strength, and Colonel Serocold called upon the Sussex, who meantime had been brought up closer in anticipation that they would be required ; by 6.30 A.M. they were deployed on his left, each battalion covering nearly eight hundred yards of front. At the same time Br.-General Bulfin threw out the Northamptonshire to the spur next to the eastward to protect the right flank. The two leading companies of the Sussex, finding that the fire came from trenches some three hundred yards to the 14 Sept. north of them, moved westward so as to take the defenders 1914. in flank. For a brief space there was a sharp interchange of rifle fire ; and then large numbers of Germans threw up their hands in token of surrender. Some of the Sussex rose to their feet to bring their prisoners in, upon which other Germans in rear opened fire indiscriminately upon friend and foe ; but, none the less, some three hundred of the enemy were captured and sent to the rear.[1] Continuing the fight, the left half-company of the Sussex succeeded in overlapping the western flank of the Germans, who, astride the road from Troyon north-west to the sugar factory, were opposing the progress of the K.R.R.C. The British marksmanship was so accurate that here also numbers of Germans threw up their hands. Thereupon, two German batteries, entrenched east of the factory, opened fire upon their unhappy comrades, who, between German shells from the east and British bullets from the south and west, were quickly exterminated. Teams then appeared near the two batteries, but in a very short time every driver, horse and gunner was shot down by British rifles, and the twelve guns remained silent and derelict upon the plateau.[2]

It was now nearly 7 A.M. The head of the 1st (Guards) Brigade had reached Vendresse, where Br.-General Maxse decided to advance and prolong the line of the 2nd Brigade to the left. The 3rd Brigade was in reserve on the right rear of the 2nd at Moulins, less the Queen's, which was on its way further east to the plateau of Paissy (2 miles east of Vendresse) to act as right flank guard and escort to the portion of the divisional artillery in readiness there. The 1st and 4th Cavalry Brigades were in observation near Paissy itself and the 2nd Cavalry Brigade in the neighbourhood of Vendresse, to which position it had fallen back after General Bulfin's force had passed through it. The 2nd Division was not ready to move, the 6th Brigade having not yet finished the passage of the Aisne. The two batteries also assigned to Br.-General Bulfin's force had not yet joined him, nor was there the slightest prospect in the fog which prevailed that they could find a target when they did arrive.

After 7 A.M. the fusillade upon the Chemin des Dames

[1] Principally men of the *16th Reserve Regiment* (*VII. Reserve Corps*) and *78th Regiment* (*X. Corps*).
[2] Zwehl, p. 73, says only one battery (*1st* of the *Reserve F.A. Regiment No. 14* on the left of the *Abteilung*).

ridge increased, and by 8 A.M. Major-General Lomax (1st Division) was satisfied that a strong German attack was developing upon the front of his 2nd Brigade, and despatched a message to the Cavalry Division at Paissy asking that his right flank should be protected. Between 8 and 9 A.M. the combat rapidly became more intense. The 1st (Guards) Brigade, led by the 1/Coldstream, was approaching the left of the 2nd Brigade, but General Lomax sent orders to Br.-General Bulfin not to push on after he had secured the high ground. Meanwhile the Loyal North Lancashire were sent up by Br.-General Bulfin from brigade reserve to support the K.R.R.C. and the Sussex in the attack upon the Troyon factory ; all three battalions then advanced, and successfully occupied the buildings and entrenched on the flat top of the ridge beyond. They had actually passed through the two abandoned batteries ; but, though they clung to the position which they had taken up, and the Northamptonshire worked forward on their right, they were unable to make further headway against the enemy, entrenched with field guns and machine guns north and east of the factory. He, on his side, made repeated counter-attacks, which were steadily repulsed. During the whole day the fight surged to and fro across some three hundred yards of ground, the fresh units which arrived as reinforcements being thrust in where they seemed most required.

Meanwhile the 1/Coldstream was struggling through a large and thick patch of wood in the Vendresse valley and up the very steep hillside which led to the top of the ridge. On reaching it, their commanding officer, Lieut.-Colonel J. Ponsonby, learnt that the Cameron Highlanders [1] and the Black Watch had discovered an easier road and were already in position. There was, however, still a space left for his battalion between them and the left of the 2nd Brigade. He accordingly deployed it and led it forward as far as the actual roadway of the Chemin des Dames, along which he aligned his men. The road for most of its length ran level with the ground and had neither bank nor ditch, but at this point was about two feet below the general surface, and afforded a little cover ; but the German artillery fire was very heavy and the Coldstream suffered severely. Finally, Colonel Ponsonby collected the equivalent of about a company and led them forward to the village of Cerny ($\frac{3}{4}$ mile

---

[1] The 1/Cameron Highlanders had taken the place of the 2/Royal Munster Fusiliers in the 1st (Guards) Brigade.

north of Troyon) on the far side of the ridge, and beyond it, 14 Sept. penetrating far into the German position. So obscure was 1014. the whole situation, owing to the fog, that at first he mistook the Germans all round him for British, while they on their part mistook the Coldstream for their own men. The Coldstream, however, were the first to realize the truth, and under their fire the enemy near them speedily disappeared. The rest of the battalion worked its way further to the east and formed on the right of the K.R.R.C., prolonging its line to the east. Still further eastwards, the Queen's, nominally the right flank guard, also crossed the Chemin des Dames, but met with no serious resistance till it reached the northern slope by La Bovelle Farm ($\frac{1}{2}$ mile north-east of Cerny). Here the battalion took up a position and engaged the German reserves in the valley of the Ailette north of it, turning its machine gun upon the flank of any German troops who chanced to pass across its front, and inflicting considerable damage. Actually, therefore, there were two separate points, a mile apart, at which the German line had been pierced with no great trouble or loss, and five companies in all of British infantry were looking down into the valley of the Ailette.

Owing to the fog, however, the confusion on the ridge was remarkable even for a modern battlefield. The Germans unfortunately enjoyed the advantage of having their guns in position and, indifferent whether they hit friend or foe, maintained a heavy fire, which caused the British considerable loss. The British batteries, on the other hand, took some time to reach their position on the plateau of Paissy, and when they arrived there did not immediately open fire, fearing to do more harm than good. Before 11 A.M., however, the 54th and 114th Batteries did signal service for the 2nd Brigade ; and the 116th, coming boldly into the firing line east of Troyon, fought alongside the infantry. Nevertheless, the general situation was unpleasant, and, for reasons which will be given later, there was no sign of the 2nd Division coming up on the left of the 1st.

Meantime the 3rd Brigade had been despatched by the divisional commander to reinforce the left of the 1st (Guards) Brigade, and it had reached its position when, about 10.30 A.M., a counter-attack of three German battalions (*25th Reserve Brigade*) south-eastwards towards Vendresse began to make itself felt. Fortunately at this time the fog lifted, so the 46th and 113th Batteries, unlimbering near

Moussy, south-west of Vendresse, opened fire on this force with deadly effect. By this and flanking fire from the 5th Brigade the advance of the Germans was checked, whereupon the 2/Welch Regiment and 1/South Wales Borderers delivered an attack upon them towards the north-west. The progress of the Borderers was much impeded by dense woods, but the Welch, having clear ground before them, pressed their assault with great determination and, carrying all before them, established themselves firmly on the south-eastern slopes of the Beaulne spur.

It was now about 1 P.M. The Welch were in the position above described, and the South Wales Borderers in rear of them, between Chivy and Beaulne. They had done their work well ; but they had hardly completed it before the Germans launched a counter-attack [1] against the entire front of the 2nd and 1st (Guards) Brigades. The first onslaught fell on the British right, and it drove the 2nd Brigade from the sugar factory and back through the two derelict German batteries to the position which it had held earlier in the day. The ground thus regained by the enemy was of no great depth, but it was sufficient to expose the right flank of the Cameron Highlanders (1st Brigade), upon whom the Germans turned a devastating machine-gun fire.

This battalion had in the morning formed for attack under cover of the wood by the head of the Chivy valley, which runs down from the Chemin des Dames to Chivy, a little to the west of Troyon. It came under rifle fire before it was clear of the trees, and on emerging into the open was immediately checked by a storm of shells from its front and left, and by enfilade fire of machine guns from the right. The right company, which came up first, was shattered almost immediately, but the remaining companies came on in succession and maintained the attack. A company of the 1/Black Watch was pushed up on the right of the Camerons and part of the 1/Scots Guards [2] on their left ; the whole, pressing steadily on, charged the German trenches on the plateau above them, and carried them in an irresistible rush. Then, attacked in flank and riddled through and through, with more than half of the men down and with ammunition failing, the Highlanders gradually dribbled back into the Chivy valley, whence they had

[1] For the German forces engaged against the 1st Division see Note at end of Chapter. In infantry they amounted to about twelve battalions.
[2] Two companies were absent as escort to artillery.

started.   A last party of fifty Camerons, under Major Hon. 14 Sept.
A. H. Maitland, clung to the ground which they had won, 1014.
until their ammunition was almost exhausted ; then they
fell back fifty yards behind the crest of the ridge.   There
they were attacked by masses of the enemy, five and six
deep, and, after beating back the first onset, during which
their commander was killed, were finally overwhelmed by
sheer numbers.

Two companies of the 1/Gloucestershire, the reserve
of the 3rd Brigade (the rest of the battalion being divisional reserve), were sent forward to cover the retirement
of the Camerons and of such of the Black Watch as were
with them, and the Highlanders were delivered from their
pursuers.   The troops between them and Troyon gradually conformed to the new front, facing north-west.   The
Queen's were still at La Bovelle, and Colonel Ponsonby's
party of the 1/Coldstream was still north of Cerny, these
forming, as it were, advanced posts in front of the right
and right centre of the British line.   The whole of the
infantry of the 1st Division except the two companies in
divisional reserve had been put into the fight.   The situation remained practically unchanged for the next two hours,
during which the Germans continued to make counter-
attacks at various points along the whole length of the line
—attacks which grew weaker and weaker after each repulse,
until by 3 P.M. they had practically died away.

Leaving the 1st Division we will now turn to the Sketch 19.
2nd Division on its immediate left.   Map 35.

The orders issued by Major-General Monro were to
continue the pursuit.   The 6th Brigade, with the XXXIV.
Brigade R.F.A. and 5th Field Company R.E., was to form
the new advanced guard under Br.-General Davies and
begin the passage of the Aisne by the pontoon bridge at
Pont Arcy at 5 A.M.   Having crossed the river under protection of the 5th Brigade in position on the line Verneuil—
Moussy—Soupir, the 6th was to advance northwards
through the 5th, and halt on the Chemin des Dames ridge
and wait for further instructions.   The 5th Brigade was
then to close and follow.   The 4th (Guards) Brigade,
with the XXXVI. Brigade R.F.A., under Lieut.-Colonel
E. F. Hall, crossing by the same bridge at 6.30 A.M. (actually, as will be seen, the bridge was not clear for it until
about 8.30 A.M.), was to turn north-westward through
Soupir and La Cour de Soupir (a farm about one mile

north by west of Soupir) and secure the summit of the
Soupir spur (marked by the figure 197, a point known as
La Croix sans Tête), about a mile further north. The rest
of the division, including two brigades of artillery, was to
follow the Guards, except the heavy battery, which was to
cross the river at Bourg and join the column north of the
river ; actually one of the brigades, the XLIV. (Howitzer),
also crossed at Bourg.

The leading battalion of the 6th Brigade began its
crossing punctually at the named hour ; but though not
molested by the enemy, the march of the troops over
the narrow floating bridge was slow ; it was 8 A.M. before
the entire brigade, with its attached guns, was assembled on
the north bank. The 1/R. Berkshire, with two companies
of the 1/K.R.R.C. thrown out upon the hills on either hand
as flank guards, and preceded by two troops of the 15th
Hussars, was then pushed north-north-west towards Braye,
up the long valley in which lies the Oise and Aisne canal.
This canal valley breaks into the main ridge so deeply
that Braye, which stands at the head of its western fork,
is hardly half a mile from the Chemin des Dames. On
the sides of spurs which jut out on the eastern side of this
valley are the villages of Verneuil and Moussy.

Shortly after 9 A.M., on reaching a line east and west
of La Maison Brûlée (about half-way between Moussy and
Braye), the Berkshire were checked by heavy shell and
rifle fire, from the high ground north of the latter village ;
there was some delay whilst the King's were brought
forward and extended to the right of the Berkshire, between them and their right flank guard. The batteries
which had crossed the Aisne at Bourg were also retarded
by a steady rain of German shells upon the road leading
northward from Bourg to Courtonne. However, at 10
A.M. the 50th and 70th Batteries of the XXXIV. Brigade
R.F.A. came into action on the southern slopes of the
Moussy spur ; and at 10.30 A.M. the 6th Brigade opened
its attack. Two companies of the 1/K.R.R.C., moving
along the summit of the Moussy spur, formed the right.
On their left, the King's entered the woods which clothe
the western slope of the spur on the eastern side of the Oise
canal ; and the Berkshire advanced on the lower ground
west of the King's, their left flank being guarded by
the two remaining companies of the K.R.R.C. on the subsidiary spur of La Bovette, immediately to the north of
Soupir village.

2ND DIVISION403

The attack appears to have been launched prematurely, 14 Sept. before the troops on Moussy spur had had time to reach their 1914. places in the line. In any case, it is certain that, whether from accident or design, the Berkshire outstripped the King's, and that the King's outstripped the two companies of the K.R.R.C. on their right. The Berkshire made their way successfully to the foot of the spur which juts southward from the Chemin des Dames just north-east of Braye village, and by noon had two companies in action on its lower slopes. But they could advance no further, finding their progress barred by fire from tiers of trenches in their front and from both flanks. The King's, though under heavy fire from howitzers, field guns and rifles, likewise advanced nearly to the foot of the main ridge of the Chemin des Dames, where they, too, were brought to a stand by fire from tiers of German trenches on the steep slope before them, from their right flank and from their rear. An effort was made, with the help of the 2/Worcestershire (the head of the 5th Brigade), to clear the trenches on the right from which the enfilade fire proceeded, but without success. Still further to the east, the two companies of the 1/K.R.R.C. pushed on to a wood, where they were counter-attacked by infantry in front, and enfiladed by machine guns from a flank. They fought vigorously and inflicted heavy losses on the enemy, but were finally forced back to the top of the spur above Moussy, and the German counter-attack spread further to the west. The Berkshire and King's were pushed back abreast of Beaulne village, only half a mile from Moussy ; but the K.R.R.C., having been reinforced by the 2/Worcestershire and the Highland L.I., were able to stem the German onslaught until, by the aid of the 46th and 113th Batteries and of the 3rd Brigade which had advanced on their right, as already described, they finally repulsed the enemy with very heavy loss.

Although the 2/Grenadiers, the leading battalion of the 4th (Guards) Brigade, which was to prolong the left of the 6th Brigade, commenced to cross the pontoon bridge at 8.30 A.M., the Irish Guards, who were the last battalion, were not all across, according to their diary, until 10 A.M. The Connaught Rangers were on the extreme left of the 5th Brigade covering line, and had taken up a position on the previous night on the outskirts of Soupir, facing north and west. Their commanding officer, Major W. S. Sarsfield, on hearing at 1 A.M. that the 4th

(Guards) Brigade was going to advance via Soupir, rightly appreciated that he would greatly assist the Guards by making good the high ground near La Cour de Soupir, instead of remaining down in the valley where he was; so he decided to move. Reaching the farm with three companies at 5.30 A.M., he pushed out small posts and ascertained that the spur above was clear of the enemy as far as Point 197. On reporting his action to the 5th Brigade headquarters, he was informed by a message which reached him about 9.45 A.M. that it would be some time before the 4th (Guards) Brigade could arrive, and that until the brigade came up and securely occupied the high ground about Point 197, he was not to leave his position. Almost at the same moment a platoon of the 2/Grenadier Guards, the point of the 4th (Guards) Brigade advanced guard formed by that battalion, arrived at La Cour de Soupir, unaware, like the rest of the brigade, that the Connaught Rangers were ahead of it. Rain was now falling, and whilst the officers were discussing the situation in the courtyard of the farm, violent rifle fire was heard a thousand yards away to the left, and immediately afterwards a N.C.O. ran in from one of the Connaught posts and reported the advance of German infantry in force. The three companies of the Connaught Rangers were at once deployed east and west of La Cour de Soupir; the detachment of the 1/K.R.R.C. was not yet in position on the crest of La Bovette, to their right. The enemy, covered by the fire of his artillery, attacked in large masses over the open, at the same time sending troops into the wood about La Bovette, to turn the flank of the Connaught Rangers. In the centre and on the left the British held their own, the whole of the 2/Grenadier Guards (Major G. Jeffreys) having been engaged as the companies came up on the left flank of the Connaught Rangers. But in the woods on the right the enemy steadily gained ground, and after an hour's sharp fighting he had advanced to within one hundred yards of La Cour de Soupir. The leading battalion of the main body of the 4th (Guards) Brigade, the 3/Coldstream (Major T. G. Matheson) was now beginning to arrive; it had suffered from shell fire after leaving Soupir, and in consequence had been ordered to leave the road. Engaging three companies on the right of the 2/Grenadier Guards, it brought the enemy advance to a halt. Arrangements were then made for the 2/Grenadier Guards and 3/Coldstream to

resume the advance and secure the high ground near
Point 197 . the 1/Irish Guards (Major H. Stepney), which
had now arrived on the scene and was clearing the woods
on the right, was to join in. About 12 noon the movement was got under way, and the first result was that about
two hundred Germans in a root field to the north of the
farm immediately stood up with their hands above their
heads. In the enthusiasm of the moment a number of
Guardsmen, with the limited outlook of the local situation, rushed forward to receive the surrender, and the
Irish Guards, hearing the cheering, began to leave the
edge of the woods. At this moment other German troops,
advancing over the sky-line about half a mile away, opened
fire on both friend and foe. Under the German artillery
and rifle fire which ensued everyone lay down where he
was. Realizing that it was impossible to restart the
attack with the same companies, Major Matheson, the
whereabouts of brigade headquarters being unknown,
left Major Jeffreys in charge, and made his way to the
Irish Guards. He arranged with Major Stepney to attack
from the wood and thus outflank the Germans, when the
Grenadiers, Coldstream and Connaught Rangers would co-
operate as opportunity offered. About 2 P.M. the movement was initiated by the Irish Guards ; but it was soon
checked by heavy rifle fire down the rides and from a
field a hundred yards from the edge of the wood. It
caused, however, considerable commotion amongst the
Germans on the ridge in front of the farm, of which the
British took advantage to inflict heavy casualties. The
1/K.R.R.C. was by this time making its presence felt
about La Bovette, and the rest of the 4th (Guards)
Brigade was rapidly coming up. Thus, by about 2 P.M.,
the 2nd Division, though unable as yet to advance very
far, was in firm possession of a line running, roughly
speaking, from Beaulne westward to La Cour de Soupir,
and thence south-west along the eastern edge of the top of
the spur towards Chavonne.[1]

To sum up the situation on the I. Corps front between
2 and 3 P.M. :—The corps was successfully holding a line
roughly facing north-west from the plateau of the Chemin
des Dames opposite La Bovelle, through Troyon, Chivy
and Beaulne, to La Cour de Soupir, and thence south-
westward to the river ; it had made appreciable headway

---

[1] The opponents of the 2nd Division were the right half of the *13th
Reserve Division* and part of the *6th Division*.

and repulsed all counter-attacks with heavy loss to the
enemy. The 1st Division batteries on the plateau of Paissy
on the right had come into action when the fog lifted at
noon, and divided their fire between the Germans who were
retiring in disorder over the Chemin des Dames and those
who were assembling for a fresh attack about Chermizy
(about three miles N.N.W. of Paissy) in the valley of the
Ailette.

Sketch 19. In the centre and on the left of the British front the
Map 35. situation was less satisfactory, and there was a gap of very
nearly two miles between the left of the I. Corps and the
right of the II. Of the 3rd Division, the 8th and 9th
Brigades were, it will be remembered, already on the north
bank of the Aisne, their line of outposts extending from a
farm called Rouge Maison (1 mile north-east of Vailly)
south-west for about a mile and a half to the southern
slopes of the Jouy spur, which runs down to the Aisne
between the villages of Jouy on the east and Sancy on the
west. The 9th Brigade held the right of this line and the
8th the left. All had orders to continue the pursuit on
the 14th. At dawn the Royal Scots, of the latter brigade,
advancing to take up a position on the crest of Jouy spur,
came under fire at close range, the German trenches being
just on the other side of the crest of the ridge. The Royal
Irish came up on their right, and the 4/Middlesex on their
left ; then the three battalions, only some fifteen hundred
strong, slowly made their way almost to the crest. The
British batteries on the south bank did their best to support them ; but the XL. Brigade R.F.A., which had crossed
the river at Vailly soon after daylight, could find no position
from which it could come into action.

For some hours the 8th Brigade clung to the ground
which it had gained ; meanwhile, about 7.30 A.M., the
enemy opened an attack, covered by the fire of artillery
and machine guns, on the Lincolnshire and Royal Fusiliers
of the 9th Brigade, to the right and left of Rouge Maison.
The German trenches, which had been concealed from the
Royal Fusiliers by the fog, were in fact less than six hundred yards away, and only two hundred yards beyond the
crest of the ridge. The Northumberland Fusiliers were
sent up to the left of the Royal Fusiliers, and the three
battalions were ordered to meet the German offensive
by a counter-attack. A successful advance here was particularly desirable, inasmuch as the Germans had placed

batteries on the flanks of the two valleys which run down to the Aisne east and west of Vailly, and were bursting shells very accurately over the pontoon bridge by that village.

Whilst the 9th Brigade was slowly forcing its way through the dripping woods against a driving mist, about 9 A.M., the Germans delivered a heavy counter-attack upon the 8th Brigade on Jouy spur, supporting it by machine-gun fire from the west ; after suffering severely, the brigade, about 10 A.M., began to fall back. Urgent messages were despatched to the 7th Brigade from 3rd Division head-quarters to come up in support ; but its commander, on nearing the pontoon bridge at Vailly, found the shell fire so heavy that he turned the head of the brigade further up-stream to the damaged railway bridge, the breach in which was traversable only by a single plank. Before, however, the brigade could pass it, British soldiers were filing back over the narrow passage towards the southern bank. The 9th Brigade, upon emerging from the woods, had been received with a murderous fire from artillery and machine guns, and after enduring it for a while and attempting to entrench, the right battalion, the Lincolnshire, had given way, and the rest of the brigade had fallen back. The Royal Fusiliers, their flank being uncovered by the retire-ment of the Lincolnshire, had been compelled to withdraw to a sunken road just south of Rouge Maison. The Fifth Fusiliers, whose leading company had advanced too far into the open whilst the remainder were still entangled in the woods, had been very severely handled, but rallied on the Royal Fusiliers. The Scots Fusiliers, the reserve of the brigade, had already been thrown into the fight, half of them on the right and half on the left, and the former, being enfiladed by machine guns while toiling over heavy beetroot fields waist deep in dripping leaves, had been driven back with heavy losses.

The situation was critical ; for owing to the gap between the I. and II. Corps, the right flank of the 9th Brigade was absolutely exposed ; had the Germans followed up their advantage the consequences might have been serious. The western side of the Soupir spur, the valley of the Ostel west of it, and the spur between that valley and St. Précord—a space fully a mile and a half wide—was open to them. The British gunners to the south of the Aisne were cut off from the battlefield by the mist. If the Germans could have advanced in force they would probably have outflanked and thus overwhelmed the 4th (Guards)

Brigade to the east, and the 8th and 9th Brigades to the west of the gap, and cut the British Army in two. There were, it is true, two regiments of the 5th Cavalry Brigade in Vailly ; they had crossed the pontoon bridge in the early morning, but the fog had lifted for a time while the third regiment, the 20th Hussars, was filing over, and it had been ordered to re-cross at once to the south bank. The Scots Greys and 12th Lancers, who remained in Vailly, were under heavy and continuous shell fire. Their five or six hundred rifles might have delayed, but could hardly have averted a catastrophe.

However, whether from dread of the British guns on the heights of Chassemy, which were searching for the concealed German batteries across the river, or from the effects of his own heavy losses, the enemy made no immediate offensive movement. By 1 P.M. the 1/Wiltshire of the 7th Brigade had crossed the Aisne by the railway bridge, deployed with its right on the Vailly—Ostel road, and now, though heavily shelled on the way, hastened to the assistance of the 9th Brigade on the spur to the east of St. Précord. Thus reinforced, the latter brigade stood fast. At 3.30 P.M., the Irish Rifles of the 7th Brigade came up on the left of the Wiltshire, bringing the intelligence that a strong German column was moving south-eastward from Ostel. Warning of this movement was at once sent to the 4th (Guards) Brigade. The remainder of the 7th Brigade continued to pass the river ; whilst the 8th Brigade fell back to the south of Jouy spur, with its right on the road that leads from Vailly to Aizy, and its left west of the chateau of Vauxelles ($\frac{3}{4}$ mile north-west of Vailly).

The 3rd Division, thus compactly drawn together, held its own without difficulty until dusk, and at 5.30 P.M. General Hamilton declared himself confident of his ability to maintain his position on the north bank of the Aisne. Nevertheless, the casualties had been serious : the 9th Brigade had lost between six and seven hundred men, and the 7th and 8th Brigades about one hundred and fifty each, losses which would not have been felt so much had not the battalions been already below establishment.

As a result of the improvement in the situation, the 5th Cavalry Brigade and the XL. Brigade R.F.A. were ordered back. The former re-crossed the pontoon bridge under heavy shell fire in single file at increased distance, a troop at a time, the passage of the bridge being kept open and controlled with the greatest coolness by Captain T. Wright,

V.C., with the assistance of a party of the 57th Field 14 Sept. Company R.E. The cavalry escaped with some forty men 1914. and half a dozen horses wounded ; but Captain Wright was killed. The three batteries, being unable to re-cross the river at Vailly, drove 5 miles up the valley to Pont Arcy, coming under fire at various points on the way, and especially at the bridge itself. Their losses were fortunately slight ; but the orderliness of their retreat, as also of that of the 5th Cavalry Brigade, under such conditions, spoke highly for their discipline.

It is now time to turn to the 5th and 4th Divisions on Sketch 19. the left of the line. Their operations, though nominally Map 35. in combination with the divisions on the right, were, as it turned out, practically distinct, owing to the barrier interposed by the promontory of Chivres. The 5th Division continued the passage of the river during the night of the 13th/14th by improvised methods, for Missy bridge was not ready and still required many hours' work before it would be serviceable. The 14th Brigade, it will be remembered, had crossed to Ste. Marguerite on the 13th September. The 15th Brigade was ferried over on rafts during the same night at Moulin des Roches (1 mile east of Venizel) and reached Ste. Marguerite by 6 A.M. on the 14th. The R. West Kent and Scottish Borderers of the 13th Brigade—the other two battalions remaining south of the river—likewise passed the river under cover of darkness, by means of rafts and boats, near the wrecked bridge of Missy, but their further advance was then stopped by fire, and they took such cover as they could find on the north bank. Ferrying was continued under fire all day until 7 P.M. by Captain W. H. Johnston and Lieut. R. B. Flint of the Royal Engineers, carrying wounded one way and ammunition the other.[1]

The operation orders of the 5th Division for the 14th September, in accordance with higher instructions, directed the continuation of the pursuit : the 15th Brigade, with the VIII. Brigade R.F.A., to march via Celles (near Condé) and thence some fifteen miles northwards to Cessières (6 miles west of Laon) ; the 14th and 13th Brigades, with the rest of the divisional troops, via Missy to Suzy (8 miles west of Laon).

It early became evident that these orders could not be

[1] The former officer received the V.C. and the latter the D.S.O. Both officers were killed in action later in the war.

carried out so long as Chivres spur remained in the hands of the enemy. This, the highest ground on the field, with the old fort of Condé on its summit, commands the valley on both sides of it for a considerable distance. It was therefore arranged that the left of the 14th Brigade, with two battalions of the 13th on its right, should attack eastward from the direction of Ste. Marguerite (which village was held by the 12th Brigade), and its right should be thrown forward so as to threaten the spur from the south. The 15th Brigade was to make its way through Missy as soon as the right of the 14th Brigade had cleared the village, and attack the spur from the south-east. The XV. Brigade R.F.A. (reduced by previous losses to two batteries of four guns apiece), together with the 37th and 61st Howitzer Batteries, was brought over the Aisne to the vicinity of Bucy le Long to support the attack.

The 14th Brigade started early, but the Germans began to burst shells in the valley near Missy, as soon as it was light. The progress of the operations was very slow. The Manchester, on the left of the 14th Brigade, were checked by enfilade fire of artillery and machine guns from the village of Chivres and the valley above it. The battalion had, in fact, got within three hundred yards of the German trenches, but once there, could do no more than hold its own. The Cornwall L.I., in the centre, and the East Surrey, on the right, however, worked their way round to Missy, very slowly, for the road from Ste. Marguerite was under artillery, rifle and machine-gun fire; by noon the East Surrey were established on the northern edge of Missy village. Thence they threw out a company to feel for the West Kent and Scottish Borderers (13th Brigade) on their right. The 15th Brigade had meanwhile also moved from Ste. Marguerite, leaving the Dorsetshire in a sunken road north of the village. At 2.30 P.M. its head arrived at Missy, and the officer commanding the Bedfordshire at once pushed a company, in co-operation with one of the East Surrey, a considerable way up the wooded spur beyond the village, where they found only a few Germans and established themselves. As Ste. Marguerite was being heavily shelled, the remainder of the brigade was unable to reach Missy until more than an hour later; it was 4.30 P.M. before the dispositions were completed for a final effort by the 14th and 15th Brigades to secure the crest of the spur.

The left centre of the 14th Brigade, having been absolutely stopped by the frontal fire from the enemy's

trenches on the western side of the spur and by the flanking
fire from the Chivres valley, the new attack was made up
the spur from the south. Ten companies (including the
two already on the spur)—three from the Norfolk, four
from the Bedfordshire, of the 15th Brigade, and three from
the East Surrey of the 14th Brigade, with supports from
the Cheshire and Cornwall L.I.—were detailed for it. As
they advanced northwards up the hill, the woods were
found to be held by the enemy with an organized system
of trenches protected by wire netting and fencing.[1] The
companies of Bedfordshire and East Surrey, on the left,
were the first to enter the woods ; they pressed on steadily,
shooting down a good many Germans and making headway
by sheer superiority of marksmanship. In fact, on the
left of the attack all seemed to be going well.

But on the right it was otherwise. Whether, in view
of the failing light, insufficient time had been allowed
for the various units to reach their several starting points,
or because the wire netting in the woods caused them to
converge, it is difficult to say—it is only certain that, in
spite of all precautions, some companies lost direction, and
that the right tended to close in on the centre, where the
overcrowding and confusion became so great that few
could tell in which direction they should fire, whilst both
British and German guns shelled the woods. The inevitable
result soon followed. Confused advance gave place to confused retirement. Br.-General Count Gleichen, the senior
officer on the spot, therefore decided to abandon the attack,
called back his battalions and broke off the fight.

Three companies of the East Surrey and a company
of the Bedfordshire, however, still stuck to the ground
which they had gained within seventy yards of the German
trenches. They were still striving to push forward when,
between 6 and 7 P.M., they received orders to fall back.
The 15th Brigade was then re-formed south of Missy, and a
line was taken up by the 14th Brigade and entrenched, starting from the left, from the eastern end of Ste. Marguerite,
across the mouth of the Chivres valley to Missy village ;
thence the West Kent and Scottish Borderers of the 13th
Brigade prolonged it to Missy bridge. The casualties had
not been heavy, but the loss of a total of one hundred men
was a serious thing to these already depleted battalions.[2]

[1] According to Bloem, his regiment reached Chivres spur on the 12th
September ; so there had been plenty of time to entrench.
[2] See page 413, f.n. 1, for the German forces opposite the 5th Division.

West of the 5th Division, the 4th had received orders to push on northward over the plateau between Vregny and Crouy, with the double object of dislodging the German heavy guns, which from Clamecy (2 miles north of Crouy) were stopping the advance of General Maunoury's right, and of helping forward the advance of the 5th Division. By 1 A.M. on the 14th, the 10th Brigade had completed its passage of the river, and an hour later it was sent up to reinforce the 11th Brigade which, secure by its own boldness, was still occupying the line of heights from Ste. Marguerite to Crouy, a front of 3 miles. The 12th Brigade held a line on the right of the 11th. Its right was thrown back into the Chivres valley, the right flank resting on the stream about five hundred yards south of Chivres village, which was the point of junction of the 5th and 4th Divisions. From here the line ran west-north-west over the valley to the northern edge of Ste. Marguerite spur, at a point immediately south of Vregny, and thence to the crest of the hill between Le Moncel and Ste. Marguerite. The 39th and 68th Batteries, with a section of the 88th, were in the open a little to north-east of Venizel—a position exposed to the fire of the German guns on Chivres spur, but the best which could be found. The 31st and 55th Howitzer Batteries also crossed the river about dawn and, in order to facilitate the advance of the French, moved to a position a hundred yards north-west of La Montagne Farm (north-east of Bucy le Long), and opened fire on German guns which were on the ridge about thirteen hundred yards north-west of Crouy.

The difficulty of giving any artillery support to a direct attack by the 4th Division was so great that Br.-General Wilson, the divisional commander, hesitated to commit himself to such an operation unless the 5th Division on his right or the French on his left should make a decided forward movement. The right of the French Sixth Army could neither force its way beyond Crouy nor establish itself on the plateau north of Pommiers (2 miles west of Soissons). The French had no heavy artillery comparable with that of the Germans, and immediately east and west of Soissons the heights on the north bank of the Aisne are, at the nearest point, over five thousand yards distant from those on the south bank. The 5th Division, for reasons already explained, was progressing very slowly. So far as infantry was concerned the numbers facing the British 4th and 5th

Divisions did not appear to be very great, though as a 14 Sept.
matter of fact the whole of the German *II. Corps* and parts 1914.
of the *III.* and *IX.* were opposite to them ; [1] but all
approaches to the enemy's position, which was entrenched
and of considerable natural strength, were swept by artillery,
in great force, and by machine guns.

At daylight intermittent fire was opened on the line
of the 4th Division and on its batteries ; work upon the
trenches of the 10th Brigade could only be carried on at
intervals, so that the shelter obtained by the battalions
was, in many cases, inadequate, and among the killed
was Lt.-Col. Sir E. Bradford commanding the 2/Seaforth
Highlanders. At noon the fire increased so greatly that
a German attack on the spur of La Montagne (west of Le
Moncel) was apprehended, and a company of the Dublins
was sent forward to make a counter-attack. This company advanced for half a mile, engaged hostile infantry
in a beetroot field at four hundred yards' range, and by
sheer marksmanship silenced its fire. This practically
ended the active work of the 4th Division for the day.
The casualties were slight for the most part ; but the 10th
Brigade lost one hundred officers and men, chiefly owing
to the fact that they had not had time to dig themselves
really good trenches.

The close of the I. Corps operations on the 14th Sep- Sketch 19.
tember can now be told shortly. News of the repulse
of the 3rd Division reached General Haig about 2 P.M. ;
the serious menace which it meant to the left flank of
the 2nd Division was instantly realized. Not a single battalion was available in corps or divisional reserve, every
one having been thrown into the fight ; but the 1st and
2nd Cavalry Brigades were at once despatched to the
left, near Soupir. After an interview with Br.-General
Perceval, R.A., who had taken over command of the 4th
(Guards) Brigade column and was at Soupir, Br.-General
Briggs pushed the 1st Cavalry Brigade on to Chavonne,
where it arrived about 3.30 P.M. Finding two companies
of the 2/Coldstream (Lieut.-Colonel C. Pereira)—the last
battalion of the 4th (Guards) Brigade, which had been
sent up from Soupir in view of the emergency—holding
the village, he forthwith sent one cavalry regiment to

---

[1] *II. Corps* held Vregny—Crouy, with the *5th Division* of the *III.
Corps* east of it, on Chivres spur. Then came Kraewel's *Composite Brigade*
of the *IX. Corps*, and next the *6th Division*, extending to Vailly, inclusive.

occupy a commanding bluff west of Chavonne and the small wood beyond, with a troop to connect it with the 3rd Division. About the same time, various reports were received tending to show that the enemy was retreating, and Major-General Monro (2nd Division) ordered the general advance on the main ridge to be resumed in the direction of Courtecon, the original objective. The commander of the 4th (Guards) Brigade thereupon ordered the 2/Grenadiers and the troops south-west of La Cour de Soupir [1] to advance and swing round, pivoting on that farm, so as to face northward. The southern edges of the foothills were so steep and the space between the river and the hills was so narrow that very few guns could be put into position north of the river. Thus the only artillery support which could be provided was a section of 18-pdrs. near Soupir, and this had speedily to be withdrawn. The right of the Irish Guards and the left of the 1/K.R.R.C., reinforced by some of the remaining platoons of the 2/Coldstream, made a little progress ; but a German counter-attack now began to develop south-eastwards from Ostel towards La Cour de Soupir, and the 2/Grenadiers and 3/Coldstream lined the road to the north of the farm, fronting north-north-west, supported by a machine gun in the farm enclosure. This position they held until dusk ; but they were unable to advance further owing to the enemy on their left flank. Ultimately the bulk of the 4th (Guards) Brigade entrenched, after the battalions had been sorted out—the right and the K.R.R.C. being drawn back into the general line—and the brigade then bivouacked where it stood. Its casualties were 21 officers and 566 other ranks killed and wounded.

The 6th Brigade on the right of the Guards fared little better ; owing to heavy shelling, it could only just hold its own, without any thought of forward movement. On its right again, Br.-General Haking (5th Brigade) with the 2/Highland Light Infantry and the 2/Worcestershire, and half the 1/K.R.R.C. of the 6th Brigade managed to advance up the eastern slopes of the Beaulne spur, and there held on. Of the two remaining battalions of the 5th Brigade, which for a time had been nominally in corps reserve, the Connaught Rangers were still with the 4th (Guards) Brigade at La Cour de Soupir, and the Oxfordshire near Soupir, where they had been sent by Sir Douglas Haig to assist in securing the left of his corps.

[1] See page 405.

On the extreme right, the situation towards evening 14 Sept. had sensibly improved. The French XVIII. Corps had 1014. begun the day badly, for by 10 A.M. it had been severely handled, and had been driven from Craonne and Craonnelle. The French Colonial Division, immediately on the right of the British, had likewise at the outset suffered a repulse ; but now the XVIII. Corps was once more in possession of Craonne, and the ridge immediately to the west of it ; and the Colonial Division was again advancing over the plateau of Paissy upon Les Creutes (2½ miles south-east of Cerny). The enemy was showing signs of hesitation, and Sir Douglas Haig felt that the time was come for a general forward movement of the I. Corps, and issued orders for it. The commander of the 2nd Division had, as we have seen, anticipated this ; in the 1st Division there had been no change in the general disposition since last described, except that Lieut.-Colonel D. Warren of the Queen's, after sharp fighting at La Bovelle, had skilfully extricated his battalion from its dangerously advanced position, and brought it back at 4.30 P.M. to the foremost of the British guns on the Chemin des Dames. The light was failing fast before the 1st Division was under way, and the Troyon factory had, after heavy bombardment, just been re-occupied by the Germans, who, under cover of a counter-attack, had carried off their abandoned guns. The 3rd Brigade pushed forward between the 2nd and 5th Brigades, and carried the line to within three hundred yards of the Chemin des Dames, the Welch capturing a hundred prisoners and a machine gun. Mistaking the Germans in the factory for British, the 3rd Brigade missed its chance of recapturing that building. Br.-General Haking, when it became dusk, continued his advance over heaps of German bodies to the top of the main ridge opposite Courtecon. The 3rd and 5th Brigades, however, were never really in touch, and, in fact, Br.-General Haking, after sending out patrols, found only the enemy on either side. Judging it imprudent to remain in his forward position he withdrew his two and a half battalions after dark to Verneuil and Moussy. The 3rd Brigade was left on the ground which it had so honour-ably won ; but, on the whole, though a final effort was fully justified, no solid advantage had been gained by it. With a few fresh battalions to put life into the fight, the results might have been widely different. Colonel Ponsonby's small party remained out in its advanced position at Cerny, with Germans all round it, until nearly midnight.

Then, in pitch darkness and heavy rain, carrying the colonel, who was wounded, the forty odd survivors, guided by an officer with a compass, made their way back into the British lines.

Sketch 19.
Map 35.
On the whole, the results of the 14th September were disappointing. The I. Corps had certainly made some progress, but at heavy cost ; for its casualties amounted to three thousand five hundred. In the 1st (Guards), 2nd and 4th (Guards) Brigades, the 1/Cameron Highlanders lost six hundred officers and men, the 1/Coldstream, 1/Loyal North Lancashire and 2/Sussex, 2/Grenadiers and 3/Coldstream, each of them, over three hundred and fifty, and the 1/ and 2/K.R.R.C. over three hundred apiece. Amongst the killed was Lieut.-Colonel Adrian Grant-Duff commanding the 1/Black Watch, who fell whilst superintending the filling of a gap in the line.[1] On the rest of the line the British force was stationary ; though the casualties of the 4th and 5th Divisions were slight, those of the 3rd Division fell little short of a thousand. Moreover, the general situation of the British was very far from secure. Apart from the one and a half mile gap between the 2nd and 3rd Divisions, covered by battle outposts of the 1st Cavalry Brigade, the 5th and 4th Divisions, separated from the rest of the Army by the promontory of Chivres, held their position on the north bank of the Aisne on a most precarious tenure. The only link between the two sections of the force was Gough's cavalry division (3rd and 5th Cavalry Brigades), which, from a position about Chassemy, on the south bank, watched the undestroyed bridge of Condé, to guard against a German counter-attack. It was still by no means certain, after the day's experience, whether the Aisne was being defended by a strong rear guard or by an enemy in position. It may be said now that, but for the determined spirit of the British attack, Bülow, who, as already mentioned, was commanding all the German Armies defending the Aisne—the *Second, Seventh* and *First*—might have succeeded, as he expected, in sweeping the French and British across the river and securing the ground on the south bank. It would seem that here, as on other occasions in 1914, the sheer audacity of

[1] As Assistant Secretary of the Committee of Imperial Defence 1910–1913, he had designed and edited the " War Book " (see page 13) and worked out the detailed co-ordination of the action to be taken by the various Government Departments on the outbreak of war.

the British in attacking with small numbers imposed on
the enemy, and made him believe that large reserves were
behind them.   Examination of prisoners and of the dead
proved that the greater part of the German *VII. Reserve
Corps* and at least one division of the *III. Corps* [1] had
been pitted against Haig's I. Corps.   It was plain that the
British were distributed on a front far too extensive for
their strength, except in defence.   Practically every battalion was in the firing line, and there was no general
reserve whatsoever.   Two of the corps in the field required
at least another division apiece, and the third, two
divisions (for the III. Corps was still a corps in name only),
besides heavy guns, if they were to do the work assigned to
them.
      Again, there was no permanent bridge over the deep
and rain-swollen waters of the Aisne : although the engineers had displayed conspicuous energy and self-sacrifice
in the laying of temporary bridges, still these were, most
of them, exposed to fire, and always in danger, owing
to the nearly incessant rain which now fell, of being suddenly carried away by a flood.   In any case, the greater
part of the valley was open to the shells of the German
artillery.   On the left of the line it was impossible to establish any depots of supplies and stores on the north bank ;
everything required had to be brought down to the river
and across it by night.   At Missy, the most dangerous
point of all, on the night of the 14th September, the supply
wagons were brought safely to within two hundred yards
of the German trenches and as safely withdrawn ; but
frequently rations could only be brought over by hand.
The wounded could not be brought in except at night ;
the stretcher bearers, who toiled with equal courage and
devotion through the hours of darkness, had to carry disabled men for one or two miles over heavy soaked ground
before they could deliver them to a horse ambulance.
Even on the south bank trains of transport were occasionally caught by the enemy's high-explosive shells—of
greater calibre than any gun which the French or British
had available, and fired from a range which forbade any
effective reply.   All ranks, however, whether of combatant
or non-combatant branches, were confident of a further
and immediate advance.   On the enemy's side there was
corresponding depression, for on the evening of the 14th
September, as will be seen below, the Supreme Command

[1] Part of the *6th Division*.   See also page 424.

issued an order for a general retirement if the *First Army* could not hold the Aisne line.

The situation of the British troops on the night of the 14th/15th September was as follows :—

Sketch 19. I. Corps : right on the Chemin des Dames, 4 miles from the
Map 35.   Aisne ; left almost on the Aisne near Chavonne.

    1st Division : From a point on the Chemin des Dames about 1,000 yards east of Troyon factory, south-west behind the factory, over the ridge to Mont Faucon and into the valley south of Chivy, with two advanced detachments at the head of the Chivy valley.

    4th Cavalry Brigade : Paissy and Geny (south of Paissy), behind the junction of French and British armies.

    2nd Division : From the southern end of Beaulne spur, across the Braye valley to the vicinity of La Bovette, and thence, by La Cour de Soupir, to Point 166 just north of Chavonne.

    1st and 2nd Cavalry Brigades : Connecting the I. and II. Corps ; from Point 166 to the mill midway between Chavonne and Vailly.

II. Corps : in two portions, barely across the river, with a gap of $3\frac{1}{2}$ miles between them.

    3rd Division : From the mill aforesaid, north-west to Rouge Maison, thence parallel with the Aisne south-west to Vauxelles Chateau and the confluence of the stream which runs southward from Aizy.

    5th Division : From Missy westward to Ste. Marguerite. Two battalions of the 13th Brigade south of the Aisne about Sermoise (south-east of Missy).

III. Corps : on the edge of the main ridge.

    4th Division : From Ste. Marguerite north-west to La Montagne Farm, thence westward to Point 151 (east of Crouy).

    19th Brigade : South of the Aisne about Venizel.

    3rd and 5th Cavalry Brigades : on the south bank of the Aisne, Chassemy southward to Augy.

THE FRENCH ON THE 14TH SEPTEMBER

Map 4.   The 14th September marked the definite end of the advance of the Fifth Army after the battle of the Marne. The X., I. and III. Corps and the right of Valabrègue's Group of Reserve divisions remained where they were, unable to gain any ground in front of the position of Bülow's Army. Conneau's cavalry corps and the portion of Valabrègue's group which had penetrated into the wide gap in the enemy front north of the Aisne, at the threat of convergent attacks from the east and north-east, " hurriedly " re-crossed to the southern bank of the river.

The XVIII. Corps, next to the British—the troops actually 14 Sept. nearest to them being the 76th Mixed Brigade of four battalions 1914. of Zouaves and four of native African Tirailleurs—made a little progress on the left, but the right of the corps after heavy fighting was driven back, evacuating Corbeny.

" In all the area of the Fifth Army, the front now remained un- " changed for a long period."

Foch's Army, on the right of the Fifth, " after hard fighting, " made only some insignificant local progress " as the Germans settled into their line.

The Sixth Army, being in close contact with the enemy, was un- able to carry out the duty assigned to it of outflanking Kluck's right. Part of the 45th Division and the Moroccan Brigade managed to cross the Aisne at Soissons, but were not able to reach the edge of the heights beyond. Lamaze's group, still south of the Aisne, the VII. Corps and Ebener's group remained in their positions of the previous day, unable to advance. The IV. Corps, by attacking north-east- wards, endeavoured, without success, to help its neighbours : only one of its brigades (16th) crossed the Oise, and joined the 37th Division, which was advancing slowly with its right on the river, the 3rd Cavalry Division being on its outer flank. The XIII. Corps nearly completed its detraining in the Creil area. Bridoux's cavalry corps (1st and 5th Cavalry Divisions) finding nothing but stragglers in front of it, pushed on nearly to the Somme near Bray, but did not turn behind the German front. General Maunoury still hoped to envelop the German right with the 37th Division, XIII. Corps and the cavalry corps, but he was too late.

15TH SEPTEMBER : THE DEADLOCK

Operation orders for the 15th September issued from Sketch 19. G.H.Q. only contained information as to the situation,[1] but Map 35. the Commander-in-Chief, at a personal interview at his head- quarters at Fère en Tardenois with the commanders of the II. and III. Corps, and the Br.-General General Staff of the I. Corps, at 11 P.M., on the 14th, ordered all troops to entrench on the positions which they then occupied. He dwelt on the importance of concentrating the 60-pdrs. of the five divisions in turn on the heavy batteries of the enemy, and instructed the I. Corps, without committing itself in any way, to render what assistance it could to the 3rd Division (which was barely across the river) by gun fire or infantry demonstration. Sir John French was confirmed in his view of the situation by the receipt at 1.15 A.M. of the following telegram addressed by General Joffre to his Army commanders :—

" It seems as if the enemy is once more going to accept " battle, in prepared positions north of the Aisne. In con-

[1] Appendix 45.

" sequence, it is no longer a question of pursuit, but of a " methodical attack, using every means at our disposal and " consolidating each position in turn as it is gained."

There was, however, little opportunity of carrying these intentions into effect : the 15th was a day not of Allied but of German attacks ; the British could do no more than repel them, maintaining their position and inflicting severe loss on the enemy. The Royal Flying Corps rendered great assistance, for, though there were showers during the day, there was no heavy rain until night. Photographs were for the first time taken of the enemy's positions, most of his batteries were located, and considerable success was achieved in assisting the ranging of the artillery. From the few movements of troops behind the German lines little could be gathered for certain, though the reports of large empty bivouacs, of movements of trains northwards, and of troops moving into massed formation north of Pancy (north of Courtecon) [1] still seemed to indicate retirement.

The 15th, however, was by no means a day without any offensive action on the part of the British. In the 3rd Division, the 7th Brigade, discovering soon after daylight that Germans were entrenching themselves between La Fosse Marguet (1 mile north-east of Vailly) and La Rouge Maison (1¼ miles N.N.E. of Vailly), attempted with two companies of the Irish Rifles to clear them out of their trenches, which lay 200 yards north of a wood. The attack was repulsed with severe loss ; still, German attacks or demonstrations on the line of the 3rd Division were all beaten back by rifle and machine-gun fire alone, and the situation remained unchanged. Vailly bridge was in spite of considerable shelling made passable for all traffic except heavy artillery. The 3rd Division, it may be noted, was on this day strengthened by the arrival of the 1/Devonshire, which replaced the remnant of the 1/Gordon Highlanders in the 8th Brigade.

Further west a final endeavour was made by the 5th Division to gain the Chivres spur. The 14th and 15th Brigades were ordered to renew their attacks from the south-west and south over the same ground as on the previous day, whilst the 13th Brigade, including the two battalions still on the south bank, struck in simultaneously from the south-east. The 2/Duke of Wellington's was therefore brought over the river at Missy on pontoon rafts,

---

[1] Probably the *2nd Cavalry Division* moving eastwards.

losing some men by German high-explosive shell fire while
approaching and crossing the river. The Yorkshire L.I.
also suffered in the same way, but did not pass the river,
as rafts were not ready in time.   About 8 A.M. the Norfolk
of the 15th Brigade led the advance, with the Bedfordshire
in support and the remainder of the brigade in reserve, over
the same ground as on the 14th September but on a narrower
front.   It was soon discovered that the Germans had
thrown up new defences in the woods, and there was half
an hour's pause during which the British batteries searched
them.   The ground before the 15th Brigade was at best
very unfavourable, for the open country ran up into a
wooded re-entrant.   On advancing once more, the Norfolk
were stopped by a wire-netting fence six feet high, through
which there was but one entrance.   Wirecutters were to
hand, but the task of making a gap was long and tedious,
and the density of the undergrowth made a flanking attack
extremely difficult.   A few outlying Germans were shot
down by flanking parties ; but the attack made no progress and gradually came to a standstill.   In the 14th
Brigade, the Cornwall L.I. had orders to advance up the
valley in touch with the 15th Brigade, with its left on the
Missy—Vregny road ; the 2/Manchester on the western side
of the Cornwall L.I. was to advance as soon as the latter's
progress enabled it to do so.   But the Germans on the end
of the Chivres spur offered a stout resistance ; the advance
was therefore stopped, and artillery support called for.   At
11 A.M. Br.-General Rolt of the 14th Brigade was placed in
command of all troops of the 5th Division on the northern
bank of the Aisne.   Meanwhile, the 13th Brigade found it
impossible to move along the road towards Condé, which
was swept by the German artillery, and could not therefore
reach its assigned position to assail the Chivres spur from
the south-east.   Thus, the whole movement was checked.
The rear battalions of the 15th Brigade and the Cornwall
L.I. of the 14th became crowded together in Missy.   A
German aeroplane, passing over the village, took note of
this congestion, and at 10 A.M. the German artillery poured
such a storm of shells upon the houses that the battalions
were compelled for a time to evacuate the village.   Gradually they returned to their original places in front of it,
always under harassing fire from German snipers at the edge
of the wood ; but there they remained until dark.   It was
then found that there were far too many men crowded together in the small space, and the 15th Brigade was ordered

to re-cross to the south bank of the river, where a temporary bridge was now available. Between 11 P.M. and midnight the Germans bombarded Missy heavily and for a short period caused some confusion ; then after a trying time the troops settled down in the positions ordered under the new arrangement. The 15th Brigade successfully completed its re-passage of the river just before the first streak of dawn on the 16th.

The casualties were not serious, though the Yorkshire L.I. paid for its unprofitable march down to the bank of the Aisne with fifty killed and wounded. It now seemed established beyond doubt that the capture of the promontory of Chivres was beyond the strength of the British force.

In the I. Corps the infantry had a comparatively quiet day. There were repeated outbursts of enemy shelling from field and heavy guns, which caused some losses among the artillery horses and disabled one field gun, and some small attacks by the enemy's infantry, which were beaten off without difficulty. Advantage was taken of the cessation of the advance to begin the construction of a very complete system of bridges and communications across the river and canal, as the enemy had spent a great deal of ammunition the previous day in trying to damage the canal bridges at Pont Arcy and Bourg.

In the 4th Division there was no change in the situation, and the day was spent in improving the trenches and collecting wire from the fences of the country round, which was converted at night into entanglements ; for except what the Field Companies carried, no barbed wire or other engineer stores were yet available.

THE FRENCH ON THE 15TH SEPTEMBER

Right and left of the British, the French had also been unable to advance. Eastward the French XVIII. Corps in the afternoon lost Craonne and Craonnelle, as a result of the arrival of German reinforcements,[1] after most gallant and strenuous fighting. The gap which had existed between the German *First* and *Second Armies* was now completely closed and all chance of turning the western flank of the *Second Army* had disappeared. Westward the French Sixth Army could make no progress along the line of the Aisne. Though there had been great hopes that the French IV. Corps might turn the right of the *First Army* at Nampcel (about thirteen miles

[1] On the 15th the German *XVIII. Corps* from the *Fourth Army* arrived, in addition to the *VII. Reserve*, *XV.* and *XII. Corps* already mentioned.

north-east of Compiègne), the enemy offered stubborn resistance in that quarter, and in addition he had been reinforced [1] 15 Sept. 1914.
The French General Staff was now satisfied that the Germans intended to stand on the Aisne. North of the river there was now no doubt that the troops who had been shaken by their defeat at the Battle of the Marne, reinforced by fresh divisions, were resting and refitting. It was becoming clear that, if any immediate progress were to be made by either side, it must be by turning movements rather than by frontal attack. Everything pointed to the probability, if not the certainty, of a deadlock on the line of the Aisne, which could only be resolved by a decisive action on the one open flank towards the west. For the moment the French General Staff hoped that it might be beforehand with the enemy in this ; for the district west of the Oise, from Compiègne to Montdidier, was now reported fairly clear of Germans, who, to all appearances, were steadily retiring. But meanwhile it was essential to hold the enemy to his ground on the existing front.

There was actually better reason for the optimistic views of the French than was afforded by the information then available.

NOTE

THE 14TH–15TH SEPTEMBER ON THE GERMAN SIDE

The attack of the Allies on the 14th September had anticipated Maps 4 and prevented the execution of Bülow's programme for driving the & 35. I. Corps and French XVIII. Corps across the Aisne and breaking the Allied front—but there were many vicissitudes.

The early part of the day, according to their own accounts, was a most anxious time for the Germans :[2]—" Nothing was to be seen " of the *XV. Corps*, in whose attack the *VII. Reserve* was to co- " operate ; far from troops coming on, part of Marwitz's cavalry " corps (which was to cover its advance) sent its baggage back in " the direction of Bruyères (south of Laon). It was very exhausted. " Strong bodies of cavalry followed and took cover behind Fort " Montbérault (4 miles north of Troyon, and Zwehl's headquarters). " It was reported and confirmed that forces considerably stronger than " our own, as it was supposed, had crossed the Aisne, moving north- " wards. The *VII. Reserve Corps* and also the *III. Corps* felt they " must confine themselves to the defensive." Kluck, for his part, repeated his orders to the *First Army* to continue entrenching its position and hold it at all costs (Kluck, p. 141).

The attack of Br.-General Bulfin's two battalions against Troyon [3] was met by three battalions of the *27th Reserve Brigade* (*14th Res. Div.*), supported by three batteries of *Reserve Field Artillery Regiment No. 14* ; but just as the situation became critical, assistance arrived in the form of 1,200 infantry reinforcements, a company of the *78th Regiment* of the *X. Corps*, and a Horse Artillery *Abteilung* of the

[1] The *7th Cavalry Division* from Alsace and the *IX. Reserve Corps* from Antwerp had arrived on the 15th. The place of the latter was taken by *Landwehr*.
[2] Zwehl, p. 71.
[3] See page 396.

9th Cavalry Division.[1] The *27th Reserve Brigade*, however, was wavering, and reported that it was attacked by very superior force. Zwehl called up the *25th Reserve Brigade* (*13th Res. Div.*) and *III. Corps* to come to its help by taking the offensive, and ordered his last reserve, the *25th Landwehr Brigade*, to its left. The *25th Reserve Brigade* attacked, but, suffering heavily, soon stopped, and " was " forced to retire behind the steep slopes of the northern face of the " Chemin des Dames " ; the *25th Landwehr Brigade*, " in consequence " of artillery fire, did not carry out the attack ordered. At this " critical moment vital support was given by the two 8-inch howitzer " batteries, which were brought into action south of Chamouille in " the valley of the Ailette. The howitzers, about 12.30 P.M., suc-" ceeded in stopping an attack threatening the left flank of the " *27th Reserve Brigade*. In spite of this, affairs became more and " more critical." Between 2 and 3 P.M., two fresh battalions arrived from Maubeuge ; they attempted a counter-attack, but failed to do more than assist in holding the line.

Meanwhile, the *13th Reserve Division* was entrenching itself on the Chemin des Dames, north of Braye. Before 9 A.M. the corps commander ordered an attack towards Moussy, where the advance of the 2nd Division had been reported. Affairs at Troyon were, however, too critical, and at 10 A.M. the flank attack to relieve the situation was begun ; this was defeated by the 1/South Wales Borderers and 2/Welch (3rd Brigade), with the assistance of the 46th and 113th Batteries.[2] The attack was carried out by three battalions and two machine-gun companies of the *25th Reserve Brigade*, and a battery. Its repulse seems to have been more complete than the British accounts indicate.[3] One battalion " had to " retire with heavy losses. The remains of it assembled under the " steep slope, south of Courtecon." The other two battalions " were " compelled to give up their positions, as the companies had got " thoroughly mixed up. . . . They assembled on the reverse slope " between Malval Farm (1 mile west of Courtecon) and Courtecon. " The brigade commander was mortally wounded."

The other brigade (*28th Reserve*, 4 battalions) of the *13th Reserve Division* made a short advance to Braye, where it had the fire fight already described with the 6th Brigade. " At 4 P.M. came the " information that the left wing of the *III. Corps* (which had " attacked the 4th (Guards) Brigade near Soupir) was going back. " At dusk the *28th Reserve Brigade* retired to the position it had held " in the morning."

Turning now to what happened in front of the French XVIII. Corps on the British right : the German *28th (Active) Brigade* of the *14th Reserve Division* at Craonne and the *2nd Cavalry Division* of Marwitz's cavalry corps on its left, standing isolated with a large gap on either side of them, were being roughly handled and driven back, when the *XV. Corps* appeared just in time to save them from destruction. The corps which thus came to the rescue had been brought by rail from Alsace. After a delay at Brussels, where part of it was detained from two to four days on account of the sortie from Antwerp,[4] it detrained at Busigny and marched to St. Quentin, the

---

[1] Zwehl, p. 73. According to Poseck, p. 121, the Machine-Gun Troop, Cyclist Battalion, *Jäger* and dismounted men of the *9th Cavalry Division* also took part.

[2] See page 399.   [3] Zwehl, p. 76.   [4] See page 357.

assembly area of the *Seventh Army*, which its leading troops reached 15 Sept. on the 12th September. It was immediately ordered east by General von Heeringen. Early on the 13th it continued its march through La Fère to near Laon, and thence on the 14th moved down the main road towards Reims. The leading division, the *39th*,[1] came up to the *28th Brigade*, now driven back north of Craonne, about 2 P.M., and there was some question of turning to the direct assistance of that brigade. General von Deimling, the corps commander, however, considered that he could best help by carrying out the original plan, and, after deployment, the *82nd Brigade* of the *39th Division*, supported very soon by one of the *30th Division*, and covered by the artillery of both divisions, attacked towards Corbeny. The advance was slow, owing to enfilade artillery fire from the Craonne plateau, now in French possession, but by dusk the two brigades had reached the heights 2,000 yards south of Corbeny "without loss." At 2.30 P.M. Bülow, quite unnecessarily, issued an order that the *XV. Corps* was not to cross the Aisne.[2]

The arrival of another corps, intact and up to strength, from a quiet part of the front, and of two rested battalions from Maubeuge, put new life into the exhausted divisions of the *VII. Reserve Corps*, and, as already narrated, a counter-attack made by them resulted in the I. Corps being driven back from its advanced positions to the southern slopes of the ridge. Opposite the French XVIII. Corps, from the British right eastward to Corbeny, there was a gap of over five miles, which much troubled General von Heeringen, although there now stood behind it, to support the remains of the *28th Brigade*, the fresh 1½ brigades of the *XV. Corps* still in reserve. East of Corbeny, between the *XV. Corps* and the right of the *Second Army*, there was another gap of eight miles; but, so far from exploiting it, the French cavalry and supporting infantry which had penetrated it had been seen retiring. To block the gap Bülow collected a number of units of all arms which were not actually in the line, to the strength of nearly a division, and placed them under Lieut.-General Steinmetz, the commander of the foot artillery of the *Second Army* ; the Supreme Command directed to the gap the *XII. Corps* of the *Third Army*, which was already on the march westward to the right of the *First Army*. By midday on the 14th, the advanced guard of this corps was at Warmeriville (12 miles east of Berry au Bac), where orders from Bülow reached it to send on its artillery and cavalry without delay to assist Steinmetz and then continue its march westwards.[3] The *Guard* and *2nd Cavalry Divisions* were also brought from the British front eastward to the gap. Thus reinforced the German line not only held its own opposite the French but Steinmetz's division made some advance and established itself on the high ground north of the Aisne, north-east of Berry au Bac. The situation had been critical, for the right of the German *Second Army* had put into the fight every man it possessed except its last reserve battalion ; even during the night of the 14th/15th there was still a gap of five miles—

---

[1] This division was one infantry regiment of the *61st Brigade* short, it having been left in Alsace. It rejoined on 21st September. (" Regt. No. 132," pp. 67-9.)

[2] Zwehl, p. 75.

[3] Its advanced guard reached the line of battle about three miles north-east of Berry au Bac at 6 A.M. next day.

soon, however, to be filled by the *XII. Corps*—between Steinmetz's division and the *XV. Corps* at Corbeny.

On this night the dispositions of the German forces in front of the British Army and the left of the French Fifth Army, from west to east were : *II. Corps*, Crouy to Vregny ; *III. Corps* thence to Ostel ; *VII. Reserve Corps* and *9th Cavalry Division* thence to Craonnelle ; the above, except the *28th (Active) Brigade* (the left of the *VII. Reserve Corps*), supported by a brigade of the *IX. Corps* and various small reinforcements, covered the British front.

Then came in succession the *XV. Corps, Guard* and *2nd Cavalry Divisions*, Steinmetz's division supported by the *XII. Corps*, and the *VII. Corps*. By morning these troops effectively closed the gap between the German *First* and *Second Armies* and it was then as strongly held as any other part of the line. There might be little hope for the Germans of driving the Allies back, but the crisis was completely over. Only on the extreme right of the line was there any anxiety. There, although Kluck stated he could hold his front, he had withdrawn his right flank to prevent envelopment from the direction of Compiègne. The Supreme Command in consequence sent off the following instructions to Bülow, which were received during the night of the 14th/15th :

" If the *First Army* cannot hold the Aisne valley, it should retire " in good time (*rechtzeitig*) in the general direction of La Fère behind " the river valley. In this case, the *Second* and *Seventh Armies* will " hold the line Laon—Reims." [1]

But no such action was found necessary. Kluck, on receiving the reinforcements of the *IX. Reserve Corps* and *7th Cavalry Division*, already mentioned, forthwith began an operation to clear his flank by an offensive movement. These operations were by no means to the taste of Bülow, who apparently feared that the *First Army* would repeat the fatal manœuvre it had made towards the Ourcq, and that he would no sooner have filled one gap than Kluck would make another. He forbade the operation, and his principal interest during the 15th September seems to have been to secure that it was stopped. It is typical of the relations of these two commanders that, although Kluck had been temporarily placed under Bülow, the latter had to appeal to the Supreme Command to enforce obedience to his orders.

The O.H.L. order quoted above was the last issued under the authority of General von Moltke, for on the evening of the 14th September, Lieut.-General von Falkenhayn, then Minister of War, was entrusted with the duties of the Chief of the Staff of the Field Army in his place. Moltke was, however, directed to remain at O.H.L. in order that the fact of his dismissal, which would be regarded by the German Army, its opponents and the world at large as admission of failure and defeat, might be kept concealed.[2]

Possibly, the German Official Account hints, he might have been forgiven by the Kaiser for the defeat on the Marne ; but since the 9th September affairs had not gone well in the Eastern theatre. On the 12th had come a report from Hindenburg that Rennenkampf's

---

[1] Bülow, p. 71.

[2] He fell sick, and was sent back to Germany in November, and died in the summer of 1916. His chief assistant, General von Stein, was also removed from O.H.L. and sent to command a Reserve corps, being replaced by General von Freytag-Loringhoven, who had been Military Plenipotentiary at the Austro-Hungarian G.H.Q.

Army, attacked since the 5th in the Battle of the Masurian Lakes, had, as a whole, escaped his clutches, and that he was bringing the pursuit to an end. Further, on the same day, came the news of the end of the struggle in Galicia, and the retreat in disorder of the whole Austrian Army from the Battle of Lemberg—Rawa Russka. Moltke had promised, before the war, to go to its assistance, after settling with the French, on the 39th day of mobilization—that is the 9th September, a day which was to be the turning point of the opening campaign, but which ended very differently to what Germany had expected. She was not in a position to fulfil the promise given by the Chief of the General Staff. Well might Falkenhayn say on taking over that the war was " as good as (*eigentlich*) lost."

15 Sept.
1914.

The German accounts speak of little more than local attacks on the 15th September, "with unsatisfactory results." The *XV. Corps* made little progress on the Craonne plateau ; the *VII. Reserve Corps,* " still exhausted by the fighting of the previous day, found it im-" possible to attack owing to the great artillery superiority of the " enemy " (G.O.A., v. 33) ; the *III. Corps* maintained its position against British attacks ; on the western flank of the *First Army,* the *10th Landwehr Brigade* and *4th Cavalry Division,* near Carlepont, were forced back, exposing the flank of the *IX. Corps* ; the situation was saved by the arrival in the afternoon of the *7th Cavalry Division* and the *IX. Reserve Corps.*

CHAPTER XXI

LAST DAYS ON THE AISNE

(Sketches 19 & 20 ; Maps 2, 3, 4, 35 & 36)

GENERAL SITUATION

Map 2. WITH the stand of the Germans on the Aisne, where they filled up the great gap which had existed in their line since the Battle of the Marne, the successful defence of the French Armies in Lorraine and the failure of the Germans by attack on the Aisne front to prevent General Joffre from shifting troops westward, an entirely new strategic situation arose. With this it now seems desirable to deal ; for it is the key to the events with which the remainder of this volume is concerned.

The front of the French Armies on the right of the British, though fighting continued sporadically, was by the middle of September practically stabilized on the ground where it was to remain so long. There was but one exception : a weak place in the line of the Third Army gave an opportunity in the latter half of September to German troops from Metz to push in and secure the St. Mihiel salient. Neither belligerent force, for the moment at least, could hope for success by frontal attack, and as their southern flanks rested on Switzerland, they could not be turned on that side. The western flank both of the Allies and the Germans, on the contrary, lay perfectly open ; it was therefore still possible to continue the enveloping movements which both sides had in turn attempted, with the result, it is true, of gain of ground and prisoners in turn, but hitherto without decisive success.

There were, however, other good and weighty reasons for pursuing operations on the western flank. In the great interval between the Oise and the Dutch frontier lay objectives of the highest importance to both sides. The Channel ports were practically defenceless ; only a

428

few scattered French Territorial battalions about Péronne, Sept.
Douai, and Lille interposed between them and the German 1914.
Armies. General von Falkenhayn has said : " It still
" seemed possible, providing the present German front
" held, to bring the northern coast of France and therefore
" the control of the English Channel into German pos-
" session." [1] Turning to the other side, the German communications were in danger : " the only line of supply of
" any use to the greater part of the western half of the
" German Armies was the railway leading from Belgium
" into the St. Quentin district. This was almost wholly
" unprotected against enemy attacks." [2] Hence, an extension of the front to the west was imperative for each
of the belligerent parties, both on offensive and defensive
grounds. Further, it was of the utmost importance to
the Allies to re-establish connection with the Belgian Army
which was still holding out in Antwerp, to secure Lille,
and to cover the Bethune coalfields.

In the latter half of September, therefore, both belligerents began to make preparations for extending their
lines westwards and northwards by withdrawing troops
from other parts of the front. Each cherished hopes of
enveloping the open flank of the other, and of rolling up
his line, and each in the meantime endeavoured by attacking on the old front to hold the foe to his ground and
prevent him transferring forces to the vital flank.

The failure of the French Sixth Army to turn the open
right flank of the German line during the advance from the
Ourcq to the Aisne and during the first days of the fighting
on the Aisne had not altered General Joffre's determination to persist in operations to that end. He had already
brought the XIII. Corps from the First Army to reinforce
the Sixth, and other corps and all available cavalry were
soon to follow. But he was careful on the 17th September,
in Instruction No. 29, to point out that " it is essential
" to maintain an offensive attitude in order to keep the
" enemy under threat of attack and thus prevent him from
" disengaging and transferring portions of his forces from
" one point to another." On the 18th September he
informed Sir John French that " the general offensive
" would be resumed as soon as a new Army that he was
" concentrating in the west was in a position to move
" forward."

To the German Supreme Command the danger to the

[1] Falkenhayn, p. 13.   [2] Falkenhayn, p. 12.

western flank of the Armies was naturally patent, nor had the commander of the German *First Army* failed to bring it to notice. On the 15th September Kluck reported that his "westward communications were in danger; " enemy column of all arms moving from Clermont reached " Compiègne at noon." He received the instructions that " in the event of the right flank of the *First Army* being " imperilled, the Army will withdraw due north."

On the evening of the 14th September General von Falkenhayn took over the duties of the Chief of the General Staff, as already stated. He devised immediate steps to prevent the continuance of the movements of French troops round to the western flank by ordering counter-attacks along the whole front, principally along the Aisne front and east and west of Reims. Many of these attacks fell, as will be seen, on the British Army. But " they did " not produce the hoped-for results, and the attempt to " prevent or divert the movement of enemy troops was " unsuccessful." [1]

Sketch 19.
Map 35.

Sir John French's operation orders for the 16th September ordered the line held by the Army to be strongly entrenched.[2] He still, however, had hopes of being able to continue the advance and added that it was his intention to assume a general offensive at the first opportunity. His orders proved to be the official notification of the commencement of trench warfare. Next day, with the same proviso as before, he ordered the line to be strengthened by every available means. Thenceforward the general situation remaining unaltered, the daily issue of operation orders ceased, and they were prepared only when some considerable change in the situation or a projected attack made them necessary. To those at the front, however, the days on the Aisne seemed a continuous battle which might at any moment develop into a decisive operation and end the war; the apathy of trench warfare had not yet set in on either side. Artillery fire, though intermittent, never ceased for long. By day, sniping made it impossible to move about or to work except under cover; constant vigilance was required to detect enemy infantry attacks in good time. Night was livelier even than day, and was made almost as bright at times by the enemy's flares and light-balls; but during darkness working parties and

[1] Falkenhayn, p. 9.   [2] Appendix 46.

supplies came up, patrols were continually on the move and Sept. 1914.
reliefs were carried out.

There was nothing novel in two armies thus facing each other, entrenched and adding daily to their defences. After the Russo-Japanese war a few writers had forecast that the next war on the Continent would be one of " siege " warfare in the field," [1] and, but for the doctrine of the offensive at all costs, held by both the French and German General Staffs, and the generally accepted theory that a war must, for financial and industrial considerations, be short, they had good reason on their side. Measuring the Franco-German frontier as about one hundred and sixty miles in length, or three hundred and twenty miles with the Franco-Belgian frontier added, and counting the heads of the trained men available in the belligerent countries, there were on both sides, for the shorter distance some 30,000 men and for the longer nearly 15,000 men, per mile available, nearly twenty or ten to the yard as the case might be. These, entrenched, were ample to hold all national territory —for 2,000 to 4,000 men a mile was the usual estimate for the requirements of a modern fortress—and to provide an enormous reserve to break through at any selected spot.

It is unnecessary to recall the fortified lines of ancient campaigns, when lack of communications made the possession of certain routes indispensable and caused turning movements to be slow and difficult. Operations of those days, if only from lack of railway and other means of rapid transport, have nothing in common with those of modern warfare. In the American Civil War, 1861–65, entrenchments were extensively used by both sides, and after the failure of Grant to force Lee's breastworks in the Wilderness campaign there had been the long period—nine and a half months, 16th June 1864 to 2nd April 1865—of deadlock in the trenches of the Petersburg lines. This genuine trench warfare ended only because the gradual extension of the lines westwards made it impossible for the Confederates to man the trenches in sufficient strength, and Grant was then able at once to outflank them and to break through their front.

Passing over the extraordinary results obtained by entrenched troops at Plevna in 1877–78, we find that in the Russo-Japanese war, twenty-six years later, both sides took to the spade, and in the four months on the Sha Ho

[1] *E.g.* " The Campaign of the Future," by Captain (later Lieut.-Colonel) C. E. P. Sankey, D.S.O., R.E., in the " R.E. Journal," January 1907.

(15th October 1904 to 27th February 1905), assisted by experiences gained at Port Arthur, developed trench warfare to a very high degree.

In the Balkan war the victorious Bulgarians were stopped before the Tchataldja Lines, which they could not turn ; the lines it is true had been magnificently sited in the leisure of peace, but were little better than earthworks. It is remarkable, therefore, that none of the belligerents entered the war prepared for trench warfare on a large scale. Digging had been encouraged by precept in the British Army, but, owing to the rapidity of the course of peace manœuvres, was seldom possible in practice, except on the oft-dug-over soil of the tiny portion of the training ground allotted for the purpose. General Lanrezac has written that so opposed to entrenching was French doctrine in 1914, that when he ordered his corps to dig in before the battle of Charleroi, some evaded the order, and others, to satisfy the written word, threw up just a *bourrelet* of earth : a parapet about the size of a window sand-bag, as an Englishman might say.

The Germans naturally had not trained their troops for, and did not expect, position warfare, because, as has been already pointed out, their General Staff believed that the decision in France would be reached in 36 to 40 days. They had however prepared for and held exercises in the accelerated attack of fortifications,[1] with a view to dealing quickly with those of Eastern France, or at any rate pretending that they were in a position to do so. They had very carefully studied the Russo-Japanese war from this point of view; and September 1914 found them in possession of heavy guns,[2] trench mortars, rifle-grenades, hand-grenades, searchlights, illuminating pistols, and periscopes, designed for the attack of fortresses, but practically comprising all the apparatus of trench warfare. Though, as the German record states,[3] these instruments " in their " present form are war-children grown large and perfected " in the storms and troubles of the times, yet they had been " so far developed in peace that the German Army in " August 1914 achieved great success with them against

[1] *E.g.* at Coblenz in 1908.
[2] Each corps took into the field two batteries of four 5·9-inch howitzers. 21-cm. (8-inch) howitzers reached the Aisne on the 14th September. (Zwehl, p. 74.) The siege train went to Liége, Namur and Antwerp, and was not available in the field until the fall of the last named fortress, when most of it was moved to the Ypres area.
[3] " Die Technik im Weltkriege," by Generalleutnant Schwarte.

" the Belgian fortresses." As the Germans relied on the Sept.
suddenness of the attack and never contemplated lengthy 1914.
operations, such matters as sound ranging, flash spotting
and camouflage [1] were absent from their original conception. Of the desirability of scattering batteries, maga-
zines, observation stations, strong points and keeps, and
interspersing them with dummies, so as to offer a multi-
plicity of small targets, the Germans were fully cognizant ;
they had for many years avoided building concrete shell-
traps like the self-contained detached forts designed after
the war of 1870-71 by the Belgian general, Brialmont, and
the French engineer, General Séré de Rivière. The precise nature of shelter necessary to resist heavy artillery had
also been decided on.[2] Such matters had been exhaustively
studied in the design and lay-out of the German *Feste*, the
super-fortresses of Metz, Thionville, Strasbourg, etc. The
arrangement of these permanently fortified areas was, as
far as the means available permitted, imitated in field warfare at the front ; thus in the course of time the German
field defences were developed on a definite plan into broad
fortified zones.

At the beginning therefore the enemy was at a great
advantage in his knowledge of trench warfare ; and he had
the material required for its practice, even if his men had
not been generally trained in its use.[3] The improvisation
by the British Army of trench warfare implements whilst
waiting for them to be manufactured and supplied from
home will be told in a later volume of this history ; the only
engineer stores which reached it on the Aisne, beyond what
the engineer companies and bridging trains carried, were
small quantities of barbed wire and sandbags, and the only
heavy artillery which arrived (apart from the 60-pdrs.
which formed part of the divisional artillery) were four
batteries of old pattern 6-inch howitzers.

The British could at first do little more than dig cover.

---

[1] Generalmajor von Gleich in " Die alte Armee," p. 19, says, " as
" regards concealment from aeroplanes, we had learnt as good as nothing
" (in peace). Even in the war we followed halting and hesitating behind
" our adversaries. ' Camouflage ' we actually only learnt from the English
" after our losses had made us wise."

[2] The ferro-concrete shellproofs at Tsingtau " which resisted perfectly
all calibres up to and including the 28 cm. howitzers " were 1·5 metres
(5 feet) thick : that is to say, the thickness of the pill boxes and other
concrete shelters used in France (see " Der Kampf um Tsingtau," pp. 57
and 194).

[3] The first German train-load of engineer stores for siege warfare
arrived on the Aisne on 14th September. (Vogel, p. 111).

Fortunately for them the soil on the slopes of the Aisne valley and on the plateau was easy—though near the river there was hard rock a foot below the surface—and as long as they were in the Aisne district—that is to say, before the first frosts—the sides of the trenches, except in one sector of the II. Corps area, stood vertical without revetment ; in fact they stood so well that it was even possible to obtain additional cover by undercutting the sides in the South African fashion, thus forming the first " funk holes." The trenches dug at this period were rarely continuous, usually a succession of pits capable of holding a few men. Generally, they were of the narrow type, eighteen inches to two feet wide, with tiny traverses, three to six feet wide. These days were afterward spoken of in jest as the " Augustan Period " (August 1914) of field fortification. The narrow trenches, though giving good cover, were easily knocked in by high-explosive shell, and proved the graves of some of the defenders, for men were occasionally buried alive in them. In siting fire trenches, when a choice was possible, concealment from the direct observation of hostile artillery became the most important factor ; on the slopes of the Aisne valley an extensive field of fire was out of the question, and it soon became evident that a short one, flanked by machine guns, was in reality more effective.

The enemy on the Aisne seemed by his shooting to have such accurate information as to movements of troops and positions of batteries, that it was for some time suspected that he was being assisted by spies ; but experience went to show that the results were due rather to the enterprise of his artillery observers. In one case a German disguised as a farmer was found with a telephone in a house between the lines in direct communication with his commander. Several others were caught actually inside the British lines connected by the field telegraph wire to their batteries. One with a week's supply of food was found inside a hay-stack ; another concealed in a tree, on being detected by an officer who looked up, promptly dropped upon him and, stunning him, escaped.

As regards our own artillery, the difficulties of employing the batteries effectively on the plateau south of the Aisne were at first almost insuperable. In order that they might be defiladed from direct view they were necessarily placed well back from the edge of the heights, where they stood four thousand yards or even further from the trenches of the British infantry. In the case of the 3rd Division, how-

ever, it was impossible to find positions on the north side
of the river.   Guns which were visible to ground observation were at once silenced by the German heavy howitzers,
and the positions of those which could be approximately
identified by their flashes or by aerial observation were
often subjected to a fire which compelled the withdrawal
of the detachments.   The British field howitzers were
occasionally able to reach the German guns, but for the
most part only the 60-pdr. batteries were of sufficient power
and range to deal with them.

On the 18th September, however, the redistribution of
the British aeroplanes and their equipment with wireless
enabled the British batteries to reply more effectively to
the German.   The system of maintaining forward observers
was also extended, though the distance of the heavy guns
to the rear, the interposition of a river and the incessant
fire of the enemy made the laying and maintenance of telephone cables a difficult and dangerous matter ; they were
continually cut and the labour of repairing them never
ceased. Communication was hampered also by the casualties
among trained men and by the instruments getting out of
order.

As the final weeks on the Aisne witnessed mainly
artillery combats and no definite battle, some description
of the normal conditions of such fighting as did take place
may be given here.

In every division an aeroplane with an artillery officer
as an observer went up early each day.[1]   The observer
noted down the positions of German batteries on a squared
map, and sent this map to the divisional artillery commander, who settled which objectives his batteries could
best engage.   When any part of our infantry line was
shelled, the batteries most capable of bringing fire to bear
on the hostile guns were immediately ordered to search
their position.   Each " group " of guns and howitzers was
under an artillery lieutenant-colonel who was responsible for
supporting a portion of the infantry line in case of attack,
and was in touch with the infantry brigadier concerned.
At certain preconcerted times, a general bombardment by
all our batteries was carried out over the whole position of
the Germans ; our aeroplanes observed this fire, and sent
corrections to each group.

Throughout the long series of encounters on the Aisne,

[1] The first occasion on which British batteries worked with aeroplanes
in war appears to have been the 13th September 1914.

the British had the greatest difficulty in finding observation stations, and in maintaining communication between them and the batteries. The Chemin des Dames, being the highest ridge in the neighbourhood, completely defiladed the German gun positions ; for after the first two days, no British soldier overlooked the valley behind it, and it made direct observation impossible, except on a few German infantry trenches ; these were dealt with by batteries near the front line. Practically all shooting was done by the map, and ranges, switches and angles of sight were calculated from measurements taken from maps.

Attempts were at first made to observe from buildings and sheds, but these were usually knocked down very quickly or set on fire. There remained haystacks and " dug-outs " in the open. These gave cover from view, and deep trenches made near them on the side away from the enemy provided shelter from shrapnel and from machine-gun and rifle fire, but not from heavy shell, which either destroyed them or blew them in. A party of observers did remain nine days in a haystack near the Tour de Paissy, and this only once received a direct hit, though many heavy shells burst close to it. Every precaution had to be taken to prevent any movement being visible from the front, such as making all orderlies and messengers stop and wait, if possible, one hundred yards short of observation posts, and insisting on absolute immobility when aeroplanes were near.

All batteries were carefully entrenched, covered from view by bushes and straw ; dummy batteries were made, and teams sent back, as a rule, at least a mile to cover. " Funk holes " were generally to be found ready made in the numerous caves, to which detachments ran when serving their guns became impossible owing to hostile fire. Replacement of ammunition was generally carried out by hand.

Any change of position found desirable was made during darkness, after reconnaissance had been previously carried out during daylight. Dummy guns made with hop-poles, branches, etc., were left in the old positions when they were vacated.

The deep mud made " switching " for change of target a matter of much labour, and any change of over 15° was impossible. The guns were left at night under a guard, with sufficient men and officers within call to work them in case of attack. Night lines were carefully marked

before dark ; lamps were used as aiming points, and Sept.
electric torches employed to read range dials when the 1914.
batteries were actually firing.

A great many different kinds of shell were fired by the
German heavy howitzers. The high-explosive shell on bursting caused a tremendous concussion, and made craters 15-20
feet across and 10 feet deep. The high-explosive shrapnel,
however, though it made a terrific noise, and produced
much green and white smoke, was comparatively harmless.
Ordinary shrapnel was generally burst too high to be
dangerous. A small high-velocity shell (" whizz-bang ")
was very accurate, the burst and report of discharge being
practically simultaneous.

Besides using forward observers inside our lines, as
already mentioned, the Germans observed artillery fire
by means of :

1. Captive sausage-shaped balloons. These were generally kept low and well out of range.

2. Observation posts very near our trenches, such as
the " Chimney " at the sugar factory on the Chemin des
Dames, ½ mile north-west of Troyon. This erection,
though continually fired on and suffering many direct
hits, was never actually demolished.

3. Aeroplanes which continually flew over the whole
battle front. If any of our troops moved or any guns
fired when these were overhead and able to observe, an
accurate heavy cross-fire was usually opened by the German
artillery very soon afterwards.

The canal, villages, bridges, and all railways and routes
behind our positions were methodically searched by shell
each day. Headquarters and roads on which it was
known that supplies and ammunition must move received
special attention from the enemy.

Nevertheless, the British gunners made their presence
felt ; and the second week of the new warfare saw them
competing on less uneven terms with the Germans. The
arrival on the 23rd September of the brigade of old pattern
6-inch howitzers tended to reduce the disparity between
them, but only to a small degree, for these weapons were
far inferior even to the enemy's 5·9-inch howitzers. In
the matter of anti-aircraft guns, the British ordnance
also fell far behind the German. For this service, light
quick-firing guns known as pom-poms were sent out from
England early in September. It is sufficient to say that
they fired a percussion shell, which, as not one in several

hundred ever hit its aerial target, fell to earth, frequently at some point in the British lines, and there burst. Not a single enemy aeroplane was brought down at this period, either by these guns or by rifle fire. Such a state of things, it is needless to say, was neither reassuring nor comfortable.

It remains before proceeding to the narrative of the operations to survey the all-important work accomplished in bridging the Aisne. On the 13th and 14th five pontoon bridges in all were built by the engineers: at Bourg, Pont Arcy, Vailly, Venizel, and a mile above Venizel, those at Vailly and Venizel being of mixed construction, partly pontoon and partly barrel piers. In addition to these, the damaged aqueduct at Bourg and the road bridge at Venizel were repaired. On the 15th a barge bridge and a trestle bridge were completed over the canal near Bourg, and on the 17th a new pontoon bridge was laid at Bourg, the repair of the permanent bridge being simultaneously taken in hand. By the 20th two more bridges at Moulin des Roches and Missy, respectively, and a foot-bridge below Venizel had been constructed; a damaged German trestle bridge at Chavonne had also been restored. On the 21st, the river being at the moment two feet above its level of the 15th, the aqueduct at Bourg was wrecked by a German shell, and for the time rendered useless. The enemy's observation must have been excellent, for he ceased firing directly after this shell had burst. A semi-permanent bridge was therefore begun at Bourg, which was supplemented by another at Soupir, of which the construction commenced on the 28th.

A wooden girder bridge to replace the broken span of the existing bridge was begun at Soissons on the 1st October and completed on the 9th. It was then handed over to the French, as the British were leaving the locality; it was known hereafter as the " Pont des Anglais," [1] and was in use continuously until destroyed in the German offensive in 1918. In addition to all these bridges, barges equipped with roadway were prepared, ready to be swung instantly across the river to form additional bridges if required.

This bald enumeration, however, gives but a slight idea of the strain borne by the engineers during the weeks that the Army was on the Aisne. Nearly all of the bridges were within known range of the German guns; most of them were constructed, and at different times all of them

[1] The permanent bridge built after the war perpetuates the name.

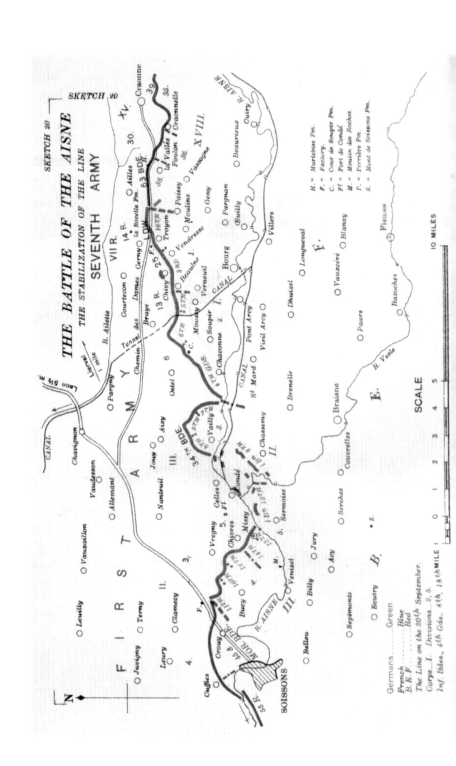

THE BATTLE OF THE AISNE

THE STABILIZATION OF THE LINE

SKETCH 20

SEVENTH ARMY

H. = Hurtebise Fm.
F. = Factory.
C. = Cour de Soupir Fm.
Ft = Fort de Condé.
M. = Moulin des Roches.
P. = Perrière Fm.
S. = Mont de Soissons Fm.

Germans........Green
French..........Blue
B.E.F...........Red
The Line on the 20th September.
Corps. I. Divisions. 2, 6.
Inf. Bdes., 4th Gds. 8th, 18th MILE

SCALE

0   1   2   3   4   5   10 MILES

repaired, under fire. At Vailly, where a permanent
bridge was much needed, the German shells prevented
even attempts to build one. The rise of the water necessitated frequent changes and modifications of level; and
the incessant rain made the task of keeping the approaches
in order most difficult and trying. Yet the engineers
contrived not only to maintain the bridges, but to make
bridgeheads and to entrench positions against the possibility of a retreat. In the course of the operations on
the Aisne, the divisional Field Companies R.E. which had
done the work were reinforced by the 1st and 2nd Bridging
Trains, and by the 20th and 42nd Fortress Companies
from the Line of Communications; but even with this
assistance the burden of work thrown upon them was
very heavy.

With these preliminary observations we may pass on
to recount rapidly the operations on the British front,
mentioning chiefly the events of the days on which infantry
attacks took place, although on every day there was an
intermittent duel of artillery. The chief centre of interest,
be it remembered, was now shifting from the Aisne to the
north-west, where, in the endeavour to out-flank each
other, the French and Germans were continually extending their sphere of operations northwards in the so-called
" Race to the Sea." Of these operations an outline will
be given in another chapter.

OPERATIONS ON THE AISNE

The general characteristics of the week which saw the Sketch 20.
beginning of trench warfare were continued wet weather, Map 35.
intermittent bombardment by both sides, steady advance
of the German trenches to closer quarters with the British,
and almost daily German attacks of a more or less serious
nature. These were made, as already explained, to hold
the Allied forces on the Aisne whilst troops were being
shifted to the western flank. The losses from the heavy
German shells were at the outset considerable, for the
British trenches were as yet so incomplete as to afford only
indifferent shelter. Thus on the 15th September the Highland Light Infantry had sixty, and on the following day the
2/Grenadier Guards seventy casualties from German shell
fire. On the 16th the Oxfordshire L.I. lost twenty-two
killed and wounded and the 1/K.R.R.C. sixty-eight;
whilst on the 17th the artillery had forty horses killed

at Bucy le Long. On the right of the I. Corps front the trenches (held by the 2nd Brigade) just south of the Chemin des Dames were subjected to a galling enfilade fire both from rifles and guns. The plateau of Paissy again was swept by artillery fire from east, north and west. German snipers were both active and troublesome against the front of the 3rd and 5th Divisions, where their possession of commanding ground combined with the proximity of the trenches gave them decided advantages. At Missy the British position seemed tactically hopeless, for it was immediately dominated by the promontory at Chivres, and had but a limited field of fire in any direction. Just east of Ste. Marguerite (1¼ miles W.N.W. of Missy) the trenches were in places only twelve yards from those of the enemy; and nowhere in the Chivres valley were they more than two hundred yards distant. Altogether during the first few days of the new warfare the situation of the British seemed anything but good.

Nevertheless the leaders and troops never for a moment lost confidence; and every day saw the situation improve. On the 16th September the 6th Division, delayed in transport by the shifting of the British base from Havre to St. Nazaire, arrived in rear of the III. Corps. It was temporarily broken up in order to provide relief to the war-worn troops of the first five divisions. The 17th and 18th Brigades were attached to the I. Corps, and the 16th to the II. Corps. The 17th Brigade became corps reserve, releasing the 1st Cavalry Division, which from the 19th September onward furnished five hundred rifles for the trenches about Chavonne. On the 17th a supply of entrenching tools reached the II. Corps, and from that date its casualties sensibly diminished. On the 19th arrived the first 18-pdrs. to make good part of the losses of the II. Corps at Le Cateau; and from that day forward a stream of drafts poured in to fill the gaps in the battalions.

It is significant of the heavy and unexpected wastage that within a month of the firing of the first shot, the supply of Regular reservists for many regiments had been exhausted, and that men of the Special Reserve—the Militia of old days—were beginning to take their place. Many stragglers, however, who had lost their regiments in. the retreat, now returned to them fresh and re-equipped, including several of the Dublin Fusiliers who had got through the German lines to Boulogne after the Battle of

Le Cateau [1] Transport wagons, which had long been 16 Sept. 1914
given up for lost, also reappeared from time to time ; one
such wagon, which had been missing since the 24th of
August, rejoining the 3rd Cavalry Brigade on the 21st
September. The reinforcements together with the improvement of the defences rendered two brigades sufficient to
defend a sector for which three had hitherto been necessary ;
as a result, on the 19th September the 1st (Guards) and
2nd Brigades were withdrawn from the trenches for a few
days' rest ; and the line, which had hitherto absorbed the
whole of the 1st Division, was defended by the 3rd and 18th
Brigades alone. Altogether as the month of September
wore on, the strain on the men was slowly but sensibly
relaxed. Considering that the weather was abominable
and the loss of greatcoats and waterproof sheets during the
retreat was not made good for some time, the health of the
troops suffered marvellously little. There was, it is true,
already trouble with their feet, many of the trenches being
deep in mud during the rains, and in the flat ground about
Chivres two feet deep in water. But constant digging kept
the men in good condition ; and, as soon as a regular
system of reliefs became possible, a course of route-march-
ing was introduced for the companies off duty to fit them
for the work of an ordinary campaign.

The 16th September was regarded by the British as
an uneventful day without change in the situation.[2] It
dawned with heavy rain and mist, but as soon as the weather
cleared about 8 A.M. artillery fire was opened by both sides
and continued with quiet intervals until the evening. It
appears, however, that the *XII.*, *XV.* and *VII. Reserve
Corps*, forming the German *Seventh Army*, and the *III.
Corps*, were ordered to renew the attack.[3] They attempted
to do so, but " the *XII.* and *XV. Corps* made no actual
" progress, the *III. Corps* declared it could not advance
" until the *VII. Reserve* attacked and in both divisions
" of the latter corps (opposite General Haig) the day
" passed in stationary fire fight."   This result, it is stated,
was due to " an overpowering artillery fire."

After a quiet night, at dawn on the 17th there were Sketch 7.
feeble attacks, all of them easily repulsed, upon the 2nd Maps 31 & 33.
Brigade on the right of the British line. Between 11 A.M.
and noon a more serious onslaught was made upon the
extreme right of the British and the left of the French next

[1] See page 197.   [2] Appendix 47.   [3] Zwehl, pp. 84, 85.

to them, which was held by Moroccan battalions.[1] These troops, having lost practically all their officers, gave way for the moment, and the two reserve companies of the 2nd Brigade were moved up to fill the gap and came under artillery fire which cost them fifty casualties. For the next three hours the Germans kept up a heavy bombardment, after which about a company of German infantry stole forward, under cover of mist and rain, to a previously abandoned trench, whence they could enfilade the British line. The Northamptonshire and the Queen's, supported by the 2/K.R.R.C., were ordered to turn the enemy out ; and the Northamptonshire, creeping up unperceived, with a single rush recaptured the trench.

Shortly afterwards a party of Germans, headed by two officers, advanced towards the 2/K.R.R.C. with their rifles slung and their hands up. An officer went out to meet them and the men stood up in their trenches, whereupon the Germans opened fire from the hip, wounding several. The trick was not forgotten by the 2/K.R.R.C. Almost immediately after this incident another body of three or four hundred Germans repeated the same stratagem against the Northamptonshire, actually driving them back a few yards in the first surprise. But the machine-gun officer of the 2/K.R.R.C. who had a gun trained on this second body, mowed them down almost, if not absolutely, to a man.[2] Both sides then made efforts to advance ; first the British, who were checked by the German guns, and then in turn the Germans, who were stopped by the rifles and machine guns of the Queen's and the 2/K.R.R.C. Finally the enemy fell back, leaving behind him forty prisoners and a large number of dead. The loss in the affair was about two hundred of all ranks.

On the British left the only noteworthy occurrence was a heavy bombardment of Bucy le Long which for a time drove the 10th Brigade from its trenches.

To the right and left of the British the French persisted steadily in their offensive. On the right Craonne and

---

[1] This attack was made by the *28th Brigade* (the " active " brigade of the *VII. Reserve Corps*), and a composite force from the *XII. Corps* :— *63rd Brigade*, 3 field batteries, and a heavy howitzer battery. (Zwehl, p. 86.)

[2] General von Zwehl, on behalf of the German *16th Reserve Regiment* (*VII. Reserve Corps*), makes on this very day similar charges against the British of pretending to surrender and then firing (p. 73). There was no doubt a misunderstanding, begun by the men of one side or the other making signs of surrender, not noticed, or resented, by their commanders or neighbouring units.

Corbeny (1½ miles north-east of Craonne) were constantly 17 Sept.
changing hands, though on the evening of the 17th they 1914.
were finally left in possession of the enemy. The arrival
of the German *XII. Corps* [1] in that quarter checked any
further progress on the part of the French XVIII. Corps.

On the left, the chief effort of the French Sixth Army Map 3.
had been made on the extreme flank at Noyon ; but there
had also been hard fighting north of Soissons, and by the
evening of the 17th the French 45th Division had gained
at least a footing on the plateau of Cuffies (1½ miles north
of Soissons). But on that same evening the point of
application of the outflanking movement was reported to
have shifted from Noyon, westward and slightly northward, to Lagny and Lassigny. As two fresh German
corps were known to be moving in that direction from
Belgium, General Joffre was preparing to meet them by
forming a new Army on the left, to be known as the Second
Army, under General de Castelnau. It was to consist of
the XIII. and IV. Corps of the Sixth Army, the XIV.
(from the First Army) and the XX. (from the old Second
Army), with the 1st, 5th, 8th and 10th Cavalry Divisions
under General Conneau. Meanwhile the left of the reduced
French Sixth Army was entrenching strongly about
Nampcel. General Joffre hoped to resume the offensive
directly the Second Army was ready to move forward.[2]

The German report for this day—and also for the 18th
—as regards the British front is, that except for the action
of the *28th Brigade*, already narrated, " the attacks ordered
did not take place." [3]

On the 18th the French Fifth Army on the British right Map 35.
was driven back a little by a German counter-attack which
gave the enemy possession of Brimont (5 miles north of
Reims).

On the British front the Germans tried to reoccupy
the trenches near the Chemin des Dames from which they
had been expelled by the Northamptonshire on the 17th.
They were, however, easily dealt with by the 1/Gloucester-
shire of the 3rd Brigade, which brought away four machine
guns as trophies.

To the west, General Maunoury's extreme right gained
a little ground near Perrière Farm north-east of Crouy, but

---

[1] See page 425.
[2] The story of the French outflanking operations is given in Chapter
XXII.
[3] Zwehl, p. 85.

achieved nothing of great importance. The need for a decisive movement on the western flank as a solution of the deadlock was becoming more and more evident.

Map 35. The 19th September brought some relief to the right of the British line, for, though the 3rd Brigade remained in position, the 1st (Guards) and 2nd Brigades, as has been mentioned, were replaced after dark by the 18th, which was quite strong enough to hold the ground occupied by both. After heavy shelling, there were one or two trifling attacks on the 2nd Division, and at dusk a rather more serious one against the 3rd Division, all of which were beaten off with considerable loss to the enemy. The German report for this day is that " there was no progress worth " mentioning as the enemy was in possession of good " observation posts on the Chemin des Dames and could " direct his field and heavy artillery fire where he desired," [1] a situation not realized by the British.

Henceforward, as will be seen, such efforts as the enemy infantry made were directed against the right of the British line. On the left Vailly, Missy and Bucy le Long were heavily shelled almost daily, particularly Missy ; and Ste. Marguerite was under continuous rifle and machine-gun fire, but no infantry attacks were made on the II. and III. Corps sectors, except on that of the 3rd Division around Vailly. Opposite the 4th Division, the enemy showed great activity in putting up wire. There were, indeed, many signs of the reduction of the infantry in the front line, but none that his heavy guns were being removed, or that he was at all inclined to retire.

The front, over eight miles, held by the 3rd, 5th and 4th Divisions, was too long in proportion to their reduced numbers, and the enemy's position too strong for any hope of progress to be made without an important diversion elsewhere. The 4th Division was able to assist the attacks of the French on its left with gun and rifle fire, but had orders not to take part in a general attack. Nevertheless, the divisions were ordered to keep the possibility of advance before them. At the same time, as a measure of precaution in the event of the II. and III. Corps being driven back, entrenchments were taken in hand on the heights on the southern side of the Aisne. The 19th Brigade and some units of the 6th Division, with the assistance of inhabitants, were employed on their construction. Later the I. Corps

[1] Zwehl, p. 86.

undertook defences on the south bank of the Aisne, so that 20 Sept. on the 30th September Sir John French was able to inform 1914. General Joffre that there was an alternative position there, entrenched from end to end and ready for occupation.

On the 20th September, General von Heeringen, commanding the German *Seventh Army,* ordered a general attack by the whole of the *VII. Reserve Corps.*[1] The day was cold and at times there were heavy showers of hail.

Soon after dawn the Germans attacked the Moroccans Sketch 20. immediately on the right of the British line and drove them Map 35. back. Lieut.-Colonel F. W. Towsey commanding the 1/West Yorkshire Regiment, which was the right battalion of the British Army, thereupon sent out a company to cover his exposed flank. The Moroccans soon rallied and came forward again, when, not knowing what had happened, they fired into this company, inflicting some thirty casualties. The line then settled down again under a heavy fire from German artillery and rifles. A second German attack made between 10 and 11 A.M. was effectively checked by the West Yorkshire. Between noon and 1 P.M. the enemy delivered a third attack under cover of a heavy storm of rain, and once again the Moroccans fell back. Once again Lieut.-Colonel Towsey threw out a company eastward to protect his right, at the same time asking help from the 2nd Cavalry Brigade at Paissy. But before this could come, the enemy, having advanced into the gap left by the Moroccans, enfiladed and, after inflicting heavy casualties, charged and captured the remnants of the right company of the West Yorkshire. Within half an hour, working down the line, the Germans were in occupation of the entire front trenches of the battalion and had swept what remained of two more companies into captivity. The officer commanding led forward his one remaining company to retrieve the situation, but being met by heavy fire on front and right flank, whereby he himself was wounded, the survivors fell back on the cavalry at Paissy.

The disaster to the West Yorkshire laid open the flank of the Durham L.I. who were next on their left, and exposed them to so destructive an enfilade fire that the East Yorkshire, on the left of the D.L.I., were sent to relieve them by a counter-attack. No sooner, however, did they leave their trenches than they were beaten back to them by overwhelming shrapnel and machine-gun fire. Meanwhile B Squadron of the 18th Hussars sent up by the G.O.C.

[1] See page 455.

446 LAST DAYS ON THE AISNE

2nd Cavalry Brigade, in consequence of a report of the attack despatched from the West Yorkshire at 7 A.M., rode to the head of the valley north of Paissy. Leaving their horses there, forty men climbed the slope to the plateau ; then learning the situation from the officer commanding the Sherwood Foresters, who were in brigade reserve at Troyon, and seeing a few infantry coming back, they went forward to what must have been the support trenches of the West Yorkshire. The news of the arrival of the cavalry ran like wildfire along the line and had the greatest possible moral effect ; as a result, the enemy's attempts to press on were foiled and the situation was saved.

A call for support had also been received by the 2nd Cavalry Brigade from the French ; but on the officer commanding the 18th Hussars riding forward to learn how he could best assist, he was informed by a French general that French reinforcements were arriving and British help was no longer required. A squadron of the 9th Lancers, however, was sent to entrench in echelon in rear of the West Yorkshire trenches in case the Africans should again give way.

About 1 P.M. a second appeal for help from the West Yorkshire reached the headquarters of the 2nd Cavalry Brigade. Br.-General de Lisle at once set his whole brigade in motion. It was followed by the 2/Royal Sussex (2nd Brigade) which was still at Paissy. The 2/Sherwood Foresters (18th Brigade reserve) had previously gone forward under Br.-General Congreve.

The 4th Dragoon Guards rallied the remnant of the West Yorkshire, and, together with the 18th Hussars, occupied the supporting trenches in rear of the captured first line. These they held successfully against heavy pressure from the enemy until the arrival of the Sussex made the position secure. The lost trenches were finally regained by a dashing counter-attack of the Sherwood Foresters, but at a cost of two hundred casualties, mostly from machine-gun fire. It was 4.30 P.M. when the situation was thus restored. The day had cost the 2nd Cavalry and 18th Brigades nearly 400 killed and wounded and 500 missing.

Sketch 20. The onslaughts of the enemy were, however, by no Map 35. means confined to the extreme right of the British line. At dawn an attack was made on the King's of the 6th Brigade and was pressed to within eighty yards of their trenches, immediately east of the Oise and Aisne canal, when the Germans finally broke and retired, having

suffered heavily. At about 9 A.M. they made a second
onset, bringing up two machine guns to the right of the
King's, near the crest of the western slope of Beaulne
spur, and advancing both through the woods and across
the open. Two platoons of the 2/Highland L.I. and six
of the 2/Worcestershire were thereupon sent to counter-
attack through the wood and to clear the ridge beyond
it. With great difficulty they made their way through
the thicket under heavy fire, and charged and carried a
German trench beyond it ; they were still advancing when
they fell into an ambush. Being enfiladed by machine
guns from their left and having lost every one of their
officers, they were driven back in disorder on to a company
of the King's. Some of these men they carried away
with them in their retreat ; but the rest stood firm. The
situation was becoming serious ; for the Connaught
Rangers on the ridge further east had been driven out of
their trenches by a heavy bombardment, and the right
flank of the King's was thus exposed. However, the flank
company threw back its right, and the other, above mentioned, quickly rallied and re-formed. The deadly fire of
these two companies was too much for the Germans,
who retired, severely punished. Seventy of their dead
and many wounded were found next day by a patrol of
the King's in a single abandoned trench ; and as the
casualties of the battalion did not exceed fifty, the honours
of the day were decidedly with it.

With the 4th (Guards) Brigade of the 2nd Division,
about Soupir, the enemy interfered little except by heavy
shelling and occasional feint attacks.

Before dawn also the Germans opened a violent bombardment on the 9th Brigade on the line south-west Map 35.
of Rouge Maison (1 mile north-east of Vailly) ; later
they brought forward first a machine gun and afterwards
a field gun to enfilade the trenches of the Royal Fusiliers.
They had already stolen forward during the night and
entrenched themselves within four hundred yards of the
Fifth Fusiliers, who were on the left of the Royal Fusiliers.
It seemed evident that an attack was in prospect. At
9 A.M., however, two howitzers of the XXX. Brigade R.F.A.
forced the Germans to withdraw their guns from the neighbourhood of Rouge Maison, and the pressure on the right
flank of the 9th Brigade disappeared. The Fifth then
counter-attacked, driving the German snipers from the
wood in their front ; and at 1 P.M. the engagement died

LAST DAYS ON THE AISNE

down. The casualties of the brigade were trifling; those of the enemy probably considerable.

The above movements, however, were but a diversion in favour of a more serious attack upon the 7th Brigade holding the eastern face of the salient of Vailly from Chavonne north-westwards, where an entirely unsuccessful attempt had been made on the previous day. Between 8 and 9 A.M. after a heavy bombardment the front held by the Wiltshire, in the centre of the brigade line, was engaged by the enemy's infantry; and a couple of hours later a party of some two hundred Germans with two machine guns contrived to push through some dense undergrowth between the right flank of the battalion and the left flank of the 3/Worcestershire, which was immediately on its right. Having thus pierced the line, thanks to the excellent cover afforded by the wooded valley, the Germans came suddenly on the reserve of the Wiltshire and carried off a few prisoners. They also fired on the 2/South Lancashire, which was coming forward from the rear to reinforce the Wiltshire; there was much confused fighting at close quarters whilst the enemy strove to make good his advantage and envelop the right of the British line. Meanwhile the Irish Rifles on the left of the Wiltshire were suffering severely from shelling; and shortly after noon the brigadier was obliged to ask assistance both from his divisional commander and from the 4th (Guards) Brigade on his right at Chavonne.

Throughout this time the three companies of the Wiltshire steadily continued to hold the enemy at bay on their front. The call for assistance had first reached the Queen's Bays at Chavonne, and they, being unable to leave their position, passed it on to the nearest battery. After a time the 2/South Staffordshire of the 6th Brigade from 2nd Division reserve were sent mid-way between Chavonne and Vailly and began to work northward up the valley against the enemy's left flank. A gun of the XXIII. Brigade R.F.A. also came into action with great effect; and shortly before 2 P.M. the hostile advance was brought to a standstill. The Germans, falling back a little, then tried to entrench themselves upon two bare knolls but were driven off them by shrapnel; and about 4 P.M. about two hundred men of the Wiltshire, Worcestershire and South Lancashire advanced, and after sharp fighting drove the enemy back to his own lines, leaving the ground behind littered with his killed and wounded. These were found

to belong to the *56th Regiment* of the *VII. Reserve* and *64th* 20 Sept.
of the *III. Corps*. The struggle in fact was sharp ; it cost 1914.
the 7th Brigade some four hundred casualties, nearly half of
which fell upon the South Lancashire. The 16th Brigade and
the 2nd Cavalry Division were during the afternoon placed
by G.H.Q. at the disposal of the II. Corps to assist the 3rd
Division, but it was not found necessary to employ them.

Altogether the 20th September was a successful day
for the British, though it cost the B.E.F. nearly twenty-two
hundred killed, wounded and missing. The Germans had
delivered four serious attacks at four different points and
had, after first gaining some little advantage, been everywhere repulsed. The French immediately to the right and
left of the British were subjected to similar onslaughts with
much the same result. The Fifth and Sixth Armies were
both forced back a little at certain points ; but the lost
ground was recovered by the latter before nightfall and
by the former within twenty-four hours.[1] The Germans
were evidently most anxious to hold the Allies to their
ground and prevent them from shifting troops to their
western flank ; for already there were indications of a
general movement of German units from east to west.

On the 20th the rain, which had been nearly continuous
since the 12th and had made life in the trenches miserable,
came to an end, and a period of fine autumn weather ensued.

On the night of the 20th/21st the posts of the South Sketch 20.
Wales Borderers and Welch Regiment of the 3rd Brigade Map 35.
were withdrawn from their advanced position at the head
of the Chivy valley to a less exposed one on the spur
south of the village, with the result that free access to
the valley was now yielded to the enemy. But, if this
ground was henceforward a source of some anxiety to the
I. Corps, it became a trap for the Germans. They were
under constant temptation to collect men there for attack ;
but each advance was the offering up of more troops as a
sacrifice to the British batteries which were able to search
every square-foot of the valley.

The 21st and 22nd were days unmarked by any event
of importance on the British front. The French Fifth and

[1] G.O.A. (v. pp. 70-1) makes no claim of any success on the Aisne
front on the 20th. The *XV. Corps* failed to storm Hurtebise Farm (west of
Craonne) ; the *XII. Corps* (part of which attacked the West Yorkshire),
in a fight of varying fortune, managed to hold its ground ; the *VII.
Reserve Corps* reported that its troops were so exhausted that, at best, it
could only hold the line ; the *III. Corps* had some local fighting without
result.

Sixth Armies kept the enemy on those fronts well occupied and both made a little progress, the left of the Fifth Army recapturing trenches near Hurtebise and Vauclerc on the Chemin des Dames immediately to the right of the British.

On the 23rd and 24th nothing of importance took place on the Aisne, although there were the usual desultory attacks and the usual bombardment. Opportunity was taken to carry out reliefs. For instance, the 17th Brigade took the place of the 5th, whose brigadier, General Haking, had been wounded, and the latter brigade was withdrawn into corps reserve. The 2nd Brigade resumed its old place as the right of the 1st Division.[1]

Sketch 20.
Maps 35 & 36.

Throughout the 25th September, the Germans showed activity in the Chivy valley—they were apparently collecting troops there—and early on the morning of the 26th, between 3.40 and 4 A.M., they made an attack against the right of the 2nd Brigade, the right of the British line, combined with a more serious effort against the left of the French XVIII. Corps, next to it. The attack was not well carried out, the enemy advanced in heavy columns which gave a splendid target to the British machine guns, so it was easily repulsed.

At the same moment as this attack was beaten back, another began to develop against the front of the 3rd Brigade on the left of the 2nd, which continued nearly until noon. First, in the early light of the morning, about a thousand men in close formation advanced against—it can hardly be called attacked—the Queen's at the head of the Moulins valley. This again gave a superb opportunity to the British machine guns, and the column was repulsed with heavy loss. Nothing was attempted against the Gloucestershire on the left of the Queen's; but against the South Wales Borderers, next to them on the spur of Mont Faucon, a force of about 1,200 Germans issued from the woods and broken ground on their front, and moved forward apparently in platoon columns covered by skirmishers.

---

[1] As regards the German side : the commander of the *Seventh Army* again ordered a general attack for the 21st, being promised support from the neighbouring corps. This, however, led to the commander of the *VII. Reserve Corps* making a personal protest that " the daily repetition " of attack orders could not obtain any success. For this the preliminary " conditions were at least a fresh division with strong artillery, if possible " a whole corps." One brigade could only put 200 rifles with nine or ten officers into the fight out of its six battalions. No success could be expected from partial attacks, " the enemy was too stubborn and used his " artillery too skilfully." " On the front of the other corps the situation was similar." (Zwehl, pp. 87, 88.)

A fire fight ensued, which lasted nearly two hours before 25 Sept. superiority over the Germans was obtained. Towards 1914. 8 A.M. a further effort was made by the Germans with increased numbers, and at one point they succeeded in penetrating the line of the Borderers. The reserve company went forward without a moment's hesitation, and, with the assistance of two companies of the Welch which were sent by the brigadier to the right round the slopes of Mont Faucon, succeeded in retaking the trenches after a hot fight. Meanwhile, the rest of the South Wales Borderers were for a time held to their trenches by heavy shrapnel fire. The East Yorkshire and Durham L.I. of the 18th Brigade were warned by the divisional staff to reinforce them, but their services were not required. The 3rd Brigade succeeded in clearing the woods on its immediate front, although the Germans did not finally withdraw until about 11.30 A.M., still covered by a heavy fire from their batteries on the heights above, which made communication with the British forward trenches impossible. The retirement of the enemy infantry up the Chivy valley, however, found the British artillery ready for it : thirty-three guns and howitzers of the 1st and 2nd Divisions concentrated their fire on the valley, and the Cameron Highlanders of the 1st (Guards) Brigade on the left of the 3rd were able to enfilade the retreating parties, who were in close formation. They were seen to suffer heavily. The total losses must have been severe : dead were lying thick before the trench the Germans had carried, and, considering the havoc wrought by the British artillery, the number of enemy killed alone must have exceeded the total casualties of the British. These were just under two hundred and fifty, four-fifths of which fell upon the South Wales Borderers. Bad luck befell the Cameron Highlanders, for a cave in which their headquarters were installed was wrecked by a high-explosive shell, which killed and buried the acting commanding officer, Captain D. N. C. C. Miers, four other officers and twenty-three other ranks.

It was found on investigation that some of the German dead and of the prisoners taken this day belonged to the *21st* and *25th Divisions*, both of the *XVIII. Corps*, parts of which, and of the *XV. Corps*, it is now known, were brought up as fresh troops to drive back the British.[1]

----

[1] The *50th Brigade* of the *25th Division* and four battalions of the *XV. Corps* were brought up to reinforce the *VII. Reserve Corps*. (Zwehl, pp. 88, 89.)

But, except for a momentary penetration at one place in the line, they achieved nothing ; as ever, the shooting of the battalions and batteries of the B.E.F. was too effective even for the German Army of 1914.[1]

On the 27th the Germans confined themselves to artillery fire until dusk, when somewhat feeble attacks upon the 2nd and 3rd Brigades were renewed and easily repulsed. Lower down the river the valley of the Aisne was alive with bursting shells ; two to three hundred fell upon Missy alone, but they did little military damage.

On this day, hand-grenades, whose revival dates from the siege of Port Arthur, were for the first time during the war thrown into the British trenches ; and, since the Expeditionary Force in France had none, the Royal Engineers were called upon to improvise, with gun-cotton, a missile with which to reply to this latest device of the Germans, until a supply of service grenades should arrive from home.

Sketch 20.
Map 36.
From this day forth offensive operations on the British front ceased, and the 1st October found the positions practically the same as on the 14th September. The activities of the infantry were henceforward confined to sniping, digging new trenches, and patrolling No Man's Land during the hours of darkness.[2] Artillery activity

[1] The German offensive on the 26th September was carried out by the whole of the *Seventh Army*. The *III. Corps* of the *First Army* should have taken part, but reported that " it could not attack, but would support " the offensive with its heavy artillery."

The attack on the right of the British line was made by the reinforced *28th Brigade*, the *63rd Brigade*, and battalions of the *132nd* and *171st Regiments* of the *XV. Corps*. The troops " became engaged in a stationary " fire fight without actual progress."

The attack near the Chivy valley was carried out by the *13th Reserve Division* and *50th Brigade*. " Chivy fell into the hands of the Westphalians " [above-mentioned division], and some ground beyond it was won " ; but later " Chivy had to be evacuated, and in general the troops had to go " back to their starting places."

Mention is also made of an attack by the *14th Reserve Division* (less *28th Brigade*), between the two above mentioned, towards Troyon. The left (east) portion of the division " struck a wire entanglement of the enemy, " certainly a poor one, but it was not expected and could not be sur- " mounted. The whole front of the division came to a standstill under " heavy hostile artillery fire."

The account ends with the words :—" This attempt at attack had also " been shattered." (Zwehl, pp. 88-90.)

[2] On 4th October the first operation in the nature of a raid took place. On the front of the 1/Coldstream, just east of the Troyon factory road, the Germans had run out a sap, and it was decided to fill it in. At 8 P.M. a platoon of the battalion, led by 2/Lieut. M. Beckwith Smith (who was wounded and subsequently received the D.S.O.), crossing the hundred yards of No Man's Land, rushed the trench with the bayonet, and finding

continued on both sides: the Germans occasionally Sept.-Oct.
managed by lucky shots to burst shells in the billets of 1914.
British units well south of the river; the 9th Lancers in
this way lost over forty officers and men at Longueval
(2½ miles south of Bourg) on the 29th. No further serious
attacks by infantry took place and there were signs of
cessation of artillery action also. The expenditure of gun
ammunition had been so enormous, and had so far exceeded the calculations of the most far-seeing, that the
British Commander-in-Chief had been for some days
anxious as to the supply of shells for his heavy artillery.
However, on the 28th it was noticed that twelve German
shells which fell among the 9th Brigade failed to burst;
and by the 6th October the proportion of " blinds " fired
by the German batteries had risen to one in two. Evidently the enemy on this part of the line was also in difficulties for ammunition and using old stock. But the time
was now coming for the British to leave the Aisne.

NOTE

THE GERMAN STRATEGY DURING THE BATTLE OF THE AISNE [1]

On the evening of the 14th September, when General von Falkenhayn took over the duties of the Chief of the General Staff, also re-
taining those of the Minister of War, he was fully acquainted with the
situation. He had been warned on the 10th August that if anything
happened to Moltke he would be appointed to replace him, and from
the outset he had been at G.H.Q. keeping touch with events. The
outlook was gloomy, and he had to come to an immediate decision
whether he would continue the offensive campaign in France, or
stand on the defence there and go to the assistance of the defeated
Austrians. The German right flank in the West was open; the
transfer of strong forces to the East would probably lead to envelopment and disaster in France. The movement to the East, Falkenhayn thought, could not be attempted until the French and British
had been defeated. He came to the conclusion that he must adhere
to the original plan of obtaining a quick decision in the West, and
determined to resume the offensive as speedily as possible. It was
quite clear that the operations would take some weeks, and the question was whether the Eastern Front could hold out so long and, without help, protect the German rear. Six and a half new Reserve corps
were being organized, but they would not be available before October.
Falkenhayn therefore directed that a *Ninth Army* should be formed
in the East of the *XI.* and *Guard Reserve Corps* and a cavalry division

another trench behind it, rushed that also, killing 17 Germans in it. These
trenches were, however, covered by a third, and it was not possible, owing
to fire from it, to fill them in.
[1] From G.O.A., v. pp. 1-143.

sent in August from France, two corps taken from *Eighth Army*
(Hindenburg), Woyrsch's *Landwehr* corps (which had already co-
operated with the Austrians), and a division of the mobile reserve of
the fortress of Posen : all told, a total of 11 divisions and one cavalry
division. This left the *Eighth Army*, with 9½ divisions and one
cavalry division. Hindenburg was directed to hand over the command of it to General von Schubert, and himself take command of the
Ninth Army, and do what could be done to help the Austrians.[1]

Map 2.   Falkenhayn's first plan, committed to writing on the night of
the 14th/15th, maintained the main idea of the Schlieffen plan : an
enveloping offensive against the Allied left wing. For this purpose,
he proposed to use the *Sixth Army* from Alsace. The place of the
Sixth and *Seventh Armies* was to be taken by various Army detachments, under Generals Strantz, Falkenhausen and Gaede, composed
mainly of *Ersatz* and *Landwehr* troops. The heads of all the advanced guards of the *Sixth Army*, however, could not arrive even
behind the *Second Army*, which did not hold the outer flank, until
the 21st. To bridge over the time, he first proposed that the *Second*,
Seventh and *First Armies* should wheel back to the line Reims—Laon
—La Fère—Artemps (7½ miles S.S.W. of St. Quentin), even further, if
pressed, until the right was on the Warnelle stream (Le Cateau).

The General Staff, however, advised Falkenhayn that the German
troops would hardly stand further rearward movements without
demoralization, and, as he was by no means desirous of opening his
tenure of command by a retirement, he abandoned his scheme. He
did so the more readily as on the morning of the 15th Colonel Tappen
(Operations Section) returned from a visit to the front with a reassuring account of the situation : the gap between the *First* and *Second*
Armies had been closed, and the *First Army* was out of danger.
Falkenhayn, therefore, decided to stand on the defensive and accept
battle whilst collecting the *Sixth Army*. Kluck proposed to counter-
attack with the *First Army* at once to stop envelopment ; but Bülow,
remembering the results of his colleague's counter-attacks on the
Marne, opposed this, and approval was given to his plan, already in
course of execution, that " the *Seventh Army* should throw the enemy
" in front of it back on to the Aisne," whilst the *First* and *Second*
Armies on either side of it assisted by attacking concentrically.
This offensive was carried out on the 16th, 17th and 18th without
any success, the results being described as "unsatisfactory " on the
15th, " essentially resultless " on the 16th, " without decisive result "
on the 17th, and "without bringing a decision any nearer " on the
18th. The efforts of the *Third, Fourth* and *Fifth Armies* to co-
operate on these days " remained without any visible result ; they
" had not succeeded in preventing French forces from moving away,
" whilst, on the other hand, they did not permit the [German] troops
" to get any rest, and wore down their physical and moral strength."

On the 16th Falkenhayn ordered the investment of Antwerp
to be changed to bombardment and siege, in order to capture the
fortress and secure the safety of the German communications. On the
18th, when the French threat of envelopment was becoming definite,

---

[1] The *Ninth Army* was sent to the left of the Austrians to give direct
assistance, whilst the *Eighth* held East Prussia. Between them, with the
help of the *XXV. Reserve Corps* which arrived in mid-October, they held
off the Russians until further assistance was sent in November after the
Battle of Ypres.

he directed Crown Prince Rupprecht (*Sixth Army*) to take over the Sept.
protection of the right flank, and use the first forces (*XXI. Corps*) 1914.
which arrived, " even battalion by battalion," to throw back the
French—assumed to be cavalry with infantry attached—who were
assembling and reported to be at Roye, Montdidier and Péronne.
To prevent the French from transferring troops from right to left,
at 9.30 A.M. on the 19th he ordered a general offensive next day from
Verdun westward, " at latest at daybreak," of the *Fifth, Fourth,
Third* and left of the *Second Armies*, which were to attack and
" overrun the French infantry positions, and capture as many as
" possible of the numerous hostile guns." The rest of the *Second*,
and the *Seventh* and the *First Armies* were to continue their offensive.
Ammunition, however, was short, the commanders of the *Fifth,
Fourth* and *Third Armies* protested, and the C.G.S. was compelled
to revoke his orders to them, and substitute the words " make
" offensive strokes " for " attack." There was severe fighting on
the 20th, as we have seen, on the front of the *Seventh* and *First
Armies*, but the other Armies made only half-hearted efforts, without
any result.

During that day Falkenhayn visited the various Army headquarters, finishing his tour at St. Quentin, where Crown Prince
Rupprecht was located. He found that the *First Army* had already
shifted the *II. Corps* to extend its right. Thoroughly alarmed at
the French transfer of troops north-west and the slowness of movement by rail and road of the corps which were to form the *Sixth
Army*, Falkenhayn on the 25th ordered another general attack of all
the other Armies for the 26th ; sending at 6.40 P.M. a special message,
" It is urgently necessary to exploit to the utmost the successes
" gained by the attacks to be made to-night." The German
Armies did their best to respond, but although they were cheered
by the news of the capture on the 25th, at the conclusion of
operations begun on the 22nd, of the Fort Camp des Romains and
the area to be known as the St. Mihiel salient, by Strantz's Army
Detachment, pushed out from Metz, there was everywhere failure,
and the Official Account records (pp. 108, 114, *et seq.*) :

" The 26th was the bloodiest battle-day of the whole of this period
" of the war. . . . Nowhere had the Armies won any ground worth
" mention, far less beaten the enemy. . . . A great part of the
" German Armies suffered irreparable loss of officers and men in
" these battles ; but what was more serious was the disappearance
" of the hitherto unshaken faith in the irresistible might of the
" German attack, which the Marne had not destroyed. . . . The
" result of the fighting from the 15th to the 27th did not come up to
" expectation. The German Army had not succeeded in beating
" the ever-lengthening western wing of the enemy. Instead, the
" *Sixth Army* itself was compelled to form front to a flank."

CHAPTER XXII

THE " RACE TO THE SEA " AND THE TRANSFER OF
THE B.E.F. TO FLANDERS

(Sketch 21 ; Maps 2, 3 & 4)

Sketch 21. It will be remembered that, shortly after the Aisne was
Maps 2, 3 reached, General Joffre had reinforced the Sixth Army
& 4. with the XIII. Corps, and impressed on General Maunoury
the importance of enveloping the German right flank ; in
consequence of which, on the 17th September, the latter
commander again took the offensive.[1] His left wing, consisting of the XIII. Corps, IV. Corps and Ebener's Group
of Reserve divisions (61st and 62nd), was ordered to outflank the German right which was bent back near Noyon,
south of the Oise ; whilst his right was to consolidate the
ground gained north of the Aisne, keep contact with the
enemy, and be ready to resume the offensive.

At the moment the forces at the disposal of the German
Supreme Command to meet the enveloping movement were
small in number.   The *IX. Reserve Corps*, which had been
brought from Antwerp, had arrived on the right of the
First Army on the 15th and had been thrust into the fight
by Kluck next day.   The *Sixth Army* could not be expected
to arrive there on that flank much before the 25th.   Bülow,
with the approval of O.H.L., after ordering Kluck to stop an
offensive [2] which, in order to prevent envelopment, he was
wildly taking south-westward with his right—the *IV.* and
IX. Reserve Corps and the *4th* and *7th Cavalry Divisions*—
instructed him to echelon these two corps behind his right
flank.   On the 16th, the *2nd* and *9th Cavalry Divisions* were
sent from the Chemin des Dames to his support.

On the 17th September, before the retrograde movement of Kluck's right could be carried out, the French
offensive began.   The French IV. and XIII. Corps advan-

---

[1] See page 443.   [2] See page 426.

456

THE EXTENSION OF THE BATTLE-LINE NORTHWARDS.
15 SEPTEMBER – 8 OCTOBER, 1914.

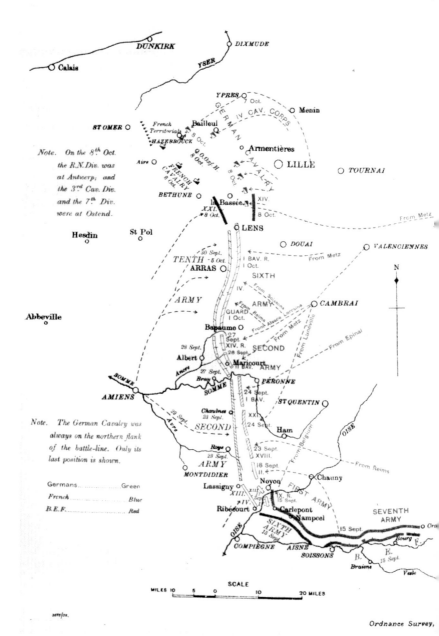

Note. On the 8th Oct.
the R.N.Div. was
at Antwerp; and
the 3rd Cav. Div.
and the 7th Div.
were at Ostend.

Note. The German Cavalry was
always on the northern flank
of the battle-line. Only its
last position is shown.

Germans................ Green
French................ Blue
B.E.F.................. Red

SCALE

MILES 10   5   0   10   20 MILES

cing up both sides of the Oise came into collision with the German right in the area Carlepont—Noyon. On the 18th, however, the French attack came to a standstill on a line south-east and north-west through Carlepont. The first attempt to outflank the Germans had failed and had only resulted in the extension of the battle front north of the Aisne.

General Joffre made his next effort with the reconstructed Second Army under General de Castelnau, and on the 26th September sent General Foch, as his deputy, to take charge of the operations on the western flank. The composition of the Second Army has already been given.[1] As a preliminary measure, its former front in Lorraine having been taken over by the French First Army—since entrenchments allowed the line to be held with fewer men—its four corps were concentrated about Amiens, the four cavalry divisions covering its left flank. On the 22nd September, this Second Army advanced across the Avre against the front Lassigny—Roye—Chaulnes ; but, by this time, new German forces had arrived and were ready to parry the envelopment. The German *II. Corps* of the *First Army* had been withdrawn from its position on the Aisne and brought to the right of the *IX. Reserve Corps*. It came into line between Noyon and Roye on the 18th/19th September. Even with the support of Marwitz's four cavalry divisions, the *II. Corps* proved insufficient to stop de Castelnau's offensive, and on the afternoon of the 23rd the French Second Army had reached the road Ribecourt— Lassigny—Roye and was threatening the German communications at Ham and St. Quentin. At this critical moment, the German *XVIII. Corps*, sent off by road on the 21st from the neighbourhood of Reims, over fifty miles away, was approaching Ham. It immediately counter-attacked westward towards Roye, and, supported by the *II. Corps*, it forced back the right wing of the French. De Castelnau's left wing, however, reached Péronne and formed a bridgehead on the eastern bank of the Somme.

The offensive force of the French Second Army was for the moment spent ; and it was not fated to make further progress, for another German Army was beginning to appear on the western flank.

At a conference between Falkenhayn and Bülow on the 21st, it had been decided to concentrate the *Sixth Army* in as great strength as possible, near Amiens ; it was to

[1] See page 443.

make a push for the coast and then turn and envelop the French left wing south of the Somme. Before however these troops could arrive de Castelnau's offensive had so materially altered the situation that the plan had to be abandoned ; for the first two corps (the *XXI.* and *I. Bavarian*) as they came up found their way to Amiens barred and they were merely used to extend the front.

The *XXI. Corps* had entrained at Blouay (Lunéville) on the 15th September, and had been railed through Belgium to Cambrai, whence it marched at once towards Chaulnes, arriving, on the right of the *XVIII. Corps*, on the 24th. The same evening the *I. Bavarian Corps* came up on the right of the *XXI.*, facing Péronne. Entrained at Glonville (east of Epinal) on the 14th/15th September, it had been railed to Namur, whence it made a forced march. These two newly arrived corps, with Marwitz's cavalry (now reinforced by the *Guard Cavalry Division*) on the right, drove the French out of Péronne and across the Somme. On the 26th after heavy fighting de Castelnau took up a strong position on the line Lassigny—Roye—Bray. The German cavalry corps moved further north to clear the front for the *II. Bavarian Corps*, which now came into line on the right of the *I. Bavarian Corps*, north of the Somme. This corps had entrained at Metz on the 18th/19th September and had travelled as far as Valenciennes by rail.

On the 27th, Marwitz's cavalry corps continued its way northwards, driving away d'Amade's French Territorials, now under General Brugère, and clearing the front this time for the *XIV. Reserve Corps*, which came up on that day on the right of the *II. Bavarian Corps* and at once moved on Albert. The two divisions of the *XIV. Reserve Corps* had detrained at Valenciennes and Cambrai.[1]

On the 25th September the German Supreme Command had moved from Luxembourg to Mezières—Charleville, and, as already recorded, had ordered the *Second, Seventh* and *First Armies* to take the offensive again, in order to hold the Allies to their position on the Aisne, and prevent the flow of reinforcements to the Somme district.

Meanwhile, the German offensive in the north was progressing. The *II. Bavarian* and *XIV. Reserve Corps* easily drove back the French Territorial division holding

[1] An account of the journey from Lorraine and the disorganization at Cambrai is given in the "Erlebnisse" of General von Stein, who commanded the *XIV. Reserve Corps*.

the Bapaume district, and were approaching Bray sur
Somme and Albert in high hopes of reaching Amiens and
Abbeville and the sea. But again reinforcements came
to the French northern flank, where General de Castelnau
was holding on to cover the detrainment of the Tenth
Army (at first called " Subdivision d'Armée ") near Arras.
There was little time to lose, and during the 25th, 26th
and 27th September the XXI. and X. Corps, which were
north of the Somme, covered on the left by Brugère's
group of Territorial divisions and Conneau's cavalry corps,
were in grave danger ; but by the evening of the 28th they
had succeeded in stopping the Germans on the line Mari-
court—Fricourt—Thiepval. Marwitz's cavalry extended
the German line further northwards to the neighbourhood
of Arras, where it was held in check by Conneau's cavalry.

The commander of the new Tenth Army, General
Maud'huy (lately commanding the XVIII. Corps), had
to deal with a totally different situation from that which
had confronted de Castelnau on his arrival in the north.
So far from being able to take the offensive in the hopes
of turning the enemy's flank, a strong German force was
already advancing and threatening Arras before the
Tenth Army was even concentrated. For the moment the
most that General Maud'huy could hope was to bring the
enemy to a standstill. On the 29th September, the X.
Corps then at Acheux, between Albert and Doullens (20
miles north of Amiens), Conneau's cavalry corps (1st, 3rd,
5th and 10th Cavalry Divisions) south-east of Arras, and
d'Urbal's provisional corps, consisting of Barbot's and
Fayolle's Reserve divisions, at Arras and Lens respectively,
were placed at his disposal.

On the 1st October, Maud'huy, having but a few hours'
breathing space to make preparations, was intending to
begin an offensive from Arras—Lens south-east against
the German flank, in the expectation of finding nothing in
front of him except cavalry.[1] But again the enemy was
able to parry the blow, for behind the cavalry three more
corps had arrived, and were already deploying preparatory
to taking the offensive. The French Tenth Army, scattered
over a wide front, was soon in imminent danger of being
itself enveloped.

It was to be expected that the Germans would make
every effort to prevent the French line from being extended

[1] An account of General Maud'huy's operations will be found in the
" Revue des Deux Mondes " for 1st August 1920.

to include Lille, and also—what would have been still
more serious for them—from joining hands with the
Belgian Army in Antwerp. This fortress, close to the
Dutch frontier, offered, apart from its intrinsic importance,
an ideal holdfast on which to secure the Allied extreme
left flank. The German Supreme Command had already
decided on its future plan. It involved three distinct
operations, in which all the troops that could be released
or collected were to be employed.[1]

First, a strong offensive was to be made on the northern
wing near Arras. The three corps selected for the purpose
were the *IV.* from the *First Army*, the *Guard Corps* from
the *Second Army*, and the *I. Bavarian Reserve Corps*, the
last remaining corps of the original *Sixth Army*. The
attack on Arras was begun on the 2nd October, in combination with an attempt to break through near Roye and
capture the French forces between the two places.

Secondly, eight cavalry divisions (the *Bavarian Cavalry
Division* had arrived and joined the others), in three corps,
the *I.* and *II.* under General von der Marwitz, and the *IV.*
under Lieut.-General von Hollen, were to cover the right
flank of the offensive and sweep across Flanders towards
the coast.[2] The two groups started on the 2nd and 4th
October, respectively.

Thirdly, the operations at Antwerp were to be accelerated, and the place captured before it could be reinforced.
The bombardment with 42-cm. howitzers was commenced
on the night of the 27th/28th September.

Map 2. It may be noticed here that, taking up a proposal
made earlier from London, General Joffre, on the 16th September, had asked that all available troops should be sent
to Dunkirk and Calais " to act effectively and constantly
" against the enemy's communications," so as to interfere
with his outflanking movements. In response, the Marine
Brigade of the Royal Naval Division was disembarked at
Dunkirk on the night of the 19th/20th September and the
Oxfordshire Yeomanry on the 22nd.[3] These troops were

---

[1] Falkenhayn, p. 12. Stegemann, ii. pp. 70-76. Vogel, p. 179.
[2] *I. Cavalry Corps : Guard* and *4th Cavalry Divisions.*
  II.   „   „   *2nd, 7th* and *9th Cavalry Divisions.*
  IV.   „   „   *3rd, 6th* and *Bavarian Cavalry Divisions.*
      (" Schlachten und Gefechte," pp. 46 and 48.)
  The Kaiser sent General von der Marwitz a message on 3rd October,
" His Majesty wishes to see the cavalry corps in the rear of the enemy
" to-morrow."
[3] How they were got across is described in " Naval Operations," vol. i.
p. 190.

under the command of Br.-General G. Aston, who had Sept.-Oct. instructions to give the impression that they were the 1914. advanced guard of a large British force. As in the case of minor landings in the past, the enemy paid no direct attention to so stingless a threat. He took measures, however, to push on with the siege of Antwerp.

The action of Br.-General Aston's force, and of other troops landed on the coast in October 1914, is related in due course in a subsequent volume. It suffices to say now that on the 28th September, the first day of the bombardment of Antwerp, Br.-General Aston sent one battalion to Lille ; the rest of his brigade moved to Cassel on the 30th, and watched the country by means of parties in motors. On the 29th, in consequence of sickness, he had handed the command over to Br.-General A. Paris. At 6 A.M. on the 3rd October the brigade was moved to Antwerp, being followed on the 6th by two new brigades of the Royal Naval Division which had landed at Dunkirk on the night of the 3rd/4th. On the 6th also the 7th Division landed at Zeebrugge, followed on the 7th by the 3rd Cavalry Division.[1]

To return to the German offensive against the French Sketch21. Tenth Army near Arras, the *Guard* and *IV. Corps* left Maps 2 their old positions on the Aisne on the 27th, and the *I.* & 3. *Bavarian Reserve Corps* entrained at Metz on the same day. The three corps came into action on the 1st October, almost simultaneously, in the above order from south to north, on the front Arras—Douai, where there were General Brugère's (formerly d'Amade's) Territorial troops. They thus encountered the Tenth Army whilst it was preparing for its offensive. Neither side was destined to achieve its ambitious aims. Very heavy fighting took place on 1st-9th October; the French gave ground gradually, but eventually brought the German onslaught to a standstill. By the evening of the 6th the front had become stabilized near the line Thiepval—Gommecourt—Blairville—eastern outskirts of Arras—Bailleul—Vimy—Souchez, on which the belligerents were to face each other for so many months.[2] The attempt to break through near Roye was an even greater failure, although continued until the 9th, when Falkenhayn ordered the battle to be broken off, as no

[1] The organization of these divisions is given in " 1914," Vol. II.
[2] It was on the morning of the 6th that General Foch said to the commander of the Tenth Army, " Fight to the last man, but hang on " like lice. No retirement. Every man to the attack " (" Revue des Deux Mondes," 15.8.1920, p. 846).

impression had been made on the French defence. To the
Germans it was " incomprehensible " that they could not
get the better of the French, and their ill-success was
ascribed to the strength of the French field fortifications
and the hitherto unappreciated power of the defence.[1]
The German hopes now rested on the three *Cavalry
Corps, I., II.* and *IV.* under Marwitz and Hollen, outflanking the French line, and so compelling a withdrawal.
They had been working north of the main battle, pushing
local Territorial troops before them, to the line Lens—Lille
(which towns still remained in French possession).

On the 2nd October, Marwitz had issued orders for a
general offensive, the objectives of which were " finally to
" break down the weakening resistance of the enemy by
" operating against his flank and rear, to block all the
" railways leading from Paris and the Lower Seine, and
" to destroy completely the railways from the lower Somme
" and the coastal railways near Abbeville." A number of
additional artillery, engineer and infantry units were
allotted to the cavalry divisions.[2]

The progress of this great cavalry raid must have been
extremely disappointing to those who had organized it.
The operation was in fact a complete failure. The *I.* and
II. Cavalry Corps advancing between Lens and Lille met
with some opposition and by evening retired behind the
Lorette heights. It was only with difficulty that they
held their ground on the 7th, for the heads of the divisions
of the French XXI. Corps, detrained near Béthune, were
moving against them.

On the morning of the 8th, however, hopes of French
success were again blighted by the arrival of the German
XIV. Corps to extricate the cavalry. Entraining at Metz
on the 4th October, this corps had marched to the field
from Mons. On its arrival the *I.* and *II. Cavalry Corps*
were sent north to penetrate between La Bassée and
Armentières and reach Abbeville.

Meantime the *IV. Cavalry Corps* moving north of Lille
had, on the 8th, passed through Ypres expecting to reach
the sea that evening.[3] General von Hollen's orders were
" to ride round the flank and rear of the enemy opposite
" the right wing, thoroughly destroy the communications,

[1] G.O.A., v. p. 148.
[2] See Reinhardt's " Sechs Monate Westfront," p. 19 ; Rutz's " Bayernkämpfe," p. 12 ; Hocker's " An der Spitze meiner Kompagnie," p. 124.
[3] Rutz's " Bayernkämpfe," pp. 16-25 ; he was with the *2nd Cavalry
Division*.

" particularly the railways which lead from the coast and Oct. 1914.
" the south to the area west of Amiens—Lille—Alost, and
" at the cost of the last horse and man ensure that the
" enemy's operations against our right flank are hindered
" in every way." The columns turned south-west from
Ypres and were soon streaming on all the roads towards
Hazebrouck. They turned back, however, on meeting
resistance from units of de Mitry's newly formed cavalry
corps,[1] and reassembled next day in and near Bailleul.

Thus by the 9th October, on both sides, the battle line
had been extended from the Aisne westwards and northwards to within 30 miles of Dunkirk and the coast.

Towards the close of September, Sir John French had Map 2.
suggested to General Joffre the transfer of the British Army
to its former place on the left of the line. Other British
troops, as already mentioned, were about to be landed in
the north of France;[2] and it was obviously desirable that
all the forces of the nation available should act in one body.
The lines of communication also of the B.E.F. would be
greatly shortened by its being near the coast. The British
were specially concerned in preventing the fall of Antwerp,
and were vitally interested in barring the way to the
Channel ports from which the Germans could threaten the
transport of troops from England to France and block the
avenues of water-borne traffic converging on London. That
the Germans had not seized Ostend, Calais and Boulogne
during their first triumphant advance, when they might
easily have done so, had been due to lack of troops;[3] but that
omission they were now desperately striving to make good.

Apart from all question of those ports, it was obvious
that if the British were restored to their old place on the
left of the new line, they could be reinforced with a swift-
ness and secrecy elsewhere impossible.

Against this movement there were the obvious objec-
tions that it must be carried out gradually, so that for a
time the British Expeditionary Force would be divided,
and that the British in their journey northward must
move right across the line of the French communications,
thus necessarily preventing the despatch of French troops
to the north for several, it was even said ten, days.
General Joffre, however, agreed to Sir John French's pro-

[1] 4th and 5th Cavalry Divisions, from the Fifth Army and I. Cavalry
Corps, respectively.
[2] See page 461.   [3] See page 48.

posal; and on the night of the 1st/2nd October was begun the withdrawal of the British troops from the valley of the Aisne. Their movements were carefully concealed; all marches were made by night and the men confined to their billets by day, so that no sign of their departure from the Aisne should be visible to enemy aircraft. These precautions were so far successful that on the 3rd October an intercepted German wireless message mentioned that all six British divisions were still on the Aisne.[1]

The II. Corps was the first to move, the I. Corps extending its left to Vailly and the III. Corps its right to Missy to cover the vacated ground. A day's rest on the south bank enabled the II. Corps to make good its deficiencies in blankets and greatcoats which had been keenly felt throughout the miserable weather on the Aisne. By the night of the 3rd/4th the entire corps had started on its march westward to the railway at Compiègne and three neighbouring stations. The 2nd Cavalry Division marched by road on the night of the 2nd; the 1st Cavalry Division on the night of the 3rd. The III. Corps, giving over its trenches to the French on the night of the 6th, moved off twenty-four hours later, also to entrain at and near Compiègne, leaving the 16th Brigade with the I. Corps.[2] This corps remained in its trenches until the night of the 12th/13th, but the evacuation was not finally completed until forty-eight hours later.

The advance of the B.E.F. into Flanders will be dealt with in the succeeding volume of this history, but the following outline of it is given to complete the narrative of the move from the Aisne. During the 8th and 9th October the II. Corps detrained at Abbeville and concentrated on both banks of the lower Authie, about twelve miles north-east of Abbeville, in the area Genne Iverny—Gueschart—La Boisle—Raye. It then received orders to advance towards Béthune. On the 9th also, the 2nd Cavalry Division arrived between St. Pol and Hesdin, with the 1st a day's march in rear of it. On the 8th, G.H.Q. moved from Fère en Tardenois to Abbeville and five days later to St. Omer.

<hr />

[1] G.H.Q. operation orders for the relief and movements are given in Appendices 48 to 51. It was not until 8th October that German air reconnaissances revealed lively traffic on the railway south of the Aisne, and the movement of lorries and marching columns westwards : a transfer of troops from the Aisne to the lower Somme was deduced. (G.O.A., v. p. 197.)

[2] The 19th Brigade took its place for a time in the III. Corps.

On the 11th October, the III. Corps began detraining Oct. 1914. and concentrating at St. Omer and Hazebrouck, and subsequently moved on the left rear of the II. towards Bailleul and Armentières.

On the 19th, a week later than the III. Corps, the I. Corps detrained and concentrated at Hazebrouck, and moved on Ypres. The 7th Division and 3rd Cavalry Division landed at Ostend and Zeebrugge, and the Belgian Army retiring from Antwerp had meantime filled the gap between Ypres and the sea.

Thus ended for the British the fighting on the Aisne Sketches in 1914 ; and the narrative may be closed with a very brief 19 & 20. review of the battle. Maps 35 & 36.

The disappointing results of the operations on the 12th-14th September, after which a deadlock ensued, seem to have been due to a failure of the High Command to appreciate the situation, and exploit the still existing gap in the enemy's line. It was at any rate partly due to the neglect to exercise control and issue orders which would have made the essential requirements of the situation clear to subordinate commanders.

The forcing of the Aisne was likely to involve a race with hostile reinforcements, in which the Germans had the advantage, as they were falling back. This race was lost mainly owing to the failure to make a resolute effort even to reconnoitre the enemy's dispositions on the river, and, except in the 4th Division, to push forward parties to seize the bridges on the night of the 12th/13th. On the 13th, when the divisions made a rather cautious and leisurely advance, they should have been reminded, in spite of their fatigue after over three weeks' continuous operations, that " sweat saves blood." In the G.H.Q. orders there was no hint whatever of the importance of time.

By the evening of the 13th September the situation had completely changed. German reinforcements were known to have arrived, and serious resistance was to be expected on the 14th ; yet the G.H.Q. orders merely repeated the formula that " the Army will continue the " pursuit . . . and act vigorously against the retreating " enemy " ; they gave no more tactical direction than to allot roads. There was no plan, no objective, no arrangements for co-operation, and the divisions blundered into battle.

The actual passage of the Aisne is likely to be remem-

2 H

bered in the annals of the Army as a very remarkable feat ; for it involved forcing a passage frontally without possibility of manœuvre. The Germans excuse their failure to stop the British at the river line by the explanation that their peace-time teaching required one single strong line and a long field of fire, and that to secure these they went back to the top of the plateau. The advance of the 11th Brigade alone across the damaged bridge at Venizel was a most audacious move ; yet at no point did the crossing of any one body of troops facilitate the passage of others, owing to the topography of the valley and the small depth of the positions gained on the north side of the river. But for the German failure to destroy the aqueduct at Bourg completely, it is possible that the British might have been unable to maintain their firm hold on the north bank. By way of that aqueduct, however, the guns of the 1st Division managed to cross the river and find effective positions at once. Thus Sir Douglas Haig, taking instant advantage of his opportunity, was able to make his bold thrust forward on the 14th and to establish his right on the Chemin des Dames, where his troops clung to the shallow holes which did duty for trenches, with a tenacity beyond all praise. For want of another division in reserve, he was unable to push his advance further ; to the west of Troyon the 2nd Division, the II. Corps and the III. Corps were pinned to their ground and could give him no help.

Regarding the Aisne in the light of the ditch of a fortress, only the I. Corps had really passed over it and could see any prospect of carrying forward its attack. The II. and III. Corps had practically made no more than a lodgment on the escarp,[1] above which they dared not show their heads. They could find no effective positions for their artillery ; and for a time could make little reply to the German bombardment except with rifle fire. Indeed, had not the enemy frequently assaulted the British lines in force and in close formation, the British would have had little to show in return for the casualties which they suffered from the German artillery. As matters fell out, the Germans gave on many occasions the very opportunity of which the British soldier could take advantage, and he did so to the full.

It is somewhat difficult to arrive at the total number of German formations which fought the British five, eventually six, divisions on the Aisne ; for single brigades from

[1] The defender's side of the ditch of a fortress.

many corps were put into the line. Thus we know [1] that, apart from the cavalry and two heavy howitzer batteries, the British I. Corps was opposed not only by the *VII. Reserve Corps*, but by a mixed detachment of the *XII. Corps* consisting of the *63rd Brigade*, three batteries and a heavy howitzer battery ; the *50th Brigade* of the *XVIII. Corps* ; five battalions of the *XV. Corps*, the *25th Landwehr Brigade*, and 1,200 men of the *X. Corps* : a total of over 20 extra battalions. The British II. Corps had opposite it the German *III. Corps* with the *34th Brigade* of the *IX. Corps* interposed between its divisions,[2] and two heavy howitzer batteries, as well as, on at least one day, a regiment of the *VII. Corps*. The four infantry brigades of the III. Corps had in front of them the German *II. Corps*, whose front was from Chivres sector (exclusive) to Cuffies.[3] Thus, recalling that German brigades contained six battalions to the British four, there were at least 100 German battalions to 78 British (including the 6th Division).

It is remarkable to note the contrast from the 16th September onward between the activity of the Germans in the new *Seventh Army* east of Celles and the apathy of the wearied soldiers of Kluck's *First Army* west of the spur of Condé. Hardly a day passed without an onslaught of some kind on some point of the line between Paissy and Vailly ; but, except on the 26th September, there was little sign of an offensive movement west of Condé. There was, of course, constant shelling of the 5th and 4th Divisions, but little more ; yet the position of the 5th Division was so precarious as positively to invite attack. Moreover, the Germans can hardly have been unaware that the battalions of the 5th Division had suffered more, perhaps, in the previous operations than any others in the Army. The 4th Division, as its trenches improved and as its ranks were refilled, showed much enterprise on the Aisne. It could do nothing on a great scale ; but by pushing trenches forward and by worrying the Germans perpetually with patrols and snipers, it established over them a well-marked ascendancy.

The British Army gained much useful experience on the Aisne, and absolute confidence in its shooting. The men learned how to entrench quickly and to appreciate the value of digging. The drafts were able to settle down, and the young soldiers of the Special Reserve had time to gather instruction from the trained officers and N.C.O.'s who,

[1] From General von Zwehl, commander of the *VII. Reserve Corps*.
[2] Zwehl's map No. 4.   [3] Kluck, p. 187.

though sadly reduced in numbers, were still fairly abundant. For the rest, the soldiers astonished even those who had trained them by their staunchness, their patience, their indomitable cheerfulness under incessant hardship, and, in spite of a fire such as no human being had ever before experienced, by their calm, cool courage at all times. Whether it was the gunner unloading ammunition almost too hot to handle, in the midst of blazing wagons ; the engineer repairing his bridge under continuous fire ; the infantryman patiently enduring heavy shell fire, patrolling No-Man's-Land in the hours of darkness, or, as sniper, lying all night on soaking clay in dripping beet-fields ; the cavalry trooper fighting on foot to hold gaps in the line ; the transport driver guiding his wagons through bursting shells ; or the stretcher-bearer toiling through the dark hours to rescue the wounded, all alike proved themselves worthy soldiers of the King. Though their dearest friends, comrades of many years, fell beside them, they fought with the majesty of their ancestors, without anger or malice, trusting always in the good cause of their country. Their good health in quagmires of trenches under constant rain of itself testified to their discipline. Sober, temperate and self-respecting, they were not to be discouraged by wounds or sickness. There could be no fear as to the final victory, if only more armies of such soldiers could be brought into being in sufficient numbers and without delay, and conveyed in security across the Channel to France.

APPENDICES

APPENDIX 1. 471

ORDER OF BATTLE

OF THE

BRITISH EXPEDITIONARY FORCE

AUGUST 1914[1]

GENERAL HEADQUARTERS

Commander-in-Chief . . Field-Marshal Sir J. D. P. French, G.C.B., G.C.V.O., K.C.M.G.

GENERAL STAFF BRANCH:
Chief of the General Staff . Lieut.-General Sir A. J. Murray, K.C.B., C.V.O., D.S.O.
Major-General, General Staff Major-General H. H. Wilson, C.B., D.S.O.
G.S.O. 1 (Operations) . . Colonel G. M. Harper, D.S.O.
G.S.O. 1 (Intelligence) . . Colonel G. M. W. Macdonogh.

ADJUTANT-GENERAL'S BRANCH:
Adjutant-General . . . Major - General Sir C. F. N. Macready, K.C.B.
Deputy Adjutant-General . Major-General E. R. C. Graham, C.B.
Assistant Adjutant-General . Colonel A. E. J. Cavendish, C.M.G.

QUARTERMASTER-GENERAL'S BRANCH:
Quartermaster-General . . Major-General Sir W. R. Robertson, K.C.V.O., C.B., D.S.O.
Assistant Quartermaster - Colonel C. T. Dawkins, C.M.G.
General

Attached :
Major-General, Royal Artil- Major-General W. F. L. Lindsay, lery C.B., D.S.O.
Brigadier-General, Royal En- Brigadier-General G. H. Fowke.
gineers

[1] The Composition of Staffs is taken from " Expeditionary Force, General Headquarters, etc.," dated 8th August 1914 ; the units from the August and September copies of the " Composition of the British Expeditionary Force." The September issue is wrongly dated " 1 August."

HEADQUARTERS OF ADMINISTRATIVE SERVICES AND DEPARTMENTS :

Director of Army Signals . Colonel J. S. Fowler, D.S.O.
Director of Supplies . . Brigadier-General C. W. King, M.V.O.
Director of Ordnance Services Brigadier-General H. W. Perry.
Director of Transport . . Brigadier-General F. C. A. Gilpin, C.B.
Director of Railway Transport Colonel J. H. Twiss.
Director of Works . . . Brigadier-General A. M. Stuart.
Director of Remounts . . Brigadier-General F. S. Garratt, C.B., D.S.O.
Director of Veterinary Services Brigadier-General J. Moore.
Director of Medical Services Surgeon-General T. P. Woodhouse.
Director of Army Postal Services Colonel W. Price, C.M.G.
Paymaster-in-Chief . . Brigadier-General C. A. Bray, C.B., C.M.G.

The Cavalry Division

G.O.C. . . . . . . Major-General E. H. H. Allenby, C.B.
G.S.O. 1 . . . . . Colonel J. Vaughan, D.S.O.
Commanding R.H.A. . . Brigadier-General B. F. Drake.

1st Cavalry Brigade

G.O.C. . . . . . . Brigadier-General C. J. Briggs, C.B.
2nd Dragoon Guards (Queen's Bays) ;
5th (Princess Charlotte of Wales's) Dragoon Guards ;
11th (Prince Albert's Own) Hussars.
1st Signal Troop.

2nd Cavalry Brigade

G.O.C. . . . . . . Brigadier-General H. de B. de Lisle, C.B., D.S.O.
4th (Royal Irish) Dragoon Guards ;
9th (Queen's Royal) Lancers ;
18th (Queen Mary's Own) Hussars.
2nd Signal Troop.

3rd Cavalry Brigade

G.O.C. . . . . . . Brigadier-General H. de la P. Gough, C.B.
4th (Queen's Own) Hussars ;
5th (Royal Irish) Lancers ;
16th (The Queen's) Lancers.
3rd Signal Troop.

APPENDIX 1 473

4th Cavalry Brigade

G.O.C. . . . . . . Brigadier-General Hon. C. E. Bingham, C.V.O., C.B.

Composite Regiment of Household Cavalry ;
6th Dragoon Guards (Carabiniers) ;
3rd (King's Own) Hussars.
4th Signal Troop.

Cavalry Divisional Troops

Artillery . . III. Brigade R.H.A.,
D and E Batteries ;
III. Brigade Ammunition Column.

VII. Brigade R.H.A.,
I and L ¹ Batteries ;
VII. Brigade Ammunition Column.

Engineers . . 1st Field Squadron, R.E.

Signal Service . 1st Signal Squadron.

A.S.C. . . . H.Q. 1st Cavalry Divisional A.S.C.

Medical Units . 1st, 2nd, 3rd and 4th Cavalry Field Ambulances.

5th Cavalry Brigade (and attached troops)

G.O.C. . . . . . . Brigadier-General Sir P. W. Chetwode, Bart., D.S.O.

2nd Dragoons (Royal Scots Greys) ;
12th (Prince of Wales's Royal) Lancers ;
20th Hussars ;
with J Battery R.H.A. and Ammunition Column ;
4th Field Troop ;
5th Signal Troop ;
5th Cavalry Field Ambulance.

I. Corps

G.O.C. . . . . . . Lieut.-General Sir D. Haig, K.C.B., K.C.I.E., K.C.V.O., A.D.C.-Gen.

Brigadier-General, General Staff — Brigadier-General J. E. Gough, V.C., C.M.G., A.D.C.

Brigadier-General, Royal Artillery — Brigadier-General H. S. Horne, C.B.

Colonel, Royal Engineers . Brigadier-General S. R. Rice, C.B.

1st Division

G.O.C. . . . . . Major-General S. H. Lomax.

G.S.O. 1 . . . . . Colonel R. Fanshawe, D.S.O.

C.R.A. . . . . . Brigadier-General N. D. Findlay, C.B.

C.R.E. . . . . . Lieut.-Colonel A. L. Schreiber, D.S.O.

¹ H Battery R.H.A. was sent out in September to replace L Battery.

APPENDIX 1

1st (Guards) Brigade

G.O.C. . . . . . . Brigadier - General F. I. Maxse,
C.V.O., C.B., D.S.O.

1st Coldstream Guards ;
1st Scots Guards ;
1st The Black Watch (Royal Highlanders) ;
2nd The Royal Munster Fusiliers.[1]

2nd Infantry Brigade

G.O.C. . . . . . . Brigadier-General E. S. Bulfin,
C.V.O., C.B.

2nd The Royal Sussex Regiment ;
1st The Loyal North Lancashire Regiment ;
1st The Northamptonshire Regiment ;
2nd The King's Royal Rifle Corps.

3rd Infantry Brigade

G.O.C. . . . . . . Brigadier-General H. J. S. Landon,
C.B.

1st The Queen's (Royal West Surrey Regiment) ;
1st The South Wales Borderers ;
1st The Gloucestershire Regiment ;
2nd The Welch Regiment.

Divisional Troops

Mounted Troops .   C Squadron, 15th (The King's) Hussars.
1st Cyclist Company.

Artillery[2] . .   XXV. Brigade R.F.A.,
113th, 114th and 115th Batteries ;
XXV. Brigade Ammunition Column.

XXVI. Brigade R.F.A.,
116th, 117th and 118th Batteries ;
XXVI. Brigade Ammunition Column.

XXXIX. Brigade R.F.A.,
46th, 51st and 54th Batteries ;
XXXIX. Brigade Ammunition Column.

XLIII. (Howitzer) Brigade R.F.A.,
30th, 40th and 57th (Howitzer) Batteries ;
XLIII. (Howitzer) Brigade Ammunition
Column.

26th Heavy Battery R.G.A., and
Heavy Battery Ammunition Column.

1st Divisional Ammunition Column.

[1] In September the 1/Queen's Own Cameron Highlanders replaced the 2/Royal Munster Fusiliers in the 1st (Guards) Brigade.
[2] An Anti-Aircraft Detachment (of 1-pdr. Pom-Poms) was added to the Divisional Artillery in September.

Engineers . .	23rd Field Company, R.E. 26th Field Company, R.E.
Signal Service .	1st Signal Company.
A.S.C. . . .	1st Divisional Train.
Medical Units .	1st, 2nd and 3rd Field Ambulances.

2nd Division

G.O.C.	Major-General C. C. Monro, C.B.
G.S.O. 1	Colonel Hon. F. Gordon, D.S.O.
C.R.A.	Brigadier-General E. M. Perceval, D.S.O.
C.R.E.	Lieut.-Colonel R. H. H. Boys, D.S.O.

4th (Guards) Brigade

G.O.C. . . . . . . Brigadier-General R. Scott-Kerr, C.B., M.V.O., D.S.O.

2nd Grenadier Guards ;
2nd Coldstream Guards ;
3rd Coldstream Guards ;
1st Irish Guards.

5th Infantry Brigade

G.O.C. . . . . . . Brigadier-General R. C. B. Haking, C.B.

2nd The Worcestershire Regiment ;
2nd The Oxfordshire and Buckinghamshire Light Infantry ;
2nd The Highland Light Infantry ;
2nd The Connaught Rangers

6th Infantry Brigade

G.O.C. . . . . . . Brigadier-General R. H. Davies, C.B. (New Zealand Staff Corps).

1st The King's (Liverpool Regiment) ;
2nd The South Staffordshire Regiment :
1st Princess Charlotte of Wales's (Royal Berkshire Regiment) ;
1st The King's Royal Rifle Corps.

Divisional Troops

Mounted Troops .	B Squadron 15th (The King's) Hussars. 2nd Cyclist Company.
Artillery [1] . .	XXXIV. Brigade R.F.A., 22nd, 50th and 70th Batteries; XXXIV. Brigade Ammunition Column.

[1] An Anti-Aircraft Detachment (of 1-pdr. Pom-Poms) was added to the Divisional Artillery in September.

XXXVI. Brigade R.F.A.,
15th, 48th and 71st Batteries ;
XXXVI. Brigade Ammunition Column.

XLI. Brigade R.F.A.,
9th, 16th and 17th Batteries ;
XLI. Brigade Ammunition Column.

XLIV. (Howitzer) Brigade R.F.A.,
47th, 56th and 60th (Howitzer) Batteries ;
XLIV. (Howitzer) Brigade Ammunition
Column.

35th Heavy Battery R.G.A., and
Heavy Battery Ammunition Column.

2nd Divisional Ammunition Column.

Engineers	. .	5th Field Company, R.E. 11th Field Company, R.E.
Signal Service	.	2nd Signal Company.
A.S.C.	. . .	2nd Divisional Train.
Medical Units	.	4th, 5th and 6th Field Ambulances.

II. Corps

G.O.C.	(1) Lieut.-General Sir J. M. Grierson, K.C.B., C.V.O., C.M.G., A.D.C.-Gen. (Died in the train, between Rouen and Amiens, 17th August 1914). (2) General Sir H. L. Smith-Dorrien, G.C.B., D.S.O. (Took over command of II. Corps at Bavai, 4 P.M., 21st August 1914).
Brigadier-General, General Staff	Brigadier-General G. T. Forestier-Walker, A.D.C.
Brigadier - General, Royal Artillery	Brigadier-General A. H. Short.
Colonel, Royal Engineers .	Brigadier-General A. E. Sandbach, C.B., D.S O.

3rd Division

G.O.C.	Major - General Hubert I. W. Hamilton, C.V.O., C.B., D.S.O.
G.S.O. 1	Colonel F. R. F. Boileau.
C.R.A.	Brigadier-General F. D. V. Wing, C.B.
C.R.E.	Lieut.-Colonel C. S. Wilson.

7th Infantry Brigade

G.O.C. . . . . . . Brigadier - General F. W. N. McCracken, C.B., D.S.O.

3rd The Worcestershire Regiment ;
2nd The Prince of Wales's Volunteers (South Lancashire Regiment) ;
1st The Duke of Edinburgh's (Wiltshire Regiment) ;
2nd The Royal Irish Rifles.

8th Infantry Brigade

G.O.C. . . . . . . Brigadier-General B. J. C. Doran, C.B.

2nd The Royal Scots (Lothian Regiment) ;
2nd The Royal Irish Regiment ;
4th The Duke of Cambridge's Own (Middlesex Regiment) ;
1st The Gordon Highlanders.[1]

9th Infantry Brigade

G.O.C. . . . . . . Brigadier-General F. C. Shaw, C.B.

1st The Northumberland Fusiliers ;
4th The Royal Fusiliers (City of London Regiment) ;
1st The Lincolnshire Regiment ;
1st The Royal Scots Fusiliers.

Divisional Troops

Mounted Troops . A Squadron 15th (The King's) Hussars.
3rd Cyclist Company.

Artillery[2] . . XXIII. Brigade R.F.A.,
107th, 108th and 109th Batteries ;
XXIII. Brigade Ammunition Column.

XL. Brigade R.F.A.,
6th, 23rd and 49th Batteries ;
XL. Brigade Ammunition Column.

XLII. Brigade R.F.A.,
29th, 41st and 45th Batteries ;
XLII. Brigade Ammunition Column.

XXX. (Howitzer) Brigade R.F.A.,
128th, 129th and 130th (Howitzer) Batteries ;
XXX. (Howitzer) Brigade Ammunition Column.

48th Heavy Battery R.G.A., and
Heavy Battery Ammunition Column.

3rd Divisional Ammunition Column.

[1] In September the 1/Devonshire Regiment replaced the 1/Gordon Highlanders in the 8th Infantry Brigade.
[2] An Anti-Aircraft Detachment (of 1-pdr. Pom-Poms) was added to the Divisional Artillery in September.

478   APPENDIX 1

Engineers . . 56th Field Company, R.E.
57th Field Company, R.E.
Signal Service . 3rd Signal Company.
A.S.C. . . . 3rd Divisional Train.
Medical Units . 7th, 8th and 9th Field Ambulances

5th Division

G.O.C. . . . . . . Major-General Sir C. Fergusson,
Bart., C.B., M.V.O., D.S.O.
G.S.O. 1 . . . . . Lieut.-Col. C. F. Romer.
C.R.A. . . . . . Brigadier-General J. E. W. Head-
lam, C.B., D.S.O.
C.R.E. . . . . . Lieut.-Colonel J. A. S. Tulloch.

13th Infantry Brigade

G.O.C. . . . . . . Brigadier-General G. J. Cuthbert,
C.B.
2nd The King's Own Scottish Borderers ;
2nd The Duke of Wellington's (West Riding
Regiment) ;
1st The Queen's Own (Royal West Kent Regiment) ;
2nd The King's Own (Yorkshire Light Infantry).

14th Infantry Brigade

G.O.C. . . . . . . Brigadier-General S. P. Rolt, C.B.
2nd The Suffolk Regiment ;
1st The East Surrey Regiment ;
1st The Duke of Cornwall's Light Infantry ;
2nd The Manchester Regiment.

15th Infantry Brigade

G.O.C. . . . . . . Brigadier-General A. E. W. Count
Gleichen, K.C.V.O., C.B., C.M.G.,
D.S.O., Eq.
1st The Norfolk Regiment ;
1st The Bedfordshire Regiment ;
1st The Cheshire Regiment ;
1st The Dorsetshire Regiment.

Divisional Troops

Mounted Troops . A Squadron 19th (Queen Alexandra's Own
Royal) Hussars.
5th Cyclist Company.
Artillery [1] . . XV. Brigade R.F.A.,
11th, 52nd and 80th Batteries ;
XV. Brigade Ammunition Column.

[1] An Anti-Aircraft Detachment (of 1-pdr. Pom-Poms) was added to
the Divisional Artillery in September.

XXVII. Brigade R.F.A.,
119th, 120th and 121st Batteries ;
XXVII. Brigade Ammunition Column.

XXVIII. Brigade R.F.A.,
122nd, 123rd and 124th Batteries ;
XXVIII. Brigade Ammunition Column.

VIII. (Howitzer) Brigade R.F.A.,
37th, 61st and 65th (Howitzer) Batteries ;
VIII. (Howitzer) Brigade Ammunition
Column.

108th Heavy Battery R.G.A., and
Heavy Battery Ammunition Column.

Engineers . .	17th Field Company, R.E.
	59th Field Company, R.E.
Signal Service .	5th Signal Company.
A.S.C. . . .	5th Divisional Train.
Medical Units .	13th, 14th and 15th Field Ambulances.

III. Corps

(Formed in France, 31st August 1914)

G.O.C.	Major - General W. P. Pulteney, C.B., D.S.O.
Brigadier - General, General Staff	Brigadier-General J. P. Du Cane, C.B.
Brigadier - General, Royal Artillery	Brigadier - General E. J. Phipps-Hornby, V.C., C.B.
Colonel, Royal Engineers .	Brigadier-General F. M. Glubb, C.B., D.S.O.

4th Division

(Landed in France, night 22nd/23rd August)

G.O.C.	Major-General T. D'O. Snow, C.B.
G.S.O. 1	Colonel J. E. Edmonds, C.B.
C.R.A.	Brigadier-General G. F. Milne, C.B., D.S.O
C.R.E.	Lieut.-Colonel H. B. Jones.

10th Infantry Brigade

G.O.C.	Brigadier-General J. A. L. Haldane, C.B., D.S.O.

1st The Royal Warwickshire Regiment ;
2nd Seaforth Highlanders (Ross-shire Buffs, The Duke of Albany's) ;
1st Princess Victoria's (Royal Irish Fusiliers) ;
2nd The Royal Dublin Fusiliers.

11th Infantry Brigade

G.O.C. . . . . . . Brigadier-General A. G. Hunter-Weston, C.B., D.S.O.

1st Prince Albert's (Somerset Light Infantry) ;
1st The East Lancashire Regiment ;
1st The Hampshire Regiment ;
1st The Rifle Brigade (Prince Consort's Own).

12th Infantry Brigade

G.O.C. . . . . . . Brigadier-General H. F. M. Wilson, C.B.

1st King's Own (Royal Lancaster Regiment) ;
2nd The Lancashire Fusiliers ;
2nd The Royal Inniskilling Fusiliers ;
2nd The Essex Regiment.

Divisional Troops[1]

Mounted Troops . *B Squadron 19th (Queen Alexandra's Own) Hussars.
*4th Cyclist Company.

Artillery[2] . . XIV. Brigade R.F.A.,
39th, 68th and 88th Batteries ;
XIV. Brigade Ammunition Column.

XXIX. Brigade R.F.A.,
125th, 126th and 127th Batteries ;
XXIX. Brigade Ammunition Column.

XXXII. Brigade R.F.A.,
27th, 134th and 135th Batteries ;
XXXII. Brigade Ammunition Column.

XXXVII. (Howitzer) Brigade R.F.A.,
31st, 35th and 55th (Howitzer) Batteries ;
XXXVII. (Howitzer) Brigade Ammunition Column.

*31st Heavy Battery R.G.A., and
*Heavy Battery Ammunition Column.

*4th Divisional Ammunition Column.

Engineers . . *7th Field Company, R.E.
*9th Field Company, R.E.

Signal Service . *4th Signal Company.

A.S.C. . . . *4th Divisional Train.

Medical Units . *10th, 11th and 12th Field Ambulances.

[1] The 4th Division were without the units marked * at the battle of Le Cateau, 26th August 1914.
[2] An Anti-Aircraft Detachment (of 1-pdr. Pom-Poms) was added to the Divisional Artillery in September.

6th Division

(Embarked for St. Nazaire 8th/9th September 1914)

G.O.C. . . . . . . Major-General J. L. Keir, C.B.

G.S.O. 1 . . . . . Colonel W. T. Furse, D.S.O.

C.R.A. . . . . . Brigadier-General W. L. H. Paget, C.B., M.V.O.

C.R.E. . . . . . Lieut.-Colonel G. C. Kemp.

16th Infantry Brigade

G.O.C. . . . . . . Brigadier-General E. C. Ingouville-Williams, C.B., D.S.O.

1st The Buffs (East Kent Regiment) ;
1st The Leicestershire Regiment ;
1st The King's (Shropshire Light Infantry) ;
2nd The York and Lancaster Regiment.

17th Infantry Brigade

G.O.C. . . . . . . Brigadier-General W. R. B. Doran, C.B., D.S.O.

1st The Royal Fusiliers (City of London Regiment) ;
1st The Prince of Wales's (North Staffordshire Regiment) ;
2nd The Prince of Wales's Leinster Regiment (Royal Canadians) ;
3rd The Rifle Brigade (The Prince Consort's Own).

18th Infantry Brigade

G.O.C. . . . . . . Brigadier-General W. N. Congreve, V.C., C.B., M.V.O.

1st The Prince of Wales's Own (West Yorkshire Regiment) ;
1st The East Yorkshire Regiment ;
2nd The Sherwood Foresters (Nottinghamshire and Derbyshire Regiment) ;
2nd The Durham Light Infantry.

Divisional Troops

Mounted Troops . C Squadron 19th (Queen Alexandra's Own) Hussars.
6th Cyclist Company.

Artillery [1] . . II. Brigade R.F.A.,
21st, 42nd and 53rd Batteries ;
II. Brigade Ammunition Column.

---

[1] An Anti-Aircraft Detachment (of 1-pdr. Pom-Poms) was added to the Divisional Artillery in September.

XXIV. Brigade R.F.A.,
110th, 111th and 112th Batteries ;
XXIV. Brigade Ammunition Column.

XXXVIII. Brigade R.F.A.,
24th, 34th and 72nd Batteries ;
XXXVIII. Brigade Ammunition Column.

XII. (Howitzer) Brigade R.F.A.,
43rd, 86th and 87th (Howitzer) Batteries ;
XII. (Howitzer) Brigade Ammunition Column.

24th Heavy Battery R.G.A., and
Heavy Battery Ammunition Column.

6th Divisional Ammunition Column.

Engineers . . 12th Field Company, R.E.
38th Field Company, R.E.

Signal Service . 6th Signal Company.

A.S.C. . . . 6th Divisional Train.

Medical Units . 16th, 17th and 18th Field Ambulances.

Army Troops

Mounted Troops . A Squadron North Irish Horse,
B Squadron South Irish Horse,
C Squadron North Irish Horse.

Medium Siege Artil- Nos. 1, 2, 3, 4, 5 and 6 Siege Batteries R.G.A.
lery [1]

Engineers . . Headquarters of G.H.Q., 1st, 2nd and 3rd Signal
Companies ;
A to E Air-line Sections ;
F to P Cable Sections ;
Q Wireless Section ;
1st and 2nd Bridging Trains.

Royal Flying Corps : [2]

Commander . . . . Brigadier-General Sir D. Henderson, K.C.B., D.S.O.

G.S.O. 1 . . . . . Lieut.-Colonel F. H. Sykes.

2nd Aeroplane Squadron.
3rd Aeroplane Squadron.
4th Aeroplane Squadron.
5th Aeroplane Squadron.
6th Aeroplane Squadron.

[1] Nos. 1, 2, 3 and 4 Siege Batteries disembarked at St. Nazaire on
19th September 1914, and Nos. 5 and 6, on 27th September 1914.   Each
battery was armed with four 6-inch B.L. Howitzers.   39 Company R.G.A.
formed Nos. 1 and 2 Batteries, 23 Company formed Nos. 3 and 4, and
107 Company formed Nos. 5 and 6.

[2] The 2nd, 3rd, 4th and 5th Aeroplane Squadrons accompanied the
first portion of the British Expeditionary Force to France in August
1914.   The 6th Squadron landed at St. Nazaire on 5th October, but did
not come into action until 16th October 1914.

Infantry	. .	1st The Queen's Own Cameron Highlanders.
A.S.C.	. . .	Army Troops Train.
Medical Units	.	19th and 20th Field Ambulances.

Lines of Communication Defence Troops

1st The Devonshire Regiment;
[1] 2nd The Royal Welch Fusiliers;
[1] 1st The Cameronians (Scottish Rifles);
[1] 1st The Duke of Cambridge's Own (Middlesex
        Regiment);
[1] 2nd Princess Louise's (Argyll and Sutherland
        Highlanders).

Lines of Communication Units

Engineers	. .	Railway Transport Establishment; 8th and 16th Railway Companies; 29th Works Company; 20th and 42nd Fortress Companies; 1st Printing Company.
Royal Flying Corps		1st Aircraft Park.
Signal Service	.	1st Signal Company, L. of C.
A.S.C.	. . .	Cavalry Ammunition Park; 5th Cavalry Brigade Ammunition Park; 1st-6th Divisional Ammunition Parks; Cavalry Supply Column; 5th Cavalry Brigade Supply Column; 1st-6th Divisional Supply Columns; Army Troops Supply Column; Base Mechanical Transport Depot; Advanced Mechanical Transport Depot; Base Horse Transport Depot; Advanced Horse Transport Depot; 1st-6th Reserve Parks (2-horsed wagons); 1st-6th Field Butcheries; 1st-6th Field Bakeries; 1st-8th Railway Supply Detachments; Central Requisition Office; Branch Requisition Office; 1st-30th Depot Units of Supply; 1st-8th Bakery Sections; Nos. 1 and 2 Advanced Remount Depots; Base Remount Depot.
Medical Units	.	1st-6th Clearing Hospitals; 1st-12th Stationary Hospitals; 1st-12th General Hospitals; 1st-6th Ambulance Trains;

[1] These four battalions were formed into the 19th Infantry Brigade, at Valenciennes, on 22nd August 1914. The command of this Brigade was given to Major-General L. G. Drummond, C.B., M.V.O.

	Nos. 1, 2 and 3 Hospital Ships ; 1st-3rd Advanced Depots of Medical Stores ; 1st-3rd Base Depots of Medical Stores ; 1st and 2nd Sanitary Sections ; 1st-11th Sanitary Squads ; Convalescent Depot.
Ordnance Units .	1st-8th Ordnance Companies.
Veterinary Units [1]	1st-7th Mobile Veterinary Sections ; 1st-8th Veterinary Sections ; Base Depot of Veterinary Stores.
Army Pay Unit .	Base Army Pay Department Unit.
Postal Units .	Base Post Office ; Advanced Base Post Office ; 1st and 2nd Stationary Post Offices.
Prisons . . .	Military Prisons in the Field.
Bases . . .	Nos 1, 2 and 3 Bases.

[1] 8th-11th Mobile Veterinary Sections were to follow as soon as they were completed.

NOTES

ON THE

ORGANIZATION OF SOME OF THE PRINCIPAL FORMATIONS AND UNITS OF THE BRITISH EXPEDITIONARY FORCE IN AUGUST 1914

Royal Flying Corps

Aeroplane Squadron = 12 Aeroplanes.

Cavalry

Regiment = 3 Squadrons = 12 Troops.

(Two machine guns were an integral part of each regiment.)

Artillery

Royal Horse Artillery :

Brigade = 2 R.H.A. Batteries and Brigade Ammunition Column.
(R.H.A. Battery = Six 13-pdr. Q.F. Guns and 12 Ammunition Wagons.)

Royal Field Artillery :

Brigade = 3 R.F.A. Batteries and Brigade Ammunition Column.
(R.F.A. Battery = Six 18-pdr. Q.F. Guns (or six 4·5-inch Howitzers) and 12 Ammunition Wagons.)

Royal Garrison Artillery :

Heavy Battery = Four 60-pdr. Guns, 8 Ammunition Wagons and Battery Ammunition Column.

Infantry

Battalion = 4 Companies = 16 Platoons.

(Two machine guns were an integral part of each battalion.)

Medical

Field Ambulance = 3 Sections = 10 Ambulance Wagons
(It accommodated 150 patients.)

Cavalry Division

4 Cavalry Brigades = 12 Cavalry Regiments, together with
Divisional Troops.

Strength   .   .   .   . 9,269 all ranks.
                            9,815 horses.
                            24 13-pdrs.
                            24 machine guns.

Marching depth (about)   .   . 11½ miles.

A Cavalry Brigade occupied nearly 2 miles of road space.

The Divisional Troops required more than 2¼ miles (Brigade
Ammunition Columns taking 1 mile).

The details of personnel and horses are as follows :

	Officers and other ranks.	Horses.
Headquarters	96	64
4 Cav. Brigades . . .	6,872	7,492
H.Q. Cav. Divl. Artillery . .	20	18
2 Horse Artillery Brigades .	1,362	1,558
1 Field Squadron . . .	191	196
1 Signal Squadron . . .	206	164
H.Q. Cav. Divl. A.S.C. . .	26	11
4 Cav. Field Ambulances . .	496	312
Total . . .	9,269	9,815

Division

3 Infantry Brigades = 12 Infantry Battalions, together with
Divisional Troops.

Strength   .   .   . 18,073 all ranks.
                       5,592 horses.
                       76 guns (fifty-four 18-pdrs.,
                          eighteen 4·5-inch Howitzers
                          and four 60-pdrs.).
                       24 machine guns.

Marching depth (about)   15 miles.

An Infantry Brigade occupied 2¼ miles of road space.

The Divisional Artillery (less Divisional Ammunition Column)
occupied 5 miles (Brigade Ammunition Columns taking
1¼ miles).

The Divisional Ammunition Column required nearly another 1½
miles.

Ambulances and Divisional Trains occupied 1⅔ miles.

APPENDIX 2

487

The details of personnel and horses are as follows :

	Officers and other ranks.	Horses.
Headquarters	82	54
3 Infantry Brigades	12,165	741
H.Q. Divl. Artillery	22	20
3 Field Artillery Brigades . . .	2,385	2,244
1 Field Artillery (Howitzer) Brigade .	755	697
1 Heavy Battery and Amm. Column .	198	144
1 Divl. Amm. Column	568	709
H.Q. Divl. Engineers	13	8
2 Field Companies	434	152
1 Signal Company	162	80
1 Cavalry Squadron	159	167
1 Divisional Train	428	378
8 Field Ambulances	702	198
Total . .	18,073	5,592

ORDER OF BATTLE

OF THE

FRENCH ARMIES IN AUGUST 1914

Commander-in-Chief   .   General Joffre.
Chief of the General Staff   General Belin.

FIRST ARMY   .   .   .   General Dubail.

VII. Corps	(14th and 41st Divisions)	General Bonneau ;
VIII. Corps	(15th and 16th Divisions)	General Castelli ;
XIII. Corps	(25th and 26th Divisions)	General Alix ;
XIV. Corps	(27th and 28th Divisions)	General Pouradier-Duteil ;
XXI. Corps	(13th and 43rd Divisions)	General Legrand-Girarde ;

44th Division ;
An Alpine Group ;
1st Group of Reserve Divisions (58th, 63rd and 66th) ;
6th and 8th Cavalry Divisions.[1]

SECOND ARMY .   .   .   General de Castelnau.

IX. Corps	(17th and 18th Divisions, with Moroccan Division attached)	General Dubois ;
XV. Corps	(29th and 30th Divisions)	General Espinasse ;
XVI. Corps	(31st and 32nd Divisions)	General Taverna ;
XVIII. Corps [2]	(35th and 36th Divisions)	General Mas-Latrie ;
XX. Corps	(11th and 39th Divisions)	General Foch ;

2nd Group of Reserve Divisions (59th, 65th and 70th) ;
A Mixed Colonial Brigade ;
2nd and 10th Cavalry Divisions.[1]

THIRD ARMY .   .   .   General Ruffey (succeeded by General Sarrail).

| IV. Corps | (7th and 8th Divisions) | General Boëlle ; |
| V. Corps | (9th and 10th Divisions) | ˙General Brochin ; |

[1] Early in September three of the cavalry divisions (2nd, 8th and 10th) of the First and Second Armies were formed into a cavalry corps under General Conneau.
[2] This corps was transferred to the French Fifth Army, and operated on the right flank of the British Expeditionary Force.

VI. Corps   (12th, 40th and 42nd Divs.)   General Sarrail ;
3rd Group of Reserve Divisions (54th, 55th and 56th) ;
7th Cavalry Division.

FOURTH ARMY .   . .   General de Langle de Cary,

XII. Corps   (23rd and 24th Divisions)   General Roques ;
XVII. Corps   (33rd and 34th Divisions)   General Poline ;
Colonial Corps   (1st, 2nd and 3rd Colonial   General Lefevre ;
                 Divisions)
9th Cavalry Division.

FIFTH ARMY .   . . General Lanrezac (succeeded by
                      General Franchet d'Espèrey.

I. Corps   (1st and 2nd Divisions)   General Franchet
                                          d'Espèrey ;
II. Corps ¹ (3rd and 4th Divisions)   General Gerard ;
III. Corps (5th and 6th Divisions)   General Sauret ;
X. Corps   (19th and 20th Divisions)   General Defforges ;
XI. Corps ² (21st and 22nd Divisions)   General Eydoux ;
37th and 38th Divisions ;
4th Group of Reserve Divisions (51st, 53rd and 69th, General
     Valabrègue) ;
52nd Reserve Division ; ²
60th Reserve Division ; ²
4th Cavalry Division.

CAVALRY CORPS   .   . General Sordet.
1st Cavalry Division .   .   .   General Buisson.
3rd Cavalry Division .   .   .   General de Lastour.
5th Cavalry Division .   .   .   General Bridoux.

¹ The II. Corps was transferred to the Fourth Army on the arrival
of the 37th and 38th Divisions from Africa.
² The XI. Corps and 52nd and 60th Reserve Divisions went to the
Fourth Army on arrival of the XVIII. Corps from the Second Army.

NOTES

ON THE

ORGANIZATION OF SOME OF THE PRINCIPAL
FRENCH FORMATIONS AND UNITS IN 1914

Cavalry

Cavalry Brigade = 2 regiments and machine-gun section.
Cavalry Regiment (32 officers, 651 other ranks, 687 horses
= 4 squadrons.
Cavalry Squadron = 5 officers, 145 other ranks, and 143 horses.

Artillery

Field :
Regiment (Divisional) = 3 *groupes.*
Regiment (Corps)   = 4 *groupes.*
Groupe   = 3 batteries.
Battery   = 4 guns, 12 wagons, etc.

Heavy : [1]
Regiment   Strength variable ; those in Second and
                            Fifth Armies consisted of six 120-
                            mm. batteries and seven 155 - mm.
                            batteries.
                            The 4th Regiment had 5 *groupes* of four
                            120-mm. batteries each.

Groupe   = three or four batteries.
Battery   = 4 guns, 8 wagons, observation wagon,
                            etc.

Infantry

Brigade   = 2 regiments.
Regiment   = 3 battalions and H.Q. company.
Battalion   = 4 companies and a machine-gun section
                (22 officers and 1,030 other ranks),
                etc.
Company   = 2 *pelotons* each of 2 *sections.*

[1] Allotted to Armies and corps.

Cavalry Division

3 Cavalry Brigades ;
1 Horse Artillery Brigade (of two 4-gun batteries) ;
Groupe cycliste (4 officers and 320 other ranks) ;
Telegraph detachment, etc.

> 4,500 all ranks and 8 guns.

Division

2 Infantry Brigades ;
1 Squadron ;
3 Field Artillery *groupes* ;
Engineer Company, etc.

> 15,000 all ranks, 36 guns and 24 machine guns.

Reserve Division

2 Brigades ;
1 Squadron ;
3 Field Artillery *groupes*, etc.

> Reserve Brigade = 3 regiments and a *chasseur* battalion
> Reserve Regiment = 2 battalions.

Corps

Normally two divisions (VI. and Colonial Corps had three) ;
1 Cavalry Regiment ;
Field Artillery Regiment ;
1 Groupe of 15·5-cm. Howitzers ;
1 Engineer Company ;
Reserve Infantry Brigade of two regiments of two battalions
each.

ORDER OF BATTLE

OF THE

BELGIAN ARMY IN AUGUST 1914

Commander-in-Chief . .	His Majesty King Albert.
Chief of the General Staff .	Lieut.-General Chevalier de Selliers de Moranville.
1st Division . . .	Lieut.-General Baix.
2nd Division . . .	Lieut.-General Dassin.
3rd Division . . .	Lieut.-General Leman.
4th Division . . .	Lieut.-General Michel.
5th Division . . .	Lieut.-General Ruwet.
6th Division . . .	Lieut.-General Latonnois van Rode.
Cavalry Division . .	Lieut.-General de Witte.

Garrisons of Antwerp, Liége and Namur.

A Belgian division consisted of three mixed brigades, a cavalry regiment, and an artillery regiment of three batteries,[1] together with engineers, telegraphists, transport, etc.

A mixed brigade consisted of two infantry regiments and an artillery group of three batteries. Each infantry regiment had three battalions, and one regiment in each brigade had a machine-gun company (6 machine guns).

The strength of a division varied between 25,500 and 32,000 all ranks, with 60 guns and 18 machine guns.

The Cavalry Division had two cavalry brigades (each of two cavalry regiments), three Horse Artillery batteries (12 guns), a cyclist battalion, a cyclist pioneer bridging company, telegraphists, and transport.

The strength of the Cavalry Division was 4,500 all ranks, with 3,400 horses, and 12 guns.

[1] Two divisions (2nd and 6th) each had three extra batteries. The batteries were all 4-gun units.

ORDER OF BATTLE

OF THE

GERMAN ARMIES

Chief of the General Staff . .	Generaloberst von Moltke.
Deputy Chief of the General Staff	General von Stein.
Chief of Operations Branch . .	Oberst Tappen.
Chief of Intelligence Branch .	Oberstleutnant Hentsch.
Chief of Secret Service . . .	Major Nicolai.
Chief of the Political Section .	Oberst von Dommes.
Director of Munitions in the Field	Generalleutnant Sieger.
Chief of Staff of Air Service . .	Major Thomsen.
Director of Field Railways . .	Oberst Groener.
General of Engineers and Pioneer Corps	General von Claer.
Director of Medical Services. .	General von Schjerning.

(1) ARMIES EMPLOYED AGAINST THE BRITISH EXPEDITIONARY FORCE, THE FRENCH FIFTH ARMY, AND THE BELGIAN ARMY IN AUGUST 1914

FIRST ARMY : Generaloberst von Kluck.

II. Corps	Gen. von Linsingen	(3rd and 4th Divisions);
III. Corps	Gen. von Lochow	(5th and 6th Divisions);
IV. Corps	Gen. Sixt von Armin	(7th and 8th Divisions);
IX. Corps	Gen. von Quast	(17th and 18th Divisions) ;
III. Reserve Corps	Gen. von Beseler	(5th Reserve and 6th Reserve Divisions) ;
IV. Reserve Corps	Gen. von Gronau	(7th Reserve and 22nd Reserve Divisions) ;
IX. Reserve Corps	Gen. von Boehn [1]	(17th Reserve and 18th Reserve Divisions) ;

10th, 11th and 27th *Landwehr* Brigades :
1 *Pionier* regiment.

[1] This corps was originally left behind in Sleswig to oppose landings, and as it hurried up behind the advance it sacked Louvain, 25th August 1914.

SECOND ARMY :   Generaloberst von Bülow.

Guard Corps	Gen. von Plettenberg	(1st Guard and 2nd Guard Divisions) ;
VII. Corps	Gen. von Einem	(13th and 14th Divisions) ;
X. Corps	Gen. von Emmich	(19th and 20th Divisions) ;
Guard Reserve Corps [1]	Gen. von Gallwitz	(3rd Guard and 1st Guard Reserve Divisions) ;
VII. Reserve Corps	Gen. von Zwehl	(13th Reserve and 14th Reserve Divisions) ;
X. Reserve Corps	Gen. von Kirchbach	(2nd Guard Reserve and 19th Reserve Divisions);

25th and 29th *Landwehr* Brigades ;
4 Mortar battalions ;
1 10 cm.-gun battalion ;
2 Heavy Coast Mortar battalions ;
2 *Pionier* regiments.

THIRD ARMY :   Generaloberst Freiherr von Hausen.

XI. Corps [1]	Gen. von Plüskow	(22nd and 38th Divisions) ;
XII. (1st Saxon) Corps	Gen. d'Elsa	(23rd and 32nd Divisions) ;
XIX. (2nd Saxon) Corps	Gen. von Laffert	(24th and 40th Divisions) ;
XII. (Saxon) Reserve Corps	Gen. von Kirchbach	(23rd Reserve and 24th Reserve Divisions) ;

47th *Landwehr* Brigade ;
2 Mortar battalions ;
1 *Pionier* regiment.

I. CAVALRY CORPS : Lieut.-General Freiherr Von Richthofen.

Guard Cavalry Division ;
5th Cavalry Division.

II. CAVALRY CORPS : Lieut.-General von der Marwitz.

2nd Cavalry Division ;
4th Cavalry Division ;
9th Cavalry Division.

(2) NOT OPPOSED TO THE BRITISH IN AUGUST–SEPTEMBER 1914

FOURTH ARMY :   Generaloberst Duke Albrecht of Württemberg.

3 Corps, 2 Reserve Corps and one *Landwehr* Brigade.

[1] These two corps (Guard Reserve and XI.) began to move to the Russian front on the 26th of August, after the fall of Namur.

APPENDIX 6

FIFTH ARMY :   Crown Prince of Germany,

3 Corps, 2 Reserve Corps, 1 Division, 2 Cavalry Divisions and 5 *Landwehr* Brigades, etc.

SIXTH ARMY :   Crown Prince Rupprecht of Bavaria.

4 Corps, 1 Reserve Corps, 4 *Ersatz* Divisions, 1 *Landwehr* Brigade and 3 Cavalry Divisions, etc.

SEVENTH ARMY :   Generaloberst von Heeringen.

2 Corps, 1 Reserve Corps, 1 Reserve Division, 2 *Ersatz* Divisions and 5 *Landwehr* Battalions, etc.

Total on Western Front :

45 divisions ;
27 Reserve divisions ;
10 cavalry divisions ;
6 *Ersatz* divisions (17 brigades) ;
14 *Landwehr* brigades ;
15 artillery battalions ;
7 *Pionier* regiments.

(3) RUSSIAN FRONTIER

EIGHTH ARMY :   Generaloberst von Prittwitz.

3 Corps, 1 Reserve Corps, 1 Reserve Division, 1 *Ersatz* Division, 1 Cavalry Division, 1 *Landwehr* Division [1] and two *Landwehr* Brigades, etc.

[1] Originally in Sleswig to oppose landings ; arrived in East Prussia on 28th August 1914.

NOTES

ORGANIZATION OF SOME OF THE PRINCIPAL
GERMAN FORMATIONS AND UNITS IN 1914

Air Forces :
Field Balloon Detachment = 2 Balloons.
Gas Column.
Flying Detachment   = 12 Aeroplanes.
(*Flieger Abteilung*)
(One Balloon Detachment was allotted to each Army, and one
Flying Detachment was allotted to each Army and corps.)

Cavalry :
Cavalry Brigade   = 2 Regiments.
Cavalry Regiment (36 officers, 686 other ranks and 765 horses)
                 = 4 Squadrons, Telegraph Detachment, and 1st
                   and 2nd line transport.
Squadron   = 6 officers, 163 other ranks and 178 horses.

Artillery, Field:
Brigade   = 2 Regiments.   (72 guns).
Regiment   = 2 *Abteilungen.*
Abteilung   = 3 Batteries and Light Ammunition Column.
Battery   = 6 guns, 6 ammunition wagons (4 of each in
               horse batteries), 1 Observation Wagon, and
               1st and 2nd line transport.

Artillery, Foot (Heavy), of the Field Army :
Regiment   = 2 Battalions.
Battalion   = 4 Batteries of 5·9-inch (15-c.m.) howitzers, or
               2 Batteries of 8·27-inch (21-c.m.) mortars.
Battery   = 4 guns.

Infantry :
Brigade   = 2 Regiments.
Regiment   = 3 Battalions and a machine-gun company of
               6 guns and one spare gun.

Battalion = 4 Companies (26 officers and officials and 1,050 other ranks) and 1st and 2nd line transport.

Battalion of *Jäger* = 4 Companies and a machine-gun company or *Schützen* (4 officers and 104 other ranks) and a Cyclist Company (3 officers and 113 other ranks).

Company = 3 Platoons (5 officers and 259 other ranks).

Cavalry Division :

3 Cavalry Brigades.
Divisional Troops :
Horse Artillery *Abteilung* (three 4-gun batteries) ;
1, 2 or 3 *Jäger* battalions, each with machine-gun company of 6 guns ;
Machine-gun battery (mounted) ;
Pionier Detachment ;
Heavy and Light Wireless Stations ;
Motor Transport Column.

5,200 all ranks.   5,600 horses.   12 guns.   6 machine guns.

Infantry Division :

2 Infantry Brigades.
Divisional Troops :
1 Field Artillery Brigade (72 guns) ;
1 Cavalry Regiment ;
1 or 2 *Pionier* Companies (3 per corps) ;
1 Divisional Bridging Train ;
1 Divisional Telephone Detachment ;
1 or 2 Medical Companies (3 per corps).

17,500 all ranks.   4,000 horses.   72 guns.   24 machine guns.

Cavalry Corps :

2 or 3 Cavalry Divisions.

Corps :

2 Infantry Divisions.
Corps Troops :
1 Foot Artillery Regiment ;
1 *Jäger* Battalion ;
1 Corps Bridging Train ;
1 Telephone Detachment ;
1 Searchlight Section ;
1 Flying Detachment ;
4 Infantry Ammunition Columns ;
9 Field Artillery Ammunition Columns ;
8 Heavy Artillery Ammunition Columns ;
12 Field Hospitals ;
6 Supply Columns ;
7 Transport Columns ;
2 Horse Depots ;
2 Field Bakeries.

Reserve Division :

Same as Active division, except it has 6 Field batteries instead of
12.

Reserve Corps :

Same as Active corps, except it has 12 Field batteries instead of
24, no heavy guns, no aeroplanes and correspondingly fewer
ammunition columns.

Landwehr Brigade :

2 Regiments of three battalions ;
1 Squadron ;
1 Battery.

INSTRUCTIONS TO SIR JOHN FRENCH
FROM LORD KITCHENER

AUGUST 1914

" Owing to the infringement of the neutrality of Belgium by
" Germany, and in furtherance of the Entente which exists between
" this country and France, His Majesty's Government has decided,
" at the request of the French Government, to send an Expeditionary
" Force to France and to entrust the command of the troops to
" yourself.

" The special motive of the Force under your control is to sup-
" port and co-operate with the French Army against our common
" enemies. The peculiar task laid upon you is to assist the French
" Government in preventing or repelling the invasion by Germany
" of French and Belgian territory and eventually to restore the
" neutrality of Belgium, on behalf of which, as guaranteed by
" treaty, Belgium has appealed to the French and to ourselves.

" These are the reasons which have induced His Majesty's
" Government to declare war, and these reasons constitute the
" primary objective you have before you.

" The place of your assembly, according to present arrangements,
" is Amiens, and during the assembly of your troops you will have
" every opportunity for discussing with the Commander-in-Chief of
" the French Army, the military position in general and the special
" part which your Force is able and adapted to play. It must be
" recognized from the outset that the numerical strength of the
" British Force and its contingent reinforcement is strictly limited,
" and with this consideration kept steadily in view it will be obvious
" that the greatest care must be exercised towards a minimum of
" losses and wastage.

" Therefore, while every effort must be made to coincide most
" sympathetically with the plans and wishes of our Ally, the gravest
" consideration will devolve upon you as to participation in forward
" movements where large bodies of French troops are not engaged
" and where your Force may be unduly exposed to attack. Should
" a contingency of this sort be contemplated, I look to you to inform
" me fully and give me time to communicate to you any decision to
" which His Majesty's Government may come in the matter. In
" this connection I wish you distinctly to understand that your
" command is an entirely independent one, and that you will in no
" case come in any sense under the orders of any Allied General.

" In minor operations you should be careful that your sub-

" ordinates understand that risk of serious losses should only be
" taken where such risk is authoritatively considered to be com-
" mensurate with the object in view.

" The high courage and discipline of your troops should, and
" certainly will, have fair and full opportunity of display during the
" campaign, but officers may well be reminded that in this their
" first experience of European warfare, a greater measure of caution
" must be employed than under former conditions of hostilities
" against an untrained adversary.

" You will kindly keep up constant communication with the
" War Office, and you will be good enough to inform me as to all
" movements of the enemy reported to you as well as to those of
" the French Army.

" I am sure you fully realize that you can rely with the utmost
" confidence on the whole-hearted and unswerving support of the
" Government, of myself, and of your compatriots, in carrying out
" the high duty which the King has entrusted to you and in main-
" taining the great tradition of His Majesty's Army."

KITCHENER,
Secretary of State.

THE FRENCH PLAN OF CAMPAIGN[1]

PLAN 17

(Translation)

Note.—Each Army Commander received on the 7th February, 1914, a copy of the section of this document that referred to his command : their receipts for it being kept in a special file by the 3rd Bureau of the (French) General Staff.   BELIN.[2]

DIRECTIONS FOR THE CONCENTRATION

General Situation.

From a careful study of information obtained, it is probable that a great part of the German forces will be concentrated on the common frontier. They may cross this frontier in places before our general operations can be developed.

Intentions of the Commander-in-Chief.

Whatever the circumstances, it is the C.-in-C.'s intention to advance with all forces united to the attack of the German Armies.

The action of the French Armies will be developed in two main operations : one, on the right, in the country between the wooded district of the Vosges and the Moselle below Toul ; the other, on the left, north of a line Verdun—Metz.

These two operations will be closely connected by forces operating on the Hauts de Meuse and in the Woëvre.

General distribution of the forces in the theatre of operations.

The First and Second Armies will at first operate between the Rhine and the Moselle below Toul, prolonged west of that place by the Marne-Rhine Canal, and the line Vaucouleurs—Gondrecourt.

The Fifth Army and the Cavalry Corps will operate north of the line Verdun—Metz.

The Third Army will act as connecting link between these two operations.

The Fourth Army will be provisionally placed in second line ready to move up either south or north of the Third Army ; an

---

[1] This was the plan in force when hostilities commenced. It is translated from Appendix III. of " La Bataille de la Frontière (Août 1914) Briey " by M. Fernand Engerand, Député de Calvados.
[2] General Belin, General Joffre's first Chief of the Staff.

alternative detrainment of part of this Fourth Army has consequently to be provided for, and eventually a change in the composition of the other Armies.

The two groups of Reserve divisions which will be at the disposal of the commander-in-chief, are at first to be placed in rear of the wings of the general front.

FIRST ARMY

Five corps (VII., VIII., XIII., XIV., XXI.). Two cavalry divisions (6th and 8th).

Five regiments of heavy artillery (six batteries of 120 B., six batteries of 155 C.T.R.) ;[1] two groups at Epinal.

General idea.

This Army will attack in the general direction Baccarat—Sarrebourg—Sarreguemines—the right of its main body following the crest of the Vosges, and its extreme right advancing into the plains of Alsace, so that the right of the whole battle front may rest on the Rhine.

By this advance it will be able to co-operate with the offensive of the Second Army which is to be made in the direction of Château Salins.

The First Army may be called upon to move out from the Meurthe on the 12th day of mobilization. As a preliminary measure it will as early as possible be in a position to drive back the enemy from the eastern slopes of the Vosges, north of the Schlucht, but at the same time it will avoid becoming engaged with any strong forces in the Alsatian plain.

A part of this Army will advance as early as possible, on the order of the commander-in-chief, into Upper Alsace by the Belfort gap, the pass of the Schlucht and the intermediate passes, in the general direction of Colmar.

Special idea for the group operating in Alsace.

The order to advance into Alsace may be given by the commander-in-chief any time after the fourth day of mobilization.

The part of the First Army to carry out this operation will consist of the VII. Corps and the 8th Cavalry Division.

Its special idea is to hold in Alsace, by attacking them, any enemy forces which may attempt to advance on the eastern slopes of the Vosges, and to assist the removal of that part of the population of Alsace that has remained faithful to the cause of France.

SECOND ARMY

Five corps (IX., XV., XVI., XVIII., XX.). Two cavalry divisions (2nd and 10th).

One regiment of heavy artillery (3rd Regiment : six batteries of 120 L.) ; seven batteries of 155 C.T.R., one group of four batteries of 120 L.[2] (of the 4th Regiment).

2nd Group of Reserve divisions (59th, 65th, 70th).

Headquarters : Neufchâteau.

---

[1] 120 B. = 120-mm. Bacquet (name of inventor).
155 C.T.R. = 155-mm. court tir rapide.
[2] 120 L. = 120-mm. long.

General idea.

This Army is to be ready to attack in the general direction Château Salins—Sarrebruck. For this purpose, it will make use of the Nancy bridgehead, for the protection of which it will be responsible. Its dispositions will be made so that it can at first occupy a front Lunéville—Grand Couronné de Nancy, from which line it may be called upon to advance on the 12th day of mobilization.

It should be possible to send the 2nd Group of Reserve divisions to the area north of Nancy as they detrain, so as to oppose any possible operation of German forces coming from Metz and to assure the protection of the left flank of the Second Army.

THIRD ARMY

Three corps (IV., V., VI.). One cavalry division (7th).

One regiment of heavy artillery (part of the 2nd Regiment : three batteries of 120 L.) ; three batteries of 155 C.T.R., three groups of four batteries of 120 L. (of the 4th Regiment).

3rd Group of Reserve divisions (54th, 55th, 56th).

Headquarters : Verdun.

Zone of operations.

To the south, bounded by the line Lerouville (inclusive)—Hauts de Meuse.

To the south-east by the line Girauvoisin—fortress of Toul (inclusive)—the Moselle below Toul.

To the north by the line (inclusive) Villosne sur Meuse—Haraucourt—Ecurey (N.W. of Damvillers)—Damvillers—Romagne sur les Côtes (E. of Damvillers).

General idea.

The Third Army forming the connecting link between the main operations to be carried out on the right bank of the Moselle, to the south, and north of the line Verdun—Metz, to the north, will be ready either to force back on to Metz and Thionville any enemy forces which may have advanced from the direction of these fortresses, or to prepare the preliminary investment of Metz.

It will be responsible for the protection of the Hauts de Meuse on which its operations will be based. For this purpose it will employ the group of Reserve divisions and the heavy artillery which are allotted to it to hold the positions the occupation of which has been planned. The same units are intended to enable the Army afterwards to organize, as mentioned above, the investment of Metz.

It will be ready to make a general offensive from a line Domèvre en Haye—Vigneulles les Hattonchatel—Ornes any time after the 12th day of mobilization ; it will at first co-ordinate its movements with the Second Army on the right and with the Fifth Army on the left.

Consequently, it will be necessary for it to keep a considerable force always in reserve in order to extend, according to circumstances, the operations of the Second Army on the right bank of the Moselle or those of the Fifth Army in the northern Woëvre.

Additional directions for the Third and Fifth Armies

1. The II. Corps will be responsible for organizing the south-eastern front, that is to say the high ground of Ire le Sec, between the Loison (Jametz district) and the Othain (Marville district).

2. The organization for defence of the Hauts de Meuse, from Ornes to Damvillers along the Côtes de Romagne and de Morimont, will be carried out by the Third Army. It will be defended by any available units of the IV. Corps, which will be relieved as soon as possible by the 54th Reserve Division.

3. The 4th Infantry Division covering the northern Woëvre will have a detachment (six companies of the 120th Regt.) in the Azannes district to keep touch with the fortress of Verdun until the arrival of the IV. Corps.

In the event of the force covering Spincourt (18th Battalion of Chasseurs à pied) being compelled to withdraw before the arrival of this force, it will retire on the detachment about Azannes to co-operate with it in holding the Côtes de Romagne.

4. From the moment the units of the IV. Corps arrive near Azannes, the Hauts de Meuse to Damvillers (inclusive) will come into the zone of operations of the Third Army.

The limit of the zones of operations of the Third and Fifth Armies may, in addition, be modified before the date (12th day of mobilization) when the main body of the Fifth Army reaches the Meuse, in accordance with the situation which may arise out of the events of the first days of the campaign in the northern part of the theatre of war.

> *Note.*—The field works to be constructed in order to organize the defences that are required will be studied in peace time. As regards the positions north-east and south-east of Montmédy, the projects have been undertaken by the II. Corps; as regards those along the Hauts de Meuse, from Ornes to Damvillers, by the VI. Corps. The projects will be sent to the IV. Corps.

FOURTH ARMY

Three corps (XII., XVII. and Colonial). 9th Cavalry Division. Heavy artillery : three batteries of 155 C.T.R. of the 2nd Regiment. Headquarters : St. Dizier.

General idea.

This Army will at first be temporarily in second line and ready to move on the . . . day of mobilization, with the object either of advancing into the southern Woëvre, between the Second and Third Armies, to co-operate ultimately in the operations of the Second Army, or of moving northwards west of the Meuse, to the left of the Third Army, in the direction of Arlon.

FIFTH ARMY

Five corps (I., II., III., X., XI.). One cavalry division. Heavy artillery : one regiment (six batteries of 120 L., seven

batteries of 155 C.T.R.), one group of four batteries of 120 L. (of the 4th Regiment).
Two Reserve divisions.
Headquarters : Rethel.

Zone of operations.

From the Argonne Forest to a line Vervins—Hirson.

Headquarters : XI. Corps at Ville sur Tourbe.
      „   X. Corps at Vouziers.
      „   III. Corps at Amagne.
      „   I. Corps at Aubenton.
      „   II. Corps : covering force at Stenay.
      „   Group of Reserve divisions, 53rd at Neufchâteau, 69th at Sissonne, 51st at Vervins.

The northern boundary of the zone of operations of the Fifth Army will vary according to circumstances, and cannot be laid down beforehand.

General idea.

This Army is to operate against the right wing of the enemy forces. The theatre of operations may be limited, to begin with, to the territories of the two belligerents ; or it may extend at once into neutral territory (Luxembourg and in particular Belgium).

In the first case it will operate northwards at once, the Third Army advancing from the Hauts de Meuse and the Montmédy bridgehead. It will deploy in the general direction of Thionville and Luxembourg, endeavouring to drive northwards any enemy forces in front of it. It should hold a part of its force in reserve behind its left wing to protect itself against any enveloping movement the enemy may attempt by violating Belgian territory, in the immediate proximity of the frontier. It will also be prepared for a strong offensive against Thionville with its Active corps, or for the investment of that place with the Reserve divisions at its disposal.

The Cavalry Corps, concentrated at first south-east of Mézières, will march on Montmédy to support the II. Corps and afterwards to co-operate in the action of the left of the Fifth Army.

In the alternative case, that of the enemy violation of neutral territory, the Fifth Army will move north-eastwards for an advance into Belgian Luxembourg by way of the Neufchâteau and Florenville districts, echeloned on its left, as before, for flank protection. This movement will however be carried out only by order of the commander-in-chief.

In this case, the Fourth Army, moving northwards by the left bank of the Meuse, will take up a position on the right of the Fifth Army and move between it and the Third Army in the direction of Arlon.

The Cavalry Corps will form the left of this mass of manœuvre.

Consequently the Fifth Army should at first be so disposed in depth that it can march either east or north-east and cross the line of the Meuse on the . . . day of mobilization.

Whatever the circumstances, it will be responsible for the protection of the Hauts de Meuse, north of Verdun (sector Azannes —Damvillers), and the bridge-head of Montmédy and will employ its Reserve divisions for this purpose.

506 APPENDIX 9

1ST GROUP OF RESERVE DIVISIONS
(58th, 63rd, 66th Reserve Divisions)
Headquarters : Vesoul

General idea.

(1) To deploy facing east in the event of a violation of Swiss territory.

(2) To move north-eastwards as a support to or eventually as part of the First Army, with the principal object of covering the right of the operations of that Army, and assisting in the investment of Neuf Brissach and Strasbourg.

4TH GROUP OF RESERVE DIVISIONS
(51st, 53rd and 69th Reserve Divisions)
Headquarters : Sissonne.

General idea.

To deploy either facing east or south-east, or else facing north-east as support to the Third, Fourth and Fifth Armies, or as part of the mass of manœuvre of the left wing.[1]

CAVALRY CORPS
1st, 3rd and 5th Cavalry Divisions
Headquarters : Charleville, Aubenton, Poix Terron.

General idea.

The corps will be at the disposal of the commander-in-chief, who is responsible for the initial covering arrangements.

In the event of the commander of the Cavalry Corps ascertaining that the enemy has crossed the Franco-German frontier in the northern Woëvre sector, or that the neutrality of Belgium or of the Grand Duchy of Luxembourg has been violated, he will immediately assemble his three cavalry divisions east of Mézières.

He will hold them in readiness either, in the first case, to march on Montmédy to support the II. Corps or, in the second case, to advance into Belgium.

The movement will only be carried out by order of the commander-in-chief ; but in either case no unit must enter neutral territory before receiving the express authority of the commander-in-chief.

In the second eventuality, such dispositions will have to be made as will enable the Cavalry Corps to advance at once, on receipt of the order, to meet the enemy's columns, more especially those moving through Belgian Luxembourg, south of the difficult country Houffalize—Saint Hubert. Its mission will be to reconnoitre these columns and delay their advance. It may employ all or a part of the 145th Infantry Regiment as a support.

The 148th Infantry Regiment, which will also come under its orders, will move as rapidly as possible on Dinant, to occupy the Meuse bridges between the fortress of Namur and the frontier, in the event of the Belgian Government not having already arranged for this.

[1] No zone of operations was indicated for this group, but on the map its billeting area was marked in rear of the Fifth Army, from Bourgogne (inclusive) to Vervins (inclusive) with Sissonne as headquarters.

NOTE

How far Maréchal Foch was responsible for Plan XVII. has not been divulged.   In a study dated 1911 (that is two years before that plan was elaborated), entitled " Emploi du terrain et de la fortification dans la stratégie," a lithographed copy of which is preserved in the library of the École Supérieure de Guerre, Paris, is to be found a project of offensive operations based on a general advance between Belfort and the Ardennes north-eastwards on Mayence, and then on Berlin.   The main lines of this are hardly distinguishable from those of Plan XVII.   In the text Maréchal Foch discounts the value of fortifications, saying " The salvation of Armies by fortifications bears the name of Metz and Sedan. . . .   Fortresses, however vast, are the tombs of Armies."   His doctrine is finally expressed in the words :

" However little ambitious are our views, however moderate our politics, solely desirous of ensuring the integrity of our territory and the independence of our country, there is only one way of defending ourselves, that is to attack—to attack as soon as we are ready."   (" Revue Militaire Française," No. 130, p. 5 et seq).

Copy No. 10.

OPERATION ORDER No. 5

BY

FIELD-MARSHAL SIR JOHN FRENCH, G.C.B., ETC.,
Commanding British Expeditionary Force.

General Headquarters,
20th August 1914.

1. Information regarding the enemy and allied troops will be communicated separately.

2. The British Army will move north of the River Sambre in accordance with the attached march table.

3. The Cavalry Division and 5th Cavalry Brigade will cover the movement, occupying approximately the positions indicated in the march table, the 5th Cavalry Brigade acting under the orders of the G.O.C. Cavalry Division.

4. The R.F.C. will act in accordance with special instructions.

5. Army Troops are allotted in accordance with the table attached.

6. Positions of H.Q. of Divisions and 5th Cavalry Brigade will be reported to G.H.Q. as soon as decided.

7. Rendezvous for Supply Columns on August 21st will be as under :

Friday, August 21st, 6 A.M.:

Cavalry Division and ⎫ Douzies.
   5th Cavalry Brigade ⎭
First Army.   .   .   .   Boue
Second Army .   .   .   Landrecies. Supply columns to be west of the meridian of Landrecies by 6 A.M.

Army Troops, G.H.Q.   Landrecies.

Saturday, 22nd August, 7 A.M.:

Cavalry Division and ⎫ Blanc
5th Cavalry Brigade ⎭ Misseron. Railway station on French side of Belgian Frontier between Valenciennes and Mons.

First Army.   .   .   .   Landrecies.
Second Army .   .   .   Onnaing.   4½ miles N.E. of Valenciennes.

Army Troops, G.H.Q.   Landrecies.

8. G.H.Q. and Army Troops attached will remain at Le Cateau, to which reports will be sent.

Issued at 1 P.M.   A. J. MURRAY,
Lieutenant-General,
C.G.S.

TABLE OF MOVES FOR 21ST AUGUST 1914

Formation.	Movement.	Roads allotted.	Outposts.	Remarks.
Cav. Div.	H.Q. to Givry. To area St. Symphorien—Harveng—Vieux Reng—Grand Reng—Faurœulx. (E. of 3rd Div.)	The Solre le Chateau—Maubeuge—Mons road and all roads E. of it.	Merbes le Chateau inclusive — Binche —Villers St. Ghislain—Mons exclusive. All under G.O.C. Cav. Div.	Maubeuge to be clear by 9 A.M. The Maubeuge — Mons road as far as Bonnet to be clear by 12 noon. *Note.*—Binche may be occupied by Belgian troops.
5th Cav. Bde.	To neighbourhood of Binche, march to be arranged by G.O.C. Cav. Div.			
II. Corps .	H.Q. to Bavai. Heads of Divisions to line Gognies—Bavai. Tails to be clear of line Avesnes —Marbaix — Maroilles — Landrecies by 11 A.M.	The La Capelle—Avesnes — Mons road and all roads W. of it.	Local protection.	
I. Corps .	H.Q. to Marbaix. Heads of Divisions to the line Avesnes—Marbaix—Maroilles—Landrecies all inclusive.	do.	do.	

TABLE OF MOVES FOR 22ND AUGUST 1914

Formation.	Movement.	Roads allotted.	Outposts.	Remarks.
Cav. Div.	H.Q. to Jurbise. To area Lens—Herchies—Erbisœul—Les Bruyères—Masnuy St. Pierre.	E. of the road Givry — Mons exclusive.	On the line Binche—Rœulx—Lens.	
5th Cav. Bde.	At Binche.	Any available between Binche and Rœulx.		
II. Corps	H.Q. Bavai. Heads of Divisions to the line Mons (exclus.)—Thulin (9 m. W. of Mons). Tails to be clear of Hautmont—Hargnies by 11 A.M.	The Avesnes—Mons road and all roads W. of it.	Local protection.	
I. Corps	H.Q. Marbaix. Heads of Divisions to line Hautmont — Hargnies both inclus.	do.		

TABLE OF MOVES FOR 23RD AUGUST 1914, TO BE COMPLETED BY 4 P.M.

Formation.	Movement.	Roads allotted.	Outposts.	Remarks.
Cav. Div.	No move.		Line Thieusies exclusive—Lens. The outposts from Binche exclusive—Thieusies will be withdrawn in evening when relieved by infantry. Local protection. Connect with outposts of 1st Div.	
5th Cav. Bde.	No move.			
2nd Corps 3rd Div.	H.Q. to Genly. To area St. Denis—Mons exclusive—Noirchin—Asquillies—Spiennes—St. Symphorien — Havré. (Prepared to move N.E. of E.)		Line Maurage (inclusive)—Thieu—Gottignies—Thieusies (inclusive). Connect with 1st Corps on right and Cav. Div. on left. Local protection and watching roads leading N. and N.E.	To be N. of the line Blaregnies — Bougnies—Villers St. Ghislain by 11 A.M. Note.—Mons is probably occupied by Belgian troops.
5th Div.	To area Nimy — Ghlin — Baudour—St. Ghislain — Boussu. (Prepared to move E.)			
1st Corps 1st Div.	H.Q. to La Longueville. Head to Estinne au Mont, tail to Mairieux.	All roads S. of line Bougnies — Villers St. Ghislain, which will be cleared by 3rd Div. by 11 A.M.	Line Vellereille les Brayeux—Maurage (exclusive), connect with French troops on right and with 2nd Corps on left.	
2nd Div.	Head to Harmignies, tail to La Longueville.			

Allotment of Army Troops.

Army Troops will be attached as follows :—

	Formation to which attached.	Remarks.
G.H.Q. 1st and 2nd Echelon. G.H.Q. Signal Co.; H.Q. and Sections A, B, C, F, N, H, J, Q. A Squadron, North Irish Horse. A.T. Inf. Bn. (1/Cam. Highlanders) less 2 Companies. A.T. Train H.Q. Printing Co. L. of C., No. 1 Section. No. 20 Field Ambulance.	G.H.Q.*	*Will receive from Staff Officer for A.T. through Camp Commandant, G.H.Q.
I. Army H.Q. I. Army H.Q. Signal Co. & Sections K, L, G, D. Printing Co. L. of C.; No. 2 Section. B Squadron, South Irish Horse. 1 Co. A.T. Inf. Bn. (1/Cam. Highrs.). No. 1 Bridging Train. No. 19 Field Ambulance, B and C Sections.	I. Army Corps.	
II. Army H.Q. II. Army H.Q. Signal Co.; H.Q. and Sections E, M, O, P. C Squadron, North Irish Horse. 1 Co. A.T. Inf. Bn. (1/Cam. Highrs.). No. 2 Bridging Train. No. 19 Field Ambulance, A Section.	II. Army Corps.	

The 5th Cav. Bde. and R.F.C. will receive orders direct from G.H.Q. similarly to Armies and the Cavalry Division.

Secret.   Copy No. 6.

OPERATION ORDER No. 6

BY

FIELD-MARSHAL SIR JOHN FRENCH, G.C.B., ETC.,
Commanding British Expeditionary Force.

G.H.Q.,
21.8.14.

1. Two hostile Cavalry columns are reported moving S. and S.W. from the neighbourhood of Nivelles and patrols have been reported as having reached the line Grammont — Ath — St. Ghislain (6 miles W. of Mons)—Mons—La Louvière (10 miles E. of Mons)—Charleroi.
   A column of all arms was reported moving on Mons from Brussels and its head may have reached the neighbourhood of Braine le Comte this evening. The French have been in contact with the enemy's infantry on the line Pont à Celles (7 miles N.N.W. of Charleroi)—Tamines (7 miles E. of Charleroi).

2. The movements of 1st and 2nd Corps and 5th Cav. Bde. ordered for to-morrow in Operation Order No. 5 of 20th instant will hold good except as regards outposts (see para. 5 below).

3. The Cav. Div. will remain in their present position until the outposts of the 2nd Corps are in position. They will then move to the area Thulin — Quiévrain — Baisieux — Audregnies —Élouges (on the left of 5th Div.). G.O.C. 2nd Corps will send a Staff Officer to Cav. Div. to lead the division across the billeting area of the corps.
   Cav. Div. H.Q. to Quiévrain.

4. Further orders will be issued to 5th Cav. Bde. during to-morrow morning.

5. *Outposts.*
   2nd Corps. The line Givry inclus.—Harmignies — Bois la Haut all by 12 noon—Nimy and the line of the canal westward, as far as bridge S. of OE in Pommerœul inclus. not later than 1 P.M.
   Cav. Div. from left of 2nd Corps along line of canal to Condé sur Escaut.

6. Reports to Le Cateau.

G. M. HARPER, Colonel, G.S.
for C.G.S.

Issued at 11.55 P.M.

CAVALRY DIVISION

O (A) 47   21st.

(1) The information which you have acquired and conveyed to the C.-in-C. appears to be somewhat exaggerated. It is probable that only mounted troops, perhaps supported by Jäger battalions, are in your immediate neighbourhood.

(2) In no circumstances, however, does the C.-in-C. wish the Cavalry Division to be seriously engaged until he is ready to support it.

(3) You will therefore move to-morrow to a position on the left of the 2nd Corps, viz. :—to the area Thulin—Quiévrain—Baisieux—Audregnies—Élouges. This movement will be carried out after the infantry outposts of the 2nd Corps have occupied the line Givry—Mons—canal bridge N. of Nimy (Mons) and the line of the canal westward, to north of Thulin. The G.O.C. 2nd Corps will send a Staff Officer to arrange as to time and route. Orders will be issued to this effect to 2nd Corps.

(4) The movements of the 1st and 2nd Corps will otherwise be as indicated in Operation Order No. 5 of 20th instant.

(5) The 5th Cavalry Brigade will remain at Binche, taking measures for its own protection. If seriously attacked the brigade will fall back on Givry ; further orders will be issued to this brigade during the morning.

(6) Cav. Div. H.Q. will move to Quiévrain.

HENRY WILSON, Major-General,
Sub-Chief of the Staff,
G.H.Q. Exped. Force.

21/8/14.
11.35 P.M.

Copy No.

OPERATION ORDER No. 7

BY

FIELD-MARSHAL SIR JOHN FRENCH, G.C.B., ETC.,

Commander-in-Chief, British Ex. Force.

Bavai,
24 Aug. 1914.

1. The Army will move to-morrow, 25th inst., to a position in the neighbourhood of Le Cateau, exact positions will be pointed out on the ground to-morrow.

2. Corps will march so that their rear guards are clear of the Maubeuge —Bavai—Eth road by 5.30 A.M.

3. Roads available :

   1st Corps (with 5th Cavalry Brigade attached). All roads east of, but excluding, Bavai—Montay road.

   2nd Corps. Bavai — Montay road (inclusive), up to but excluding the road Wargnies—Villers Pol—Ruesnes—Capelle sur Ecaillon—Vertain—Romerie—Solesmes.

   Cavalry Division, with *19th Infantry Brigade* attached, the last-named road inclusive and all roads to the westward.

4. Two brigades of the Cavalry Division with Divisional Cavalry of the 2nd Corps, under command of a brigadier to be named by G.O.C. Cavalry Division, will cover the movement of the 2nd Corps.
   The remainder of the Cavalry Division with the 19th Inf. Brigade, under command of the G.O.C. Cavalry Division, will cover the west flank.

5. Reports to H.Q. Bavai up to 5 A.M., then to H.Q. Le Cateau.

6. A Staff Officer from Corps and Cavalry Division will report to G.H.Q. Le Cateau at 5 A.M. to receive orders as to positions.

Issued at   A. J. MURRAY,
    8.25 P.M.   Major-General,
                                      C.G.S. for
                                   F.M. C.-in-C.

OPERATION ORDER No. 8

BY

FIELD-MARSHAL SIR JOHN FRENCH, G.C.B., ETC.,

Commanding British Expeditionary Force.

G.H.Q.
25/8/1914.

1. The enemy followed our movement this morning and is also passing troops of all arms to the West and South.

2. It is the intention of the C.-in-C. to continue the retirement to-morrow with a view to covering his advanced base and protect his L. of C.

3. For this movement the 19th Brigade will be taken from the Cavalry Division and placed under the orders of the II. Army.

4. The retirement will be carried out from left to right.

5. The 4th Div. will fall back on the western flank in the general direction of Péronne, the western column moving along the line indicated roughly by the line Seranvillers—Le Catelet.
   The movement to commence at 7 A.M.
   The billeting area for to-morrow night being around Le Catelet—Beaurevoir.
   Boundary roads for this force being :
   On the East.
   Fontaine — Ligny — Caullery — Elincourt — Serain — Beaurevoir inclus.
   On the West.
   Such roads as the G.O.C. 4th Div. wishes to use.

   The II. Corps, with the 19th Bde., will move in echelon and fall back in the general direction of Beaurevoir — Prémont — La Sablière.[1]
   Boundary roads for this force :
   On the West.
   Fontaine — Ligny — Caullery — Elincourt — Serain — Beaurevoir exclus.
   On the East.
   All roads between the above and the Le Cateau—Busigny road exclusive.

   [1] La Sablière is not marked on any map issued with this Volume. It is on the French 1 : 80,000 (Cambrai sheet) issued to the B.E.F. It is a wood 2 miles S.S.W. of Busigny, *i.e.* midway between Busigny and Bohain.

The billeting area for to-morrow night being from Beaurevoir (exclus.) to La Sablière.

7. The I. Corps will start at 5.30 A.M. and march to the area of Busigny, and connect with the II. Corps at La Sablière.
The I. Corps can use the Le Cateau—Busigny road and roads to the East.
Billeting area in Busigny and to the N. and E.

8. The Cav. Div., with the 5th Cav. Bde. attached, will cover the movement on the N. and W. and will arrange their billets outside those already allotted.

9. G.H.Q. to St. Quentin at 7 P.M. to-night.

A. J. MURRAY,
Lieut.-General,
C.G.S.

Issued at ꞵ P.M.[1]

[1] The II. Corps War Diary states that G.H.Q. Operation Order 8 was received about 9 P.M. Two copies of the order were preserved as appendices to this diary ; of these one bears no time of issue, and the other is marked " Issued at ꞵ P.M." like the G.H.Q. copy, and also the I. Corps copy.
The 4th Division copy of the order is marked " Issued at 7.30 P.M." This is no doubt the correct time. That the time was later than 3.45 P.M. is proved by the following autograph letter from the Sub-Chief of the General Staff to Sir Horace Smith-Dorrien preserved in the G.H.Q. G.S. War Diary :

25th/8/14
3.45 P.M.

Dear Sir Horace,
The C.-in-C. has decided to continue the retirement to-morrow, the left (probably the 4th Division) being directed towards Péronne.
He told me to let you have this private note of his intention.
Orders will follow as soon as the details can be worked out.

v. s. yrs.

HENRY WILSON.

Copy No. 6.

OPERATION ORDER No. 1

BY

MAJOR-GENERAL T. D'O. SNOW, C.B.,
Còmdg. 4 Div.

Cambrai Sheet.

Aug. 25,
Pt. 129.

1. 1st and 2nd Corps are taking up a position approximately on the line Avesnes—Le Cateau—Caudry (incl.). Third Div. on the left.

2. The Fourth Division will take up a position Caudry (excl.)— Fontaine au Pire—Wambaix—knoll just West of Seranvillers, and will commence entrenching as soon as it is light to-morrow.

8. Disposition of units will be :

   (a) *11th Brigade* Caudry (excl.) to station on railway between Fontaine au Pire—Wambaix (incl.). *Tempy. H.Q.* Carrières, just south of Fontaine au Pire. *Route* from present position Briastre—Viesly—Bethencourt—Beauvois.

   (b) *12th Brigade* station on railway between Fontaine au Pire and Wambaix (excl.) to knoll West of Seranvillers. *Tempy. H.Q.* Longsart. *Route* from present position Bethencourt— Cattenières—Wambaix. The ½ Bn. R. Innis. Fus. must remain in position until the Tenth Brig. has passed through Beauvois. It may withdraw its detachment from Bevillers to Beauvois.

   (c) *10th Brig.* Haucourt (in reserve). *Route*—any route west of Caudry.

   Order of March of Inf. Brigs. :
   12th Brig., 11th Brig., 10th Brig.

   (d) *Irish Horse* Haucourt.

   (e) *Div. H.Q.* Haucourt.

   (f) *Div. Arty.* (less 32 Bde.) Ligny en Cambrésis.

   Tempy. H.Q. The Mairie at Ligny en Cambrésis.

   (g) *Fd. Ambces.* (on arrival) one at Ligny en Cambrésis, one at Mn. d'Haucourt.

4. Outposts will be found by 11th and 12th Brigades:
   11th Brig. Caudry (excl.) to the line Estournel—Longsart.
   12th Brig. from the line Estournel—Longsart to Masnières.

5. Refilling point will be notified later.

6. Sick will be taken back with units in impressed wagons and will be handed over to the Fd. Ambces. when they arrive.

7. Meeting place for the 2nd Line Transport:
   10th Brig. East exit of Haucourt.
   11th Brig. Railway Bridge on road Fontaine au Pire—Ligny en Cambrésis road.
   12th Brig. North exit of Esnes.
   Arty. Stand fast at Ligny en Cambrésis.

8. All First Line vehicles not required can be sent back at once to the position given in para. 3.

9. Troops will *not* move from their present position to those mentioned in para. 3 until they receive further orders, but reconnaissances will be made with a view to carrying it out in the dark.

J. E. EDMONDS,
Colonel,
G.S. 4th Division.

Issued at 5 P.M.

Note.—This is the only Divisional Operation Order available for Le Cateau.

An amendment to this Order, sent out at 6.40 P.M. in consequence of instructions from G.H.Q., reduced the length of front as follows:

11th Infantry Brigade:
" From Fontaine au Pire (inclusive) to railway station, instead of Caudry (exclusive) to railway station."

12th Infantry Brigade:
" From railway line at Station between Fontaine au Pire and Wambaix (exclusive) to Wambaix (inclusive)."

Copy No. 9.

2ND CORPS

OPERATION ORDER No. 6

2nd Corps Headquarters

Reference Map F.T. 13.   25th August 1914.

1. Information regarding the enemy is that he followed our movements to-day and is also passing troops to South and West.

2. The Army will continue its retirement to-morrow.

3. The 19th Infantry Brigade is placed under the orders of G.O.C. 2nd Corps.

4. Order of Columns from East to West :
   1st Corps.
   2nd Corps (and 19th Infantry Brigade).
   4th Division.
   The Cavalry Division, with 5th Cavalry Brigade, will cover the movement on the North and West.

5. The 2nd Corps and 19th Infantry Brigade will march to the billeting area Beaurevoir (exclusive)—La Sablière.

6. Roads allotted to 2nd Corps :
   (a) 5th Division and 19th Infantry Brigade (under command of G.O.C. 5th Division) : the Le Cateau—Maretz—Estrées road, and the Troisville—Reumont road leading to it.
   (b) To 3rd Division :
       the Audencourt—Montigny—Elincourt—Malincourt (West of the Church)—Beaurevoir road.
   (c) Corps Headquarters and Corps Troops will march by the 5th Division road.

7. Each Division will detail a rear guard of one Infantry Brigade, two Brigades R.F.A., and the Cyclist Companies and Divisional Squadrons.

8. (a) All impedimenta (moving by Divisional roads) will start at 4 A.M. using divisional roads.
   (b) Main bodies will start at 7 A.M.
   (c) Corps Headquarters and Corps Troops will join the 5th Divisional Column one mile South-West of where the road crosses the railway.

9. Railhead to-morrow will be Péronne.

10. (a) Rendezvous for Supply Columns, S. Quentin 2 A.M.
    (b) Rendezvous for Ammunition Park, Maretz at 5 A.M.

11. Report to Bertry until 10 A.M., and after that hour to crossroads half mile South-East of Serain.

G. F. WALKER,
Brigadier-General, General Staff,
2nd Corps.

Issued at 10.15 P.M.

OPERATION ORDER No. 9

Issued at 8 P.M. Noyon.

27.8.14.

O (a) 326.

Eventually took the form of a message to
    Cavalry Division ;
    I. Corps ;
    II. Corps.

Copies of the messages are p.a. in above files in O (a).

Note.—Message concluded with an order to throw away unnecessary impedimenta and ammunition not absolutely required and carry exhausted men on vehicles.

The above is the record in the G.H.Q. Files. Copies of the messages to the Cavalry Division and I. Corps cannot be found ; that sent to the latter was in cipher. The original order, given below, was, however, received by the II. Corps.

OPERATION ORDER No. 9

BY

FIELD-MARSHAL SIR JOHN FRENCH, G.C.B., ETC.

G.H.Q.,
27/8/14.

1. It is reported on good authority that German Forces are in or near St. Quentin.

2. The 3rd and 5th Divisions and 19th Bde. will clear Ham and the other canal bridges by daylight, and will then march on Noyon and cross to the left bank of the R. Oise.

3. The 4th Division, under orders of II. Corps, will move to ground north of the bridges at Ham, starting immediately on receipt of order.

4. The I. Corps has been ordered to Pierremande (8 miles S.W. of La Fère), passing the R. Oise at La Fère, starting as soon after receipt of this order as possible.

5. The Cav. Div. now under orders of the C.-in-C. will cover the retirement of the II. Corps and 4th Division.

6. All ammunition on wagons not absolutely required and other impedimenta will be unloaded and officers and men carried to the full capacity of all transport, both horse and mechanical.

7. G.H.Q. will move to Compiègne at Y (*sic*) A.M. to-morrow.

H. WILSON, Major-Genl.,
Sub-Chief of Staff.

Issued at 8.30 P.M.

Secret.   Copy No. 6.

OPERATION ORDER No. 10

BY

FIELD-MARSHAL SIR JOHN FRENCH, G.C.B., ETC.,

Commanding British Expeditionary Force.

G.H.Q.,
28th August 1914.

1. (*a*) The enemy advanced to within 6 miles of St. Quentin last night and appears to have taken up a flank position with 1 corps a few miles north of St. Quentin to-day, to cover a general movement to the westward of a considerable portion of his 1st Army, with a view to checking the advance of French troops from the west, some of whom have been successfully engaged with him last night and during to-day.

(*b*) The approximate position of our troops is as follows :

Cavalry Division :

1st Brigade and 4th Brigade	Cressy.
3rd Brigade	Jussy.
5th Brigade	covering I. Corps.
2nd Brigade	not reported.
H.Q.	Moyencourt.

I. Corps. Area Charmes (1 mile S.E. of La Fère)—Amigny—Barrisis. H.Q. St. Gobain (6 miles S.E. of La Fère).

II. Corps (including 4th Division and 19th Brigade). Area Noyon—Carlepont—Cuts. H.Q. Cuts.

R.F.C. Vicinity of Compiègne.

2. It is the Field-Marshal Commanding-in-Chief's intention that the Army should halt to-morrow to rest, but all formations must be south of the line Vendeuil (4 miles N. of La Fère)—Jussy—Ham—Nesle, and will take steps for local protection.

3. The 4th Division and 19th Infantry Brigade will remain for the present under the orders of the G.O.C. II. Corps. The 5th Cavalry Brigade will remain under the orders of the G.O.C. I. Corps.

G.O.'s C. Corps and Cavalry Division will report the position of their formations to G.H.Q. to-morrow at 12 midday.

4. Railheads for Supplies, August 29th:

I. Corps	Attichy.
Cavalry Division	Lamotte Breuil.
5th Cav. Bde.	do.
II. Corps	Compiègne.
4th Division	do.
19th Brigade	do.
G.H.Q.	do.
Flying Corps	do.
L. of C. Units	do.

Railheads will be regarded as the rendezvous, and formations will consequently be responsible for conducting the supply columns to and from the railheads.

5. Reports to G.H.Q. Compiègne.

Issued at 11.30 P.M.

A. J. MURRAY, Lieut.-General,
C.S.O.

[*Note.*—The draft copy of this Order (Copy No. I.) is endorsed in pencil "Despatched 5 A.M. 29.8.14."]

Secret.   Copy No. 6.

OPERATION ORDER No. 11

BY

FIELD-MARSHAL SIR JOHN FRENCH, G.C.B., ETC.,

Commanding British Expeditionary Force.

G.H.Q.
29th August 1914

1. Information as to the enemy has been communicated personally to G.O.'s C. Corps and Cavalry Division.

2. The Army will retire to a line Soissons—Rethondes to-morrow.
   The Corps Commanders will arrange the hours of starting.
   The 5th Cavalry Brigade will remain attached to the 1st Corps.
   The 2nd Cavalry Brigade will come under the orders of the 2nd Corps. The 4th Division and 19th Inf. Bde. will remain under the orders of the 2nd Corps.
   The Cavalry Division, less 2 cavalry brigades, will cover the left of the retirement moving on Compiègne.
   Corps Commanders will as far as possible destroy all bridges as they retire, taking care that the cavalry is not cut off.
   The dividing line between the two Corps will be St. Paul—Selens —Nouvron—Fontenoy, the roads passing through these places being assigned to the 1st Corps.

3. Railheads for 30th August 1914.

Formation.	Railhead and Rendezvous.
1st Corps	Béthisy St. Pierre.
Cavalry Division	Verberie.
5th Cavalry Brigade	Verberie.
2nd Corps	Pont Ste. Maxence.
4th Division	do.
19th Brigade	do.
G.H.Q.	do.
Flying Corps	do.
L. of C. Units	do.

Railheads will be regarded as the rendezvous, and formations will consequently be responsible for conducting the supply columns to and from the railheads.

4. Reports to G.H.Q. at Villers Cottérêts after 10 A.M. 30/8/14, up to that hour to Compiègne.

A. J. MURRAY, Lt.-Genl.,
C.G.S.

Issued at 9 P.M.

Secret. Copy No. 6.

OPERATION ORDER No. 12

BY

FIELD-MARSHAL SIR JOHN FRENCH, G.C.B., ETC.,

Commanding British Expeditionary Force.

G.H.Q. 30/8/14.

1.   Yesterday the 2nd Corps was attacked south of Ham by the VII. German Corps which had advanced from St. Quentin that morning, but which met with but little success. The pressure, such as it was, was relieved by a French advance in force on our right which met with great success in the neighbourhood of Guise, where the German Guard and X. Corps were driven back into the Oise. On our left French forces were engaged with the enemy in the direction of Péronne, but the action was not pressed by the Germans, who had slightly withdrawn during the early hours of the afternoon.

2.   The Army will move west to-morrow in accordance with the attached table.[1]
Corps Commanders will fix the hour of starting which will be communicated to G.H.Q. as soon as decided.

3.   The 4th Division and 19th Infantry Brigade will become the 3rd Corps and will pass under the command of Lieut.-Gen. W. P. Pulteney, C.B., D.S.O., at a date and hour to be arranged by G.O.'s C. the 2nd and 3rd Corps.
The 3rd Corps will be the northern column.
The Cavalry Division will cover the northern flank of the movement, marching down the right bank of the R. Oise.

4.   Railheads :

Formation.					Railhead and Rendezvous.
1st Corps	.	.	.	.	Plessis Belleville.
5th Cav. Bde.	.	.	.	.	do.
2nd Corps	.	.	.	.	do.
3rd Corps	.	.	.	.	Senlis.
Cav. Div.	.	.	.	.	do.
G.H.Q.	.	.	.	.	do.
Flying Corps	.	.	.	.	do.
L. of C. Units	.	.	.	.	do.

[1] Marginal note in pencil: "Order changed later and Army moved south. H. Wake, G.S."

Railheads will be regarded as the rendezvous, and formations will consequently be responsible for conducting the Supply Columns to and from the railheads.
This order will remain in force until cancelled.

5.   Reports to Dammartin en Goële at 6 A.M., 12 miles S.E. of Senlis and 15 miles S.W. from Crépy.

                                A. J. Murray, Lt.-Gen., C.G.S.
Issued at 5.15 P.M.

[*Note.*—The Cavalry Division and I. and II. Corps copies of this order are endorsed "issued at 6.15 P.M."]

MARCH TABLE FOR 31ST AUGUST

Formation.	Roads Allotted.	Billeting Area.	Remarks.
Cav. Div. . .	To cross R. Oise at Port de la Croix St. Ouen.	Rivecourt — Bazicourt—Sarron.	
4th Div. 19th Bde.	To be allotted by II. Corps Commander.	Verberie — Pontpoint — Saintines — St. Sauveur.	These formations will form III. Corps.
II. Corps . .	The road Mortefontaine—Taillefontaine — Eméville —Feigneux—Duvy inclusive and all roads N. and W. of it.	Morienval — Béthisy —Néry — Crépy — Feigneux — Fresnoy.	
I. Corps and 5th Cav. Bde.	Roads S. of that allotted to II. Corps. Bulk of force to move by Soissons—Villers Cottérêts—Nanteuil road.	Soucy — Haramont—Vez — Vaumoise — Villers Cottérêts —Puiseux.	

Secret.

OPERATION ORDER No. 13

BY

FIELD-MARSHAL SIR JOHN FRENCH, G.C.B., ETC.,

Commanding British Expeditionary Force.

G.H.Q. 31/8/14.

1. The enemy appears to have completed his westerly movement and was to-day pivoting round to the south, large columns having been observed advancing in a general southerly or south-easterly direction on the front Noyon—Compiègne from about Roye—Montdidier. This advance is covered by at least two Cavalry Divisions who reached the Oise this afternoon.

2. The Army will move to-morrow in accordance with the attached table.

3. The 4th Div. and 19th Infantry Brigade will constitute the 3rd Corps under the command of Lieut.-General W. P. Pulteney, C.B., D.S.O.

4. The Cav. Div. will continue to cover the 3rd Corps.

5. The 3rd Cav. Bdc. will come under the orders of I. Corps.

6. Railheads and Rendezvous :

Formation.	Railheads.	Rendezvous.
1st Corps	Plessis Belleville.	Betz.
2nd Corps	do.	do.
5th Cav. Bde.	do.	do.
Cav. Div.	St. Mard (near Dammartin).	
3rd Corps	do.	
Flying Corps	do.	
G.H.Q.	do.	
L. of C. Units	do.	

7. Reports to Dammartin en Goële.

A. J. MURRAY, Lieut.-General,
C.G.S.

Issued at 8.50 P.M.

MARCH TABLE FOR 1st SEPTEMBER

Formation.	Billeting Area, Aug. 31/Sept. 1.	Roads Allotted.	Billeting Area, Sept. 1st/2nd.
1st Corps H.Q. Villers Cottérêts	Vauxbuin—Pernant —Soucy—Verte Feuille.	Vauxbuin—Villers Cotté-rêts—La Ferté Milon—Mareuil (inc.) on east. Vivières—Villers Cottérêts — Boursonne — Antilly (inc.) on west.	La Ferté Milon—Ivors — Betz—Mareuil.
2nd Corps H.Q. Crépy.	Coyolles — Crépy — Lévignen.	Vaumoise — Lévignen — Fresnoy—Villers St. Genest (inc.) on east. Duvy—Ormoy—Nanteuil (inc.) on west.	Villers St. Genest —Nanteuil— Silly — Brégy —Bouillancy.
3rd Corps . .	St. Jean aux Bois —St. Sauveur.	Gilocourt—Crépy—Auger St. Vincent—Rozières —Bois du Val (inc.) on east. Verberie—Raray—Rully —Baron (inc.) on west.	Bois du Val—Baron — Montagny.
Cav. Div. H.Q. Plessis Villette.	South bank of Oise.	Roads west of Verberie—Rully—Baron (exclus.).	Montépilloy—Mont l'Evêque.

G.H.Q. MESSAGES TO I. CORPS

1st September 1914

1st September.

No operation orders—retirement ordered by messages.

H. W.   G. S.

The above is the record in the G.H.Q. file.   The messages sent to I. Corps are given below ; similar messages were sent to II. and III. Corps and Cavalry Division.

To) 1st Corps ·

O.A. 530   1st.   C. in C. wishes it to be borne in mind that it is of paramount importance that march S.W. should be carried out. Therefore general engagement must not be entered upon if possible to avoid it and all fighting should be rear-guard action covering retirement to billets ordered.

from) G.H.Q.   11.5 A.M.

To) 1st Corps :

O.A. 533.   1st.   If further retirement is ordered for to-morrow roads allotted to you La Ferte Milon—Varreddes—Meaux Bridge— Couilly Road to road Betz—Acy en Multien—Vincy—Etrepilly— Barcy—Meaux Station—Villenoy—Esbly Bridge both inclusive. Probably rear of fighting troops will halt on line Dammartin— Etrepilly—Mary.

from) G.H.Q.   1.20 P.M.

To) 1st Corps :

O.A. 539.   1st.   Some enemy cavalry are between II. Corps and G.H.Q.   Have ordered II. and III. Corps to retire down their respective roads as soon as they can.   March south on roads allotted as soon as possible gaining touch with II. Corps.   All information points to considerable enemy forces along the whole of our northern front with possibility of night attack.   G.H.Q. move Lagny on Marne now.

from) G.H.Q.   7 P.M.

CORRESPONDENCE

WITH REGARD TO HALTING ON THE MARNE
AND THE RETREAT BEHIND THE SEINE[1]

I.

General Joffre to Fd.-Marshal Sir J. French.

G.Q.G.. 2nd Sept. 1914.

Monsieur le Maréchal,

I have the honour to thank you for the proposals that you have kindly made to the Government of the Republic relative to the co-operation of the British Army, which have been communicated to me.

In view of the events which have taken place during the past two days, I do not believe it possible actually to carry out a combined manœuvre on the Marne with all our forces. But I consider that the co-operation of the British Army in the defence of Paris is the only one which can produce advantageous results in the situation described in the attached letter which I am addressing to the Minister of War, of which I have the honour to send you a copy.

Please accept, Monsieur le Maréchal, the expression of my high consideration and of cordial sentiments of comradeship.

JOFFRE

II.

The General Commanding-in-Chief to the Minister of War.

G.Q.G., 2nd Sept. 1914.

I have received the proposals of Fd.-Marshal Sir J. French, which you kindly communicated to me ; they suggest organizing a line of defences on the Marne which should be held by forces sufficiently dense in depth and particularly strong behind the left flank.

The actual position of the Fifth Army does not permit of the realization of the programme traced by the Fd.-Marshal and at the same time of assuring effective aid on the right of the British Army at the proper time.

On the other hand, the support of General Maunoury's Army, which is to move to the defence of the north-east fronts of Paris, is always assured on the left of the British Army ; under these conditions the latter would be able to stand on the Marne for a certain time, then retire on the left bank of the Seine, which it should hold from Melun to Juvisy ; thus the British forces would participate

[1] Translated from the G.H.Q. Records.

in the defence of the capital and their presence would greatly cheer the troops of the Entrenched Camp.

I may add that instructions have just been given to the Armies in order that their movements may be co-ordinated, and that it would not be advantageous to modify these instructions; they are intended to place our troops in a situation which will permit them to take the offensive in a very short time. The date of this movement will be communicated by Fd.-Marshal Sir J. French so as to allow the British Army to take part in the general offensive.

The General Commanding-in-Chief, JOFFRE.

III.

Special Instruction No. 4.

G.Q.G., 1st Sept. 1914.

(1)   In spite of the tactical successes won by the Third, Fourth and Fifth Armies from the Meuse to Guise the outflanking movement against the left of the forces, insufficiently arrested by the British Army and the Sixth Army, constrains the forces as a whole to pivot on our right.

As soon as the Fifth Army has escaped the menace of envelopment, the Armies will resume the offensive.

(2)   The withdrawal may lead the Armies to retire in a north-south direction. The Fifth Army must not on any account allow its left to be held fast. The other Armies will be able to oppose the enemy, the Army Commanders being careful not to uncover the neighbouring Armies and keeping in liaison.

(3)   Lines of demarkation :

between the Fourth and Fifth Armies (Foch's Detachment); road Rheims—Epernay (Fourth) ; road Montmort—Romilly (Fifth) ;

between the Fourth and Third ; road Grandpré—Sainte Ménehould—Revigny (to the Fourth Army).

In the zone allotted to the Fourth Army, Foch's Detachment will keep in liaison with the Fifth Army. The gap between Foch's Detachment and the Fourth Army will be watched by the 7th and 9th Cavalry Divisions (Fourth Army) supported by infantry detachments.

The moment that the Armies are in the following situations may be regarded as the limit of the retirement, without any implication that this limit must necessarily be reached :

Cavalry Corps (new formation),[1] south of Bray ;

Fifth Army, behind the Seine, south of Nogent sur Seine ;

Fourth Army (Foch's Detachment), behind the Aube, south of Arcis sur Aube ;

Fourth Army (main body), behind the Ornain east of Vitry le François ;

---

[1] Conneau's.

Third Army, north of Bar le Duc; it should then be re-inforced by the Reserve divisions, which will leave the Hauts de Meuse to take part in the offensive movement.

If circumstances permit, portions of the First and Second Armies will be brought at an opportune moment to take part in the offensive. Finally the mobile troops of the Entrenched Camp of Paris may likewise be able to participate in the general action.

JOFFRE.

Secret. O (*a*). Copy No. 7.

OPERATION ORDER No. 14

BY

FIELD-MARSHAL SIR JOHN FRENCH, G.C.B., ETC.,

Commanding British Expeditionary Force.

G.H.Q., 2nd September 1914.

1. On the 1st September the 1st Cav. Bde. was in action at an early hour with the 4th German Cavalry Division, it was supported by units of the 3rd and 2nd British Corps, with the result that twelve German guns and a number of prisoners were captured.

The 2nd Division was engaged during the afternoon of the 1st September with the advanced guard of the 3rd German Corps, whose attack was checked and has not been pressed to-day.

An engagement has been taking place to-day between what is probably a German cavalry division, perhaps supported by the artillery of the leading division of the 2nd German Corps, posted about Montépilloy, and the French about Senlis. By the middle of the afternoon no infantry attack had been developed.

The 4th German Corps was this morning about Crépy en Valois and the 3rd German Corps about Villers Cottérêts.

2. The Army moves to-morrow to a position indicated personally by the C.-in-C. to Corps Commanders.

(*a*) 1st Corps using Trilport Bridge and bridges up stream, to move to ground about 2 miles south of Jouarre.

(*b*) 2nd Corps using Trilbardou, Isles les Villenoy and Meaux bridges, the latter being cleared by arrangement with the 1st Corps (Note: it is reported that Trilbardou bridge is only suitable for light transport), move to a position in the neighbourhood of Signy Signets—Vaucourtois inclusive.

(*c*) 3rd Corps by Lagny bridge to a position in the neighbourhood of Vaucourtois exclusive—Coutevroult.

(*d*) Cavalry Division by Lagny bridge, in rear of the 2nd and 3rd Corps to a position on the right of the 1st Corps.

3. The 3rd and 5th Cav. Bdes. remain under orders of I. Corps until the Cav. Div. has reached its position, when 3rd Cav. Bde. will come under orders of Cav. Div.

4. Corps Commanders will be responsible for the destruction of bridges over the Marne as follows :

1st Corps, Changis to Trilport both inclusive, and as far up-stream as possible.

2nd Corps, Trilbardou inclusive, and all upstream thence to Trilport exclusive.

3rd Corps, Trilbardou exclusive, and all downstream thence to Lagny inclusive.

It is understood that preparations have been made by the French to destroy bridges between Isles les Villenoy inclusive and Lagny inclusive and that they have detachments posted at them for the purpose, but these detachments will act only on receipt of orders from British commanders.

5. Railheads for to-morrow :

1st Corps ⎫
2nd Corps ⎬ Marles.
5th Cav. Bde. ⎭

Cavalry Division ⎫
3rd Corps . . ⎪
G.H.Q. . . ⎬ Tournan.
L. of C. Units . ⎪
Flying Corps . ⎭

6. Signal Offices established at Civil Post and Telegraph Offices at Meaux and at Lagny will remain open until ordered to close.

A Signal Office will be established at Mortcerf south of Crécy by 7 A.M.

Mortcerf will become the report centre for G.H.Q. from 7 A.M.

G.H.Q. will remain at Melun.

A. J. MURRAY, Lieut.-General,
C.G.S.

Issued at 7.30 P.M.

Secret.   O (a).   Copy No. 7.

OPERATION ORDER No. 15

BY

FIELD-MARSHAL SIR JOHN FRENCH, G.C.B., ETC.,
Commanding British Expeditionary Force

G.H.Q., 3rd September 1914.

1. The Army was not attacked during its movement to-day.

The enemy has been moving in an easterly and south-easterly direction during the day on Chateau Thierry where the left of the French was attacked this morning from which it retired to about Montfaucon.

The position of the German troops this afternoon was approximately as under :

(a) 1 corps (? IX.) about Chateau Thierry.

(b) 1 division (? III. Corps) at 2 P.M. in Marigny.
   1 division (? III. Corps) at 2 P.M. at La Ferté Milon.

(c) 1 division (? IV. Corps) at 2 P.M. head about May en Multien.
   1 division (? IV. Corps) not identified, but probably between Marigny and Mareuil.

(d) 1 division (? II. Corps) at 2 P.M. about Chèvreville.
   1 division (? II. Corps) head about Nanteuil at 2.20 P.M.
   Cavalry at Dammartin at 2.20 P.M., St. Soupplets (two sqdns.) at 2.40 P.M. and between right flank of marching column and Marne.

There are indications that perhaps one additional corps (? VII.) may be advancing on Chateau Thierry from the N.N.W.

2. The Commander-in-Chief is most anxious to give the Army a complete day's rest to-morrow, but he feels very strongly the necessity for Army Corps Commanders to be ready to retire at short notice, the right of the Army being thrown back pivoting on its left and eventually resting along the left bank of the R. Seine.

3. All arrangements will be made for retirement as follows :

The movement will not commence without orders.

The general line to be reached by rear guards on the first day's march will be :

Mauperthuis (S.W. of Coulommiers) — Faremoutiers — Tigeaux —Chanteloup

The roads allotted are as follows :

1st Corps. Signy Signets — Pierre Levée — La Haute Maison — Maisoncelles—Mortcerf—Marles—and all roads to the east.

2nd Corps. Quincy Ségy — St. Germain — Villiers sur Morin — Villeneuve le Comte—Tournan—and all roads between that and 1st Corps.

3rd Corps. Chanteloup—Ferrières—Pontcarré and all roads between that and 2nd Corps.

4. The 3rd and 5th Cavalry Brigades under Brig.-General H. Gough acting under instructions from 1st Army Corps will reconnoitre to the east and if possible gain touch with the French Cavalry starting early to-morrow. All information as to the enemy's movements to be transmitted to G.H.Q. as rapidly as possible.

5. The R.F.C. will as early as the light permits carry out reconnaissances in the direction of Chateau Thierry and to the north.

6. All bridges in front of the Army will be destroyed forthwith. See para. 4 of Operation Orders No. 14 (d) of 2nd September 1914.

7. Railheads :

Cavalry Division	Verneuil.
5th Cavalry Brigade	Mormant.
1st Corps	Mormant.
2nd Corps	Marles.
3rd Corps	Chaumes.
Flying Corps	do.
G.H.Q.	do.
L. of C. units	do.

Railhead for Ammunition, Villeneuve St. Georges (Goods Station) 10 miles S.E. of Paris.

8 Mortcerf will remain the report centre for G.H.Q.

G.H.Q. will remain at Melun.

HENRY WILSON,
Major-General,
Sub-Chief of the Staff

Issued at 11.50 P.M.

LETTER
OF
GENERAL JOFFRE
TO
FIELD-MARSHAL SIR J. FRENCH

Grand Quartier Général
des
Armées de l'Est.   Au G.Q.G. le 4 septembre 1914.

État-Major.

3e Bureau.

Le Général Commandant en Chef,
au Field Maréchal Sir John French,
Commandant en Chef les Forces Britanniques.

Mon cher Maréchal,
 Je viens de recevoir votre lettre du 3 septembre et je tiens à vous adresser mes remerciements pour les sentiments cordiaux qu'elle renferme. Ils m'ont vivement touché.
 Mon intention, dans la situation actuelle, est de poursuivre l'exécution du Plan que j'ai eu l'honneur de vous communiquer et de n'engager le combat sur les lignes choisies, que toutes forces réunies.
 Au cas où les Armées Allemandes poursuivraient leur mouvement vers le Sud-Sud-Est, s'éloignant ainsi de la Seine et Paris, peut-être estimerez-vous comme moi, que votre action pourrait s'exercer plus efficacement sur la rive droite de ce fleuve, entre Marne et Seine.
 Votre gauche appuyée à la Marne, étayée par le Camp retranché de Paris, serait couverte par la garnison mobile de la capitale qui se portera à l'attaque dans la direction de l'Est par la rive gauche de la Marne.
 J'ai l'honneur de vous confirmer la nouvelle que je vous avais annoncée hier de la nomination du Général Franchey d'Esperey, au Commandement de la 5e Armée. Je suis certain qu'il résultera de votre collaboration au combat les meilleurs résultats.
 Croyez-moi, mon cher Maréchal, votre très sincèrement dévoué

J. JOFFRE.

Received 2.15 P.M.

LETTER

OF

FIELD-MARSHAL SIR JOHN FRENCH

TO

EARL KITCHENER

Headquarters,
[Monday] 7th September 1914.

My dear Lord K.

Thank you for your letters of September 5th received late last night.

I am very sorry to seem to have allowed you to lack information in the previous two days, but, as I explained to you in my telegram, the situation and the arrangements for our advance were so uncertain on Saturday that I was afraid of misleading you. For instance, late on Friday night Joffre asked me to retire 12 miles in order to make room for his 5th Army south of the Marne. I had half completed the movement when he determined to keep the 5th Army north of the river and asked me to retrace my steps and get touch with that Army.

I think this was unavoidable, and on the whole his conception and his dispositions are really quite good. He tells me of the success in the advance of the 5th Army yesterday on my right and adds, " This result is certainly due to the advance of the English Forces " towards the East. The continuation of your offensive will be of " the greatest assistance to the attack of the 5th Army during the " movement to-morrow."

He asked me to direct the march to-day a little more to the north, so as to be in closer touch with the 6th Army on the left.

As regards this latter Army, they have in front of them the 4th German Reserve Corps which has retreated north of the Marne and which they appear to be hammering pretty freely.

The 2nd German Corps was moving north all yesterday and at nightfall was watched by the aeroplanes into a large forest just south of the Marne from which we supposed them to be debouching, through Lizy, north of the wood to the north of the river.

Joffre tells me that the 5th French Army have parts of the 9th and 3rd German Corps opposite them, and in rear of them are the 4th Regular Corps and parts of the 10th Corps.

As I told you, we pushed back considerable detachments of the enemy yesterday and hope to reach a much more forward line to-day.

I have been a great deal amongst the men and I find them in excellent spirits and good heart. Most of our casualties have now been replaced. I enclose you the returns for the 4th, 5th and 6th

September ; they have, of course, gone officially through the Lines of Communication.

We are refitting as quickly as we can, having regard to the forward movement and to the awful congestion of trains in the rear. This is now getting better, but it will be some days before we get our full requirement and our maxims and guns.

I am delighted to hear about the Indian Divisions. Who is to be the Indian Corps Commander ?

Thank you for all your trouble about the 6th Division. I have not worried you about it because I know very well you are doing all you possibly can, and I much hope to get a wire from you to-night or to-morrow morning to say it is coming.

.   .   .   .[1]

You ask my opinion as to German fighting characteristics. I will write to you on this subject in a day or two, as I must get this letter off by the messenger ; but I may say at once that it will never do to oppose them with anything but very highly trained troops led by the best officers. All their movements are marked by extraordinary unity of purpose and mutual support ; and to undergo the fatigues they have suffered they must be under an absolutely iron discipline. However, more of this to-morrow. At the same time I will tell you what I think of Gwynn's very useful letter.

I return the Prime Minister's note.

I have tried to write a bit of my despatch on every day when I could spare a few minutes. I have got the story fairly complete and accurate in despatch form up to our retirement from St. Quentin on Friday the 28th. That is practically when we threw off the bulk of the enemy after our first fight on the Mons position.

This shall be finished off at once and will be with you in about three days ; and it might be published on Thursday or Friday.

You say in your note enclosing P.M.'s letter,

" I only sent one man to write."

No one for writing purposes has arrived at the front. I should be delighted to have Percy.

Yours very truly,
J. D. P. FRENCH.

[1] Some personal remarks on a general have been omitted.

Secret.

OPERATION ORDER No. 16

BY

FIELD-MARSHAL SIR JOHN FRENCH, G.C.B., ETC.,

Commanding British Expeditionary Force

G.H.Q., 4th September 1914.

1. Columns of the enemy, probable strength 3½ Corps and 4 Cavalry Divisions, have been marching all day across our front in a south-easterly direction, their left on Chateau Thierry, their right on La Ferté sous Jouarre. By noon the leading troops had begun to attack the XVIII. Corps of the 5th French Army at St. Barthélemy. The enemy's right flank guard, directed on Barcy, may be expected to cross the Marne to-night or to-morrow morning near Germigny.

2. The Army will move S.W. to-morrow—September 5th—pivoting on its left.

The general line to be reached by rear guards of 1st, 2nd and 3rd Corps will be :

Ormeaux (7 miles S.W. of Coulommiers)—Les Chapelles Bourbon —Ozoir la Ferrière.

Roads Allotted :

> 1st Corps. The road Pierre Levée—Gde. Loge Farm— Maisoncelles—La Celle—Mortcerf—La Houssaye—Fontenay and all roads east of this.
>
> 2nd Corps. The road Quincy Ségy—St. Germain—Villiers sur Morin—Villeneuve le Comte—Tournan—Coubert and all roads between this and 1st Corps.
>
> 3rd Corps. The road Chanteloup—Ferrières en Brie— Pontcarré—railway crossing 1½ miles east of Ozoir la Ferrière—Chevry—Brie Comte Robert and all roads between this and 2nd Corps.
>
> The Cavalry Division (less 3rd and 5th Cav. Bdes. under 1st Corps) will move from Gournay by any roads west of those allotted to 3rd Corps to the area Brie Comte Robert (exclus.)—Limoges, consulting with 3rd Corps as to clearing Brie Comte Robert.

The Cavalry Division will be required to move S.E. early on the 6th so as to clear the eastern flank of the army.

3. Hours of starting will be arranged by Corps and Cav. Div. Commanders.

4. Railheads :

5th Cav. Bde.	Melun.
1st Corps	do.
G.H.Q.	do
L. of C.	do.
R.F.C.	do.
2nd Corps	Lieusaint.
3rd Corps	do.
Cavalry Division. . . .	Bruncy.

Ammunition railhead, Villeneuve St. Georges (Goods Station) about 10 miles S.E. of Paris.

5. Reports to Melun.

A. J. MURRAY, Lieut.-General,
C.G.S.

Issued at 6.35 P.M.

LENGTH OF MARCHES[1]

(In miles)

	I. Corps.		II. Corps.		III. Corps.[2]	
	1st Div. (1/Glouc. R.).	2nd Div. (35th Heavy Batty. R.G.A.).[3]	3rd Div. (From various War Diaries).	5th Div. (From various War Diaries).	19 Inf. Bde. (Brigade Diary).	4 Div. (G.S. Diary).
Advance						
August 20	8½	..	2	..	..	..
,, 21	13	..	21	15	..	..
,, 22	22½	20	17	15	..	..
Battle of Mons						
August 23	..	22	5	3	7	..
Retreat						
August 24	17	14	15	10	13	..
,, 25	15½	24	25	24	19	6
,, 26	15	16	14	15	} 40 (26–27)	21[4]
,, 27	23	15	17	23		10
,, 28	21	20	27	20	17	20½
,, 29	Rest day	2	} 25 (29–30)	4	Rest day	12½
,, 30	10	23		12	15	14
,, 31	18	12	15	15	19	15
September 1	19	19	15	12	14	11½
,, 2	18½	21	13	14	13	9½
,, 3	16½	18	10	18	22	17½
,, 4	11½	8	Rest day	Rest day	Rest day	Rest day
,, 5	15	16[3]	16[5]	16[5]	14[5]	14[5]
	244	250	237	216	193	151½

[1] In many cases, on certain days, particular units greatly exceeded the distances given in the above table, which represent the bare minimum done on the roads.

[2] The IIIrd Corps, consisting of the 4th Division and the 19th Infantry Brigade, was only formed on 31 August.

[3] In this same period the battery fired 76 rounds.

[4] This includes both the retirement to the Le Cateau position in the early morning (8¾ miles) as well as the continuation of the Retreat after the conclusion of the action (12¼ miles).

[5] March carried out during night of 4/5 September.

Note.—It is hoped that some officers in the 3rd and 5th Divisions will be able to furnish a complete record of the marches carried out by their units between 20 August and 5 September 1914.

GENERAL JOFFRE'S INSTRUCTION
FOR THE BATTLE OF THE MARNE[1]

INSTRUCTION No. 6

G.Q.G., 4th September 1914. 22 hours.

(1) The time has come to profit by the adventurous position of the German First Army and concentrate against that Army all the efforts of the Allied Armies of the extreme left.

All dispositions will be made during the 5th September for beginning the attack on the 6th.

(2) The following will be the positions to be attained by the evening of the 5th :

(*a*) All available forces of the Sixth Army north-east of Meaux, ready to cross the Ourcq between Lizy sur Ourcq and May en Multien in the general direction of Chateau Thierry.

The available portions of the I. Cavalry Corps which are at hand will be placed under the orders of General Maunoury for this operation.

(*b*) The British Army, established on the front Changis—Coulommiers, ready to attack in the general direction of Montmirail, the II. Cavalry Corps ensuring liaison between the British Army and the Fifth Army.

(*c*) The Fifth Army, closing slightly to the left, will be established on the general front Courtacon—Esternay—Sézanne, ready to attack in a general south-north direction.

(*d*) The Ninth Army (General Foch) will cover the right of the Fifth Army, holding the southern exits of the Marshes of St. Gond and sending a part of its forces on to the plateau north of Sézanne.

(3) These various Armies will take the offensive on the morning of the 6th September.

———

On the morning of the 5th September, the following orders were given to the group on the right formed by the Fourth and Third Armies :

FOURTH ARMY :

To-morrow, 6th September, the Armies of the left will attack the front and flank of the German First and 2nd Armies.   The

[1] F.O.A. i. (ii)., Annexe No. 2332.

Fourth Army, ceasing its movement towards the south, will turn and oppose the enemy, linking its movements with those of the Third Army, which, debouching north of Revigny, will take the offensive commencing towards the west.

THIRD ARMY :

The Third Army, covering itself from the north-east, will debouch towards the west in order to attack the left flank of the enemy forces which are advancing west of the Argonne. It will link its action with the Fourth Army which has been ordered to turn and oppose the enemy.

(No time of issue stated.)

OPERATION ORDER No. 17

BY

FIELD-MARSHAL SIR JOHN FRENCH, G.C.B., ETC.,

Commanding British Expeditionary Force

General Headquarters,
5th September 1914.

1.   The enemy has apparently abandoned the idea of advancing on Paris and is contracting his front and moving south-eastward.

2.   The Army will advance eastward with a view to attacking.
    Its left will be covered by the 6th French Army also marching east, and its right will be linked to the 5th French Army marching north.

3.   In pursuance of the above, the following moves will take place, the Army facing east on completion of the movement :

1st Corps { Right on La Chapelle Iger.
          { Left on Lumigny.
          Movement to be completed by 9 A.M.

2nd Corps { Right on La Houssaye.
          { Left in neighbourhood of Villeneuve.
          Movement to be completed by 10 A.M.

3rd Corps facing east in neighbourhood of Bailly.
          Movement to be completed by 10 A.M.

Cavalry.
    (1) Cavalry Division to guard the front and flank of 1st Corps on the line Jouy le Chatel (connecting with 5th French Army)—Coulommiers (connecting with 3rd & 5th Cavalry Brigades).
    (2) 3rd and 5th Cavalry Brigades will cease to be under the orders of 1st Corps and will act in concert under instructions issued by Brigadier - General H. Gough.   They will cover the 2nd Corps connecting with Cavalry Division on the right and with French 6th Army on the left.
    Trains south of railway Nangis—Verneuil l'Etaing—Ozoir.

4. Roads allotted :—

　　1st Corps.　Guignes—Chaumes—Fontenay—Marles—
　　　　　　　Lumigny inclusive and all roads to E.

　　2nd Corps.　Coubert — Tournan — Villeneuve le Comte in-
　　　　　　　clusive and all roads between this and 1st Corps.

　　3rd Corps.　All roads W. of 2nd Corps.

5.　Railheads for 6th September 1914 :—

Cavalry Division	Melun.
5th Cavalry Brigade	do.
G.H.Q.	do.
L. of C.	do.
1st Corps	Lieusaint.
2nd Corps	do.
3rd Corps	Brunoy.
R.F.C.	do.
Ammunition Railhead	Villeneuve St. Georges (Goods Station).

6.　G.H.Q. remains at Melun.

　　Reports centre G.H.Q., Tournan from 8 A.M.

A. J. MURRAY,
Lieut.-General,
Chief of the General Staff.

Issued at 5.15 P.M.

Copy No. 16.

OPERATION ORDER No. 11

BY

MAJOR-GENERAL E. H. H. ALLENBY, C.B.,

Commanding Cavalry Division

5th September 1914.

1. (a) The enemy has apparently abandoned the idea of advancing on Paris and is contracting his front and moving south-eastward.

   (b) The Army will advance eastwards to-morrow with a view to attacking. The right of our Ist Corps will be about La Chapelle Iger at 9 A.M.

2. The Cavalry Division will advance north-east. 1st bound, Gastins. Advanced guard, Pécy. Reconnaissances, Jouy le Chatel and Vaudoy. A special Officers' patrol detailed from the 2nd Brigade will accompany the former and get touch with the French Cavalry on our right. March table for the Division attached (not reproduced).

3. The Cavalry Field Ambulances & Ammunition Column will park at Mormant and be ready to move at 8 A.M. The Transport and spare horses will park between the road Mormant—Guignes, south-east of Pecquex, and be ready to move at 10 A.M.

   These formations will remain until they receive orders to move.

4. Units will parade as strong as possible, and leave as few spare horses as possible with the transport.

5. Reports to the *mairie* at Mormant till 8 A.M., after that hour to Gastins.

J. VAUGHAN,
Colonel, G.S.

Issued at 9.15 P.M.

Copy No. 14.

1ST CORPS OPERATION ORDER No. 10

5th September 1914.

1. The proximity of the Allied and hostile forces is believed to be approximately as shown on the accompanying sketch map. [not reproduced.]

2. It is believed that the French Armies are going to take the offensive. The Expeditionary Force is to co-operate, and will to-morrow be disposed in the following positions with a view to attack.

   The front allotted to the 1st Corps is from La Chapelle Iger to Lumigny.

3. The 2nd Corps will be in echelon behind our left with its right at La Houssaye.

   The 3rd Corps will be in echelon behind the left of the 2nd Corps.

   The Cavalry Division will cover the front and right flank of 1st Corps.

   The 3rd & 5th Cavalry Brigades will cover the left flank.

4. The following moves will be completed by 9 A.M., at which hour the 1st Corps will be ready to advance ; general direction Montmirail.

   (a) 1st Division front Courpalay to Rozoy, both inclusive, with one infantry brigade in reserve behind the right flank.

   (b) 2nd Division less one infantry brigade, 1 brigade R.F.A., & 1 troop Divisional Cavalry, Rozoy (exclusive) to Chateau de la Fortel (inclusive). One infantry brigade in echelon on the left flank.

   (c) Reserve—one infantry brigade, one brigade R.F.A., and troop Divisional Cavalry, 2nd Division, will be placed near Chaubuisson Farm under the orders of G.O.C., 1st Corps.

   (d) Army troops to Chaubuisson Farm.

5. *Trains* will be parked until movements of troops are completed. At 9 A.M. they will be moved south of the Nangis—Verneuil—Ozoir railway.

6. Reports to Chaubuisson Farm after 9 A.M.

J. E. GOUGH,
Brigadier-General,
S.G.S.O., 1st Army Corps.

Issued at 8.30 P.M.

Copy No. *6*

2ND ARMY CORPS

OPERATION ORDER No. 15

2nd Army Corps Headquarters,
5th September 1914.

1. The advance of the enemy's main forces in a south-easterly direction continues. The right flank of this advance appears to be a column, variously estimated at a division and a corps, moving south-east from La Ferté sous Jouarre.

No hostile forces had been reported in our immediate vicinity up to 4 P.M. to-day.

The French forces to the north and east are taking the offensive.

2. The British Army will advance against the enemy to-morrow as follows :—

(a) 1st Corps to line La Chapelle Iger—Lumigny.

(b) 2nd Corps to line La Houssaye—Villeneuve.

(c) 3rd Corps massed about Bailly.

(d) Cavalry Division (less 3rd & 5th Brigades) to line Jouy le Chatel—Coulommiers. 3rd & 5th Brigades connecting with the Cavalry Division on the right and with French VI Army on the left, covering our 2nd Corps.

3. Heads of main bodies of Divisions of 2nd Corps will reach the line La Houssaye—Villeneuve by 10 A.M.—3rd Division starting at 6 A.M., 5th Division at 5 A.M.

Corps Headquarters & Corps Troops to Tournan, starting at 9 A.M.

4. The following roads are allotted :

3rd Division—

(a) Châtres — Chau. des Boulayes — Champrose Fe. — La Houssaye.

(b) Champrose Fe:—Pt. 120 ($\frac{1}{2}$ mile south of T of Bois de Fauvmet.

(c) Any roads between (a) and (b).

5th Division—

(d) Tournan—Favières—Villeneuve.

(e) Any roads between (d) and (b).

550   APPENDIX 34

5. Divisions will find their own advanced guards ; 3rd Division in communication with 1st Corps, 5th Division with 3rd Corps.

6. On arrival, on the line given in paragraph 3, Divisions will bivouac in depth on the roads on which Divisional Columns have been marching, the actual roads being kept as clear as possible.

7. After arrival, the outpost line will be on the general line Crève-cœur (connecting with 1st Corps)—Obelisque—Croix de Tigeaux —L'Ermitage Fe.—Villeneuve St. Denis (connecting or communicating with 3rd Corps).
   Divisional mounted troops to observe during daylight northeast of the Forest to the line Mortcerf—Tigeaux—Romain Villers.

8. (a) Only ½ rations to be issued to units this evening—the other ½ being kept in Supply Sections of Trains, which are to be given the best horses.

   (b) Baggage Sections of Trains will remain in the Brigade areas when the troops march ; and, when roads are cleared, be parked at some central place in the rear of to-day's billeting area under orders issued by Divisional Commanders.
   Subsequent orders will be issued by Corps H.Q.

   (c) The head of the Ammunition Park will be at the road junction just north of the last S in Presles at 10 A.M.

   (d) Railhead for supplies—Lieusaint.
   Railhead for ammunition—Villeneuve St. Georges.

   (e) Rendezvous for Supply Columns—Lissy, at 3 P.M.

9. Reports to Chau. Villepateur up to 9 A.M., and after that hour to Chau. Combreux (¾ mile south of Tournan).

G. F. WALKER,
Brigadier-General,
General Staff,
2nd Army Corps.

Issued at 7 P.M.

Copy No. 11.

3RD CORPS OPERATION ORDER No. 7

Ref. Paris—Meaux—Melun
  & Provins Sheets,   Brie Comte Robert
1·26 miles to 1 inch (1/80,000)   5th September 1914.

1. The bulk of the German forces which have been following the British troops in their retirement has moved south-east against the left of the French 5th Army about St. Barthelemy.

 The British Force is about to assume the offensive to the north-east against the German right flank, in conjunction with the 6th French Army.

2. The 3rd Corps will advance to-morrow towards Serris, acting in conjunction with the 2nd Corps on its right.

3. Starting Point—Railway crossing 1½ miles east of Ozoir la Ferrière.

 Time—5 A.M.

 Route—Pontcarré—Ferrières—Jossigny—Serris.

 The 4th Division will furnish the advanced guard consisting of 1 Infantry Brigade and attached troops.

 On reaching Ferrières a left flank guard of 2 battalions and 1 battery will be provided by the 4th Division.

 The 19th Infantry Brigade will follow the 4th Division.

4. Trains are to be parked in the vicinity of Ozoir la Ferrière by 11 A.M.

5. Railhead for supplies to-morrow, 6th September, Brunoy.

 Rendezvous for Ammunition Parks to-morrow, 6th September, Brie Comte Robert at 10 A.M.

6. The Commander 19th Infantry Brigade will detail half a battalion to proceed to Ozoir la Ferrière to provide for the security of the train, and half a battalion to proceed to Brie Comte Robert to provide for the security of the Ammunition Parks.

7. Report centre—Brie Comte Robert up to 6 A.M., after that hour Ferrières.

J. P. Du Cane,
Br.-General,
General Staff.

Issued at 7.45 P.M.

SPECIAL ORDER OF THE DAY

BY

FIELD-MARSHAL SIR JOHN FRENCH, G.C.B., G.C.V.O., K.C.M.G., Commander-in-Chief, British Army in the Field.

6th September 1914.

After a most trying series of operations, mostly in retirement, which have been rendered necessary by the general strategic plan of the Allied Armies, the British forces stand to-day formed in line with their French comrades, ready to attack the enemy.

Foiled in their attempt to invest Paris, the Germans have been driven to move in an easterly and south-easterly direction, with the apparent intention of falling in strength on the V French Army. In this operation they are exposing their right flank and their line of communication to an attack from the combined VI French Army and the British forces.

I call upon the British Army in France to now show the enemy its power, and to push on vigorously to the attack beside the VI French Army. I am sure I shall not call upon them in vain, but that, on the contrary, by another manifestation of the magnificent spirit which they have shown in the past fortnight, they will fall on the enemy's flank with all their strength and in unison with their Allies drive them back.

J. D. P. FRENCH, Field-Marshal,
Commander-in-Chief, British Army in the Field.

(From a copy among the G.S. papers of the III Corps.)

O (a)
Secret. Copy No. 13.

OPERATION ORDER No. 18

BY

FIELD-MARSHAL SIR JOHN FRENCH, G.C.B., ETC.,

Commanding British Expeditionary Force

G.H.Q., 7th September 1914.

1. During to-day the enemy's forces in our front have been retreating towards the north all along the line.

On our right the French 5th Army are pursuing the German corps to the line of the Petit Morin, after inflicting severe losses upon them, especially about Montceaux which was carried at the point of the bayonet.

In our front, the enemy's retreat has been covered by his 2nd and 9th Cavalry Divisions who have suffered severely.

On our left flank two hostile corps, that were withdrawing northwards across the Marne, have been heavily attacked by the French 6th Army on the line of the Ourcq.

2. The intention of the Field-Marshal Commanding-in-Chief is to continue the pursuit in the direction of the Marne, with the right of the Army on Nogent, attacking the enemy wherever met.—

3. Roads are allotted as follows :—

1st Corps. The road St. Remy—Rebais (eastern road)—La Trétoire—Boitron—La Noue—Pavant—Charly to Breuil —Sablonnières—Hondevilliers—Nogent l'Artaud road, in- clusive. Roads east of this will be used by the French.

2nd Corps. The road Boissy le Châtel—Doue—St. Cyr— Saacy and all between this and 1st Corps.

3rd Corps. Will march on Jouarre, using roads west of 2nd Corps.

Heads of columns will cross the line St. Remy—Boissy le Châtel—La Haute Maison at 6 A.M.

The Cavalry Division and 3rd and 5th Cavalry Brigades will continue the pursuit, keeping touch on the right with the Corps of Cavalry of the 5th French Army, and on the left with the 6th French Army.

4. Supply railheads for 8th September 1914 :—

Cavalry Division	Chaumes.
5th Cavalry Brigade.	do.
1st Corps	do.
G.H.Q.	do.
L. of C. Units	do.
Royal Flying Corps .	do.
2nd Corps	Marles.
3rd Corps	Tournan.
Ammunition Railhead	Verneuil.

5. Reports to Melun.

HENRY WILSON, for
Lieut.-General, C.G.S.

Issued at 9 to 10 P.M.

Secret. Copy No. 13.

OPERATION ORDER No. 19

BY

FIELD-MARSHAL SIR JOHN FRENCH, G.C.B., ETC.,

Commanding British Expeditionary Force

General Headquarters, 8th Sept. 1914.

1. The enemy are continuing their retreat northwards and our Army has been successfully engaged during the day with their rear guards on the Petit Morin, thereby materially assisting the progress of the French Armies on our right and left, which the enemy have been making great efforts to oppose.

2. The Army will continue the advance north to-morrow at 5 A.M., attacking rear guards of the enemy wherever met.

   The Cavalry Division will act in close association with the 1st Corps and gain touch with the 5th French Army on the right.

   General Gough, with the 3rd and 5th Cavalry Brigades, will act in close association with the 2nd Corps and gain touch with the 6th French Army on the left.

3. Roads are allotted as follows :—

   1st Corps. Eastern road—Sablonnières—Hondevilliers—Nogent l'Artaud—Saulchery—eastern side of Charly—Le Thiolet.

   Western road—Le Trétoire—Boitron—Pavant—western side of Charly—Villiers sur Marne—Domptin—Coupru, both inclusive.

   2nd Corps. Western road—St. Ouen—Saacy—Méry—Montreuil inclusive, and all roads between this and western road of 1st Corps exclusive.

   3rd Corps. Western road—La Ferté sous Jouarre—Dhuisy inclusive, and all roads between this and western road of 2nd Corps exclusive.

4. Supply railheads for 9th September 1914 :—

Cavalry Division	Chaumes.
Brig.-Gen. Gough's Command . .	Chaumes.
1st Corps	Coulommiers.
2nd Corps	do.
3rd Corps	Mortcerf.
L. of C.	Chaumes.
G.H.Q.	do.
R.F.C.	do.
Ammunition Railhead . . .	Verneuil.

5. Reports to Melun till 9 A.M., after that hour to Coulommiers.

A. J. MURRAY, Lt.-Gen.,
Chief of the General Staff.

Issued at 7.30 P.M.

Copy No. 13.

OPERATION ORDER No. 20

BY

FIELD-MARSHAL SIR JOHN FRENCH, G.C.B., ETC.,

Commanding British Expeditionary Force

General Headquarters, 9th Sept. 1914.

1.   The Army to-day forced the passage of the Marne. The 1st and 2nd Corps have reached the line Le Thiolet—Montreuil. 3rd Corps, opposed by the enemy's Guard and 2nd Cavalry Divisions, holds the north bank of the river at La Ferté.

During the pursuit the enemy suffered heavy loss in killed and wounded ; some hundreds of prisoners have fallen into our hands and a battery of eight machine guns was captured by 2nd Division.

The 6th French Army has been heavily engaged to-day along the line Crégy—Marcilly—Puisieux—Bouillancy—Betz, and has successfully resisted all attacks.

The left of the 5th French Army was expected to reach Chateau Thierry this evening.

2.   The Army will continue the pursuit northwards to-morrow at 5 A.M. and attack the enemy wherever met.

3.   The 3rd Corps will bridge the Marne during the night so that the corps may be in a position to cross at 5 A.M., and march on Cocherel, maintaining touch with the French Cavalry Brigade on its left.

The Cavalry Division will act in close association with 1st Corps and gain touch with 5th French Army on the right.

General Gough, with 3rd and 5th Cavalry Brigades, will act in close association with 2nd Corps and keep touch between 2nd and 3rd Corps.

4.   *Roads allotted :*

      1st Corps. Eastern road. Le Thiolet—Lucy le Bocage—Torcy—Priez—Neuilly St. Front.

      Western road. Coupru—Marigny en Orxois—Bussiares—Hautevesnes—St. Gengoulph—Monnes—Passy en Valois—Noroy sur Ourcq, both roads inclusive.

2nd Corps. Western   Road.   Montreuil—Dhuisy—Germigny sous Colombs –Brumetz—St.   Quentin—La Ferté Milon, inclusive, and all roads between this and western road of 1st Corps, exclusive.

3rd Corps. Roads west of those allotted to 2nd Corps.

The Cav. Div. Transport and Supply Columns will use the eastern road allotted to the 1st Corps.

The 2nd Corps will arrange with General Gough regarding the road to be used by the transport of the 3rd and 5th Brigades.

5. Supply Railheads for 10/9/14 :

Cavalry Division	Jouy sur Morin.
1st Corps	St. Siméon.
2nd Corps	Chailly Boissy.
Gen. Gough's Command . .	Coulommiers.
3rd Corps	do.
L. of C.	do.
G.H.Q.	do.
R.F.C.	do.
Ammunition Railhead . . .	Verneuil.

6. Reports to Coulommiers.

HENRY WILSON, for
Lieut.-General, C.G.S.

Issued at 8.15 P.M.

OPERATION ORDER No. 21

BY

FIELD-MARSHAL SIR JOHN FRENCH, G.C.B., ETC.,

Commanding British Expeditionary Force

General Headquarters, 10th September 1914.

1.　During the advance to-day the 1st and 2nd Corps have been opposed by strong rear guards of all arms, and assisted by the Cavalry Division on the right, 3rd and 5th Cavalry Brigades on the left, have driven the enemy northwards.　Seven guns, many machine guns, well over 1,000 prisoners, and much transport have fallen into our hands.　The enemy left many dead on the field.

2.　The Army will continue the pursuit in a north-easterly direction to-morrow at 5 A.M., and crossing the Ourcq will reach the line Bruyères—Cugny—St. Remy—La Loge Ferme (north of Chouy).

　　The Cavalry Division and General Gough's Command will carry out the same rôle as to-day.

3.　Roads will be allotted as follows :

　　1st Corps.　Eastern　road.　Monthiers — Grisolles — Rocourt St. Martin—Fère en Tardenois (inclusive).　Western road.　Priez — Latilly — Oulchy le Chateau—Beugneux (inclusive).

　　The road Dammard—Neuilly St. Front and all roads to the west will be cleared by the 1st Corps by 8 A.M.

　　2nd Corps.　Western road.　Passy en Valois — Montron —Neuilly St. Front—Vichel Vanteuil—Billy sur Ourcq —St. Rémy—Hartennes (inclusive), and all roads between this and the western road of the 1st Corps.

　　3rd Corps.　Roads between western road of 2nd Corps (exclusive) and the road La Ferté Milon—Troesnes—Longpont (exclusive), the latter being used by the French 6th Army.

　　The 3rd Corps will arrange with the 2nd Corps

for the use of the road Brumetz—Chézy en Orxois —Passy en Valois—Chouy, which will be cleared by the 2nd Corps as early as possible.

4. The Cavalry Division transport and supply columns will use the eastern road allotted to the 1st Corps.

   The 2nd Corps will arrange with General Gough regarding the road to be used by the transport of the 3rd and 5th Cavalry Bdes.

5. Railheads for September 11th will be the same as for to-day.

6. Reports to Coulommiers.

A. J. Murray, Lieut.-Gen., C.G.S.

Issued at 8.15 P.M.

Secret.   Copy No. 17.

OPERATION ORDER No. 22

BY

FIELD-MARSHAL SIR JOHN FRENCH, G.C.B., ETC.,

Commanding British Expeditionary Force

General Headquarters, 11th September 1914.

1.　　The 1st German Army appears to be in full retreat north and east before our advance.

2.　　The Army will continue the pursuit to-morrow. Every endeavour will be made by the Cavalry, in co-operation with the French Cavalry on the right and left, to harass the retreating enemy.

3.　　Heads of corps will cross the road Saponay—Grand Rozoy— St. Rémy—Louatre at 6 A.M.

4.　　The crossings over the Aisne will be seized, and the columns will reach the high ground overlooking the river.

5.　　Roads will be allotted as follows :

> *I. Corps.* Eastern road. Rocourt—Fère en Tardenois— Loupeigne—Bazoches—Longueval—Bourg (inclusive).
> 　　　　　　Western road. Latilly—Oulchy le Chateau— Arcy Ste. Restitue — Jouaignes — Courcelles — Pont Arcy (inclus.).
>
> *II. Corps.* Western road. Billy sur Ourcq—St. Rémy— Hartennes—Chacrise—Serches—Vailly (inclusive), and all roads between this and western road of I. Corps exclusive.
>
> *III. Corps.* Western Road. Chouy—La Loge Fe.— Villers Hélon—Septmonts—Venizel—Bucy le Long (inclusive), and all roads between this and the western road of II. Corps (exclus.).

6.　　The Cavalry Division transport and supply columns will use the eastern road allotted to the 1st Corps.
　　　　The 2nd Corps will arrange with General Gough regarding the road to be used by the transport of the 3rd and 5th Cav. Bdes.

Cavalry Supply columns will have precedence over those allotted to corps.

7. All supply railheads for 12th September will be the same as for the 11th September.

An advanced ammunition depot has been formed near Nogent l'Artaud where corps Ammunition Parks can replenish.

8. Reports to Coulommiers till 2 P.M., after that hour to Fère en Tardenois.

A. J. MURRAY, Lieut.-General,
Chief of the General Staff.

Issued at 6 P.M.

GENERAL JOFFRE'S INSTRUCTION
OF 12TH SEPTEMBER 1914 [1]

SPECIAL INSTRUCTION No. 23

G.Q.G., 12th Sept. 1914.

The enemy has been forced to retreat before the front of the Ninth and Fourth Armies ; if the enemy continues to give way before our Armies of the left and the British Army the following dispositions will be made after the passage of the Aisne :

In order to outflank the enemy by the west, the Sixth Army leaving a strong detachment in the west of the Saint Gobain forest [2] to ensure liaison, in all circumstances, with the British Army, will send the bulk of its forces to the right bank of the Oise.

The British Forces should be directed northward ; in order to facilitate their passage through the wooded hill region south-west of Laon, the zone included between the road Soissons—Coucy le Chateau—Saint Gobain—La Fère (inclusive) and the road Longueval—Bourg and Comin—Chamouille—Bruyères—Athies (inclusive) is placed at their disposal.

The Fifth Army, likewise maintaining close liaison by a detachment with the right of the British forces, will cross the Aisne with its left as soon as possible so as to be astride of that river.

No modification has been made in Special Instruction No. 22, as far as the other Armies are concerned.

The General Commanding in Chief
(sd.) J. JOFFRE.

True copy
The Major General
F. BELIN.

[1] Translated from the copy in the G.H.Q. Records.
[2] " dans le massif de Saint Gobain " is corrected in MS. to " dans l'ouest du massif de Saint Gobain."

Copy No. 17.

OPERATION ORDER No. 23

BY

FIELD-MARSHAL SIR JOHN FRENCH, G.C.B., ETC.,

Commanding British Expeditionary Force

General Headquarters,
12th September 1914.

1. The enemy continued retreating to-day. There was some opposition south of Soissons and on the line of the Vesle.

   The Army is halted to-night in close touch with the French 6th Army on our left and 5th Army on our right.

2. The Army will continue the pursuit to-morrow at seven A.M.

3. Heads of Corps will reach the line Lierval—Chavignon—Terny.

4. Roads allotted :

   1st Corps :
   Eastern road.   Longueval — Bourg — Chamouille — Bruyères—Athies (inclusive).
   Western road.   Braine — Presles (2 miles south - east of Vailly)—Chavonne—Lierval—Presles (2 miles southwest of Bruyères)—Laon (inclusive).

   2nd Corps :
   Western road.   Chacrise—Missy sur Aisne—Vregny—Pont Rouge—Bascule—Pinon—Anizy le Chateau—Suzy (inclusive) and all roads between this and the western road of the 1st Corps (exclusive).

   3rd Corps :
   Courmelles — Soissons — Terny — Coucy le Chateau — St. Gobain (inclusive) and all roads between this and western road of 2nd Corps (exclusive).

5. The Cavalry Division will use the eastern road allotted to the 1st Corps.

   The 2nd Corps will arrange with General Gough as to the allotment of roads for transport of the 3rd and 5th Cavalry Brigades. Cavalry transport will have precedence over that of corps.

6. Supply columns will fill up on the 13th from Reserve Parks as follows :

Cavalry Division 1st Corps R.F.C. L. of C. Units	Main road between Fère en Tardenois and Coincy.
Genl. Gough's Command 2nd Corps	Main road between Latilly and Neuilly St. Front.
3rd Corps	Main road between Monnes & La Ferté Milon, at a point about south-west of Passy.

Ammunition Parks replenish at Nogent l'Artaud and all empty lorries of the Parks should be sent there to replenish as early as can be arranged.

7. Reports to Fère en Tardenois.

A. J. MURRAY,
Lieutenant General,
Chief of the General Staff.

Issued at 7.45 P.M.

Copy No. 17.

OPERATION ORDER No. 24

BY

FIELD-MARSHAL SIR JOHN FRENCH, G.C.B., ETC.,

Commanding British Expeditionary Force

General Headquarters,
13th September 1914.

1. The Army has succeeded in obtaining a footing on the North side of the Aisne in face of considerable opposition by strong rear guards of the enemy's 3rd Corps supported by one or two cavalry divisions.

    The 5th and 6th French Armies have also succeeded in crossing on our right and left respectively, working in close touch with us.

2. The Army will continue the pursuit to-morrow at 6 A.M., and act vigorously against the retreating enemy.

3. Heads of corps will reach the line Laon—Suzy—Fresne.

4. Roads allotted :

    1st Corps.
    Eastern road. Bourg—Chamouille—Bruyères—Athies in-
    clusive.
    Western road. Presles — Chavonne — Lierval — Laon in-
    clusive.

    2nd Corps.
    Western road. Missy sur Aisne—Pont Rouge—Pinon—
    Anizy le Chateau—Suzy inclusive, and all roads be-
    tween this and western road of 1st Corps.

    3rd Corps.
    Western road. Venizel—Bucy le Long—Crouy—Braye—
    Clamecy—Terny—Coucy le Chateau—St. Gobain in-
    clusive, and all roads between this and western road
    of 2nd Corps.

5. The Cavalry Division will advance in the general direction Courtecon—Laon.
    Communication must be maintained with 1st Corps.

General Gough's Command in the general direction Allemant—Wissignicourt.

Communication must be maintained with 2nd Corps.

Every effort must be made to harass the enemy's retreat.

6. Arrangements will be made between 1st Corps and Cavalry Division and between 2nd Corps and General Gough's Command, with regard to cavalry billets and roads to be used by cavalry transport and supply columns, which in all cases will have precedence over transport allotted to corps.

7. Supply railheads for 14th September will be :

1st Cavalry Division . .	Fère en Tardenois.
1st Corps	do.
G.H.Q.	do.
R.F.C.	do.
L. of C. Units . . .	do.
General Gough's Command .	Oulchy—Breny.
2nd Corps	do.
3rd Corps	Neuilly St. Front.

Ammunition Parks will continue to replenish at Nogent l'Artaud.

8. Reports to Fère en Tardenois.

A. J. MURRAY,
Lieutenant General,
Chief of the General Staff.

Issued at 6 P.M.

Secret.   Copy No. **33.**

OPERATION ORDER No. 25

BY

FIELD-MARSHAL SIR JOHN FRENCH, G.C.B., ETC.,

Commander-in-Chief, British Forces in the Field

General Headquarters, 14th September 1914.

1.   The situation as far as known along the whole line from left to right is as follows :

6th French Army.   The 6th French Army is engaged along the right bank of the Aisne from Soissons to Attichy.   On the extreme left the 4th Corps was marching with its left on Nampcel this afternoon.

3rd Corps :   The 3rd Corps holds the spurs north-west and north-east of Bucy le Long having been closely engaged with the enemy all day.

2nd Corps :   The 5th Division is on the line south of S. of Chivres— Ste. Marguerite to-night where it has been engaged during the day.

The 3rd Division holds a position from the railway bridge south-east of Vailly—north of Vailly—knoll west of Vailly.   It has been heavily engaged all day.

1st Corps :   The 1st Corps advanced this morning from Bourg supported by the Cavalry Division on its right ;   the 2nd Brigade of the 1st Division was attacked near Cerny, but drove off the enemy and captured twelve guns ;   several hundred prisoners were also taken.

During the day both 1st and 2nd Divisions successfully drove off the hostile counter attacks and in the afternoon the 2nd Division was holding the plateau south of Ostel supported by the 4th Cavalry Brigade on its left and the 2nd Cavalry Brigade on its right.

5th French Army.   On the right of the 1st Corps the 18th French Corps was heavily attacked at Craonnelle and has been ordered to maintain itself in its present position.

On the right of the 18th Corps the group of Reserve Divisions is at Berry au Bac, and with the 3rd Corps on its right holds the line of the canal through Loivre to La Neuvillette near Reims.   The 1st Corps occupies Reims.   The 10th Corps is on its right.

At 4.30 P.M. the French 5th Army (less the 18th Corps) were ordered to take the offensive along the whole front.

2. The Army will operate to-morrow according to instructions issued personally by the Commander-in-Chief to G.O.C. Corps and Cavalry Divisions.

3. Supply railheads for the 15th September will be :

1st Cavalry Division . .	Fère en Tardenois.
1st Corps	do.
G.H.Q.	do.
R.F.C.	do.
L. of C. Units . . .	do.
General Gough's Command .	Oulchy—Breny.
2nd Corps	do.
3rd Corps	Neuilly St. Front.

Ammunition Parks will continue to replenish at Nogent l'Artaud.

4. Reports to Fère en Tardenois.

HENRY WILSON, for
Lieut.-Gen., Chief of the General Staff.
Issued at .¹

¹ The II. Corps copy of this order is endorsed " recᵈ 9.15 P.M."

OPERATION ORDER No. 26

BY

FIELD-MARSHAL SIR JOHN FRENCH, G.C.B., ETC.,

Commander-in-Chief, British Forces in the Field

General Headquarters,
15th September 1914.

1. On the right of the British Army the French have made some progress.

The 18th Corps has occupied Craonne and the high ground on the left and is in touch with the right of our 1st Corps.

On the left the French have reached the general line Soissons—Noyon and are making progress on their left.

Our Army has successfully maintained its position and has repulsed numerous counter-attacks inflicting severe loss on the enemy.

The 6th Division has to-day reached Rocourt and is marching early to-morrow morning to join 3rd Corps.

2. The Commander-in-Chief wishes the line now held by the Army to be strongly entrenched, and it is his intention to assume a general offensive at the first opportunity.

3. Supply Railheads for the 16th September will be :

1st Cavalry Division . .	Fère en Tardenois.
1st Corps	do.
G.H.Q.	do.
R.F.C.	do.
L. of C. Units . . .	do.
General Gough's Command .	Oulchy—Breny.
2nd Corps	do.
3rd Corps	Neuilly St. Front.
Ammunition Railhead .	Fère en Tardenois Rly. Station.

4. Reports to Fère en Tardenois.

A. J. MURRAY, Lieut.-General,
Chief of the General Staff.

Issued at 8.30 P.M.

Copy No. 18.

OPERATION ORDER No. 27

BY

FIELD-MARSHAL SIR JOHN FRENCH, G.C.B., ETC.,

Commander-in-Chief, British Forces in the Field

General Headquarters, 16th September 1914.

1. The enemy in our front appears to be holding approximately the same position as yesterday, but in some cases has withdrawn guns to positions further North. Six batteries are also reported to have moved east along the Chemin des Dames north-east of Aizy.

The 5th French Army on our right has maintained its position and on our left the 6th French Army has continued a vigorous offensive, the result of which is not yet known.

2. The intention of the Commander-in-Chief is that the Army should continue to hold its present line which should be strengthened by every available means, and that a general offensive should be resumed on the first opportunity.

3. The 6th Division is placed in General Reserve at the disposal of the Commander-in-Chief. The Artillery of this Division now in action will not, however, be withdrawn without further orders from the Commander-in-Chief.

4. Supply Railheads for the 17th September 1914 will be :

1st Cavalry Division	Fère en Tardenois.
1st Corps . . .	do.
G.H.Q. . . .	do.
R.F.C. . . .	do.
L. of C. Units . .	do.
2nd Cavalry Division	Oulchy—Breny.
2nd Corps . . .	do.
3rd Corps . . .	Neuilly St. Front.
Ammunition Railhead .	Fère en Tardenois Railway Station.

5. Reports to Fère en Tardenois.

HENRY WILSON,
Major-General,
Sub-Chief of the Staff.

Issued at 8.30 P.M.

Secret.   Copy No. 18.

OPERATION ORDER No. 28

BY

FIELD-MARSHAL SIR JOHN FRENCH, G.C.B., ETC.,
Commander-in-Chief, British Forces in the Field

General Headquarters, 1st October 1914.

1. Reports indicate the continued movement of troops from in front of the 5th and 6th French and the British Armies to the north and north-west.

2. It is the Commander-in-Chief's intention to withdraw the 2nd Corps from the defensive line and concentrate it in rear.

3. The following changes in the disposition of the Army will take place under cover of darkness this evening and will be carried out as rapidly as possible subject to tactical considerations. The movements will be completed by daylight on October 3rd.

4. The defensive line *now allotted to the 3rd Division* will be taken over *by the 1st Corps* with the 16th Infantry Brigade attached.
    The 1st Cavalry Division will be in reserve to 1st Corps.
    The defensive line now occupied by the 5th Division will be taken over by the 3rd Corps less the 16th and 17th Infantry Brigades of the 6th Division (see para. 8).
    The 19th Infantry Brigade will remain for the present in reserve under the 3rd Corps, but will not be used for duty in the trenches.
    The 17th Infantry Brigade will be in general reserve.

5. To enable this readjustment to be carried out:
    The 17th and 18th Infantry Brigades and 38th Field Co. R.E. will be relieved in the trenches by troops of 1st Corps and will be concentrated at a place to be selected by 1st Corps.
    The position of the 17th Infantry Brigade will be notified to General Headquarters and that of the 18th Infantry Brigade to 3rd Corps.
    The 18th Infantry Brigade will be moved from there under orders of 3rd Corps.
    The 17th Infantry Brigade will remain in general reserve.
    The 9th Infantry Brigade and 12th Field Co. R.E., will be withdrawn from the trenches at Vailly and relieved by troops of the 1st Corps.

Arrangements for taking over the artillery positions of 2nd Corps will be arranged between 2nd Corps and 1st and 3rd Corps respectively.

The artillery of the 6th Division will be moved under orders of 3rd Corps.

The XXXII. Field Artillery Brigade will come under orders of 3rd Corps.

The artillery of the 2nd Corps will be concentrated under corps arrangements.

The 6-inch howitzers and Fortress Companies R.E. will remain in their present positions and will come under the command of the corps responsible for the areas in which they are situated.

The 3rd Corps will arrange with 2nd Corps to hand over sufficient pontoon equipment from 2nd Bridging Train to complete the bridging establishment of the Field Companies of the 5th Division. The Field Companies of the 3rd Division will be completed from the half bridging train allotted to 2nd Corps ; the remainder of this train will come under the orders of 1st Corps.

6. As soon as relieved the 2nd Corps will concentrate in the area Cuiry Housse—Nampteuil sous Muret—Muret—Droizy—Oulchy le Chateau—Cramaille—Arcy Ste. Restitue, disposed with a view to marching on Compiègne by the Vierzy—Vivières—Pierrefonds—Compiègne road inclusive and roads to south.

7. The order in which the foregoing moves will be carried out generally will be as follows :

    (a) Relief of trenches.
    (b) Concentration of infantry of 2nd Corps.
    (c) Readjustment of artillery and reserve troops.

8. The 3rd Corps from this date will consist of the 4th and 6th Divisions with the 19th Infantry Brigade temporarily attached.

9. Railheads for supplies and ammunition remain unchanged.

10. Reports to Fère en Tardenois.

A. J. MURRAY,
Lieut.-General,
Chief of the General Staff.

G.H.Q.,
3 P.M.

Secret.   Copy No. 18.

ARMY OPERATION ORDER No. 29

BY

FIELD-MARSHAL SIR JOHN FRENCH, G.C.B., ETC.,

Commander-in-Chief, British Forces in the Field

General Headquarters, 2nd October 1914.

1.   The 2nd Cavalry Division will move in accordance with attached march table via Amiens and St. Pol to Lille.

2.   The II. Corps will move in accordance with attached march table to the area Longueil Ste. Marie—Pont Ste. Maxence and will commence entraining there on October 5th.

Paragraph 6 of Operation Order No. 28 is modified accordingly.

3.   *Roads allotted :*

2nd Cavalry Division.   Hartennes—Long Pont—Bonneuil—La Croix St. Ouen—Montdidier—Amiens—St. Pol—Bethune inclusive, and roads south or west.

2nd Corps.   Serches—Hartennes—Long Pont—Villers Cottérêts—Bonneuil—La Croix St. Ouen—Longueil Ste. Marie inclusive and roads to south.

4.   The first two marches at least will be carried out by night. Great care must be taken to conceal the troops and columns of transport during the day.

5.   Reports to Fère en Tardenois.

A. J. MURRAY,
Lieut.-General,
Chief of the General Staff.

G.H.Q., 11 A.M.

[TABLE

APPENDIX 49

MARCH TABLE

FOR MOVEMENT OF

2ND CAVALRY DIVISION AND II. CORPS

Date.	2nd Cav. Div. Head of Column.	II. Corps. Heads of Columns to reach the approximate line.
Oct. 1st/2nd	Hartennes.	Oulchy le Chateau—Serches.
„ 2nd/3rd	Fleury—Troesnes.	Troesnes—Long Pont.
„ 3rd/4th	Verberie.	Crépy en Valois—Béthancourt.
„ 4th/5th	Le Ployron.	Pont Ste. Maxence—Longueil.
„ 5th/6th	Thennes.	Begins entraining on 5th.
„ 6th/7th	Villers Bocage.	
„ 7th/8th	Frevent.	
„ 8th/9th	Houdain.	
„ 9th/10th	La Bassée.	
„ 10th/11th	Lille.	

Secret.   Copy No. 18.

ARMY OPERATION ORDER No. 30

BY

FIELD-MARSHAL SIR JOHN FRENCH, G.C.B., ETC.,

Commander-in-Chief, British Forces in the Field

General Headquarters, 4th October 1914.

1. The 1st Cavalry Division will move via Amiens and St. Pol to the neighbourhood of Lille. Move to commence this evening and the first two marches to be carried out under cover of darkness or fog. Great care must be taken to conceal the troops and columns of transport during the day.

2. Roads allotted : Hartennes — Longpont — Bonneuil — La Croix St. Ouen—Montdidier—Amiens—St. Pol—Bethune inclusive and roads south or west.

3. *Table of Marches :*

Date.	Heads of Columns to reach the Approximate Line.
4th/5th	Longpont—St. Rémy.
5th/6th	Morienval—Crépy en Valois.
6th/7th	Hémévillers—Estrées St. Denis.
7th/	La Neuville Sire Bernard.
8th/	Villers Bocage.
9th/	Nuncq.
10th/11th	Bethune.
11th/12th	Lille.

4. Railheads will be notified later

5. Reports to Fère en Tardenois.

A. J. MURRAY,
Lieut.-General
Chief of the General Staff.

G.H.Q.,
8 A.M.

ARMY OPERATION ORDER No. 31

BY

FIELD-MARSHAL SIR JOHN FRENCH, G.C.B., ETC.,

Commander-in-Chief, British Forces in the Field

General Headquarters, 5th October 1914.

1. The 19th Infantry Brigade will move in accordance with the following march table to the area Longueil Ste. Marie—Pont Ste. Maxence, and will commence entraining there on October 8th at an hour to be notified later.

The move will commence this evening, and the first two marches will be carried out under cover of darkness. Great care must be taken to conceal the troops and columns of transport during the day.

2. Roads allotted :
Septmonts—Villers Cottérêts—Béthancourt—Verberie—Pont Ste. Maxence.

3. Table of marches :

Date.			Head of Column to reach.
5th/6th	.	.	.	Villers Cottérêts.
6th/7th	.	.	.	Béthancourt.
7th/8th	.	.	.	Longueil Ste. Marie—Pont Ste. Maxence.

4. The 19th Infantry Brigade will cease to be under 3rd Corps from the commencement of the movement.

5. Reports to Fère en Tardenois.

A. J. MURRAY, Lieut.-General,
C.G.S.

Issued at 8.30 A.M.

ADDENDA AND CORRIGENDA TO VOLUME I

ADDITIONAL TO THOSE ISSUED WITH VOL. II.

(Kindly pointed out by various correspondents,[1] and extracted from the French and German Official accounts.)

[1] In consequence of some errors as regards the German Army having been pointed out by critics in the German press, the Director of the Reichsarchiv was asked, and kindly indicated, where the correct information could be found.

Note.—Where two references are given the first is to the FIRST EDITION ; that in brackets to the SECOND EDITION.

Page 3, line 8 from bottom. After " and the like " add footnote :
 " An assurance has been received from the Reichsarchiv that neither in the Marine Archiv (Navy Historical Section) nor in the Military Section and the Espionage Section has anything of the nature of the sabotage system mentioned in the text been discovered."
 Doubtless the arrangements detected in the Empire were the work of irresponsible individuals. An unequivocal case of individual action took place on the 1st January, 1915, near Broken Hill, South Australia, when two Turks armed with rifles ambushed a picnic train, killing three men and one woman and wounding seven.

Page 7, line 13 from bottom (12 from bottom). For " twenty guns " read : " twenty-four guns ".

Page 14, line 7 from bottom. After " The frontier had no natural protection " add : " both banks of the Rhine and the crest of the Vosges being in German hands ".

Page 15. Add to footnote 3 : " See footnote correction to page 21 ".

Page 21, lines 3-9. Add footnote :
 " The German Official History of the War, Military Operations on Land, Volume I., pages 38-39 gives the following totals for Germany :

Peace strength	847,000
Trained officers & men (excluding Navy)	4,900,000
Total available for military service .	9,750,000 "

 " The same source gives for France :

Peace strength (including coloured troops and Foreign Legion) .	1,052,000
Trained officers & men (excluding Navy)	5,067,000
Total available for military service .	5,940,000 "

ADDENDA AND CORRIGENDA TO VOL. I 2

Page 22, lines 6-15. For the paragraph " In peace . . . divisions."
substitute :
" The *Ersatz* brigades and divisions of 1914 were not
formed from untrained men of the *Ersatz Reserve*,[1] but from
trained men supernumerary to the numbers required for the
Active and Reserve formations. They were organized like
the Reserve formations but had not the full establishment of
machine guns, cavalry, or artillery, and were entirely without field
kitchens, medical units, train and ammunition columns. They
were therefore not equivalent to other brigades and divisions
in open warfare. (Correction furnished by a German officer.) "

[1] This consisted of men temporarily unfit, or fit and liable for military service but not
called up for training either because they were supernumerary to the annual contingent,
or for family reasons, or on account of minor physical defects.

Page 23. Add to footnote :
" The Reichsarchiv states that no mobilization took place
in Germany before the 1st August and that the *Landsturm*
in the frontier districts was called out on the same date, not
on the 31st July ; the troops employed against Liége were
at peace strength. Movements of men and troops were those
in consequence of the proclamation of *drohende Kriegsgefahr*
(see correction to page 24)." Some local authorities, however,
did not wait for this ; for General von Moser (Commander
of the 53rd Brigade) in his " Kampf und Siegestage 1914 "
(published by Mittler of Berlin 1915), page 1, says :
" ' On 29th July early the order " Return to garrison "
' reached us on the troop training ground where we had
' assembled on the previous day for regiment and brigade
' training. [This signifies that one of the precautionary
measures (see correction to page 24) was taken 2 days before
the Precautionary Period *(drohende Kriegsgefahr)* was pro-
claimed]. On the 1st August " Last preparations for taking
' the field." On the 2nd August (1st day of mobilization) the
' brigade reinforced by a squadron and 3 batteries left at 9 A.M.
' on frontier protection duty.' "

Page 24. At end of 3rd paragraph (11 lines from bottom) after " Belgrade."
add the paragraph :
" In order to avoid the possibility of a frontier incident
the French government ordered that ' no individual, no
' patrol, should under any pretext pass a line between Hus-
' signy (on Luxembourg frontier, east of Longwy) and Delle '
(on Swiss frontier, south-east of Belfort), described by a
precise enumeration of localities. This line on an average
was 10 kilometres inside the frontier." [3]

[3] French Official Account, Tome I., Vol. I., page 76. This particular order was
repeated on 31st July :—
" This prohibition applies to the cavalry as well as to the other arms. No patrol, no
" reconnoitring party, no post, no individual, must be east of the said line. Anyone who
" crosses it will be liable to court-martial. It is only permitted to transgress this order
" in case of a very definite attack ". (Idem p. 81.) The restriction was withdrawn at
2 P.M. on the 2nd August on account of German violation of the French frontier. (Idem
p. 85.) (See below, page 26.)

Page 24, lines 10 and 9 from bottom.   For " On the 31st July Austria
and Russia . . . whereupon " substitute: " At 1 P.M. on the
30th July the ' Berlin Lokalanzeiger ' issued a special number
(*Extrablatt*), announcing that mobilization had been ordered.
The statement was soon contradicted but it was telegraphed
to Petrograd and at 6 P.M., before contradiction arrived,
Russia ordered general mobilization.⁴ On the 31st Austria
followed suit, and ".

⁴ See Renouin, " Les origines immédiates de la Guerre ", p. 146 ; General Daniloff
(Quartermaster General of the Russian Army), " Russland in Weltkrieg 1914-15, p. 25-6 ;
General Suchomlinow (War Minister), " Erinnerungen ", pp. 365-7.

Page 24, lines 7 to 4 from bottom.   For " which meant . . . classes of
the Reserve ; "
substitute : " which enabled precautions similar to those of
the British ' Precautionary Period ' to be taken ; " ⁵

⁵ On the proclamation of *drohende Kriegsgefahr*, the following precautionary measures
had to be taken in all Army Corps districts :—
Protection of important railway structures :—bridges, tunnels, etc.
Recall from leave of all members of the active army.
Recall of troops, if away, to their garrisons.
Control of railway and other traffic.
Execution of the measures laid down for protection of the frontier.
Move of garrisons of active troops and fighting equipment to the islands of the North
Sea coast.
In addition, in the frontier districts :—
Guard of railway lines ; defence of large bridges and important railway junctions, air-ship
sheds and establishments important to aircraft and wireless, against attempts at demolition,
including attacks by aircraft ; removal of sick into the interior of the country.
" If a hostile attack is made before definite mobilization, or it is evident that such an
" attack is imminent, the Army Corps commanders must take all necessary measures to
" remove inland from the threatened districts and protect all men liable to service, and
" all men found fit for military service, as well as all serviceable horses. They must also,
" as far as possible, remove all material resources from reach of the enemy, particularly
" depots of supplies, the monies of the State, petrol. In case of necessity measures must
" be taken to destroy them." (Correction furnished by the Reichsarchiv.)

Page 26, line 3 from bottom.   After " four different points " add footnote :
" They are enumerated in the French Official History,
Tome I., Vol. I., page 83, which adds that ' at Petit Croix
' German cyclists fired on French custom house officers '.
" According to the Reichsarchiv : ' There were trans-
' gressions of the frontier by small detachments, contrary
' to the will of the High Command.' "

Page 27.   Add to footnote : " The German Official History of the War,
Military Operations on Land, Vol. I., pages 104 footnote 2,
and 105 footnote 1, revives the charges, although Freiherr
von Schoen, German ambassador in Paris in 1914, in his book
translated as ' The Memoirs of an Ambassador ', p. 201, has
declared the alleged air attacks to be ' merely the product
' of highly overwrought imagination '. He adds : ' How such
' false reports could have been given the weight of facts in
' our responsible quarters, and of such momentous facts, is
' inconceivable.' "

Page 155, lines 7-8. For " the 12th Infantry Brigade was resting on its
position . . . Esnes." substitute :
    " in the 12th Infantry Brigade, which was on the left of
the 11th, the Lancashire Fusiliers and two companies of the
Essex Regiment had from 4 A.M. onwards been preparing a
position near Longsart and doing what digging was possible
with their ' grubbers '. The King's Own had been delayed
on the march, but towards 6 A.M. were seen approaching over
the hill in quarter column."

Page 155, lines 12-13. Delete " The King's Own were formed up preparatory to entrenching ".

Page 155, line 17. After " fire of machine guns ", add, between commas,
" after opening on the outpost at the railway crossing north
of Wambaix ".

Page 166, line 16. For " 3.30 P.M." read " 4.30 P.M.".

Page 246, first line of footnote 2. For " These orders seemed to have
been altered, for " substitute : " In consequence of an air
report that the enemy had already reached Villers Cotterets,
General von der Marwitz decided not to continue the march
eastwards, but to strike south (German Official Account,
Vol. III., p. 194)."

Page 251. Add to footnote 2 : " The German Official Account, Vol. III.,
p. 203, adds that it was a I. Corps operation order captured
by the German *III. Corps*."

Page 333, last line but 3 (last line).
    For " Brigadier-General H. F. M. Wilson that his brigade
(the 12th) " read :
    " Lieut-Colonel F. G. Anley, then commanding that
brigade, that he ".

Page 355, last line but 6 (Page 356, line 27).
    For " Bucy le Long " read : " Ste. Marguerite ".

Page 403, lines 5-2 from bottom (Page 404, lines 5-2 from bottom). For
" the Marine Brigade . . . night of the 19th/20th September."
read : " the Marine Brigade of the Royal Naval Division was
disembarked at Dunkirk on the night of the 19th/20th
September and the Oxfordshire Yeomanry on the 22nd."

Page 404, line 14 (Page 405, line 14). For " On the 2nd October " read :
" At 6 A.M. on the 3rd October ".
    line 17 (Page 405. line 17). For " night of the 4th/5th." read :
" night of the 3rd/4th."

MAPS
No. 11 (Le Cateau). The position of the 134th Battery R.F.A. (with the
4th Division) should be 850 yards E.N.E. of the position
shown on the map. It was in action astride the Ligny-
Caullery road, facing north-west.

ADDENDA AND CORRIGENDA TO
" 1914 " Vol. I (1933 Edition)

(Kindly pointed out by various correspondents)

*Page xxvi. Under " F.O.A." At end, after " Battle of the Marne." add : " the positions shown being those it was supposed by French G.Q.G. to be occupying at the time."

*Page 60, line 36 (3rd para., line 3). For " defeat " read " repulse ".

*Page 117, line 14. For " disorganized " read " partially disorganized ".

*Page 218, lines 31-2. For " saved the left flank of the French Army." read, in inverted commas, " powerfully contributed to ensure the safety of the left flank of the French Army."

Page 256, line 1. After " word of explanation." add : " to the III. Corps or 4th Division, in accordance with a personal agreement made between Major-General Allenby (Cavalry Division) and General de Cornulier (Provisional Cavalry Division) at Compiègne, which assigned Verberie to the British left."

*Page 326, line 24. For " which, as will be seen, it failed to do." read " which was eventually done, but only in the afternoon of the 9th."

*Page 328, line 3. For " The I. Corps also did little during the day " read " The I. Corps could only progress a short distance during the day "

*Page 328, line 21. For " The Ninth Army had a disastrous day." read " The Ninth Army had been severely assailed and compelled to fall back, but though badly shaken had kept its line unbroken."

*Page 330, lines 11-12. For " fell back in panic, or was driven back, although the French make no claim to have done so." read " was driven back in panic by a night attack of the French 36th Division (XVIII. Corps)."

*Page 342, lines 20-31. For " General Franchet d'Espèrey, too, had contributed little . . . well under way." it was proposed by General Halbwachs to substitute : " General Franchet d'Espèrey's share in the victory might have been greater had he not been obliged to assist Foch's left wing, and even

---

* *Indicates corrections suggested by General Halbwachs when head of the " Service Historique " of the French General Staff in 1935.*

ADDENDA AND CORRIGENDA

to succour it by the loan of his X. Corps. His I. and III. Corps had wheeled to the right, following the right of Bülow's Army, which had swung back eastwards ; by so doing they widened and maintained open the gap between Kluck and Bülow into which the B.E.F. was successfully progressing. His XVIII. Corps and Conneau's cavalry corps had kept touch with the right wing of the B.E.F. and safeguarded its flank."

It must be pointed out, however, that General Joffre directed that General Franchet d'Espèrey's Army should attack " south-north ", whilst Foch covered its flank (see " 1914 " Vol. I. (3rd edition) p. 543), that is, its task was offensive : it was not " obliged " to diverge from its purpose to assist the defensive wing.

Page 65, lines 13-14. After " the bridge at Obourg " add footnote :
" Whilst D Company of the 4/Middlesex was engaged in throwing up entrenchments at Obourg it was fired on by cavalry and the fire was returned. The cavalry in question was the *6th Squadron* of the *16th Dragoons* (three squadrons of which formed the divisional cavalry of the *18th Division, IX. Corps*). The following is the account given in the regimental history, pp. 145-6 :
' At midday [on the 22nd August] the *6th Squadron* ' received orders to reconnoitre the canal crossings east of ' Mons and Obourg. At 4.30 P.M. the squadron lay north- ' west of Obourg engaging with fire a strong enemy, who ' held the canal crossings [cyclists and British cavalry]. ' As the object of the reconnaissance was achieved, the ' fight was broken off and a report sent back. Two squad- ' rons returned to Gottignies. Unfortunately there were ' notable losses on the reconnaissance : 2 men had fallen, ' 4 were missing and many horses were killed and wounded.'
The divisional cavalry of the *17th Division* (the other three squadrons of the *16th Dragoons*) was ordered to send out two officer's patrols, one towards Villers St. Ghislain and the heights north of Harmignies (six miles S.S.E. of Mons), the other towards Houdeng and Maurage (six miles east of Mons). They encountered the cavalry which was covering the I. Corps front. The first patrol heard from inhabitants that there were British in front, and was fired on ; the second actually saw troops in British uniform near Maurage, before being driven off by fire. These reports reached divisional headquarters about 10 P.M. There is no mention of them reaching General von Kluck."

Page 220, line 2 from foot. Delete " 1/Black Watch ". This battalion was in reserve to the front line and dug a trench across the Oisy—Etreux road.

Page 335, line 5 from foot. For " by the 65th (Howitzer) Battery " read " by two guns of a German field battery ", and delete the last line and first three lines of p. 336, adding footnote :
" Recent investigations (see Colonel Pugens in *Revue de Cavalerie*, January 1933, p. 127, and ' Lauenburgisches Feldartillerie Regiment Nr. 45 ', p. 29) make it clear that it was a section of *No. 5 Battery* of the *45th Field Artillery Regiment* which fired on the Lincolnshire. The diary of the latter unit states it was fired on with shrapnel, whilst the 65th (Howitzer) Battery was firing H.E."

ADDENDA AND CORRIGENDA TO
" 1915 " Vol. I

(Kindly pointed out by various correspondents)

Page 220, line 10 (end of first para.). Addendum issued with " 1915 "
Vol. II should be amended to read :
Add footnote :
" The second order did not reach the battalions concerned
until much later, for it was about noon when the 5/Durham
L.I. crossed the canal and the 5/Green Howards followed
some time afterwards."

Page 276, line 22.   After " next day." add footnote :
" With regard to the supersession of General Sir H.
Smith-Dorrien by General Sir H. Plumer see General Sir C.
Harington's ' Plumer of Messines ' containing an extract
from one of Lord Plumer's letters, dated 30th April 1915, in
which he says :
' It is not fair because Smith-Dorrien and I were in
' absolute agreement as to what should be done, and I am
' only doing now exactly what I should have been doing if
' I had remained under Smith-Dorrien.' "

Issued with " 1918 " Vol. II.

ADDENDA AND CORRIGENDA TO
" 1916 " Vol. I

(Kindly pointed out by various correspondents)

Page 486, footnote 1, line 1. For " entirely " read " almost entirely "
and not as stated in the Addenda and Corrigenda issued with
" 1918 " Vol. I.

ADDENDA AND CORRIGENDA TO
"1918" Vol. I

(Kindly pointed out by various correspondents)

Page 47, line 9 from foot. For " (Lieut.-General Sir R. H. K. Butler) " read " (Lieut.-General Sir W. Pulteney) ".

Page 55, line 16. Delete " , in England,".

Page 86, line 12. For " councillor " read " counsellor ".

Page 99, footnote 1. Add at the beginning :
" It is stated by a C.R.E. that nearly every man had been wounded, some three times ; all were in a weak condition, many still convalescent."

Page 123, footnote 1, para. 3. At end, after " notice boards.", add :
" The position was to be completed by the troops who occupied it, and to indicate its approximate site to them it was considered best to dig a continuous line ".

Page 126, line 10. For "Le Catelet" read "Catelet (14 miles N.W. of St. Quentin)".

Page 144, footnote 3. For " Coursing " read " Hare Drive ".

Page 195, line 30. For " south-west " read " south-east ".

Page 204, lines 5-6. For "the howitzer battery" substitute "five guns of one battery".

Page 209, footnote 1. Add at the beginning :
" There were also some belts of wire along the canal, at Jussy in particular, with shallow trenches including a support line, made by the French. They were not shown on the defence maps."

Page 228, footnote 2, last line. For " It had never been in any serious action " substitute :
" It suffered heavy losses 26th September-3rd October 1917 in the Battles of Menin Road and Polygon Wood ".

Page 267, line 5 from foot. For " Noreuil " read " Noureuil ".

Page 280, line 3 from foot. For " 20th Division " read " 30th Division ".

ADDENDA AND CORRIGENDA

Page 282, line 10 from foot. For " Br.-General R. W. Morgan " substitute : " Lieut.-Colonel C. J. Wyatt (temporarily commanding the brigade) ".

Page 343, line 14. For " 36th Division " read " 30th Division ".

Pages 343, line 4 and 501, line 22. For " Griffiths " read " Griffith " and make corresponding correction in Index.

Page 347, lines 6-5 from foot. For " Wyatt, commanding the engineer company," substitute : " Wyatt, commanding it, the engineer company ".

Page 348, footnote 1, lines 3 and 7. For " F. G. Bayley " read " G. F. Baylay ".

Page 390, lines 19-20. For " in converting trenches . . . semblance of a position. It " read " in improving the reserve position, on which they had fallen back. By the care of the XVII. Corps it was a good one, consisting of two lines of trenches well wired, with excellently sited machine-gun defences and deep dug-outs. But its completion ".

Page 445, last line of footnote. For " 127th " read " 126th ".

Page 471, footnote 2, line 1. Delete " (less artillery) " and for " on the 25th " read " on the 25th-26th ".

Page 524, line 7 from foot. For " 19th Divn." read " 9th Divn."

Page 534, line 13. After " headquarters back." add : " In others a notification from them of the signal route prepared, by which the divisions were to fall back, was mistaken for an order to retire."

Page 551. Index. For " Lieut. F. G. Bayley " read " Lieut. G. F. Baylay ".

Page 551. Index. Under " Butler, Lieut.-Gen." delete " 47 ".

Page 562. Index. Under " 9th Division " add " 524 ; "
Under " 19th Division " delete " 524 ; "

Page 563. Index. Under " 4th Australian Division " for " relieves 19th " read " relieves 9th ".

Sketch 6, in left hand top corner. For " Coursing " read " Hare Drive ". The German is *Hasenjagd*—coursing is forbidden by law in Germany.

Map 9, in area of 66th Division, near Biaches. For " 2/4th E. Lan " read " 2/5th E. Lan ".

SPECIAL ADDENDUM TO "1918" VOL. II.

The comments of the Portuguese military authorities were received by H.M.'s Embassy at Lisbon in December 1936, but owing to the time taken at Lisbon to translate them, they were not received in the Historical Section until the 24th February 1937, when the volume had gone to press. The general criticisms offered in them are :—

(1) No attention was paid until the 6th April to the reports sent in by the Portuguese of the various signs of preparation for attack which they had observed since the beginning of March.

(2) The British 55th and 40th Divisions, on either side of the Portuguese 2nd Division, formed defensive flanks prematurely, " which resulted in both "flanks of the Portuguese Division being left unprotected, thus allowing "the penetration of the Germans through these open breaches ".

(3) Portuguese units, side by side with the British, contributed assistance particularly in the defence of Marais S. Post until after 4 p.m., of La Couture, which did not surrender until 11 a.m. on the 10th April, and in the holding of the Lawe line.

(4) The artillery, as a whole, held its positions until rushed by the enemy.

The corrections suggested are as follows :

Page 141, line 4. After " surprise attack " add : " —of which the Portuguese had detected signs for some weeks and duly reported— ".

Page 147, lines 3-4. For " was a quiet sector " substitute : " had been a quiet sector " .

Page 147, line 12. After " informed him " add : " in view of the wideness of its front " .

Page 147, line 18. After " British troops." add : " A suggestion made by Colonel Sinel de Cordes, Chief of the Staff of the Portuguese Corps, that each division should be distributed in depth, with a brigade in each of the three lines, was not accepted."

Page 148, line 9. After " the front was not reduced " add : ", although General da Costa informed his corps commander, General Tamagnini, that he declined all responsibility for what might happen as the result of manning so wide a front with weakened effectives ; "

Page 161, line 8 from bottom. After " breastworks." add : " , which, however, were in a bad state owing to constant shelling."

1

2 SPECIAL ADDENDUM TO "1918" VOL. II.

Page 165, line 9 from bottom. For "a mounted A.D.C." substitute: "an A.D.C. in a car"; and for "an hour" substitute: "half an hour".

Page 165, lines 6-5 from bottom. For "occupy . . . Battle Zone." substitute: "man the Village Line."

Page 166. The paragraph beginning "About 6 a.m." should be placed later in the narrative, as the second paragraph on page 173; for it was, it is said, not until 11 a.m. that General da Costa took this action.

Page 167, line 18. Delete the words: "with rifles taken from the Portuguese".

Page 167. Add to footnote 2: "Later Portuguese accounts would make the time between 9 and 10 a.m."

Page 167, last line. "A party of thirty". Portuguese accounts say: "Almost the whole of the 13th Infantry Battalion and three platoons from the 15th".

Page 171, line 21. For "crowds" substitute: "considerable numbers".

Page 172, lines 14-23. "By 6 a.m. . . . immunity." As regards this incident, the Portuguese account is to the effect that "after 9 a.m. the Portuguese left was attacked by groups of Germans coming from the British sector."

Page 173, line 5 from bottom. Delete "with most of its artillery".

Page 175, line 14 from bottom. After "a couple of hundred Portuguese" add: "of the 15th Infantry Battalion".

Page 177, line 5. After "Horse" add: "the men of the Portuguese 13th and 15th Battalions".

Page 177. Add to footnote: "The casualties of the Portuguese are stated to have been 12 killed and 168 taken prisoner."

Page 179, line 21. After "8/Durham L.I." add: "and men of the Portuguese 12th Battalion with it,"

Page 185, line 4 from bottom. Delete "taking their artillery with them."

Page 187, lines 8-4 from bottom. For "with no special interest . . . bombardment" substitute: "uncertain of their flanks, the officers and men did their duty as far as they could, and their retirement after a bombardment of exceptional severity."

ADDENDUM TO " 1914 " Vol. I (1933 Edition)

Page 280, penultimate line. After " further south " add new footnote :
" It is now accepted in France that the British retirement
on the night of the 4th/5th September was in accordance
with the instructions from General Joffre in force at the
time and not a ' dérobade '. See ' Joffre et Galliéni à la
Marne ', pp. 65-7, by Capitaine P. Lyet, published in 1938
by the ' Service Historique ' of the French General Staff
with a preface by General Gamelin, Chief of the General Staff
of National Defence, who was one of General Joffre's General
Staff officers at the time of the Battle of the Marne 1914."

SKETCH 3A.

THE EVE OF MONS

22ND AUGUST 1914.

GERMANS . . . GREEN
FRENCH . . . BLUE
BRITISH . . . RED
Fort . . . x

Ordnance Survey, 1924.

SKETCH 3 B.

THE EVE OF LE CATEAU.
25TH AUGUST 1914.

SCALE

10 MILES

MILES 5

GERMANS

ADVANCE OF GERMAN CAVALRY

FRENCH — GREEN
BRITISH — BLUE
RED — FORT

Bohain

N.

RICHTHOFEN

Binche

SECOND ARMY

THIRD ARMY

Florennes

Pedigny

Mariembourg

Couvin

Chimay

Forest of Chimay

Rance

GD.

Beaumont

Sivry

Bodre le Chateau

X.R.

Belgian Franco-

Forest of Trelon

Forest of St. Michel

Hirson

X.

4 CAV. DIV.

ARMY

Rocroi

Gué d'Hossus

MONS

CANAL

Dour

Quievrain

Condé

From Ath

VALENCIENNES

Onnaing

St. Amand

Orchies

Marchiennes

FIRST

II.

Scarpe

IV. R.

ARMY

MAUBEUGE

Pont sur Sambre

Aulnoye

Bavai

IX.

VII.

VIII.

le Quesnoy

IV.

7

8

II

9

Selle

Villers

St. Hilaire

Beauvois

Bevillers

Solesmes

Forest of Fontaine

Landrecies

le Cateau

Neuvilly

Beaumont

INF. BDE.

E.

B.

Bazuel

Busigy

Noyelles

Dompierre

Mathaix

Maroilles

le Grand Payr

Tannieres

I.

Prinches

VALABREGUE

F.

XVIII.

Le Nouvion

Forest of Nouvion

Avesnes

FIFTH

III.

Fourmies

Etreux

Wassigny

Bohain

Oignies

Beaurevoir

Maissemy

Hargicourt

SORDET

MARWITZ

CAMBRAI

TERRT'L. DIV.

Bouchain

Sensée

Scheldt

Mory

Esnes

Mortu

CANAL

Oise

Guise

Maromme

LE CATEAU

SKETCH 3 C.

WEDNESDAY, 26TH. AUGUST 1914.

Ordnance Survey, 1924.

Croix
Forest
P.M.
Montay
Basuel
St. Benin
3 (at 9 A.M.)
LE CATEAU
½ 14 (at 6.30 A.M.)
5TH. DIVISION (27.I&II.)
Beaumont
Honnechy
Escaufort
Reumont
G. Tree
19
Troisvilles
Maurois
Bertry
Viesly
Bethencourt
Inchy
Beaumont
Audencourt
Candry
Clary
Bevillers
Beauvois
Montigny
Ligny
Fontaine
Quarries
Haucourt
Cauroir
Caudry
Chatterbriere
Longsart
Esnes
Selvigny
Wambaix
Seranvillers
Crevecoeur
Lapinin

Warnelle Ravine
11 at 3 P.M.

SORDET

Cambrai 2 miles

SKETCH 3 C.

SCALE

Contours at 20 metres v.i.

N

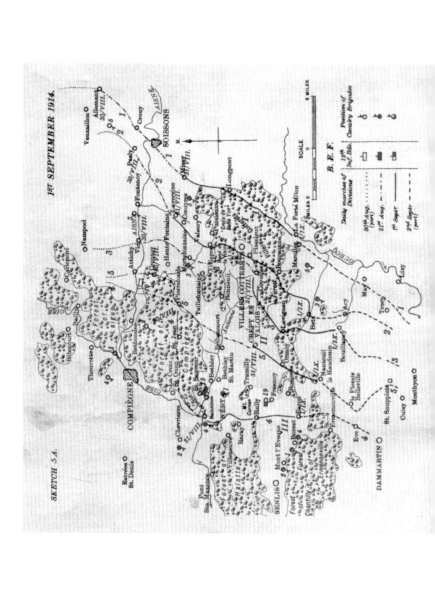

SKETCH 5A.

1ST SEPTEMBER 1914.

B.E.F.

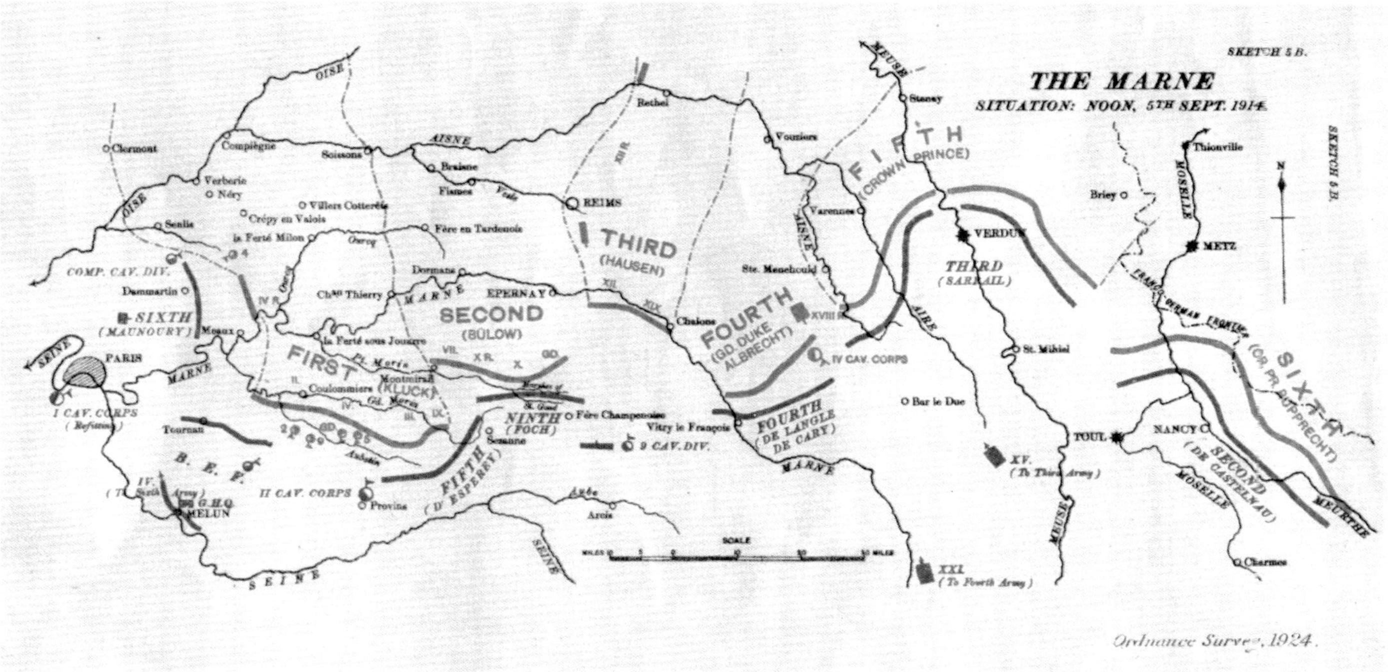
SKETCH 5 B.
THE MARNE
SITUATION: NOON, 5TH SEPT. 1914.
Ordnance Survey, 1924.
SIXTH (MAUNOURY)
FIRST (KLUCK)
SECOND (BÜLOW)
THIRD (HAUSEN)
FOURTH (GD. DUKE ALBRECHT)
FIFTH (CROWN PRINCE)
SIXTH (CR. PR. RUPPRECHT)
FIFTH (D'ESPEREY)
NINTH (FOCH)
FOURTH (DE LANGLE DE CARY)
THIRD (SARRAIL)
SECOND (DE CASTELNAU)
B. E. F.
G.H.Q.
COMP. CAV. DIV.
I CAV. CORPS (Refitting)
II CAV. CORPS
IV CAV. CORPS
9 CAV. DIV.
XV. (To Third Army)
XXI. (To Fourth Army)
PARIS
MEAUX
MELUN
REIMS
EPERNAY
VERDUN
METZ
TOUL
NANCY
Clermont
Compiègne
Soissons
Braisne
Fismes
Verberie
Néry
Senlis
Villers Cotterêts
Crépy en Valois
la Ferté Milon
Fère en Tardenois
Dammartin
Dormans
Chau Thierry
la Ferté sous Jouarre
Montmirail
Coulommiers
Tournan
Provins
Sezanne
Fère Champenoise
Vitry le François
Chalons
Ste. Menehould
Varennes
Vouziers
Rethel
Stenay
St. Mihiel
Bar le Duc
Briey
Thionville
Arcis
Charmes
OISE
AISNE
Vesle
Ourcq
MARNE
SEINE
Aube
AIRE
MEUSE
MOSELLE
MEURTHE
FRANCO-GERMAN FRONTIER
SCALE
MILES

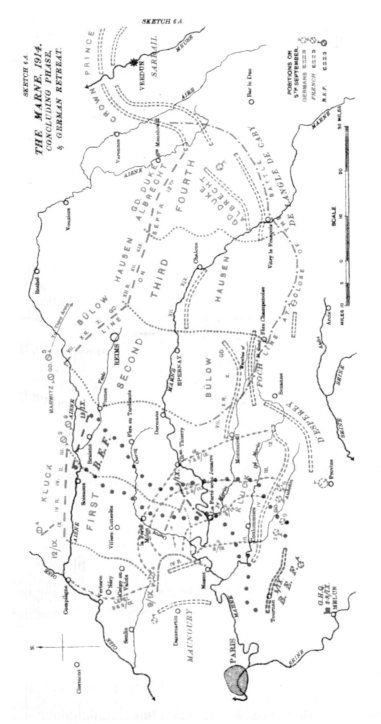

SKETCH 6A.

THE MARNE, 1914.
CONCLUDING PHASE,
& GERMAN RETREAT.

SKETCH 6A.

POSITIONS ON
5TH SEPTEMBER.
GERMANS
FRENCH
B.E.F.

SCALE

MILES 10 0 5 10 20 30 MILES

Ordnance Survey, 1924.

GENERAL INDEX

Abercrombie, Lieut.-Col. A. W., 202
Ailette, 389, 399
Air reconnaissance, advance to Mons, 50, 51, 52, 63, 66, 67 ; at Mons, 92 ; retreat, 118, 123, 125, 129, 216, 217, 230, 241, 248, 265, 270, 273, 281, 282 ; at Le Cateau, 193 ; at the Marne, 298, 299, 301, 309, 311, 313, 319, 324, 329, 332, 333, 340; pursuit to the Aisne, 359, 362, 365, 366 ; at the Aisne, 384, 389, 420
Aisne, battle of the, 377-427; German position, 377 ; Allied orders, 378 ; 13th Sept., 379-94 ; gap entered by French cavalry, 391 ; German reinforcements, 393-4 ; 14th Sept., 395-419 ; preparations for German retirement, 418, 426, 430, 454 ; French cavalry retire from gap, 418 ; 15th Sept., 419-423 ; German movements, 423-7 ; last days, 428-55 ; British withdrawal, 464 ; retrospect, 465-7
Aisne, the, reached, 370-1 ; description, 371 ; German retirement to, 373-4 ; French cross, 373 ; 11th Brigade crosses, 378-9
Albert, H.M., King of the Belgians, 28, 38
Albert of Württemberg, Duke, 43
Alexander, Major E. W., V.C., 111
Allenby, Major-Gen. E. H. H., 31, 51, 66, 103, 107, 121, 126, 140, 143, 226, 246, 297, 359, 378, 472
Alsace offensive, 39
Ammunition, shortage, 452
Anley, Lieut.-Col. F. G., 144, 185, 387
Ansell, Lieut.-Col. G. K., 140, 258
Anti-aircraft guns, 437
Antwerp, Belgian retirement to, 36, 50 ; sorties from, 151, 356-7, 424, 429, 454, 460, 461
Armin, Gen. Sixt v., 206, 351
Army Council, 2

Army Service Corps, Royal, changes of organization, 1900–1914, 5
Artillery observation, improved methods, 434
Asquith, Right Hon. H. H., 14, 27
Aston, Br.-Gen. Sir G. G., 232, 461
Austrian guns at Namur, 37

Balfour, Right Hon. A. J., 13
Ballard, Lieut.-Col. C. R., at Elouges, 107-11
Barstow, Major J. B., 242
Base, change of, 232, 286-7
Bauer, Major, 251
Bécherelle, 321, 322
B.E.F., 6 ; embarkation, 29 ; destination, 30 ; arrival in France, 49. (See also Battles and Place-Names)
Behnke, Admiral, 54
Belgian Army, 18, 19 ; concentration, 33 ; retires into Antwerp, 36, 50, 465
Belgium Conversations, 14 f.n. ; war plan, 18
Belin, Gen., 18, 254
Bellot, 320, 327
Berchtold, Count, 24
Bertie, Sir F., 264
Bethmann-Hollweg, Herr v., 55
Bingham, Br.-Gen. Hon. C. E., 103, 473
Bird, Lieut.-Col. W. D., 183
Boëlle, Gen., 392
Boger, Lieut.-Col. D. C., 111
Boileau, Col. F. R. F., 476
Bois la Haut, description of, 72
Bond, Lieut.-Col. R. C., 175
Bourg, 380, 385
Bowes, Col. W. H., 148
Boys, Lieut.-Col. R. H. H., 475
Bradbury, Captain E. K., V.C., at Néry, 256-8
Bradford, Lieut.-Col. Sir E. R., Bt., 413
Braisne, 368-9
Brantes, Col., 313

Bray, Br.-Gen. C. A., 472
Brécard, Lieut.-Col., 306
Brett, Lieut.-Col. C. A. H., 161
Bridging, 339, 381, 382, 385, 386, 438-9
Bridoux, Gen., 326
Briggs, Br.-Gen. C. S., 103, 257, 413, 472
Brugère, Gen., 458
Buckle, Major M. P., 243
Bulfin, Br.-Gen. E. S., 73, 220, 396-397, 423, 474
Bülow, Generaloberst von, 41, 46, 47, 114, 129, 130, 170, 233, 234, 249, 250, 253, 254, 288, 289, 305, 315, 316, 330, 348, 349, 353, 373, 374, 375, 377, 393, 394, 416, 425, 426, 454, 456

Camouflage, 433
Campbell, Lieut.-Col. D. G. M., 108, 308, 309
Campbell, Lieut. J. D., 256
Campbell-Bannerman, Rt. Hon. Sir H., 14
Capelle, Admiral, 54
Captured documents, 244, 248, 287, 317
Cardwell's System, 5
Casualties, at Mons, 91, 106, 112 ; Landrecies, 134 ; Le Cateau, 159, 165, 176, 181, total, 191 ; 23rd-27th Aug., 238 ; Néry, 258 ; Villers Cottérêts, 262 ; in retreat from Mons, 286 ; at the Marne, 324 ; 10th Sept., 362-3 ; 6th-10th Sept., 363 f.n. ; at the Aisne, 408, 411, 413, 416, 422, 439, 446, 447, 449, 451, 453
Cavalry charges, 108, 229, 309
Cavalry, divisional, taken from divisions, 147 f.n., 164
Cavendish, Col. A. E. J., 471
Cérizy, fight at, 227-9
Cerny, 398
Channel ports, not attacked, 48
Charleroi, battle of, 66, 92 ; retirement from, 93, 118
Charly, 333, 334
Charrier, Major P. A., 221, 222, 223, 225, 226
Chateau Thierry, occupation, 340, 341, 346, 358, 364
Chavonne, 380, 385, 405
Chemin des Dames, 389, 390, 391, 393, 394, 395, 398, 403, 406, 415
Chetwode, Br.-Gen. Sir Philip, Bt., 51, 220, 228, 229, 272, 276, 360, 473

Chivres spur, 381, 382, 387, 388, 409, 410, 416, 420, 422
Chivy valley, 400
Collisions on roads, 122, 124, 128, 131, 202, 327, 365
Committee of Imperial Defence, 13
Communications, line of, 286 f.n.
Concealment, 80, 94, 275, 433, 436
Condé, 370, 381, 410, 416
Congreve, Br.-Gen. W. N., V.C., 446, 481
Cornulier-Lucinière, Gen., 239, 326, 329
County Associations, 7, 8
Cover, shell-proof, 433
Crépy en Valois, fight at, 259
Cuthbert, Br.-Gen. G. J., 74, 260, 478

d'Amade, Gen., 42, 458
Davies, Br.-Gen. R. H., 475
Dawkins, Col. C. T., 471
Dease, Lieut. M. J., V.C., 85
de Castelnau, Gen., 16, 303, 443, 457, 458, 459
Declarations of War, 23, 28, 29
de Galbert, Captain, 306, 307
Deimling, Gen. v., 425
de Langle de Cary, Gen., 16, 42, 93, 296, 304
de Lartigue, Gen., 311, 313
Delay in issue of Joffre's orders, 306-7, 308, 341, 344, 358, 391
Deligny, Gen., 328, 345
de Lisle, Br.-Gen. H. de B., 52, 103, 108, 212, 213, 380, 446, 472
de Mas-Latrie, Gen., 63
de Mitry, Gen., 463
Demolitions, 72, 85, 86, 87, 240, 242, 248, 273, 275, 276, 312, 324, 329, 380, 381, 382
Dinant, fight at, 38
Diversions, R. Marine landing, 232
Division, Cavalry, composition, 7
Division, composition, 6
Dominion forces, 11
Doran, Br.-Gen. B. J. C., 73, 82, 89, 91, 477
Doran, Br.-Gen. W. R. B., 481
Dorrell, Sergt.-Major G. T., V.C., 257, 258
Doughty, Major E. C., 161
Drain, Dvr. J. H. C., V.C., 174
Drake, Br.-Gen. B. F., 472
Drummond, Major-Gen. L. G., 50, 171, 483
Dubail, Gen., 16, 303, 304
Du Cane, Br.-Gen. J. P., 479
d'Urbal, Gen., 459
Dykes, Lieut.-Col. A. M., 165

Edmonds, Col. J. E., 143, 173, 479
Eichhorn, Gen. v., 41
Elles, Captain H. J., 149
Elouges, fight at, 107
Emmich, Gen. v., 33, 34, 254
Entente, pre-war military arrangements, 13, 26, 30 *f.n.*
Entrenching, 73, 98, 101, 102, 129, 144, 154, 155, 159, 162, 164, 430, 432
Ersatz, 22
Etreux, fight at, 221-6
Ewart, Lieut.-Gen. Sir J. Spencer, 14

Falkenhausen, Gen. v., 454
Falkenhayn, Lieut.-Gen. v., 342, 426, 427, 429, 430, 453, 454, 455, 457, 461
False reports, 218, 226
Fanshawe, Col. R., 473
Feilding, Col. G. P. T., 385
Ferdinand, Archduke Franz, 23
Fergusson, Major-Gen. Sir Chas., Bt., 31, 73, 103, 105, 107, 143, 172, 173, 175, 478
Feste, 433
Findlay, Br.-Gen. N. D., 360, 473
Flanders, B.E.F. moves to, 463
Flares, first use of, at Mons, 92
Flint, Lieut. R. B., D.S.O., 409
Flying Corps (R.F.C.), concentration, 49 ; co-operation with artillery, 435
Foch, General, 43 ; to command Ninth Army, 277 ; at the Marne, 293, 295, 303, 304, 314, 328, 346 ; on western flank, 457, 461
Fog of war, 68, 95, 149, 170, 205, 233, 236, 248, 305, 328, 367
Forestier-Walker, Br.-Gen. G. T., 68, 97, 100, 476
Fowke, Br.-Gen. G. H., 471
Fowler, Col. J. S., 472
Frameries, 100, 115
France, defence problems, 14, 15, 16 ; war plan, 17
Franchet d'Espèrey, General, to command Fifth Army, 277 ; 278, 279, 280, 281, 282 ; at the Marne, 295, 296, 297, 302, 313, 328, 340, 342, 344, 345 ; at the pursuit to the Aisne, 372, 391
French Army, numbers, 15 ; guns, 16 ; concentration zones, 16, 38, 39 ; enters Belgium, 38 ; change in dispositions, 40 ; final plan, 41. (*See also* Index to Arms, Formations and Units)
French Government, leaves Paris, 267

French, Field-Marshal Sir John, 7, 31, 48, 49, 50, 68 ; at Mons, 72, 92, 93 ; after Mons, 97 ; 118, 120, 123, 135, 139 ; at Le Cateau, 142, 184 ; confers with Joffre, 26th Aug., 199 ; 201, 216, 217 ; promised reinforcements, 230 ; orders rest day, 232 ; 240 ; his anxiety to withdraw B.E.F., 241, 244, 245 ; 242 ; orders continuation of retreat, 249 ; correspondence with Kitchener, 263 ; interview with Kitchener, 264 ; 265, 268, 271 ; orders retreat across Marne, 272 ; 273, 275, 277, 278, 280, 282, 284, 287 ; Joffre's orders for advance arrive late, 296 ; 297 ; at battle of the Marne, 299, 300, 301, 307, 309, 310, 325, 332, 334, 339, 341, 343 ; at battle of the Aisne, 358, 389, 419, 429, 430, 445 ; his anxiety regarding ammunition supply, 453 ; suggests transfer of B.E.F. to Flanders, 463
Freytag-Loringhoven, Gen. v., 426
Frightfulness, German, 78
Furse, Col. W. T., 481

Gaede, General, 454
Galliéni, General, Military Governor of Paris, 267, 273, 277 ; visits G.H.Q., 278 ; outlines plans, 278, 293, 294 ; 280, 281 ; orders Sixth Army advance, 282 ; 283, 300, 306
Gallwitz, Gen. v., 37, 130
Gandelu, fighting at, 361-2
Garnier, Gen. v., 258
Garratt, Br.-Gen. F. S., 472
General Staff, 3, 4, 10 ; Imperial, 12
German aeroplanes, artillery, 178, 179, 214, 437
German Army, no study of, 11 ; numbers, 15, 20 ; guns, 16 ; attack on Liége, 33 ; concentration, 45 ; plan, 46
German artillery fire on own infantry, 102 *f.n.*, 171
German artillery, heavy, 161 *f.n.*, 181 (*f.n.* 2), 395, 417, 424, 432, 437
German marches, 316, 329, 350, 393
German Supreme Command. *See* O.H.L.
German swerve past Paris, 270, 273, 282
Germany, preparations for war, 15 ; movements before mobilisation, 54 ; plan, 56 ; financial readiness, 56 (*f.n.* 1)

Gette, fighting on the, 35, 36
G.H.Q., composition, 471 ; moves to France, 48 ; at Le Cateau, 68 ; conference after Mons, 97 ; at Bavai, 118 ; orders for 26th Aug., 123, 135, 139 ; at St. Quentin morning of Le Cateau, 142 ; order *re* divisional cavalry, 147 *f.n.*; move to Noyon, 199 ; conference with General Joffre, 199 ; instructions for I. Corps retirement, 201 ; pessimism, 218 ; leaves Dammartin, 265 ; Galliéni's visit at Melun, 278 ; receipt of Joffre's orders for the Marne, 306-7 ; at Fère en Tardenois, 419 ; moves to Abbeville and St. Omer, 464
Gifford, Lieut. J., 256
Gilpin, Br.-Gen. F. C. A., 472
Gleichen, Br.-Gen. A. E. W., Count, 75, 105, 143, 411, 478
Glubb, Br.-Gen. F. M., 479
Godley, Private S. F., V.C., 85
Gordon, Col. Hon. F., 475
Gordon, Col. W. E., V.C., 194, 195
Gough, Br.-Gen. H. de la P., 53, 103, 227, 228, 229, 276, 297, 298, 300, 318, 472
Gough, Br.-Gen. J. E., V.C., 68, 97, 123, 361, 378, 473
Gower, Lieut. E. W., 226
G.Q.G. *See* Joffre
Graham, Major-Gen. E. R. C., 471
Grant-Duff, Lieut.-Col. Adrian, 416
Great Britain, mobilization scheme modified, 25 ; mobilization ordered, 4th Aug., 29 ; declares war on Germany, 5th Aug., 28 ; general mobilization and despatch of B.E.F., 31
Grenfell, Captain F. O., V.C., 111
Grey, Rt. Hon. Sir Edward, Bt., 24, 25, 28, 29
Grierson, Lieut.-Gen. Sir J. M., 14, 31, 50, 476
Gronau, Gen. v., 209
Grossetti, Gen., 347
Guise, battle of, 217, 231, 237, 239, 241, 251 (*f.n.* 4) ; note on, 252-4, 285
Guns, loss of, at Mons, 92 ; at Le Cateau, 172-3, 177, 181, 183, 190 ; Étreux, 225

Hache, Gen., 327, 345
Haelen, fight at, 35
Haig, Lieut.-Gen. Sir D., 31, 64, 82, 97, 98, 105, 120, 122, 123, 132, 135, 140, 141, 193, 200, 201, 232,

242, 245, 268, 276, 277, 299, 310, 321, 333, 334, 362, 380, 390, 413, 414, 415
Haking, Br.-Gen. R. C. B., 90, 203, 414, 415, 451, 475
Haldane, Br.-Gen. J. A. L., 138, 146, 168, 191, 243, 479
Haldane, Rt. Hon. Viscount, 3, 4, 7, 8
Hall, Lieut.-Col. E. F., 401
Hamilton, Major-Gen. H. I. W., 31, 73, 82, 141, 143, 183, 335, 386, 408, 476
Hand-grenade, 10, 452
Harper, Col. G. M., 471
Hausen, Gen. v., 46, 47
Headlam, Br.-Gen. J. E. W., 478
Heeringen, Gen. v., 41, 393, 394, 425, 445
Helfferich, Herr (German Foreign Secretary), 289
Henderson, Col. C. F. R., 8
Henderson, Br.-Gen. Sir D., 31, 67, 482
Hentsch, Lieut.-Col., 292, 330, 338, 348, 350, 351, 352, 355-6, 373, 374
Hildebrand, Br.-Gen. A., 142
Hindenburg, Gen. v., 237, 317, 356, 426, 454
Hogg, Lieut.-Col. J. G., 260
Hollen, Gen. v., 460, 462
Horne, Br.-Gen. H. S., 98, 104, 105, 110, 226, 228, 473
Hötzendorf, Field-Marshal Conrad v., 61
Huguet, Col., 14, 30, 185, 201, 217, 218, 245, 273, 295, 306, 307
Hull, Lieut.-Col. C. P. A., 84
Hunter-Weston, Br.-Gen. A., 145, 146, 182, 191, 214, 215, 379, 480
Hutier, Gen. v., 253

Imperial General Staff, 12
Indian Army, 12, 30
Ingouville-Williams, Br.-Gen. E. C., 481
Interpreters, 215
Italy proclaims her neutrality, 28

Jackson, Lieut.-Col. S. C. F., 214
Jäger, uniform, 158 *f.n.*
James, Lieut.-Col. H. L., 161
Jarvis, Lce.-Corpl. C. A., V.C., 86
Jeffreys, Major G., 404, 405
Joffre, General, 17, 30, 31, 38 ; his tactical note, 44 ; 48 ; orders general advance, 50 ; admits failure of French offensive, 139 ; 185, 199, 211, 217, 231 ; congratulates B.E.F., 238 ; 240, 241, 244, 245, 246, 249, 252, 263, 267,

270, 271, 273, 278, 279, 280, 283 ; plans and order for battle of the Marne, 293, 306 ; begs British co-operation, 296; 308 ; further instructions, 312, 314, 315, 326, 341, 343, 344 ; 339 ; instructions during pursuit to the Aisne, 358, 364, 367, 372 ; instructions during battle of the Aisne, 378, 389, 390, 391, 419 ; new plans for enveloping German right, 429, 443, 456 ; 460, 463
Johnston, Captain W. H., V.C., 409
Jones, Lieut.-Col. H. B., 148, 479
Jouannic, Gen., 327

Kaiser Franz Joseph, 24
Kaiser Wilhelm II., 54, 235, 289, 317, 347, 426, 461
Keir, Major-Gen. J. L., 31, 481
Kemp, Lieut.-Col. G. C., 481
King, H.M. the, 26 ; message to his troops, 32
King, Br.-Gen. C. W., 472
Kitchener, Field-Marshal Earl, 4, 12, 29, 51, 249, 263, 264, 280
Kluck, Generaloberst von, 45, 53, 69, 92, 95, 110, 114, 119, 136, 169, 170, 204, 210, 216, 233, 234, 244, 248, 250, 251, 275, 287, 288, 292, 304, 305, 315, 328, 340, 341, 350, 351, 352, 355, 374, 375, 393, 423, 426, 430, 454, 456
Kraewel, Gen. v., 329, 337, 340, 351, 353, 354, 373
Krafft v. Dellmensingen, Gen., 60, 352
Kuhl, Gen. v., 351, 352, 353

La Cour de Soupir, 401, 404, 405, 414
La Ferté sous Jouarre, 319, 323-4, 329, 337-8, 339
La Forge, bridge, 317, 321
Landon, Br.-Gen. H. J. S., 73, 474
Landrecies, action at, 133-6, 150, 200
Lanrezac, General, 16, 39, 42, 44, 48, 49, 50, 66, 68, 92, 93, 94, 136, 199, 201, 232, 242, 243, 248, 249, 252, 272, 273, 274 ; superseded in command of Fifth Army, 277
La Trétoire, 320
Le Cateau, battle of, 152 et seq. ; remarks on, 192-3 ; reorganization after, 198 ; G.H.Q. orders for retirement after, 201 f.n. ; German accounts, 204 ; French help, 185, 210 ; German movements after, 233-7
Le Grand Fayt, action, 203

Leman, Gen., 34
Lemberg, battle of, 237, 356, 427
Leopold II., H.M., 58
Liége, siege, 33
Lille, evacuation of, 117 ; garrison of, 118
Lindsay, Major-Gen. W. F. L., 471
Linsingen, Gen. v., 209, 351, 353, 354
Lister, Captain G. D., 79
Liveing, Major C. H., D.S.O., 190
Lochow, Gen., 207, 351, 353
Lomax, Major-Gen. S. H., 31, 73, 135, 398, 473
Longley, Lieut.-Col. J. R., 322
Lovat, Lord, 4
Ludendorff, Major-Gen., 34, 59, 237, 348, 355
Luke, Dvr. F., V.C., 174
Luxembourg, Germans enter, 27

McCracken, Br.-Gen. F. W. N., 74, 180, 183, 477
Macdonogh, Col. G. M. W., 92, 279, 280, 471
Machine gun jams, 165
Macready, Major-Gen. Sir C. F. N., 471
Maitland, Major Hon. A. H., 401
Malplaquet, 52, 65
Mangin, Gen., 38, 302
Maps, 152, 246 f.n.
Marches, 218, 219, 220, 242, 247, 254, 269, 283, 284 (f.n. 2)
Marne, genesis of the battle of the, Sir J. French's proposal to defend the, 271 ; air reports, 274, 277 ; Galliéni's visit to G.H.Q., 278 ; Wilson's visit to Franchet d'Espèrey, 278-9 ; Joffre confirms the retirement, 280 ; continued German advance, 282-3 ; Kluck disobeys orders, 288 ; O.H.L. orders before the battle, 290-1 ; German situation on 5th Sept., 292 ; Germans surprised, 292 (f.n. 2) ; note on genesis, 293 ; Joffre's orders, 295-6 ; Joffre visits G.H.Q., 296 ; delay in issue of Joffre's orders, 306-7
Marne, battle of the, 6th Sept., 295-305 ; French movements, 302 ; German movements, 304 ; 7th Sept., 308-15 ; belated receipt of Joffre's orders, 308 ; short advance, 310 ; arrival of French 8th Division on British left, 311, 313 ; Joffre's orders, 312 ; French movements, 313 ; Franchet d'Espèrey's slowness, 314 ; Ger-

man movements, 315 ; 8th Sept., 318-326 ; Joffre's orders, 326 ; French movements, 326-8 ; German movements, 328-31 ; passages of the river abandoned, 330 ; 9th Sept., 332-341 ; 11th Hussars cross on night 8th-9th, 327 ; false alarm and halt, 333-4 ; results of day, 340 ; retrospect, 341 ; French movements, 344-7 ; German retirement, 347-56

Maroilles, action at, 132-3, 150

Marwitz, Gen. v. d., 34, 53, 67, 69, 114, 117, 126, 149, 150, 170, 193, 204, 205, 209, 238, 248, 251, 292, 298, 299, 311, 316, 348, 350, 353, 354, 373, 394, 423, 457, 459, 460, 462

Massy-Westropp, Lieut. R. F. H., 196

Masurian Lakes, battle of, 356, 427

Matheson, Major T. G., 404, 405

Mauberge, investment of, 130, 150 ; capitulation, 366, 393

Maude, Col. S., 284

Maud'huy, Gen., 327, 346, 362, 459

Maunoury, Gen., 40, 231, 239, 245, 265, 278, 293, 296, 313, 325, 326, 340, 341, 344, 345, 364, 392, 456

Maurice, Lieut.-Col. F. B., 100

Maxse, Br.-Gen. F. I., 73, 220, 221, 222, 223, 396, 397, 474

Mesnil, French fight at, 231

Miers, Captain D. N. C. C., 451

Militia, 1, 2, 5, 6

Millerand, M., 263, 267, 271

Milne, Br.-Gen. G. F., 147, 167, 189, 479

Missy, 379, 382, 386, 409, 417, 421

Mobilization, 9, 25, 29, 31

Moffitt, Major F. W., 338

Moltke, Generaloberst von, 45, 47, 56, 59 ; misled by Kluck's report on Le Cateau, 206 ; decision on 4th Sept., 291 ; 317, 330 ; supersession of, 342, 426 ; 347, 356 ; visit to Armies, 11th Sept., 374

Monro, Major-Gen. C. C., 31, 73, 321, 334, 385, 401, 414, 475

Mons, battle of, 71-94 ; German account, 94 ; summary of retreat from, 283-7

Mont Faucon, 450-1

Montgomery, Lieut.-Col. A. A., 138

Montmirail, fighting before, 314, 327-8, 344-5

Montrésor, Lieut.-Col. E. H., 396

Montreuil aux Lions, 329, 335-6, 362

Moore, Br.-Gen. J., 472

Moratorium, 28

Morhange, battle, 43, 47

Morin, Grand, forced by 1/Wiltshire, 300 ; fighting on, 309-10 ; French arrival at, 314

Morin, Petit, 312 ; forcing of, 318-321, 327-8

Morland, Lieut.-Col. C. B., 221, 222

Mormal, forest of, 64, 119-20, 132, 140, 150

Morris, Lieut.-Col. Hon. G. H., 260, 261

Motor transport, 5, 6

Moulton-Barrett, Lieut.-Col. H. P., 188

Moussy, 402, 403

Muller, Comdt., 294

Mundy, Lieut. L. F. H., 257

Murray, Lieut.-Gen. Sir A. J., 68, 97, 278, 279, 280, 471

Musketry, British, effect of, 77-81, 83-85, 88, 94, 100, 106, 115, 166, 176, 181, 183, 309, 336, 361, 396, 411, 413, 447

Namur, 36, 131

National Reserve, 11

Navy, Royal, measures taken at outbreak of war, 23, 27

Neish, Lieut.-Col. F. H., 194

Nelson, Sergt. D., V.C., 257, 258

Néry, fight at, 248, 256-8, 266

Nogent, 332, 334

Officers' Training Corps, 4

O.H.L., operation orders, 46, 129, 234-6, 250, 288, 290-1 ; none issued 6th and 7th Sept., 317 ; 10th Sept., 373-4 ; moves from Luxembourg, 458

Orly, fighting at, 319, 324 f.n.

Ostend, landing, 232, 292, 393

Ourcq, battle of the, 296, 302, 304 ; march of German II. and IV. Corps to, 305, 311 ; march of German III. and IX. Corps to, 315-16, 325-6, 328, 333

Oven, Major-Gen. v., 135

Packs, carriage of, 200, 268

Paget, Br.-Gen. W. L. H., 481

Papen, Captain v., 56

Paris, Br.-Gen. A., 461

Parker, Major R. G., 196, 214

Pau, General, 39

Pearce Serocold, Lieut.-Col. E., 396

Pennycuick, Lieut. J. A. C., D.S.O., 243

Perceval, Br.-Gen. E. M., 413, 475

Pereira, Lieut.-Col. C., 413

Péronne, French fight at, 216, 230, 231
Perry, Br.-Gen. H. W., 472
Pétain, Gen., 302
Phipps-Hornby, Br.-Gen. E. J., V.C., 479
Photographs, air, first, 420
Plans of campaign, French, 16 ; German, 45
Plumer, Lieut.-Gen. Sir H. C. O., 50
Poincaré, M., 263
Ponsonby, Lieut.-Col. J., 398, 415
Pont Arcy, 380, 385, 409
Pontoise bridge, demolition, 242 *f.n.*
Poole, Major A. J., 196
Potsdam Conference, 54
Pourtalès, Count, 26
Price, Col. W., 472
Priez, fighting at, 360, 363
Prittie, Captain Hon. H. C. O'C., 214
Prittwitz, Gen. v., 237
Prowse, Major C. B., 191, 214
Proyart, French fight at, 239
Pulteney, Major-Gen. W. P., 31, 243, 255, 337, 479
Pursuit from the Marne to the Aisne, 358, 363, 364 ; 11th Sept., 364-366 ; 12th, 366-372

Quast, Gen. v., 208, 315, 316, 329, 351, 353, 354

Race to the sea, 429, 439, 456-463
Raids, French cavalry, 326, 329 ; first trench, 452 (*f.n.* 2) ; German cavalry, 462
Rapid fire, 80, 81, 85, 87, 309. (*See also* Musketry)
Reinforcements, ten per cent, 286, 301 ; shortage, 440
Rennenkampf, Gen., 317
Retirement threatened by Sir J. French, 245, 249, 263 ; Lord Kitchener intervenes, 264
Retreat, French plans, 199, 217, 231, 241, 245, 249, 271-2, 273, 284
Reynolds, Captain D., V.C., 174
Rice, Br.-Gen. S. R., 473
Richthofen, Gen. Fr. v., 38, 120, 130, 149, 150, 224, 248, 305, 311, 316, 348, 350
Rifles, clogged, 88
Robb, Major-Gen. F. S., 241, 287
Robertson, Major-Gen. Sir W. R., 286, 471
Roe, Captain S. G., 371
Rolt, Br.-Gen. S. P., 74, 421, 478
Romer, Lieut.-Col. C. F., 100, 478
Rosières, French fight at, 239

Rouge Maison, 406
Rowley, Major F. G. M., 257
Royal Defence Corps, 11
Ruffey, Gen., 16, 41
Rupprecht, Crown Prince of Bavaria, 46, 47, 61, 250, 303, 317, 347, 455
Ruses, 78, 134, 405
Russia, despatch of German corps to, 236

Sablonnières, fighting at, 318, 320
Saglier, Captain, 211
St. Cyr, 319, 321, 322
St. Gond, Marshes of, 303, 314, 316, 328, 330, 346, 349, 364
St. John, Captain B. T., 78
St. Leger, Major S. E., 84
St. Mihiel, 428, 455
St. Ouen, 322
Ste. Marguerite, 387, 409, 410
Sandbach, Br.-Gen. A. E., 476
Sanders, Major G. H., 186
Sarrail, Gen., 267, 296, 304
Sarrebourg, battle, 43, 47
Sarsfield, Major W. S., 403
Sazonov, M., 26
Schlieffen Plan, 56, 251, 454
Schreiber, Lieut.-Col. A. L., 473
Schubert, Gen. v., 454
Schulenberg, Col. v. d., 350
Scott-Kerr, Br.-Gen. R., 98, 135, 261, 475
Selle, river, 153
Semoy, battle of the, 44, 47
Shaw, Br.-Gen. F. C., 74, 85, 143, 180, 334, 335, 477
Shell shortage, 453, 455
Shewan, Major H. M., 196, 197
Short, Br.-Gen. A. H., 476
Smith, 2nd Lieut. M. Beckwith, 452
Smith-Dorrien, Gen. Sir H. L., 50, 52, 90, 99, 135 ; decision to stand at Le Cateau, 140, 149 ; at Le Cateau, 152, 155, 169, 172, 173, 177, 184, 185, 192, 193, 199, 206, 210 ; 200, 215, 216, 240
Snow, Major-Gen. T. D'O., 31, 121, 135, 138, 139, 142, 146, 148, 149, 192, 218, 379, 479
Soissons, 373, 392, 419
Solesmes, 4th Division sent to, 121, 124, 126 ; 127, 128, 136
Sordet, Gen., 38, 184, 326
Soupir, 401, 403, 413
Spears, Lieut. E. L., 66, 92, 93
Special Reserve, 5, 6
Spies, 434
Stein, Gen. v., 426
Steinmetz, Gen. v., 425
Stepney, Major H., 405

Strantz, Gen., 454
Stuart, Br.-Gen. A. M., 472
Swayne, Lieut.-Col. E. H., 190
Sykes, Lieut.-Col. F. H., 482

Tannenberg, battle of, 236, 237, 246
Tappen, Col., 60, 454
Territorial Force, 7, 28
Tew, Major H. S., 128
Towsey, Lieut.-Col. F. W., 445
Train, 5
Training in peace, 8
Trench warfare, beginning of, 396, 430 ; apparatus, 432, 433, 434
Triple Alliance, 15
Troyon factory, 396, 398, 399, 415
Tulloch, Lieut.-Col. J. A. S., 478
Twiss, Col. J. H., 472

Uniforms, colour of, 22

Vailly, 370, 381, 386, 407, 408, 420
Vallentin, Major H. E., D.S.O., 190
Vaughan, Br.-Gen. J., 68, 298, 472
Vendresse, 396, 397, 398, 399
Venizel, 371, 379, 382, 383, 386
Vesle, the, passage of, 368, 372, 374, 391
Villers Cottérêts, fight at, 260-2
Virton, battle, 44, 47
Volunteer Corps, 1, 4, 7

Walcot, Captain B., 149

Waldersee, Gen. v., 237
Waldersee, Graf, 56
" War-book," the, 13, 416
Ward, Lieut.-Col. B. E., 186
Warnelle, stream, 147, 150
Warren, Lieut.-Col. D., 415
Weigeit, Major, 55
West, Lieut. R. R. F., D.S.O., 243
White flag incidents, 397, 405, 442
Wilding, Major C. A., 370
Wilhelm, Crown Prince of Germany, 43, 44, 352
Wilson, Lieut.-Col. C. S., 476
Wilson, Br.-Gen. H. F. M., 166, 167, 379, 387, 413, 480
Wilson, Major-Gen. H. H., 14, 142, 278, 280, 306, 471
Wing, Br.-Gen. F. D. V., 476
Wire, barbed, none available, 422, 433
Wireless, aeroplane, 435
Wireless communications, German, fail, 317, 330
Woodhouse, Surgeon-Gen. T. P., 472
Wormald, Lieut.-Col. F., 229
Wright, Captain T., V.C., 86, 408, 409
Wyatt, Lce.-Corpl. G. H., V.C., 134

Yate, Major C. A. L., V.C., 176
Yeomanry, 1, 7

Zwehl, Gen. v., 233, 393, 423, 424

INDEX TO
ARMS, FORMATIONS AND UNITS

Artillery—
Batteries, Field—
6th—88, 91, 162, 183, 477 ; 9th
—260, 262, 476 ; 11th—159,
161, 172, 478 ; 15th—476 ;
16th—321, 476 ; 17th—260,
262, 476 ; 22nd—82, 475 ;
23rd—88, 91, 477 ; 24th—
482 ; 27th—167, 190, 480 ;
29th—477 ; 30th (How.)—
385, 474 ; 31st (How.)—190,
412, 480 ; 34th—482 ; 35th
(How.) — 189, 480 ; 37th
(How.)—101, 154, 160, 172,
174, 337, 410, 479 ; 39th—
167, 412, 480 ; 40th (How.)
—360, 474 ; 41st—127, 137,
156, 163, 183, 477 ; 43rd
(How.)—482 ; 45th—477 ;
46th—220, 399, 403, 424,
474 ; 47th (How.)—476 ; 48th
—476 ; 49th—83, 84, 381,
477 ; 50th—402, 475 ; 51st
—474 ; 52nd—160, 173,
218, 478 ; 54th—399, 474 ;
55th (How.)—190, 412, 480 ;
56th (How.)—476 ; 57th
(How.)—474 ; 60th (How.)
—134, 323, 476 ; 61st (How.)
—154, 178, 410, 479 ; 65th
(How.)—154, 155, 162, 335,
479 ; 68th—167, 383, 387,
412, 480 ; 70th—82, 402,
475 ; 71st—476 ; 72nd—
482 ; 80th—172, 335, 478 ;
86th (How.)—482 ; 87th
(How.)—482 ; 88th—167,
412, 480 ; 107th—155, 180,
362, 477 ; 108th—155, 180,
477 ; 109th—85, 100, 213,
477 ; 110th—482 ; 111th—
482 ; 112th—482 ; 113th—
276, 399, 403, 424, 474 ;
114th—276, 399, 474 ; 115th
—474 ; 116th—399, 474 ;

117th—320, 474 ; 118th—
221, 225, 320, 474 ; 119th—
101, 107, 109, 110, 112, 179,
259, 320, 479 ; 120th—74, 79,
80, 92, 479 ; 121st—101, 102,
179, 322, 382, 479 ; 122nd—
160, 173, 174, 187, 479 ;
123rd—173, 479 ; 124th—
173, 479 ; 125th—480 ; 126th
—480 ; 127th—480 ; 128th
(How.)—477 ; 129th (How.)
—477 ; 130th (How.)—477 ;
134th—167, 480 ; 135th—
167, 182, 190, 480
Batteries, Garrison (Heavy)—
24th—482 ; 26th—474 ; 31st
—370, 382, 480 ; 35th—321,
402, 476 ; 48th—74, 155,
477 ; 108th—148, 154, 160,
171, 177, 178, 186, 187, 323,
382, 479
Batteries, Horse—
D—63, 109, 110, 157, 158, 268,
319, 359, 473 ; E—63, 109,
110, 177, 178, 186, 213, 228,
268, 276, 319, 473 ; H—359,
473 ; I—156, 257, 359, 381,
473 ; J—98, 228, 318, 359,
361, 380, 473 ; L—104, 107,
109, 111, 113, 177, 178, 186,
247, 256, 258, 473 ; Z—359,
360
Brigades (Field)—
II.—481 ; VIII. (How.)—101,
107, 409, 479 ; XII. (How.)
—482 ; XIV.—167, 189, 480 ;
XV.—124, 154, 155, 159, 179,
218, 410, 478 ; XXIII.—74,
155, 162, 180, 448, 477 ;
XXIV.—482 ; XXV.—385,
396, 474 ; XXVI.—224, 474 ;
XXVII.—101, 103, 106, 154,
479 ; XXVIII.—101, 107,
154, 159, 160, 479 ; XXIX.
—167, 189, 319, 370, 480 ;

586 INDEX TO ARMS, FORMATIONS AND UNITS

Brigades (Field) (*continued*)—
XXX. (How.)—74, 156, 447,
477 ; XXXII.—138, 167,
190, 380, 480 ; XXXIV.—
333, 361, 401, 402, 475 ;
XXXVI.—98, 226, 320, 401,
476 ; XXXVII. (How.)—167,
179, 260, 480 ; XXXVIII.—
482 ; XXXIX.—474 ; XL.—
73, 156, 183, 406, 458, 477 ;
XLI.—98, 320, 321, 476 ;
XLII.—73, 156, 477 ; XLIII.
(How.)—474 ; XLIV. (How.)
—321, 402, 476
Brigades (Horse)—
III.—473 ; VII.—473
Cavalry—
Brigades—
1st—103 ; at Elouges, 109 ;
125, 127 ; at Solesmes, 137 ;
at Le Cateau, 156, 157, 159,
177, 198 ; 212, 213, 216, 219,
230, 240, 243, 247 ; at Néry,
256 ; at the Marne, 298, 318,
332 ; pursuit to the Aisne,
359, 368 ; at the Aisne, 380,
385, 397, 413, 416, 418 ; 472
2nd—52, 62, 103, 104 ; at
Elouges, 107, 108, 111 ; 113,
125, 126 ; at Solesmes, 137 ;
at Le Cateau, 156, 198 ; 212,
213, 216, 219, 230, 240, 243,
247, 263, 268 ; at the Marne,
298, 308, 318, 321, 334 ; at
the Aisne, 380, 381, 384, 397,
413, 418, 445, 446 ; 472
3rd—53, 63, 103 ; at Elouges,
107, 109, 110 ; 125, 127 ; at
Solesmes, 137 ; at Le Cateau,
156, 159, 188, 198 ; 212, 213,
216, 219, 227, 230, 240, 243,
246, 247 ; at Villers Cottérêts, 260, 262 ; 268, 270,
275, 281 ; at the Marne, 297,
298, 310, 319, 322, 339 ; at
the Aisne, 418, 441; 472
4th—75, 103 ; at Elouges, 111 ;
125, 126, 127, 128 ; at Le
Cateau, 141, 156, 189 ; 214,
216, 219, 230, 240, 243 ; at
Néry, 257 ; 263, 276 ; at the
Marne, 298, 308, 318, 320,
321, 332, 346 ; at the Aisne,
397, 418 ; 473
5th—7, 51, 53, 62, 64, 66, 67,
73, 96, 98, 100, 113, 121, 123 ;
at Le Grand Fayt, 201, 203 ;
at Étreux, 220, 224, 226 ; at
Cérizy, 228, 229 ; 230, 242,
243, 247 ; at Villers Cot-

térêts, 260, 262 ; 268, 270,
272, 275, 277, 281 ; at the
Marne, 297, 310, 321, 339 ;
pursuit to the Aisne, 361 ; at
the Aisne, 408, 409, 418 ; 473
Divisions—
1st (The Cavalry Division)—
composition, 7 ; 30, 31 ; position in general line, 49, 51 ;
advance to Mons, 52, 53 ; at
Mons, 64, 66, 87, 96, 103 ; at
Elouges, 107, 110, 112, 113 ;
121, 124, 126, 129, 136 ; at
Le Cateau, 140, 156, 174, 198,
201, 210 ; 212, 216, 217, 219,
230 ; casualties, 23rd-27th
Aug., 238 ; 242, 246, 255,
263, 265, 269, 270, 273, 275,
277, 281 ; at the Marne, 297,
300, 301, 308, 310, 318, 321,
324 ; 327, 334, 339 ; pursuit
to the Aisne, 359, 363, 365,
371; at the Aisne, 378, 380,
388, 390, 398, 418, 440 ;
move to Flanders, 464 ; 472
2nd (3rd and 5th Brigades)—at
battle of the Marne, 297, 300,
301, 308, 310, 318, 324, 339 ;
pursuit to the Aisne, 361, 362,
363, 366, 369, 371 ; at the
Aisne, 378, 386, 388, 390, 416,
418, 449 ; move to Flanders,
464
3rd—lands at Zeebrugge, 461,
465
Yeomanry—on East coast defences, 30, 121
Regiments—
Household, Composite, 212, 473
Dragoon Guards, 2nd (Queen's
Bays), 186, 198, 256, 448, 472
—— 4th, 52, 62, 69, 107, 108,
111, 113, 198, 318, 321, 446,
472
—— 5th, 110, 137, 140, 256,
258, 318, 359, 369, 472
—— 6th (Carabiniers), 75, 214,
215, 473
Dragoons, 2nd (R. Scots Greys),
62, 66, 70, 228, 276, 318, 361,
408, 473
Hussars, 3rd, 247, 473
—— 4th, 127, 137, 227, 260,
369, 472
—— 11th, 188, 198, 256, 257,
327, 332, 472
—— 15th, 82, 132, 221, 224,
225, 402, 474, 475, 477
—— 18th, 103, 107, 108, 113,
309, 445, 472

Regiments (continued)—
Hussars, 19th, 76, 79, 147, 157, 188, 478, 480, 481
—— 20th, 228, 361, 408, 473
Lancers, 5th, 157, 319, 369, 472
—— 9th, 52, 103, 107, 108, 111, 113, 198, 213, 308, 396, 446, 453, 472
—— 12th, 228, 361, 362, 408, 473
—— 16th, 63, 127, 239, 369, 472
Special Reserve—
North Irish Horse, 148, 482
South Irish Horse, 482
Yeomanry—
Oxfordshire, 461
Corps—
I.—31 ; concentration, 49, 51 ; advance, 52, 64, 65 ; at Mons, 68, 71, 73, 81, 90, 94 ; on 24th Aug., 96, 99, 100, 105, 112, 113, 115 ; on 25th Aug., 121, 131 ; 132 ; at Landrecies, 133, 135 ; 139, 141, 142, 149 ; during Le Cateau, 152, 155, 156, 162, 170, 192, 200, 217 ; on 28th Aug., 219, 226, 227 ; 229, 230, 233 ; casualties, 23rd-27th Aug., 238 ; 242, 245, 246, 247, 255 ; at Villers Cottérêts, 260, 266 ; 265, 268, 269, 273, 275, 277, 281, 286 ; at the Marne, 296, 298, 301, 310, 314, 321, 324, 325, 333, 337, 339, 363 ; casualties, 6th-9th Sept., 363 ; pursuit to the Aisne, 366, 370, 371, 372 ; at the Aisne, 378, 380, 384, 388, 390, 393, 396, 405, 407, 413, 415, 417, 418, 419, 422, 423, 425, 440, 444, 464, 466 ; casualties, 14th Sept., 416 ; move to Flanders, 465 ; 473
II.—31 ; concentration, 49, 51 ; advance to Mons, 52, 53, 64 ; at Mons, 68, 72, 73, 90, 93, 96 ; casualties, 23rd Aug., 91 ; on 24th Aug., 99, 100, 102, 105, 113 ; 121, 123, 135 ; at So-lesmes, 136, 139 ; at Le Cateau, 140, 143, 152, 156, 171, 172, 173, 177, 184, 192, 199, 204 ; 212, 217, 218, 220, 227, 229, 231, 233 ; casualties, 23rd-27th Aug., 238 ; 240, 243, 246, 247, 255, 265, 268, 270, 275, 277, 281, 286 ; at the Marne, 296, 297, 299, 311, 323, 324, 334, 339 ; casualties, 6th-9th Sept., 363 ; pursuit to the Aisne, 363,

366, 370, 371 ; at the Aisne, 378, 381, 386, 388, 390, 406, 418, 444, 466, 467 ; move to Flanders, 464, 465 ; 476
III.—31 ; formation, 243 ; during retreat, 246, 247, 255, 268, 270, 275, 277, 281, 286 ; at the Marne, 296, 297, 299, 300, 301, 309, 311, 312, 324, 337, 339, 340; pursuit to the Aisne, 362, 363, 365, 366, 370, 371 ; casualties, 6th-9th Sept., 363 ; at the Aisne, 378, 382, 389, 390, 417, 418, 419, 440, 444, 464, 466, 467 ; moves to Flanders, 465 ; 479
Cyclists—
1st Div.—474 ; 2nd Div.—475 ; 3rd Div.—477 ; 4th Div.—379, 382, 480 ; 5th Div.—322, 323, 478 ; 6th Div.—481
Divisions—
1st—30, 31 ; concentration, 49 ; advance to Mons, 52, 64, 67 ; at Mons, 73, 76, 96, 97, 98, 113 ; 121, 123 ; at Le Grand Fayt, 135, 200, 202 ; 197 ; at Étreux, 220, 223 ; 227 ; casualties, 23rd-27th Aug., 238 ; 242, 247 ; at Villers Cottérêts, 260 ; 273, 276 ; at the Marne, 299, 333, 334 ; pursuit to the Aisne, 360, 362, 365, 369 ; at the Aisne, 380, 384, 388, 390, 396, 398, 406, 415, 418, 441, 450, 466 ; 473
2nd—30, 31 ; concentration, 49 ; advance to Mons, 52, 64 ; at Mons, 68, 73, 76, 81, 96, 98, 113 ; 121, 122, 123, 135 ; at Le Grand Fayt, 200, 203 ; at Étreux, 220, 224 ; 227 ; casual-ties, 23rd-27th Aug., 238 ; 242, 243, 247 ; at Villers Cot-térêts, 260, 262 ; 273, 276 ; at the Marne, 320, 333, 334, 350 ; pursuit to the Aisne, 361, 362, 369 ; at the Aisne, 380, 385, 390, 397, 399, 401, 405, 413, 415, 418, 424, 444, 451, 466 ; 475
3rd—30, 31; concentration, 49 ; advance to Mons, 52, 64, 65 ; at Mons, 73, 82, 89, 94, 96, 99 ; at Elouges, 110 ; casualties, 24th Aug., 112 ; 113, 114, 123, 124, 125, 127 ; at Solesmes, 136, 139 ; at Le Cateau, 140, 143, 148, 149, 155, 173, 180, 188, 194, 196, 198, 200 ; 212,

588 INDEX TO ARMS, FORMATIONS AND UNITS

Divisions (*continued*)—
213, 216, 218, 230 ; casualties,
23rd-27th Aug., 238 ; 240, 245,
247, 262, 273 ; at the Marne,
300, 323, 334, 337, 350 ; pursuit to the Aisne, 361, 369 ; at
the Aisne, 381, 386, 406, 413,
416, 418, 419, 440, 444, 449 ;
476
4th—on East coast defences, 29 ;
31 ; arrival in France, 50, 121 ;
advance to Solesmes, 123, 124,
126, 128, 135, 136, 137, 138 ;
at Le Cateau, 140, 141, 144,
146, 156, 164, 167, 170, 173,
182, 184, 189, 192, 194, 196,
198, 200, 204, 210 ; 212, 213,
216, 217, 218, 219, 229, 230 ;
casualties, 23rd-27th Aug., 238 ;
239, 240, 243, 245, 262, 266,
273 ; at the Marne, 319, 323,
339 ; casualties, 6th-9th Sept.,
363 ; pursuit to the Aisne, 365 ;
at the Aisne, 379, 382, 388, 390,
392, 412, 416, 418, 422, 444,
465, 467 ; 479
5th—30, 31, 32 ; concentration,
49 ; advance to Mons, 52, 65 ;
at Mons, 74, 76, 78, 89, 91, 94,
96, 100, 101 ; at Elouges, 104,
105, 107, 110, 116 ; casualties,
24th Aug., 112 ; 113, 123, 124,
128 ; at Solesmes, 137 ; at Le
Cateau, 140, 143, 148, 154, 156,
157, 171, 172, 174, 175, 179,
180, 188, 191, 192, 193, 197,
200, 204 ; 212, 216, 218, 230 ;
casualties, 23rd-27th Aug., 238 ;
240, 243, 245, 247 ; at Crépy en
Valois, 259 ; 262, 266, 273 ;
at the Marne, 300, 301, 323,
334, 336 ; pursuit to the Aisne,
362 ; at the Aisne, 381, 382,
409, 411, 412, 416, 418, 420,
440, 467 ; 478
6th—29, 31, 32, 205, 230 ; at the
Aisne, 440, 444 ; 467
7th—lands at Zeebrugge, 461, 465
Royal Naval—lands at Dunkirk,
460
Engineers—
Bridging Trains—
1st—439, 482 ; 2nd—439, 482
Field Companies—
5th—401, 476 ; 7th—480 ; 9th
—480 ; 11th—476 : 12th—
482 ; 17th—87, 382, 479 ; 23rd
—224, 276, 475 ; 26th—277,
475 ; 38th—482 ; 56th—155,
478 ; 57th—85, 86, 409, 478 ;

59th—87, 174, 176, 186, 243,
382, 386, 479
Field Squadron—
1st—87, 475
Fortress Companies—
20th—439, 483 ; 42nd—439,
483
Printing Company—
1st—483
Railway Companies—
8th—483 ; 16th—483
Signal Companies—
1st—475 ; 2nd—476 ; 3rd—
478 ; 4th—480 ; 5th—479 ;
6th—482
Signal Squadron—
1st—473
Works Company—
29th—483
Flying Corps (R.F.C.)—
2nd, 3rd, 4th, and 6th Squadrons
—482 ; 5th Squadron—69, 482
French Army—
Armies—
First—16, 39, 41, 42, 47, 60,
285, 303, 368, 429, 443,
457
Second—16, 39, 41, 42, 46, 60,
285, 303, 443, 457
Third—16, 39, 40, 42, 44, 47,
60, 118, 253, 267, 278, 283,
296, 304, 311, 313, 342, 364,
428
Fourth—16, 38, 39, 41, 42, 44,
47, 60, 93, 118, 237, 252, 277,
295, 296, 304, 328, 343, 349,
364, 367, 368, 392
Fifth—16, 38, 42, 44, 48, 50,
53, 60, 68, 70, 92, 118, 130,
131, 136, 204, 217, 219, 226,
231, 234, 237, 239, 241, 242,
244, 245, 247, 248, 250, 252,
265, 266, 270, 271, 274, 275,
277, 278, 281, 288, 289, 292,
293, 295, 297, 299, 301, 302,
305, 306, 308, 311, 312, 313,
316, 325, 328, 333, 342, 343,
344, 349, 352, 356, 358, 364,
366, 368, 372, 374, 377, 385,
388, 391, 418, 426, 443, 449,
463
Sixth—200, 211, 231, 239, 241,
244, 245, 247, 248, 249, 250,
254, 263, 265, 267, 270, 273,
274, 278, 279, 281, 282, 292,
293, 294, 295, 296, 299, 301,
302, 306, 311, 313, 325, 334,
340, 341, 343, 344, 350, 354,
358, 363, 364, 366, 367, 372,
373, 374, 378, 382, 388, 391,

INDEX TO ARMS, FORMATIONS AND UNITS 589

Sixth—(continued)—
412, 419, 422, 429, 443, 449,
450, 456
Ninth—277, 280, 293, 295, 303,
306, 312, 314, 325, 326, 342,
343, 344, 346, 358, 364, 366,
367, 372, 391, 419
Tenth—459, 461
Army of Paris—267, 273, 278,
280, 282, 293, 294
Bridoux's Cavalry Corps—326,
359, 364, 366, 371, 373, 419
Conneau's Cavalry Corps—270,
277, 282, 302, 314, 325, 327,
340, 342, 344, 345, 358, 359,
360, 364, 366, 368, 372, 378,
384, 391, 418, 443, 459
De Mitry's Cavalry Corps—463
Sordet's Cavalry Corps—38, 40,
49, 50, 53, 62, 63, 66, 67, 118,
122, 123, 128, 136, 139, 141,
142, 144, 153, 164, 184, 185,
189, 209, 210, 214, 216, 217,
230, 239, 245, 263, 270, 282,
313, 326. (See also Bridoux's
Cavalry Corps)
d'Urbal's Provisional Corps, 459
Reserve Divisions—
Ebener's Group—118, 216, 231,
282, 392, 419, 456
Lamaze's Group—267, 303, 313,
389, 392, 419
Valabrègue's Group—16, 40, 42,
48, 49, 66, 67, 94, 118, 131,
132, 201, 203, 204, 227, 231,
237, 252, 253, 372, 378, 391,
418
Territorial Divisions—
Brugère's Group—458, 459, 461
d'Amade's Group—51, 103, 116,
118, 119, 125, 127, 136, 139,
185, 204, 205, 210, 227, 230,
231, 233, 234, 439. (See also
Brugère's Group)
Infantry Brigades—
1st (Guards)—64, 73, 122, 170 ;
at Le Grand Fayt, 202 ; at
Étreux, 220, 224 ; 286 ; at the
battle of the Marne, 299, 320 ;
advance to the Aisne, 360 ; at
the battle of the Aisne, 384,
396, 397, 399, 400, 441, 444,
451 ; casualties, 14th Sept.,
416 ; 474
2nd—64, 73, 122 ; at Le Grand
Fayt, 202 ; at Étreux, 220, 224,
227, 276 ; advance to the
Aisne, 360, 363 ; at the battle
of the Aisne, 380, 384, 396, 398,
399, 400, 415, 440, 441, 442,

444, 446, 450, 452 ; casualties,
14th Sept., 416 ; 474
3rd—64, 73, 82, 122 ; at Le Grand
Fayt, 202 ; at Étreux, 222,
223 ; 242, 243 ; at the battle
of the Marne, 310, 333 ; advance to the Aisne, 360 ; at
the battle of the Aisne, 384,
397, 399, 401, 403, 415, 424,
441, 443, 444, 449, 450, 452 ;
474
4th (Guards)—81, 90, 96, 98, 104,
122 ; at Landrecies, 132, 135,
193 ; 201 ; at Le Grand Fayt,
202 ; at Étreux, 220, 226 ; at
Villers Cottérêts, 260 ; casualties, 1st Sept., 262 ; at the
battle of the Marne, 310, 320,
322 ; at the battle of the
Aisne, 385, 388, 390, 401, 403,
407, 408, 413, 424, 447, 448 ;
casualties, 14th Sept., 414 ; 475
5th—82, 90, 96, 101, 102, 104,
122 ; at Le Grand Fayt, 201,
202 ; at Étreux, 220, 226 ;
262 ; at the battle of the Marne,
321, 323, 334 ; advance to the
Aisne, 369, 370 ; at the battle
of the Aisne, 381, 385, 388, 400,
403, 414, 450 ; 475
6th—82, 96, 100, 122, 132 ; at Le
Grand Fayt, 201, 202 ; at
Étreux, 220 ; 246 ; at Villers
Cottérêts, 261 ; casualties, 1st
Sept., 262 ; at the battle of the
Marne, 333 ; advance to the
Aisne, 360, 362, 363 ; at the
battle of the Aisne, 385, 388,
390, 397, 401, 414, 424, 446,
448 ; 475
7th—65 ; at Mons, 74, 86, 89, 96,
100, 104 ; 124, 125, 127, 129 ;
at Solesmes, 136, 137 ; at Le
Cateau, 142, 143, 155, 163, 168,
182, 184, 188 ; 216 ; at the
battle of the Marne, 300 ; at the
battle of the Aisne, 386, 388,
407, 420, 448 ; casualties, 14th
Sept., 408 ; casualties, 20th
Sept., 449 : 477
8th—65, 67 ; at Mons, 73, 82, 89,
91, 96, 97, 100, 104, 124, 128 ;
at Le Cateau, 143, 155, 163, 183,
188, 194, 216 ; at the battle of
the Marne, 321, 323 ; at the
battle of the Aisne, 381, 386,
388, 406, 420 ; casualties, 14th
Sept., 408 ; 477
9th—52, 65 ; at Mons, 73, 78, 82,
84, 87, 89, 96, 97 ; at Frameries,

Infantry Brigades (continued)—
100, 104 ; 124, 128 ; at Solesmes, 137 ; at Le Cateau, 143, 155, 162, 176, 180, 188, 213, 216 ; 240 ; at the battle of the Marne, 323, 334, 340 ; advance to the Aisne, 362, 369 ; at the battle of the Aisne, 386, 388, 406, 407, 447, 453 ; casualties, 14th Sept., 408 ; 477
10th—at Solesmes, 126, 138, 139 ; at Le Cateau, 146, 147, 168, 189, 191, 198, 214 ; 240, 243, 257 ; at the battle of the Marne, 339 ; at the battle of the Aisne, 383, 387, 412, 442 ; casualties, 14th Sept., 413 ; 479
11th—30 ; at Solesmes, 126, 138 ; at Le Cateau, 144, 146, 147, 149, 156, 164, 166, 168 ; 180, 182, 190, 199, 213, 215 ; 258, 262 ; at the battle of the Marne, 323, 337, 339 ; at the battle of the Aisne, 379, 383, 412, 466 ; 480
12th—at Solesmes, 127, 138 ; at Le Cateau, 144, 147, 156, 164, 166, 167, 180, 185, 189, 190, 198, 214 ; 219, 262 ; at the battle of the Marne, 319, 323, 337, 339 ; at the battle of the Aisne, 382, 387, 388, 410, 412 ; 480
13th—65 ; at Mons, 74, 78, 80, 86, 89, 90, 96, 97, 106 ; at Elouges, 107 ; 128 ; at Le Cateau, 154, 162, 172, 175, 178 ; 243 ; at Crépy en Valois, 259 ; at the Marne, 322, 336 ; at the Aisne, 382, 386, 388, 409, 411, 418, 420 ; 478
14th—65 ; at Mons, 74, 81, 87, 90, 96, 97, 106 ; at Elouges, 107 ; 124, 128 ; at Solesmes, 137 ; at Le Cateau, 154, 157, 172, 175, 186 ; 212 ; at the Marne, 322, 335, 336 ; at the Aisne, 382, 386, 388, 409, 410, 420, 421 ; 478
15th—at Mons, 75, 90, 96, 97, 101; 128, 143 ; at Le Cateau, 154, 162, 178, 186 ; at the Marne, 336, 338 ; at the Aisne, 409, 410, 420, 422 ; 478
16th—arrival on the Aisne, 440 ; 449, 464 ; 481
17th—arrival on the Aisne, 440 ; 450 ; 481
18th—29 ; arrival on the Aisne, 440, 441 ; 446, 451 ; 481
19th—formation, 50 ; at Mons,

72, 75, 87, 90, 96, 97, 103 ; at Elouges, 107 ; casualties, 24th Aug., 112 ; 113, 121, 123, 124, 125, 126, 127, 128, 129, 135 ; at Solesmes, 137 ; at Le Cateau, 153, 156, 159, 161, 171, 174, 176, 186, 188, 198, 200 ; 216, 217, 230 ; casualties, 23rd-27th Aug., 238 ; 243 ; at the Marne, 319, 323, 339, 353 ; casualties, 3rd-10th Sept., 363 ; at the Aisne, 388, 390, 418, 444, 464 ; 483
Royal Marine L.I., 232, 393, 461
Infantry Regiments—
Coldstream Guards, 1st Bn., 220, 223, 398, 401, 415, 452, 474
—— 2nd Bn., 260, 262, 321, 323, 381, 413, 475
—— 3rd Bn., 133, 260, 320, 404, 414, 416, 475
Grenadier Guards, 2nd Bn., 134 ; at Villers Cottérêts, 260, 262 ; 321, 404, 416, 439, 475
Irish Guards, 260, 262, 320, 323, 403, 405, 414, 475
Scots Guards, 1st Bn., 220, 224, 400, 474
Argyll and Sutherland Highlanders, 2nd Bn., 50, 159, 161, 171, 172, 174, 176, 178, 186, 188, 483
Bedfordshire, 1st Bn., 90, 96, 101, 102, 105, 162, 179, 180, 410, 421, 478
Berkshire, Royal, 1st Bn., 133, 150, 262, 361, 402, 443, 475
Black Watch (Royal Highlanders), 1st Bn., 220, 224, 225, 320, 398, 400, 474
Buffs (East Kent), 1st Bn., 481
Cameron Highlanders, 1st Bn., 286, 320, 398, 400, 401, 416, 451, 474, 483
Cameronians (Scottish Rifles), 1st Bn., 50, 87, 171, 173, 177, 186, 188, 483
Cheshire, 1st Bn., 101 ; at Elouges, 107, 109, 112 ; 180, 411, 478
Connaught Rangers, 2nd Bn., 96, 104 ; at Le Grand Fayt, 202, 203 ; 233, 323, 403, 405, 414, 447, 475
Devonshire, 1st Bn., 420, 477, 483
Dorsetshire, 1st Bn., 96, 101, 102, 105, 162, 179, 180, 336, 410, 478
Dublin Fusiliers, Royal, 2nd Bn., 147, 190, 191, 196, 197, 257, 413, 440, 479
Duke of Cornwall's L.I., 1st Bn., 74, 81, 87, 90, 128, 135, 157,

Infantry Regiments (*continued*)—
159, 177, 186, 188, 322, 335,
336, 353, 410, 411, 421, 478
Duke of Wellington's (West Riding), 2nd Bn., 80, 101, 102 ;
casualties at Mons, 106 ; 175,
178, 259, 420, 478
Durham L.I., 2nd Bn., 445, 451,
481
East Lancashire, 1st Bn., 145,
146, 169, 180, 191, 258, 339,
480
East Surrey, 1st Bn., 74, 81, 87,
90, 128, 154, 157, 158, 159, 175,
177, 186, 188, 332, 336, 387,
410, 478
East Yorkshire, 1st Bn., 445, 451,
481
Essex, 2nd Bn., 144, 164, 166,
185, 190, 324, 338, 387, 480
Gloucestershire, 1st Bn., 202,
401, 443, 450, 474
Gordon Highlanders, 1st Bn., 73,
83, 84, 88, 89, 91, 181, 183, 188,
192, 194, 195, 233, 321, 420,
477
Hampshire, 1st Bn., 145, 146,
164, 166, 169, 191, 214, 258,
339, 480
Highland L.I., 2nd Bn., 102, 220,
403, 414, 439, 447, 475
Inniskilling Fusiliers, Royal, 2nd
Bn., 138, 144, 148, 166, 167,
181, 182, 190, 324, 339, 370,
380, 480
Irish Fusiliers, Royal, 1st Bn.,
147, 168, 189, 191, 196, 479
Irish Rifles, Royal, 2nd Bn., 89,
91, 127, 137, 143, 155, 163, 181,
183, 408, 448, 477
King's (Liverpool), 1st Bn., 262,
402, 446, 475
King's Own, 1st Bn., 144, 156,
164, 165, 166, 168, 190, 192,
196, 214, 324, 339, 480
King's Own Scottish Borderers,
2nd Bn., 67, 74, 76, 80, 87, 89,
101, 154, 162, 175, 178, 179,
386, 388, 400, 410, 411, 478
King's Own Yorkshire L.I., 2nd
Bn., 74, 80, 90, 101, 102, 106,
154, 159, 160, 162, 175, 194,
421, 422, 478
King's Royal Rifle Corps, 1st Bn.,
361, 402, 405, 414, 416, 439, 475
—— 2nd Bn., 396, 399, 416, 442,
474
Lancashire Fusiliers, 2nd Bn.,
144, 164, 165, 167, 190, 338,
387, 388, 480

Leicestershire, 1st Bn., 481
Leinster, 2nd Bn., 481
Lincolnshire, 1st Bn., 52, 74, 85,
115, 155, 180, 335, 363, 406, 477
Loyal North Lancashire, 1st Bn.,
360, 398, 416, 474
Manchester, 2nd Bn., 75, 90, 106,
128, 137, 161, 162, 174, 178,
335, 336, 387, 388, 410, 421,
478
Middlesex, 1st Bn., 50, 87, 161,
171, 176, 186, 188, 257, 321,
406, 483
—— 4th Bn., 73, 76, 77, 82, 87,
91, 163, 183, 477
Munster Fusiliers, Royal, 2nd Bn.,
at Étreux, 221, 225, 226, 234 ;
286, 398, 474
Norfolk, 1st Bn., 101, 107, 108,
110, 111, 112, 177, 186, 187,
336, 411, 421, 478
Northamptonshire, 1st Bn., 223,
396, 398, 442, 443, 474
North Staffordshire, 1st Bn., 481
Northumberland Fusiliers, 1st
Bn., 74, 78, 86, 179, 180, 334,
406, 447, 477
Oxford and Bucks L.I., 2nd Bn.,
102, 332, 369, 414, 439, 475
Queen's (R. West Surrey), 1st
Bn., 333, 397, 399, 401, 415,
442, 450, 474
Rifle Brigade, 1st Bn., 145, 146,
147, 164, 169, 180, 191, 214,
258, 262, 339, 383, 387, 480
—— 3rd Bn., 481
Royal Fusiliers, 1st Bn., 481
—— 4th Bn., 74, 76, 77, 82, 85,
180, 406, 407, 447, 477
Royal Irish, 2nd Bn., 73, 77, 82,
87, 89, 91, 163, 183, 188, 194,
321, 386, 406, 477
Royal Scots, 2nd Bn., 73, 83, 89,
90, 163, 181, 183, 188, 194, 381,
386, 406, 477
Scots Fusiliers, Royal, 1st Bn.,
52, 74, 76, 77, 85, 137, 176, 180,
407, 477
Seaforth Highlanders, 2nd Bn.,
146, 168, 189, 191, 413, 479
Sherwood Foresters, 2nd Bn., 446,
481
Shropshire L.I., King's, 1st Bn.,
481
Somerset L.I., 1st Bn., 145, 146,
169, 190, 214, 258, 262, 339,
480
South Lancashire, 2nd Bn., 86,
100, 115, 127, 136, 155, 309,
448, 477

Infantry Regiments (continued)—
South Staffordshire, 2nd Bn., 361,
448, 475
South Wales Borderers, 1st Bn.,
224, 400, 424, 449, 450, 474
Suffolk, 2nd Bn., 75, 81, 128, 137,
154, 158, 159, 160, 162, 171,
174, 175, 194, 478
Sussex, Royal, 2nd Bn., 360, 396,
398, 416, 446, 474
Warwickshire, Royal, 1st Bn.,
147, 165, 166, 191, 196, 257, 479
Welch, 2nd Bn., 220, 221, 224,
400, 415, 424, 449, 451, 474
Welch Fusiliers, Royal, 2nd Bn.,
50, 171, 173, 177, 186, 187, 188,
248, 324, 483
West Kent, Royal, 1st Bn., 74,
76, 78, 87, 89, 95, 101, 102, 173,
175, 178, 243, 259, 382, 386,
388, 409, 410, 411, 478

West Yorkshire, 1st Bn., 445, 446,
449, 481
Wiltshire, 1st Bn., 127, 136, 137,
155, 300, 309, 408, 448, 477
Worcestershire, 2nd Bn., 102, 321,
369, 403, 414, 447, 475
—— 3rd Bn., 127, 147, 155, 163,
180, 448, 477
York & Lancaster, 2nd Bn.,
481

Lines of Communication units, 483

Medical—
Field Ambulances—
1st, 2nd, 3rd—475 ; 4th, 5th,
6th—476 ; 7th, 8th, 9th—
478 ; 10th, 11th, 12th—480 ;
13th, 14th, 15th—479 ; 16th,
17th, 18th—482 ; 19th, 20th
—483
See also L. of C. units

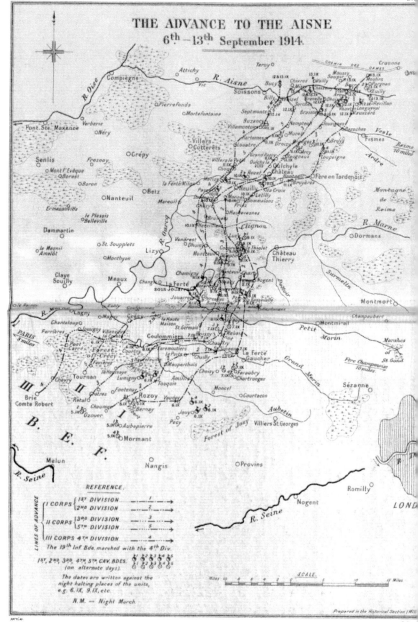

THE ADVANCE TO THE AISNE
6th –13th September 1914.

REFERENCE.

LINES OF ADVANCE	I CORPS	1ST DIVISION	1
		2ND DIVISION	2
	II CORPS	3RD DIVISION	3
		5TH DIVISION	5
	III CORPS	4TH DIVISION	4

The 19th Inf. Bde. marched with the 4th Div.

1ST, 2ND, 3RD, 4TH, 5TH, CAV. BDES.
(on alternate days).

The dates are written against the
night halting places of the units,
e.g. 6.IX, 9.IX, etc.

N.M. — Night March.

SCALE.

Miles 10   5   0   5   10   15 Miles

Prepared in the Historical Section (Mil...)

Ordnance...